D0872175

THE RISE AND FALL OF
CLASSICAL GREECE

FRONTISPIECE   *Temple of Apollo at Bassae, in the mountains above the polis of Phigalia in the region of Arcadia (northern Peloponnese).*

Engraving is plate 1 of Thomas Leverton Donaldson, *Description of the Temple of Apollo Epicurius at Bassae, Near Phigalia.* London: Priestly and Weale, 1830 (Vol. 5 of James Stuart and Nicholas Revett, *Antiquities of Athens:* London, 1762 and following).

THE
RISE AND FALL
OF
CLASSICAL
GREECE

JOSIAH OBER

PRINCETON UNIVERSITY PRESS
Princeton & Oxford

PUBLISHED BY PRINCETON UNIVERSITY PRESS

41 William Street, Princeton, New Jersey 08540

IN THE UNITED KINGDOM: PRINCETON UNIVERSITY PRESS

6 Oxford Street, Woodstock, Oxfordshire OX20 1TW

PRESS.PRINCETON.EDU

JACKET IMAGE: Engraving of northeast view of the Temple of Apollo Epicurius at Bassae near Phigalia, by Thomas Leverton Donaldson, from *The Antiquities of Athens* (London, 1830). Image courtesy of Aikaterini Laskaridis Foundation.

Library of Congress Cataloging-in-Publication Data

Ober, Josiah.

The rise and fall of classical Greece / Josiah Ober.

pages cm. — (The Princeton history of the ancient world)

Includes bibliographical references and index.

ISBN 978-0-691-14091-9 (hardcover : acid-free paper)   1. Greece—Civilization—To 146 B.C.   2. Social change—Greece—History—To 1500.   3. Greece—Politics and government—To 146 B.C.   4. City-states—Greece—History.   5. Greece—Economic conditions—To 146 B.C. I. Title.

DF77.O24 2015

938—dc23

2014037623

BRITISH LIBRARY CATALOGING-IN-PUBLICATION DATA IS AVAILABLE

This book has been composed in Garamond Premier Pro and Penumbra Flare Std

Printed on acid-free paper. ∞

PRINTED IN THE UNITED STATES OF AMERICA

1 3 5 7 9 10 8 6 4 2

for ADRIENNE

CONTENTS

IMAGES and TABLES

TABLES

PREFACE

I live in exceptional times. I can take for granted a global order defined by many independent states, some of them wealthy democratic federations governed ultimately by their citizens. Freedom, equality, and dignity are widely shared values. In states where citizens keep rulers in check, public authority protects individual rights and the rule of law pertains most of the time. These political conditions promote economic growth. The conjunction of democratic politics and a strong economy is, in practice, available only to affluent citizens of highly developed countries. But many people who do not yet enjoy those conditions aspire to them. Democracy and growth define the normal, although not yet the usual, conditions of modernity: Autocracy, while still prevalent, is regarded as aberrant, so that most autocrats pretend to be democrats. Economic stagnation is seen as a problem that demands a solution.

These conditions were *not* normal, or even imaginable, for most people through most of human history. But, for several centuries in the first millennium BCE, democracy and growth *were* normal for citizens in ancient Greece. How that happened, and why it matters, is what this book is about.

New scholarship—much of it written by my colleagues at Stanford—has helped to show *why* the political and economic conditions of modernity are, historically, so exceptionally rare. For the past several thousand years of human history, and until the eighteenth century, most people lived under the rule of autocrats who claimed a special relationship to divinity. The most successful of these rulers were masters of extensive empires, but most of their subjects lived perilously close to bare subsistence. Rulers stayed in power by extracting surplus from their subjects and distributing the loot to a ruling coalition. Under these conditions, access to institutions is limited, rights remain vestigial, and economic growth is usually low.[1]

This *premodern normal* can be summed up as "domination"—so long as we remember that some subjects had input into government, through consultative assemblies or petition rights, that autocracy was sometimes limited by tradition or religious institutions, and that subjects often accept the legitimacy of royal authority. Domination pertained across most of the world until the eighteenth century. Then things began to change, first in a few Atlantic countries and later across much of the world. The result is our modern political normal, a condition that may be summed up as "democracy"—so long as we keep in mind that many people in democratic societies are in fact dominated in various ways.[2]

The modern world is exceptional for its economic development *and* for its political development: not only for being (overall) wealthy, but also for the prevalence of democratic politics and the values that democracy sustains. I assume that few readers of this book would choose to live in premodern normal conditions of domination, even if their economic circumstances could be guaranteed. I assume that equally few would choose to live at the median economic level of a normal premodern society, even were it democratic. The citizens of modern developed countries need not make the choice between wealth and democracy. As we now know, democratic states are quite capable of achieving high levels of economic growth.

My colleague, Ian Morris, has shown that relatively high levels of development have historically been achieved under various political systems.[3] The question of what institutional conditions are necessary or sufficient to sustain growth remains hotly debated. But what is *not* in question is that many people—including those not lucky enough to be affluent citizens of developed countries—have a strong preference, not only for affluence over poverty but also for democracy over domination. This is a *normative* preference, predicated on deeply held assumptions about the *value* of democracy relative to that of domination. I believe that there are good reasons for that normative preference. I assume that many readers of this book share my preference for democracy, even though your reasons may be different from my own.[4]

If we prefer our modern political and economic conditions to the premodern normal, we have good reason to inquire how we got here and to ask how likely it is that democracy plus wealth will become *usual* as well as normal. How is it that historically exceptional economic and political conditions came to be regarded as normal? Ought we to expect these conditions to persist where they currently pertain and to spread to the rest of the world? The prehistory of political and economic exceptionalism offers one relatively unexplored avenue by which we may address those questions.

The exceptional political conditions that I have summed up under the rubric of democracy—a social ecology of many independent states, federalism, citizen self-governance with its associated values—were indeed rare before the eighteenth century. But they were not unknown. Societies with these features include the Dutch republics of the sixteenth century, the Italian city-states of the fourteenth and fifteenth centuries—and classical Greece in the fifth and fourth centuries BCE. In each case, the era of economic exceptionalism was limited, and in no case did premodern political rights or economic growth reach levels comparable to those enjoyed by many citizens of the most highly developed states in the past 150 years. But these early societies each experienced an extended period of economic growth and cultural achievement in the context of a historically remarkable extension of citizenship.

A comparative analysis of these (and other) historical cases of political and economic exceptionalism would go a long way toward answering important questions about the origins and sustainability of our modern condition. Before that ambitious comparative project can be undertaken, however, we need to know more about each of the relevant cases. We need to explain how each historically exceptional society arose when and where it did and how and why its political and economic exceptionality was terminated. By offering a new political and economic history of ancient Greece, this book contributes to that project.

This is *not* a book about a putative "great divergence" between East and West, nor does it claim that democracy is either necessary or sufficient to sustain economic growth. It traces the rise of a society in which the normatively valued political conditions of democracy for an extensive body of citizens (although decidedly *not* for all residents) were conjoined with economic growth whose benefits were widely shared and with cultural achievements that had a lasting impact on the world. It measures growth, traces the causal relationship between Greek political and economic development, narrates the conquest of citizen-centered states by an autocratic empire, and explains why so much is still known about ancient Greek society.

It would be absurd to claim that ancient Greeks, who owned slaves, denied rights to women, and glorified war, offer an off-the-shelf model for us. The Greek transition from domination to democracy was incomplete, and it left a great many people behind. It would be equally absurd to claim that our modernity has all, or even most, of its roots in what happened in Greece some 2,500 years ago. But if we are interested in the conjunction of political and economic exceptionalism, we must start somewhere, and classical Greece was the society in which the wealth-and-democracy package first emerged in a form that can be studied in depth.

Classical Greece was not a state or a nation; it was an extensive social ecology of many independent city-states with citizen-centered governments. While the Greeks never fully formulated the concept of *human* rights, they did develop the basic democratic values of liberty, political equality, and civic dignity. The Greeks experimented successfully with federalism. Some Greek states practiced the rule of law, and some went a long way toward opening access to institutions. Political reforms were self-consciously enacted by Greek legislators, who sometimes left records of what they intended. Political development was critically analyzed in incisive and groundbreaking works of Greek political theory.

Because of the rich literary and documentary record surviving from classical antiquity, subsequent theorists and practitioners, eager to break with the norm of domination, were able to draw on Greek experience. For their own part, while they learned a great deal from other societies, the Greeks themselves had few precedents to build upon when devising democratic institutions and values. If we can explain the rise of classical Greece, we may gain a better sense of what it took to bootstrap the wealth and democracy package in the first place. If we can explain the fall of the Greek political order—that is, why major city-states did not maintain full independence for longer than they did—we may better understand democratic fragility.

My approach to explaining the rise and fall of classical Greece is that of a historian and political scientist. These are not the only ways to elucidate the Greek past. Scholars from the fields of anthropology, sociology, and literary studies have advanced our understanding of Greek culture in ways that are compatible with the results offered here. But there are ways to think about the ancient Greek world, associated with these three disciplines, that in their strongest forms, would render my project incoherent: First is an assumption that the Greek world was *not* actually exceptional. Next is a claim that Greece's exceptionalism makes it analytically irrelevant. Third is an assertion that the exceptionalism of the Greek world has nothing to do with modern politics or economics.

The first assumption, that Greece is not exceptional because the Greek world shared various features with other premodern societies, seems to me insufficiently attentive to historically salient distinctions: It is certainly true that the Greek economy remained primarily based on arable agriculture; that Greeks practiced various sorts of morally repugnant status-based hierarchy, including slavery and other forms of coerced labor; and that polytheistic religion was an important part of the ordinary Greek's worldview and daily practice. But the Greek economy was also, as we will see, fundamentally based on specialization and exchange; real wages (including the wages of at least some slaves) were much higher than the premodern norm. Religion was very important in Greece, as it was (and is) elsewhere. Yet classical Greece stands out among documented premodern societies, as the Oxford Greek historian Oswyn Murray has emphasized, in the prominence of formal rationality and explicitly political reasoning in the decisions and decision-making processes that set the course of its history.[5]

The second claim, that Greek exceptionalism renders the Greek case analytically meaningless, seems to me to place too much interpretive weight on historical prevalence. When studying some feature of a given society, a social scientist may (under some circumstances) discard "outliers" on the ground that the relevant sample is in the middle of the distribution. But in this case, the features that made the historical outlier exceptional are of great interest because the outlier appears quite similar, in salient ways, to *our* normal and because of its normative significance to us. Perhaps the city-state ecology was, as the Cambridge historical sociologist W. G. Runciman claimed, "doomed to extinction" because the Greek city-states were "without exception, far too democratic."[6] But the city-state ecology lasted for a very long time before it went extinct. All ancient empires, most of which proved more ephemeral than the city-state ecology, are likewise extinct. Insofar as we value democracy, and insofar as Greek democratic exceptionalism did anticipate exceptional conditions of modernity, we have strong reasons to want to know whether Greece's "doom" must also be our own—and if not, why not.

The third assertion is based on the premise that, because each society is in some ways distinctive, societies are strictly incomparable. The strong version of the historicist argument rejects quantification and focuses on the contextual specificity of the societies in question and their cultural products.[7] Historicists embrace the idea that comparative analysis highlights *differences* by showing how desperately foreign each society is when viewed from the perspective of the other. Comparison of *similarities*, on this argument, yields only false analogies. The historicist approach is, however, incomplete insofar as patterns of human behavior *are* fundamentally similar across societies widely separated in time and space. Social science (like natural science) is predicated on the possibility of determining regularities that underpin apparently diverse phenomena. The goal of much contemporary social science is to infer the causes of observed social, political, and economic phenomena, based on parsimonious "micro-foundations"—minimal and at least potentially testable assumptions about the motivations of individual and collective human action under specifiable conditions.

This book is both history and social science. As history, it may be characterized as *middle-range* in the sense of being neither global nor local, neither big nor micro-level. I do not attempt to match the breadth of global history or the level of generalization of recent "big histories," which look at change and continuity over tens of thousands or millions of years.[8] I am concerned to explain change and continuity in a society of several million people, in about a thousand states, over a period of several hundred years. I will sometimes focus on the doings of individual legislators or leaders, but more often I try to explain collective action at both the level of the state and at inter- and multi-state levels. My approach is, therefore, at a much higher level of generalization than local or microhistory.[9]

As social science, my approach is also middle-range, straddling quantitative and qualitative methods. A good deal of the argument draws on quantified data. My discussion of Greek economic growth over time is necessarily quantitative, and I believe that it is possible to make substantial advances by using original data sets (compiled in conjunction with colleagues and students) based on recent monumental collections of evidence for the ancient Greek city-state ecology. I also make some use of simple game theoretic models, drawing on well-established social-scientific theories of political behavior and development. Although only one formal game is presented in full (appendix II), throughout the book readers are invited to think of Greek social relations in the form of games whose background rules induce individual players to make relatively cooperative choices. The aggregate of those prosocial choices was the "thumb on the scale" that tipped classical Greece toward sustained economic growth.

When addressing complex questions of long-term social development in a society that flourished in the distant past, it is impossible to employ a perfectly clean identification strategy—that is, to strictly distinguish independent (explanatory) variables from dependent variables and to rigorously test hypotheses through natural, lab, or survey experiments. The data I use are inevitably noisy, although, as I argue, not so noisy as to preclude valid conclusions. More generally, the social systems I address are sufficiently complex and the time spans long enough to introduce what social scientists call the problem of *endogeneity*—that is, feedback between causes and effects. Many of my results are based in part on qualitative analysis of literary and documentary sources. The conclusions of this book assume that quantitative and qualitative methods can be conjoined in ways that are rigorous enough to pass muster as causal explanation.[10]

My goal is to use the tools of the historian and the social scientist to explain two phenomena that seem to me especially relevant to the larger project of understanding political and economic exceptionalism: First is the sustained economic and cultural growth of the Greek world from 1000 to 300 BCE: "the rise of classical Greece." The second phenomenon is "the fall of classical Greece": the defeat of a coalition of Greek city-states by imperial Macedon in the late fourth century BCE, an event that ended the era in which fully independent city-states determined the course of Mediterranean history. I explain the economic rise by tracing the development of civic institutions and political culture in an environment of interstate and interpersonal competition and rational cooperation. I demonstrate how and why political development drove exceptionally high individual and collective investments in human capital, high levels of economic specialization and exchange, continuous technical and institutional innovation, high mobility of people and ideas, low transaction costs, and ready transfer of both goods and ideas. I distinguish the role played by these same political and economic developments in the political fall.

The rise and fall of classical Greece can be explained without special pleading involving a mystical Hellenic spirit and without spurious assumptions about inherent differences between the peoples of the East and West.[11] The answers to the questions of why and how Greece rose, fell, and persisted in the cultural memory of the world are of intrinsic interest. They bear on central issues in social science, including the problem of collective action without central authority and the role of political institutions in economic development. Those answers also bear on some of the biggest challenges and most promising opportunities that democratic citizens are now confronting in our own decentralized world.

In the chapters that follow, after posing the question of why Greece rose and fell, I present new data for answering that question. This new evidence shows just how far Greece had come from the age of Homer to the age of Aristotle, both politically and economically. I formulate new hypotheses concerning specialization and innovation to explain both rise and fall through a causal relationship between political and economic developments. I then offer a new narrative of Greek history, from the Early Iron Age to the Hellenistic period. The narrative expands and tests the explanatory hypotheses. Tracing the histories of great and small Greek city-states alike, the unfolding story reveals how the ecology of city-states grew so dramatically, over such a long period of time, how it was finally conquered, and how Greek culture became a world culture.

Chapter 1 introduces the puzzle of classical Greek exceptionalism. Chapters 2–4 explore the contours of a decentralized ecology of hundreds of small states; develop a theory of how high-level cooperation, and therefore stable political order, is achieved in the absence of central authority; and document ancient Greek economic growth. Chapter 5 suggests two primary drivers of Greek growth: First is the establishment of fair rules that encouraged investment in human capital and lowered transaction costs. Next is competition among individuals and states, driving continuous institutional and technological innovation, and motivating rational cooperation.

Chapters 6–9 tell the story of the rise of classical Greece: the historical development of citizen-centered politics and economic growth from the age of Homer to Aristotle. We focus on a few particularly successful and influential states but also attend to the historical development of less prominent and less powerful communities. The rise of Hellas is illuminated by similarities and differences among Athens, Sparta, and Syracuse and by the differential historical trajectories of many Greek states of different sizes and levels of prominence. Comparing the internal development of great and small city-states reveals how innovative political institutions and culture stimulated specialization and fomented creative destruction. The failure of Athens to sustain its fifth century BCE empire demonstrates the robustness of the decentralized Greek social ecology, while dense populations and high per capita incomes in the postimperial era demonstrate that empire was not a precondition for continued economic growth.

Chapter 10 narrates the political fall, showing how the products of Greek specialization, especially military and financial expertise, were taken up by leaders of states on the frontiers of the Greek world, and how Philip and Alexander of Macedon, the most talented of these entrepreneurial opportunists, terminated the era in which independent city-states determined the course of Greek history.

Chapter 11 concludes by explaining the surprising robustness of the polis ecology and continued high economic performance in the postclassical era. Because Hellas did not collapse after the political fall of the major independent city-states, the memory of Greek political exceptionalism has been preserved as part of the world's cultural heritage. As a result, classical Greece remains a resource for theorists of decentralized social order, and both an inspiration and a cautionary tale for those who aspire to practice citizen-centered politics.

ACKNOWLEDGMENTS

I have been thinking about and working on the subject matter of this book since I first fell in love with Greek history. That was in an introductory class at the University of Minnesota taught by Thomas Kelly, who, after overcoming his skepticism about my seriousness of purpose, sent me on to earn a Ph.D. under the direction of Chester Starr at the University of Michigan. Kelly's high standards for writing history and Starr's belief that Greek historians must seek to understand social, political, and cultural change (and not just continuity) have guided my studies ever since.

I have been extraordinarily lucky in my subsequent career to have colleagues eager and able to help me as I struggled to make sense of the Greek past and with the question of why it ought to matter to anyone who was not convinced, as I always have been, that it is the most fascinating possible subject of inquiry. I learned a great deal about history beyond antiquity from colleagues in the Department of History and Philosophy at Montana State University; about classical studies beyond history and about political theory from colleagues in the Department of Classics and the University Center for Human Values at Princeton; and, most recently, about political institutions and behavior, quantitative methods, and causal inference from my colleagues in the Departments of Political Science and Classics at Stanford.

Along the way, I have been equally lucky in having the chance to teach and to learn from extraordinary students, undergraduate and graduate alike. A list of those who influenced the ideas and arguments in this book would, in its length, grossly violate the norms governing expressions of academic gratitude. Many who deserve mention here are unnamed but not unremembered.

This book began as a presidential address on the topic "Wealthy Hellas," presented to the American Philological Association ("Wealthy Hellas" © 2010 American Philological Association). An earlier version of chapter 4 first appeared in *Transactions of the American Philological Association,* Volume 140, No. 2, Autumn 2010, pp. 241–286, published by Johns Hopkins University Press (Ober 2010c). "Wealthy Hellas" was then the topic of a two-term classics graduate seminar at Stanford. I learned much from the students, from Rob Fleck and Alain Bresson, who, as faculty visitors to Stanford, regularly sat in, and especially from Ian Morris, with whom I codirected the seminar. I have also had the opportunity to present work related to the book to well-informed and helpfully critical audiences at conferences and by invitation—in most detail at Cornell University as the Townsend Lectures in Classics, and also at Aarhus University, Bergen University, Cambridge University, University of Brussels (Franqui Conference), University of Chicago, University of Florence (ISNIE Conference), Fudan University, University of Indiana, Lund University, McGill University, Ohio State University, Princeton University, University of Rome (Sapienza), St. Andrews University, Stanford University, and Zheijiang University.

Special thanks are due to those who read various drafts. John Ma, Adrienne Mayor, Michelle Maskiell, Ian Morris, and an anonymous reader for Princeton University Press read drafts of the entire manuscript and made erudite, thoughtful, and detailed suggestions that have substantially improved the final result. Peter van Alfen, Ryan Balot, Sarah Ferrario, Rob Fleck, Stephen Haber, Eero Hämeenniemi, Andy Hanssen, James Kierstead, Carl Hampus Lyttkens, Emily Mackil, Walter Scheidel, Matt Simonton, Barry Strauss, David Teegarden, and Greg Woolf commented helpfully on parts of the manuscript and raised my occasionally flagging spirits with their enthusiasm. I owe special thanks to Deborah Gordon for introducing me to the world of ant science and for discussions of information exchange, evolution, and behavior; to Steve Haber and Barry Weingast for many long and deep discussions concerning institutions, economics, game theory—and much else. Eleni Tsakopoulos, Markos Kounalakis, and Yan Lin have supported my work at Stanford, both materially and through their ardent belief that Greek culture and democratic politics belong together as matters of the greatest possible import.

My profound indebtedness to the work of the Copenhagen Polis Center (CPC), and especially to its former director, Mogens Hansen, will be evident throughout. David Teegarden, Tim Johnson, and Bailey McRae entered some of the published results of the CPC onto spreadsheets, thereby making those results available as data for quantitative analysis. Those data were made publicly accessible on an interactive Web page (http://polis.stanford.edu) created and designed by Maya Krishnan, a Stanford undergraduate whose talents range from history and philosophy to computer science. Michele Angel transmogrified crude versions of the maps and figures into their present forms. Stanford University, through its School of Humanities and Science, provided substantial material, as well as intellectual, support for this project from the beginning. I hardly need say that, while whatever merit this book possesses is due in large measure to others, its errors of omission and commission are my own.

Rob Tempio, who is my editor at Princeton University Press, along with my literary agent Jill Marsal, played a formative role in the book's genesis and a major part in its subsequent development. The editorial, production, and marketing staff at Princeton University Press have also been outstanding throughout. In an age in which scholarly books are sometimes regarded as exotic luxury goods, their passion for academic book publishing is an inspiration and offers hope for the future of a uniquely deep and powerful form of intellectual communication.

This book is dedicated to Adrienne Mayor—my life partner, intellectual companion, closest friend, my heart's desire—who once warned me that autodidacticism has its limits and urged me to try a few university courses.

ABBREVIATIONS

NOTE: Ancient Greek authors, whose works are available in the Loeb Classical Library and other modern editions, are cited by book, chapter, and section, according to the ordinary practice of classical historians.

Ath. Pol. *Athenaion Politeia* ("The Constitution of Athens"). Two literary works by this title have come down to us, one attributed to Aristotle (probably by one of his students) and the other by an anonymous author of the later fifth century BCE, alluded to as Pseudo-Xenophon and nicknamed "The Old Oligarch" by twentieth century classical scholars.

BCE Before common era.

CAH *Cambridge Ancient History* (Cambridge: Cambridge University Press). 2nd edition (vols. 3–14) or 3rd edition (vols. 1–2), 1970–2005.

CE Common era.

cm centimeter. 1 cm = 0.39 inches.

dr drachma—basic unit of Greek silver coinage. Attic drachma = 4.3 grams of silver. Approximately one day's wage for an unskilled laborer in late fifth century BCE Athens.

FGrH *Fragments of Greek Historians*, English edition, edited by Ian Worthington (Leiden, Netherlands: E. J. Brill), multiple volumes.

EIA Early Iron Age, in the Greek world, ca. 1100–750 BCE.

GDI Gross domestic income.

GDP Gross domestic product.

Inventory Hansen, Mogens Herman, and Thomas Heine Nielsen. 2004. *An Inventory of Archaic and Classical Poleis*. Oxford: Oxford University Press. i# (e.g., i361) refers to the inventory number of a polis listed in the *Inventory* (i361 = Athens).

km kilometer. 1 km = 0.62 miles. 1 km² = 0.39 square miles, or 247 acres.

L liter. 1 L = 0.25 U.S. gallons, 0.22 imperial gallons.

LBA Late Bronze Age, in Greek world, ca. 1600–1200 BCE.

m meter. 1 m = 3.28 feet. 1 m² = 10.7 square feet, or 1.2 square yards.

T Talent: Basic unit for measuring large amounts of money in the Greek world. 6,000 drachmas. 1 Attic talent = ca. 25.725 kilograms of silver. Very approximately, a lifetime's income for an Athenian laborer in the fifth century BCE.

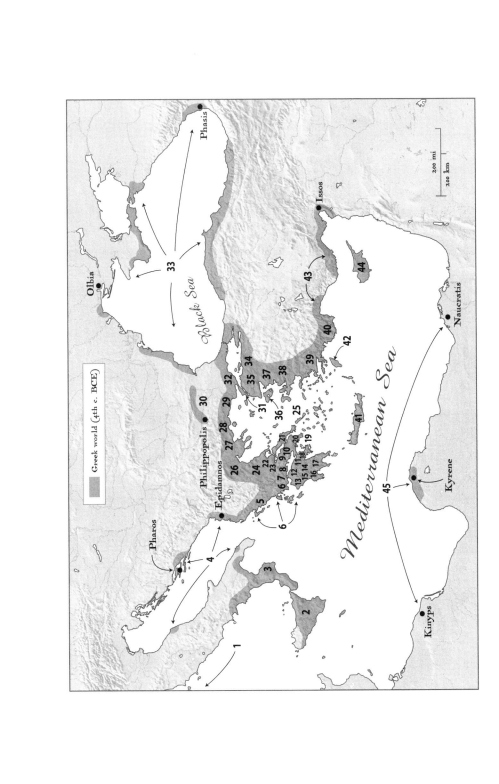

Greek world (4th c. BCE)

Mediterranean Sea

Black Sea

Phasis

Issos

Olbia

Naucratis

Kinyps

Kyrene

Pharos

Epidamnos

Philippopolis

44

43

42

40

39

45

41

38

37

35

34

32

31

36

25

30

29

28

27

26

24

23

22

21

20

19

18

17

16

15

14

13

12

11

10

9

8

7

6

5

4

3

2

1

33

200 mi

200 km

MAP 1 *The 45 regions of the Greek world.*

Regions (indicated by numbers on the map) are per order in the *Inventory*, based on 907 of 1,035 total city-states with known (or plausibly inferred) locations. Polis numbers are per the *Inventory*. See further appendix I. Known or plausibly hypothesized locations of individual poleis: http://polis.stanford.edu/. Most but not all of the poleis listed in the *Inventory* were in existence in the later fourth century BCE; some had, however, gone out of existence before that time. 128 of 1,035 poleis in the *Inventory* have not been located with enough confidence for mapping. Note that region 1 is off the map to the left—for locations of region 1 poleis, see map 3.

MAP KEY

region number (poleis in the region: *Inventory* numbers), region name

1	(1–4)	Spain & France	
2	(5–51)	Sicily	
3	(52–74)	Italy & Campania	
4	(75–85)	Adriatic	
5	(86–111)	Epirus	
6	(112–141)	Acarnania & Ajacent	
7	(142–156)	Aetolia	
8	(157–168)	West Locris	
9	(169–197)	Phocis	
10	(198–223)	Boeotia	
11	(224–228)	Megaris, Corinthia, Sikyonia	
12	(229–244)	Achaea	
13	(245–265)	Elis	
14	(266–303)	Arcadia	
15	(304–311)	Triphylia	
16	(312–322)	Messenia	
17	(323–346)	Lakedaimon (Laconia)	
18	(347–357)	Argolis	
19	(358–360)	Saronic Gulf	
20	(361–364)	Attica	
21	(365–377)	Euboea	
22	(378–388)	East Locris	
23	(389–392)	Doris	
24	(393–470)	Thessaly & Adjacent	
25	(471–527)	Aegean	
26	(528–544)	Macedonia	
27	(545–626)	Thrace: Axios—Strymon	
28	(627–639)	Thrace: Strymon—Nestos	
29	(640–651)	Thrace: Nestos—Hebros	
30	(652–657)	Thrace: Inland	
31	(658–672)	Thracian Chersonesos	
32	(673–681)	Propontic Thrace	
33	(682–734)	Black Sea	
34	(735–764)	Propontic Asia Minor	
35	(765–793)	Troas	
36	(794–799)	Lesbos	
37	(800–835)	Aiolis & SW Mysia	
38	(836–869)	Ionia	
39	(870–941)	Caria	
40	(942–943)	Lycia	
41	(944–992)	Crete	
42	(993–1000)	Rhodes	
43	(1001–1011)	Pamphylia & Cilicia	
44	(1012–1021)	Cyprus	
45	(1022–1035)	Syria to Pillars of Herakles	

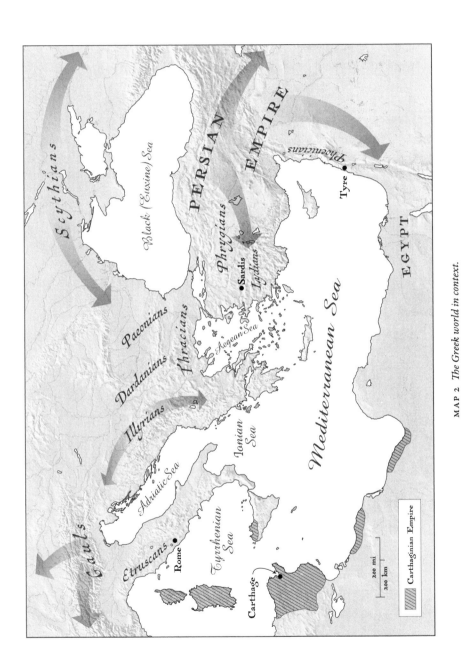

MAP 2   *The Greek world in context.*

THE RISE AND FALL OF CLASSICAL GREECE

1

THE EFFLORESCENCE OF CLASSICAL GREECE

In 1812, Lord Byron published a poem that made him the hero of a world poised at the brink of modernity and ready for romance. It included these poignant lines:

> Fair Greece! sad relic of departed worth!
> Immortal, though no more! though fallen, great![1]

With just fourteen words, Byron illuminated the stark contrast between Greek antiquity and the Greece he had observed during his travels in 1809 and 1810. Byron knew a lot about Greece. As an educated English nobleman, he had read classical literature. As an intrepid traveler, he had personal experience of early nineteenth century Greece. By Byron's day, the Greeks had suffered as subjects of the Ottoman Empire for more than 300 years, and, more recently, from the rapacity of European collectors. But Greece was already a "relic of departed worth" when Pausanias, a travel writer of the Roman imperial age, described Greek antiquities in the second century. Neither Byron nor Pausanias could have guessed that at the dawn of the twentieth century, Greece would be the poorest country in Europe or that in the early twenty-first century, two centuries after Byron wrote his memorable lines, Greece would be sadder yet—wracked by a political and economic crisis that immiserated millions of Greek citizens and threatened the financial stability of Europe.[2]

Byron's vision of greatness was inspired by ancient Greek cultural and intellectual achievement: art and architecture, literature, visual and performance art, scientific and moral thought. A generation later, the British banker-scholar George Grote published his monumental *History of Greece* (12 volumes: 1846–1856), a work that came to define, for the English-speaking world, the greatness of classical Greece in terms of a unique set of values and institutions: democracy, freedom, equality, dignity—conjoined with a dedication to reason, critical inquiry, and innovation.

Despite its brevity and limited frame, Byron's romantic couplet, with its sharp contrast between the fortunes of ancient and modern Greece and its explosion of exclamation points, captures the mystery that this book explains: Why and how did the ancient Greeks create a culture that became central to the modern world? If Hellas had once been great, why was it no longer? Why, once fallen, was Greece so long and well remembered?

Those questions remain vitally important in the twenty-first century, and they can be answered. Hellas—the ancient Greek world that, even before the conquests of Alexander the Great, extended east into western Asia, north to the Black Sea, south to North Africa, and west to Italy, France, and Spain— was great indeed. Hellas was great because of a cultural accomplishment that was supported by sustained economic growth. That growth was made possible by a distinctive approach to politics.

CLASSICAL GREEK EFFLORESCENCE

In a spirited diatribe against the habit of dividing world history into dichotomous eras of premodern economic stagnation and modern growth, the historical sociologist Jack Goldstone has shown that a number of premodern societies experienced more or less extended periods of *efflorescence*—increased economic growth accompanied by a sharp uptick in cultural achievement. Efflorescence is characterized by more people (demographic growth) living at higher levels of welfare (per capita growth) and by cultural production at a higher level. It is not signaled merely by treasure heaped up in palace storerooms or by monumental architecture. Concentrations of state capital and grand building projects may or may not be accompanied by a dramatic rise in population, welfare, and culture.

Efflorescence is impermanent by definition, but some efflorescences are more dramatic and longer lasting than others. Modernity—the experience of the developed world since the early nineteenth century—is the most dramatic, but not (yet) the longest lasting efflorescence in human history. It remains an open question whether the historically exceptional rate of sustained economic growth that some parts of the world have experienced in the past two centuries is merely the most recent and biggest (by many orders of magnitude) of a long series of efflorescences—or whether "this time it's different," so that modernity represents a fundamental and permanent change of the direction of human history. Goldstone focuses on examples of efflorescence

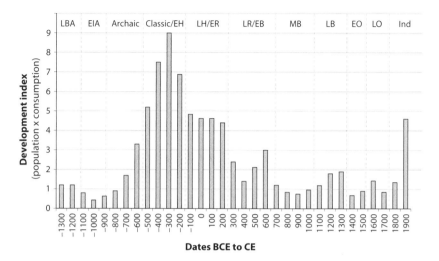

FIGURE 1.1 *Development index, core Greece, 1300 BCE–1900 CE.*

NOTES: The development index multiplies a population estimate (in millions) × median per capita consumption estimate (in multiples of bare subsistence). Population and consumption estimates are discussed in chapters 2 and 4, and broken out in figure 4.3. Core Greece = The territory controlled by the Greek state in 1881–1912 (*Inventory* regions 6–25: see map 1). LBA = Late Bronze Age. EIA = Early Iron Age. EH = Early Hellenistic. LH = Late Hellenistic. ER = Early Roman. LR = Late Roman. EB = Early Byzantine. MB = Middle Byzantine. EO = Early Ottoman. LO = Late Ottoman. Ind = Independent Greek state.

after 1400 CE, but he notes in passing that classical Greece was among a handful of societies that experienced efflorescence long before that date.[3]

The Greek efflorescence that peaked by around 300 BCE lasted several hundred years, from the Archaic, through the Classical, and into the Hellenistic eras of Greek history. Figure 1.1, based on evidence presented in chapter 4, illustrates efflorescence in terms of economic development (measured by population and consumption) in "core Greece" from the Late Bronze Age to the dawn of the twentieth century. Because, by my definition, core Greece is limited to the territory controlled by the Greek state in the late nineteenth century CE, the graph *understates* the total population of the wider Greek world at the peak of the classical efflorescence by a factor of about three—so the chart captures only part of the rise. But the main implication is clear enough: it was not until the twentieth century that the number of people living in the Greek core, and their material welfare, returned to levels comparable to those achieved some 2,300 years before.[4]

The ancient Greek efflorescence was exceptional in premodern world history. While ancient Greek economic growth fell far short of the growth rates

3

experienced by the globe's most highly developed countries since the nine-teenth century, the ancient Greek efflorescence was distinctive for its dura-tion, its intensity, and its long-term impact on world culture. The Greek ef-florescence took place in a social ecology of hundreds of city-states. "Greeks," for our purposes, are the residents of communities that were, in antiquity, substantially (not homogeneously) Greek in terms of language and a distinc-tive suite of cultural features.[5] While wealth and incomes remained unequal in those communities, a substantial part of the Greek population experi-enced relative prosperity. The growth of the Greek economy was driven, at least in part, by the ability of an extensive middle class to consume goods and services at a level well above mere existence.[6]

Ancient Greek society was unlike our modernity in important ways: Among other things, slavery was taken for granted and women never held political participation rights. Yet the most developed states of classical Hellas in some respects tracked conditions typical of developed modern states as late as the mid-nineteenth century. Residents of the most developed ancient Greek states experienced aspects of a precocious "modernity before the fact." As Byron's lines remind us, the classical efflorescence was not sustained indefinitely. Yet, by the same token, it was never forgotten.[7]

We can answer questions about Greece that remained mysterious for Byron because we have better data. We now know *much* more about ancient Hellas than he could have known. Happily for the contemporary investigator seek-ing to explain the changing fortunes of Hellas, a great deal of primary evi-dence for Greek history has come down to us from antiquity—it survived the fall for reasons we will explore in chapter 11. Moreover, from the age of Byron onward, classical Greece was such a hot field of inquiry that many of the Western world's most brilliant intellects devoted their lives to investigat-ing its every facet. After generations of exploration and reconstruction by historians and archaeologists, there is now an unrivaled historical record for the Greek world in the first millennium BCE.

Equally important, that massive and detailed record has been organized by encyclopedic projects and thereby made available for systematic analysis. The most important of these, for our purposes, is the monumental *Inventory of Archaic and Classical Greek Poleis* (hereafter "the *Inventory*"), compiled by an international team under the direction of the preeminent Danish his-torian of the Greek world, Mogens H. Hansen.[8] The *Inventory* collects de-tailed information for 1,035 Greek states known to have existed in the ex-tended Greek world, across 45 regions, during the 500-year period from the eighth through the later fourth century BCE. Each state has a separate entry and a corresponding inventory (i) number. These numbers (e.g., Athens =

i361) help us to be clear about which Greek states are being discussed in the pages that follow (some Greek names are shared by more than one state, others are Anglicized in various ways). The 45 *Inventory* regions are illustrated in map 1.

Meanwhile, the archaeological and some relevant documentary evidence for the long history of the Greek world, from the Bronze Age to modernity, has been recently summarized and reassessed in a magisterial volume by John Bintliff of the University of Leiden. Bintliff's detailed survey, which includes analyses of demographic change over time, enables us to assess the data for archaic and classical Greece against a much broader chronological context.[9]

The mass of quantifiable evidence assembled in the *Inventory*, and in other recent collections of data on Greek history, archaeology, and geography, has made it possible to employ the sharp analytical tools of contemporary social science when we seek to explain Greek history. By quantifying evidence, we can estimate the total population of the classical Greek world and of each of its regions. We can study comparative state and regional development across the Greek world, and we can compare the Greek world to other premodern societies. All of this comparison allows us to test competing explanations for the rise to greatness of Hellas, for its fall, and for its enduring influence. The data on which my statistics are based are publicly available at http://polis .stanford.edu.[10]

The twenty-first century has seen a renaissance in the study of ancient Greek and Roman economic history. Following a generation of scholarship grounded on the premise that a unitary "ancient economy," lasting for millennia, was defined by a deep social structure inherently resistant to change, economic historians are now attempting to measure and to explain economic growth and decline in specific times and places within the premodern world. Much recent scholarship on Greek and Roman economies is predicated on the "new institutional economics" pioneered by the Nobel Prize–winning economist and political scientist, Douglass North and exemplified by recent work by the MIT and Harvard social scientists Daron Acemoglu and James Robinson. Their insistence that institutions (the "rules of the game") and organizations (including, but not only, states), along with markets and networks, are fundamental determinants of economic change, grounds the arguments of this book. Scholars working in the institutional economics field seek, first, to develop a plausible theory of how specific institutions in a given society affected social choices, and then to test the theory against competitor theories by reference to a substantial body of evidence. At its best, institutional economics offers bold, new, and defensible explanations for important developments in historical and contemporary societies.[11]

Along with a theory of social choice under conditions of decentralized authority, and data for testing the theory, this book presents a new narrative history of Greek political and economic development. It does not pretend to offer a comprehensive account of every major event of ancient Greek history. I focus more on formal institutions and civic order than on the politically salient informal cultural performances that have been wonderfully elucidated by Sara Forsdyke, a classical Greek historian at the University of Michigan.[12] I will have little to say about the Greek family, religion, gender, sexuality, ethnicity, childhood, aging, sport, or other important areas of social history. Other books, by scholars more knowledgeable than I, cover each of these areas well. Nor do I describe in detail the cultural accomplishments that so impressed Byron. While cultural accomplishment is an important part of the efflorescence I seek to explain, this terrain has been brilliantly elucidated by others. I assume that it is uncontroversial to say that in the areas of visual art, architecture, drama, historiography, philosophy (ethics, politics, epistemology, metaphysics, logic), and natural science (geometry, geography, astronomy, medicine), classical Greece provided enduringly important resources for world culture. Finally, although promising recent collaborations between historians and geneticists have demonstrated that, as a result of colonization and mobility, ancient Greeks had a profound and enduring impact on the genetic makeup of populations in the western, as well as eastern Mediterranean, I will not seek to address the genetic legacy of Hellas.[13]

My goal is to *measure* the classical Greek efflorescence and to *explain* how political institutions and culture enabled the Greek world to rise to greatness from humble beginnings, how the great states of Greece fell to a predatory empire, and how Greek culture was subsequently preserved for posterity.

SMALL STATES, DISPERSED AUTHORITY

After two centuries of intensive scholarly research and with the aid of the *Inventory,* we can now grasp, much more clearly than Byron or his contemporaries could have, the extent and development of ancient Hellas. First and foremost, it was a world defined by a startlingly large number of surprisingly small states—there were about 1,100 Greek states by the end of the third quarter of the fourth century BCE—when Aristotle was writing his masterpiece on *Politics* and his student, Alexander the Great, was completing the conquest of western Asia. The extended Greek world of city-states stretched from outposts in Spain and France, through southern Italy and Sicily, to the Greek peninsula; east and north to Thrace (modern Bulgaria), to the shores of the Black Sea and western Anatolia; then south to eastern and southern outposts in Syria and North Africa (map 1). By Alexander's day, the total population of Hellas—that is, the residents of small states that were substantially Greek in language and culture—was in excess of 8 million people.[14]

Individual Greek states varied tremendously in their size and influence. Athens, Sparta (i345), and Syracuse (i47), which provide focal points for developing the ideas in this book, were among the largest and most influential states in Hellas. Athens boasted a territory of some 2,500 km²—about the size of Luxembourg or Orange County in southern California—and a population of perhaps a quarter-million people. A more typical Greek polis, Athens' northwestern neighbor, Plataea (i216), had a territory of ca. 170 km², with a population below 10,000. And a great many Greek states were considerably smaller than that. At the lower end of the range, Koresia (i493), the smallest of four poleis on the modest-sized (129 km²) island of Kea, possessed a territory of roughly 15 km²—about one-fifth the area of the island of Manhattan or one-seventh the area of Paris. Yet in important ways, the Greek states were *peer polities*, interacting with one another diplomatically, militarily, and economically as equals in their standing as states, if not in power, wealth, or influence.[15]

These small Greek states were *city-states*—in ancient Greek, *poleis* (singular *polis*). By Aristotle's day, a polis was characterized by a well-defined urban center, typically walled, in which lived perhaps half of the polis' population. The urban center was surrounded by a rural hinterland. The hinterland of larger poleis featured small towns, as well as villages, and farmsteads. Near the borders were pastureland and tracts of near wilderness. Boundaries between the many states of Hellas were quite clearly defined, although not always respected by neighboring states: Disputing borders was a major source of conflict between poleis, and wars among the Greek states were frequent. As a result of warfare, and of diplomatic negotiations carried out in the shadow of war, some poleis went out of existence altogether. Close to 100 Greek states, about one in ten of the known poleis, are known to have disappeared, through extermination or assimilation, by the time of the death of Alexander the Great in 323 BCE. Many other poleis were less than fully independent in terms of their authority to determine their own foreign policy. But, by definition, each polis had considerable local authority to set and to enforce the rules by which its residents lived.[16]

There have been dozens of small-state, "dispersed-authority" cultures in world history—prominently including ancient Renaissance northern Italy and the Hanseatic League of late medieval/early modern northwestern Europe. Other city-state cultures are documented in Europe, Asia, Africa, and the New World. When juxtaposed to "centralized authority" cultures—most obviously in the form of empires (imperial Rome, Han China), and nation-states (Europe after 1500)—that have tended to dominate the political history of the premodern world, these small-state cultures are sometimes disproportionately influential in terms of their long-term impact on world history. Examples of small-state cultures that "punched over their weight" include, in addition to the two examples above, the city-states of early Mesopotamia, which pioneered many of the basic elements of urban civilization, the commercial city-states of Phoenicia, and the Etruscans of northwestern Italy (see map 2).

Small-state, dispersed-authority systems can be compared to a natural ecology, characterized by a rich variety of plant and animal species, none of which is dominant. Large, highly centralized states more closely resemble the ecology of a modern large-scale factory farm, which efficiently produces great quantities of a single crop by eliminating diversity. Hellas was a strikingly extensive and long-lived small-state, dispersed authority culture—and it was by far the largest and the longest lived city-state culture in documented world history.

Among the central questions raised by ancient Greek history is how and why such an extensive small-state system persisted, in such a flourishing condition, for such a long time. In an inversion of, for example, European history from 1500 to 1900 or Chinese history from ca. 700 to 200 BCE, there were many *more* independent states in the Greek ecology by the height of the classical efflorescence than there had been several hundred years previously. Despite repeated attempts, no classical-era Greek city-state succeeded in creating a centralized empire (chapter 8). Why, during the era of efflorescence, did the many states of Hellas not consolidate into a unitary empire, on the model of Persia, Carthage, or Rome? Or, failing that, into several large competitor states, on the model of ancient Phoenicia, or Warring States China, or Europe ca. 1500–1900?[17]

All workable social systems are predicated on creating reliable forms of cooperation among an extensive population and then distributing the fruits of that cooperation across the population in ways that prevent the outbreak of catastrophic levels of violence. Centralized authority systems work according to the simple and powerful logic of command-and-control: Cooperation is achieved through obedience to a central coercive authority. With a unified authority structure capable of enforcing cooperation, and a distribution plan designed to ensure that those who are capable of destabilizing society through violence have no incentive to do so, conflict is effectively reduced.[18]

The basic logic of centralized authority has long been appreciated; Thomas Hobbes, in his great mid-seventeenth century work of political theory, *Leviathan* (1996), remains among the most astute and influential of its expositors. Hobbes famously argued that the choice faced by all societies is between a centralized authority system and the anarchy of "war of all against all"—a condition in which human life is inevitably, "poor, solitary, nasty, brutish, and short." Although modern social scientists usually do not see the history of human development in such stark terms, the tendency to associate economic and cultural development with the emergence and persistence of highly centralized bureaucratic states remains pervasive, not least in discussions of premodern state formation.[19]

In a centralized system, people know just where they stand (or kneel) in a hierarchical social order, and that order determines who *does* what in the production of goods, and who *gets* what in the distribution of goods, services, and privilege. The system is centered on a ruler (or a small group of rulers), typically, in the premodern world, a monarch to whom divine or quasi-divine powers are attributed. Authority devolves from the godlike ruler through a pyramidal chain of authority. The residents of the state are the subjects of the ruler. Wealth and power are concentrated at and distributed from the center. Social privileges and access to important institutions (e.g., law, property rights) are determined by social proximity to the ruler. The pyramidal organizational structure allows commands to be passed down from the apex of the hierarchical system to its base, and thus, ideally at least, everyone knows exactly what is expected of him or her and what he or she can expect to get in return. As long as those expectations are met, and no one who could disturb the order of society has reason to do so, the system is stable.

The great majority of the ruler's subjects are situated at the base of the pyramid; they provide the productive labor that sustains the system. They take orders and pass most of the surplus to those above them, in the form of rents or taxes. With most of his or her surplus appropriated, the median individual thus lives quite close to the level of bare subsistence. Because wealth is concentrated at the center and at the top, and because conflict is suppressed, a well-organized centralized state can sustain both a bureaucracy and military forces—thereby allowing the ruler to manage the state, pay off his or her coalition, and make war against rivals. An especially large and successful centrally organized state eventually subordinates its local rivals and thereby becomes an empire.[20]

How premodern small-state systems function is less well understood. How can a system in which authority is dispersed create adequate opportunities for cooperation at scale, redistribute the fruits of cooperation in ways that promote stability, and thereby accumulate resources sufficient to preserve itself over time? Why do small-state systems not quickly collapse into Hobbes' "war of all against all"? The puzzle of how dispersed-authority systems are sustained is exacerbated when the stakes are high: How could a small-state system like Greece survive, much less flourish, when it was endemically threatened by a large, well-managed, and predatory empire like Achaemenid Persia?

In small-state systems authority is decentralized. There is no overarching hierarchy, no central point at which wealth and influence can readily be concentrated. As a result, as Hobbes confidently predicted, conflict remains endemic within the system. The many wars between the small states of ancient Greece are typical of other dispersed-authority ecologies, for example in early Mesopotamia, Warring States era China, or Renaissance Italy. Nor is the answer to the question of how small-state systems manage to flourish necessarily to be found in local centralization. Individual states within a small-state system may be ruled by kings and their elite coalitions. But a number of small-state systems included states with republican, citizen-centered, forms of government.[21]

In the most influential states of Hellas, authority was widely distributed, not only at the level of the multistate ecology but also at the level of the individual state. In the typical Greek polis, the adult male native residents were citizens, rather than subjects. In a Greek *democracy*, a form of government that became increasingly prevalent in Hellas after the late sixth century BCE, free and politically equal citizens collectively governed themselves. While political authority was concentrated in state institutions, power was dispersed *among* institutions; many citizens held offices and participated actively in both legislation and adjudication. Once again, in an inversion of the experience of state-building in early modern Europe, where, by the seventeenth century, centralized royal authority had succeeded in weakening the power of deliberative institutions, individual Greek states and the ecology of states became *more* democratic during the era of classical efflorescence.[22]

Some of the most influential and most democratic of the individual Greek states diverged markedly from the model of social order that political scientists Douglass North, John Wallis, and Barry Weingast call the "natural state"—and which they argue has been the basic form of centralized state-level social order throughout most of recorded human history. The natural state is ultimately based on domination and governed by a leader and the members of his or her elite coalition. Leader and elites cooperate to create and sustain, in their own interest, a system of production, distribution, and conflict suppression.

Natural states are not democratic; they seek to restrict access to institutions; they tend not to extend rights to secure possession of property or other privileges beyond the small and tightly patrolled ambit of the ruling coalition. But, so long as it distributes the fruits of cooperation to the right people (i.e., those with potential for violence) in the right proportion (the greater the potential for violence, the bigger the share), the natural state can be very stable. The unitary empire is one historically important kind of natural state, but the natural state, as a basic form of social order, can be scaled up or down.

While economically inefficient, when compared to modern open-access orders, the emergence of ever-larger limited-access states with ever more highly centralized authority, has, historically, been associated with political and economic development. In the light of the stubborn refusal of the Greek small-state ecology to coalesce into either an empire or a few large states ruled by strong leaders and narrow elite coalitions, the greatness of ancient Hellas becomes more mysterious. It also becomes more interesting to those who prefer democracy, freedom, and dignity—even in the incomplete form in which they were manifest in ancient Greece—to the kinds of domination typical of most premodern states.

Ancient Greek history points to a possible alternative to the dominant narrative of political and economic development, based primarily on the history of early modern Europe, as "*first* (and necessarily) the big, centralized, and autocratic state, and only *then* (sometimes) democracy and wealth."[23]

SPECIALIZATION, INNOVATION, CREATIVE DESTRUCTION

One of the keys to unlocking the puzzling success of the polis ecology is economic specialization and exchange. In the Greek world, as in other times and places through history, specialization was based on developing and exploiting a local advantage, relative to other producers, in the production of some valued good or service. Assuming that costs of transactions are low enough to make exchanges mutually beneficial, specialized goods (e.g., olive oil, fine pottery) and services (of, e.g., mercenary soldiers, poets) are distributed through networks of exchange so that the products of specialized endeavor become available across a large ecology of diverse local specialists.

The powerful role that specialization and cooperative (mutually beneficial) market exchange can play in promoting economic growth was recognized and described in the later eighteenth century by Adam Smith in the *Wealth of Nations* (1981 [1776]). Greek specialization was often more horizontal (workshops and individual craftspeople specializing in the production of specific goods) than vertical (factories employing specialist labor at each phase of a production process). And ancient Greek writers never produced a work of economic analysis to rival Smith's hugely influential book.

Yet it is now very clear that specialization and exchange flourished at different levels in Hellas and, moreover, that the core principles of relative advantage and rational cooperation were understood by the ancient Greeks.[24]

Individual Greek states developed specialties based on natural resource
endowments relative to other poleis—for example, the fine white marble at
the Aegean island-state of Paros (1509), or favorable wheat-growing conditions in the cities of southern Italy and Sicily (chapter 6). Other poleis developed advantages by perfecting industrial processes—e.g., manufacture of
painted vases and warships in Athens (chapters 7 and 8). Competition and
conflict among poleis served to sharpen the recognition of the necessity of
exploiting relative advantages, whereas a recognition of the value of lowering
transaction costs pushed in the direction of opening access and interstate
cooperation. Meanwhile, within poleis, individuals specialized in a wide range
of endeavors. Within a given specialization, individuals competed with one
another ("potter vies against potter," as the poet Hesiod remarked in his
Works and Days, line 25), once again sharpening the recognition of the value
of relative advantage and leading to the deepening and multiplication of
subspecializations.

The upshot of the cycle of competition, specialization, and cooperation in
creating conditions for mutually beneficial exchange was a high premium on
innovation and entrepreneurship. Innovation—the process whereby novel
solutions were developed to meet new requirements or existing needs—in
turn drove a dynamic that the Austrian-American economist and political
scientist Joseph Schumpeter famously described as "creative destruction":
Advances in artistic and productive technique drove out earlier techniques;
new institutions marginalized traditional forms of social organization; poleis that exploited relative advantages absorbed their less innovative rivals,
while new poleis were continuously being created on the ever-expanding
frontiers of Hellas.[25]

The products of local specialization were readily distributed, within poleis,
across the extensive small-state ecology, and then beyond the Greek world,
through increasingly dense networks of exchange and interaction. Local markets grew into regional markets, and some poleis succeeded in creating major
interstate emporia where goods from across the Mediterranean and Black Sea
worlds could be bought and sold. Experts in various arts and crafts migrated
to new homes and established new centers of specialized production. Meanwhile, the costs of transactions were driven down by continuous institutional
innovations, notably by the development and rapid spread of silver coinage as
a reliable exchange medium, the dissemination of common standards for
weights and measures, market regulations and officials to enforce them, and

increasingly sophisticated systems of law and legal mechanisms for dispute resolution. Competition and conflict between poleis and between the Greeks and their non-Greek neighbors temporarily disrupted local networks of exchange. But those disruptions only served to motivate poleis and individuals to seek out new markets for their goods and services, to deepen and broaden their exchange networks, and to develop cooperative solutions whereby conflict could be reduced or at least rendered less disruptive.

Specialization in production of goods and exchange of the goods and services produced by specialists are common features of complex societies. If we are to explain the efflorescence of Hellas, we need to answer the question of why and how, in the Greek world, specialization and exchange achieved such high levels, and how they become so strongly intertwined with continuous innovation and creative destruction—thereby driving a sustained level of economic growth that proved high enough to overcome the costs of conflict among many small states.

Geography and climate are certainly one part of the answer. Specialization and exchange in the Greek world were encouraged by distinctive geographic and climatic features of the Mediterranean basin, a region characterized by a great variety of microclimates, diverse soil conditions, and unevenly distributed concentrations of natural resources. Moreover, the geophysical conditions that were common to the states of Hellas disfavored large-scale standardization directed from a distant imperial center. Agriculture in Hellas was primarily based on sparse but adequate rainfall in relatively small valleys and terraced hillsides, rather than large-scale irrigation in extensive plains. Unlike Mesopotamia, Egypt, or China, for example, Hellas had no great river systems that could be cooperatively managed by a centralized bureaucracy so as to create the conditions favorable to maximizing the production of a few staple crops. The geographic and climatic conditions typical of Hellas were conjoined with a highly variegated coastline and a seascape featuring many islands, which facilitated overseas trade and lowered the costs of transport. Nearby empires (Persia) and less developed societies (Thrace, Scythia) provided ready markets for the goods and services produced by Greek specialists; those societies in turn produced goods (notably food and slaves) imported by the Greeks.[26]

These exogenous factors, important as they were, ultimately fail to explain how specialization, innovation, and creative destruction drove the classical Greek efflorescence. That failure is manifest simply by comparing classical Hellas to earlier and later eras in Greek history. The Greek world remained geophysically similar over the millennia, and Hellas has always had more and less developed neighbors. And yet, as Byron believed and modern scholarship confirms, the classical-era efflorescence of the first millennium BCE was unique: Neither before nor after the first millennium BCE did Greece experience a world-class efflorescence. The geophysical and climatological conditions of the Mediterranean world obviously *permitted* high levels of economic growth and the distinctive forms of cultural flourishing that characterized classical Greece. But if those factors were primary drivers of Greek greatness, we would expect greatness to recur over time.

Natural conditions favoring specialization and exchange were reinforced by favorable cultural conditions: As the Greek polis system expanded in the eighth century BCE and thereafter, a common language and other commonly shared cultural attributes (religion, diet, marriage practices) lowered the cultural barriers to efficient exchange and thereby lowered transaction costs. But the dynamic expansion of the Greek world is one of the remarkable features of the Greek efflorescence that we are seeking to explain. Although there was no doubt a degree of productive feedback in the system, an expanding common culture cannot at once be an adequate cause *and* a primary effect of Hellenic greatness.[27]

KNOWLEDGE, INSTITUTIONS, CULTURE

In order to understand the relationship between specialization, innovation, creative destruction, and the classical Greek efflorescence, we will need to step back from Adam Smith's early industrial-era conception of the relationship between specialization and economic growth to consider the roles played by individual exchanges of information and by the aggregation of diverse forms of useful knowledge. Smith's prime example of vertical specialization was a pin factory. Smith vividly illustrated the advantages to be reaped from specialization by comparing the output of an efficient factory, in which workers specialize in different parts of the production process, to the output of pins that could be expected from that same number of workers if each were making pins on his or her own, from scratch. Knowledge is certainly part of Smith's story: Someone with the relevant knowledge of how pins are made needs to set up the factory. But diverse forms of local knowledge that might be possessed by and exchanged among the workers is irrelevant—each needs to be properly trained in his or her specialized job; the rest of what he or she happens to know is not a positive factor in the performance of the factory—and indeed it may be thought of as a liability.

The idea that specialization implies that the information and knowledge component of production ought to be separated from its manual part was deeply embedded in industrial-era thinking: Henry Ford, who famously employed Smith's core insight to create a sophisticated industrial production system for automobiles, is said to have bemoaned the fact that when he hired a pair of hands, they came with a head attached. The conjunction of specialization of production and centralization of the management of knowledge for rational planning was one of the hallmarks of the industrial era of the nineteenth and twentieth centuries. This conjunction might help us to understand how highly centralized societies function, but it does not explain the powerful role of specialization, innovation, and creative destruction in the decentralized world of ancient Greece.[28]

To explain the world of the Greek poleis, we need to move forward in time, beyond the industrial era into the contemporary world of self-consciously knowledge-based enterprises. It is now widely understood that exchanging and aggregating diverse and dispersed forms of knowledge is a key factor to the success of contemporary purposeful organizations—whether for-profit business firms (professional service and software firms are canonical examples) or not-for-profit organizations of various kinds (e.g., modern research universities).

The challenge of the knowledge-based enterprise is not detaching hands from heads à la Ford but rather providing conditions in which the different forms of useful knowledge embedded in many minds will be voluntarily disclosed and effectively organized so as to address the problems that must be solved in order for the organization to further its purposes. This system typically requires creating conditions of mutual trust and a sense of shared purpose. Those conditions are in turn facilitated by the development of the relevant forms of common knowledge—that is, the situation in which person A knows something, and B knows that A knows it, and A knows that B knows that A knows it . . . and so on. Under conditions of common knowledge, people are better able to align their efforts. Under conditions of effective aggregation of diverse types of knowledge, the group may effectively be wiser than any of its individual members, and important innovations may be the product of group effort rather than individual genius.[29]

When common knowledge and dispersed and diverse knowledge are brought together under the right conditions, and when the results are codified, the effect is to increase over time the total stock of useful knowledge. By "the right conditions," I mean conditions of shared interests and purposes, rational trust, and fair competition (level playing field, equitable rewards), such that people voluntarily choose to share what they know with others in their organization in a timely and appropriate manner, thereby allowing for their knowledge to be applied to complex problems—that is, to problems that demand for their solution many different kinds of knowledge.

Moreover, under the right conditions, individuals voluntarily choose to deepen their own special knowledge and sharpen their skills: In other words, they invest in the development of their own relative advantages and turn those relative advantages to cooperative, prosocial ends. This process of building human capital and social capital is manifest in the operations of modern science and engineering and is therefore at least indirectly responsible for, inter alia, the dynamic growth of modern economies. As the managers of modern organizations have found, however, getting the conditions right is not easy. In the Greek world, the right conditions were achieved and sustained by innovative political institutions and a robust civic culture.[30]

The greatness of the Greek world that inspired Byron and so many other Hellenophiles before and since was driven by a set of political institutions and a civic culture that are historically rare—indeed, at the time of their emergence in Hellas, those institutions and that culture were probably unique. The political institutions found in many citizen-centered Greek states, but especially in democratic states and most especially in democratic Athens, put specialization and innovation on overdrive because those institutions and that culture encouraged individuals to take more rational risks and to develop more distinctive skills. They did so by protecting individuals against the theft by the powerful of the fruits of risk-taking and self-investment.

Today we typically think of such protections as "rights." The Greeks did not have a fully modern conception of *universal human rights*. But they did develop a strong tradition of *civic rights*—immunities against arbitrary action by powerful individuals or government agents. These immunities guaranteed for each citizen the security of his or her body against assault, the security of his or her dignity against humiliation, and the security of his or her property against confiscation. It is important to remember that many residents of a polis were not citizens and so were not full participants in the regime of immunity and security. And yet, in some of the most highly developed poleis, these immunities were extended to at least some noncitizens.

Citizens, who themselves collectively held the authority to make new institutional rules, in turn were more likely to trust the rules under which they lived to be basically fair. Judgments, by citizens who were empowered (by vote or lottery) to settle disputes and to distribute public goods, were made on the basis of established and impartial rules, rather than on the basis of patronage or personal favoritism. With these guarantees in place, and because successful innovation was well rewarded, individuals had strong incentives to invest in their own special talents, to defer short-term payoffs, and to accept a certain level of risk in anticipation of long-term rewards. The end result of those rational choices, made by individuals in many walks of life in the common context of clear rules and a level playing field, was a historically unusual level of sustained economic growth and an equally unusual rate of sustained cultural productivity and innovation.[31]

Attention to the political foundation upon which the growth of human and social capital was predicated helps to solve an apparent paradox: In classical Hellas the benefits of specialization were reaped in such abundance because specialization did not go "all the way down" in the ways that are typical of centralized authority systems. Much of the work of governance in a democratic polis was done by *amateurs*—by citizen-farmers and citizen-shoemakers, and citizen-soldiers who chose to dedicate themselves, part-time, to the tasks of rule-making, judgment, and administration. The costs associated with amateurs spending part of their productive energies on the business of governance (loss of productivity in the nongovernment sector, steep learning curves) were more than made up for by the benefits that arose from the assurance that the incentives of decision-making bodies were aligned with those of the citizen population.[32] Further benefits accrued from exchanging and aggregating diverse local knowledge resources and from a rising stock of social and human capital, as citizens came to trust in one another and in a political system that they collectively created and collectively managed.[33]

The logic of centralized authority places specialization at the heart of the system of social order: The rulers are specialists in ruling, and no one who is not a specialist in ruling has a legitimate role to play in governing the state. Rulers are supported by a military class of violence specialists, who monopolize the use of force and support the rulers in exchange for a share of the rents extracted from the rest of society. This situation of specialist-rulers was certainly conceivable to the Greeks. Indeed, "each does his own specialized job and strictly avoids interfering in the specializations of others" is the primary principle of justice in the most famous work of Greek political philosophy, Plato's *Republic*. In Plato's ideal state, that principle leads inevitably to the absolutist rule of philosopher-kings, who are described as perfectly and uniquely competent expert rulers. The philosopher-kings are supported by the auxiliary guardians, specialists in violence who enjoy a monopoly on the legitimate use of force, both internally against rule-breaking locals and for purposes of external warfare.

In practice, however, the Greek poleis rejected this kind of hyperspecialization at the level of governance and violence. In most Greek states, it was the citizens who were the warriors: either infantrymen or rowers in warships. Violence was a specialization, but not of a small military elite. Meanwhile, the embrace of collective self-governance by amateurs and the rejection of governance by experts alone played a fundamental role in making the Greek efflorescence so extraordinary, so durable, and so memorable. This embrace of amateurism did not mean that expert knowledge was excluded from the processes of decision and judgment in the making of public policy. But it did mean that no individual or small group could legitimately monopolize authority to govern the state. As we will see, when the right institutional and cultural conditions had been achieved, the many actually did prove to be adequately wise.[34]

The historically distinctive Greek approach to citizenship and political order, and its role in driving specialization and continuous innovation through the establishment of civic rights, alignment of interests of a large class of people who ruled and were ruled over in turn, and the free exchange of information, was the key differentiator that made the Greek efflorescence distinctive in premodern history. The emergence of a new approach to politics is what propelled Hellas to the heights of accomplishment celebrated by Byron. By the same token, however, the dynamic combination of political institutions, innovation, specialization, and low-cost distribution of goods and services across an expanding exchange network helps to explain how an authoritarian ruler was able to terminate the era in which major city-states set the course of Mediterranean history.

FALL AND PERSISTENCE

The dynamic process of creative destruction, driven by specialization and knowledge-based innovation, was central in the rise of the Greek world. It was also a key factor in the defeat of a coalition of independent poleis of mainland Greece by imperial Macedon in the later fourth century and in the subsequent conquest of the whole of the Greek world by imperial Rome in the second century BCE. The fall of most of the great Greek city-states from their dominant position in Mediterranean affairs was precipitated, at least in part, by the successful adaptation of Greek innovations by some of the Greeks' neighbors.

Among the most notable products of Greek specialization in the fourth century BCE were new forms of expertise, notably in warfare and in state finance. While developed within a civic context, to further the purposes of Greek city-states as civic communities, military and financial expertise proved to be readily exportable. Relevant forms of expertise migrated across the borders between poleis—but also outside the classical world of the poleis, to emerging states at the frontiers of the Greek world. In the fourth century BCE, certain of these states self-consciously adopted products of Greek culture and adapted them to the expansionist needs of centralized authority systems. By the middle decades of the fourth century BCE, the kingdom of Macedon had proved the most successful of these "opportunist" states.[35]

In the Macedon of King Philip II (who reigned 359–336 BCE) and his son Alexander III ("the Great": 336–323 BCE), Greek expertise in finance and warfare were conjoined with ethnonationalism, rich natural resource endowments, and a level of military and organizational skill that may legitimately be described as genius. The result was the emergence of state military capacity that was unequaled in the prior history of the Mediterranean or west Asian worlds: In the course of a single human generation, Macedon conquered not only the poleis of mainland Greece, but also the vast Persian Empire. Rome later proved spectacularly adept at borrowing expertise and technology from its various neighbors, including the Greeks, and putting those elements together into a highly effective military and administrative system. That system eventually allowed the Romans to govern an empire of some 75 million people that encompassed much of Europe, the Middle East, and North Africa.

If full independence of most major Greek states was ended by the Macedonian and Roman conquests, the classical economic and cultural efflorescence continued into the postclassical era as a result of an equilibrium struck between ambitious Hellenistic monarchs and the city-states within their kingdoms. After Alexander's death, the sprawling Macedonian empire was carved up by Alexander's most competent lieutenants. They quickly found in the polis system the economic and social underpinnings for their own newly created kingdoms. In the administrative systems perfected in the most advanced poleis, they found some of the tools that allowed them to manage their kingdoms.

The early Hellenistic kings often acted as predatory warlords, but the fortified, federalized, and democratic Greek poleis proved to be hard targets. The kings were constrained to allow considerable independence to the city-states and to tax them at moderate rates. Democracy became more prevalent than ever in the Greek world; public building boomed; science and culture were codified and advanced. The perpetuation of efflorescence in the Hellenistic era, long past the moment of political fall, made possible the "immortality" of Greek culture.[36] The material conditions of non-elite Greeks and the population of core Greece declined after the consolidation of the Roman imperial order and fell precipitously after the collapse of the Roman Empire. But by then Greek culture had been codified and was so widely dispersed that much of it survived—enough for Byron to admire and for us to explain what made it possible.

2

ANTS AROUND A POND

AN ECOLOGY OF CITY-STATES

In Plato's dialogue, *Phaedo* (109b), Socrates describes the corner of the Earth that was in his day occupied by his fellow Greeks. He employs what initially appears to be a peculiar analogy: "The Earth is very large and we . . . live in a small part of it about the sea, *like ants or frogs around a pond.*" Although Plato himself knew little about the lives of ants, new research on ant behavior by evolutionary biologists suggests that his seemingly far-fetched simile was in some ways startlingly apt: Greek society developed, through the historical mechanisms of cultural-institutional innovation, certain features that mimic social behavior developed through evolutionary adaptation by ants. Just as self-conscious biomimicry has, in modernity, inspired technological break-throughs (e.g., Velcro fasteners and drag-reducing "shark skin" swim suits), so too focusing on the unconscious biomimicry by the Greeks of certain behavioral patterns typical of social insects may help us to understand the under-pinnings of the classical Greek efflorescence.

In this chapter, we establish some basic facts about the social ecology of the Greek city-state world—its extent, topography, and climate; its demography; and the ways in which the states of Hellas resembled and differed from one another. Our survey of the city-state world poses a basic question: How do certain human societies manage to cooperate at scale and over time without resort to centralized systems of authority? As we will see in chapter 3, Plato's student Aristotle answered that question for us by pursuing Plato's analogy of Greeks to social insects.

POPULATION AND DISTRIBUTION

If the conclusions reached in chapter 4 are on the right track, the total Greek population in about 1000 BCE, during the Early Iron Age nadir, was about

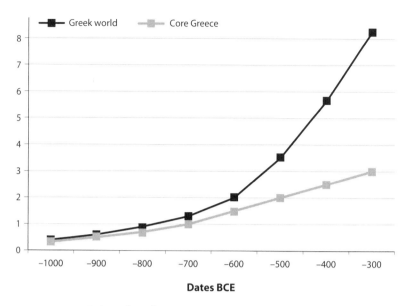

FIGURE 2.1 *Estimated populations, core Greece and the Greek world, 1000–300 BCE.*

NOTES: The data points at the far left (1000 BCE) and far right (300 BCE) of the chart are based on evidence discussed in chapters 2, 4, and 6. Points in between (900–400 BCE) are interpolated. Core Greece = the territory controlled by the Greek state in 1881–1912 (mainland from Thessaly south, Ionian islands, Cycladic islands). Core Greece figures after 800 BCE are reduced at least marginally by migration to other parts of the Greek (and non-Greek) world. Greek world figures include Hellenized populations, per discussion in chapter 4.

Morris 2004 models Greek population growth from 900 to 300 BCE across a region larger than "core Greece" but smaller than "Greek world" and assumes less dense population for some regions. These assumptions result in a population growth curve that lies between the two curves illustrated here.

330,000 people. At the height of the classical efflorescence in the later fourth century BCE, the population of "core Greece" (mainland south of Macedonia, Cycladic and Ionian islands) had risen to about 3 million. The total population of polis-dwelling Greek-speakers in the extended Greek world was in the neighborhood of 8.25 million people (figure 2.1). That was something like 10–15% of the population of the Roman Empire in the high imperial first and second centuries CE. Hellas in the fourth century BCE accounted for perhaps 3–4% of the world's total population—roughly comparable to the percentage of the world's population currently made up by residents of the United States.[1]

The land area occupied by the Greek city-state culture (excluding unclaimed territory and wasteland between poleis and non-Greek populations interspersed among the poleis, as in Sicily, Anatolia, and around the Black

Sea) was about 190,000 km²—about one and a half times the total territory claimed today by the Greek state today. The overall population density of the ancient Greek world was, based on these calculations, about 44 persons per km²—very close to that of two of the most highly developed European states of the sixteenth and seventeenth century: Holland (in 1561) at 45.3/km² and England and Wales (in 1688) at 44/km².[2] Ancient Greek population density resembles that of modern South Africa, Lithuania, or Panama—or (coincidentally) the contemporary world (47/km²—land area only); it falls about midway between the population density of the United States (35/km²) and Mexico (60/km²).

The surface area of the interconnected Mediterranean and Black Seas is roughly 15 times the land area occupied by ancient Greeks: about 3 million km² (approximately a third of the land area of the United States or Europe). The combined length of the coastline of the two seas is about 50,000 km— approximately equivalent to the coastline of Indonesia and 2.5 times that of the United States. On and near the shores of these two very considerable bodies of water, and on the many habitable islands of the Mediterranean, there were, in Plato's and Aristotle's time, something in the order of 1,100 Greek poleis.

The Greeks were unevenly distributed along the shores of the Mediterranean and Black Seas (map 2). The great majority of the Greek states—more than nine in ten poleis, and at least seven-eighths of the total Greek population—were concentrated in just one corner of Plato's pond: the northern and eastern quadrant of the Mediterranean basin: Sicily, southern Italy and the Adriatic islands, mainland Greece, the Aegean islands, western Anatolia. A handful of poleis were located on Mediterranean coasts west of Sicily (Emporion (i2) near modern Barcelona in northeastern Spain, Massalia (i3 = modern Marseilles) in southern France. A few were located south of Crete, notably African Kyrene (i1028) and Egyptian Naukratis (i1023). Most of the rest of the poleis that lay outside the intensely Greek eastern Mediterranean (a total of 92 known communities) were to be found along the shores of the Black Sea, including the Sea of Marmara (Propontis) (see map 1).[3]

Plato's analogy of polis-dwelling Greeks to ants or frogs around a *pond* points immediately to one of the most striking features of the Greek city-state ecology: Greek poleis were very seldom to be found far from the seashore. The majority of the poleis were located within 25 km in a straight line from the coast, and most of the rest within 50 km from the coast.[4] Of course, the overland routes of Greece were rarely straight, and travel to the coast was sometimes arduous due to the rugged terrain. Not every Greek state had easy access to the sea. Nevertheless, the pattern of polis location near the coasts is very striking, and Plato's pond analogy is quite apt in this sense, as (we shall see) in others.

The Greek world was (and is) famously mountainous: About 80% of the land area of the modern Greek state is covered by mountains; Sicily, south Italy, and the regions of western Asia in which the Greeks settled in antiquity are similarly mountainous. In a few regions of the Greek world, a substantial number of poleis lay far above sea level—high-elevation poleis were especially prevalent in Arcadia, where 28 of 39 poleis with measured elevation lay above 500 m and only 3 below 200 m. Sicily, Thessaly, Caria, and Crete also sported relatively high concentrations of poleis at higher elevations. Throughout most of the Greek world, however, most poleis were located at relatively low elevations: Well over half of the 902 poleis with a measured elevation (507: 56%) were located at elevations under 100 m above sea level, and fewer than a quarter (205: 23%) were located over 300 m. The distribution of poleis by region and by elevation is illustrated in figure 2.2.

Although there are notable examples of large and prominent high-elevation poleis (e.g., Kyrene at 616 m, Mantinea [1281] at 629 m, and Megalopolis [1282] at 406 m), higher elevation is negatively correlated, weakly overall but more strongly in some regions (notably Sicily), to both polis size and prominence.[5] The general preference of ancient Greeks for locating their states at lower elevations within their ruggedly mountainous homelands can be explained in part by the attraction to coastal regions for purposes of trade, and in part because much of the best arable land of Greece was relatively close to sea level. Both the fact that there was considerable intra- as well as interregional variation in polis elevation and the fact that most poleis were *not* situated in inaccessible mountaintop locations are relevant to the development of the Greek economy. Both of these features of polis distribution also had a very significant bearing on the Greek way of war.

The distribution of poleis is noteworthy in respect to climate. With the exception of about 50 poleis around the Black Sea proper (north and east of the Sea of Marmara), the Greek city-states were located almost entirely within a particular and rare (in global terms) climatic zone characterized by a temperate, hot and dry summer, "Mediterranean" climate.[6] Moreover, if we look more closely at modern climate maps, we will see that (again the Black Sea poleis excepted) almost all Greek poleis were located in only one band of the Mediterranean climate zone: Greeks lived almost uniquely in places in which winter lows now average between–1°C to 4°C (30–40°F) and 7–15°C (45–60°F). They almost never lived in the relatively "frigid" parts of the Mediterranean near-coastal zones, where winter lows now average below–1°C (30°F). In terms of rainfall, Greeks strictly avoided desert regions, that is, areas with average rainfall in the range of 15–25 cm per year or less.

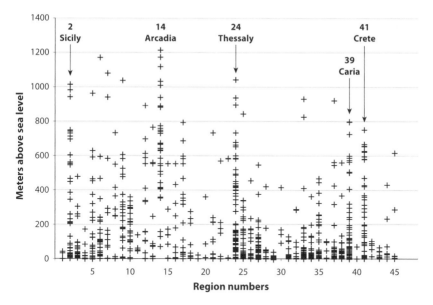

FIGURE 2.2 *Elevations of 902 poleis, by region.*

NOTES: Based on polis locations specified in http://polis.stanford.edu/. Some locations, and thus some elevations, are only approximate. High outliers deleted = Sollion (i137): 1,577 m, Chedrolioi (i566): 2,044 m, Smila (i611): 2,044 m, and Kerasous (i719): 1,922 m.

More surprisingly, perhaps, Greeks seldom settled in regions that, today, see *any* substantial rainfall in the summer months. Although a fair part of the Mediterranean climate zone receives between 2.3 and 5.0 cm of rain per month in the summer (e.g., most of the west coast of Italy from Naples north, and the south coast of France), almost all Mediterranean Greek poleis—and thus the great majority of all poleis, were located in regions that currently receive less than 2.3 cm of rain in each of two consecutive summer months. This region was, in antiquity, unsuited to irrigation—there are few major rivers in Greece. Those that there are did not lend themselves, as did the Nile and Tigris/Euphrates systems, to large-scale irrigation in antiquity. Without irrigation, and with very low summer rainfall, most plants are dormant in the midsummer months. Most crops were therefore planted during the wet months and harvested before the driest part of the summer.[7]

By the classical era, the Greeks had occupied virtually *all* of the territory in Eurasia (all of it is near the Mediterranean) that falls in the specific moderate temperature and "dry but not too dry" rainfall bands described above—

except, that is, for those regions that were claimed and successfully defended by another highly developed city-state culture. The Phoenicians and their kinsmen, the Carthaginians, occupied the relevant parts of the coastal Levant, the Mediterranean coast of Africa from the Tunis peninsula west, the big islands of Sardinia and Corsica, the smaller western Mediterranean islands, parts of western Sicily, and the Hispanic Mediterranean coast south of Barcelona/Emporion (see map 2).

Evidently the Greeks—not unlike particular species of ants—tended to occupy a very particular ecological niche. Their niche was characterized both by its proximity to seacoasts and by a specific climate of above-frigid winter temperatures and very (but not excessively) dry summers. By the classical period, Greeks had occupied all the territory in that niche that was available to them. In thinking about the potential significance of the geographic distribution of Greek poleis, we need to answer several related questions: First, since virtually all of the relevant (temperate and dry but not too dry) climate zone is to be found near the Mediterranean coasts, was the striking coastal, "around the pond," distribution of poleis simply an epiphenomenon of a climate preference? Next, why were the Greeks so attached to (or so limited by) a particular coastal/climate niche? And finally, did the narrow ecological niche in which Greeks mostly lived serve to promote or to inhibit the rise of the Greek world?[8]

We have, in a sense, already answered the first question: the Black Sea and outlier Greek settlements show that climate is not strictly determinative. Evidently a good location on a coast could sometimes, if not often, trump a less-than-ideal climate. The second question, why the Greeks lived where they did, is harder and may benefit from Plato's ant analogy. Suppose that an ant nest is established by accident (say the queen was blown a long way from her home nest) in a new region with abundant resources that the particular ant species is well adapted to exploiting. Suppose further that this new region lacks rival nests (or other species) to exploit the same resources, and that it is relatively free of anteaters. We may expect the nest to flourish and to spawn other nests. The descendants of the original nest will eventually occupy the entirety of the region with the desirable features of resources, absence of rivals, and low predation. The basic settlement history of the Greek world fits that scenario tolerably well. Starting out from their homeland in mainland Greece, in the course of the later Bronze Age, through the Early Iron Age, and especially in the archaic and classical periods, Greek speakers occupied all places available to them with the right natural features that lacked effective competition from rival cultures and offered security from predatory cultures.[9]

The "right natural features" were, in the first instance, the climatic conditions that made it possible to grow grain (especially wheat and barley), which was the staple of the Greek diet, grapes for wine, and olives whose oil was used for lighting and cleaning as well as for food. These three basic crops make up the so-called "Mediterranean triad" (see below): the basis of the Greek diet. Of the three crops, the olive is by far the most demanding in terms of where it can be cultivated. Nutritious grains can be grown under a wide variety of climatic conditions. Grapes (of the sort suited to wine production) are pickier, requiring average annual temperatures in the range of 10–20°C. Olives grow only under the conditions specific to the generic "Mediterranean" climate, as described above.

We have yet to specify *why* Greeks were so culturally wedded to the grain/olive/grape triad—obviously humans (unlike a given species of ant) can live on a wide variety of diets. But accepting for the moment that Greeks *were* attached to the triad, we have an explanation for their territorial distribution. As the Black Sea settlements show, under the right conditions, i.e., favorable conditions for lucrative trade with other cultures, olive cultivation could be foregone. But through the classical era, Greeks almost never established communities outside the zone of ready cultivation of grain and grapes.

In regions with the right resources, and lacking militarily effective competitors, the Greeks were able to push aside, assimilate, or exterminate local populations—the history of Greek colonization (as with other colonial histories) conjoined accommodation, assimilation, and organized violence (ch. 6). Effective competition for regions with the right resources came, as we have seen, in the form of the Phoenicians and Carthaginians, who tended to occupy exactly the temperate "dry but not too dry" subset of the Mediterranean zone particularly favored by the Greeks. Given that grain, olives, and grapes can be grown throughout the Mediterranean climate zone, it seems possible that Greeks might have settled more of the somewhat wetter parts of the Mediterranean zone had those areas not been occupied by other competitor cultures: for example, by Latins and Etruscans on the central and northern parts of the western coast of Italy. Possibly, in the absence of competitors, Greeks would have extended their range into very low rainfall regions in which agriculture was made possible through large-scale irrigation and drainage systems—places like Egypt and Mesopotamia. But these areas were settled by highly organized cultures and for the most part were unavailable (until Alexander the Great's conquests) for Greek settlement. Naucratis (i1023), a trading port in the Egyptian Nile Delta, was a notable exception.

Dangerous human predators came in the form of expansionist imperial states (notably, in the classical period, Persia and Carthage) and in the form of the nomadic steppe cultures of central and western Eurasia—the people the Greeks called Scythians and Cimmerians. Predations by peoples from the steppes was an endemic problem for even the largest and best-organized premodern imperial states—including Rome and China. While the Greek communities in western Anatolia and especially around the Black Sea were exposed to steppe-nomad predation, the European Greeks, those located west and south of the Bosphorus, were effectively insulated from the steppes by the nature of the terrain. Most of the territory occupied by Greeks lay outside the dry and frigid grassland zone in which the horse-centered culture of the steppe nomads flourished. In much of the Greek world, lack of grazing land meant that cavalry could not readily operate at the grand scale required by the steppe cultures.[10]

The third question posed above—did the restriction to a narrow climatic/coastal zone limit or promote Greek growth?—will be considered in more detail in later chapters. I suggest that, far from inhibiting Greek growth, the conditions typical of the particular zone in which Greeks lived provided a firm foundation for the development of the institutions and cultural features that drove the classical efflorescence. Among other things, subtle variations within the distinctive Greek climate zone created opportunities for subregions to specialize in one or another or the "triad" crops: Low-rainfall regions, like Athens' territory of Attica, where relatively low-value barley grew better than high-value wheat, could, for example, export olive oil and import wheat. The very dry summers created a natural break in the agricultural year, a window that was available for long-distance travel—and for war. Moreover, as we have seen, the poleis of the northeastern Mediterranean quadrant, where resources were right and competitors absent, were tightly packed together. Arable land was at a premium within that quadrant, and rival poleis were typically within a short march or a shorter sea voyage of one another. These conditions created ample opportunity for conflict but also rewarded intensification, specialization, and cooperation—primary drivers of the classical efflorescence.

SIMILARITY

The Greeks states around the shores of the Mediterranean and Black Seas manifested notable regional differences, some of which we consider below (for the 45 regions of the Greek world, see map 1 and appendix I). But the many poleis of Hellas shared some important cultural similarities, including language; religion and death rituals; ways of war-making and peace-making; styles of architecture and city planning; and modes of dress, games, and food ways.

By definition all Greeks spoke the same language (albeit with many dialectical variations). The standard Greek definition of "barbarian" was one who did not speak Greek. To be Greek was, at a minimum, to be a speaker of the Greek language and a sharer in some key aspects of a common culture typical of the Greek city-states. The Greek world expanded so dramatically in the period 800–300 BCE in part because so many of the Greeks' neighbors learned the Greek language and adopted other aspects of Greek culture. In some cases, this process of Hellenization was well enough advanced by the latter part of the fourth century BCE for formerly "barbarian" cities to be categorized, by residents, by other Greeks, and by the editors of the *Inventory*, as Greek poleis. Their shared language and culture enabled Greeks from across the extended Mediterranean–Black Sea world to communicate easily with one another— even as marked regional and ethnic dialects and local cultural peculiarities made it readily apparent from where in the Greek world a traveler originally hailed.

Although they varied greatly in size and splendor, Greek poleis resembled one another in salient ways. Greek sacred and civil architecture took roughly the same form across the Greek world: Temples, stoas, theaters, gymnasia, council-houses, and fortifications would readily be identified by any experienced Greek traveler. Post and lintel construction (famously, colonnaded public buildings and temples) was standard. Stone (especially limestone and conglomerate, but sometimes marble) and plastered brick were the primary building materials; wood was generally reserved for roofs and superstructure. Moreover, Greek cities tended to be laid out in a similar way, typically featuring a central public square (the *agora*) in which no private building was allowed, public wells for water, and public sanctuaries for the gods. Beginning in the eighth century BCE, a number of Greek towns were laid out in a strict grid pattern. The primary conurbation was, by the fourth century, typically surrounded by a substantial city wall (see below). Greek houses were, by the fourth century, relatively large (ch. 4) and tended to be built on a standard pattern around a courtyard. A special room was often reserved for entertaining male guests at drinking parties (*symposia*). Women and men tended to center their activities in different parts of the house, but gendered private spaces are difficult to distinguish archaeologically.[11]

The standard Greek diet was based on the "Mediterranean triad" of grain (especially wheat but also barley), olives (mostly for oil used for cleaning and light as well as for food), and grapes (for wine) discussed above. This basic fare would be complemented by seasonal vegetables and occasionally by fish. Meat was commonly consumed at public occasions, after animal sacrifices. In elite households, with adequate leisure and hounds, meat might also be obtained by hunting—rabbits were the most common quarry.[12]

Religion was an important shared cultural feature: A common poetic tradition (beginning with the Homeric epics in the eighth century BCE and continuing with lyric, and then tragic poetry) helped to forge a rich shared mythology. Gods, goddesses, and heroes had the same names across the Greek world, and some of the same stories were told of them, although heroes and deities took on very different roles in the rituals and narratives of different regions and towns. The growing popularity of several great Panhellenic religious sanctuaries—at Delphi, Olympia, Isthmia, Nemea, and elsewhere—became important nodes in extended interpolis social networks and encouraged the emergence and continuity of a repertoire of shared cultic practices. The rituals defining local expressions of religious life were diverse, but animal sacrifice (followed by distribution of meat), processions, initiation into sacred mysteries, consultation of oracles, and formalized kin-group-centered death rituals were standard features. An attentive Greek traveler, like the historian Herodotus in the fifth century BCE, or the polymath travel writer Pausanias seven hundred years later, would be repeatedly struck by the unity in diversity of the religious practices in the Greek Mediterranean/Black Sea culture zone.[13]

Warfare was, from the perspective of understanding rise and fall, a particularly important shared cultural feature. Throughout much of the Greek world and over most of our period, the dominant mode of Greek land warfare centered on combat between phalanxes of hundreds or even thousands of heavily armed infantrymen (hoplites), often supported by lighter armed foot soldiers and sometimes by light cavalry. Meanwhile, the standard Greek warship was the trireme: a triple-banked, oared ship with a crew of about 200. Like an individual hoplite, an individual warship was quite vulnerable, but deployed in ranks, both hoplites and triremes were formidable (ch. 6).

Wars were traditionally fought in the midsummer months, which, due to plant dormancy (above) was a slack time in the agricultural calendar; it was also the least dangerous time for warships (as well as trading vessels) to ply the seas. The Greek way of war demanded the mobilization of many men. Bigger forces were in general better because a large formation of men or ships could outflank and thereby overwhelm a smaller one. Greek warfare favored larger poleis, or coalitions of poleis, over smaller or isolated states—and thus helped to place a premium on political innovations that allowed poleis and coalitions to grow and to remain big. We consider, in chapter 6, why the process of "growing big" was truncated, so that only a few of the very biggest poleis measured their total populations in the hundreds of thousands or their territory in the thousands of square kilometers.

A major Greek state might be able to launch a few thousand hoplites and a few dozen triremes; the very greatest of the poleis numbered their warriors in the tens of thousands and their warships in the hundreds. On land and sea alike, Greek warfare was centered on many men, similarly equipped, wielding spears or oars, all operating together in close formations. The key differentiator, in addition to size, was training that forged groups of individual soldiers and rowers into reliably similar and skillful fighting units. Marching or rowing in echelon and meeting the shock of an enemy line without losing unit coherence took a great deal of practice. Training in the use of spear and shield or oar was a common experience for Greek men. In the fifth century BCE, Sparta and Athens stood out as premier land and sea powers, respectively, not only because they were, compared to their Greek rivals, especially big and coherent states and thereby able to mobilize big forces but also because they were innovators in techniques of standardized military training.[14]

Just as Greek states typically shared many characteristics in common, so too many of the inhabitants of a given polis (especially the adult male citizens) would have appeared to an outsider to be quite similar to one another. In contrast to, for example, medieval European society in which kings, nobles, merchants, and peasants were readily distinguished by dress and manner, as well as by occupation, classical Greek citizens tended to dress and behave (at least in public) more or less alike. In aristocratic Sparta, the similarity in dress and lifestyle was taken to an extreme among citizens, but there were clearly marked distinctions in dress and behavior between citizens and noncitizens. In democratic Athens, however, it could be difficult to distinguish a free citizen from a slave or foreign visitor (Pseudo-Xenophon, *Ath. Pol.* 1.10). Moreover, in most poleis each of the apparently similar citizens took on a variety of quite different social roles.

In the *Republic*, Plato argued that all real-world city-states fell short of his ideal highly regulated community in regard to the organization of work. In Plato's ideal society, each individual was perfectly specialized, in that he or she did only one task: farmers did the farming, guardian-auxiliaries did the fighting, philosopher-kings did the ruling. No guardian ever took up a hoe, nor did a farmer wield a spear. In contrast, in every real Greek city-state, as in a nest of ants, individuals took on different tasks at different times. Whereas in a few poleis, notably Sparta (ch. 6), specialization was taken quite far, in Athens, as in many other Greek poleis, the same citizen might labor in his fields as a farmer in the spring, fight as a heavy-armed warrior in the summer, and officiate over religious ritual as a priest and conduct public business as a civic magistrate at almost any time of the year. In this crucial respect, as in others, the ants/Greeks analogy gains some purchase, as it would not if we were comparing ants to societies in which social and occupational roles were less fluid. We pursue that line of thought in the next chapter.

TABLE 2.1 *Territorial Sizes and Population Estimates for 1,100 Greek City-States*

Polis Size	Area (km²)	Estimated Population Range	Estimated Average Population	Polis Count Known Size	Polis Count Total (est.)	Total Pop. (1,100 poleis)	% Total Pop. (1,100 poleis)	% Polis Count (1,100 poleis)
1	25 or fewer	525–2,500	1,000	148	277	277,000	0.03	0.25
2	25–100	875–10,000	3,500	256	483	1,690,500	0.20	0.44
3	100–200	3,500–25,000	7,000	95	144	1,008,000	0.12	0.13
4	200–500	7,000–50,000	17,000	107	124	2,108,000	0.26	0.11
5	500–1,000	17,500–75,000	35,000	53	59	2,065,000	0.25	0.05
6	1,000–2,000	35,00–100,000	65,000	10	10	650,000	0.08	0.01
7	More than 2,000	75,000–250,000	150,000	3	3	450,000	0.05	0.003
TOTAL				672	1,100	8,248,500		

NOTES: The total of 1,100 poleis is hypothetical, based on models developed in Hansen 2006b and 2008. Polis sizes 1–5 are based on the *Inventory*. Size 6 = Argos, Byzantion, Elis, Eretria, Kyrene, Megalopolis, Miletus, Pantikopaion, Rhegium, and Rhodes. Size 7 = Athens, Sparta, and Syracuse. "Estimated average population" is based on Hansen 2006b, modified by results in Hansen 2008. "Polis count known size" includes 636 poleis in the *Inventory* whose size is known or plausibly estimated, along with 32 additions in Hansen 2008 and 4 additions from Emily Mackil (personal communication). 109 "size 1 or 2," 37 "size 2 or 3," 11 "size 3 or 4," 8 "size 4 or 5" (including Pergamum and Xanthos from Hansen 2008) are divided evenly between the two relevant categories. "Polis count total" assumes that the distribution of known-size poleis is modeled in the total count as follows: size 1 and 2: 53% of total are known; size 3: 65% of total are known; size 4: 86% of total are known; size 5: 89% of total are known; sizes 6 and 7: 100% of total are known. N.B. Hansen 2008 additions to the *Inventory* list of sized poleis includes 29 size 4 poleis and 3 size 5 poleis but no size 1–3 poleis.

DIFFERENCE

The notable similarities between Greek states can be juxtaposed to equally striking differences. Most obviously, Greek states varied greatly in size—albeit, the variation in scale does not equal that found among the nation-states of the contemporary world.[15] While all Greek poleis were tiny in comparison to most modern nation-states, within the world of the poleis, it is reasonable to speak of small, middling, and large states. In terms of territorial extent, Greek states range across two to three orders of magnitude, from tiny Koresia (1493) on Kea with a territory of about 15 km² to Syracuse, which may at one point have controlled as much as 12,000 km². Although some very small poleis had large populations (notably Aigina [1358]), across the entire sample, territorial size can be taken as a rough proxy for population. The population estimates adopted here, and summed up in table 2.1 are based primarily on the data in the *Inventory* and on the estimation methods developed by Mogens Hansen.[16]

Of the 672 poleis whose territorial area is known or can be plausibly estimated, 148 were relatively tiny, with territories estimated at 25 km² or less and estimated populations of 1,000 or fewer; at the other end of the distribution, only three classical-era poleis—Athens, Sparta, and Syracuse—had territories over 2,000 km², with estimated populations ranging up to a quarter million people or more. Polis size also varied by regions: In Phocis (region 9), the region around Delphi (map 9), the average polis territory is about 65 km², whereas in Arcadia (region 14: map 4), in the central Peloponnese, it is ca. 120 km²; on the north Aegean island of Lesbos (region 36: map 9) in the fourth century, it was about 320 km².

We return to the implications of demographic distribution in chapter 3. The key point for now is that although most (about 8 in 10) poleis were small (under 200 km²), most Greeks (about 2 in 3) lived in middling (200–500 km²) to large (more than 500 km²) poleis. Table 2.1 models the distribution of an assumed total of 1,100 classical poleis by territory size and estimated population size. Figure 2.3 graphically illustrates the distribution of polis territory sizes. The truncated bell curve, with no left-side tail and long right-side tail shows the extent to which the distribution of polis territory sizes was skewed toward the small-polis end of the scale.[17]

Poleis also varied greatly in their relative prominence. The effect of state prominence on individual and collective lives was keenly appreciated by the Greeks. The Roman-era biographer Plutarch (*Life of Themistocles* 18.2) records an exchange between an anonymous citizen of the small Aegean island polis of Seriphos (1517: size 2) and the renowned Athenian general and politician of

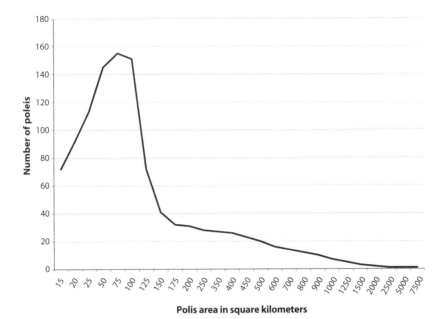

Polis area in square kilometers

FIGURE 2.3 *Polis territory sizes, 1,100 poleis.*

NOTES: Based on 672 poleis whose size is known or can be estimated with some confidence. Count for each size is based on estimated total number of poleis in each of seven general size categories, and the range of km² area sizes within each general category. For data, see table 2.1. Horizontal scale is compressed on the right side.

the early fifth century BCE, Themistocles: "When [Themistocles] was told by the Seriphian that it was not due to himself that he had got his reputation, but to his polis, 'True,' said he, 'but neither should I, had I been a Seriphian, have been famous, nor would you, had you been an Athenian.'"[18]

Lacking an ancient Greek's fingertip feel for the relative prominence of Greek states, I use the amount of space (measured in columns of text) allotted to each polis in the *Inventory* as a proxy for individual polis prominence. This "fame" proxy is obviously rough: It indicates what is *now* known about a given polis, and thus is sensitive to the loss of knowledge since classical antiquity. On the other hand, the *Inventory* includes all that is now known about obscure poleis, whereas many volumes have been written about the most prominent states (e.g., Athens, Sparta, Syracuse). Over all, given the intensity of scholarly investigation to which the Greek world has been subjected, it seems plausible to assume that most poleis that are famous or obscure today were also relatively famous or obscure in antiquity.[19]

Table 2.2 and figure 2.4 show that we know, individually and in the aggregate, very little about more than half of all known poleis (fame categories 1 and 2: 567/1,035 poleis = 55%). Yet for several hundred "middling" poleis (fame categories 3 and 4, 442/1,035 = 43%), we do have a fair amount of historically relevant information, and many of these poleis would have been quite widely known in antiquity. Seriphos, the polis whose relative obscurity would have doomed the ambitions of Themistocles, falls at the low end of this middling group, with a fame rank of 3. We may guess that many of the 158 poleis whose constitutional histories were collected by Aristotle, and which provided some of the data for his *Politics* (see below, ch. 3) fell in the upper end of the middling-fame range.

The hypothesis that a low fame score likely reflects (albeit imperfectly) the limited prominence of a state in antiquity, and is not simply an artifact of lost knowledge, can be tested by the evidence of coinage. Literary evidence and archaeological evidence are subject to the vagaries of preservation and exploration. Yet, because silver coins minted by a given state usually circulated outside the territory of the polis of origin, and because they remain valuable and are recovered through a variety of methods (including amateurs with metal detectors), if an ancient state *did* mint silver coins in any quantity, we are likely to know it. Of the middling-fame group of poleis, 60% (264/442) are known to have minted silver coins, compared to only 9% (51/567) of the

TABLE 2.2 *Fame Scores for 1,035 Poleis*

Fame Rank	Columns Range	Polis Count	Aggregate Columns	% Total Poleis	% Total Text
1	0.12–0.37	238	63	0.23	0.05
2	0.5–0.87	329	216	0.32	0.15
3	1–2.87	355	539	0.34	0.39
4	3–5.87	87	354	0.08	0.25
5	6–10.5	22	165	0.02	0.12
6	12–20.87	4	60	0.004	0.04

NOTES: Fame is measured by number of columns of text assigned to the polis in the *Inventory*. Granularity = to 1/8 column. "Aggregate columns" figures are rounded to whole numbers. Total columns of text for 1,035 poleis: = 1,396. 1 column = ca. 425 words. Total words = ca. 600,000.

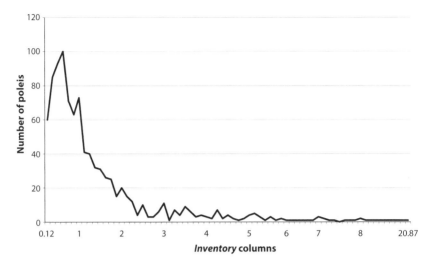

FIGURE 2.4 *Fame scores, 1,035 poleis.*

NOTES: Fame measured by columns of text devoted to each polis in the *Inventory*. Granularity is at level of 1/8 column. Horizontal scale is compressed on the right side.

low-fame group. In another test of the evidence: 15% of the poleis in the middling group (68/442), are known to have had at least one victor in one or more of the great Panhellenic games, as opposed to only 1% (6/567) in the low-fame group.[20]

We know, relatively speaking, a great deal about a couple of dozen Greek poleis (26/1,035: fame categories 5 and 6). All of these high-fame poleis, except (notoriously) Sparta, coined silver, and 20 of the 26 recorded victors in the games. These high-fame poleis would certainly have been almost universally well-known in classical antiquity, and likewise very influential. Although there may have been significant exceptions, we may guess that their institutions were more likely to be imitated by other poleis, and they were more likely to take dominant roles in regional systems of hegemony.[21]

Table 2.2 documents the distribution of fame scores, and their relationship to the aggregate of our knowledge of the world of the poleis, as it is measured by the *Inventory*. Figure 2.4 illustrates the distribution graphically; the "long right tail" of relatively high-fame poleis is where most of the attention of historians of ancient Greece has traditionally tended to focus. Our goal will be to keep in view the relatively greater historical impact of the most prominent poleis, *and* the reality that there were a great many poleis that were prominent enough to be significant players on the stage of Greek history, *and* that there were even more small and obscure poleis that were an essential part of the ecology, even if they were individually less likely to be major players on the stage of Greek history. Grasping the dynamics of the decentralized ecology of classical Hellas requires attention to the interplay between the most prominent poleis and all the rest.[22]

Prominence is obviously related to polis size: Figures 2.3 and 2.4, which graphically illustrate the distribution of poleis by size and fame, respectively, trace similar truncated bell curves, with similarly sharp peaks on the left side of the chart (many small size, low fame) and similar long right tails (few large size, high fame). The three outstandingly famous poleis—Athens, Syracuse, and Sparta—were also the largest poleis. The average high-fame (category 5–6) polis was substantially larger (average size category about 4+ = ca. 500+ km²) than was the average middling-fame polis (fame category 3–4, average size category 2+ = ca. 100+ km²) and much larger than the average low-fame polis (fame category 1–2, average size category 1+ = ca. 25+ km²). Yet a number of small poleis were very well known: Delphi (1177: fame 5, size 2) and Delos (1478: fame 4, size 2) were associated with major sanctuaries, but Italian Neapolis (163: fame 4, size 1) and the island-polis of Aigina (fame 4, size 2) were famous for quite different reasons. At the other end of the scale, Kereneia (11015), Byblis (192), and Tyrodiza (1687) register low fame scores of 2 but boasted large, category 5, territories. The overall correlation between size and fame for the 672 poleis whose size can be estimated (Pearson = 0.58, r^2 = 0.34) is quite strong but does not support the assumption that the prominence of a given Greek polis was a simple function of its size.

The substantial differences in polis size and prominence, along with the important roles that manpower, training, and wealth played in military operations, were factors in the emergence of various voluntary and hegemonic forms of interstate cooperation among the Greek states. In the fifth century BCE, most of the poleis of the Peloponnese (continental Greece south of the Isthmus of Corinth: map 4), along with a number of poleis in central Greece, were members of the Peloponnesian League, a defensive–offensive military alliance dominated by Sparta. In the mid-fifth century, Athens had transformed a defensive league of poleis into an eastern Mediterranean empire that, at its greatest extent, extracted tribute from between a quarter and a third of the states of Hellas (map 7). In the age of Plato, most of the 200+ Greek states on the west coast of Anatolia were under at least the nominal control of Persia. Meanwhile, by Aristotle's day, about half of the poleis of mainland Greece were members of one of several federal leagues (*koina*).[23] These leagues were increasingly influential voluntary associations of states. Federation enabled smaller poleis to compete more effectively in an environment potentially

TABLE 2.3 *Limits to Polis Independence: Some Examples*

Organization	Century BCE	No. of Poleis (approximate)	Population (estimated millions)
Peloponnesian League	5th	150	1.1
Athenian empire	mid-5th	300+	2.5
Persian Empire	late 6th	100	0.7
	mid 4th	200+	1.8
Federal league	5th or 4th	200+	1.6

NOTES: Data for Peloponnesian League: *Inventory* regions 9–11, 13–17, 22, plus Ambrakia, Anaktorion, Leukas, Pallene (see Thucydides 2.9.2); for Athenian empire: *Inventory* Index 18; for Persian empire in late 6th century BCE: *Inventory* regions 35–38, total population reduced by 170,00 to account for later growth; for Persian empire in mid-4th: *Inventory* regions 34–40; for federal leagues, *Inventory* individual entries, with corrections by E. Mackil (personal communication). Population estimates for Peloponnesian League, Persian Empire, and Federal league derived from estimated regional populations (see Appendix I). Athenian empire population = Delian League poleis (*Inventory* Index 18), excluding Attica; total population reduced by 400,000 to account for 4th century growth. Athenian empire and Federal league populations estimated by methods described in Appendix I.

dominated by aggressive and successful big states. We look at each of these systems in more detail in later chapters. Table 2.3 estimates the total numbers of poleis and estimated Greek populations that were involved in each of these state-autonomy-limiting systems of interpolis dependency.

Dependency relations, voluntary and coerced, create some blurriness at the margins when we ask the question: Is a given Greek settlement actually a city-state?—in the sense of being an urban center connected organically to a specific rural hinterland, and in the sense of being an political unit that is sufficiently autonomous, as a system of territorially defined authority, to qualify as a state. The editors of the *Inventory* recognized and addressed the issue. While standing behind the claim that each of the 1,035 settlements listed in the *Inventory* as poleis does in fact deserve to be called a city-state in a territorial and political sense, the editors also assign each polis a score from A to C meant to measure the strength of the claim that a community was actually a polis—with A indicating those communities (about half the total) unambiguously attested to in ancient sources as poleis. Category C is reserved for 217 settlements for which the evidence for polis status is weakest and the status of the settlement as a polis can only be regarded as likely or possible. The upshot is that for about two in ten of the communities considered to be poleis in the

TABLE 2.4 *Certainty of Attribution of Settlement as a Polis and Degree of Hellenization for 1,035 Poleis*

Polis-Certainty Rank	Polis Count	% Total Poleis	"Hellenicity" Rank	Polis Count	% Total Poleis
A	506	0.49	α	822	0.79
[A]	112	0.11	β	85	0.08
B	200	0.19	γ	44	0.04
C	217	0.21	?	84	0.08

NOTES: Source data = *Inventory*, individual polis entries. A = community is called *polis* in an ancient source. [A] = community is subsumed under the heading *poleis* alongside other communities. B = community is believed to be a polis based on its known activities that are characteristic of a polis. C = known activity characteristic of a polis but identification as a polis is less certain or only a possibility. α = Hellenic polis with few or no elements of non-Greek civilization. β = mixed community in which Greeks and non-Greeks live side by side. γ = predominantly barbarian community with some elements of Hellenic civilization. N.B. Many type β and γ poleis became fully Hellenized after the classical period (*Inventory*, p. 7).

Inventory there is reason for hesitation in considering the settlement to be a city-state in the most robust sense of the term. Table 2.4 sums up the distribution of *Inventory*-listed sites according to this "polis-certainty" measure.[24]

Despite any limitations upon its full autonomy, each Greek city-state sought political distinction, or at least local independence, and to be an entity unto itself. Each had its own code of law (written or unwritten), its own ritual calendar, its own peculiar social customs. Although weights and measures were becoming increasingly standardized across the Greek world, by the time of Plato most of the larger and more prominent poleis minted their own silver and (later) bronze coins. These coins typically proclaimed the name of the state (often abbreviated) along with some suitable image: Athena's owl for Athens, a sea turtle for maritime-trading Aigina, an ear of wheat for grain-rich Metapontum, and so on. Almost 100 Greek states were already minting their own distinctive silver coinage by the end of the sixth century BCE and, by 323 BCE, a third of all known poleis were minting silver coins.[25]

Just as each city-state cherished its own laws and customs, so too each remembered and recounted its own local history. Among the distinctive shared features of Greek culture was a concern with historical narrative. By the time Aristotle began collecting polis constitutional histories, local polis identity was manifest in a flourishing literary genre of local and regional historiography.[26]

The many diverse but at least partially overlapping local Greek narratives, oral and written, were the raw materials that enabled Herodotus, Thucydides, and other classical Greek historians to write histories, not just of individual poleis, but of Hellas. These master narratives concerned interaction among individuals within Greek states and conflict and cooperation among the Greek states—but they also took in the relations, by turns friendly and hostile, of the Greeks with their non-Greek neighbors.

Among the issues prominently addressed by historians, local and "panhellenic" alike, was the emergence, endurance, and change of political regimes. Although most Greek political regimes are startlingly citizen-centered by comparison with other premodern states, the diversity of regimes among the poleis was a constant theme of Greek historical and philosophical literature. No doubt every state's government had its own peculiarities, but by the early fifth century BCE, the Greeks had settled on a canonical list of three regime types: The rule of one man was tyranny (or in a benign form, monarchy); the rule of a restricted part of the adult native male population in a state was oligarchy (or, when spoken of approvingly, aristocracy). The rule of all, or almost all, the free adult native males was democracy.

Herodotus and Thucydides, along with many other Greek writers, regarded the question of the emergence and collapse of regimes in specific poleis to be among the most important events in a state's history, and they considered the regime to be a primary determinant of state behavior. The question of how specific social conditions and institutions preserved or undermined regimes was a major concern of Greek theoretical writing on politics: both Plato (*Republic* and *Statesman*) and Aristotle (*Politics* and Pseudo-Aristotle *Constitution of the Athenians*—probably written by one of his students) treated the question of regime persistence and change as a primary issue for political philosophy.

At any given point in the sixth through fourth centuries BCE, a political map of the Greek world would have resembled a mosaic of regime types, but the mosaic would have looked substantially different depending on the moment chosen. Overall, tyranny would have appeared less prevalent in the fifth or fourth century, compared to its two citizen-centered rivals, oligarchy and democracy. Moreover, by the later fourth century BCE, democracy had gained a good deal of ground over oligarchy. Yet regional differences persisted. For example, tyranny remained a major factor in Sicily long after it had become less common in the central and southern mainland of Greece. Both the general Greek drift away from tyranny and toward democracy, and the persistence of regional specificity of regime distribution played a role in the classical efflorescence, and we return to these topics in later chapters.

The history of a given polis was often traced (whether historically or mythologically) back to a founder-hero. Some founders were thought to have magically sprung from the Earth (as in the case of Athens); other founders were more plausibly remembered as having been natives of another city-state who led expeditions from their homeland in the hope of creating a new and independent state in some other land. It was through the process of colonization that the Greek world grew outward from the Greek peninsula, first to Anatolia, then Sicily, Italy, southern France, northern Africa, and the shores of the Black Sea (map 3 and ch. 6).

Some 81 Greek states (8% of all known poleis) are known to have served as "mother-cities" in that they colonized, or participated in the colonization, of one or more of hundreds of other "colonial" poleis—some of which themselves became major colonizers. Several especially prominent states (Athens, Miletus i854, Syracuse, Corinth i227, Samos i864, and Thasos i526) were involved in 10 or more colonizing expeditions; 25 other poleis were involved in establishing 3 or more colonies. Greek colonial settlements typically developed into independent poleis; a few (like Syracuse, a colony of Corinth) became preeminent poleis. Yet relations between colony and mother-city sometimes remained strong, and some mother-cities took a proprietary interest in the doings of their former colonies. The question of how much deference a colony ought to show to its mother city helped spark the conflicts leading to the outbreak of the Peloponnesian War in 431 BCE (ch. 8), whereas aid sent by a mother-city to a former colony sparked the economic resurgence of Sicily after its decline in the mid-fourth century (ch. 9).[27]

Colonization was one important route by which Greeks came to live among non-Greek peoples, in ways that make obvious the error of imagining that the "Greek world" was ever purely Greek in ethnicity, culture, language, or history. Some 10–20% of known "Greek" poleis—mostly located in Sicily, Thrace, and Anatolia—are best understood as hybrids, manifesting strong non-Greek cultural features. Of these poleis, 44 (4% of all known poleis) were primarily non-Greek in their culture and only became substantially Hellenized after the end of the classical era. The degree of Hellenization of the 1,035 known poleis is summed up in table 2.4.

Moreover, and obviously, the Greeks of the city-states shared their extended Mediterranean/Black Sea world with non-Greek peoples (map 2). Some of these peoples (for example Lydians, Phrygians, Persians, Egyptians, and Phoenicians) lived in highly developed, state-based societies. Others (for example, some Thracians and most Scythians) were seminomadic tribe- or clan-based societies, and at least part-time pastoralists. Yet others (native Sicilians, Anatolians, North Africans) lived in towns and villages interspersed

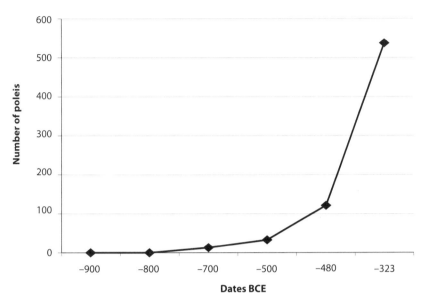

FIGURE 2.5 *Walled poleis, 900–323 BCE.*

NOTES: Numbers are of poleis believed to be walled on the basis of literary or archaeological evidence. Source data = Frederiksen 2011, except for –323 (323 BCE) = *Inventory*, Index 23.

among Greek poleis. Greeks learned many things from their neighbors—borrowing their alphabet, for example, from the Phoenicians and the idea of coined money from the Lydians. Non-Greeks, for their part, borrowed some of the cultural features of the poleis. The Greeks engaged intensively in cooperative trade relations with non-Greek peoples. Yet competition for resources periodically led to conflicts between Greek states and their non-Greek neighbors as well as between Greek states.

Failure in war could, and sometimes did, mean destruction of urban infrastructure or even state death (extermination, enslavement, or forced migration of the population). In the Early Iron Age of the eleventh and tenth centuries BCE, Greek settlements were unwalled. But in subsequent centuries, along with developing forms of social organization that promoted effective mobilization of soldiers, Greek poleis increasingly invested in substantial fortifications: urban circuits, and later in long walls connecting cities to harbors, and forts and towers to protect rural populations and assets. The preference for strong walls was not universal: Sparta remained unwalled throughout the classical period, believing that "our men are our walls." Some Greek political theorists, notably Plato in the *Republic,* argued against wall-ing the city on the grounds that brave men ought willingly to fight their enemies in the open field. But by the end of the classical period, this was a minority position; Aristotle thought it badly outdated (ch. 11). Fortification policy was one way in which Greek poleis became more similar to one another over time.

Fortification walls were costly. The Danish classicist, Rune Frederiksen, is surely right to say that, "city walls belong to the category of public architecture and must have constituted the most expensive and laborious undertaking for the communities that built them."[28] Yet the no-wall option clearly became less attractive over time, as Greek poleis grew wealthier. Fortifications figured in early stages of Greek state formation and, from the early fifth century BCE to the later fourth century, more Greek cities were increasingly heavily fortified. Late classical city walls were on the whole more substantial (built of stone, rather than mud-brick), more highly developed (towers, crenellations, indented trace), and in many cases augmented with outworks and elaborate systems of rural defense (forts, watchtowers, pass-control walls).[29] Figure 2.5 shows the growth in the number of known (to modern scholarship) fortified poleis in the Greek world, from 900 to 323 BCE. Table 2.5 shows that by 323 BCE almost all large and prominent Greek cities were fortified.

Finally, circling back to the physical conditions of the Greek world, different poleis, and even different subregions within the territories of large city-states, had quite different resource endowments. In addition to the uneven

TABLE 2.5 *Greek City Fortifications, by 323 BCE*

	City Walls	N =	%
All poleis	537	1,035	0.52
Size 3+	199	249	0.80
Size 5+	56	63	0.89
Fame 3+	352	469	0.75
Fame 4+	103	113	0.91

NOTES: Source data = *Inventory*, Index 23. Evidence of city walls may derive from literary, epigraphic, or archaeological investigation. Size 3 = 100–200 km²/population range 3,500–25,000. Size 5 = 500–1,000 km²/population range 17,500–75,000. Fame 3 = 1–2.87 *Inventory* columns. Fame 4 = 3–5.87 *Inventory* columns. On size and fame, see further, tables 2.1 and 2.2.

distribution of valuable minerals (iron, silver, gold), regional differences in elevation (figure 2.2) and in rainfall (above, note 7) produced areas better suited to one or the other of the triad of basic crops (grain, olives, grapes), or to specific grains (wheat or barley), or to some specialty crop (e.g., silphium, at Kyrene, a now-extinct plant used both as a seasoning and as a medicine). While much of the Greek world had abundant building stone, fine marbles, suited for sculpture, were located only in particular regions (most famously on the island of Paros). Moreover, the core Greek world lacked certain essential metals, most notably copper and tin, the components of bronze. These valuable raw materials had to be imported into the Greek core from Cyprus, Anatolia, and western Asia. Resource diversity and scarcity provided a further impetus to specialization and cooperative exchange, to competition, and to conflict—both within Hellas and with neighboring cultures. Those conditions in turn helped to drive the classical efflorescence.

3

POLITICAL ANIMALS

A THEORY OF DECENTRALIZED
COOPERATION

At the heart of the mystery of classical efflorescence lies the question of how the Greeks, in an ecology of many small states, solved problems of decentralized cooperation and thereby ruled one another, as citizens—rather than being ruled as dominated subjects of centralized royal authority in a large state.

Decentralized cooperation is among the most important and pervasive features of life. It plays a major role in the activity of, for example, bacteria, ants, birds, and humans—and it defines a research area for the social and biological sciences alike. Yet many aspects of cooperation have long resisted explanation. Why do organisms cooperate? And how does local cooperation among individuals produce higher order, system-level effects? In biology, explaining *emergent* phenomena associated with decentralized cooperation, exemplified by the complex and rapidly changing formations of large flocks of birds in flight or schools of swimming fish, remains a research frontier.[1]

The behavior of flocks and schools is minutely coordinated; the shapes produced by that coordination are things of startling beauty and great complexity. No bird in the flock, nor fish in the school, issues commands to others, yet huge flocks and schools move as one—resembling at times a single, gigantic, shape-shifting superorganism. Biologists have recently shown that relatively simple algorithms can go a long way toward explaining how large groups of birds and fish coordinate their movements.[2] Explaining decentralized cooperation in ants is harder because their collective activities are more complex. Explaining decentralized cooperation in humans is hardest of all, yet it is imperative if we are to understand the efflorescence of classical Hellas.

For social scientists, the research agenda for the problem of "human cooperation at scale" was set a half century ago by the political economist,

Mancur Olson, who posited that cooperation without coercion (i.e., a centralized system of authority, backed by a credible threat of force) was only possible in small groups of not more than a few hundred people. This is because, in small groups, individuals can readily monitor one another's behavior and can act quickly to sanction aberrant behavior by those who stray from the path of cooperation. As Olson famously argued, once a human group exceeds a certain size, it becomes impossible for group members effectively to monitor *free riding*—i.e., strategically defecting from the cooperative regime by refusing to pay the costs of cooperation, yet continuing to share in the collective benefits accruing through others' cooperation. As a result of the failure of monitoring, and because of the costs associated with punishing defectors, sanctioning of defection will be foregone. Given that everyone has the same incentive to defect by free riding, we can expect that a cascade of rational defection will doom the cooperative regime: In Olson's words, "unless the number of individuals is quite small, or unless there is coercion or some other special device to make individuals act in their common interest, *rational, self-interested individuals will not act to achieve their common or group interests.*"[3]

Olson's argument was backed by an impressively strong theory of human behavior (often called rational choice or rational actor theory) that posited the pursuit of self-interest, expressed as expected utility maximization, as the primary motivator of human social action. Yet rational choice theory, in its original strong form, notoriously fails to account for some evident facts about the world—including the success of large and democratic Greek poleis and the efflorescence of Greek polis ecology as a whole. The question of how certain human communities have managed to solve the problem of cooperation at scale, without the creation of centralized authority, is obviously important. There is now a large and growing scholarly literature that seeks to conjoin natural and social science to explain the motivation for human cooperation and the mechanisms that would allow well-motivated cooperation to be effective in producing valued goods. This literature is based on hypotheses about human sociability that weaken the strong assumptions of rational behavior on which Olson predicated his theory.[4]

Plato's star student, Aristotle, anticipated the "natural and social science" approach to the problem of human cooperation. Aristotle took up Plato's light-hearted "Greeks and social insects" analogy and transformed it into a theory of politics as collective social action. Following Aristotle, we may seek the answer to the puzzle of decentralized cooperation in the ancient Greek polis ecology by asking why self-consciously rational and highly communicative humans would be motivated to cooperate, and how, once motivated, they could produce goods that would be comparable, on an expansive human scale of value, to those produced by colonies of ants.

Despite flaws in certain of his premises—notoriously, the existence of "slaves by nature," the inherent weakness of deliberative reasoning in women, and the inevitable corruption of virtue through other-directed labor—Aristotle's theory of human collective activity offers much of what we need to explain the cooperative behavior that underpinned the classical Greek efflorescence.[5] It also has the virtue, for our purposes, of being a theory that was devised by a Greek at the height of the classical efflorescence and that was tested with reference to a mass of (now mostly lost) empirical data on the observed behavior of city-states and their residents. Like the editors of the *Inventory*, Aristotle was convinced that gathering a great deal of information about a great many poleis would further the endeavor of making sense of the development of the Greek world. Of the 158 constitutional histories that were gathered in Aristotle's school, we now have only one—known to classical scholars as "Pseudo-Aristotle's *Constitution of Athens*" because it is generally thought to have been written by one of his students, rather than by Aristotle himself. But happily we do have the major work of political theory and institutional design that was, at least in part, based on the empirical data of many other constitutional histories: Aristotle's *Politics*.

ARISTOTLE'S POLITICAL ANIMALS

Aristotle was at once a naturalist (the author of works on animals and their behavior), a moral philosopher, and a political theorist. Moreover, he was very interested in conjoining aprioristic theorizing about social order, of the sort perfected by Plato, with empirical observations of natural and social phenomena. For our purposes, the most notable example of his conjunction of natural science with the science of morals, and social theory with empirical observations of human behavior, is his political philosophy. In his *Politics,* Aristotle used his knowledge of the behavior of nonhuman social animals, and especially social insects, to help explain the distinctive forms of cooperation that he observed among his fellow Greeks. Moving beyond Plato-style simile ("like ants around a pond") to behavioral taxonomy, Aristotle noted that the kingdom of animals, ranging from insects to mammals, could be organized according to social behavior, rather than mere physical appearance (figure 3.1). This allowed him to see why humans and ants belong, behaviorally, in the same category of animal, and how their behavior is affected by their natural capacities. Thinking with Aristotle about the social insects/classical Greeks comparison that was introduced in chapter 2 helps us to grasp

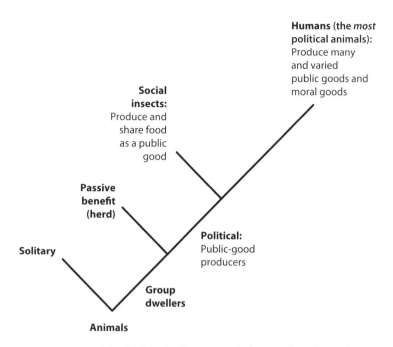

FIGURE 3.1 *Aristotle's behavioral taxonomy of solitary and social animals.*

NOTE: Up and to the right: more communication, more richly social (i.e., political) behavior, more public goods.

some of the distinctive institutional and civic features that were characteristic of the marketlike ecology of city-states.[6]

In one primary category of animals, Aristotle placed those species whose members lived essentially solitary lives, without need for complex forms of intraspecies cooperation—we may think, for example, of orangutans, many species of wild feline, bumblebees, or spiders. In a second category were those species whose members always lived in groups—for example, flocks of birds, schools of fish, herds of herbivores, and bands of primates. Within the broad category of the social, group-dwelling animals, he observed that the individuals of some species gained an essentially passive benefit from their sociability. Many herbivores, for example (think of antelope, bison, or zebra), benefit from the multiplication of individual senses. If a single antelope in the herd sees, hears, or smells the approach of a predator and therefore takes flight, all the rest in the herd may take his or her flight as a signal and flee to safety. But antelope do not create or share goods in common.

Aristotle's second subcategory of group-dwelling animals was made up of species whose members live more actively social lives, in that they cooperate in the production of some tangible good that is publicly shared by all members of the community. The behavior of these public-good-producing creatures was designated by Aristotle as "political." Social insects provided Aristotle with his prime examples of nonhuman political behavior. In the *Politics*, he singled out honey bees, although he might just as well have referred to ants. In his major work on zoology, the *History of Animals* (1.1.20), he includes ants among political animals, along with bees, wasps, and cranes. He notes that, of these species "some submit to a ruler, others are subject to no governance; so, for instance, the crane and the several sorts of bee submit to a ruler, whereas ants and numerous other creatures are every one his own master." Aristotle erroneously thought that each beehive had a "king" who directed the other bees' activity. But, as we will see, he was right to believe that the ants of a given nest cooperate to produce public goods without a master. Like honey bees, harvester ants process and store food that is shared by all individuals in the nest. All creatures that live in clearly defined communities, producing and sharing public goods, are, in Aristotle's behavioral taxonomy, "political animals," whether they "submit to a ruler" or live "every one his own master."[7]

Humans, according to Aristotle, fell into the public-good-producing subcategory of social creatures, which is the basis of his famous claim that "the human being is a political animal" (*Politics* 1253a). Indeed, for Aristotle, humans were the *most* political of animals—that is, we are, in behavioral terms like social insects, only more so. Although, as we will see, Aristotle was well aware of the human propensity to engage in strategic behavior, the hypertrophy of human political nature was not, according to his behavioral theory, due to humans' capacity to act strategically in pursuit of their own selfish interests. Rather, humans are, for Aristotle, the most political of animals because of our uniquely human capacity to employ reason in pursuit of common ends and to communicate complex prosocial plans through the use of language.

The unique conjunction of reason and complex language enables humans to produce public goods that are greater, in abundance, variety, and (as Aristotle confidently believed) moral worth, than those produced by any other species. Our hyperpolitical nature is, for Aristotle, the relative advantage that humans enjoy in comparison to other animals—some of which are obviously stronger, faster, and have more acute senses of sight, smell, and so on than any human. Our political nature is the reason, we might then add, that the human race is so prevalent on the face of the Earth—why humans as a single species have recently (in evolutionary time) become, as ants as a taxonomic family have long been, a very large part of the total biomass of land animals.

Aristotle's discussion of humans as political animals was intended not only descriptively, as a naturalistic explanation of why humans behave as we do, but also normatively, as a moral argument for how we *ought* to behave. Unlike the philosopher David Hume, who famously claimed that it was a fundamental error to seek to derive an *ought* from an *is*, Aristotle supposed that certain moral duties arise directly from the specifics of human nature. In the *Politics*, Aristotle sought to explain to his readers, first, that the wellsprings of human behavior *do* lie in our ontological status as a certain sort of social creature. And next, he sought to show that, as a consequence of having an inherently social—indeed political—nature, humans *ought* (that is, have a moral duty) to behave in specific prosocial (public goods creating and preserving) ways. In a properly ordered Aristotelian society, then, cooperation would rightly (as a matter of justice, not merely of expediency) be praised and rewarded, while defection from cooperation would rightly be blamed and punished. He supposed that this felicitous condition could be achieved only in a polis, and moreover, only in a polis that was provided with the right resources.

Aristotle's moral "ought" served, and was clearly meant to serve, to distinguish polis-dwelling Greeks from their non-Greek neighbors—and very much to the favor of the former. Aristotle's attempt to show that the Greek polis was the most natural, and thus the best, system of social organization for humans was put to blatantly ethnocentric purposes. It led him into what we must now regard as a reprehensible attempt to justify slavery as both natural and moral. But despite these failings, it is worth our while to pursue Aristotle's naturalistic argument because it can help us to see what actually *is* historically distinctive about the citizen-centered social order developed in the classical Greek world, and how that social order contributed to the efflorescence of the classical era.

Aristotle's thought was strongly teleological. Human beings, Aristotle supposed, are like all other beings in that we have a proper end (in Greek, a *telos*). Achieving its end, in fullness, is what, in Aristotle's teleological naturalism, is best for each sort of being. Ends differ according to species: Each distinctive kind of being's end is specific to the kind of thing it is. Thus antelopes, ants, and humans all have their proper ends, but not the same ends. Our proper end as humans—and therefore what is best for us as humans—is, in Aristotle's account, hard-wired into the hyperpolitical sort of social beings that we are by nature. Aristotle supposed that it is only by attaining the highest and fullest form of its own proper end that a being (or a collectivity of social beings) could truly flourish. Human flourishing—construed as true well-being, genuine happiness, in Greek: *eudaimonia*—required the production of and access to a wide range of public goods. Human flourishing thus required behavior on the part of each individual human that was appropriately hyperpolitical in the sense of orientation to provision of the requisite public goods through cooperative social activity.

Aristotle knew, of course, that many individual beings and communities exist, and have long existed, in a state that could not appropriately be described as flourishing. There are, for example, individual ants and ant nests that are alive but in a self-evidently poor physical state, and likewise individual humans and human communities. Aristotle posited that certain species-appropriate material conditions are necessary for any creature or community of social animals to flourish. As a contingent matter of luck, these material conditions might, or might not, be adequately abundant in a given local environment. Obviously enough, every animal needs, at a minimum, enough oxygen, water, and food of the proper sort. For many species, appropriate shelter will also be necessary. For all political animals, the necessary conditions include access to raw materials from which the right sort of public goods (pollen to make honey for the bees, grain for harvesting and storage for the harvester ants) can be produced. If by bad luck resources are inadequate, the political community fails to flourish.

Assuming that the right resources *are* available, the flourishing of individual political animals requires that the right public goods be produced from raw materials and that each member of the community has access to public goods once they are produced. That, in turn, meant that individual flourishing required living in the right sort of community—not only one with the right resources but also with the right systems of production and distribution. For honey bees or ants, then, the conditions necessary for flourishing included living in a well-located and well-functioning hive or nest.

For humans, the conditions necessary for flourishing, according to Aristotle, prominently included living in a well-located and well-functioning city-state. The city-state was, he argued, a natural communal environment for humans, just as the hive was for bees or the nest for ants. This is a startling claim, and on the face of it an implausible one, when we consider how relatively rare extensive and long-lived city-state ecologies are in human history. But Aristotle's argument was about ultimate flourishing, not about historical prevalence. His argument hinged on the unique advantages that were offered to humans, as hyperpolitical animals, by life in a community large enough to be self-supporting but small enough to enable effective communication of important information among its members.

According to Aristotle, in every community of political animals, the individuals (bees, ants, or humans) constituting the group should be thought of as *parts* of a community *whole* (hive, nest, or polis). In each case, the right activity for each individual part (that is, what the bee, ant, or person ought to do) was to act for the common good of the community as a whole. Choosing to act cooperatively in ways that promoted the common good through the production of public goods was thus, for Aristotle, one way to define the ethical value of justice. Aristotle's second definition of justice was fairness in respect to the distribution of the public goods produced through social cooperation. These two aspects of justice link his moralized conception of human flourishing to collective material flourishing—and potentially, at least, to the high level of sustained collective flourishing that we are calling efflorescence. A well-ordered Aristotelian community produced enough public goods so that all of its members, through sharing fairly (each receiving goods according to his or her desert: a combination of need and virtue), could achieve their highest ends. The requirement that all members of the community have the chance to flourish up to their highest potential thus meant that the community as a whole must be highly productive and must divide the fruits of that productivity fairly.[8]

Ants, like humans, make mistakes, but ants are incapable of injustice in the Aristotelian senses of ignoring the common good or engaging in unfair distribution of public goods. In the case of social insects, there is no meaningful gap between the natural *is* and the moral *ought*: The nest is the only environment in which individuals of the relevant species of ants can survive. Cooperation in the production of essential public goods, and fair distribution of those goods among the members of the nest, is hard-wired. Individual ants have little, if any, capacity (much less desire) to behave strategically in order to pursue private advantage at the expense of their productive roles in the community, and so ants act justly by nature. But the vistas opened by reason and language give humans many more options—both in terms of the kinds of communities (city-states, empires, nomadic societies, nation-states) in which they may potentially live, and in terms of how individuals contribute to and benefit from those communities.

Aristotle knew that many peoples in the world lived in societies that were *not* organized as independent city-states. And, assuming that he consulted the 158 constitutional histories of mostly Greek city-states that were collected for him by his students, he certainly had at hand a great deal of evidence that showed that some residents of city-states failed to produce their fair share of public goods for the community. Much of Aristotle's *Politics* is devoted to squaring his naturalistic moral theory with readily observable facts about human history and sociology. He needed to explain to his readers how and why the *actual* behavior of humans, unlike that of social insects, deviated so often from what was *naturally and normatively* the right course for them as political animals—that is, the course that would lead to the collective achievement of the highest human ends by the members of a polis community, and thus to the flourishing of individuals and community alike.

His answer, in brief, was that human sociability was not enough to produce consistently cooperative behavior, in light of the human capacity and tendency to use our capacities for reason and communication to identify and exploit gaps between the good of the whole community and the interests of the individual or subgroup. If human political nature produced naturally just individuals, there would be no need for laws and education—which feature prominently in the description of the best possible city-state, "the polis we should pray for" that is the subject of books 7 and 8 of Aristotle's *Politics*. The purpose of political institutions in a well-ordered state was, in Aristotle's view, to close that gap—to align individual and factional interests with the collective good of the state as a whole. Much of the *Politics* is devoted to showing how specific mechanism designs could help achieve that salutary purpose—not only in the best possible state but also in the imperfect poleis of the real Greek world.

Unlike Aristotle in the *Politics*, my concern in this book is *not* to show that organizing human society into Greek-style city-states is the only, or even the most obvious, or even (in modernity) a feasible way to move forward toward collective human flourishing. We need not pursue Aristotle's sometimes tortuous explanations for why it is that so many human societies deviated from the one path that he supposed could promote true flourishing. Nor need we concern ourselves with his diagnosis of the origins of social-psychological pathologies that led polis-dwellers to ignore the common good.[9]

Our goal is to explain why and how, despite the various obstacles to large-scale efficient cooperation that are seemingly intrinsic to life in the Greek city-states, the communities and individuals that constituted the ancient Greek world did in fact flourish, materially and culturally. Much in Aristotle's teleological naturalism is clearly (in light of evolutionary science) mistaken and unhelpful in achieving our goal. But Aristotle's basic insight about the potentially beneficial role of political institutions in sustaining high levels of social cooperation in a community of citizens—that is, that good institutions could and should align the motivations of citizens with the collective good of the community, and that it was within the abilities of real-world states to make institutional changes that would go some ways to achieving that alignment—does help to explain the classical efflorescence. My proposed solution to the puzzle of decentralized cooperation in the ancient Greek world is based on Aristotle's basic insight and on several related Aristotelian ideas.

I propose that Aristotle was right about the following things: Humans are like other political animals in our production and distribution of public goods.

We are distinctive among social animals in our natural capacities to use reason and our ability to communicate complex ideas and information through language. Well-ordered human communities produce and distribute public goods through the development and prosocial use of human capacities of reason and communication. Societies that offer individuals especially rich opportunities to use those distinctive capacities are (all other things being equal) especially conducive to both individual and collective flourishing. Unlike bees (which Aristotle erroneously believed were subject to monarchical rulers) or ants (which he correctly believed were "each [her] own master"), Aristotle knew that human societies can be either autocratic or citizen-centered. But citizen-centered communities are (once again, all other things being held constant) more likely to enable individuals to use reason and communication in the pursuit of public goods than are highly hierarchical societies.[10]

The efflorescence of the city-states of Hellas was, as I argue in chapter 5, promoted by high levels of specialization and innovation. Those were in turn made possible through the reliable production and fair distribution of bountiful and varied public goods. All of this was accomplished through self-governance, by citizens: individuals who, like ants, were their own masters and not under the command of a centralized, third-party governmental authority. The political structure of the Greek polis was well adapted—by the use of reason, history, and learning rather than by nature alone—to the production and application of new knowledge and the exchange of information among many of the community's members. Institutions and culture promoting communication of useful knowledge among citizens (and sometimes noncitizens) sustained a complex set of activities and thereby potentially allowed for high levels of collective and individual flourishing.[11]

DISPERSED VS. CENTRALIZED COOPERATION

If the Aristotelian claims sketched in the previous section are right, and if, counterfactually, Greeks had been more like masterless ants, in terms of having an unproblematically hard-wired propensity to cooperate in the effective production of public goods for their local communities, the answer to why Hellas flourished in the classical era would be obvious. But the Greeks were certainly no more *inherently* cooperative than are the people of any other society. Indeed, competition—between individuals and communities—was a hallmark of ancient Greek culture. Hellas, with its agonistic values, its multiplicity of small states, its lack of centralized authority, its emphasis on the value of independence for states and of freedom of choice for the individual, seems on the face of it poorly positioned for an efflorescence based on cooperation. Why, given the salient differences between Greeks and most other great civilizations in terms of the centralization of authority, did the little corner of the Earth that was the Mediterranean/Black Sea Greek world do so well for so long?[12]

For all the obvious disanalogies, what makes the ants around a pond analogy useful as a starting point for an investigation of Greek flourishing—more useful than Plato or Aristotle could have guessed, given their limited knowledge of the actual behavior of social insects—is precisely the absence of central authority. In this crucial respect, the Greeks of Hellas appear rather like ants, and rather unlike most of the other highly civilized peoples of the premodern world. It would not make much sense, for example, to analogize the Egyptians of the Old, Middle, or New kingdoms with "ants along the banks of the Nile." Aristotle was right that the Greeks were, in this salient way, unlike their civilized neighbors.[13]

Unlike social insects, and unlike Plato's and Aristotle's contemporary Greeks, ancient Egyptian society was oriented around a unitary and legitimate central authority: a king (pharaoh). The Egyptians expected the king to manifest in his person, and to maintain through his rule, the order of their world. Most Egyptians indeed lived in many villages scattered along the banks of the Nile. But the king of Egypt decided, for example, when the unified kingdom of Egypt went to war, and with whom: It was not left up to a process of distributed or collective decision-making in the villages. The king's will (at least in principle) was law and determined many aspects of the activity of each individual Egyptian. Egyptian literature celebrated the authority of the king and registered the deepest dismay when the centralization of authority was temporarily disturbed. While there were practical limits to the extent of centralization, the political and social organization of ancient Egypt is inexplicable without reference to centralized royal authority.[14]

So it was, with relevant modifications for local cultural specificities, for many of the great civilizations of western Asia with whom the Greeks shared their extended world, for example, ancient Persia, Phrygia, and Lydia. Yet others of the Greeks' neighbors, notably the Etruscans of northwestern Italy and the Phoenicians of the Levantine coast, lived in vibrant and commercially oriented city-states. The Etruscans, massive importers of sixth and early fifth century BCE Athenian painted vases, were ruled first by aristocrats and later by republican oligarchies. The political organization of a Phoenician city-state may in some ways have resembled that of a citizen-centered Greek polis, although most of the ca. 50 cities of the Phoenician Levant were under the control of just four powerful city-states. Although early Phoenician states were palace-centered and ruled by kings, the king's authority was probably limited by a council, and by the eighth century, wealthy traders were politically powerful. From the mid-eighth century BCE, the Phoenician city-states were incorporated into one or another of the great empires of western Asia, but it is not implausible to think that the emergent poleis of eighth century BCE Greece were influenced by the institutions as well as the culture of the Phoenician states. The highly successful Phoenician North African colony of Carthage was ruled by a wealthy oligarchy, headed by a king. Carthage was similar enough in constitutional order to a Greek state to be included in the catalogue of poleis whose constitutional history was collected by Aristotle's students. By the sixth century BCE, the government of Carthage served as a centralized authority for an extensive empire.[15]

By contrast, with the partial and ephemeral exception of the unified Macedonian empire at the end of the fourth century, Hellas was never brought together as an empire with a unified center—although it was not for want of effort: Syracuse acted as an imperial sovereign in Sicily for parts of the fifth and fourth centuries, and Athens built a regional Aegean empire, incorporating hundreds of Greek states for much of the fifth century BCE (ch. 8). There was never an emperor of Hellas—although near the end of our period, Philip II of Macedon and his son Alexander the Great came close (ch. 10). In their wake, several large kingdoms competed for power and wealth in the Hellenic world, but many poleis continued to function as independent states (ch. 11). Finally, few Greek city-states were ruled by a single family for more than two consecutive generations. Despite attempts by would-be imperial poleis and by tyrants to "normalize" the polis world through centralized authority, Hellas remained, in classical antiquity, distinctively and peculiarly "antlike" in the dispersed and decentralized nature of political authority. The pattern held at the level of the Greek world as a whole and at the level of the individual polis.

The highly complex activities carried on by most middling or large Greek city-states, and especially by large democracies, were the products of communication and choice-making on the part of many individual citizens who did not know one another as individuals. Given that most Greeks lived in middling or large poleis (table 2.1 and ch. 4), we cannot resort to Mancur Olson's small-group exception to explain decentralized Greek cooperation. Choices were strongly influenced by formal and informal rules, but the rules of the community were not given or enforced from above, by a supreme ruler or by divine dispensation. The rules governing each polis, laws and customs alike, were self-consciously devised and often revised, by the citizens themselves. The citizens of each polis acted as a collectivity—as a more or less coherent group agent.[16]

Likewise, the higher level interpolis coordination between Greek states that was sometimes achieved in the recognition of common regional interests, or in the face of common threats (ch. 9) was a matter of interstate communication and cooperation. With a few exceptions (most notably the relatively short-lived Syracusan and Athenian empires: ch. 8), there was no central authority structuring when or how a number of city-states would choose to collaborate on common projects, or whether and how they would oppose common enemies.

In sum, it is the combination of a coherent and extensive Greek cultural zone, around the shores of the two great seas, and the lack of cohesive central authority, either for the cultural zone or in the individual communities that comprised it, that makes Hellas appear in some ways so strikingly like Plato's ants around the pond and that renders Hellas so unusual in premodern history. In light of Olson's theory of collective action, which posits that large-scale noncoercive cooperation is simply not possible, the distinctive Greek form of geopolitical organization poses a puzzle: How did the residents of city-states manage to act as an effective group agent in the absence of centralized authority? It is fine and well for Aristotle to claim that people *ought* to act cooperatively, but why would they be motivated to do so, and how did they manage to do so in ways that were highly productive?

HOBBES VS. ARISTOTLE

Group agency and collective action are easier to explain in political systems featuring strong individual leadership and centralized authority—which is why the relative success of ancient Egypt, Lydia, or Persia is less of a puzzle: A unitary royal will determined (at least in principle) the choices of the community. A centralized-authority community, although in fact made up of many individuals possessing unique sets of preferences and diverse interests, is in principle an extension of a single intelligence and will.[17]

If the king's preferences are coherently ordered; if his choices, expressed as commands, reflect his preferences; and if the individuals making up the community act on the basis of his choices via a hierarchical system by which orders are passed down in a chain of command to the base of the social pyramid, then the community may be regarded as functioning like a rational individual.[18] If we further suppose that the king has a good sense of what needs to be done (e.g., in the way of public works necessary for basic state security), then we can readily grasp why the state that he rules does adequately well. The same may be said to be true of a society ruled by a cohesive junta of like-minded rulers. The result (ch. 1) is the centralized and autocratic "natural state." As we have seen, a natural state is not optimally productive, but it does solve the problem of the motivation and mechanism of cooperation. The necessity of a ruler (or unified ruling junta) to provide coherent direction for an extended community of individuals with diverse preferences and interests is the core assumption of many influential accounts of political authority. Among these, in the Anglophone European tradition, Thomas Hobbes' *Leviathan* (1996) holds pride of place.

Hobbes, who was fluent in ancient Greek, was well versed in Aristotle's political philosophy, and he engaged directly with Aristotle's vision of humans as political animals, taking the comparison to social insects head on: "It is true that certain living creatures, as bees and ants, live sociably one with another (which are therefore by Aristotle numbered amongst political creatures), and yet have no other direction than their particular judgments and appetites; nor speech, whereby one of them can signify to another what he thinks expedient for the common benefit." Hobbes acknowledged that "therefore some man may perhaps desire to know why mankind cannot do the same" (*Leviathan* 17.7).

Hobbes' answer was, he supposed, decisive:

1 Humans, unlike social insects, were "continually in competition for honour and dignity,"
2 For social insects, common and private goods were identical, "But man, whose joy consisteth in comparing himself with other men, can relish nothing but what is eminent."
3 Social insects, lacking reason, do not find fault with one another, whereas men habitually do.
4 Lacking language, social insects cannot misrepresent reality to one another, as men do.
5 Social insects make no distinction between injury and damage, as men do.
6 "Lastly, the agreement of these creatures is natural," whereas humans can have agreement only by "artificial" covenants between them, and thus they require a third-party coercive enforcer of agreements: an absolute ruler, standing above and outside the law (*Leviathan* 17.8–12).

In short, the production and fair distribution of public goods was simply impossible absent a central authority. Moreover, without central authority, human life was utterly miserable.

Hobbes famously argued that the only alternative to highly centralized political authority was a grim state of nature—one in which human existence would necessarily be "solitary, poor, nasty, brutish, and short." Hobbes countenanced a direct form of majoritarian democracy (in which whatever was decided by direct vote of the majority, no matter how prejudicial to any minority, was law) and an equally tyrannical form of aristocracy among the possibilities for central authority. But he clearly favored monarchy as the most efficient solution. Hobbes' core argument, that only a strong, legally unconstrained, central government can bring the order necessary to civilized life in a complex society, has seemed intuitively convincing to many of his readers ever since. His line of thought has a very long history; the basic notion that order is both essential for decent human life and impossible without central authority was prominent in political thinking long before Hobbes (cf. Egyptian wisdom literature, cited above) and has remained influential despite many attempts to show that Hobbes was wrong.[19]

Strong centralized authority not only helps to explain how a group may function as a collective agent through the guidance of a single will but also explains why the individual members of an extensive group rationally choose to cooperate with one another. As we have seen, modern social scientists have identified cooperation as a fundamental problem confronting any relatively large human society. If we assume that individuals are at least to a degree rationally self-interested (i.e., each will under some circumstances seek to maximize his or her expected utility), cooperation at scale becomes problematic. Why, as Mancur Olson asked, does each individual not choose to free ride on the cooperative behavior of others by contributing as little as possible to the public good while taking from it as much as possible? And if some are free riding, then why ought anyone else cooperate? This problem is not just a fiction of modern social science; it was well understood by the ancient Greeks themselves. The Hobbesian tradition has a very good answer.[20]

In a centralized-authority state, a king or ruling junta has both the incentive (rent-seeking) and the means (the rational cooperation of violence specialists who share the rents) to establish a system of monitoring and sanctioning such that free riders were likely to be caught, and, when caught, punished. Moreover, many centralized-authority societies have the means to develop and promote ideologies that discourage free riding. If there is a general belief that the king is divine or has a unique access to divine will, if the divine order is believed to punish disobedience (perhaps in the afterlife), and if free riding is regarded as disobedience, each member of society has good reason to obey the king by obeying his commands. Moreover, and just as important, each individual has good reason to believe that everyone else has good reason to obey. And thus, ideally, no one will free ride: All cooperate through obedience to the dictates of the king.

Of course in the real world, no system of monitoring is perfect and no ideology is seamless. But even though the command-and-control/ideological system is imperfect, it may be good enough to prevent a cooperation-destroying race to the bottom. This is, presumably, why centralized-authority political systems are historically common. It is also, with a few tweaks (more monitoring, less belief in a divine order, with the Party standing in place of the King), why highly centralized forms of political authoritarianism remain so common in the contemporary world—long after the apparent victory in much of the world of Enlightenment ideals of democracy, individual freedom, and equality.

The Greek city-states for the most part failed to establish command-and-control bureaucracies. Nor did the Greek world develop an integrated master social or theological narrative that would have provided ideological support for the necessity of individual obedience to central authority. It was to correct that ideological lacuna that Plato, in the *Republic*, proposed to introduce a "Myth of Metals" (each resident will be told that he or she was born with a gold, silver, bronze, or iron soul and is duty-bound to act accordingly) as a foundational Noble Lie that would sustain the rule of philosopher-kings in an ideal, highly hierarchical polis. As we have seen, there was no divine king capable of commanding obedience, either in Hellas or in the individual city-states. The laws of the Greek states were, for the most part, recognized by the Greeks themselves as products of human invention. While the Greeks did see their gods as a source of justice, and certain forms of criminal behavior were thought likely to incur divine wrath, there was nothing like the full-featured ideology of necessary obedience to a divine order that helped to sustain cooperation within societies predicated on a centralized royal authority.

Outside philosophical circles, the idea of setting up an absolute ruler in the interests of promoting order was limited to would-be tyrants. Greek oligarchs and democrats alike sought to prevent the emergence of tyrants, but the Greek world had enough experience with tyrants to allow a rough natural experiment that tests Hobbes' theory of necessary absolutism. If Hobbes was right, poleis run by tyrants should consistently have outperformed citizen-centered oligarchies and democracies and, over time and across the ecology, tyranny should have driven out citizen-centered regimes. Although the history of Greek Sicily shows that tyranny was sometimes associated with local prosperity (ch. 8), tyranny certainly did not drive out oligarchy, much less democracy (chs. 9–11), and there is reason to believe that the highest performing democracies (notably Athens and Syracuse in its democratic era, 465–412 BCE) outperformed even the highest performing tyrannies. Again, we are faced with the puzzle of why and how that could have been. One way to solve the puzzle is to dig more deeply into the behavior of the "masterless" ants.[21]

ANTS AND INFORMATION EXCHANGE

I suggested above that Aristotle's theory of humans as political animals can help to explain the classical efflorescence. But Aristotle's natural and moral account of politics lacks an adequate "micro-foundation": an explanation of individuals' motivation for cooperation. Nor does it describe an underlying mechanism that would account for how it is that, once motivated, many individual social insects or humans could produce complex public goods in the absence of centralized direction. In the case of social insects, modern biological science fills the gap, providing explanations of both motivation and mechanism. Ants belonging to a single nest are motivated to cooperate by their close genetic kinship. In regard to the mechanism, ants are able to achieve their complex ends because they constantly and actively exchange information with one another. Albeit these are very simple bits of information, the aggregate effect of the many information exchanges is high-level coordinated behavior much more complex than the movements of schools of fish or flocks of birds—animals that are "gregarious but not political" in Aristotle's scheme.

The discussion of ant behavior in this section (and elsewhere in this book) is based on the work of my Stanford colleague Deborah Gordon, a leading evolutionary biologist, who directs a long-term study of the behavior of nests of harvester ants at a site in the Chiricahua Mountains of southeastern Arizona. Gordon's research explores how ant nests function as quasi-organisms, sustaining highly complex forms of collective activity without resort to anything remotely resembling centralized control. Gordon demonstrates how the collective behavior of the nest emerges and adapts over time in response to environmental change. It does so through countless exchanges of simple bits of information among thousands of individual ants.

In the following paragraphs, the world of harvester ants, as described by Gordon, is adapted to Plato's simile, and thus to the physical world of the Greek city-states, by situating the nests in the immediate proximity of a pond, rather than in a desert. The imaginary "Platonic pond ants" discussed below have the behavioral traits of Gordon's desert-dwelling harvester ants. Thinking about nests of ants as an extended thought experiment in collective action, imaginatively getting down on our hands and knees to peer more closely at the miniature ant world into which Plato's simile and Aristotle's taxonomy invite us, highlights for us what is most historically distinctive about the city-states of ancient Greece and offers us information exchange as a basic mechanism underpinning decentralized productive cooperation.[22]

Ants, as a taxonomic family of something like 14,000 species, have been extremely prevalent across most of the land surface of the Earth for tens of millions of years. Today ants comprise a large, if not accurately measurable, part of the total biomass of land animals. Ants have, in short, flourished. One key to their flourishing is their social behavior: Ant nests are hives of collective activity. The obvious point is that antlike social behavior is one route (of course not the only route) to collective flourishing for social animals. Comparing Greeks to ants risks confusing analogy with explanation. Yet if we employ the analogy carefully, as a heuristic device, it can help us to distinguish more clearly why the political and social organization of the Mediterranean/Black Sea world of the Greek city-states produced a historically remarkable efflorescence.

Entering the microrealm of ants dwelling around a pond, we notice that some of the anthills that interest us are located right on the shore of the pond, others lie back a ways, but all are quite close to the water. Once we move any distance from the pond's edge, we find that all the ant nests belong to other species. These other ant species are in some ways quite different from the pond ants with which we are primarily concerned. The nests of ants of different species differ in appearance and behavior—the various ant species go about food gathering in distinctive ways, treat their dead differently, use different means to attack their enemies, and so on. By the same token, the nests of each species are alike in many salient ways. The species that we are focused upon has adapted to the immediate environs of the pond as its unique ecological niche.[23]

The nests of our pond ants vary considerably in size: Each nest is inhabited by several thousand to several hundred thousand ants. All ants belonging to a given nest recognize one another as nest-mates. They interact with their nest-mates in specific ways, behaving quite differently toward all other ants. Each nest has its own more or less well-defined territory. Within that territory, the ants belonging to a given nest work cooperatively; their activity prominently includes foraging to extract resources from their environment. Because there are many nests, because the nest territories are not perfectly well defined, and because resources are limited, there is periodic violent conflict among the ants from neighboring nests. The conflicts are both intra- and interspecies: The pond ants of a given nest protect their territory against pond ants from other nests—that is, against animals that are behaviorally like themselves—as well as against ants of other species, animals that differ substantially from them.

The nests constructed by our pond ants are all superficially alike in that each has a standard physical infrastructure. Yet each nest is a world of its own, with its own history, beginning from the day its founder-queen flew away from her home nest, mated, came to Earth in a new place, and began the new colony. If all goes well, the new nest will live for dozens of years, although no given ant, other than the queen, lives longer than a year. A successful nest grows in size over time. As the nest matures, the collective behavior of its ants changes in subtle ways—most notably, the instances of violent clashes with same-species ants of neighboring nests are likely to decline.

The ants of a given nest take on very different tasks: foraging for food, properly disposing of dead nest-mates, attending to the immature ants, and working on the tunnels and other infrastructural features of the nest. If we observe closely and manage to distinguish one individual ant from another (perhaps, as Deborah Gordon's research assistants do, by daubing them with spots of nontoxic paint) we notice something remarkable: An individual ant takes on different tasks at different times of day and on different days. Yet their physical appearance and genetic makeup is very similar: Most of the ants of the nest are morphologically almost identical. There is only one possible conclusion: The role assumed, day by day, by each ant in the work of the nest is specified by something supplementary to its genetic makeup. Yet, try as we may, we will not be able to find any form of top-down organization in any given nest, much less in the larger ecology of the ants living around the pond. No ant ever undertakes to organize the nests around the pond into a pond-ant empire.[24] Nor does an individual ant ever determine what goes on within a given nest. In each nest, a single queen lays eggs. She is the common mother of all the ants of the nest, and the nest will die soon after she does. But she does not give orders, or advice, or direction of any kind.

As Gordon has documented, the extragenetic something that determines the behavior of individual ants, and organizes a mass of individual behavioral choices into productive collective activity that is responsive to changes in the external environment, is the information exchanged among thousands of individuals, through a plethora of binary interactions. If we pay close enough attention, we see that the ants of a given nest are constantly interacting with one another. When an ant encounters a nest-mate, she will typically touch the other's antennae with her own, rather than ignoring her or trying to bite her head off, which are the two primary choices when encountering a same-species non-nest-mate. The result of each touch is the transfer of a discrete bit of information. It is through the multitude of these individual encounters, and the information that is exchanged in them, that the seemingly highly organized activity of the nest is brought about.[25]

Each bit of information exchanged by two ants meeting is very simple. Yet the sum of those many bits of simple information is profoundly powerful: It conditions what happens in the nest—which ant does what and when, and thus what collectively gets done by the nest acting as a quasi-organism. The aggregation of a great many very simple bits of data ("ant now leaving nest to forage," "ant now arriving in nest with food," "ant now arriving at nest without food")—in a process that in some ways mimics certain forms of machine-computational intelligence—enables the nest to adjust its collective rate of foraging, for example. And if, as a result, the ants of a nest forage at a rate that is well suited to the environmental conditions, the nest does well as a collectivity: It brings in more in the way of essential resources (e.g., food, water) than is consumed by the energy-burning activity of the foraging individuals.

It is through many individual information exchanges that, collectively, the nest "knows" what needs to be done and thus is able to respond to environmental change. It knows to change its collective behavior based on a changing environment (e.g., more or less rainfall), and it "assigns" the necessary tasks to individuals in ways that conduce to the collective flourishing of the community. This emergent and decentralized collective intelligence, all the product of a mass of very simple information exchanges, is the secret to the ants' success.

The "Platonic pond ant" thought experiment offers a way to think about natural collective self-organization, through information exchange, as a way for an extensive ecology of beings to flourish over time in a challenging and changing environment. It suggests that there is nothing preternatural about the efflorescence of the decentralized world of the Greek city-states. I would suggest, as a working hypothesis to be tested in the chapters to come, that the ancient Greeks reproduced the ants' process of successful decentralized organization through constantly reiterated information exchange. The reproduction may be thought of as a sort of unconscious biomimesis, keeping in mind, of course, the very different scales of time and size that were involved and the great increase in complexity of outcomes that are made possible by human reason and communicative capacity. If this information-centered hypothesis is right, the key to effective decentralized human cooperation in the context of a state is enabling a wide variety of valuable (at a minimum: accurate and pertinent) information to be exchanged with great frequency by the residents of the state. The hypothesis would be falsified, of course, if, relative to central-authority systems, citizen-centered Greek poleis tended to discourage information exchanges. The evidence of Greek history does not, as we see, support the falsification condition.

LIMITS TO THE ANTS–GREEKS ANALOGY

Even at the highest level of imaginative generality, the ants–Greeks analogy can take us just so far. We must also attend to the striking disanalogies. Start with the pond itself: Although some species of ants are able to cross small streams by creating living ant bridges, ants do not intentionally venture out onto the water by choice. By contrast, the Greeks constantly went down to the sea in ships and did business in the great waters that defined their corner of the world. They exploited the bounty of the Mediterranean and Black Seas for fish and other marine products (e.g., shellfish for high-value purple die), but even more importantly they used the sea as a means of easy transport from one port of call to another—and thus as a means of facilitating exchanges. Travel by land in the mountainous geography that defined much of the Mediterranean–Black Sea zone was notoriously difficult, slow, and expensive. But the Greeks moved readily and rapidly across the surface of the two seas, in sailed ships powered by wind and oared ships powered by the strength and skill of men. Moving goods and people over the water vastly facilitated mercantile trade and information exchange. Overseas travel enabled the Greeks to take advantage of the diversity of their Mediterranean–Black Sea world, interweaving the crazy quilt of geographic, climatic, and social microzones into a complex network of cultural communication and economic interdependency.[26]

Next and at a more basic level, although, as we have seen, individual ants do exchange information and act accordingly, and although the behavior of the nest changes over time, ants do not learn in ways that would enable self-conscious innovation. The ant nest has no long-term collective memory, no knowledge of its own history, no access to an accumulated nongenetic store of useful knowledge. Although the physical infrastructure of the nest persists across many year-classes of ants, each year-class is on its own; there is no inherited wisdom to call upon; no narratives of past successes or failures. Each year-class makes do with its genetic inheritance and with the emergent properties of simple-information exchange. The experiences of each successive year-class die with it. This makes explaining behavioral changes in the collective behavior of a nest over time a major puzzle for students of ant behavior. But there is less mystery about how and why the behavior of a Greek polis changed, sometimes radically, over the generations or even within a single human generation, through the iterated processes of information-based innovation and learning.[27]

Innovation, in the world of the ants, is dependent upon the standard evolutionary mechanism of random mutation and adaptation. Unlike groups of humans, ants cannot innovate culturally. By contrast, human culture may change quickly, based on immediate experience, on a new idea, or on the interpretation of historical experience. The citizens of a Greek polis learned from the accumulated historical memory of their polis. They also learned from the historical experience of other city-states, and they borrowed and adapted institutions and cultural traits accordingly. Moreover, they learned from their non-Greek neighbors in ways that proved to be profound and persistent. Finally, the unique human capacity to use reason and to communicate complex ideas through language potentially enables very extensive forms of cooperation among as well as within communities. Although ants engage in complex forms of social cooperation with nest-mates, same-species ants of different nests are unable to cooperate on common projects that would be mutually beneficial to several nests, nor can they unite against common threats. In short, communities of ants cannot know, nor can they make, nor can they make use of their own histories, as communities of humans can and do—for good and ill.

The human capacity to employ information of complex kinds, historical as well as current, to innovate and thus to drive big changes over short time horizons explains differences in ant and human timescales: The rise and fall of the polis ecology happened over a span of hundreds of years. Ant development must be measured across the span of millions of years. Nevertheless, if the analogy holds (albeit at a very high level of generality), the information-exchange-driven collective social behavior of ants will help us to understand how the decentralized ecology of Greek poleis might have produced a remarkable efflorescence in the absence of the centralized organization that, as we have seen, is often taken as the necessary condition of human flourishing.

Before that conclusion can be accepted, however, we still need to explain motivation: Why is quasi-antlike cooperation at scale chosen by the individuals who make up human communities? Hobbes supposed that, absent a third-party enforcer, humans could never manage to cooperate at scale.[28] Even Aristotle, despite his teleological naturalism, declined to attribute human cooperation in complex communities simply to the fact of natural sociability—as we have seen, he supposed that law and education were essential to the successful maintenance of the kinds of social cooperation that conduced to human flourishing. The motivation (as opposed to the operational mechanism) of cooperation among ants is now regarded by natural scientists as unremarkable, insofar as all nest-mates are close relatives, and, as such, share a sociobiological "genetic interest" in collective flourishing. Moreover, lacking individual strategic rationality, ants have no way to distinguish individual from collective flourishing. If the ant analogy is to be of value, we need to explain how cooperation in a Greek polis, or even between poleis, might be well enough motivated to enable the mechanism of information exchange to gain traction among many individuals who were not closely related to one another genetically and who were quite capable of distinguishing individual from common interests.

MOTIVATING COOPERATION AMONG NONRELATIVES

All ants of a given nest are daughters of the queen, either sisters or half-sisters.[29] Given their shared genetic inheritance and thus their shared reproductive interest, cooperation among ants is, in evolutionary terms, adaptive. Although ants do not use reason, we may say that ant cooperation is, in terms of expected utility maximization, rational. The flourishing of the nest ensures the survival of each ant's genetic inheritance—there is, in Aristotle's terms, no gap between the good of the whole and the good of each individual part. Residents of a given Greek polis were not, of course, genetically related to one another at anything approaching an ant-nest level of genetic closeness. So how could active cooperation have been motivated among the residents of a polis—who *shared* with the ants a lack of direction from any central authority, but who *lacked* the ants' strong genetic reasons for ongoing cooperation?

Ideology may provide a partial answer. Some city-states, prominently including Athens in the imperial mid-fifth century, tried, through the medium of culture, to promote an ethnic origins narrative that claimed something like the biological kinship of the ant nest. According to one strand of Athenian mythology, all native Athenians (and indeed, by extension, all Ionian Greeks) traced their ancestry back to a single Earth-born queen (Creusa: the story is told in Euripides' tragedy, *Ion*). So Athenians might suppose that by acting for the good of their fellow citizens, they were also acting for the good of close kin. But in the Greek polis, this fictive kinship story did not enjoy a monopoly among narratives of origin. The "all Athenians as kin through a common mother" myth faced rivals in competing and contradictory stories that emphasized that the population of Athens was heterogeneous, the result of immigration from many different regions of the Greek world (Thucydides 1.2.6). Many Athenians and their imperial subjects certainly recognized the myth of shared ancestry as a fiction. Ideologies of fictive kinship presumably gave some Greeks some reason to choose to cooperate with their fellows, but an ideology of kinship cannot, in and of itself, account for the phenomenon of general cooperation.[30]

Another possible answer lies in attending to scale. As we have seen, the political economist Mancur Olson claimed that the problem of collective action does not arise, or not, at least, with the same urgency, in a very small, face-to-face community. In a community small enough for everyone to know everyone else, each can also keep an eye on what the others are up to. Free riding cheaters are likely to be caught out, and just as likely, to be promptly punished. I suggested above that smallness of scale might help to explain cooperation in the many very small Greek city-states, but that most Greeks lived in city-states that were too large to operate as face-to-face societies in which mutual monitoring would be reliably effective.

One of the challenges faced by large poleis, and most especially, superpoleis like Athens, was managing scale by creating and encouraging face-to-face subcommunities, and doing so without loss of polis-level coherence. That challenge was met at Athens through quasi-federal institutional reforms in the aftermath of a democratic revolution (ch. 7). Federalism was widely adopted in mainland Greece in the fourth century BCE (ch. 9). Federalist and quasi-federalist institutional experiments allowed Greek states to operate as extensive "networks of social networks"—and thereby contributed to solving the problem of monitoring and punishing free riders.

Why self-interested individuals would ever choose to take the potentially costly option of punishing cheaters long remained a puzzle. But recent work by social scientists on "altruistic punishment" suggests that in a given population, there are always a certain number of individuals who have a low tolerance for unfairness, and who therefore *enjoy* punishing doers of injustice. Although their choice to punish cheaters is *not* truly altruistic, the result of their choice is the important public good of rule enforcement. Those whose pleasure in dishing out just punishment is high enough willingly assume the costs of punishing. The frequency of voluntary choices to engage in socially beneficial punishment of cheaters can be increased if the community offers rewards for those who lead efforts to punish malefactors.[31]

The social rewards offered to punishers can be material or in the form of honors and recognition. In the latter case, the reward is greater if the community has successfully promoted an ideology that emphasizes the virtue of cooperative participation in monitoring and punishment, and the rightness of punishing defectors. That sort of ideology was common in large and successful Greek poleis—including Athens and Sparta (chs. 6, 7). The classicist and political theorist, Danielle Allen has shown how, in classical Athens, judicial institutions and political culture developed in tandem to create a "politics of punishment" that served to reward successful prosecutors, to generate collective anger at malefactors, and thereby to include the whole community in acts of public punishment. Where there is known to be a ready supply of punishers, the society as a whole benefits because, knowing that they are likely to be caught and punished, would-be cheaters are discouraged from cheating in the first place. And thus the community can sustain the sort of imperfect but workable cooperative order that we posited, above, pertains in efficient centralized-authority societies.[32]

Neither ideology nor smallness of scale nor altruistic punishment fully solves the puzzle of why Greeks were motivated to cooperate at scale, but together these conditions help to explain motivation. Another part of the solution can be found by attending to the endemic nature of intercommunity conflict in the city-state world. Each of the ca. 1,100 Greek city-states was a potential rival of each other city-state and therefore a potential threat to its neighbors. Conflict among neighboring poleis was common, and conflict could have deadly results. States that lost wars with their neighbors risked losing control of valuable resources. Victors would seize, as plunder, as much movable property as they could carry away. They might also take control of economically productive borderlands. If the defeat were severe enough, the defeated polis might become a dependent ally of the victor. Or the winners might simply dissolve the state of the defeated rival, incorporating its territory and population into their own polis. In the worst case, if the victors breached the city walls or otherwise forced an unconditional surrender, they might eliminate the rival polis entirely, killing the men and enslaving the women and children. The general point is that, under the conditions of limited interstate cooperation that reigned for much of Greek history across much of the Greek world, the stakes of intra-Greek, intercommunity conflict were high. When the choices are "costly cooperation" or "loss of livelihood and possible extermination," intracommunity cooperation becomes a rational choice.

Success in high-stakes regional conflicts is at least part of the explanation for the emergence, in the archaic period of Greek history, of the superpoleis that are one primary focus of subsequent chapters. While remaining small compared to the major states of early modern Europe, superpoleis grew at the expense of Greek communities that were, or might have become, fully featured poleis. The takeover by Athens of the town of Eleusis (home of an important mystery cult), and other major towns in the territory of Attica, was remembered in legend. The Spartan takeover of the southwestern portion of the Peloponnesus, in the hard-fought Messenian Wars of the early archaic period, was a defining event for Spartan history (ch. 6). Syracuse became the dominant Greek state of Sicily in the early fifth century through forcible relocation of the populations of Sicilian poleis (ch. 7). And, in the late fifth and early fourth centuries BCE, Thebes twice destroyed the small polis of Plataea, in an ultimately futile attempt to force all the poleis of the region of Boeotia into a single state (ch. 9).

The continuing attempts of bigger poleis to coerce their weaker neighbors gave the residents of both aggressor-states and potential victim-states more incentive to cooperate with one another. In some cases, cooperation meant voluntary submission to the superior power. In the introduction to his history of the Peloponnesian War, Thucydides notes that in early times, Greek coastal communities rationally acquiesced to the rule of a hegemonic power, the (semimythical) Cretan King Minos, and, in the long run, they benefited materially as a result (1.8.3: "love of gain would reconcile the weaker to the dominion of the stronger").

Yet classical Greek communities often failed to see it that way. Despite all the fierce fighting and periodic destruction of communities, the consolidation of the Greek world went only so far. The failure of attempts of Athens, Sparta, Syracuse, and Thebes to sustain stable empires was due in part to the unwillingness of the citizens in would-be imperial city-states to dilute their civic privileges by radical extension of quasi-citizenship (on the Roman model) to imperial subjects, in part to the strength of local polis identities and the effectiveness of local resistance (ch. 8). The emergence of the kingdom of Macedon in the mid-fourth century BCE ended the centrality of major independent poleis in Mediterranean history (ch. 10) but left most polis institutions intact. Macedonian warlords threatened the local independence of Greek cities but found the poleis hard targets when they sought submission rather than negotiation (ch. 11). The endemic risk posed to Greek communities by would-be predatory states, Greek and non-Greek alike, fostered decentralized cooperation by rewarding the high levels of mobilization that were facilitated by federalism and democracy.

We now have a theory of effective collective action with decentralized authority. The theory is based on a conception of human nature as at once social, interdependent, justice-seeking, self-interested, and strategic. That conception is consistent with contemporary social science and with ancient Greek thought. The theory explains (through a mix of ideology, federalism, "altruistic" punishment, and existential threats) individual motivation to cooperate in the absence of a unitary sovereign as third-party enforcer. It provides (through information exchange) a mechanism that enables many individuals to accomplish common goals and to produce public goods without requiring orders from a master.

The theory of cooperation developed in this chapter shows that a complex but decentralized social order is *possible* at the level of the individual state and across an extensive ecology of small states. The next chapter demonstrates that the classical Greek world actually *did* flourish economically; chapter 5 then proposes two hypotheses, grounded in our theory of collective action, to explain *how* citizen-centered political development contributed to the economic development of the Greek world.

4

WEALTHY HELLAS

MEASURING EFFLORESCENCE

In the later fourth century BCE, as Aristotle was writing the *Politics*, Hellas reached the peak of its classical efflorescence. This chapter documents the material conditions that provided the foundation for the cultural greatness celebrated by Lord Byron. Thanks to recent work by archaeologists, economists, and historians, we can specify, in considerable detail, how wealthy Hellas actually was. But first we need to establish a baseline: Just how wealthy ought we to *expect* classical Hellas to have been, if, counterfactually, it had reached only the median level of development of core Greece during the three-plus millennia from ca. 1300 BCE to 1900 CE? What is the *premodern normal* by which we can measure the divergence of the classical Greek economy from the expected path?

THE PREMODERN GREEK NORMAL

We may start our investigation of the premodern normal in the era shortly after Byron proclaimed contemporary Greece a sad relic. In the nineteenth and early twentieth centuries, Greece was, when compared with the more developed states of Europe, or to any premodern state in an era of efflorescence, a very poor country. In 1830, upon finally achieving independence from Ottoman Turkey, the population of Greece—comprising the Peloponnessus, the Ionian and Aegean islands, and central Greece south of Thessaly—was about 750,000 people. Life expectancy at birth was about 35.5 years in the early 1860s, by which time the population had grown to more than 1.1 million; life expectancy was undoubtedly lower in 1830 and before.

By 1890 (after territorial expansion that added the region of Thessaly), the population of the Greek state had reached about 2.3 million. By this time, Greece was experiencing severe Malthusian pressure. The population had exceeded its mostly agricultural resource base. The result was labor surplus, chronic unemployment, and widespread poverty, only partially alleviated by extensive overseas emigration, especially by adult men. In the decades before World War II, Greece was, per capita, the poorest nation in Europe. In the nineteenth and early twentieth centuries, much of the population of Greece was living quite close to subsistence.[1]

There is no reason to suppose that living conditions had been substantially better in the previous 1,500 years. The Greek core (defined as the territory controlled by the Greek state in 1890) had already declined from the classical peak by the Roman imperial era (first century BCE to second century CE). The third and fourth centuries CE saw further decline as the Roman Empire began to come apart. After a robust recovery in the early Byzantine period of the fifth and sixth centuries, Greece fell into an economic doldrums that lasted until the ninth century. The middle Byzantine period of the eleventh to fourteenth centuries saw some economic recovery. Yet in the late twelfth century, at a high point in medieval Greek history, Michael Choniates (later Metropolitan of Athens) wrote these poignant verses—anticipating Byron's sentiments by more than half a millennium:

> Though I live in Athens, I see Athens nowhere,
> Only dust, sorrowful and empty, blessed.
> Where is your magnificence, wretched city?
> All vanished, as if become a myth . . .

By around 1400, the population of Greece and median consumption had fallen to new lows. The early Ottoman period once again saw improvement; in ca. 1600, the population of the Peloponnesus was up to about 250,000. This was, however, no more than a quarter of the population of the same area around 300 BCE. The same 1:4 "early Ottoman to late classical" ratio holds for sixteenth century Boeotia. In much of Greece, these demographic gains were lost in the grim later Ottoman era of the seventeenth century. By 1685, the population of the Peloponnesus had dropped by half, to 125,000, approaching the Early Iron Age nadir of ca. 1000 BCE. While there was improvement in the eighteenth century, it was not until the later nineteenth century that the population of Greece began to climb toward the late classical peak, and even then incomes remained low enough to encourage large-scale emigration.[2]

At the other end of our historical spectrum, during the Late Bronze Age (LBA), known to historians as the Mycenaean period (1600–1200 BCE), Hellas (roughly the area of the Greek state in 1890 but including the island of Crete) was divided into approximately 15 small states; the median territorial extent of these LBA states has been estimated at ca. 1,500 km². Each state consisted of a primary urban area, centered on a fortified palace, surrounded by a number of secondary settlements (close to 300 such centers have been located archaeologically) and a scatter of smaller rural occupation sites. The Mycenaean states of Greece appear to be quite centralized, ruled by kings who controlled considerable military might (notably horse-drawn chariots) and ruled through a fairly elaborate bureaucracy. The economy of a Mycenaean state was directed from the palace, which served as a center of production and distribution of goods. Palace records, inscribed by scribes on clay tablets, tracked the movement of raw materials and other imports into the palace and of locally manufactured goods out of the palace.

The population of Hellas in the Mycenaean period (including Thessaly and Crete) was somewhere in the range of 600,000 people, suggesting that the overall population was less dense than it would be in Greece's "sad relic" era around 1830 CE. Judging by skeletal evidence for their health and the rich goods with which they were buried, the palace elite evidently lived well in the LBA. Wealth was concentrated in the palace and in the hands of local elites in secondary centers. Rents were extracted from industrial labor at the palace and from a rural population of agriculturalists and pastoralists. This is what we would expect from premodern autocratic states. There is little reason to suppose that, outside the palatial elite and the local elites who governed the territory in the name of the king, much of the population of Greece in the mid to later second millennium BCE lived substantially above subsistence.[3]

Economic conditions for some residents of the Aegean world were probably better before the Late Bronze Age. Crete and some of the Aegean islands experienced a notable efflorescence during the Middle Bronze Age of the seventeenth and sixteenth centuries BCE—the central era of the Minoan period. The palace-based Minoan culture was an early high point of Aegean civilization, marked by considerable wealth that may have extended beyond a narrow elite. The Minoan culture was weakened by natural disaster in the mid-fifteenth century, and Crete was conquered by the Mycenaeans of the mainland by ca. 1400 BCE. Although the Minoan efflorescence was not at the scale of the later classical efflorescence, it demonstrated the potential of the Aegean region for development, and, like the robust recovery of the fifth and sixth centuries CE, that an advanced level of economic development was possible under political conditions very different from the citizen-centered institutions characteristic of the classical Greek efflorescence.[4]

On the mainland, the LBA Mycenaean era marked the early peak of Greek population size and economic development. After the collapse of the Mycenaean civilization in ca. 1200–1100 BCE, Greece entered the Early Iron Age

(EIA, also known as the Greek Dark Age). At the start of this period, population and living standards declined sharply. The population of Greece reached a low of perhaps 330,000, about half of the LBA figure, around 1000 BCE. The early EIA was an era of general impoverishment: Imports of goods from outside Greece, while never falling to zero, declined even more precipitously than did the population. The palaces were abandoned, the bureaucracy withered away, writing was no longer used, and Greece fell back into illiteracy. There were many fewer urban settlements, and they were smaller than the palace centers of the Mycenaean era. Houses were small and poorly furnished.[5]

By most indications, the Early Iron Age nadir around 1000 BCE was an exceptionally poor era. That has considerable implications for thinking about the classical efflorescence. On one side, the low EIA bottom left a great deal of room for improvement: Simple reversion to the mean of premodern normal population and consumption, as represented by, say, the Late Bronze Age and Greece in 1830, would represent major progress. On the other hand, the economy of classical Hellas did not have much of a springboard from which to jump off.

The premodern Greek normal represented by the LBA and the early nineteenth century CE was considerably above the EIA nadir—but very far below the classical efflorescence. Demographically, the premodern normal was a population of fewer than a million people for the Greek core of the mainland south of Macedonia and Epirus, along with the Aegean and Ionian Sea islands—the territory defined by the late nineteenth century Greek state. By the last decade of the nineteenth century, the population of core Greece had reached 2.3 million. Yet median non-elite per capita consumption hovered uncomfortably near subsistence—which is, as we will see, the ordinary fate of premodern non-elite populations elsewhere in the world. Greeks responded to Malthusian pressure by emigration.

During the classical efflorescence, Greece was much more densely populated than the premodern norm. In the later fourth century BCE, the population of the part of Hellas occupied by the Greek state in 1890 (ignoring the extended Greek polis world to the west, north, east, and south) was in the range of 2.75 million (my lower bound estimate) to 3.5 million people (Mogens H. Hansen's upper bound, with discussion below). The population density of modern Greece did not equal that of the extended Greek world in the later fourth century until the 1920s (figure 4.1).

Even the low estimate of classical era population is several times the premodern normal. Moreover, during the same period, there is every reason to believe that, at least in the most highly developed ancient Greek states, many,

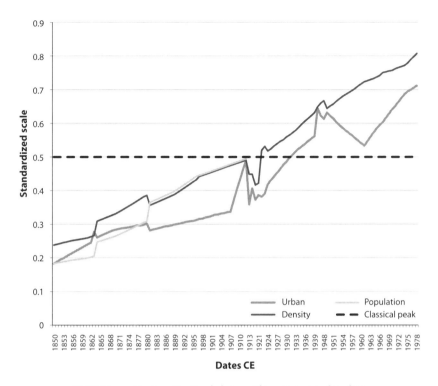

FIGURE 4.1 *Comparative Greek demographics, ancient and modern.*

NOTES: Modern data adapted from Country National Time Series (CNTS) Greece data (Banks and Wilson 2013). Normalized 0–1 scale. 1 = twice the classical peak.

URBANIZATION: Classical peak for Greek world = 32% of total population in towns of >5,000. CNTS data for percentage of population living in cities of more than 10,000 is available for 1919 to 1978; cities of more than 20,000 from 1850. "Over 5,000" figures estimated for 1919–1978 by adding the difference between the 10,000 and 20,000 figures (median 4.7%) to the 10,000 figure; estimate for 1850 doubles the median difference (9.4%) and adds that to the over-20,000 figure. DENSITY: Classical peak for Greek world = 44 per km². Modern density = CNTS population divided by area. POPULATION: Classical peak for core Greece = 2.75 million (Ober baseline estimate; Hansen 2006b, 2008 is higher). CNTS population is truncated at 1912 due to discontinuity in 1913. CNTS does not include data from 1914 to 1918.

perhaps most non-elite people were consuming well above the level of subsistence. By the later fourth century BCE, per capita consumption was well above the premodern normal and about twice what it had been 500 years earlier. In sharp contrast to the situation in Greece of the late nineteenth century CE, in the late fourth century BCE there was no evidence of a Malthusian trap: Development was not being constrained by limited resources, and there was no need to export surplus labor through emigration. Indeed, in the era of Plato and Aristotle, Hellas was a net importer of labor (slaves), food, and raw materials—and a net exporter of manufactured goods, cultural products, and expert services. In a word, Hellas, in the era of the classical efflorescence, was wealthy when compared to any point in Greek history before the twentieth century.[6]

OTHER STANDARDS OF COMPARISON

The notion that classical Hellas was wealthy comes as a surprise. Among the assumptions about the classical Greek world with which I grew up as a student of ancient history in the 1970s, was that the world of the Greek city-states was poor. This assumption was based in the first instance on what we can call the *standard ancient premise*. That premise is stated succinctly by the "Father of History"—the fifth century BCE Greek historian Herodotus: "Hellas has always had poverty as its companion." (7.102.1). In Herodotus' history, this statement is put into the mouth of Demaratus, a deposed king of Sparta, in the context of a conversation with Xerxes, the Great King of Persia. It has been cited frequently by later historians of the Greek world. Herodotus' quotable line, along with other passages in Greek authors to a similar effect, contributed to the formation of a *standard modern premise*. In the pungent early twentieth century prose of the British classical historian and political scientist Alfred Zimmern, "the pioneers who created our European civilization were stricken with poverty all of their days . . . it was the doom of Athens that Poverty and Impossibility dwelt in her midst from first to last."[7]

Along with the familiar claim that it was the Greeks who pioneered European civilization, Zimmern's comment is notable for its assumption of Athenian exemplarity: For Zimmern, "Athens" stands for "Greece." How exemplary or exceptional Athens really was, and how much we can extrapolate from Athenian economic performance to the wider Greek economy, remain important questions to which we will return in this and in subsequent chapters. In the imperial fifth century, but also in the postimperial fourth century, Athens was certainly among the most prosperous of the Greek poleis. For our present purposes, it suffices to say that if classical Athens really was impoverished, as Zimmern claimed, then it is highly likely that the rest of the Greek world fared poorly. If Athens was relatively wealthy, it is reasonable to suppose that residents of the most developed states of the Greek world were quite well off.[8]

It has long been recognized that the poverty claim in the standard ancient premise must be understood in comparative rather than absolute terms. In

Herodotus' key passage, Demaratus compares the quotidian life of ordinary citizens in Greece (and especially Sparta) with the court of Xerxes, the Great King of Persia. When the lifestyle of the King of Persia is the standard, everyone in classical Greece was certainly comparatively poor. But, equally obviously, when we are attempting to compare the overall performance of ancient economies, "ordinary Greeks vs. court of Xerxes" is the wrong standard of comparison.[9]

I have suggested above that the right standard of comparison is the premodern Greek normal. But an alternative standard of comparison for the ancient Greek economy might be sought among the most advanced economies of the nineteenth to twenty-first centuries of our era. If Xerxes is self-evidently the wrong comparison for, say, ordinary-citizen Tellus of Athens (later in this chapter), then how about middle-class American John Doe? When we compare median income (in standardized dollars) or consumption (measured, e.g., in per capita energy use) in ancient Greece with the United States or with the most developed countries of western Europe in the nineteenth to twenty-first centuries, the Greek world, once again, looks impoverished.[10]

As in the case of Demaratus of Sparta's pointed contrast of ordinary Greeks to ultra-elite Persians, comparing ancient Greek and modern developed-country levels of income or consumption tells us *something*—but nothing that we do not already know. It is hardly news that median levels of consumption in contemporary developed economies are much higher than median consumption levels in any premodern economy: Tellus of Athens did not shop at Walmart. It is certainly worth investigating just *how much* higher modern consumption levels actually are. But using contemporary developed-country economies as a standard of comparison is not particularly informative if we are seeking to learn something new about the relative economic performance of premodern societies. Neither the Tellus/Xerxes nor the Tellus/John Doe comparison gives a satisfactory answer to the question, "Are the standard ancient and modern premises right?"

Rather than seeking to determine how much poorer Tellus was than Xerxes or John Doe, when we ask, "Are the standard ancient and modern premises concerning Greek poverty right?" what we want to know is how much better or worse off the ordinary Greek in the classical period was, when compared to the ordinary individual in the Greek premodern normal situation discussed above, or in other relatively well documented premodern societies. While we cannot answer the comparative welfare question directly, we can provide answers to questions that will in turn give us an indirect way to approach the question of comparative economic performance:

Was the rate of classical Greek economic growth high or low, relative to other premodern economies?

Was the classical Greek world more or less densely populated, and more or less urbanized, than other premodern societies?

Was the distribution of wealth and income across the classical Greek population relatively more or less equitable than that of other premodern populations? What part of the classical Greek population lived at a level high enough above subsistence to qualify as at least minimally decent?

Using these questions as proxies for investigating comparative general welfare, the answer to the question, "Was classical Greece impoverished?" is "obviously not"—Greeks in the age of Plato and Aristotle were not poor when compared to the Greek premodern norm or to people in other ancient or medieval societies. The Greek economy grew briskly in the period 800–300 BCE. By the later classical period, the Greek world was densely populated and highly urbanized. A high percentage of Greeks (or at least of Athenians) lived comfortably above the near-subsistence level of consumption that has been the economic fate of most people for most of human history. By the standards of other premodern economies, Hellas was wealthy. Moreover, despite the Demaratus–Xerxes exchange and similar passages in the *Histories*, there is reason to think that Herodotus (and by extrapolation, his original classical Greek readers) knew it.

The "Eastern monarch discusses comparative welfare with a wise Greek" motif of the Demaratus–Xerxes interchange is anticipated in a scene near the beginning of Herodotus' *Histories* in which King Croesus of Lydia (in western Anatolia) interviews Solon of Athens. The imagined date of this (perhaps imaginary) interview would have been some time in the sixth century BCE. The subject of their conversation is human happiness, and the context is relative wealth. Croesus expects Solon to acknowledge that Croesus is outstandingly happy on the basis of his superabundant wealth. But to Croesus' surprise, Solon instead names as the happiest person ever to have lived Tellus of Athens, "who came from a prosperous city ... and the circumstances of his life were likewise prosperous, by our standards" (Herodotus, *Histories* 1.30.4–5).

Tellus is not portrayed by Herodotus' Solon as a member of a privileged elite pulling down big rents as a result of his violence potential in a natural state. Quite to the contrary, he is depicted as a reasonably but not exceptionally well-to-do, Greek citizen of a reasonably well-to-do Greek polis. Tellus was, in Solon's pithy account, an ordinary Greek man who had been especially fortunate in his progeny (healthy and excellent children and grandchildren) and in his demise (timely, heroic death in victorious battle in defense of his homeland). Reasonably prosperous material conditions constituted a necessary precondition for Tellus' exceptional happiness, but the clear implication of the story is that many of Tellus' fellow-citizens enjoyed a similar prosperity. It was Tellus' relative advantages in respect to his descendants and death, not his wealth, that made Tellus' life an especially happy one. It is, however, the background material conditions of that life that concern us here: Tellus and his large and healthy family evidently lived comfortably above the level of bare subsistence, in a community in which living at that level was not regarded as remarkable.

For our purposes, the important point is this: If, as Herodotus' story implies, the material conditions enjoyed by Tellus and his family were fairly typical, then a decent level of income (i.e., enough to live well above subsistence) must have been fairly common in Athens, and by extrapolation, in other developed Greek states. A society featuring a substantial body of ordinary people, living in decent conditions, consuming well above the level of bare subsistence, would be, by ancient standards, an exceptionally wealthy society. Of course Croesus was vastly richer than Tellus. But, if we think about Lydia as an autocratic state, and the sociopolitical conditions sustaining the great wealth of Croesus and his court, we will have reason to doubt that many non-elite Lydians lived at Tellus' moderately prosperous level. The figure of "ordinary, relatively prosperous Tellus" was not merely a Herodotean fiction. As we will see, some 40–60% of classical-era Athenian residents (and perhaps of Greeks generally) fit a profile of Tellus-like moderate prosperity. Although a few premodern societies, notably Mesopotamian cities in sixth century BCE Babylonia, paid wages high enough to allow the presumption of quite extensive non-elite prosperity, there are very few documented cases of high-wage societies before the early modern period.[11]

We still lack the detailed studies of the economies of ancient Middle Eastern societies that would allow meaningful comparisons to the economy of Hellas. But it seems very unlikely, on the face of it, that the Lydian empire, or the Persian Empire, or indeed any other ancient empire substantially outperformed the Roman Empire of the first and second centuries CE in terms of per capita consumption or urbanization. We now have reasonable estimates of Roman imperial economic performance. Based on those estimates, Rome appears, by ancient standards, to have been an exceptionally prosperous and urbanized empire. The Roman economy was much bigger, and much more diverse, than the Greek economy. Comparisons can be misleading, but, by certain measures (aggregate and per capita economic growth, urbanization, and income distribution), the overall Greek economy of ca. 500–300 BCE appears to have outperformed the overall Roman economy of ca. 100 BCE–200 CE.[12]

If it is true that Rome economically outperformed other ancient empires and that Hellas performed well relative to Rome, then it is fair to say that the society of Hellas was, in fact, relatively wealthy by ancient standards. Moreover, certain features of the Greek economy (or at least the Athenian economy) of the fifth and fourth centuries BCE compare favorably with the most advanced premodern European economies—Holland and England in the fifteenth to eighteenth centuries CE.[13]

The explanation I advance in chapter 5 for the comparative wealth of Hellas in the classical era is, in the first instance, political and institutional. The point of the comparisons is to falsify the standard ancient and modern premises about Hellenic poverty, to highlight the role of politics in Greek social and economic development, and thus to begin to solve the puzzle of the remarkable efflorescence of classical Hellas.

Here are three premises that, if correct, give us good reasons to believe that classical Hellas was indeed comparatively wealthy:

Premise 1   The Greek economy grew steeply and steadily from 1000 to 300 BCE, both in its aggregate size and in per capita consumption.

Premise 2   By the fourth century BCE, Greece was densely populated and remarkably urbanized, yet living standards remained high.

Premise 3   Wealth was distributed relatively equitably across Greek populations; there was a substantial middle class of people who lived well above bare subsistence yet below the level of elite consumption.

The three premises, in the form of descriptive statements about the Greek economy, are based on economic models that are in turn based on extensive collections of empirical evidence for ancient Mediterranean and early modern European economies.

The rest of this chapter offers evidence that tests, and ultimately supports, the validity of each of the three premises. In the next chapter (ch. 5), drawing on the theory of decentralized cooperation developed in chapter 3, I offer two hypotheses to explain how and why the Greek economy performed comparatively well. The historical narrative that follows (chs. 6–11) tests those hypotheses.

HIGH AGGREGATE AND PER CAPITA GROWTH

My Stanford colleague, the archaeologist and historian Ian Morris, has assembled an impressive array of data for measuring Greek economic growth in the period 800–300 BCE.[14] The first factor to consider in measuring Greek economic growth is demographic change. It is uncontroversial to state that the population of Hellas grew substantially in the half-millennium 800–300 BCE. On the basis of J. K. Beloch's late nineteenth century surveys of literary evidence, supplemented by recent work in survey and excavation archaeology, Morris posits that the population of "the Aegean and the colonies in southern Italy and Sicily" rose from under 500,000 people in the ninth century to perhaps 4 million people in the fourth century. If this is correct, the Greek population of this part of the world increased about tenfold and the per annum demographic growth rate was over 0.4%. As Morris points out, this is a comparatively high rate of sustained demographic growth in a premodern society.[15]

Morris' figures are only estimates, but in order for Morris' posited demographic growth rate to be much too low, we would have to assume that the population of the Aegean/Italian–Sicilian Greek world in 800 BCE was much larger than 500,000, or that in 300 BCE the relevant parts of the Greek world had a population much less than 4 million. Neither counterfactual is plausible: For the early period, archaeologists have expended a great deal of time and effort searching for and analyzing sites from the Greek Early Iron Age (also known as the Dark Age), and they have done their best to show that the Dark Age was not so dark as all that (ch. 6). Despite their best efforts, known Early Iron Age Greek occupation sites remain comparatively sparse and small; as noted above, the nadir of Greek population, around 1000 BCE, was probably about 330,000.

At the other end of the time period, Morris' estimate of the population of the Greek world in ca. 300 BCE is in line with other demographic estimates since the nineteenth century. Moreover, it is substantially *lower* than the more recent, detailed, and highly plausible estimates of the Danish historian, Mogens Hansen, who uses different estimation methods, addresses a substantially larger geographic area, and includes communities that were incompletely Greek in culture. My own model of Greek demographic growth, based on Hansen's estimates, is illustrated in figure 2.1. Morris' claim of a tenfold increase should be regarded as a minimum.[16]

If we accept Hansen's mid-range figure of more than 8 million for the total population of the world of the poleis in the fourth century, meaning that (as well as accepting the modeling technique) we define "Greek" as a person living in a community that was substantially Greek in culture (rather than "Greek by ancestry"), it appears that the Greek population increased by a factor of 25 in the 700-year period between the Early Iron Age nadir and the peak of the classical efflorescence.[17] The geographic expansion of the Greek world accounts for more than half the rise in total population; see figure 2.1. The figures for "core Greece," discussed below, suggest a nadir-to-peak local population density increase in the range of eight- to tenfold, but this discounts all colonization and emigration.

The second key factor in estimating aggregate economic growth is per capita consumption. Morris sought to estimate changes in per capita consumption over the same 500-year period, 800–300 BCE. While there is no way to measure consumption directly, the proxies employed by Morris are telling. Morris assembled a substantial data set ($n = 405$) of Greek house plans. The median Greek house in the ninth century was small and squalid. Over the next 500 years, the median house became both much bigger and much better built. Looking at square footage alone, when account is taken of probable second stories, the change of the median house is more than 350%—from ca. 80 m² to ca. 360 m². Given the striking improvement in building standards, the total increase in the economic value of a house would actually have been substantially greater. Morris notes the difficulty of measuring the change in other consumption goods, but based on archaeological evidence of sites destroyed suddenly, he posits that, over the period 800–300, "a five- to ten-fold increase . . . seems reasonable."[18]

Moving from these numbers to total per capita consumption is a complex problem; a big part of premodern consumption was in the form of food and (where applicable) taxes and rents. Morris argues, on very reasonable grounds, that per capita consumption in ninth century Hellas must have been close to the subsistence minimum. By 300 BCE, however, he suggests that consumption had increased by at least 50% and perhaps as much as 95%. Thus, by 300 BCE, a typical Greek household was consuming half again to twice what an ordinary household had been consuming 500 years before. This range yields a per annum growth rate in per capita consumption of 0.07–0.14%. By comparison, the growth in the Roman per capita growth rate has been estimated at 0.1%.[19] I return to the question of Greek per capita growth below, showing that Morris' upper-range estimate is more likely than any lower estimate and that the actual rate of Greek per capita growth during 800–300 BCE was probably about 0.15%—one and a half times the estimated Roman growth rate.

Combining his estimate of demographic growth with his estimated growth in per capita consumption, Morris posits that total aggregate consumption growth (number of people × rate of consumption) in Hellas increased roughly

15-fold (assuming his lower per capita rate) to 20-fold (assuming the higher per capita rate) in the period 800–300 BCE, for an annual aggregate economic growth rate of 0.6–0.9%. As Morris points out, Holland is the gold standard for a high-performing early modern economy. The annual aggregate growth rate for Holland in 1580–1820 was about 0.5%. And so, as Morris notes, even if we were to cut his estimate of growth *in half* (and, per above, we have no reason to think we ought to do that), the Greek economy compares favorably with an exceptionally high-performing premodern economy.[20]

Morris' conclusions about relatively high per capita and aggregate Greek economic growth are consistent with other indirect proxies that point to substantial growth in the late archaic and classical periods. Based on data made available in the on-line version of the Oxford-based *Lexicon of Greek Personal Names*, I calculate that the number of known (from literary or archaeological sources) names of people in Attica (the territory of Athens) grew from ca. 1,200 in the sixth century to ca. 17,000 in the fourth century, an approximately 14-fold increase in less than 300 years. The increased visibility of individuals is obviously the product of multiple variables, notably growing rates of literary and epigraphic production. This high rate of growth in name visibility is consistent with a world in which many more people were consuming substantially more. Counterfactually, a world with a declining population in which most people lived at a level of bare subsistence would clearly be less conducive to rapid growth in the literary and epigraphic visibility of people's names.[21]

Based on data taken from the *Inventory of Greek Coin Hoards*, David Teegarden and I estimate (in an unpublished study) that the volume of coined money circulating in the Greek world increased substantially as well. Between the sixth and fourth centuries BCE, the median size of a Greek coin hoard (an indirect proxy for per capita rather than aggregate growth) roughly doubled, from 23 coins to 48 coins per hoard. Meanwhile, the average hoard size quadrupled, from 52 coins to 213 coins, reflecting the increasing incidence of some exceptionally large hoards.[22]

When looking at the total number of hoards, and at the total number of coins in all known hoards (which ought to be indicative of aggregate growth), the sixth century numbers are misleading since coinage was introduced in the Greek world in the course of that century. Yet even when we restrict our survey to the classical period, the numbers are suggestive. The number of hoards more than doubled from the fifth century to the fourth, from 238 to 564 hoards, while the number of total coins in all hoards grew threefold, from about 34,000 coins to about 109,000. These numbers cannot readily be translated into a given annual growth rate. Short-term growth in hoarding

TABLE 4.1 *Summary of Proxy Indicators of Economic Growth*

	Start Date (T1)	End Date (T2)	Multiplier (T2/T1)
Population	9th	4th	10–20
House floor plan	9th	4th	3.5
Household goods	9th	4th	5–10
Per capita consumption	9th	4th	1.5–2
Aggregate growth	9th	4th	15–20
Names (Attica)	6th	4th	14
Hoard size, median	6th	4th	2
Hoard size, average	6th	4th	4
Coins in hoards	5th	4th	3
Hoards, number	5th	4th	2

NOTE: Dates represent centuries BCE.

may, in fact, indicate economic crisis.[23] But over the long term, the substantial growth in both hoard size and numbers of hoards is likely to reflect a world in which there was more money in circulation and in which more people could afford to save some part of their income in the form of cash. This ought, in turn, to mean a world in which more people were living substantially above the level of bare survival.

Table 4.1 sums up the evidence for change over time in the proxy indicators discussed in this section: They all move in the same positive direction; they all point to substantial growth over time in the classical Greek economy.

DENSE, HEALTHY, URBANIZED POPULATION

In addition to the relative measures of growth over time, we can evaluate population and welfare in a given era in absolute terms and thereby compare societies over time and space. Denser populations and high levels of urbanization tend to be correlated with higher economic performance and are, therefore, commonly employed by economic historians as proxies for economic growth.[24] Among the important results achieved by the Copenhagen Polis Center, directed by Mogens Hansen, has been to give us a better sense of the total population of the extended Greek world in the late classical period and the distribution of that population. As we have seen (ch. 2), by the later fourth century, there were an estimated 1,100 poleis in the Greek world. The territorial size of about two-thirds of all documented poleis (672/1,035) is now known or can be plausibly approximated.

Beginning with the extensive empirical evidence of his inventory of poleis, Hansen uses what he calls a "shotgun method" to estimate late fourth century Greek population and distribution. The method employs the evidence of the physical size and estimated population densities of relatively well-documented poleis, along with the size and estimated densities of intramural areas and the known distribution of poleis across a range of sizes, to arrive at overall estimates of population. On the basis of his shotgun method, and in comparison with 22 poleis for which there is literary and documentary evidence for individual polis populations, Hansen offers new estimates for the minimum total population of the Greek world, the distribution of the Greek population among large, middling, and small poleis, and the relative scale of urban and extraurban populations.[25]

It is based on this method that Hansen estimates that the extended Greek world in the late fourth century BCE had a population of at least 7.5 million, and more probably 8.5–9.5 million people. The extended Greek world considered in Hansen's estimate includes regions of Greek settlement excluded from Ian Morris' estimate of ca. 4 million for the Aegean, Sicily, and southern Italy, but Hansen also argues for a somewhat denser population overall. As we have seen, assuming a late fourth century population of 8.25 million means that the number of Greeks, taken in toto, had—through a combination of natural growth, immigration, enslavement, and the Hellenization of formerly "barbarian" towns—multiplied by a factor of about 25 in 700 years, from the Early Iron Age nadir in ca 1000 BCE to the classical peak in ca. 300 BCE. As noted in chapter 2, using these figures we can estimate that by the late fourth century the Greek world had an overall population density of ca. 44 people per km²—very similar to that of Holland in the mid-sixteenth century and to England and Wales in the late seventeenth century.[26]

Hansen argues that what I am calling "core Greece," the parts of Hellas defined by the extent of the Greek state in the later nineteenth century, had a population of at least 3–3.5 million people.[27] By way of comparison, in 1889 a census by the state of Greece counted 2.2 million people—this should probably be corrected upward to 2.3 million, per discussion at the beginning of this chapter. As Hansen points out, and as is confirmed by historical demographer Vasilios Valaoras' analysis of the causes of Greek unemployment and large-scale emigration, there is reason to believe that the population of Greece in the late nineteenth century had already exceeded Greece's agricultural carrying capacity. The land of Greece simply could not produce enough food to feed any more people. If these figures are in the right range and if the assumptions about carrying capacity are correct, it has considerable bearing on the performance of the ancient Greek economy.[28]

Unless we are willing to assume that fourth century BCE Greece was much more agriculturally productive than nineteenth century CE Greece (which seems on the face of it unlikely—although it would be interesting if true), if we adopt Hansen's figures, we must suppose that a substantial part of the fourth century Greek mainland population was fed from food imported from abroad. Something like 0.7–1.2 million Greeks, i.e., roughly a quarter to a third of core Greece's population in the fourth century BCE, thus may have lived on grain imported (e.g.) from the western Mediterranean, from the Bosphorus/Crimea, or from North Africa.

Once again, even if we were to cut the number of Greeks (derived from Hansen's estimates) who must be presumed to have lived on imported food *in half*, we would still be left with some 350,000–600,000 people in excess of the presumed carrying capacity of core Greece.[29] This means, in turn, that Athens cannot have been the only major grain-importing Greek polis. And so, the core Greek world can no longer be regarded as entirely defined by subsistence agriculture or local exchange. The imported food had to be paid for somehow—by commodity exports (oil, wine, silver), manufactured goods, services, or the extraction of rents (i.e., by the use of power to obtain resources at prices lower than those that would pertain in a competitive market).[30] The general point is that by the fourth century BCE, the mainland Greek world evidently pushed back the standard premodern limiting factor: the "low Malthusian ceiling" of resource constraints.

Total population is only one part of the equation. If we are to understand the conditions of Greek economic growth, it is important to determine how the population was distributed. My calculations, based on Hansen's analysis of the numbers of large, middling, and small poleis that ever existed in the Greek world shows that most poleis (ca. 900 of ca. 1,100) were small (sizes 1–3), with populations of ca. 1,000–7,000 people. Yet only about a third (36%) of the total Greek population lived in these small poleis. Another quarter of the population (26%) lived in fairly large poleis, that is, in communities with a median population of about 17,000 people (size 4). About 4 in 10 (38%) of the polis-dwelling Greeks lived in very large poleis (sizes 5–7), with a median population of about 35,000 people or more. The results are tabulated in table 4.2.[31]

Along with population density, the rate and level of urbanization are commonly used by economic historians of premodernity as a proxy for eco-

TABLE 4.2 *Estimated Distribution of Greek Population by Polis Size*

	Small Rank 1–3 (1,000–7,000)	Middling Rank 4–5 (median 17,000)	Large Rank 5–7 (median 35,000+)
Poleis %	82	11	7
Population %	36	26	38

NOTE: Based on ranking of polis size distribution modeled in table 2.1.

nomic growth. Among Mogens Hansen's most striking claims, based once again on the shotgun estimation method, is that about half of the population of late fourth century Greece lived in intramural "urban" centers.[32] Combined with the distribution into small, middling, and large poleis, this suggests that about a third (32%) of all Greeks lived in towns of 5,000 people or more: the standard for "urban" that is used by many demographers studying premodernity. A 32% urbanization rate means that, across the Greek world, about 2.5–3 million Greeks lived in what modern demographers define as cities. Assuming that these estimates are in the right ballpark, the Greek world of the fourth century BCE had a much higher urbanization rate, overall, than the Roman imperial world of the first and second centuries CE, in which some 10–12% of the population (7–8.5 million people) lived in similarly large towns. Rome's urbanization rate was roughly similar to that of England and Wales in the seventeenth century, or France in the eighteenth century.[33] Classical Hellas was less urbanized than mid-seventeenth century Holland (45%); but England and Wales reached classical Greek urbanization levels (and a similar number of total of urban dwellers) only in the first years of the nineteenth century (table 4.3). Modern Greece did not equal the fourth century BCE urbanization rate until the 1930s (figure 4.1). The picture does not change significantly when we use a more demanding standard of urbanization.[34]

The high urban population of classical Hellas fits comfortably with the conclusion that a good many Greeks living in the core areas of Hellas (as defined by the frontiers of the late nineteenth century Greek state) consumed imported rather than locally grown food. It would be wrong to imagine that the set "urban residents" completely overlapped with the set "imported food consumers"; a substantial number of urban Greeks may have lived in "agrotowns" from which residents commuted to their fields. Some very extensive intramural areas may have enclosed gardens or even fields. Nevertheless, the estimate that about a third of the Greek world lived in urban areas is

TABLE 4.3 *Comparative Urbanization Levels and Populations*

	Urban %	Urban Total (millions)
Hellas 350–300 BCE	32	2.5–3
Rome 100–200 CE	10–12	7–8.5
Holland 1651	45	0.44
England and Wales 1688	13	0.74
France 1788	12	2.8
England and Wales 1801–1803	30	2.78

NOTES: Urban = Town of more than 5,000 people. Figures for Rome: Wilson 2011. Figures for Holland, England and Wales, and France: Milanovic, Lindert, and Williamson 2011: Table 1.

compatible with the finding that roughly a quarter to a third of the core Greek population was fed from imported food. Both results push against the standard modern premise, which assumes that the ancient Greek economy was overwhelmingly defined by subsistence agriculture; together the two demographic results point to a relatively sophisticated and diversified economy, one in which many people lived well above bare subsistence. These population figures are, in turn, in line with recent work, notably by the Chicago-based economic historian, Alain Bresson, to the effect that trade, in commodities as well as luxury goods, was much more important in the Greek economy than was long thought to be the case.[35]

Higher levels of urbanization correlate, historically, with higher incomes and economic intensification,[36] but not necessarily with improved health and welfare: Rapid growth of urban populations has historically been associated with the spread of disease, and, e.g., in nineteenth century England and Holland, with squalid living conditions in crowded tenements. There is no evidence that these dismal conditions pertained in fourth century Greek towns. While the data on change over time in the health of Greek populations are difficult to interpret, and in some ways contradictory, it is clear enough from studies of human bones found in Greek archaeological excavations that the average life span of Greek men and women reaching adulthood increased substantially from the end of the Dark Age to the fourth century BCE. Based on the more recent (1990s) analyses, the ages at death of individuals surviving childhood seem to have increased by about 10 years for both men and women over this period: from about 26 to 36 for women, and from under 30 to about 40 for men.[37]

Life expectancy at birth (which in all premodern populations is much lower than average age at death for those surviving into adulthood, due to high levels of infant and child mortality and to the effects of disease) in fourth century Greece would still have been very low by modern standards, perhaps not exceeding the mid- to upper twenties.[38] But it was certainly substantially better than it had been 500 years previously, in Early Iron Age Greece, when there was probably no town of as many as 5,000 people. Moreover, despite intensive archaeological exploration, there is not as yet any evidence in excavations of classical Greek towns for extensive tracts of small and squalid urban dwellings. As we saw above, the median Greek house, urban as well as rural, tended to become much larger and better built in the five hundred years after 800 BCE. Given the intensity of the archaeological exploration of Greece, it seems unlikely that slums have simply escaped notice.[39]

In sum, by the late classical period, Hellas was relatively densely populated. The number of Greeks who lived in urban areas was remarkably high by premodern standards. They lived in much bigger settlements, in much bigger houses, and in substantially healthier conditions than their ancestors could have dreamed of. A good part of the population of mainland Greece was fed from imported food. The classical Greek world had not fallen victim to the Malthusian trap, and its economy cannot adequately be explained by reference to subsistence agriculture alone.

EQUITABLE DISTRIBUTION OF WEALTH AND INCOME

A third measure of economic development is the distribution of wealth and income. Historically, all complex societies have been characterized by economic inequality. Yet when wealth and income are distributed extremely inequitably, such that society is bimodally segmented into a tiny elite of the very wealthy and a great mass of individuals living at subsistence, there is correspondingly little room for sustained economic growth. It is only with the emergence of a substantial and stable middle class of people living well above the level of subsistence, and therefore willing and able to purchase goods unnecessary for their mere survival, that societal consumption becomes a driver of economic growth.[40]

How equitably was the wealth of Hellas distributed across its relatively dense and urbanized population? Once again, house sizes can be used as an indirect proxy. Ian Morris shows that archaic/classical Greek settlements were never characterized by a few mansions and many huts. Rather, across the entire half-millennium from 800 to 300 BCE, the distribution of Greek houses tends to cluster around the median house size. The size of larger houses (the top quartile in floor plan) failed to diverge markedly from that of smaller houses (the bottom quartile). The size of larger and smaller houses grew more or less in lockstep across the period: by 300 BCE, houses in the 75th percentile of the distribution were only about one-fifth again (roughly 50 m²) as large as those in the 25th percentile.[41]

A comparative survey of house sizes at Olynthos (1588) and other well-preserved Greek urban areas by Geoffrey Kron of the University of Victoria confirms this general picture: unlike (e.g.) nineteenth century England, the distribution of house sizes at mid-fourth century BCE Olynthos describes a bell curve: most houses fall in the middle, rather than on the far left (tiny house) side, of the distribution. Overall inequality among house sizes at Olythos was very low.[42] Not every Greek family could afford to buy a substantial house—which may have cost something in the neighborhood of 6–15 years of income.[43] But many could afford to own a home: Based on recorded house costs and the Athenian census of 322 BCE in which some 9,000 citizens (of a presumed total of ca. 31,000) owned property amounting to more than 2,000 drachmas, Kron estimates at least nearly a third, and possibly as many as three-quarters, of Athenian citizen families could afford to purchase a house.[44]

Kron has attempted to calculate wealth distribution in late fourth century Athens more directly by reference to the standard Gini index: a coefficient (from 0 to 1) of inequality in a given population. The lower the Gini coefficient, the more equitably the good in question is distributed across the population (so 0.1 is very equal; 0.9 very unequal). The Gini coefficient may also be displayed visually by a Lorenz curve; the further below a line describing a 45-degree angle (perfect equality), the greater the level of inequality. In Kron's calculation, the good is household wealth; we calculate the Gini index and Lorenz curve for Athenian household income below.

Athenian private wealth was certainly not distributed with anything approaching perfect equality. Based on reports of the census of 322 BCE and other sources, Kron calculates that in late fourth century Athens the richest 1% of the population owned about 30% of all private wealth; while the top 10% owned about 60% of the wealth. This yields a Gini index of 0.708. Kron compares this figure to the Gini wealth coefficients for several modern societies. The late-classical Athenian level of total-wealth inequality is roughly comparable to that of the United States in 1953–1954 (0.71). It is less equal than Canada in 1998 (0.69) but more equal than Florence in 1427 (0.788) or the United States in 1998 (0.794). It is much more equal than the United States or England in the early twentieth century (0.93 and 0.95, respectively).[45]

Kron's conclusion on the comparatively equitable distribution of private wealth in late classical Athens is consistent with estimates of landholding in Athens: Two independent studies by British classical scholars concluded that about 7.5–9% of citizens owned about 30–35% of the land of Attica; some 20% owned little or no land. Excluding those at the top and bottom of the distribution, we are left with roughly 60–65% of the land being owned by about 70–75% of the citizen population.[46] Ian Morris points out that the resulting range of Gini coefficients, 0.382–0.386, is strikingly low in comparison to estimated distributions of landholding for other ancient and medieval societies. Although the baseline Athenian figures do not tell us anything about some relevant factors affecting the value of land, e.g., distribution of especially productive land or financial encumbrances on landholdings, Morris is certainly right to conclude that, "the basic point is clear: landholding was unusually egalitarian in Classical Athens."[47]

Economists typically assess material inequality by measuring income. Although it is not possible to calculate an income Gini for all Hellas, on the basis of what I take to be a plausible model of wealth distribution for later fourth century Athens (table 4.4, with discussion below), I estimate the income Gini for the whole of Athenian society (*including* slaves and resident foreigners) in the later fourth century to be in the region of 0.40–0.45, based on two models (an optimistic model assuming lower inequality and a pessimistic model assuming higher inequality). The corresponding Lorenz curves are illustrated in figure 4.2. This is similar to the income Gini estimate of 0.42–0.44 suggested by the ancient economic historians, Walter Scheidel and Steven Friesen for the high Roman Empire. Yet, based on the relevant income distribution models, the shapes of the Lorenz curves for the two societies are quite different; the difference arises from the substantially larger Athenian population of people who fall in the middle range, between the richest and poorest.[48]

What we really want to know about income in a premodern society is how many people lived near, or well above, subsistence. Stanford's Walter Scheidel has analyzed the real wages of unskilled workers (i.e., those at the lower end of the economic distribution) in a number of ancient and medieval communities. Scheidel's approach is to convert daily income into a "wheat wage"—a well-established method of assessing the level of income in different currencies or in kind by reference to a single standard of liters of wheat per diem. The wheat wage can then be used to estimate the proximity of the wage earner to the base level of bare survival. Scheidel's figures show that in most premodern societies in which daily wages can be calculated (and thus converted into liters of wheat per day), wheat wages fell in a fairly narrow "core" or "customary wage range" of 3.5–6.5 L of wheat/day with a median of 5.5 L/day.[49]

TABLE 4.4 *Athens, Late Fourth Century BCE Income Distribution Models*

	Elite	Middling	Subsistence	Total
Optimistic				
Citizen men	400	24,500	5,000	29,900
Citizen women	400	24,500	5,000	29,900
Children of citizens	1,000	61,250	12,500	74,750
Metic men	200	7,500	2,500	10,200
Metic women	200	3,750	500	4,450
Children of metics	500	9,375	1,250	11,125
Slaves (total)	0	8,000	72,000	80,000
TOTAL	2,700	13,8875	98,750	240,325
% OF TOTAL	1.1	57.8	41.1	100
Pessimistic				
Citizen men	400	19,500	10,000	29,900
Citizen women	400	19,500	10,000	29,900
Children of citizens	1,000	48,750	25,000	74,750
Metic men	200	4,500	5,500	10,200
Metic women	200	2,250	1,100	3,550
Children of metics	500	5,625	2,750	8,875
Slaves (total)	0	0	80,000	80,000
TOTAL	2,700	100,125	134,350	237,175
% OF TOTAL	1.1	42.2	56.6	100

NOTES: Elite = liturgical fortune, which is >3–4 T (Davies 1971), and >10× subsistence. Subsistence minimum = 100 dr/year. Middling = 2.4–10 × subsistence (Scheidel and Friesen 2009).

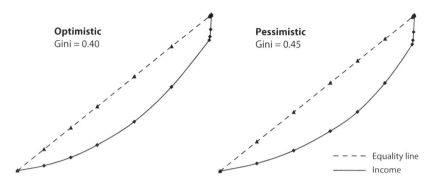

FIGURE 4.2 *Athenian inequality, late fourth century* BCE *(Lorenz curves).*

NOTE: Based on income models in table 4.4.

Scheidel suggests that 3.5 L/day defines the lower limit of the customary wage range—this level of adult male wage cannot have been far above bare subsistence (i.e., close to the edge of survival).[50] If we take that level as a baseline "head of household" contribution, below which it is not possible to fall very far or for very long, if an ordinary family were to survive (3.5 L/day adult male income = subsistence baseline = 1S), we can then calculate more generous income regimes, featuring higher wheat wages, as multiples of that baseline. Thus the median of the "customary wage range," at 5.5 L/day, is about 1.6 × bare existence (= 1.6S). This is enough to get by but is still not far enough above the level of survival to be described as comfortable, or even decent conditions of life.

Scheidel and Friesen suggest that wages in the 1–2.3S range (i.e., up to about 8 L/day) may be regarded as constituting the general category of living at the level of subsistence.[51] Adult male incomes of 2.4–10S (about 8–35 L/day) are considered to define a decent, "middling" existence—families with an income earner at this level could be expected to consume some goods not necessary for bare existence. This suprasubsistence-level consumption is an important driver of economic growth if the "middling" families constitute a substantial part of the total population. Those whose incomes were greater than 10S (more than 35 L/day) are categorized as elite. This elite group was a very small part of every premodern population. Thus, the conversion of wages to wheat wages allows the possibility of estimating the distribution of the population of a given society across the broad, but analytically useful categories of subsistence, decent/middling, and elite levels (table 4.5).

Distributing populations into three income tiers (subsistence, middling, elite) is obviously artificial and reductive; it obscures meaningful differences

TABLE 4.5 *Per Diem Income (Real Wages Expressed as Wheat Wages)*

	Customary Range	Subsistence	Decent Middling	Elite
Wheat wage (liters/day)	3.5–6.5 (median 5.5)	3.5–8	8–35	>35
Multiplier × suvival (S)	1–1.9 (median 1.6)	1–2.3	2.4–10	>10

NOTE: Based on Scheidel 2010 and Scheidel and Friesen 2009.

in levels of welfare and ignores how people defined themselves relative to others. Yet it is analytically useful in assessing and comparing the economic performance of ancient societies. As noted above, if a given society is divided into a tiny wealthy elite on one end and a mass of people living at subsistence at the other, there is relatively little social surplus, and so economic performance is correspondingly low. If there is a substantial "middling" population of people living comfortably above subsistence, then there is correspondingly more demand for surplus production, making possible relatively higher economic performance.

Scheidel and Friesen argue that Roman wages fell within the low "customary wage range" and that most Roman laborers thus remained at the subsistence level.[52] On the basis of these assumptions, they offer two simple models for the distribution of income across Roman imperial society. Their "optimistic" model is based on assumptions pointing to a relatively more egalitarian income distribution (and thus, per above, to more consumer demand and a correspondingly higher expected rate of economic growth); the "pessimistic" model employs assumptions that lead to a less egalitarian distribution (and so less demand and less growth). The goal is not to specify a single distribution (we do not have the evidence to do that) but to develop a general range into which the actual distribution of incomes can reasonably be assumed to have fallen (table 4.6).

The key point here is that even on the optimistic scenario, only a small percentage of the total Roman population fits into the middling category; most residents of the empire lived close to subsistence and thus had relatively little surplus to spend on nonessential goods. On the basis of this model, Scheidel and Friesen argue that imperial Rome, overall, failed to generate a sufficiently large social surplus to push back the Malthusian constraints that, as we have seen, limit the growth of subsistence-level economies. Once again, however, it

TABLE 4.6 *Income Distribution, Roman Empire*

Assumption	Elite	Decent Middling	Subsistence
Optimistic %	1.5	12	86.5
Pessimistic %	1.5	6	92.5

NOTE: Based on Scheidel and Friesen 2009.

is important to keep in mind that the Roman Empire was very large and that there must have been considerable regional economic variation.[53]

Athens is the only pre-Hellenistic Greek community for which we have figures for daily wages.[54] On the basis of the available evidence, classical Athens appears to be one of the very few known societies in the period 1800 BCE–1300 CE in which daily wages were substantially above the subsistence-level "customary wage range."[55] Construction-work wages and military wages in Athens in the later fifth century BCE averaged 1 drachma/day; the wheat price was about 6 drachmas/medimnos (1 medimnos = 52–54 L), yielding a daily wheat wage of 9 L and thus a baseline multiplier of 2.6S. This is just above the "middling" floor of 2.4S. In the 320s, unskilled laborers were paid 1.5 drachmas/day; wages for skilled laborers were up to 2.5 drachmas/day; the wheat price was 5–6 drachmas/medimnos. This yields a range of wheat wages of 13–16 L/day and a baseline multiplier of 3.7–4.6S: thus solidly within the "middling" range of 2.4–10S.[56] By way of comparison, median wages in Holland, ca. 1500–1800, translate to a wheat wage ranging from 10–17 L/day, and thus a baseline multiplier of 2.9–4.9S (table 4.7).

The evidence for late fourth century Athenian wages is anecdotal, but it is consistent with what Athenians were being paid for especially important forms of public service: Citizens attending a meeting of the Athenian Assembly (which typically lasted a half-day) were paid 1dr (30 annual ordinary meetings) or 1.5 dr (10 annual principal meetings).[57] The key point is that both in later fifth century BCE and, a fortiori in the later fourth century, Athenians who were engaged in unskilled as well as skilled labor (at least on construction of state-sponsored buildings) were paid wages sufficient to elevate them to a decent, middling premodern standard of living: They no longer hovered at a subsistence level perilously close to bare survival. Based on data currently available, this was rare anywhere in the world before the nineteenth and twentieth centuries.[58]

If we assume that the available data about Athenian wages is more or less accurate, we can make informed guesses about the distribution of the late

TABLE 4.7 *Athens and Holland, Wheat Wages*

Place and Time (century)	Pay (dr/day)	Wheat Price (dr/medimnos)	Wheat Wage (L/day)	Multiplier × Survival
Athens 5th BC	1	6	9	2.6
Athens 4th BC	1.5–2.5	5–6	13–16	3.7–4.6
Holland 16th–18th CE			10–17	2.9–4.9

NOTE: Based on Scheidel 2010.

fourth century Athenian population into the three general income categories of subsistence, middling, and elite. The figures on which the following estimates are based are detailed in table 4.4. Following the lead of Scheidel and Friesen, I posit two possible distributions: a "pessimistic" (less equitable, ergo lower consumption, lower expected growth) distribution and an "optimistic" (more equitable, higher consumption, higher expected growth) distribution. For each distribution, I assume a total population for Athens of just under a quarter million people, of which about a third were slaves, and about a tenth were resident foreigners.[59]

Elite status in Athens can be defined by a liturgical fortune of 3–4 talents.[60] Assuming a conventional annual return of 1:12, such a fortune would in fact yield a living standard of roughly 10 times bare survival. The elite population of Athens amounts to a little over 1% of the total. In the optimistic scenario, I assume that most citizens and metic (resident alien) males, and even a small number slaves (those who "dwelled apart" from their masters) would be able to make at least one drachma/day on average and so would achieve middling status. In the pessimistic scenario, I assume that only about two-thirds of citizens, a minority of metics, and no slaves received regular wages at or above the one-drachma/day level. In this simplified model, I do not take into account women's or children's paid labor; the middling women and children in table 4.4 are assumed to be members of "middling" families. Nor do I make any allowance for the historically exceptional absence of heavy taxes or steep rents paid by Athenian citizens below elite status.[61] Both productive labor by women and children and the low-tax/rent regime may push in the direction of more optimistic scenarios than I have presented here.

The results are tabulated in table 4.8 and illustrated in figure 4.2.

Table 4.8, based in the first instance on the evidence for relatively high Athenian wages, incorporates a number of assumptions, some of which may be too pessimistic (per above). Other assumptions may be overly optimistic, notably that the wages recorded in our sources represent something approximating the market standard and that unemployment and underemployment were not rampant. On the other hand, because achieving middling status required average wages of only 1 drachma/day (rather than the reported late fourth century wage level of 1.5–2.5 drachmas/day) there is a fair amount of discounting already built in—even without taking the relative absence of exploitative taxes or rents into account. In sum, it appears likely that a substantial number of residents of fourth century Athens lived far enough above subsistence to enable them to live decent lives. The surplus consumption capacity of a comparatively large middling population would have been a major driver of the Athenian economy.

Assuming that my model of income distribution in later fourth century Athens is more or less correct, can we extrapolate from Athens to the wider Greek world? Were high Athenian wages at all typical of the Greek world generally? The answer to that question will depend on how we imagine Greek labor markets as operating. If (counterfactually) we assume labor markets with zero transaction costs (i.e., that there was no restriction or cost, material or psychic, to movement from one part of the Greek world to another and that people would choose to move to where wages were highest), then Athenian wages would reflect the equilibrium conditions of the Greek world and we could assume that high Athenian wages reflected Hellenic norms. The no-transaction-cost assumption is, of course, false: the value of the Athenian evidence for the rest of the Greek world depends on how high the transaction costs associated with moving from one labor market or polis to another actually were.[62]

Many non-Athenians *did* choose to live in Athens as metics, and at least some of them did so for economic reasons. Indeed it is likely that most Greek poleis had populations of noncitizen residents. Thus, the costs of moving were not so high as to preclude all economically motivated movement.[63] It is, therefore, at least a plausible starting hypothesis that the Athenian wages reflect a Hellenic wage regime that is substantially higher than the 5.5 L/day

TABLE 4.8 *Income Distribution, Late Fourth Century BCE Athens*

Assumption	Elite	Decent Middling	Subsistence
Optimistic %	1.1	58	41
Pessimistic %	1.1	42	57

NOTE: For model on which these figures are based, see table 4.4.

wheat wage postulated by Scheidel as the ancient/medieval "customary wage range" median.

Suppose, for the sake of the argument, that in modeling the distribution of consumption across the Greek world, we cut the percentage of middling people in the *pessimistic* Athenian model *in half*. The resulting percentage of "middling" Greeks (a little over 20%) would still nearly double the estimated middling percentage in Scheidel and Friesen's *optimistic* Roman Empire model (12%). Moreover, as we have seen, the late classical Greek world was highly urbanized (table 4.3), and modern studies have demonstrated a high correlation between urbanization and real wages.[64] All of this suggests, in turn, that there is quite likely to have been, at least by the later fourth century, a substantial number of Greeks living well above subsistence, and thus that there was likely to have been a correspondingly substantial social surplus produced by the Greek economy. This conclusion is compatible with the two premises of strikingly high per capita and aggregate economic growth and a remarkably dense and healthy urban population, discussed above.

In light of the evidence about income in Athens and what it might have to say about income distribution in the Greek world, I posit that Morris' upper range estimate about Greek per capita economic growth is more likely than his lower range. Morris' upper range assumes that consumption roughly doubled from 800 to 300 BCE. This assumption makes sense when translated into wheat wages. If we assume that in 800 BCE an ordinary family's per capita daily consumption was fairly near the subsistence minimum (1.5*S*), and thus that the adult male wage earner contribution was about 5.25 L/day, doubling consumption would mean that by the later fourth century BCE the adult male wage earner contribution would be 10.5 L/day (3*S*). Given that fourth century Athenians were being paid at roughly 13–16 L/day, a late-classical Greek median daily income for adult male workers of more than 10 L seems plausible. Under this model, the rate of per capita Greek economic growth in the half-millennium 800–300 BCE would have been around 0.15% per annum, compared to ca. 0.1% per annum for the early Roman Empire.[65]

CONCLUSIONS

When the whole of Hellas is compared to the whole Roman Empire at its height, or when the presumptively most advanced Greek state (Athens) is compared to the most advanced early modern European states (Holland and England), Hellas, in the classical era, may reasonably be described as wealthy. The classical efflorescence was the high point of Greece's premodern economic history—both population and consumption were much higher than the premodern normal and exceeded the levels of the Middle Bronze Age efflorescence centered on Crete and the robust Greek economic recovery of the fifth and sixth centuries CE.

Figure 4.3, which breaks out the development index of figure 1.1 into its population and consumption components, illustrates the long history of economic development in "core Greece." Although the figures on which the chart is based are only rough estimates, if the main arguments of this chapter are on the right track, they must be of the right order of magnitude. The premodern normal population of "core Greece" (the territory controlled by the Greek state in 1881) was under a million; premodern normal median consumption probably hovered at 1.5 to 2 times subsistence. When we multiply population (in millions) by consumption (in multiples of subsistence) to create a simple development index, the premodern normal range is 0.5 to 2

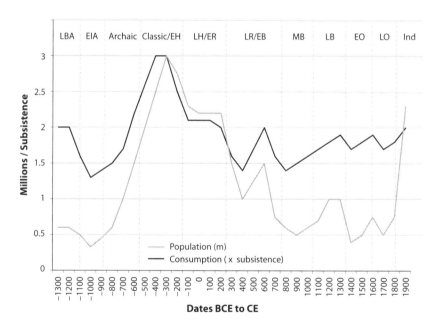

FIGURE 4.3 *Population and consumption estimates, core Greece, 1300 BCE–1900 CE.*

NOTES: Population estimated in millions. Median per capita consumption estimated in multiples of subsistence minimum. LBA = Late Bronze Age. EIA = Early Iron Age. EH = Early Hellenistic. LH = Late Hellenistic. ER = Early Roman. LR = Late Roman. EB = Early Byzantine. MB = Middle Byzantine. EO = Early Ottoman. LO = Late Ottoman. Ind = Independent Greek state. Core Greece = Territory controlled by the Greek state 1881–1912. Estimates based on evidence discussed in chapters 2, 4, and 6.

(figure 1.1). The classical peak, from about 600 to 200 BCE is, in each instance, much higher.[66]

Developing similar graphs that would trace long-run changes in population and consumption, for the whole of the territory occupied by Greeks in ca. 300 BCE, or for non-Greek regions of the Mediterranean/western Asia worlds, currently appears unfeasible: The intensity and quality of archaeological fieldwork and the availability of documentary evidence, across the many regions (and today, many countries) that constituted the classical Greek world and its neighbors, vary too greatly for plausible estimates. If, counterfactually, such charts *could* be produced, I believe that the "Greek world" chart would show a pattern somewhat similar to that of figure 4.3—although certainly not identical to it in light of diverging trajectories of development in different regions (e.g., Crete, eastern Sicily, Black Sea coast). By contrast, hypothetical long duration population/consumption graphs for most regions outside the Greek world would, I believe, look very different from figure 4.3.

The rest of this book explains how Hellas became wealthy in the archaic/classical era, why the wealth of Hellas did not prevent the Macedonian conquest of the late fourth century, and how efflorescence was sustained and Greek culture preserved after the loss of full independence by most of the great city-states.

5

EXPLAINING HELLAS' WEALTH

FAIR RULES AND COMPETITION

TAKING STOCK

The evidence presented in the previous chapter shows that in the 700 years between 1000 and 300 BCE Hellas experienced a sustained era of economic growth, culminating in a strikingly high level of development. By the later fourth century BCE, the Greek world was unusual in the extent and density of its population, its level of urbanization, the material conditions of life (including housing), and the health of the adult population. In comparison with other premodern societies, wealth and income were quite equitably distributed. Many Greeks lived between the extremes of affluence and poverty and well above the level of bare subsistence. There is good reason to believe that consumption by a substantial middle class drove classical Hellas' economic growth.

While there is room for debate about just *how* wealthy classical Hellas actually was, all the evidence discussed in chapter 4, drawn from a variety of primary sources and modeled in different ways, points in the same direction—and away from standard ancient and modern premises about Greek poverty. Classical Hellas was wealthy in ways that are unparalleled in earlier or later pre-twentieth century Greek history and rare in the documented premodern history of the world.

It remains to explain the phenomenon of exceptional economic performance. Why and how did Hellas become wealthy? The solution to the puzzle of Greek economic exceptionalism is political exceptionalism: *institutions*, understood as action-guiding rules, conjoined with *civic culture*, action-guiding social norms. Citizen-centered rules and norms promoted relatively open markets, enabling the constant exchange of information among many diverse people, and thereby drove continuous innovation and learning.

The institutions and civic culture that underpinned efflorescence arose in the context of dispersed authority, both at the level of the ecology of small states described in chapter 2 and at the level of individual poleis. We saw in chapter 3 how decentralized social cooperation in the form of a plethora of marketlike exchanges of information could ground high-level political order. It is because relevant information kept getting better—taking the form of greater assurance of aligned interests, more useful knowledge, and more innovative ideas, that the classical Greek world experienced dynamic and sustained efflorescence, rather than settling into a low-performing premodern normal equilibrium. But why did the quality of information keep improving? A plethora of choices leading to greater specialization is an important part of the answer. Those choices were framed by *rules* that served to regulate competitive markets in information, goods, and services.[1]

In chapter 1, I posited that specialization—along with the cooperative exchange of goods and ideas, and conjoined with innovation-driven creative destruction—was a key to the rise (as well as to the fall) of classical Hellas. The number of economic specializations that are known from classical Greek sources is striking. Edward Harris has documented 170 different nonpublic-sphere Athenian occupations, most of them from outside the agricultural sector, and many involved in one form or another with production or exchange. While acknowledging that farmers made up the most numerous single occupational category, Harris argues that, at least in Athens, most resident foreigners and about half of the citizens worked outside agriculture. Assuming that this is correct, and—as the evidence for urbanization and population density (ch. 4) seems to suggest—if Athens was not entirely exceptional in having a substantial nonagricultural population, we will need to revise, or at least to reinterpret, long-prevalent assumptions about the Greek economy.[2]

In the words of the Cambridge historian, Paul Cartledge, "the ancient Greek world was massively and unalterably rural."[3] This was no doubt true, in the sense that agriculture did remain the single biggest sector. Highly specialized, relatively urbanized, trade-intensive classical Greece certainly remained much more oriented around agricultural production than is the case in any developed-world modern economy. But what I take to be the ordinary connotations of the phrase "massively and unalterably rural" will need to be adjusted if we hope even to describe, much less to explain, the efflorescence of classical Hellas.

EXPLANATORY HYPOTHESES

In chapters 6–11, we will examine in detail historical examples of choices leading to classical Greek specialization, innovation, and creative destruction. Here, based on the theory of decentralized cooperation set out in chapter 3 and the evidence for Hellas' wealth presented in chapter 4, I offer two related hypotheses to explain how and why a particular set of political institutions typical of the classical Greek world (especially, but not uniquely, manifest in democratic Athens) provided Greeks with good reasons to make choices that resulted in Hellas growing wealthy.[4]

Hypothesis 1 Fair rules (formal institutions and cultural norms) promoted capital investment (human, social, material) and lowered transaction costs.

Hypothesis 2 Competition within marketlike systems of decentralized authority spurred innovation and rational cooperation. Successful innovations were spread by learning and adaptive emulation.

The first, "fair rules, capital investment, low transaction costs," hypothesis is related to the second, "competition, innovation, rational cooperation," hypothesis. Each requires (per ch. 3) valuable information to be actively and regularly exchanged and shared among many individuals. Egalitarian institutions, by creating a fair playing field and limiting expropriation by the powerful, fostered competition and innovation. Lowering transaction costs lowered the costs of movement, learning, emulation, and thus of technological and institutional transfer. Learning in turn increased human capital and local and collective stocks of useful knowledge. Capital investment, competition, innovation, and rational cooperation, in a context of low transaction costs, drove increased economic specialization. Although, for purposes of testing, it is useful to look at each hypothesis individually, the two hypotheses can be combined into a general explanation for the classical Greek efflorescence:

Fair rules and competition within a marketlike ecology of states promoted capital investment, innovation, and rational cooperation in a context of low transaction costs.

I suggested in the preface that among reasons to care about classical Greek efflorescence is that it emerged in the context of *democratic exceptionalism*—rules, civic culture, and values that have a more-than-superficial similarity to attractive features of contemporary democratic society. It is, however, necessary to keep in mind that classical Greek rules, even in the most developed states, favored adult male citizens. Rules were fair only in a relative sense—when compared with the norms typical of premodern states. They fall far short of the demands of contemporary moral theories of "justice as fairness."[5] Likewise, the level of classical Greek innovation was not high enough, nor transaction costs low enough, to satisfy a modern market economist.

Per the argument developed in chapter 3, the high-level phenomenon of Hellas' wealth is causally related to the microlevel of more or less rational choices made by many social, interdependent, justice-seeking individuals. Efflorescence was not a result of central planning, nor did any Greek have the conceptual means to measure or to explain the phenomenon. Like the collective behavior of ant nests as quasi-organisms, classical Greek wealth was an emergent phenomenon. That phenomenon was shaped by social-evolutionary processes that tended to select functionally efficient rules in a highly competitive environment. Rules were made self-consciously, by legislators, individual and collective. But the process by which rules were selected and distributed across the ecology was outside the control of any individual agent. The wealthy Hellas effect arose from uncounted individual choices but was not readily predicted by them.[6]

Before turning to the role of fair rules, capital investment, competition, and rational cooperation, other often-cited features of the classical Greek world—geography, climate, location, and exploitation of non-Greeks—deserve further attention. It seems unlikely that a marketlike ecology of citizen-centered Greek city-states would have arisen under various imaginable conditions of geography, resource distribution, and climate very different from the conditions that in fact pertained in the Greek world. Nor could the classical Greek social ecology have arisen without the prior collapse of Mycenaean civilization—a collapse that was both of the right sort (severe, long duration) and at the right time (the dawn of the Iron Age) to set the stage for a new social order.[7] By the same token, natural conditions and exogenous shock were insufficient, in and of themselves, to bring about the phenomena we are seeking to explain.

My explanation of classical efflorescence is illustrated schematically in figure 5.1. "Nature" provides the inherent human capacity for decentralized cooperation through information exchange (discussed in ch. 3) and a framework of geography, resources, climate, and collapse.[8] In this chapter, I focus on the causal role played by fair rules and competition—that is, on the political inputs of institutions and civic culture that arose *after* the accidents of nature established humans as beings with certain political capacities, provided a specific geophysical framework, and threw in a powerful shock with the Early Iron Age collapse. Before proceeding, we should consider whether natural

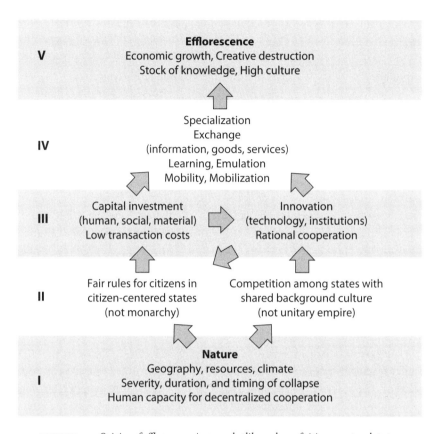

V   **Efflorescence**
Economic growth, Creative destruction
Stock of knowledge, High culture

IV
Specialization
Exchange
(information, goods, services)
Learning, Emulation
Mobility, Mobilization

III
Capital investment   Innovation
(human, social, material)   (technology, institutions)
Low transaction costs   Rational cooperation

II
Fair rules for citizens in   Competition among states with
citizen-centered states   shared background culture
(not monarchy)   (not unitary empire)

I
Nature
Geography, resources, climate
Severity, duration, and timing of collapse
Human capacity for decentralized cooperation

FIGURE 5.1 *Origins of efflorescence in a marketlike ecology of citizen-centered states.*

NOTES: The two hypotheses developed in chapter 5 are intended to explain how, after nature has set the framework at level I, the political inputs of level II and behavioral choices of levels III–IV lead to the outcomes of level V. At levels II and III, Hypothesis 1 is on the left side, and Hypothesis 2 on the right side. The two hypotheses are integrated at level IV. The early emergence of the basic polis framework during the Early Iron Age and archaic period, in response to the accidents of "nature" (level I) are discussed in chapter 6. The economic outcomes (level V) are detailed in chapter 4.

conditions, along with the factor of exploitation, might, in and of themselves, explain enough to relegate politics to the realm of epiphenomena.

CLIMATE, LANDSCAPE, LOCATION, EXPLOITATION

The Greek world's geophysical conditions and location—including topography, climate, natural resources, and exposure to disease pools—unquestionably played a role in Greek history over the long run. As we have seen (ch. 2), most of the territory once occupied by ancient Greeks shares a rare (in global terms) "Mediterranean" climate. A substantial change in the climate of the Mediterranean basin has sometimes been invoked to explain ancient Greek population growth. A recent metastudy of rainfall and temperature changes in the eastern Mediterranean over the past 8,000 years has documented a long-term drying trend beginning around 2600 BCE. The study showed no evidence of a sustained regional trend toward the consistently cooler and wetter conditions that have been posited as a driver of long-term Greek population growth. Within the general frame, however, there appears to have been an especially arid period from around 1450 to 850 BCE, roughly coinciding with the Early Iron Age (EIA) collapse.[9] Other recent studies suggest that this era of aridity precipitated the EIA collapse.[10] At the other end of our era, the centuries from ca. 100 BCE to 200 CE—the height of the "Roman Warm," which may have begun as early as ca. 350 BCE—were an era of relatively moister and warmer conditions. These centuries are coincident with the height of the Roman Empire. Within every climatic period there was subregional and short-term variation in temperature and rainfall, but the Roman Warm era seems to have seen much less variation than the periods preceding and following it.[11]

It is certainly plausible that aridity was a precipitating factor in the EIA collapse and that the end of a period of exceptional aridity enabled the population of Greece to climb back toward the premodern normal. Other, less pronounced, changes in temperature and rainfall may have had some effect on general or regional Greek social development. But, in contrast to the Roman Warm, there is as yet nothing in the known climate record of the first millennium BCE that would readily explain the intensity or duration of the classical Greek efflorescence, much less its historically distinctive framing in an extensive system of decentralized authority.[12]

As we have seen (ch. 2), the Mediterranean world is naturally subdivided into many microregions, each with distinct resources and microclimates. Microclimatic diversity, along with the uneven distribution of important natural resources (e.g., copper, silver, timber) contributed to making the Mediterranean basin especially well suited for the emergence of complex networks of short- and medium-distance trade. Mainland Greece has striking geophysical features: notably, a highly indented coastline with many offshore islands and a topography characterized by small agricultural plains amid rugged but not impassable mountains. The Mediterranean world was relatively easy for maritime traders to move around in. But by the same token it was quite difficult for would-be conquerors to master, especially those who (like the Achaemenid Persians or steppe nomads) relied heavily on cavalry. The mountainous Greek terrain offers certain of the geophysical features that the political anthropologist James C. Scott has documented as contributing to "the art of not being governed" by inhabitants of upland southeast Asia.[13]

The geography and climate of Greece were certainly potential assets, but focusing on these relatively invariant conditions leaves us with the question, raised in chapter 1, of why Greece experienced a remarkable efflorescence *only* beginning in the period 800–300 BCE. Why, if climate and geophysical conditions were the drivers of efflorescence, was Greece not similarly prosperous long before or long after that era? As we have seen (fig. 1.1 and ch. 4), although there were earlier (Middle Bronze Age Minoan) and later (fifth-sixth centuries CE) periods of efflorescence, there was nothing in Greek antiquity comparable to the efflorescence of the classical era. Greece did not have a particularly high-performing economy in the medieval or early modern periods; Greece's modern economic record has been mixed at best. So, if geography and climate are to explain the phenomenon of wealthy Hellas, we need to know why these conditions proved especially valuable in 800–300 BCE and why they did not produce equally remarkable and sustained growth in much earlier and later eras.

The classical Greek world benefited from its location among extensive and well-integrated economic zones managed by great empires (notably Persia and Carthage). Classical Greek authors, for their part, claimed that mainland Greece (and especially Athens) occupied a particularly advantageous location in respect to trade.[14] There were profits to be reaped by Greeks who served as Mediterranean middlemen, exploiting a favorable location between the environmentally and economically diverse regions of western Asia (especially after the consolidation of the Persian Empire in the sixth century BCE), northeastern Europe, and northern Africa (with its two great civilizations, Egyptian and Phoenician). A somewhat similar situation pertained in the Roman, Byzantine, and Ottoman periods. Yet in those later periods, Greece was no longer even nominally politically independent—and Greeks were therefore subject to paying rents to an external imperial center.

Political independence may have helped classical Greeks to benefit from their location relative to big imperial economies, which might help to explain the efflorescences of the Minoan and late Roman periods.[15] But, *pace* the standard ancient premise, which linked independence with poverty, sustained classical-era Greek political independence, in the face of Persian imperialism, was at least in part a product of Greek wealth: Large numbers of oared warships and many well-trained infantrymen, all financed by a thriving economy, proved essential to the preservation of Greek independence (ch. 7). So here we confront what social scientists call "the problem of endogeneity." It is the exceptional wealth of classical Hellas that we are seeking to explain. If wealth is part of the location-based explanation (because wealth helps sustain political independence and independence conspires with location to create exceptional wealth), then location, in and of itself, is no longer an adequate explanatory factor. Location may, of course, be part of a causal explanation, but even in conjunction with geophysical conditions and climate, location cannot be *the* cause, pure and simple.[16]

Exploitation (in the strong sense of rent-seeking, rather than the weak sense of benefiting from favorable market conditions, on which see ch. 9) provides another possible explanation: The wealth of classical Hellas was certainly based in part on rents. The economic performance advantage of classical Greece, relative to other premodern societies, might be explained if we could show that the Greeks extracted more rents at a lower cost than did other premodern societies. There is no doubt that Greeks extracted substantial rents. In the period of classical efflorescence (as before and for a long time thereafter), Greeks employed various forms of nonfree labor, including historically innovative forms of chattel slavery.[17] Athens gained very substantial revenues from subject states in the fifth century BCE, during the acme of the Athenian Empire.[18] Moreover, the classical Greek world gained indirectly from forms of political domination and economic exploitation in regions at its periphery. In at least some cases, domination and exploitation in these peripheral regions arguably emerged because of, and were sustained by, Greek consumption. Grain exported to Athens at below-market prices by friendly Thracian dynasts may be construed as Athenian rents.[19]

Yet if we are to explain Greek economic performance by reference to rent extraction via exploitation and domination, we need to answer a prior question: Why were the Greeks (or the Athenians in the imperial period) able to extract more rents than other premodern societies? It seems implausible to explain this (hypothetical) rent advantage as a matter of will, by claiming that Greeks (or Athenians) had fewer moral qualms about exploiting and dominating in their own interest than did people in other premodern societies. If, on the other hand, something distinctive in Greek institutional development facilitated more effective rent extraction, then we are back to square one: If we posit that exceptional growth was based on exceptionally effective rent extraction, we must explain how the Greeks managed to gain rents that were "left on the table" by other societies, which were no less willing to dominate and exploit.

One explanation of why Greeks were able to exploit others as slaves or serfs is that the relatively large "middling" population of the Greek world rendered exploitation more efficient, because close cooperation among many middling citizens enabled them to dominate outsiders and control slave populations more efficiently. Sparta, with its many helots (ch. 6), and democratic Athens, with its many chattel slaves and (for a time) imperial subjects (ch. 8), might be cited as two, somewhat different, cases in point. Similarly, we might suppose that high real wages and a large "middling class" of consumers made widespread slave-owning more economically feasible.[20] Yet we are, once again, confronted with an endogeneity problem: The large middling (suprasubsistence) population of the Greek world is an aspect of the general wealthy-Hellas phenomenon we are seeking to explain. So to the extent that coordination among middling citizens and high real wages are parts of the exploitation-based explanation, exploitation becomes inadequate as a standalone causal factor.

Due attention to geography, climate, geophysical conditions, location relative to other societies, and exploitation must be part of any serious attempt to explain the performance of the Greek economy. Yet even in the aggregate, these factors are inadequate to explain the phenomenon of wealthy Hellas. In the rest of this chapter, I develop the two explanatory hypotheses introduced above. Here the hypotheses are laid out in general terms, at the level of social theory. If it is to be believable as an explanatory account of the real world, a social theory must be empirically testable—in this case, by reference to the evidence of history. In subsequent chapters, we will test the two hypotheses by reference to the narrative of Greek history, from the Early Iron Age to the Hellenistic era. This method allows us to ask whether or not actual changes, over time and in different parts of the Greek world, are parsimoniously explained by the theoretical framework. The test of the theory is how well its predictions are confirmed by the actual historical record.

I do not claim that the hypotheses sketched above and developed below are fully adequate, in and of themselves, to explain the classical efflorescence. I am aware that each of my hypotheses suffers from the same problem of endogeneity that I raised above, in reference to other explanations. That is to say, the phenomenon I am seeking to explain, Greek wealth and cultural achievement, eventually became a driver, as well as a product, of fair rules and of competitive innovation. Institutions and civic culture productive of specialization, continuous innovation, and learning cannot be the whole story behind the classical efflorescence. But without understanding how distinctive Greek institutions promoted increases in productivity and in the value of exchanges, we cannot explain why and how classical Hellas became exceptionally wealthy.

In the following two sections, I illustrate the hypotheses with a few examples of Greek, mostly Athenian, institutional history. As we see in subsequent chapters, Athenian institutional development was exceptional in many particulars, and we need to juxtapose development in Athens with other paths to (and away from) development in other Greek poleis. Yet the institutional features highlighted here were not unique to Athens, or to other superpoleis; they are what made the classical Greek efflorescence such a distinctive chapter in world history.

FAIR RULES, CAPITAL INVESTMENTS, AND TRANSACTION COSTS

The first hypothesis for explaining the phenomenon of Hellas' wealth during the era of classical efflorescence centers on the general Greek (and especially democratic Athenian) commitment to what I will call "rule egalitarianism." Rule egalitarianism means in practice that many people within a society, rather than just a few elite people, have equal high standing in respect to major institutions: e.g., to property, law, and personal security. They have equal access to information relevant to the effective use of those institutions and to the information produced by institutions (e.g., laws, public policy). They are treated as equals by the public officials responsible for enforcing institutional rules. In sum, they can expect to be treated fairly. In an ideal rule-egalitarian society, all people subject to the rules would be treated as equals. In the Greek world, those enjoying equal high standing were, in the first instance, the adult male citizens—although, in some poleis, equal standing in respect to certain institutions was eventually extended beyond the citizen body.

Rule egalitarianism drove economic growth, first by creating incentives for investment in the development of social and human capital, and next by lowering transaction costs. A rule-egalitarian regime produces rules that respect individual equality of standing, as opposed to establishing a strictly equal distribution of goods. Yet rule egalitarianism has substantial distributive effects: Equality in terms of rules pushes back against extremes of inequality in the distribution of wealth and income. Rule egalitarianism may best be thought of as a limited form of opportunity egalitarianism. It is limited because equality of access and treatment is in respect to institutions and public information, not to all valuable goods. Of course someone committed to rule egalitarianism might *also* be an outcome egalitarian and/or a full-featured opportunity egalitarian—but the classical Greeks were neither. The key points are, first, that it is possible for a society to be committed, as the most developed states of classical Greece were, to equality for citizens in respect to rules governing standing without being committed to complete equality of outcomes or all social opportunities, and, next, that more equal rules tend to moderate extremes of wealth and income inequality through progressive taxation and limiting opportunities for rent-seeking by the powerful.[21]

It is uncontroversial to say that classical Greek society was characterized by historically exceptional levels of equality in terms of access of native males to key public institutions. The norms and rules of Greek communities tended to treat native males as deserving of some level of standing before the law, association in decision-making, and dignity in social interactions. No Greek community was ever rule-egalitarian "all the way down"—women, foreigners, and slaves were never treated as true equals. But among native males, the level of equality was remarkable when compared to other premodern (indeed pretwentieth century CE) societies. A turn to relatively stronger forms of egalitarianism in Greece began in the eighth century, and the general trend continued (although not without interruption) through the classical era.[22]

In many classical Greek poleis, rule egalitarianism among native men was codified as citizen-centered government. In focusing on the citizen, Spartanstyle citizen aristocracy and Athenian-style participatory democracy may be regarded as strikingly different versions of the same general regime type (chs. 6 and 7). Some Greek communities were, in George Orwell's memorable phrase, more equal than others. But even Greek oligarchies were strikingly egalitarian by the standards of most other premodern societies. The constitutional development of individual polis communities was certainly not uniformly in the direction of greater equality of access and treatment for natives. Yet, with the increasing prevalence of democracy (chs. 9–11), the median Greek polis was *more* rule-egalitarian in the later fourth century BCE, at the height of the classical efflorescence, than it had been 500, 300, or even 100 years previously.[23]

Social norms and rules that treat individuals as equals can have substantial effects on economic growth by building human capital—that is, by increasing median individual skill levels and by increasing the aggregate societal stock of knowledge. Relative equality in respect to access to institutions (e.g., law and property rights) and to the expectation of fair treatment by officials within institutions encourages investments by individuals in learning new skills and increases net social returns to employment of diverse skills. It does so because norms and rules that protect personal security, property, and dignity lessen fear of the powerful.

When I believe that my person, property, and standing are secure (in that I have ready institutional recourse if I am assaulted, robbed, or affronted), I am less afraid that the fruits of my efforts will be expropriated arbitrarily by those more powerful than I. In this case, I have better reasons to seek my fortune and to plan ahead. It is rational for me to invest in my own future by seeking out domains of endeavor in which I can do relatively better—that is, to seek a relative economic advantage through specialization. I also have a higher incentive to invest effort in becoming more expert within that specialized domain, insofar as I believe that there is a market for that sort of expertise—so that the return on my self-investment will have a good chance of being positive. Under these conditions, I will rationally choose to defer some short-term returns by spending time and energy gaining information and developing skills that I believe will enable me to do better in the long run.[24]

The Greeks were not strangers to the idea of incentives and pursuit of rational self-interest, and they certainly understood the correlation between ambition, achievement, and equality of standing. When Herodotus sought to explain the break-out of Athenian military capacity after the democratic revolution of 508 BCE, he argued that "while [the Athenians] were oppressed, they were, as men working for a master, cowardly, but when they were freed, each one was eager to achieve for himself."[25] If we are to judge by their literature, ancient Greeks had a solid "folk" understanding of how individuals make choices in light of strategic calculations of interests centered on expected utility and anticipation of others' behavior. Although the Greeks lacked a general theory of prices and markets, rules protecting individuals from exploitation, and subsequent individual choices to invest in human and social capital, led to the emergence of a vibrant market-based economy.[26]

Rationally chosen individual investment in human capital development can, in the aggregate, have powerfully positive economic effects through increasing societal levels of specialization and productivity. By investing in learning, each individual becomes correspondingly better at whatever endeavor in which he or she is engaged. Individuals who choose to invest in themselves, who have freedom to seek out different domains, and who have specific natural capacities (e.g., high intelligence) have reason to seek out those domains in which their capacities can be more effectively exercised. So, for example, an intelligent individual may pursue some sort of knowledge-intensive work rather than manual labor-intensive subsistence farming. Societal productivity increases because greater specialization of economic function produces more diverse goods more efficiently and because workers in each specialized domain, having invested in gaining expertise, are individually more productive. If information about the quality and availability of goods is widely shared, then better goods are produced at a lower cost, enabling more people to consume a diverse range of goods at a higher level.

Even in the absence of a general economic theory, little of this notion was lost on the classical Greeks. In the introductory section of Plato's dialogue, *Protagoras*, for example, a young Athenian citizen named Hippocrates (not

the famous medical writer) expresses his hope of receiving specialized training from the sophist Protagoras. Hippocrates' boundless eagerness to learn
something of value, and his willingness to pay for it, points to a culture of
self-conscious investment in one's own education. In Xenophon's *Memorabilia*, Socrates urges a friend to recognize the human capital represented by
the skills possessed by his female dependents and their motivation to employ
those skills: "everyone works most easily, speedily, best, and most pleasantly
when they are knowledgeable in respect to the work."[27] In the fifth and
fourth centuries BCE and continuing into the Hellenistic era, the Greek
world saw a spate of technical writing in a variety of fields: basic introduc-
tions to areas of expertise (for example, medicine, warfare, and public speaking) aimed at an audience eager to learn—and especially at potential students, like young Hippocrates, who might be willing to pay expert teachers
in their drive to improve their own special skills.

Meanwhile, per the discussion of exploitation, above, specialization was
also a way for the Greeks to increase gains from the forced labor of slaves.
Greek states (see ch. 9) and individual slave owners alike invested in human
capital by buying skilled slaves and training slaves in specialized skills.[28] But
slaves were not mindless machines. As the Greeks realized, slaves made behavioral choices that affected productivity. Writing in the later fifth century,
the anonymous author known to classical scholars as Pseudo-Xenophon
(also known as the Old Oligarch) notes that slaves in Athens would not be
economically productive if they feared arbitrary expropriation. Moreover, he
claims that the Athenian citizens who owned slaves recognized this behavioral fact and passed laws protecting slaves from arbitrary mistreatment accordingly (*Ath. Pol.* 1.11–12). We do not know how much practical protection this legislation actually afforded Athenian slaves, but the general point
is that the economic value of increasing human capital, by establishing appropriate rules governing conduct, was manifestly appreciated by the classical Greeks.

Along with providing citizens, and at least certain noncitizens, with institutionalized security against arbitrary expropriation, some Greek states encouraged investment by citizens in learning skills relevant to the provision of
valuable public goods, notably security and public services (e.g., clean water,
drainage, reliable coinage, honest market officials) that conduce to the general
welfare. Public goods benefited all citizens, and in, some cases, all members of
the community.[29] In Athenian-style Greek democracies, incentives, in the
form of pay and honors, were offered for providing public goods through
public service. The opportunity to perform public service was made readily
available to all citizens by opening access to decision-making assemblies and

by the use of the lot for selection of most magistrates and all jurors. At Athens, by the fifth and fourth centuries BCE, incentives included pay for service as a magistrate, a juror, or an assemblyman. Incentives offered to citizens who gained the skills necessary to be an effective provider of public goods included not only pay but also honors and sanctions. Those individuals whose service was deemed especially valuable by the community were rewarded with public proclamations and honorary crowns. Those whose service fell short, on the other hand, faced the potential of both legal punishment and social opprobrium.[30]

A third set of rule-egalitarian incentives for human capital investment came in the form of institutions that limited certain forms of individual risk.[31] All things being equal, people are more likely to make capital investments with potential upside benefits when the risk of downside loss is limited. Suppose, for example, that I am a subsistence farmer; my family has a median income that translates into 5.5 L of wheat per day: i.e., 1.6 × basic subsistence (see ch. 4). I have the opportunity to take on a potentially lucrative new enterprise, but only if I invest in myself and/or members of my family learning some new skill. I have reason to believe that there is a good chance that the enterprise will be successful and if it is successful, it will elevate my family to the relatively greater security of middling status (say, an income of 3 × basic subsistence). But the new enterprise means less time spent on subsistence farming. If there is a realistic risk that the failure of the new enterprise will leave my family beneath the level of subsistence (i.e., threatened with annihilation), I am unlikely to take on the new enterprise. If, however, I believe that the worst that can happen is that my family will fall to say, 1.3 × the level of subsistence (we will consume less but will not starve), I am more likely to take on the new enterprise.

Likewise, if a non-elite family knows that its own resources are its only protection against famine, accidents resulting in loss of working capacity, or death of the head of family in war, the required risk-buffering strategies usually preclude capital investments that offer potential long-term gains. Along with the high rents imposed by landlords and rulers, the high cost of private risk insurance is a structural impediment to the growth of most premodern economies.

State institutions that insure citizens against potentially catastrophic losses may enable individuals and families to invest more capital in enterprises with the potential for increasing individual welfare. Such policies raise the specter of *moral hazard*—that is, privatizing the gains of risk-seeking by distributing profits to the risk taker, while socializing losses by requiring others to pay for gambles that fail. But if a risk-limiting insurance institution is properly designed (i.e., part of the loss is borne by the risk taker), it serves an equalizing function that may have the effect of increasing aggregate welfare. Aggregate welfare is promoted because the state, unlike a single family, can spread risk of crippling accident or death in war across a large pool and can stabilize food prices in the face of local crop failure by encouraging imports from distant markets and by diplomatic agreements with producer-states. Getting the overall institutional design right is no simple task. But if the design challenge is met, the playing field is leveled because, for the poor, the stakes of embarking on a path of attempted self-improvement are lowered from potential disaster to survivable loss. And so the poor family can reasonably afford to take a risk that would previously have been open only to a wealthier family.

Assuming (as we have in the hypothetical scenario sketched above) that high-benefit enterprises are readily available and that the chances of success are better than even, the right policies, over time, lead to more people advancing from relative poverty to middling status. Although some risk takers will suffer losses, and so their families will be poorer, and some producers will be negatively affected by paying higher taxes, the net effect is positive for overall economic growth. Greek "public insurance" institutions (best documented for Athens, but not unique to Athens) included grain price stabilization and subsidization (reducing the risk of famine), welfare provisions for invalids (reducing the risk of loss of work capacity), and state-supported upbringing of war orphans (reducing the risk of military service by heads of families). Finding the right balance, such that the rules allowed risk-taking without inflating moral hazard, and such that the incentives of producers were not dampened by excessively heavy taxation, was a matter of institutional innovation and experimentation. We look at how public insurance institutions were developed and how they worked in practice in chapters 9 and 11.[32]

Examples of economically valuable individual human capital investments in the Greek (and a fortiori Athenian) world that could plausibly have been promoted by rule equality include literacy, numeracy, and mastery of banking and credit instruments. Other, perhaps less obvious, investments in human capital included military training, mastering various aspects of polis governance (e.g., rhetoric and public speaking, public finance, civil and criminal law), and individual efforts to build bridges across localized and inward-looking social networks.[33]

Another centrally important determinant of economic performance is the cost of exchanging goods and services. Voluntary transactions enhance social welfare insofar as they benefit both parties to the exchange (without harming others), that is, insofar as each party fares better than if the transaction had not taken place. Under such conditions, the more transactions that are undertaken, and the greater the benefit to each party, the better the economy performs as a whole. All things being equal, the more it costs each party to undertake a transaction relative to the expected benefits, the less likely it is that a mutually beneficial transaction will take place. So, once again holding all other factors steady, higher transaction costs depress economic growth; lowering transaction costs, by the same token, promotes growth.[34]

Rule egalitarianism can be a major factor in lowering transaction costs because inequality, in respect to access to information relevant to a transaction, or in respect to access to and fair treatment within the institutions potentially affecting a transaction, drives up transaction costs. Relevant sorts of information include, for example, the laws governing market exchanges; weights, measures, and quality standards; and the reliability of the currency in circulation. Institutions relevant to transaction costs include property rights, contracts, and dispute resolution procedures.

In the case of unequal access to information or to fair institutions, the disadvantaged party must raise the price of the goods or services in question to discount for the missing information or lack of institutional support. As the price goes up to cover these "inequality costs," the benefit of the exchange to the other party drops accordingly. And thus, either the transaction between the parties is carried out with less aggregate benefit, or it fails because no mutually beneficial price could be arrived at. In the opposite situation, where information and access to fair institutions are more equal, transaction costs are lower and thus economic growth is (at least potentially) higher. As the political scientists Douglass North, John Wallis, and Barry Weingast demonstrate, the high transaction-cost, access-limiting social order that they call the "natural state" is historically common. Such societies can be stable, but they tend to be economically unproductive relative to societies characterized by more open access to information and institutions.[35]

Relatively egalitarian institutional regimes, like those of Greek city-states, ought, according to the transaction-cost argument sketched here, to be (all else being constant) more economically productive than rule-inegalitarian regimes. Moreover, the transaction-cost benefit ought to increase if access is made more equal over time. In fact, Greek weights and measures were standardized in several widely adopted systems in the archaic and classical periods (chs. 6–9). In the case of democratic Athens, access to information and institutions did become somewhat more open and equal as the laws were increasingly standardized (e.g., in the legal reforms of 410–400 BCE), better publicized (e.g., by being displayed epigraphically), and more efficiently archived (chs. 8–9). The Athenian state provided traders with free access to market officials and specialists in detecting fraudulent coins. Parties to certain commercial transactions were put on a more equal footing with the introduction of the special "commercial cases" in which resident foreigners, visitors, and probably even slaves had full legal standing. These developments are discussed in more detail in chapter 9.

COMPETITION, INNOVATION, AND RATIONAL COOPERATION

The second hypothesis for the wealth of classical Hellas is that economic growth was fostered by competition, innovation, and rational cooperation. Innovation and cooperation were driven by competition. Competition among individuals to create more high-value goods and services and to provide more valued public goods (and to be compensated accordingly with pay and honors) was promoted by the even playing field created by fair rules equalizing access to institutions and information. Meanwhile, competition between states within the decentralized city-state ecology created incentives for cooperation among many individuals with shared identities and interests. Competition also promoted innovation in institutions faciliating interpersonal and interpolis cooperation. Innovation and cooperation, in the context of low transaction costs, encouraged interstate learning and borrowing of institutional best practices.

Continuous innovation is a primary driver of sustainable economic growth; the economist William Baumol emphasizes that societies dependent on stable regimes of rent extraction, rather than continuous innovation, face low and hard ceilings restricting growth. Today we often think of economically productive innovations as technological; improved energy capture (use of fossil fuels) was, for example, a major driver of the historically remarkable rates of economic growth enjoyed by some relatively highly developed countries in the nineteenth and twentieth centuries. Highly successful technological advances that spread quickly through the Greek world and beyond include the oil lamp, terra cotta roof tiles, and wine.[36]

Although the classical Greek world unquestionably benefited from these and other technological advances, technological development does not seem likely on the face of it to account adequately for the intensity and duration of the classical efflorescence. Technology is, however, only one domain in which continuous growth-positive innovation is possible. The Greek world was arguably a standout in its development of new public institutions that served to increase the level and value of social cooperation without resort to top-down command and control. Valuable institutional innovations were spurred by high levels of local and interstate competition, and they were spread by the circulation of information and learning.

Just as it is uncontroversial to say that the Greek world was, when compared to other premodern societies, comparatively egalitarian in its norms and formal rules, so too it is uncontroversial to say that the Greek world was characterized by high levels of competition. The competition among Greek communities could be a high-stakes affair, potentially ending in the loss of independence, loss of important material and psychic assets, or even annihilation. The high level of competition between rivals placed a premium on finding effective means, institutional and cultural, to build and to sustain intracommunity cooperation. One of the basic lessons that the fifth century BCE Greek historian and political theorist Thucydides offers his readers (positively in Pericles' Funeral Oration in book 2, negatively in the Corcyra civil war narrative in book 3) is that communities capable of coordinating the actions of an extensive membership had a better chance to do well in high-stakes intercommunity competitions.[37]

Social institutions can provide both incentives for cooperation and mechanisms for facilitating coordination, and classical Greeks were well aware of this potential.[38] One result of endemic Greek intercommunity competition was, therefore, a proclivity to value cooperation- and coordination-promoting institutional innovations: A state that succeeded in developing a more effective way to capture the benefits of cooperation across its population gained a corresponding competitive advantage vis-à-vis its local rivals. Notably, as has recently been demonstrated in detail, and contrary to the "standard modern premise," in the classical era many Greeks (and a fortiori the Athenians) had freed themselves from "the grip of the past" in that they were quite willing to embrace the positive value of novelty in many domains.[39]

Greek communities readily learned from one another. Every new institutional innovation was tested in the competitive environment of the city-state ecology. Many innovations were presumably performance-neutral—that is, they had no significant effect on the community's relative advantage in competitions with rivals. Other innovations would, over time, prove to be performance-negative. If, however, an innovation adopted by a given polis was believed to have enhanced that polis' performance, there would be prima facie reason for other poleis to imitate it.

There were, of course, many reasons for polis B *not* to imitate polis A's performance-positive institution. Most obviously, the new institution might be disruptive to polis B's existing social equilibrium, a disruption that would, among other undesired outcomes, result in a net loss of cooperative capacity. Classical Sparta was a case in point. The Spartan social system was overall resistant to disruptive innovation, which proved a disadvantage in the early phases of the Peloponnesian War.[40] Yet in other cases, the perceived chance to improve polis B's performance, and thus do better relative to its rivals, would be a sufficient incentive to adopt polis A's innovation. The Spartans eventually recognized the need to adapt; they did so by developing a substantial navy in the later phases of the Peloponnesian War (ch. 8).

Some innovations, such as the federal leagues of central Greece, were widely adopted across certain regions (ch. 9). Other highly successful innovations were adopted across the polis ecology. Widely (although never universally) adopted institutional innovations that we consider in the next chapters included coinage, euergetism, the "epigraphic habit," diplomatic arrangements, theater, and cult.

Of course not all Greeks, and not all Greek communities, were equally innovative or equally willing to emulate successful innovations developed elsewhere. But the Greek world overall saw what appears to be a strikingly high level of institutional innovation and emulation across the ecology of states over the 500 years from the beginning of an age of expansion in about 800 BCE to the classical peak in the late fourth century. Major domains of institutional innovation, considered in the next five chapters, include citizenship, warfare, law, and federalism. In the domain of state governance, both democracy and oligarchy were especially hot areas of institutional innovation and interstate learning. And, ominously for the continued independence of the leading Greek poleis, interstate learning readily jumped from city-states to potentially predatory central-authority states, through the medium of highly mobile Greek experts. Several such states were developing quickly on the frontiers of the Greek world in the fourth century BCE, an era in which expert mobility seems to have reached new peaks.[41]

Within the city-state ecology, a regional hegemon might encourage or discourage adoption of a given institution. Oligarchical constitutions were required by Sparta of the ca. 150 states of the fifth century BCE Peloponnesian League (Thucydides 1.19). Meanwhile, in the later fifth century, Athens imposed monetary and weight standards on the 300+ states of the Athenian empire.[42] Yet, as we have seen, there was no general central authority in the classical Greek city-state ecology to mandate when or how widely a given innovation was adopted across the ecology as a whole. The extended city-state environment thus operated as something approaching an open market for institutions. Opportunities for imitation were facilitated (transaction costs lowered) by the ease of communication across polis borders, which was in turn facilitated by the shared culture of the Greek world. Some impediments to institutional learning between modern nations, e.g., differences of language and religion, were much less salient in the Greek world.[43] Because this "market in institutions" favored the development and dissemination of more effective modes of social cooperation, Hellas grew wealthier—and meanwhile, Hellenism grew increasingly attractive to some of Greece's neighbors.[44]

The "fair rules, capital investment, low transaction costs" and "competition, innovation, rational cooperation" hypotheses, taken together, suggest an explanation, not only for why Hellas grew wealthy through increased specialization, but also for the creative destruction of inefficient rule-inegalitarian institutions and for the high culture of the archaic and classical periods—the new and influential forms of art and architecture, literature, visual and performance art, and scientific and moral thought that so impressed Byron. The classical efflorescence is at least partially explained by the conjunction of deep investment in human and social capital, low transaction costs, continuous competitive innovation and rational cooperation—all of which increased incentives to specialize, exchange, and learn.

Individuals and communities alike obviously benefited from higher levels of economic specialization and higher value exchanges of goods and services. The chance to gain greater payoffs—fame and honor as well as wealth—drove incremental improvements in existing domains (heavy-infantry tactics, lyric poetry) and led innovators to pioneer new domains (light-armed infantry tactics, tragedy and comedy). Innovations spread readily across the ecology (Doric and Ionic architectural orders, epic poetry).

Advances in communications technology (alphabetic writing) were quickly adapted to multiple domains (poetry, philosophy, law, contracts). Goods and services developed in the high human capital/low transaction cost/innovation-and-learning-driven Greek context were readily exported to regions on the periphery of the Greek world (red-figure pottery; mercenary soldiers, doctors, architects). In return, the Greeks imported grain, raw materials (timber, tin, copper)—and labor in the form of slaves.

In order to be of real explanatory value, hypotheses must be testable and at least potentially falsifiable. The two hypotheses offered here as explanations for classical Greek efflorescence can be tested by examining changes over time in individual poleis and the Greek world as a whole, differences among communities within the Greek world, and differences between Hellas and other premodern socieites. The *explanandum* (i.e., the thing we are seeking to explain; in the language of social science, the dependent variable) is the rapid and sustained growth of wealth, in Hellas as a whole and in individual poleis, across the period 1000–300 BCE. The "fair rules, low transaction costs" hypothesis would be falsified as an explanation (i.e., as an independent or explanatory variable) if, as wealth increased, rule-egalitarian institutions declined across the Greek world. Likewise, it would be falsified if, when we compare poleis, there proved to be a negative correlation between wealth and egalitarian rules. If the least egalitarian poleis were also the wealthiest, the hypothesis must be wrong. The "competition, innovation, rational cooperation" hypothesis can be falsified by showing a negative correlation between innovation and wealth: If the poleis that were most institutionally conservative were also the wealthiest, then continuous innovation cannot be the right explanation for why Hellas was wealthy. The narrative of Greek history traced in the next six chapters supports neither falsification condition.

Two final questions remain before we turn to historical narrative. First, do we really need *two* explanatory hypotheses? Social science values parsimony in explanation. Assuming chapter 4's claims about the extent and growth of Hellas' wealth are right, are both hypotheses developed in this chapter actually needed to explain the phenomena? Can we reductively dispense either with fair rules, capital investment, and low transaction costs or with competition, innovation, and rational cooperation as an explanatory variable?

The answer, I believe, is no. Although, as noted above, the two hypotheses can be conjoined into a single statement, in order to account for the phenomenon of the growth of wealth in the context of what we know about the history of the Greek world, we must invoke both fair rules/capital investment/low transaction costs *and* competion/innovation/rational cooperation. But this in turn means that we ought to be able to test the *interdependence* of the hypotheses. One preliminary test is to ask whether especially important and widely adopted institutional innovations tend to push toward or away from fair institutions featuring equality of access to information. The development of democracy and federalism, as, respectively, particularly strong forms of rule-egalitarian *intra-* and *inter*polis cooperation, offer us particularly salient test cases. In the coming chapters, we consider how prevalent democracy and federalism actually became across the Greek city-state ecology in the classical and immediate postclassical eras.

Finally, how was the Greek efflorescence sustained for so long? The basic answer (illustrated in figure 5.1) is that ongoing advances in exchange and specialization were driven by continued innovation and capital investment, provoked by unrelenting competition and sustained by strong institutions. However, as the example of independent medieval cities shows, under some conditions civic institutions that *initially* produce high levels of innovation and growth, over time, predictably lead to stagnation.

David Stasavage, a political scientist at New York University, has recently demonstrated that an autonomous (citizen self-ruled) city in medieval Europe could expect a *higher* rate of population growth (Stasavage's proxy for economic growth) than a comparable dependent city under the control of monarchical states—for about 100 years following the onset of independence. Thereafter, the growth rate of autonomous cities was *slower* than that of dependent cities. Stasavage suggests that this fast-then-slow growth pattern was a product of how institutions affected rates of innovation and trade. Initially *stimulated* by strong property rights and protection from outside interference, innovation and trade in autonomous medieval cities was, in the long run, *stifled* by restrictions on competition and limits on entry to institutions. Those restrictions and limits were enacted by citizen-rulers who were members of merchant and craft guilds, eager to protect their own monopolistic interests. Since kings had different interests, they imposed fewer restrictions and limits in cities under their control. We might expect independent Greek city-states, in which self-interested citizen-rulers controlled access to institutions, to have followed a similar fast-then-slow innovation, trade, and growth trajectory. Yet the evidence suggests that they did not.[45]

There are many differences between the governments of medieval European and classical Greek cities and between the contexts in which they operated. Among the salient differences is the tendency of some of the most developed Greek cities to *increase* access to institutions over time. Access was opened both by expanding the percentage of the adult male population exercising active citizenship and by broadening civil rights for at least some noncitizens. In the next six chapters, we trace the historical factors that led citizen-rulers in Greek cities to make choices in respect to access that were quite different from those made by the rulers of independent medieval cities. Those choices had profound consequences for the level and duration of the classical efflorescence.

6

CITIZENS and SPECIALIZATION
before 500 BCE

Sparta, Athens, and Syracuse were the biggest, most prominent, most powerful, and arguably the most influential states of the classical Greek world. Assessing the rise of these three poleis allows us to test the hypothesis that political exceptionalism, in the form of fair rules (resulting in capital investment and lower transaction costs) and competition (promoting innovation and rational cooperation) were primary causes of dramatic growth across the decentralized ecology of city-states. This chapter and the next trace how each of these "superpoleis" developed innovative rules that led to bold new forms of social order, in each case based on establishing an extensive body of citizens who shared equal high standing. The present chapter concentrates on Sparta and Athens in the seventh to later sixth centuries BCE. Chapter 7 focuses on Athens and Syracuse in the late sixth and early fifth centuries BCE.[1]

Each of the three superpoleis followed its own historical trajectory. Each gained advantages, relative to once-potent regional rivals, as a result of being a successful early mover. Each adopted bold institutional designs that were later adapted to the local needs of other states. The striking similarities and the sharp divergences between the historical trajectories of the three superpoleis in an Age of Expansion—an era of demographic growth, state formation, colonization, increasing trade, and scaled-up conflict—set up the question of how historically distinctive rule-egalitarian regimes came to define the Greek world and produced a long and brilliant efflorescence.

In both archaic Sparta and Athens, institutional innovations, historically remembered as the legislative initiatives of wise lawgivers, resulted in a highly original citizen-centered regime. In both Athens and Sparta, as in other less well documented Greek states, new forms of citizenship, as "civic membership and identity," were invented as highly consequential kinds of social belonging. In each case, the status of citizen was brought about by new rules that also served to reorient individuals' incentives toward specific kinds of specialization and cooperation. In the case of the Lycurgan reforms at Sparta, hyperspecialization in heavy-infantry warfare was an integral part of the citizenship reform. The result was the most effective and most feared fighting force in the Greek world. In the case of the Solonian reforms at Athens, specialization took the form of increased economic activity outside the realm of grain-intensive subsistence agriculture. The long-term result was the emergence of Athens as a center of Mediterranean production and exchange.[2]

In each case, reform was implemented against a background of social crisis. In Sparta, an ambitious expansionist project risked collapse in the face of determined local resistance. In Athens, the ruling coalition faced the prospect of fragmentation and a civil war in which elites stood to lose control of their clients and their land. In both Sparta and Athens, innovative institutions addressed an immediate threat to social order. In each case, the solution had long-term effects that the original lawmakers could not possibly have intended or imagined—but that we, with hindsight, can both describe and explain.

BEFORE CITIZENSHIP: BRONZE AGE AND EARLY IRON AGE GREECE

To understand the crises confronted by Sparta and Athens, and the originality and boldness of their institutional solutions, we must briefly review the history of the Greek world in the Bronze Age—an era that saw the first flowering of high civilization in the Aegean—and in the Early Iron Age that followed the collapse of that civilization.

When it is compared to the eras that preceded it, the Bronze Age (ca. 3000–1200 BCE) stands out as a glorious era in which high culture emerged in city-states and imperial states from Egypt, to Anatolia, Syria-Palestine, Mesopotamia, and beyond. Some regions of the Bronze Age world remained characterized by small independent communities. Others saw the rise of the first great empires. A Bronze Age state was typically ruled by a king (or queen) whose authority lay in military leadership and his (or occasionally her) claim to a special relationship to divine forces. The king and his palace, along with temples to the gods with whom he was associated, lay at the center of the social order. Palaces and temples extracted rents from subjects, who received in turn a measure of security and welfare—along with the assurance that their obedience to royal authority was in harmony with the divine cosmos. The king's godlike status legitimated high rents, which ensured that most of the population would remain fairly near subsistence. Surpluses extracted as rents were distributed to the ruling coalition: warriors, priests, bureaucrats, and local governors. Much, but not all wealth was concentrated in and near the palace and temple.[3]

Greece lay at the margins of the Egyptian and western Asian centers of Bronze Age civilization. Through networks of exchange that had crossed the Aegean long before the Bronze Age, local Greek elites became aware of these momentous technological and institutional developments and sought to benefit by copying them. The Greek rulers of Bronze Age Greek states mimicked many of the methods and legitimacy claims of Egyptian and western Asian kings, albeit on a reduced scale. Unlike Egypt or Mesopotamia but like the early city-states of western Syria, Bronze Age Greeks remained divided into small kingdoms.[4] The mountainous Greek landscape that later was to support the many independent poleis of the archaic and classical eras was already proving inimical to imperial centralization. As we have seen (ch. 4), in the seventeenth and sixteenth centuries BCE, Crete and some of the Aegean islands saw the Greek world's first efflorescence, during the Minoan era. But the Minoan kingdoms, weakened by natural disaster, had been conquered by the Mycenaean Greeks of the mainland by 1400 BCE.

Each of the Late Bronze Age–Mycenaean kingdoms was centered on a fortified palace complex, managed by a royal bureaucracy and defended by a warrior elite, men who fought from horse-drawn chariots and in oared ships. The king owned much land outright, levied taxes on others' land and flocks, and could perhaps confiscate land at will. The high-ranking personnel of local religious sanctuaries may have controlled some of their own resources, but there was overlap between the hierarchies of sanctuary and palace. Sanctuaries may not have been directly controlled by the king, but neither were they fully independent. The king ruled his kingdom through local delegates: He appointed provincial governors with administrative responsibilities for tax-paying towns. Economic specialization (e.g., chariot-making, arms and armor) was driven in large part by the needs of the palace, and much but not all industrial production was located in the palace. Records, kept on clay tablets in an early form of written Greek (in the syllabary known as "Linear B"), tracked raw materials and finished goods as they entered and left the palace. While the palace clearly did not direct all economic activity, the Mycenaean king seems to have stood at the center of a fairly typical Bronze Age ruling coalition of warriors, religious officials, bureaucrats, and local officials. The Mycenaean kingdoms were, in the terminology of the political scientists North, Wallis, and Weingast, "natural states."[5]

Athens and Sparta were sites of Bronze Age settlements, although far from the most important of them. The most prominent palace of Late Bronze Age Greece was Mycenae, in the Argolid region of the southeastern Peloponnese.

By the classical era, Mycenae (i353: size 2, fame rank 3) was a minor polis in the orbit of the major state of Argos (i347, see map 4). But in the Late Bronze Age, Mycenae was a major center, perhaps for a time even exercising a loose hegemony over some of the other Greek kingdoms. Bronze Age Sparta and Athens participated in extensive trade networks that connected the relatively small kingdoms in Greece with one another and with the great empires to the south and east, as well as with trading outposts stretching west across the Mediterranean.

The Bronze Age kingdoms were, compared to anything that had come before them in the Greek world, sophisticated in social organization, advanced in culture, and rich in treasure. But they fell victim to a system-level crisis that shattered most of the great eastern states and threatened to overwhelm even ordinarily stable Egypt. With multiple challenges to established political authority and social order came major dislocations and movements of peoples. In Greece, the crisis ended in a collapse of Bronze Age palace society. Greek speakers, probably originally raiding bands from the Aegean islands and mainland, migrated to the western coast of Anatolia where the Mycenaeans had earlier established a few outposts. Some of the raiders settled down, founding communities that would, several hundred years later, become prominent Greek city-states.[6]

Mainland Greece was hit hard. Life in the Early Iron Age (EIA, also known as the Greek Dark Ages, ca. 1100–750 BCE), the historical era that followed the collapse, was very different from the Bronze Age. By 1000 BCE, the networks of trade that had helped to sustain the thriving palace hierarchies of the Bronze Age kings were in tatters. The palaces were burned and mostly abandoned. The palace bureaucracies were no more. With no royal accounts to record, the technology of writing was lost. Reduced to the basics, life at the nadir of the EIA must have in some ways resembled Thomas Hobbes' grim vision of humanity in the state of nature: although not solitary, it was certainly, compared to what came before and after, poor and short. As we have seen (ch. 4), in the Early Iron Age the total population of Greece declined to about half of its Bronze Age peak. Communities were relatively tiny and isolated. Houses were mostly small; material possessions were relatively few and poor; life expectancy was low. Monumental building was not unknown but was rare and on a scale much reduced from the Bronze Age palaces.[7]

With the collapse of the Bronze Age Greek kingdoms and their eastern models, the way was opened for new forms of social and political organization: The strong-king-based system of centralized authority withered away, along with the systems of patronage and hierarchy that the palace-centered system had helped to maintain. Many of the economic specializations that had been sustained by the palaces and by palace-supported trade networks simply disappeared. Although pottery and metalwork remained somewhat specialized skills, the great majority of the population of any EIA community was necessarily employed in subsistence agriculture or pastoralism. When almost everyone lived near subsistence, there was little surplus to distribute. Leadership in an EIA Greek community was provided by coalitions of local chiefs. Although they may have claimed some special relationship to the gods, the chiefs lacked the capacity to capture substantial rents. While some chiefs lived in somewhat larger houses, and their houses may have been centers of cult, the circumstances of their lives were, compared to the Bronze Age kings, only marginally removed from the rest of the population.[8]

In some communities, one of the chiefs might claim preeminence, but there were no godlike rulers. If they were to retain even a marginally superior social position, Iron Age elites were compelled to consult with other adult males in the community. With only a very limited surplus of goods to control and distribute, the chiefs could not hope to create a narrow coalition capable of monopolizing the means of violence: Bronze Age war chariots were now just a memory, and the military might of each small community was measured by how many men were capable of arming themselves and mobilizing against threats from neighbors. Fighting men might double as foot soldiers and, by the later EIA, as oarsmen on ships used for local trade, piracy, and war—activities that were not yet clearly demarcated.[9]

We may assume that just as there was some distinction between the chiefs and the other armed men, there were distinctions between the fighting men and the rest of the community's male population. But once again, in the absence of substantial surpluses, distinctions could not be reinforced by great material inequality. Just how porous social distinctions were in a given community no doubt varied from place to place. Very occasionally, an individual was given a spectacular funeral: The "Hero of Lefkandi" was buried in about 950 BCE in a cemetery on the island of Euboea with what appears to be a big part of his community's stock of high-value goods and in a burial mound that required a great deal of labor. We remain in the dark as to why he was so finely treated after his death, but in any event this sort of large-scale community investment in commemorating an individual was evidently rare.[10]

The survival of an EIA community required cooperation, and its price appears to be recognition by the chiefs of relatively high standing for at least some other local men. This was still a long way from citizenship, but it provided the background norms from which historically distinctive approaches to citizenship were later devised.

The Greek Early Iron Age was neither static nor culturally homogeneous. In the generations after the great collapse, Greek material culture (pottery, weaponry, burial practices) changed over time and varied by region. Yet some elements of a shared culture extended across local communities: Regionally distinctive but recognizably Greek styles of pottery and distinctive ways of speaking the shared Greek language both distinguished and integrated networks of larger and smaller communities. By the eighth century, some more substantial towns were on their way to becoming poleis. Smaller settlements were being incorporated or subordinated by larger neighbors; social norms crystallized into more formal (if not yet written) rules; leadership positions were institutionalized as offices.

MODELING THE EMERGENCE OF THE POLIS FRAMEWORK

As the Dark Age lightened in the later ninth and eighth centuries BCE and the Greek world became relatively more prosperous, the basic framework of the decentralized ecology of citizen-centered city-states was set into place. But why did it happen that way? Viewed from of a neo-Hobbesian perspective or from the perspective of the other great civilizations of antiquity, post-Bronze Age Greek state formation might be characterized as lacking in adequately centralized authority. Why were Iron Age Greek rulers unable to create more centralized social orders that would be ripe for consolidation into a few larger states (on the model of the Bronze Age city-states of western Syria, or the Iron Age Phoenician city-states: ch. 3), or perhaps into an extensive imperial state (on the model of Carthage or Rome)? How can we explain the emergence and persistence of such a large number of small states within a single cultural zone? And why, in these many small states, was authority so often distributed among a relatively large body of citizens, rather than being concentrated within a narrow ruling elite? Why, historically, did Greece go so wrong, or so right—depending on whether the point of view is that of Hobbes, or of Aristotle (ch. 3)?

The answer may be sought in a combination of distinctive *geography*, the *nature* of the EIA collapse, and the *timing* of the collapse. Geography certainly played its part. We have considered (ch. 5) the role played by the mountainous geography of Greece in inhibiting imperial consolidation on the Greek mainland, as well as in helping to protect Greece against the endemic threat of predation by steppe nomads. We have also seen (ch. 3) that city-state ecologies remained viable in other parts of the Mediterranean world of the first millennium BCE. But geography and the general viability of ancient city-state culture does not explain the sheer number of Greek states or the failure of elites in many of the emerging Greek states to gain a stable monopoly on political authority. The palace-based society of the Bronze Age shows that Greek geography was not political destiny: citizen-centered poleis were decidedly not the only option for ancient Greek communities.

The collapse that terminated Bronze Age societies in western Asia was especially severe in Greece—severe enough to overthrow large-scale social order. The collapse eliminated the Bronze Age Greek palace economies, along with economic specializations and social relationships based on formalized and assymetrical exchanges between palace-based patrons and their clients. The collapse also lasted long enough to drown out positive memories of Bronze Age monarchy. The end of the organized Mycenaean kingdoms allowed for the development of new and highly localized social identities. The difficult conditions of the era fostered local interdependence along with relatively low levels of political and economic inequality: Everyone was poor, elite control was weak, and the threats of famine and piracy were endemic.

Along with its severity, the timing of the collapse precluded the possibility of further consolidation of the Mycenaean world. The Mycenaean states seem to have been coalescing near the end of the Bronze Age, with Mycenae taking an increasingly prominent position. But Bronze Age Greece never coalesced into anything resembling a unitary imperial state, or even into a few large states. Unlike Egypt and Mesopotamia, for example, there was, therefore, no deep imperial ideology available for would-be rulers to draw upon during the recovery era. Had the Mycenaeans counterfactually enjoyed another few centuries in which to fight their way toward consolidating the palace-states into an empire, with an ideology to match, the postcollapse Greek social order might have looked quite different.[11]

The timing of the collapse coincided with two technological innovations with huge social implications. The most obvious was the increasingly widespread use of iron across western Asia and the Mediterranean. Known, but very rarely used before the mid-eleventh century BCE, iron became increasingly common over the next several centuries. The influential Cambridge archaeologist Antony Snodgrass very plausibly argues that the shredding of the Bronze Age trade routes after the collapse led to a severe scarcity of bronze in the eastern Mediterranean world. As a consequence, ironsmiths—first on Cyprus, but soon thereafter in Aegean Greece—were motivated to improve iron technology. Iron ore was readily mined at a number of locations across the Mediterranean, and so, once they had proved their capacity to produce good tools, the smiths had no lack of raw material with which to work their craft. One unanticipated result of the collapse was, therefore, the increasingly ready availability of superior tools.[12]

Whereas bronze—an alloy of copper and tin, neither of which was mined in core Greece—was costly, iron was cheap. Moreover, as iron-working technology improved, iron implements were increasingly effective. Iron weapons were, therefore, both deadly and inexpensive. In the Bronze Age, expensive bronze weaponry had been the monopoly of a warrior elite. In the Iron Age, given the right social will on the part of the community's leaders, it was relatively easy for many local men to be outfitted with the basic infantry equipment of iron-tipped spear, wooden shield, and headgear—the equipment that was eventually elaborated and canonized as the "hoplite panoply." The ready availability of iron thus made it more difficult for Iron Age elites to monopolize the potential for organized violence.

A second technological innovation, developed in western Asia during the Early Iron Age and adopted by the Greeks, was the alphabet. Like iron weapons, alphabetic writing had potential egalitarian implications: Once the Greeks had a renewed social need for writing, the availability of alphabetic technology meant that basic literacy could be attained by ordinary people— quite unlike the complex Linear B syllabary writing systems employed by specialized palace scribes of the Bronze Age. Since the severity of the collapse had ended the occupation of scribe, and with it Linear B literacy, there was no "path dependency or legacy system" problem to overcome, that is, no body of people with a vested interest in resisting adoption of the new writing technology because of their investment in the old one.

The severity, duration, and timing of the EIA collapse in Greece, along with Greek geography, conspired to blaze a distinctive variant on a relatively familiar city-state path to state formation, a strongly *citizen-centered* path that led toward the political and economic developments that are the subject of this book (see figure 5.1). It is not possible, given the state of our evidence, to trace in detail the actual emergence of a marketlike ecology of a great many citizen-centered states in various parts of the Greek world over the half-millennium ca. 1000 to ca. 500 BCE. But the emergence of the framework can be modeled in ways that are consistent with the evidence that we do have—for example, the histories of the major poleis that are discussed in this and the next chapter. The following scenario is hypothetical. But it conforms to the known evidence, presented in subsequent chapters of this book, and I believe that it captures the main lines of early Greek historical development.

In the first part of the Early Iron Age, in the immediate aftermath of the collapse, Greek communities were relatively egalitarian.[13] But beginning in the later EIA, local elites in certain Greek communities sought to increase their social distance from other local adult males and thereby to establish themselves as an exclusive and closed order of rulers and warriors. Other Greek communities, however, rejected the claims of local elites to special status, choosing to retain, reinstate, or even to strengthen egalitarian norms that had arisen after the fall of the Bronze Age palaces. These more citizen-centered regimes were stabilized when rules (in the form of social norms) were adopted that allowed citizens to coordinate their actions against violators (see ch. 7, on tyrants). Coordination was achieved when citizens used their common knowledge of the rules as bright-line trigger points for precipitating action and as focal points for mobilizing collective action. In some places, certain of these norms were codified as early forms of formal law.[14]

Meanwhile, intercommunity armed conflicts constantly erupted over disputes concerning control of border territories, stock raiding, and so on. The victor in any given battle might be determined by a number of factors, including charismatic leadership, superior planning, and luck. But states that were able to mobilize more men with higher morale had an advantage over their rivals. Because iron technology had lowered the cost of weaponry, it was social choice rather than economic constraint that determined how many of a community's men could be mobilized. I assume that, under these conditions, higher mobilization rates and superior morale were positively correlated with citizen-centered institutions and negatively correlated with the rule of small and exclusive bodies of elites. Over a long period of time, there were many conflicts fought over by many local communities. Assuming that innovations in equipment and tactics (notably the weapons and tactics typical of hoplite heavy infantry) were quickly disseminated and that other success factors tended to wash out, a quasi-Darwinian process of selection would therefore have favored the more citizen-centered states. Citizen-centric politics was, under these conditions, adaptive.[15]

Some intercommunity conflicts would result in larger communities absorbing local neighbors (in the process the Greeks called *sunoikismos*—"coming to dwell together"). But local territorial expansion was limited by the very norms of citizenship that gave citizen-centered regimes an adaptive advantage over regimes dominated by narrow elites. Because (by hypothesis) citizen-centered poleis had beaten the most dangerous of their elite-dominated neighbors by the time that citizen norms were sufficiently advanced to inhibit further growth in polis size, the scaling advantage that might have accrued to centralized, elite-dominated regimes was preempted. The result was a marketlike ecology of citizen-centered states.

Athens and Sparta were among these emerging city-states. The villages and smaller towns of the culture zone of Attica were, in the eighth century, mostly located along the coasts. But they increasingly looked to the larger town of Athens as a center of trade, cult, and political authority. In later generations, this process of unification and pacification of the Attic countryside would be mythologized as the work of an order-bringing hero-king named Theseus, but there is no historical evidence for strong monarchical authority in early Athens. Meanwhile, a similar process was under way in Laconia, where the Spartans, the residents of a cluster of villages near the Eurotas River, were exerting greater authority over nearby settlements and claiming the region of Laconia as their own.[16]

AGE OF EXPANSION

Historians of ancient Greece generally refer to the era that followed the Early Iron Age as the Archaic period. The historian Chester Starr more evocatively dubbed it the Greek Age of Expansion. In the eighth century BCE, the low ceiling that had kept Greece below the demographic and material level of the Bronze Age seems suddenly to have lifted. Farmers across the Mediterranean climate zone may have benefited by the ending of an unusually dry period and a return to the somewhat wetter and cooler weather that had been the norm since the middle Holocene. Greek growth was certainly pushed by the revival of trade with the advanced civilizations to the east and south.[17]

By the eighth century, Greece was growing rapidly; there were more people and more wealth. Higher quality luxury goods were, once again, being produced by Greek artisans. Athenian potters were, for example, now capable of turning out huge vases, beautifully decorated in the Geometric style and used in elaborate funerary rites by prominent families with enough surplus wealth to expend some part of it for dramatic public display. Literacy returned to Greece, after the alphabet was borrowed from the Phoenicians— the dynamic, trade-oriented city-state culture centered in what is now Lebanon. The Greeks modified the Phoenician alphabet by adding vowels; the Greeks' writing system would eventually be adopted and adapted to a wide variety of purposes by Etruscans, Romans—and us. Unlike the Bronze Age, when literate scribes used an arcane writing system to keep palace accounts, the new alphabet-based Greek literacy was used widely by creative writers and political innovators: by poets, lawmakers, and later by historians, philosophers, scientists, traders, and many others.

The Age of Expansion was powered, in the first instance, by demographic growth. Yet the growth of the population of Greece was not yet matched by a comparable broadening and deepening of economic specializations—most Greeks continued to focus their efforts on pastoralism or diversified subsistence agriculture. More people therefore required more land to be brought under cultivation. In some parts of the Greek world, as populations approached Bronze Age peaks, local territories soon reached and then threatened to exceed their carrying capacity. As emergent poleis contested control of productive agricultural land with neighboring poleis, the organizational demands of war contributed powerfully to the processes of state formation. According to later traditions, the first great war of the Greek world, the war over control of the fertile Lelantine Plain in central Eubeoa, was fought in the eighth century BCE between coalitions led by Chalkis (i365), and Eretria (i370), two poleis that were in the forefront of the early post-Dark Age breakout.[18]

A burgeoning population led to increased Malthusian pressure in the most developed parts of the Greek world, pressure that could not readily be alleviated within the nascent institutional and economic structures of the early city-states. The short-term solution, anticipating the response to Greek demographic conditions in the late nineteenth century CE, was emigration: The choice to assume the risks of moving abroad was made more reasonable by limited opportunities at home. The result, beginning in the mid-eighth century BCE and continuing for the next 200 years, was a wave of colonization that expanded the world of the Greek city-states into Sicily, Italy, North Africa, and later around the Black Sea (map 3). The colonization movement, initially led by men from Chalkis, Eretria, and a handful of other relatively advanced poleis in central Greece and western Anatolia, was eventually joined by residents of many other poleis. The impetus to form a new colony may often have come from individual social and economic entrepreneurs, rather than a formal decision by a single state's government. But at least some early colonies in the western Mediterranean, and then around the Black Sea, were strongly identified with a specific "mother city." State involvement at some level seems likely.[19]

Greek colonies were founded at sites well suited for trade (Pithekoussai: i65), or agriculture (Metapontum: i61), or both (Syracuse). Although the numbers of colonists must initially have been modest, the long-term effect of Greek colonization on populations in the western Mediterranean was profound, both culturally and genetically. While initially driven by growing Malthusian pressure as a result of rapid population growth in a society with a relatively low level of economic specialization, one of the striking knock-on

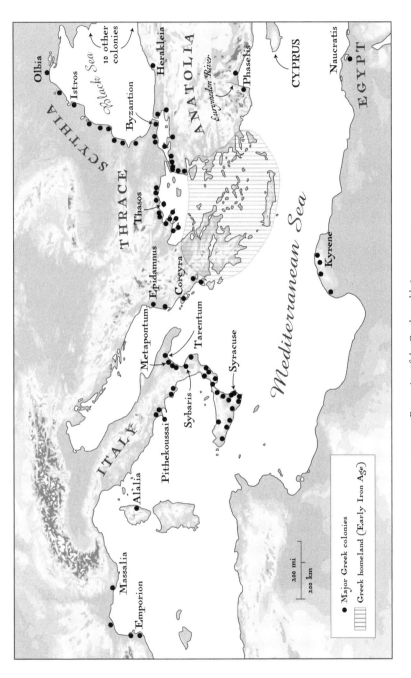

MAP 3 *Expansion of the Greek world, 800–300 BCE.*

Labels on map:

Massala
Emporion
Alalia
Pithekoussai
ITALY
Metapontum
Sybaris
Tarentum
Syracuse
Epidamnus
Corcyra
Thasos
THRACE
SCYTHIA
Olbia
Istros
Black Sea
Byzantion
10 other colonies
Herakleia
ANATOLIA
Eurymedon River
Phaselis
CYPRUS
Naucratis
EGYPT
Kyrene
Mediterranean Sea

200 mi
200 km

• Major Greek colonies

Greek homeland (Early Iron Age)

effects of colonization was increased economic specialization. The new colonies soon proved to enjoy some striking advantages relative to their mother cities—for example, ready access to new markets (with the establishment of Massalia in the early sixth century, the ancestors of the French first learned to drink wine) and climates better adapted to the large-scale production of grain—spectacularly so at Metapontum in south Italy, which was probably already exporting grain by the end of the eighth century.[20]

Meanwhile, the homeland retained some advantages relative to the new colonies: initially in production of olive oil—under ancient conditions of cultivation, olive trees take at least a human generation to begin producing olives in harvestable quantities—and later in terms of cult and culture, notably the major interstate festivals at Olympia and Delphi. Differential relative advantages stimulated exchange and rewarded deeper specialization and wider networks of exchange. As the Greek world grew, the Greeks further intensified their contacts with the great civilizations of Egypt and western Asia. Technologies and artistic styles innovated by advanced societies outside the Greek world were quickly incorporated into rapidly developing Greek manufactures of pottery, stonework, leather, textiles, and metallurgy. Some new crops and agricultural techniques were adopted and adapted to the Greek milieu.[21]

The political systems characteristic of the emergent poleis in the early Age of Expansion can best be described, using the social-scientific typology of North, Wallis, and Weingast, as weak natural states. As in the EIA, elites provided a modicum of political authority, subject to constraints arising from egalitarian norms. With the growth of trade, there was more surplus available to be extracted as rents. Where those rents were concentrated in the hands of the elite and used to buy off those with a potential for disruptive violence, egalitarian constraints were weakened. Yet most archaic Greek elite coalitions remained fragile. In an age of rapid population growth, just as in the EIA, the defense of a community's territory against incursions by rivals depended on mobilizing as many local adult men as possible. Greek elites in the Age of Expansion needed the support of armed men to ensure state security, but they lacked technological–tactical conditions favoring the monopolization of violence potential by small bodies of warriors (e.g., chariots, cavalry). Moreover, they lacked the ideological justification that might have legitimated their own superior position, for example, a privileged relationship to the divine order.

Whatever special relationship to the gods the EIA chiefs had been able to claim seems to have blown away as the ceiling came off at the dawn of the Age of Expansion. From the eighth century through the classical era of the fifth and fourth centuries BCE, Greek society was distinctive for its *lack* of leaders who were able to claim divinely ordained public authority. By the seventh century, Greek temples and sanctuaries had become important sites of social ritual and elite display, featuring rich dedications and monumental architecture. Yet, in stark contrast to other premodern societies, the priests of Greek cults failed to translate their religious authority into a position of outstanding social privilege or political power. Cults belonged not to a closed caste of priests but to the wider community of worshippers—whether they were the people of a polis, a region encompassing several poleis or, in the case of the great sanctuaries at Delphi and Olympia, the whole of the Greek world.[22]

Greek elites likewise failed to secure unique access to military technology and tactics (e.g., Bronze Age style chariots or medieval-style armor and warhorses) that would allow a few men securely to dominate many potential opponents. By the seventh and sixth centuries BCE, the technology and tactics of Greek warfare had converged on contests between organized bodies (phalanxes) of infantrymen (hoplites), fighting in close order, using a standard panoply of thrusting spear and large round shield (hoplon). A fine bronze helmet and sculpted body armor were at once the most expensive and the least essential pieces of the hoplite's panoply. Wooden shields and iron-tipped spears, the irreducible minima of hoplite arms and armor, were, as we have seen, relatively cheap. All other things being equal, a bigger phalanx could threaten to outflank, and therefore likely defeat, a smaller phalanx. There was, therefore, a strong incentive for states with aggressive neighbors, or expansionist ambitions, to mobilize fighting men at the social margin, even if their headgear and armor were rudimentary. This in turn gave subelite men who were able to provide themselves with shield and spear a stronger bargaining position.[23]

Local men who felt that they were not being treated fairly by the local ruling coalition had little incentive to support that coalition when the going got tough. This is the situation envisioned by the early Greek poet, Hesiod, who was affronted by the unwillingness of "gift-gobbling rulers" to judge disputes fairly. Hesiod advised his reader to avoid public spaces—which is, of course, where military mobilization would take place. It is perhaps not surprising that Hesiod's Askra never became a state in its own right; in the classical period, Askra was a village in the territory of the polis of Thespiai (i222: map 5). The opposite situation is imagined (ch. 4) by Herodotus' Solon in his tale about happy Tellus of Athens. Given the context of Solon's story in Herodotus' narrative, Tellus is not a plausible candidate for a privileged rent-seeking member of an elite coalition. Yet clearly his willingness to "come to help" when there was an incursion across the Athenian border was essential to Athens' security. If Tellus and his fellow moderately prosperous Athenians were to take Hesiod's quietist message to heart, the Athenian ruling coalition would quickly find itself in trouble.[24]

The stakes in interstate warfare were increasingly high. Meanwhile, the resources that might allow a defecting member of the elite to change the game were increasingly abundant. The opening up of trans-Mediterranean trade made it possible for a lucky family to make a substantial fortune in a short span of time. That fortune could be transformed into disruptive violence potential through a growing market in military expertise: The Greeks had discovered that, relative to neighboring cultures, hoplite warfare provided them with a relative advantage as violence specialists. By the seventh century BCE, a good number of Greeks were serving as mercenaries outside of the Greek world; Greek mercenaries in seventh century Egypt, for example, tagged ancient monuments with inscribed graffiti. But mercenaries might also be employed within the Greek world. As the development of Greek warfare yielded increased dividends in terms of innovations in arms, armor, and tactics—and as skilled Greek fighters became a "commodity" available to anyone with the wealth to pay them—the possibility of hiring a small army capable of displacing a fragile ruling coalition made it possible for an ambitious man to imagine establishing his family as sole rulers. And so a path to tyranny was blazed.[25]

Caught between the threat of elite defection (in the form of attempts at tyranny) and non-elite defection (in the form of refusing to mobilize against external threats), Greek ruling elites walked a tightrope. Unsurprisingly, many fell: Short-lived tyrannies replaced established aristocratic coalitions in a number of Greek poleis. Elsewhere, large Greek states proved incapable of securing their borders against smaller, more cohesive, local rivals. This was the context in which the nascent elitist social orders of both early Sparta and early Athens were creatively destroyed by the enactment of new citizen-centered rules.

SPARTA: LYCURGAN REFORMS, SEVENTH TO SIXTH CENTURY BCE

In the classical era of the mid-fifth century BCE, Sparta was an unprepossessing cluster of villages occupying a stunning mountain-girded setting in the fertile valley of the Eurotas River in the south-central Peloponnese (map 4). Like other Peloponnesians, Spartans spoke Greek with a distinctive Dorian dialect and traced their ancestry, in myth, to the ancestral claim on the Peloponnesus by the sons of the Greek superhero, Herakles. In addition to their core homeland in Laconia (also known as Lakonike, Lakedaimon), the

MAP 4 *Peloponnesus.*

Spartans had seized the territory of Messenia to the southwest—a region, now centered on the town of Kalamata, that remains among the most agriculturally productive areas of the Greek mainland. The estimated combined population of Laconia and Messenia was, in the later fourth century, in excess of 250,000 (appendix I: regions 16 and 17); the population may well have been similar in size in the late sixth and fifth centuries. By the fifth century BCE, Sparta dominated most of the other states of the Peloponnese and could mobilize large armies through its leadership of a coalition of southern and central Greek states with a combined population of more than a million (table 2.3).[26]

The key to Sparta's classical era power was its highly professionalized land army. At its peak, Sparta mobilized perhaps 9,000 citizen soldiers. Sparta's army was centered, as were the armies of other archaic and classical Greek states, on a phalanx of heavy-armed hoplite infantrymen. But the Spartans were exceptional in their level of training, discipline, and in their capacity to execute complex battlefield maneuvers. Spartan citizens were, to a man, specialists in violence: trained from childhood in the skills and the mind-set thought by the Greeks to be especially appropriate to hoplite warriors. That army was long believed to be invincible in a standard phalanx versus phalanx battle on open terrain. The certainty that fighting Sparta meant crushing defeat on the field of battle became a consequential factor in the calculations of other Greek states.

Spartan citizen-soldiers could hyperspecialize in military affairs because Sparta effectively outsourced the agricultural activities that would otherwise have been demanded of them. Sparta's economy was based on the labor of tens of thousands of state-owned serfs, known as helots. They were, in effect, specialists in subsistence agriculture. Helots farmed much of the land of Laconia and all of Messenia, turning over the surplus, as rents, to their Spartan overlords. Organized violence ensured that the "reservation price" for helot labor remained very near bare subsistence, thus maximizing rents. Sparta annually declared war on the helot population, rendering the helots not only the economic foundation of, but also official and highly vulnerable enemies of the Spartan state. Helots who stood out in any way were subjected to attack by a state-sponsored terror organization, known as "the Hidden" (*krypteia*), as well as to occasional state-organized mass killings. The net effect of state-sponsored violence was to limit helot mobility and to eliminate laborers' chance of bargaining with individual landowners for better wages. Violence, internal and external, was, therefore, an intrinsic part of Sparta's social order and essential to its perpetuation.[27]

The non-Spartan, nonhelot population of Laconia, known as *perioikoi* ("marginals"), lived in some two dozen small and dependent poleis. They did the Spartans' bidding in peace and augmented the ranks of the Spartan army in times of war. With the exception of a colony at Tarentum (171) in south Italy (settled, in Greek legend, by the bastard offspring of Spartan women whose husbands were fighting in Messenia), Spartans did not participate in the colonization movement of the Age of Expansion. The Malthusian trap faced by other leading Greek states seems to have been addressed by successful expansionism—the incorporation of Laconia and conquest of Messenia—conjoined with the distinctive approach to military hyperspecialization that resulted from a set of social and political reforms traditionally associated with the lawgiver Lycurgus.

The historicity of Lycurgus, the chronology of the reforms, and some of the details of the Spartan social order are matters of scholarly debate; I refer in this book to "Lycurgus" and "Lycurgan reforms" simply for convenience. What is most important for our purposes is that by the mid-sixth century

BCE, if not before, the social order of Laconia and Messenia had taken on the highly distinctive form that enabled classical Sparta to achieve and long sustain superpolis status.

Sparta's social order was designed for waging war. That order emerged against the background of military conflicts, beginning in the eighth and seventh centuries BCE, over the control of the territory and population of Messenia. We cannot precisely date the Lycurgan reforms; even in antiquity Lycurgus was regarded as a semimythical figure. We do not know how, or how quickly, the new order was instituted. The origin story told by the Roman-era biographer Plutarch in his *Life of Lycurgus*—that new social order was consolidated in the wake of a revolt by the Messenians, and that there was violent, although ultimately futile resistance to the new order on the part of Sparta's established ruling elite—is plausible if not demonstrable. Some details of the Lycurgan social order remain debatable, not least because the Spartans were notoriously secretive about themselves and hostile to overly inquisitive visitors. Yet the outlines of the mature Spartan system are tolerably clear.[28]

The Lycurgan order was a set of rules governing social and economic relations among Spartan citizens, the education of young Spartans and their induction into citizenship, and the governance of the state. The system was premised upon equality among citizens. Although much property was privately possessed by individual Spartan families and landholdings became increasingly unequal over time (ch. 9), each citizen was in principle the equal of every other citizen in his ability to provide for a minimum regular and mandatory contribution of food to his regimental mess: A Spartan's baseline income came, again in principle, via a tract of land that may have once been given to his family as part of a distribution of conquered lands and the agricultural enterprise of a number of privately managed but collectively controlled helots. Each Spartan citizen's civic and social standing was predicated on his sustained capacity to provide enough income from the rents of his land to provide a specified share of the food consumed by his military unit. Those who failed to provide their share were summarily dropped from the ranks of citizens and demoted to the humiliating social status of "Inferior."[29]

Based on the estimated populations of Laconia and Messenia (appendix I), there may have been something like 40,000 adult male helots, which would mean (at the high point of Sparta's citizen body and counterfactually assuming equitable distribution) about four or five helot families for each Spartan citizen.[30] Certainly by the later classical era, the distribution of land and helots was *not* equal, and probably never had been. So, even accounting for the decline in the number of Spartans, we must suppose that some Spartans controlled fewer than a "full share" of four to five helot families. The total rents that could be extracted from, say, one or two farming families engaged in subsistence agriculture might have been enough to maintain a Spartan family but cannot have been enough to provide for much luxury.[31]

The Lycurgan system was predicated on extracting rents from helots, distributing those rents among the citizens, and sustaining an appearance of lifestyle equality among many men with an equal capacity for violence. Thus, although individual Spartans reaped substantial revenues from private properties, so that they had enough private wealth to dedicate rich offerings to the local deities and to compete in high-status chariot races at Olympia, the unequal wealth accruing from private property could not be publicly displayed in everyday life. The upper bound of the quotidian lifestyle of every Spartan was set by the rent available to the least wealthy citizens. The limited rent available to the poorer Spartan citizens was, therefore, the basis of the famous "virtuous austerity" of Spartan society. That mandatory austerity became, in light of Sparta's fame, an important part of the "impoverished Hellas" mirage, in antiquity and modernity alike.[32]

The limited rent available to poorer Spartans was a potential weakness of the Lycurgan system: If mischance or malice (e.g., targeted terror killing of an enemy's helots by one of the Hidden) were to deprive a Spartan of the helot labor force necessary to cultivate his land, he would be expelled from the ranks of the citizens. This dynamic both threatened the demographic integrity of the citizen army and provided a strong individual incentive to seek private wealth as a backstop. That, in turn, might be an incentive to free ride on the system by reaping the benefits of low-cost helot labor without contributing to perpetuating the system of violence that kept labor costs low. The incentive to private wealth-seeking undercut the Lycurgan system's ostensible goals of equality among citizens and of producing citizen-specialists who focused entirely on military affairs. The system remained reasonably stable, in spite of this structural problem, as a result of the famously intense mutual monitoring among all Spartan citizens; the Spartan social panopticon was facilitated by the orientation of citizen life around public spaces and military units. Any observed deviation from the norms of citizen behavior was, in principle, immediately publicized and punished.[33]

In addition to their time-consuming military training, every Spartan was expected to devote substantial efforts to the perpetuation of the social order by contributing to the education of the young. The goal of Spartan education was the maintenance, generation by generation, of a distinctive pattern of behavior (including courage in battle and violence toward helots) and a distinctive set of attitudes (including despising cowards and helots as inherently unworthy of respect). Spartan boys were raised from childhood to be warriors and were subjected to a strict regimen aimed at making them tough, self-reliant, and loyal to their units. Upon completing his training, a Spartan youth was inducted into a combination dining club and military unit, which became, in principle, the focus of his life.[34]

As we have seen, Spartans were expected to maintain at least a public façade of austerity and simplicity in their style of life. They lived in relatively humble houses, dressed alike in simple clothing, and ate simple food. They were expected to defer, socially and politically, to elders and to their leaders: two hereditary kings (descendants of two families who traced their ancestry to Herakles; leaders in war and ritual, they were treated in ways that were decidedly heroic but far from godlike), a council of 28 elected elders selected from prominent families, and five *ephors*, who served as general enforcers of the austerity regime. Policy decisions were in practice made by the leaders and were affirmed by the citizens via public acclamation in occasional assemblies.

The Lycurgan system did not encourage economic specialization beyond the divide into citizen-soldiers and helot-farmers. Although Laconian artisans among the perioikoi continued to produce and to export some fine metalwork and pottery, Spartan citizens were, in principle, not permitted openly to engage in trade or industry. Moreover, the Spartan state, uniquely among the major poleis of Greece across the whole of the classical era, declined to coin silver and discouraged (and at one point at least forbade) the circulation of other states' coinage within their territory.[35] As silver coins increasingly became the standard of exchange across and beyond the Greek world, this restriction dampened internal and external trade. Laconia and Messenia never became a fully closed economic system, but, once the Lycurgan system was in place, Spartans were at least partly insulated from the imperatives of economic specialization, innovation, and creative destruction that was typical of much of the rest of the Greek world. One result was the conservatism for which the Spartans became famous in the classical era (ch. 8). Yet because that insulation was never perfect, there was always the danger that individual Spartans would find ways to defect from the Lycurgan system, a tendency that eventually contributed to the collapse of the system in the mid fourth century BCE (ch. 9).

The Lycurgan system was predicated around the conjoined principles of distinguishing Spartan citizens (and their families) sharply from all other residents, and of hyperspecialization in respect to strictly delimited social roles. Spartan citizens were full-time warriors and occasional governors; helots were full-time farmers. The system was sustained by systematic acts of terroristic violence and ritualized humiliation of the helots and by intense mutual supervision by the citizens. There was, in principle, little to no upward mobility: Helots did not become citizens, although they might occasionally be offered the chance to become perioikoi. On at least one such occasion, those helots who took up the offer were "disappeared," and presumably killed; the spurious offer served to cull the ambitious.[36]

There was, on the other hand, ample opportunity for downward mobility: An individual Spartan could be stripped of citizenship for failing in his military duties as a warrior (coming back from war "neither with his shield, nor on it"), as well as for failing in his economic duty to share with his military unit a sufficient quantity of extracted rents. As a result of the quickening pace of downward mobility, which clearly increased with intensifying inequality and concentration of wealth in the hands of a few elite families, the total numbers of Spartan citizens declined over time. By the late 370s BCE, there were insufficient Spartan citizens to sustain Sparta's military dominance. The tipping point was, however, slow in coming. Sparta was a dominant state for two centuries, from the early- to mid-sixth century to well into the fourth.[37]

The Lycurgan reforms created a strong and unusually broad-based "natural state" ruled by an extensive and stable coalition of citizens. Through their specialization in the arts of war, the citizens held an effective joint monopoly on the means of organized violence. The *proportionality principle*, under which rent shares are distributed in a natural state according to capacity for violent disruption of the social order, was also respected: The norms of hoplite warfare rendered thousands of citizens functional equals in their violence potential, and the public system of apportioning Messenian land and extracting the surplus from helot labor treated citizens as equals in the distribution of rents. Within the citizen body, laws were strictly enforced, and all citizens—even the kings—were, in principle, equals before the law. The citizens, as collective and, in principle, equal power holders and rent-seekers, were credibly committed to mutually sustaining the system. They shared a very high incentive to preserve the current regime and to mobilize against internal or external threats to it. The incentives were matched by sanctions for deviation, which was reliably detected and reported by the social panopticon of Spartan citizen society.[38]

Sparta's hyperspecialization on infantry tactics and training proved extremely successful in an era in which interstate contests were decided by phalanx warfare. In the wake of adopting the Lycurgan reforms, Sparta saw a string of successes in foreign affairs. With the incorporation of Messenia, Sparta was securely established as a superpolis, outstanding in size of population, size of territory, and influence. Sparta's attempt to replicate the successful incorporation of Messenia in mountainous Arcadia faltered when the Spartan army suffered a defeat at Tegea (1297) in the sixth century (see map 3).

Rather than continuing the imperial project, Sparta turned to cooptation: The poleis of southern Greece were brought into a Sparta-dominated Peloponnesian League. The league was stable so long as Sparta credibly protected the interests of local elites by suppressing would-be tyrants and, later, democrats. Potential rivals to Spartan power, notably the major polis of Argos in the northeastern Peloponnese, were handed crushing military defeats by the formidable Spartan army.[39]

By the mid-to-late sixth century BCE, with the Lycurgan system up and running, Sparta was the leading state of mainland Greece. Moreover, Sparta long maintained its first-mover advantage over potential rivals in respect to organized violence based on hyperspecialization in military affairs. Other poleis found it unpalatable (most Greek elites had little taste for austerity and a lifetime of military training) or simply too difficult (helotization of neighbors was a costly undertaking) to adopt the full Lycurgan package. It was a very long time before another Greek state found a way to replicate Sparta's excellence in land warfare.

ATHENS: REFORMS OF SOLON, 594 BCE

In the mid-fifth century BCE, the city center of Athens presented a stark contrast to the unprepossessing villages of Sparta: Great temples and public buildings were prominent features of the cityscape, and the big, densely populated city was surrounded by a massive circuit wall. Thucydides (1.10) quipped that, were some later observer to judge on the basis of infrastructure, the power of Athens would be much overestimated, while that of Sparta would be badly underestimated. The Athenian home territory of Attica was extensive, at 2500 km²—about a third of the size of Laconia and Messenia combined. The total population of the polis of Athens in the fourth century, after massive war casualties, is estimated at 250,000—thus roughly comparable to the combined population of Laconia and Messenia. Like Laconia and Messenia, Attica featured villages and more substantial towns, but Attica was much more densely settled. A number of the settlements of Attica boasted their own mythic histories and distinctive cults associated with particular gods: In addition to the major cult of Athena on the Acropolis in the city center, there were Demeter at Eleusis, Artemis at Brauron, Nemesis at Rhamnous, Dionysus at Ikaria—among many others (map 5). Athens' dispersed pattern of cult distribution contrasts with, for example, Peloponnesian Argos with its single important "border cult" dedicated to Hera.[40]

By the seventh century, the many native residents of Attica were regarded by other Greeks and by one another as Athenians and, as such, sharers in a

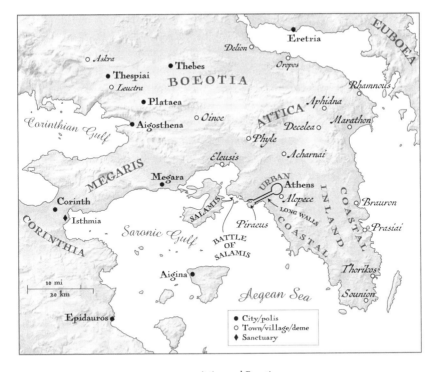

MAP 5 *Attica and Boeotia.*

distinctive common dialect and homeland. Unlike Laconia, none of the towns or villages of Attica sustained a separate polis identity into the classical period.[41] By the seventh century, the authority of Athenian public officials—notably the treasurers of the Athena cult and the archon who gave his name to the year in the Athenian civic calendar—extended, in principle, across all Attica. Yet, in the era before the reforms of the lawgiver Solon in 594 BCE, it remained unclear whether a shared Athenian heritage and the rudiments of government had as yet created a coherent state that would be capable of competing with smaller but better organized local rivals.

The Athenians, like the Spartans, and unlike residents of some smaller central Greek states—Eretria, Chalkis, Megara (1225)—were not active participants in the first great waves of Greek colonization. Nor, however, did the Athenians seek to incorporate extensive neighboring territories, on the model of Sparta's takeover of Messenia. The Athenians focused on internal colonization and intensification of agricultural enterprise in their large and still ill-defined homeland, over external colonization or regional expansionism. The choice may have been predetermined: In the era before Solon, it was probably impossible for Athenian elites to mobilize social resources for large-scale enterprises like foreign colonization or territorial expansion. Athens before Solon was not yet a cohesive community.

The Kerameikos cemetery, which lies just outside the classical-era city wall of Athens, offers a diachronic material record of Athenian social development. The graves clearly point to a striking demographic increase in the eighth century. As Ian Morris has shown, in that same era Athenian burial practice became more inclusive: More women and children were given formal burial (i.e., they were buried in graves that are readily identified and studied by modern archaeologists) than had been the case in the Early Iron Age. It is probable that a higher percentage of subelite males were now properly buried as well. But the eighth century expansion of access to dignified burial, and the generally greater social inclusiveness that formal burial implies, was followed by a seventh century reaction, as an Athenian elite seemingly consolidated its hold on the society and sought to limit access accordingly. Compared to social developments in other Greek poleis, restricting access was not a particularly successful strategy. Athens in the seventh century punched well under its weight, suffering military setbacks at the hands of smaller neighboring poleis.[42]

Herodotus' Solon (ch. 4) described Athens in the bygone age of happy Tellus as reasonably prosperous. Yet pre-Solonian Athens was clearly a very long way from the great imperial state of the fifth century BCE or the thriving commercial center of the fourth century. In Herodotus' tale, Tellus' Athens struggled not against great eastern kingdoms, like Lydia or Persia, or against grand coalitions of states led by the superpolis of Sparta, but rather against incursions from Megara, the city-state that bordered Athens to the west. Megara (size 4, with an estimated peak population of 40,000) was less than one-fifth the size of Athens, and yet Megara clearly constituted a real threat to the territorial integrity of its much larger neighbor. The story of "Tellus coming to give aid" suggests that the Megarians were capable of entering Athenian territory in arms and threatening the important Athenian border town of Eleusis. The security threat faced by Athens was not from neighboring Megara alone. Sea raiders from Aigina (1358), a small (size 2) but densely populated (perhaps 40,000 in the fifth century) and well-organized island polis in the Saronic Gulf, were capable of attacking Athenian coastal communities with relative impunity. Solon gained an early reputation with poems exhorting the Athenians not to abandon the struggle with their neighbors for the control of Salamis, a strategic island lying close to the southwestern coast of Attica.[43]

In the first decade of the sixth century, Athens faced a severe test of its tenuous cohesion as a polis. Athenian population growth, along with intensification of agricultural enterprise in Attica, in the context of the new opportunities of the Age of Expansion, led to a growing gap between relatively wealthy and relatively impoverished Athenians. In the absence of out-migration through colonization, demographic growth seems to have led to a local labor surplus, and thus to lowering the value of Athenian labor. A family with little land of its own, and therefore dependent upon selling its labor surplus in order to make ends meet, could, under these conditions, face catastrophe. Starvation was apparently fended off, in some cases at least, first by borrowing from more prosperous neighbors and then, when loans went unpaid, by self-enslavement. The hypothesis that Athens had a farm-labor surplus and that returns to agricultural labor in Attic were considered low is supported by the choice of some Athenian owners of self-enslaved Athenians to sell their human property abroad.[44]

Depressed labor costs would, in turn, have increased the rents available to the owners of large estates. Those costs could be driven even lower by using free laborers' indebtedness to create conditions of peonage, whereby local men were bound to the land of major owners by agreements that rendered them effectively serfs. Reducing the mobility of the remaining ostensibly free laborers would reduce whatever slight bargaining power they might have gained when legally enslaved Athenians were sold abroad—thereby allowing the maximum surplus to be creamed off by the rentier elite. Reducing mobility of free laborers meant that the wealthy could sell off some of their fellow Athenians without pushing up their labor costs.

With bigger rents available to corral and to distribute, ambitious Athenian elites, like elites in states throughout premodern history, sought to limit access to institutions that might widen the pool of would-be rentiers or that might protect rent-payers from rent-seekers. Athenian elites saw that if they successfully monopolized access to decision-making, dispute resolution, and sharing as equals in cult, they would be well situated to maximize their rents. Monopolizing political, legal, and religious authority was thus the obvious route to gaining and securing greater wealth. Yet, on the other hand, the proportionality principle meant that the ruling coalition must distribute rents to all those with the potential to disrupt the system. And therein lay the rub: By the end of the seventh century, there was no very obvious way for a handful of the very wealthiest Athenians to monopolize the means of violence.

As the sixth century dawned, several possible developmental paths lay open, but none looked promising. A hypothetical "Athenian Lycurgus" could have sought to unite an extensive minority of Athens' native males into a cohesive military elite, while pushing the rest of the native population into serfdom. But, as we have seen, the Spartan model was a very difficult one to follow, and halfway measures would not solve the problem of the need for mobilization against external threats and the widely distributed internal capacity for violence. Alternatively, the elite coalition might have fragmented, enabling the rise of a tyrant capable of mobilizing enough armed men to seize control of the state. In fact, a generation earlier, in the late seventh century, an Olympic victor named Kylon had seized the Acropolis of Athens in a failed attempt at establishing a tyranny. The bloody aftermath of the botched coup eventuated in the impious slaughter of some of Kylon's supporters at a sacred altar of Athena. This was the context for Athens' first formal and written laws, established in about 610 BCE by a lawgiver named Drakon. The only surviving section of the law concerns the rules for reintegrating perpetrators of involuntary manslaughter back into the community. It remains unclear what (if any) other matters were addressed in the laws of Drakon, although in later Athenian legend, he was believed to have prescribed death for a wide range of offenses. Whatever their scope and intent, the Drakonian laws did not lead to a stable social order.[45]

By the year 594 BCE, pressed by external rivals and internal conflict, the still-emergent polis of Athens seemed poised at the verge of losing any vestige of high-order cohesion it had achieved. Athens faced fragmentation along regional lines into several small poleis, or even a devolution to primitive economic conditions reminiscent of the Dark Age. It was evidently to forestall the collapse of the state, and in hopes of avoiding the rough expedients of Spartan or tyrannical solutions to social order, that Athens' ruling coalition chose Solon as archon and endowed him with special lawmaking authority.

If we are to believe the ancient tradition and the evidence of Solon's own poetry, in the event the elite got a more extensive set of reforms than they had bargained for—Solon's reforms amounted to nothing less than the creative destruction of Athens' prior system of rules. Yet Solon characterized himself in his poetry, and was remembered by Greek posterity, as a moderate. According to the tradition, Solon's reforms were attempts to find a middle way between the ambitions of greedy rent-seeking elites who sought to use the power of the state to further enrich themselves, and the hopes of a mass of relatively impoverished Athenians, who dreamed of a world of resource equality and urged revolutionary confiscation and redistribution of the agricultural land of Attica. Indeed, Solon's reforms may best be understood as seeking to create an Athenian "middling class" of moderately prosperous, Tellus-like, independent citizens: men who would stand between the very rich and very poor and who could be mobilized against external enemies.

Although Solon is a more historical figure than Lycurgus, there remains substantial scholarly uncertainty about the precise nature of the crisis leading to Solon's reforms and about exactly what "Solonian" measures were passed, when, and by whom. Yet the social and political reforms that have come down to us under Solon's name, and that were widely believed in antiquity to have been put into place in response to a social crisis during his archon-year of 594 BCE, appear to be a coherent set of rules. Those rules served to create a distinctive form of polis citizenship predicated on equalizing certain legal immunities and participation rights, while at the same time providing individuals with powerful incentives for investment in human capital and experiments with economic specialization. In the long run, the new rules convinced a significant number of Athenians to move out of the low-profit activity of subsistence agriculture and into potentially more lucrative endeavors. [46]

Solon's first move was a one-time cancellation of debts; debtors were allowed to "shake off their burdens" by declaring bankruptcy without penalties; creditors received no advance notice or reimbursement. This use of the fiat power of the state to cancel private obligations had obvious dangers, in terms of increasing moral hazard (incentivizing speculative risk-taking by some by passing the costs of failure on to others) and lowering the willingness of Athenians to lend on credit. Stories circulated claiming that Solon's opportunistic friends had used advance word of his reform plan to take out loans that were swiftly forgiven by the new law. On the other hand, Solon refused even to consider a wholesale redistribution of land. Presumably this line in the sand reassured some potential lenders. It meant, however, that the underlying conditions that led poorer Athenians to fall into crippling debt were not directly addressed, insofar as Athens' economy remained primarily agricultural. Unlike Lycurgus, Solon did not make citizens even notional equals in material terms by distribution of land and labor resources.[47]

Solon's next major innovation was to forbid the enslavement of one Athenian by another. He did not abolish slavery. Instead, he established a fundamental civil immunity against the ultimate status degradation—a "civic right" of citizens, rather than a "human right" of people as such. The civic right came with a corresponding legal duty: As a result of the new law, Athenians lost actual and potential property rights to other Athenians' persons. Thus, for the first, time, "being an Athenian" gained a substantial content beyond long-term residency and dialect: Solon had, in essence, invented citizenry as a distinctive civil status that was guaranteed by written law.

Athenians who were currently slaves of other Athenians were freed (there is no evidence to suggest that the owners or the slaves were compensated); at least some Athenians who had been sold abroad and had lived away from their homeland for long enough to "lose their Attic tongue" were repatriated. Again we lack details about how this was accomplished in practice and how many people were involved. But it is difficult to see how Solon could publicly boast, as he did, of repatriating citizens in his postreform poems unless at least some Athenians were indeed brought home.[48]

In a puzzling, but celebrated, passage of his poetry, Solon speaks of disestablishing the *horoi* (singular *horos*) that had formerly encumbered the Earth, so that the land of Attica, once enslaved, now was made free. The horoi are often taken to be records of indebtedness: "disestablishing the horoi" would, on this interpretation, simply mean "canceling debts." But the Greek word "horos" ordinarily meant "access-governing boundary marker" (i.e., "do not cross this line unless you are among those entitled to do so"). "Horos" was not used as a term for "record of indebtedness" until much later in Greek history. It seems more natural, therefore, to read Solon's "abolition of the horoi" reform as referring to boundary markers that limited territorial access. This suggests that the horoi had constrained movement by some Athenians to and from certain parts of Athenian territory—perhaps including the central city and its institutions—thereby enforcing the conditions of peonage and the elite monopoly on both political and ritual power. Disestablishing the horoi was thus a way of equalizing physical access, eliminating the insidious use of debt to enforce vicious forms of inequality, and creating de facto freedom of movement and association for Athenians within their home territory.[49]

On this interpretation, abolishing the horoi established an equal right of free citizens to move about at will within a country now understood as a collective possession of the Athenian people. With the constraining boundary markers removed, Athenians might move to and live wherever they believed they could do best for themselves. They were free to travel to the central city and to make use of state legal, political, and religious institutions, on something approaching equal footing. Of course, this newfound freedom (like the abolition of debts and the rule forbidding enslavement of fellow Athenians) was gained at the expense of the rent-seeking elite, who might attempt to reestablish conditions of monopoly control under new auspices. This possibility provides a plausible context for another Solonian law, forbidding acts of *hubris*—behavior aimed at humiliation and intimidation—against *any* resident of Attica. Among the hubris law's targets would have been rent-seeking elites who might have sought to mimic the Spartans by using threats and intimidation to reimpose limits on the free movement of poor citizens.[50]

In order to give the citizenship reforms teeth, Solon created a new procedure whereby the citizens of Athens, gathered in formal assembly, could sit as a collective court of law to pass judgment on certain categories of malefactors. State officials who abused their power by acting outside the proper purview of their office could now be indicted before the people and subsequently punished. Powerful officials thus became the equals of ordinary citizens before the law, a development with profound implications for public order. Moreover, Solon extended the right of legal standing in various criminal actions (including hubris cases) to every citizen on behalf of every other. Thus, if a powerful individual mistreated a weak individual, he might be hauled before the people's court by another powerful citizen, acting on the weak person's behalf. In a society in which "helping friends and hurting enemies" was a conventional definition of justice, and in which there were high levels of intraelite rivalry and competition, this was not an empty gesture.[51]

Taken together, these three legal reforms—written law defining bright-line violations, institutionalization of the citizenry as a legal body with authority and capacity to act jointly in response to violations, and incentives for individuals to initiate legal process against violators—created the foundations for a political order in which citizen immunities could potentially gain purchase on public behavior, and thus the equal standing of citizens might really matter. Athens had taken the first steps on the road to being a state governed not only by rules, but by fair rules.

Other of Solon's reforms augmented the "negative" value of citizenship as legal immunity from status degradation with specified "positive" participation rights. All citizens were formally granted the opportunity to vote in public assemblies. The right to stand for office (whether by election or lottery) was, however, determined by an individual's annual income: Depending on his income (denominated as "wet and dry" products of agriculture), each Athenian was assigned to one of four standardized income classes. Certain offices, notably magistrates who handled substantial public funds, were reserved to the highest income class; other offices were distributed to the two middle classes. The poorest Athenians were left with votes on policy as assemblymen and votes as jurors when the assembly met as a court. This four-classes reform seems to point to the effort by Solon, the self-described "man of the middle," to build a middling class of citizens, juridically distinguished both from the richest and poorest, unwilling to join the elite in oppressing the poor but ready and willing to be mobilized against Athens' external enemies—or against revolutionary attempts to redistribute private property.[52]

For all its boldness, the Solonian system might seem, on the face of it, to lack the essential egalitarian feature that made the Lycurgan system so successful: Athenian citizens had gained a substantial measure of legal and political equality, but inequality persisted in the economic realm—and indeed material inequality was formally recognized in the distribution of public offices. By failing to provide poor Athenians with material capital, in the form of redistributed land, while stripping them of the collateral represented by bodies that could be sold, Solon's legal reforms might have ended in strengthening bonds of patronage and increasing dependency and clientalism. This might in turn have ended in a stronger state but one with a narrower ruling coalition. Given the generally low productivity of such regimes, Athens would not be a likely contributor to the dramatic classical efflorescence.[53]

The ancient tradition concerning Solon's reforms suggests, however, that the issue of the long-term economic welfare of citizens was addressed by laws that reoriented Athenian society away from low-productivity forms of subsistence agriculture and toward potentially more productive forms of specialized agriculture and industry. A law attributed to Solon banned the export of agricultural produce other than oil from Attica (Plutarch, *Solon* 24.1). As one of the driest areas of mainland Greece, Attica was on the whole better suited for growing relatively low-value (and drought-resistant) barley than relatively high-value (and drought-sensitive) wheat. Athens had no hope of developing a comparative advantage in high-value grain production relative to other regions of the Greek world: Exports of grain from Attica might further immiserate the poor by producing local shortages but would not much improve Athenian GDP (gross domestic product). On the other hand, Attica is well suited for olive production, and the same Solonian law explicitly permitted the export of high-value olive oil. The law both encouraged entrepreneurs to invest in "exportable" high-value crops and guarded local food supplies when drought lowered yields elsewhere. Yet another law encouraged families to invest in human capital by stripping fathers who failed to teach their sons a useful skill of their traditional right to expect support from their sons in old age. Still other Solonian laws paved the way for immigration by foreigners with specialized skills and clarified certain property rights.[54]

Taken as a package, Solon's reforms represent a major rebooting of Athenian society, one that set Athens on a path that, as we now know, eventuated in democracy and prosperity. But at the end of Solon's year as archon, that outcome lay far in the unforeseeable future. In the immediate aftermath of Solon's reforms, both elite and ordinary Athenians were disgruntled; everyone, it seems, felt either that his reforms had gone too far in equalizing access to institutions and legal protection, or not far enough in equalizing property. The fragmentary poems by Solon that have come down to us were, for the most part, written after the enactment of his program, in what must have seemed at the time a vain attempt to justify it to the Athenians.[55]

The three generations following Solon's reforms (593–510 BCE) were an unsettled era in Athens' political history, marked by short-lived experiments in reorganizing state offices and by three tyrannical coups d'état. With the support of mercenaries, the third of these coups was successful. The family of Peisistratus dominated Athens from 546 to 510 BCE, while, for most of this period, carefully preserving at least the forms of the Solonian legal order.

During the same three-generation period, Athens became a notable producer and exporter of fine painted pottery, as well as of olive oil and wine. Peisistratus and his sons introduced certain innovations that had the effect of furthering some aspects of the Solonian reforms: The state extended development loans to farmers and established traveling "circuit judges" who offered alternatives to clientalistic dispute resolution by local elites. The tyrants also sought to buttress Athenian identity by the sponsorship of religious festivals. Notable among these was the great Panathenaia—an "All Athens" festival that included Olympics-like contests in which athletes and musicians from around the Greek world competed for prizes. Those prizes prominently included large, finely painted Athenian vases, in the form of transport amphorae employed in overseas trade and filled with fine Athenian olive oil. The symbolism was clear enough: Athens was being promoted as an exporter of specialized agricultural products, fine pottery, and high culture.[56]

CITIZEN STATES

By the middle of the sixth century BCE, much of the Greek world had moved toward citizenship. The world of the poleis had become remarkable on two dimensions of decentralization. First, there was the proliferation of a great number of peer polities within a single extensive culture zone. Next, many poleis were defined by an extensive body of citizens who treated one another as equals within specified domains, rather than by a tiny ruling elite dedicated to monopolizing access to institutions and rents through coercion and ideology. While increasing access to institutions *within* the body of citizens, citizenship potentially enabled tighter restrictions on noncitizens. It remained to be seen whether, where, and when access would be opened beyond the confines of the citizen body.

Although it is not possible fully to disentangle the webs of influence, the relative success of prominent poleis in weathering social crises and consolidating large territories, by expanded citizenship and promoting egalitarian rules for citizens, helped to spread citizen-centered institutions across the Greek world. The relevant context of the rise of the citizen state included a military environment that rewarded those states capable of mobilizing many highly motivated and skilled soldiers, and also the relative ease of institutional and technological transfers between states. Across the ecology of city-states, bodies of citizens were more or less extensive and citizens enjoyed more or less extensive systems of political equality. But Greek native men were, in most cases, more equal and more actively engaged in state governance than was the norm in the premodern world. Even Greek tyrants were constrained to respect salient aspects of equal citizenship. No Greek tyrant ever established himself as a godlike king. Indeed, as the historical economists Rob Fleck and Andrew Hanssen have shown, through the institution of policies favorable to economic growth, Greek tyrants appear inadvertently to have fostered conditions that also favored democratization.[57]

By 550 BCE, the Greek world had diverged in significant ways from standard premodern paths of state development. Even when compared to other ancient city-state ecologies (e.g., Etruscan and Phoenician), the Greek world was unusual in the strength and pervasiveness of citizen-centered public authority, as well as in the great number of states, on three continents, that shared a common core culture. While we know much more about Athens and Sparta than we do about other poleis, it is certain that other Greek states had also embarked on a path of bold institutional reform. A tantalizing sixth century inscribed document from the island polis of Chios (i840), for example, mentions a "popular council" as an important body of government. In order to mobilize volunteers willing to "bring aid" (like Tellus) in times of emergency, local elites were increasingly compelled to open access to some institutions to local men capable of arming themselves. Poleis that narrowly limited access to state institutions risked losing wars to neighboring states with more extensive citizen bodies.

There remained considerable social tension within Greek states: Elites in many poleis still commanded considerable property-power; some dreamed of narrowing access and thereby increasing rent shares. Meanwhile, the logic of citizenship led non-elites to seek to expand their access to institutions and to increase their collective influence on public policy. Many Greek poleis experienced violent ongoing struggles between elites who sought to shrink the functional role of citizenship in the distribution of political and social power and poorer male natives who sought to grow it. Rivalries among elites, and the constant quest for innovative paths to gaining social prestige, led ambitious aristocrats to seek support among non-elites. In the most successful Greek states, the trend was toward an equilibrium in which male citizens, elite and non-elite alike, found compelling reasons to cooperate in a political regime that was strikingly inclusive by any premodern standard.[58]

Lycurgan Sparta and Solonian Athens offered contrasting approaches to creative destruction of earlier forms of social order and the formation of the "Greek citizen state." In each state, major constitutional reforms created a large body of citizens who were distinguished from other residents by clearly defined legal and participation rights. In each, the invention of new forms of citizenship allowed for the potential (Athens) or actual (Sparta) mobilization of large bodies of armed men.

The Athenian model made strong distinctions between citizens and others and allowed for substantial social inequality among citizens. On the other hand, Athens now extended certain legal immunities to all native males and even, in the case of the hubris law, to all residents. It allowed citizens much greater freedom of choice in the conduct of their private lives, and allowed for upward, as well as downward, social and status mobility.

The Spartan model emphasized strictly enforced social, political, and (notional) material equality among citizens whose monopoly position was secured by the rents extracted, through violence and threat of violence, from other natives in their home territory and maintained by a hyperspecialization in warfare. While perioikoi presumably had some legal rights, the helots, against whom war was declared each year, were denied the protection of even minimal norms of civilized propriety. The Spartan citizenry was homogeneous in principle, and its potential for growth was strictly limited by the ease of downward mobility out of the ranks of the citizens and the impossibility of upward mobility.

By the later sixth century BCE, Sparta's revolutionary social order had achieved an equilibrium that enabled Sparta to extend its influence across a substantial part of the Greek world through its Peloponnesian League. It remained unclear how far Sparta's League might extend beyond the Peloponnese. In Athens' case, it was unclear whether the combination of a citizen-centered social order, established by Solon, with the autocratic leadership of the tyrants would find a stable equilibrium. The answer to both questions was revealed in the last decade of the sixth century, in the aftermath of a political murder arising from a love triangle within the ranks of the Athenian tyrant's ruling coalition.

7

FROM TYRANNY TO
DEMOCRACY, 550–465 BCE

TYRANT SLAYERS

The liberators' knives struck home; the tyrant fell; Athens, freed from despotism, went on to democracy and greatness. Or so the Athenians sometimes liked to imagine. The real story of tyranny, its demise, the origins of democracy, and Athens' rise to prominence in the Greek world was more complicated and, from the viewpoint of explaining efflorescence, much more interesting. It becomes even more interesting when compared to the experience with tyranny and democracy of Sicilian Syracuse, a polis that seemed in some ways to be Athens' twin.[1]

What the Greeks called tyranny was, outside the Greek world, a historically prevalent form of political order in which the head of a given family rules as an autocrat with the collusion of an elite coalition of specialists in government, ritual, and violence.[2] What is surprising about the political history of the Greek poleis is not that tyrants arose as complex states crystallized but that tyranny failed to become the Greek norm. While many prominent Greek poleis experienced tyrannical interludes, a given tyrannical regime seldom outlived two human generations. When Greek tyrants were overthrown, they were typically replaced, not by another ruling family with its own coalition, but by citizen-centered government. This is surprising in light of the challenge of achieving and sustaining decentralized social cooperation at scale (ch. 3).

By the mid-fifth century BCE, both Athens and Syracuse had solved the challenge of scaling up without tyranny through the development of democracy as an especially strong form of citizen-centered self-government. Athens and Syracuse were, in the later fifth century, in some ways strikingly similar superpoleis (ch. 8). But the trajectories and institutional forms of tyranny and democracy in Athens and Syracuse were very different. Autocrats and democrats alike must answer the fundamental question of distribution: "Who gets what—and why?" Greek tyrants failed to answer that question in a way that gained them a stable position of exclusive authority. The inability of Greek tyrants to create a powerful ideology of rulership is testimony to the enduring strength of egalitarian values in Greek society. But democracy did not automatically provide a stable alternative. Achieving a workable set of democratic institutions was a matter of constant experimentation—and some experiments failed. The experience with tyranny and democracy at Athens and Syracuse offers a further test of the explanatory power of the two hypotheses (fair rules/capital investment/low transaction costs and competition/innovation/rational cooperation) developed in chapter 5.

In the long generation of consolidated tyrannical rule (546–510 BCE), the Athenian state developed a more elaborate material infrastructure (water supply, public monuments, temples) and a more robust and diversified economy. Particularly notable was the flowering of the Athenian ceramics industry. By the mid-sixth century, Athens had replaced Corinth as the primary Mediterranean center for production of painted pottery. Athenian vases were exported throughout the Greek world and beyond—some of the finest surviving examples of Athenian vase painting come from graves in Italy, where they were buried with wealthy Etruscans. Although ceramics can never have been a big part of Athens' GDP, fired pottery is extremely durable and thus highly visible in archaeological contexts. The increasing prevalence of fine Athenian painted pottery at sites across the Mediterranean provides us with a proxy for the growth of Athens' nonagricultural economic sector. Like most other Greek poleis, agriculture remained the largest single employer of Athenian labor—but it was no longer the only game in town.[3]

For most of their 36-year reign, Peisistratus and his sons were diligent in maintaining the appearance of ruling by the law. It was noted by the Athenians (and remembered by subsequent historians) that when Peisistratus was summoned to appear before a magistrate after being accused of a legal infraction, he dutifully arrived in the magistrate's office as a private citizen and without his armed retainers or trappings of office. It was also noted that his accuser did not pursue the case. The tyrants sought to expand their coalition by allowing, perhaps encouraging, members of other elite families to hold the highest public magistracies—including the archonship, the office that had been the platform for Solon's reforms. Looking beyond the elite, the tyrants sought to strengthen ordinary Athenians' sense of civic identification with the state through promotion of new and reorganized festivals. In addition to the "all Athens" festival of the Panathenaia, these included the Dionysia, a multiday celebration of the wine god Dionysus that was the venue for the development of tragedy and comedy.

While the tyrants did not undertake imperial enterprises on the level of the fifth century Athenian state (ch. 8), Athenian control over disputed border territories was more effectively asserted, and members of prominent Athenian families became leading players in the northern Aegean. Like other major Greek states, Athens began building trireme warships and sought access to the timber and other resources necessary for their construction. Overall, Athens seemed to be coming into its own under the tyrants, beginning to fulfill the potential of its large territory and population. Yet serious weaknesses persisted. Athens still lacked a true national army of the sort Sparta was already using to great effect. The tyrants had inaugurated their regime by disarming as many of their opponents as possible, and they continued to rely on a force of mercenary cavalrymen recruited from Thessaly. Meanwhile, sea raiders from the Saronic island-polis of Aigina remained a local threat to Athenian coastal settlements, and Sparta seemed interested in extending its Peloponnesian League north of the isthmus.[4]

A more distant but greater threat was the kingdom of Persia—which had emerged with startling rapidity as the dominant power in western Asia. By the end of the third quarter of the sixth century, the Iranian Persians had absorbed Lydia, Mesopotamia, Egypt, the Greek poleis of western Anatolia, and parts of central Asia into the largest and most cohesive empire the western world had ever known. The Achaemenid Persian Empire was run by and in the interest of its dominant ethnoelite, and most especially by a handful of elite families, "the Sons of the House," closely associated with the Great King. Meanwhile, in North Africa, at the site of modern Tunis, the Phoenician colony of Carthage was now a dynamic and expansionist city-state, intent on controlling trade in the western Mediterranean. The larger world of which the Greek poleis were a part (map 2) was changing in ways that would soon threaten the independence of Greek states of the Anatolian coast, the Aegean islands, the mainland, and Sicily.[5]

Hipparchus, son of Peisistratus, was killed in 514 BCE at the Panathenaic festival. The assassins were two prominent Athenian citizens, Harmodius and Aristogeiton. This was the "tyrant killing" that the Athenians later celebrated as signaling their liberation. The historians Herodotus and Thucydides pointed out, however, that the killing actually arose from a personal quarrel: Harmodius and Aristogeiton were lovers. Hipparchus, whose amorous advances had been rebuffed by Harmodius, publicly insulted the young man's sister. Moreover, the killing itself was bungled, in that Hipparchus' brother, Hippias, the dominant figure in the tyrannical coalition, had escaped harm. Harmodius was cut down by the tyrants' bodyguards; Aristogeiton died under harsh interrogation. The most notable immediate result of the assassination was the hardening of autocratic rule. Hippias consolidated his position as sole ruler, relied more heavily than before on mercenaries, and generally began to behave like a standard-issue despot. Some Athenian elites who had formerly been reconciled to the tyranny now went into exile.[6]

One prominent Athenian family in exile, the Alcmaeonids (descendants of the men who had killed the supporters of the would-be tyrant, Kylon, a century before: ch. 6), sought to build a wider base of support in the Greek world by conspicuously underbidding the contract for repairs of the temple of Apollo at Delphi—undertaking to build in marble for the price of limestone. Apollo was properly appreciative: The Spartans found that when they consulted Apollo's oracle at Delphi about any matter of public import, they were told, "first free Athens." They did not need much persuading. Athens would be a substantial addition to Sparta's growing league, and the tyrant looked vulnerable. In the event, it took two invasions of Attica and a siege of the Acropolis that almost failed, but in 510 BCE, Hippias the tyrant was driven from Athens by a Spartan expeditionary force. He escaped to Persia, which offered a warm welcome to potentially useful exiles from countries that might some day be incorporated into the Persian Empire.[7]

ATHENIAN REVOLUTION

The Spartan army left Attica immediately after deposing the tyrant. Given that Athens had a population matching that of Sparta's home territories and given their continual need to maintain control of the helots, the Spartans could not hope to rule Athens directly. They must, however, have expected that elite Athenians, like elites in the Peloponnesian poleis of the league, would see the value of being able to call on Sparta's military might if faced by internal or external threats. Yet in the aftermath of tyranny, the Athenian elite were deeply fragmented. In the ensuing power struggle, Cleisthenes, the leader of the Alcmaeonid family, found his faction losing ground to Isagoras, a prominent aristocrat with particularly strong connections to the Spartan leadership. Nasty rumors claimed that Isagoras had pimped his wife to one of the two Spartan kings: Cleomenes, ominously nicknamed "The Mad."

At this point, Cleisthenes made a bold play that precipitated a sequence of revolutionary events: According to Herodotus, he "brought the demos into his coalition" (Herodotus 5.66.2). Based on Cleisthenes' later reforms, it appears that he promised to further the Solonian project of giving ordinary citizens a more substantial role in the affairs of the state. In 508 BCE, Isagoras, who held the archonship, responded by calling in the Spartans. Cleisthenes fled into exile, followed by his core supporters—700 families, according to Herodotus.

When Cleomenes duly arrived from Sparta at the head of a smallish mixed-nationality (i.e., mostly mercenary) force, Isagoras attempted to install 300 of his own partisans as a new ruling coalition. Yet when Isagoras ordered the sitting council to disband, the councilors balked and "the rest of the Athenians, being of one mind," rose up in arms (Herodotus 5.72.1–2). Cleomenes and Isagoras soon found themselves on the defensive and retreated to the Acropolis stronghold. After a three-day siege, Cleomenes surrendered on terms; he departed Athens for Sparta with Isagoras in tow, but he left some of his mercenaries behind, to be summarily executed by the victorious Athenians.

This revolutionary series of events signaled a sea change in Athenian politics. By the prerevolutionary norms of political factionalism, when Cleisthenes and his closest allies fled Attica, the field should have been left open for Isagoras, supported by the Spartans, to reunite the rest of the Athenian elite around his own now-dominant coalition. But by "bringing the demos into his coalition," Cleisthenes recognized that the game was changing. Civic identity and aspirations of ordinary citizens had become a determining factor in Athenian political struggles. Even the departure of Cleisthenes and his core group of partisans from Athens and the support of a Spartan-led mercenary force failed to pave the way for a smooth takeover by Isagoras because the Athenian people proved willing and able to act against him as a collectivity. In Cleisthenes' absence and without organized elite leadership, the ordinary citizens rose up in arms and carried out the three-day siege. They evidently did so in response to a bright-line rule violation: Isagoras' attempt to dissolve an existing council. Why did the violation trigger a mass revolt?

We cannot securely identify the council that Isagoras sought to overthrow, but it was certainly part of the existing Athenian constitutional system. By ordering its dissolution, Isagoras signaled (intentionally or not) his willingness to go further than had the Peisistratid tyrants in overturning the Solonian constitution. If Isagoras could chase citizens into exile en masse, as he had, and could dissolve state institutions at will, as he now sought to do, what was to prevent him from stripping citizens of both their legal immunities and participation rights? Among Solon's earlier reforms was reportedly a law that required Athenians either to take sides when a civil conflict erupted or to lose their citizenship when it was over. At the moment that Isagoras sought to dissolve the council, most citizens clearly chose to side with the absent Cleisthenes. Moreover, contrary to Isagoras' "elite politics as usual" expectations, the mass of ordinary citizens proved capable of coordinating their actions effectively enough to force the Spartan-led force to retreat to the sacred Acropolis. While besieged on the Acropolis, Cleomenes was said to have committed sacrilege. No doubt the rumor added fuel to the flames of collective fury against Isagoras, and to the people's determination to continue the siege to its successful conclusion.[8]

In the aftermath of the expulsion of Cleomenes and Isagoras by the citizen masses, there could be no quick return to prerevolutionary elite coalition politics. Recalled from his exile, Cleisthenes was now expected by the members of his hugely expanded coalition to make good on his promise to expand citizen rights. He had also to face the likelihood that the vengeful Spartans would soon return to Attica in force. Cleisthenes' reforms, quickly enacted as emergency measures, built on the earlier laws of Solon, and on the growth of Athenian civic identity under the tyrants. The reforms also introduced novel features that reconceptualized Athenian citizenship on a federalist model. Like the American Founders in 1787, Cleisthenes invented democratic federalism as an experimental response to a postrevolutionary crisis that had no other obvious solution. And like the American Constitution, the new Athenian regime proved more successful than its inventors could have dared to hope.[9]

With its many substantial towns, the region of Attica was huge as a city-state, demographically comparable to Boeotia (region 10: 26 poleis, total fourth century BCE population ca. 200,000), Euboea (region 21: 14 poleis, 140,000), or Elis (region 13: 20 poleis, 140,000). Two Athenian towns, Aphidna (population ca. 8,000) and Acharnai (population ca. 11,000) would, if independent, have counted as size 3 poleis; another 18 would count as size 2 poleis (population of 3,500 or greater) (table 7.1).[10] Among the challenges faced by Cleisthenes was, therefore, managing scale: building a strong state in a territory that might easily have supported a number of independent poleis (see map 5).

Under Cleisthenes' reformed constitutional order, 139 villages, towns, and neighborhoods of Attica were designated "demes." An average deme had a free adult male population of 150–250, although some were smaller, and others, notably Aphidna and Acharnai, much larger. The original Greek for the Anglicized term "deme" is *demos*. Just as the citizens of Athens were, collectively *the Demos—the People of Athens*, so too the native male citizens of each village and neighborhood were now acknowledged as *the People* of that place: Each Athenian was thus treated as a citizen at different levels: locally in his deme and at the federal level of the polis. All free adult males resident in Attica in the year of the reform were, in the immediate aftermath of the revolution, considered to be citizens of Athens and of their deme of residence. Moreover, the deme would hereafter be the fundamental unit of Athenian citizenship: To be a citizen of Athens, a male resident of Attica must be

TABLE 7.1 *Twenty Largest Athenian Demes*

Deme/Town	Tribe	Council Quota	Pop. Est.	Polis Size	"Third"
Acharnai	VI	22	11,000	3	Inland
Aphidna	IX	16	8,000	3	Inland
Kydathenaion	III	11.5	5,750	2	Urban
Paiania, Lower	III	11	5,500	2	Inland
Eleusis	VIII	11	5,500	2	Coast
Euonymon	I	10	5,000	2	Urban
Marathon	IX	10	5,000	2	Coast
Alopeke	X	10	5,000	2	Urban
Anaphlystos	X	10	5,000	2	Coast
Lamptrai, Lower	I	9	4,500	2	Coast
Phrearrhioi	IV	9	4,500	2	Coast
Kephale	V	9	4,500	2	Coast
Piraeus	VIII	9	4,500	2	Urban
Phaleron	IX	9	4,500	2	Urban
Aixone	VII	8	4,000	2	Coast
Rhamnous	IX	8	4,000	2	Coast
Thria	VI	7	3,500	2	Coast
Melite	VII	7	3,500	2	Urban
Phyla	VII	7	3,500	2	Inland
Xypete	VII	7	3,500	2	Urban

NOTES: Polis size 2 = average population of 3,500; polis size 3 = average population of 7,000. Deme populations are estimated based on a total population for Attica of about 250,000. Each deme's council quota (the number of representatives sent annually to the Council of 500) was based on population (at the time of Cleisthenes); we thus assume that one member of the boule represents 500 persons (of all statuses). These numbers are necessarily stylized: In the time of Cleisthenes, the population was probably less than 250,000. By the fourth century BCE, because deme membership was hereditary and internal migration was a well-known phenomenon in Athens, some of any given deme's members would not have lived in their ancestral demes. The basic point stands: There were, from the time of Cleisthenes on, a number of towns in Attica large enough to function as small or medium-sized poleis.

Fachard 2014 estimates the territorial extent of the Attic demes, concluding that 107 demes had territories of < 24 km² (ergo polis size 1 or less); 18 are 24–48 km²; 5 are 66 km², with the largest at about 85 km². Thus, some 23 of the demes would achieve polis size 2 standing in territorial terms, but none would be size 3 in terms of its territorial extent. The disparity arises because of relative population density: Athens, with a population density of ca. 100 people/km² was considerably more densely populated than the Greek world average of ca. 44 people per km².

formally recognized by an assembly of citizens in his deme as having been born to an Athenian father who was himself a citizen of the deme, and as being at least 18 years of age.[11]

Two intermediate levels of belonging connected the demes to the federal state. Citizens of each deme were assigned to one of ten newly created artificial "tribes." Each tribe enrolled roughly a tenth of the citizens, drawn from three distinct regions of Attica. Several geographically contiguous demes (or occasionally one very large deme) constituted a *third* of a given tribe. Each tribe was made up of three roughly equal-sized thirds located, respectively, in the coastal zone of Attica, the inland zone, and the city or its immediate suburbs. Each tribe was, therefore, regionally diverse in its membership. These mixed-region tribes were the basic unit for Athenian civic affairs: The Athenian army and its leadership were organized by tribes, as were civic festivals, and much else in Athenian public life.

Perhaps most importantly, the membership of the new central state Council of 500, which conducted Athens' day-to-day public affairs and set the agenda for the legislative citizen assembly, was recruited through the new deme/tribe system. In later years, at least, councilors were aged 30 and older, were chosen by lot, and were paid for their service. Each of the 10 tribes annually provided 50 councilors. The members of each tribal contingent of 50 were chosen at the deme level, each deme sending a certain number of councilors according to population. The deme of Prasiai, one of the four coastal demes of Tribe III Pandionis, for example, sent three councilors annually (figure 7.1 and map 5). A very small deme would send only one councilor each year; a very large deme might send a dozen or more. The 50-man tribal teams undertook much of the work of the Council, and took turns directing meetings of the Council and citizen assembly.

Each of the 10 tribal teams of 50, like the Council of 500 overall, was geographically representative of the population of Attica. But Cleisthenes had not introduced to Athens what we think of today as "representative government" because councilors were not expected to represent the particularistic interests of their deme, regional third, or tribe. Nor were they accountable to local voters. Rather, the councilors served, collectively, as a microcosm of the Athenian citizenry. They represented what, in the aggregate, the Athenian people knew and the skills and information the Athenians could bring to bear on problems confronting the state.

Public and private incentives encouraged councilors to disclose potentially valuable private information in deliberations on public issues. Given the realities of ancient demographics, and because service was limited to two nonconsecutive years, serving on the Council was a common experience of mature

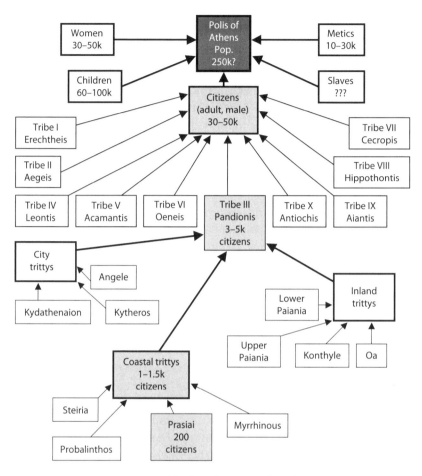

FIGURE 7.1 *Athenian tribe system, after 508 BCE.*

NOTES: Adapted from Ober 2008: Figure 4.2. The chart features the example of Tribe III Pandionis and the coastal deme of Prasiai.

Athenian men. Even the philosopher Socrates, famously uninterested in day-to-day politics, served for a year on the Council—albeit at the advanced age of 63—alongside nine of his fellow demesmen from the big deme of Alopeke (Tribe X Antiochis). Estimates vary, but within a generation after the reform probably at least one in three Athenians over age 30 had served a year as a councilor. As a result, not only was the aggregate "knowledge base" of the Council representative of that of the citizen body as a whole, but knowledge of the day-to-day workings of Athenian government was very widely distributed across the Athenian citizen population.[12]

A second council, the Areopagus (named for the hill in central Athens on which it met), whose membership was drawn from ex-magistrates, continued to play a significant role for a long generation after the reforms.[13] But the new Council of 500, with its unique control of both agenda setting and essential executive functions, quickly became the most important single body of Athenian government, after the citizen assembly itself. Given that the membership of the Council of 500 was, in any given year, broadly representative of the whole of the demos of Athens, and given that legislative authority lay with the citizen assembly, it is fair to say that in the immediate aftermath of the revolutionary uprising of 508 BCE, Athens had become, in practice if not yet in name, a democracy.[14] This was among the first, if not the first, historical experiments with true collective self-governance by citizens in a community with a total population reaching six figures, and thus vastly too large to be regarded as a simple face-to-face society.[15] The immediate question was whether the experiment would succeed.

ATHENIAN INSTITUTIONS AND STATE PERFORMANCE, 506–478 BCE

That question was answered quickly and positively. In 506 BCE, Athens' enemies launched a three-pronged attack on Attica. Along with their Peloponnesian allies, the Spartans invaded Attica from the west, through the territory of Megara. Meanwhile, armies from Boeotia and from Euboean Chalkis threatened Athens from the north and east. Yet before the first battle could even be engaged, the Peloponnesian army dispersed, beginning with the Corinthians, who suddenly found reason to be elsewhere. The Athenian army was now free to march north and east, delivering decisive defeats to the Boeotians and Chalkideans. The unraveling of the invasion and the unexpected Athenian victories can best be explained by assuming that Athens was now, for the first time, able to mobilize a national army worthy of its size. Presumably, its rivals, expecting a much smaller force, were caught off guard. We may guess that many of the Athenian fighting men of 506 were, compared to the highly professional Spartan army, ill-equipped, poorly trained, but highly motivated.[16]

Herodotus makes much of the Athenian victory in 506, noting that

> The Athenians at this point became much stronger. So it is clear how worthy an object of attention is equality of public speech (*isēgoria*), not just in one respect but in every sense. Since when they were ruled by tyrants, the Athenians did not stand out from their neighbors in military capability, but after deposing the tyrants, they became overwhelmingly superior.

This, then, shows that while they were oppressed, they were, as men working for a master, cowardly, but when they were freed, each one was eager
to achieve for himself.

—*Histories 5.78 trans. Stanton (1990) adapted*[17]

For Herodotus, the end of the tyranny was the beginning of Athens' truly
exceptional performance as a state. He specifically connects performance to
motivation and attributes the high motivation of the Athenians to their new
political standing. The implication is that men who must serve a master, and
who must turn over some of the fruits of their labors to him, are not well
motivated to take risks. Without a master, or rather, once they were the collective masters of their own collective fate, each Athenian was eager to do
well for himself.

Political liberation resulted, in Herodotus' assessment, not in a cascade of
free riding, but in the coherent collective military action that defeated the
Spartan coalition. Moreover, Herodotus claims that the Athenian leap forward in state strength demonstrates the general value of "equality of public
speech." This claim is initially puzzling.[18] But if we attend to the reform of
the deliberative Council, and the ways in which equality of public speech
could, under the right conditions, pay out in bold and innovative new policies, Herodotus' comment becomes perfectly comprehensible. The history of
Athens through the era of the Persian Wars (490–478 BCE), which followed
close on Cleisthenes' reforms, provided Herodotus with considerable evidence for the value of equality of public speech in state policy-making.

In the generation following the reforms of Cleisthenes, the Athenians expanded and refined the institutions of their democracy. These changes are
sometimes difficult to date precisely, and it is not always clear which changes
were "original Cleisthenic" and which were subsequent adjustments. But the
upshot was that collective self-governance was put on an increasingly solid
footing, as the legislative, judicial, and executive functions of the new democratic regime were expanded and consolidated within specific institutional
loci. The Athenian citizenry elected their military leaders; many other state
officials were, however, chosen by lottery. All officials, elected or lotteried,
were subject to *ex ante* public scrutiny and held publicly accountable, on an
annual basis, for their performance.

Each year, the Athenian assembly decided whether to conduct an ostracism;
if the decision was positive (as it was only 15 recorded times in Athenian history), the citizenry chose, by plurality written ballot, which prominent member of the Athenian elite to expel from the community for 10 years. The Council met almost daily to consider policy and to devise the agenda for a legislative

assembly open to all citizens. The assembly met regularly—in the fourth century four times each month. The Solonian people's court was subdivided into a number of courts, so that many more cases could now be judged by panels of citizens, chosen by lottery. Public business was carried out in new civic buildings constructed in a democratic building boom in and around the agora.[19]

The democratic regime was soon tested by another foreign invasion, this time at a scale unprecedented in mainland Greek history. Persia had taken umbrage at material support offered in 499 by Athens and Eretria (1370: the major polis on the big island of Euboea that was Chalkis' rival in the War of the Lelantine Plain) to a botched revolt by the Anatolian Greek poleis against Persian rule. A Persian naval expeditionary force swept across the Aegean. The Cycladic islands fell one by one. Eretria was successfully besieged in 490 BCE; the city was sacked, its main temple burned, and at least part of its population deported to Mesopotamia. The Persian forces then moved across the narrow straits to Attica, where they made landing at the plain of Marathon in northeastern Attica. The former tyrant, Hippias, was with them. Clearly the Persians hoped that his presence would divide the Athenian elite, making the conquest that much easier.

In response to the invasion, Athens dispatched its full levy of 10,000 hoplites, organized now by tribal regiments and led by elected generals, to meet the invaders. The defenders were joined by a small force from Boeotian Plataea, a close Athenian ally, but they remained badly outnumbered. Yet the outcome of the ensuing battle was the rout of the Persian forces and the slaughter of thousands of the invaders. In an act reminiscent of heroic Tellus' public burial (ch. 4), Athens buried the 192 Athenians who fell at Marathon beneath a great earthwork tumulus. They sent word of their victory to the rest of the Greek world—notably to the Spartans, who had promised aid but had been delayed, as they explained, by religious duties.

Although Marathon only deferred Athens' Persia problem, it was a remarkable victory, and never forgotten. John Stuart Mill memorably opined that "The battle of Marathon, even as an event in British history, is more important than the battle of Hastings." The battle was won by Athens' phalanx of hoplites. Yet the decade that followed the great infantry victory of Marathon was especially remarkable for the buildup of the Athenian navy. A rich vein of silver ore running through south Attica, was now, for the first time, efficiently mined. Since mineral rights belonged to the state, this resulted in a substantial windfall. A proposal to divide the unexpected surplus evenly among the citizens was rejected by the assembly. Instead, the citizen assembly adopted the proposal of a political leader, Themistocles, who earlier had championed the fortification of Athens' port town of Piraeus. Themistocles argued that the silver windfall should be turned to public purposes, financing the construction of a large number of warships that might be used against Aiginetan raiders. Athens thus added at least 100 (perhaps 200) modern trireme warships to its fleet and thereby became, almost overnight, the greatest naval power in the Greek world.[20]

The silver windfall was no doubt a key factor in the Athenian decision to turn to sea power in such a big way in the 480s. But it was not the only factor: With its large, well-motivated citizen body and active overseas trade, Athens was in a strong position to specialize in military operations requiring a manpower-intensive navy. Classical Greek triremes were three-banked oared galleys, powered by large (ca. 180-man) crews of rowers. The manpower for the newly constructed ships was recruited from the ranks of the poorer citizens (the lowest Solonian income class), who thereby became full participants in the Athenian defense establishment. There is no hint in our sources that the proposal to enhance Athenian sea power was opposed by the middle-class infantrymen who manned the land army. That in turn suggests that the level of trust across social classes in the Athenian citizen body was high enough that the hoplites felt no need to protect a monopoly on the employment of organized violence in the state's interest. By the 480s, and probably well before, it was clear that decisions about the Athenian military, how it would be developed, and how deployed, were being made by the citizenry and not by a closed coalition of specialists in violence.

Matters with Persia came to a head again in 481; a massive overland invasion of Greece, through Thrace and Thessaly, was imminent. Athens had to decide what to do before the Persians neared Attica. After considerable debate, the Athenians adopted a plan, advocated by Themistocles, to evacuate the population of the polis to the Peloponnese, and, in conjunction with other Greek states, to challenge the Persians at sea. The result was the dramatic Greek victory at the naval battle of Salamis, off the coast of Athens, in 480. Salamis set up a decisive land battle the next year at Boeotian Plataea, in which the infantrymen of Athens, Sparta, and the Peloponnesian League states defeated an elite Persian force of infantry and cavalry. A final naval battle, at Point Mycale on the central Anatolian coast (map 7), sealed the Greek victory. It was obvious to everyone in the Greek world that the war against Persia could never have been won without Sparta's expert citizen-infantry and its ability to muster the Peloponnesian League. But neither could it have been won without Athens' big citizen-navy. Athens had, over the course of a generation, joined the ranks of the Greek superpoleis.[21]

EXPLAINING ATHENIAN STATE PERFORMANCE

As Herodotus astutely noted in the passage quoted in the previous section, Athens' quick ascent to the status of superpolis was correlated with the end of tyranny and the institution of more egalitarian democratic rules. In order to draw a causal arrow from democratic reforms to superior performance, however, we need to explain just how the relevant changes made Athens more capable and ultimately wealthier as a polis. If that arrow can be drawn, and if it can be shown that the rise of democratic Athens furthered a general classical Hellenic efflorescence, through emulation by other poleis of performance-enhancing Athenian institutions, the fair rules/capital investment/low transaction costs hypothesis would be supported—if not yet proved. Here I focus on three related, and readily adaptable, features of the new democratic system that may be causally related to superior state performance: federalism, expertise, and elite incentives.

Federalism

The federalist deme and tribe system, along with the proliferation of voluntary associations that flourished alongside it, was an important part of what made democracy work. After the reforms of Cleisthenes, each Athenian was a citizen at three ascending levels, of a deme, a tribe, and a polis. Federalism enabled trust among citizens, arising from local interactions at the deme level, to be leveraged at the level of the tribe and then at the level of the polis. Within the general framework of the Solonian laws, Athenian citizens now worked together in their demes toward collective local ends (confirming young men as citizens, appointing councilors, managing local finances) that had important higher level effects. Collective action in an average deme was facilitated by smallness of scale: Without resorting to a Spartan-style social panopticon, the citizens of a deme could monitor and, when necessary sanction, one another's behavior relevant to the production of public goods. They could thereby credibly commit to common enterprises, ranging from the management of deme property to the mustering of units for the army.

At the tribal level, trust was built by reiterated interactions. Each adult male tribe member engaged with men from diverse geographic backgrounds (the coast, inland, and urban regions of Attica) in common enterprises aimed at important public ends that could be gained only though joint action. Coordinated tribe-level activity included performance in competitive contests (against other tribes) in state-sponsored cultural events (notably 50-person men's and boys' singing-and-dancing choruses at the Dionysia), work on tribal teams in the Council, mustering in tribal regiments in the army, and collective oath-taking.[22]

Tribe-level interactions in civic, religious, and military domains served to bring men from different parts of Attica into contact with one another in common enterprises and thus encouraged them to build more extensive and more socially diverse social networks. As men's lives extended beyond their home deme to the level of the tribe and the polis, possibilities opened up for the formation of "weak ties" that bridged the gaps between deme-level "strong-tie" networks, which were trust-based, but potentially exclusivist and parochial. By identifying "structural holes" in the burgeoning web of Athenian social interactions—that is, by making connections linking local networks that had formerly been isolated from one another—social entrepreneurs could gain material benefits for themselves (e.g., potentially lucrative marriage alliances). Weak-tie bridges between local networks thus benefited individuals who, in a sense, became specialists at networking. As a positive externality, their bridge-building helped to increase the flow of social knowledge and useful information across the citizen body as a whole.

The deme-tribe-polis federal system helped to make the mass meetings of the Athenian assembly both less daunting and less clientalistic, as ordinary citizens developed social networks that extended at least to the tribe level. Men attending the assembly, who lacked experience in institutional procedures or the substantive matters under consideration, could now appeal "laterally" to more experienced and trusted fellow tribesmen who were also in attendance. In this way, the naïve citizen gained guidance horizontally, from civic peers, rather than having to make vertical appeals to elite patrons. Moreover, networks that began at the tribe level would increasingly have been extended to the level of the polis—as members of different tribes interacted with one another on boards of magistrates, in the Council, in the assembly, on juries, in "all Athens" cult activities, and through military service.[23]

Expertise

As citizens gained in trust and confidence of the political system and of one another, the Cleisthenic order was better able to aggregate and to organize useful knowledge in ways that enabled better policy-making. Like all purposeful organizations, democratic Athens had to make many decisions on questions concerning collective security and welfare. Even when the general policy goal was tolerably clear as a matter of common interest (securing the continued existence of the community in the face of external threat, increasing collective welfare without compromising the standing of individual citizens), the right answer to the question "what policy will best promote the goal?" was far from obvious.

Information relevant to the decision was dispersed, and in some cases, might be privately owned and jealously guarded. Complex and difficult decisions called for the input of experts in various domains: A foreign policy choice might, for example, require the testimony of experts in the domains of diplomacy, finance, logistics, strategy, and geography—among others. With historical memories of the tyranny and revolution still vivid, the Athenians were attentive to the danger of elite capture—and therefore unwilling to turn over important decisions to a small body of elite experts. And yet, there remained a real danger that decision-making by a large Council and a mass assembly would devolve to a lowest common denominator of collective ignorance.[24]

As it turned out, Athenian citizens proved to be quite good at identifying and attending to experts and quite capable of using the knowledge of experts for the ends of policy-making without turning state management over to them. Plato, who was highly critical of democracy on many dimensions, readily conceded the point in his dialogue, *Protagoras* (319b–c). Plato noted that when, for example, the assembly was discussing the construction of warships, the "wise Athenians" listened only to the relevant experts; ignorant citizens who wasted the assembly's time with ill-informed opinions were quickly hooted from the speakers' platform.

Plato regarded the ends of increasing wealth and security as inferior to, and a distraction from, the ethical project of advancing individual moral excellence and therefore criticized Athenian democratic leaders for cluttering the polis with "harbors and shipsheds and walls and imperial tribute-payments and suchlike trash" (*Gorgias* 519a). But we are concerned here, in the first instance, with explaining economic growth. The capacity of many citizens to attend to experts in matters that were relevant to the wealth and security of the state was clearly, and plausibly, linked in Plato's assessment with Athenian growth. But *how* did the Athenians actually know who was expert in each domain relevant to decisions on matters concerning state wealth and power? And how did they persuade experts to divulge what might have been regarded as proprietary information?

The organization and procedures of the Cleisthenic Council of 500, in conjunction with the final decision authority of the citizen assembly, provide at least a partial answer to the Athenians' collective capacity to identify relevant experts and to persuade experts to disclose proprietary information in the public interest. As the Councilmen in each tribal team of 50, and eventually in the plenary body of 500, came to know one another better, through the extension of social networks and through deliberations on public matters, they also came to recognize who among the membership was more or less expert in any given domain. Incentives, at each level of citizenship (deme, tribe, and polis), in terms of chances to gain reputation, honors, and material rewards—or, alternatively, to incur sanctions and opprobrium—encouraged those with useful information and skills to disclose what they knew, if and when it was relevant to the issue at hand. Competition among experts for public recognition encouraged disclosure, while forestalling collusion and elite capture.

Of course, properly identified expertise in various domains of knowledge was only useful to public decisions insofar as particular domains were relevant to specific policy issues and insofar as the right weight was given by the decision-makers to each domain in addressing the matter at hand. Over time, the collective experience of the Council, passed down through annual year-classes of Councilors via increasingly dense social networks, helped to define the domains of expertise relevant to various areas of state policy and the relative significance of each relevant domain to certain kinds of issues.

Insofar as (1) decision-makers properly identified experts in each domain relevant to the issue, (2) experts sincerely disclosed their knowledge, (3) decision-makers appropriately deferred to experts within their domain, and (4) they properly weighted the significance of each domain to the overall decision, the outcome was likely to be a better decision—that is, one that better promoted the common interest in security and welfare. The process of seeking and using information and expertise remained subject to error and to manipulation. But over time, the intersection of growing trust and aggregate social knowledge among citizens, increasing specialization in various domains of endeavor, and institutional learning pushed in the direction of collective wisdom.

Athenian collective wisdom seems manifest, at least after the fact, in the decision to expand the navy of warships and then in the decision to fight the Persians at sea. Herodotus' (7.140–144) detailed account of the assembly meeting at which the decision was made to fight at sea makes it clear that a different (and presumably worse) decision would have been made had the Athenians counterfactually followed the advice of traditional sources of authority: supposed experts in oracle interpretation or community elders—both of whom urgently warned against the sea fight. In the new institutional order, however, the democratic value of "equality in respect to public speech" ensured that the opinions of neither oracle interpreters nor elders would be dispositive. Because the advice of experts in relevant domains was given proper weight, both by the Council and by the assembly, the choice of "fight at sea" was selected over the other options. The outcome was the victory that preserved Athenian, and in general Greek, freedom. That victory set up the both the cultural "golden age" of the mid-fifth century BCE and Athens' bold if ultimately unsuccessful attempt to create its own Mediterranean empire (ch. 8).[25]

Elite Incentives

Along with increasing trust and using diverse forms of expert knowledge, the new democracy avoided both disruptive civil conflict and elite capture. Ostracism is a particularly dramatic example of an accountability procedure that helped to push back against each of these threats to democratic government. The annual decision whether or not to hold an ostracism—and thus to put the most prominent men in the state at risk of expulsion from the community for 10 years—was in and of itself a very public reminder to the elite, collectively, of the authority exercised by the citizenry over civic standing. Ostracism allowed the demos to step in, decisively, when elite rivalry threatened to burgeon into violent civil strife. Ostracism, in effect, allowed the Athenians to answer, through a peaceful institution, the demand of Solon's supposed law requiring citizens to take sides in a civil war.[26]

Ostracism also served a highly salient role as a kind of knowledge-aggregating "preemptive prediction market" that allowed Athens to identify and eliminate possible internal threats to civic order. The new democratic regime confronted the problem of how to address behavior that put the internal stability of the polis at risk without creating an intrusive and unwieldy police apparatus and without unduly crushing entrepreneurial initiative on the part of talented elites. The annual decision about whether to hold an ostracism aggregated the collective judgment of the citizens regarding the level of danger facing the state from rival elites. This first vote answered a question about how a present state of affairs might play out in the future: "Is there in the polis an individual whose continued presence would put the state enough at risk to justify his expulsion without evidence of criminal wrongdoing and without trial?" If Athenians were, collectively, oversensitive to the danger posed by ambitious elites, resulting in many "false positives," the institution would be overused, and presumably elites would become overcautious. In the event, the Athenians voted to hold an ostracism only 15 times in the 180-year history of the classical-era democracy, and there was never a shortage of skilled and ambitious men vying for positions of influence in the state.

On the rare occasions on which more than half the citizens did believe that the danger level was high enough and enough of them voted accordingly, the ostracism itself was held: On the appointed day, each citizen went to the agora with a sherd (*ostrakon*) inscribed with the name of one man. These votes were cast without formal deliberation, counted, and the name of the man with the most votes was announced. This second vote aggregated many independent judgments about prominent individuals to answer a second question: "*Whose* continued presence would be most likely to put Athens at risk?" The vote by ostraka both identified and preempted what the plurality of voters saw as the least preferable, because most dangerous, alternative future for the polis—the future in which a given person X remained in the polis.

Unlike a genuine prediction market (held in advance of an election, for example), Athenian voters could not know, *ex post*, whether the collective *ex ante* choice had been right—i.e., that it had accurately identified a dangerous alternative future: Would things *actually* have gone badly if X had remained in Athens? Nor could they know that the most dangerous alternative had been eliminated: Perhaps the presence of Y, unostracized, actually presented a greater danger. Nor could they even be sure that the ostracism had not increased the danger: With X out of the way, Y might be more able to cause trouble. What they *did* know is that the process represented the aggregated judgment of the community on this highly consequential matter and, as time went on, that the democracy seemed to be proving robust to the endemic problem of internal strife arising from intraelite rivalry.

Cleisthenes himself could not have predicted the full effects of his reforms, any more than could Solon before him. But building on the laws of Solon, the Cleisthenic package changed the rules of the Athenian state in ways that seem to have oriented individual behavior of elite and ordinary citizens alike in an overall growth-positive direction. If the arguments developed here are on the right track, the federalist features of the system had the effect of increasing trust and widening social networks. The organization of the Council provided new avenues for the identification and gainful employment of expertise. Ostracism dampened the most dangerous aspects of elite rivalry, without reducing socially valuable forms of elite competition. And so we can begin to fill in Herodotus' somewhat telegraphic statement about why, in the era after the end of the tyranny, Athens rose to greater prominence in the Greek world.

SICILY IN THE LATE SIXTH AND EARLY FIFTH CENTURIES BCE

By the later sixth century, some of the Greek colonial poleis of southern Italy and Sicily were growing rich—or at least their ruling elites were. Along its coasts, Sicily boasted a dozen major Greek poleis (size 4 or larger) and another dozen smaller poleis. Inland, in the central, western, and northwestern highlands, there were perhaps two dozen substantial settlements of native Sikels, Sikans, and Elymians (map 6). Some of these inland settlements, notably Segesta in the northwest, had already taken on cultural features characteristic of Greek poleis. Thanks to robust natural population growth and very substantial ongoing flows of new immigrants from the Greek homeland—including new colonists, homesteaders, pirates, mercenaries, and other adventurers—the Greek population of Sicily was rising impressively from its modest beginnings. The total population of the island may have reached a peak of ca. 650,000 (appendix I: region 2) by the mid-fifth century.[27]

The prosperity and population growth of Sicily were driven in the first instance by the agricultural productivity of the island.[28] Greek Sicily produced major surpluses of grain, which was shipped west to the Greek mainland, and of wine, which was sent south to Carthage. Because of these ready markets, the Sicilian coastal cities were able to specialize in production of food staples for export and to import goods from the Greek homeland—as well as from Carthaginians, Etruscans, and others. Indirect taxes on imports and exports provided substantial state revenues that could be used for various purposes—among them the construction of magnificent temples, some of which, by the fifth century, rivaled the most ambitious architectural projects of the mainland Greek states.

Perhaps because their locations directly on the coast (Leontini: i33, about 10 km inland from Sicily's east coast, was the exception) gave them ready access to one another via convenient sea lanes, the major Sicilian Greek poleis seem to have formed an especially tight regional network. Institutional innovations in one polis tended to spread quickly across Greek Sicily. Tyranny is a notable case in point. Within 20 years after 505 BCE, when a tyrant named Cleander seized control of Gela (i17: size 5), every major Greek polis in Sicily was dominated by a tyrant. The tyrants, variously collaborating and competing with one another, effectively divided Greek Sicily into three mini-empires (often called *epicracies* by historians), centered on Akragas (i9: size 5) in the west, Zancle–Messana (i51: size 4) in the northeast, and Syracuse in the southeast. The expansionist tyrants put pressure on native settlements and thus extended the zone of Greek-dominated territory inland, while at the same time driving native state formation. Meanwhile, on the northwestern coast, the Carthaginians had close relations with the Punic towns of Motya, Panormus, and Soloeis. These places remained outside the tyrants' imperial ambitions.[29]

The tyrants of Sicily came to power in the context of incipient or actual civil strife. Although some Sicilian poleis may, at their foundation, have sought to establish a degree of material equality among colonists, by the later sixth

MAP 6 *Sicily.*

century BCE, elites held most of the best agricultural territory and controlled polis governments. Recent immigrants and less-successful long-term residents were pushed into conditions approaching peonage and were increasingly restive. As we saw in chapter 6, an elite coalition at Athens, when faced with a similarly fraught situation, granted Solon legislative authority to change the constitution. Elites in Sicilian poleis, by contrast, failed to coordinate on a plan that might have forestalled tyranny.

The Sicilian tyrants of the late sixth and fifth centuries BCE acted as super-elites. Already members of the very wealthiest families in their respective cities, they used control of public revenues to place themselves in a new and exalted tier of wealth and power within communities with growing economies. They were not social reformers, in that they did little to address problems arising from inequality. They did not need to appeal to the masses for continued support—instead, they used their control of public moneys to buy the services of bodyguards and then large, well-trained mercenary armies. With a near monopoly on the efficient use of violence, the tyrants turned to social engineering to create new coalitions of men dependent on tyrannical rule.

For a long generation, the grandiose plans and relatively immense power wielded by the tyrants remade Sicily's human geography. Like the great kings of Mesopotamia, the tyrants of Sicily moved populations about at will; they emptied cities of their residents, filled established cities with new residents, and founded new poleis while destroying others or leaving them to languish. The driving motivation behind these grand schemes was the desire of the tyrants to increase and to display their power rather than to grow local economies through long-term economic planning. The tyrants were able to do much as they pleased so long as they controlled the very substantial revenues of the Sicilian cities and so long as they maintained power through the support of well-compensated specialists in violence. Mercenaries had a stake in the continuation of the tyrant's rule that exceeded their daily pay, in that they were treated by the tyrants as citizens of the cities they garrisoned. As we have seen, citizenship really mattered to the Greeks.

SYRACUSE UNDER THE TYRANTS

The first tyrant of Gela was succeeded in 498 by his brother, Hippocrates, who immediately embarked on a campaign of imperial expansion. Within a few years, he controlled much of eastern Sicily. In 492 BCE, Hippocrates set his sights on Syracuse. The polis of Syracuse was already the biggest city-state in Sicily, with a territory of perhaps 5,000 km²—twice the size of Athens' home territory of Attica. But, like Athens in the early sixth century, Syracuse in the early fifth century punched below its weight, in large part because of endemic social strife. The dominant elite coalition, the Gamoroi ("They Who Divide the Land"), were probably descendants of original colonists. They ruled over a much larger population that included Killyrians—native Sikels reduced to the status of slaves or sharecroppers—and an increasingly discontented non-elite Greek population, probably mostly composed of relatively recent immigrants. Hippocrates defeated the Syracusan army in battle, but rather than risk a siege, he accepted a mediated settlement that gave him control of much of Syracuse's territory, including the important (size 4) dependent town of Camarina (i28).

A year later, Hippocrates was succeeded as tyrant of Gela by a core member of his coalition, the cavalry commander Gelon. Like the other Sicilian tyrants, Gelon belonged to a wealthy and prominent family; he soon contracted an alliance, through marriages of kinfolk, with the tyrant of Akragas. This left him free to complete the conquest of Syracuse. As it turns out, it was not a difficult job.

The loss of Camarina had exacerbated non-elite Syracusan dissatisfaction with the ruling Gamoroi. An uprising by a revolutionary coalition of free Greeks and Killyrians drove the Gamoroi from the city. This first Syracusan popular uprising did not result in a viable new regime. The Gamoroi took refuge in Kasmenai (129), a dependent town whose territory abutted that of Camarina—now controlled by Gelon. In a move reminiscent of Isagoras' appeal for Spartan aid after Cleisthenes brought the demos into his coalition, the elite Gamoroi appealed to Gelon for help against their fellow Syracusans. Gelon happily complied. The Killyrian and free Syracusan forces proved incapable of withstanding the well-organized army of the tyrant. The Gamoroi were momentarily restored to power, but Gelon had bigger plans for Syracuse.

Leaving control of Gela to his brother, Hieron, Gelon took up residence in Syracuse and proceeded to remake the city as a tyrannical capital worthy of his very considerable ambitions. Most saliently, he radically increased the city's size by enforced immigration at the expense of other Sicilian poleis. First, the entire population of Camarina was transported to Syracuse, where they were added to the citizen body. Next came Megara Hyblaea (136: size 4), defeated by Gelon in a siege. Megara's elites were transported to Syracuse as new citizens; the non-elite population was enslaved and sold abroad. A similar fate befell Sicilian Euboea (115). Finally, half the population of Gela was deported to Syracuse. Gelon may have borrowed the idea of transportation of populations from the Persians, who (following a well-established west Asian imperial tradition) had punished not only Eretria in 490 but also Miletus (1854) in 494 for its leadership in the Ionian revolt by razing the town, killing many of the men, and transporting the survivors to a settlement on the Persian Gulf. But Gelon's motivation was clearly constructive rather than merely punitive: He meant to create a superpolis as the center of his east-Sicilian mini-empire.

The structural problem faced by any would-be superpolis was how to be at once big as a city-state and coherent as a citizen-state. Both Sparta and Athens had devised distinctive solutions to the problem: Sparta created an extensive and homogeneous citizenry, dedicated to specializations in violence and government that would enable them to dominate a much larger subject population. Athens created a system of laws and then a networked federal system that allowed an extensive citizen body to remain socially and economically diverse while pursuing common ends through aggregated knowledge. Gelon brought about the first of the imperatives of the superpolis, being big, by tyrannical fiat—by transporting Greeks, and especially elite Greeks, to be citizens in his new imperial capital. Whether he would be able to achieve the second condition, of coherence, was yet to be seen.

The relative standing of the new and old citizens of Syracuse under the tyrants remains murky. What we can say is that the Gamoroi as such disappeared from history: Their monopoly on high standing was evidently overthrown by the new immigrants, many of whom were elites in their own right. Because Gelon seems systematically to have preferred *elite* immigrants (explicity so in the case of Megara), he seems to have had in mind the creation of a new, supersized imperial elite that would owe its very existence to the tyrant himself. Although we can say nothing for certain, it seems likely that the new citizens of Syracuse were allowed to keep their movable possessions and were given land grants from confiscated territories within the tyrant's extensive domains. Meanwhile, the Killyrians were left in serfdom.

It is certain that Syracuse was now among the most populous city-states of the Greek world. As the tyrant's capital, it also became one of the wealthiest. While Gelon was a bold social engineer in some domains, he seems to have done nothing to interfere with the highly profitable agricultural base of Sicilian prosperity: The tyrant skimmed enough rents to become immensely wealthy, but he kept the wealth-oriented elites in his extensive coalition content by sharing enough of the rents and suppressing the dangerous ambitions of the poorer Greeks and natives. This policy paid off handsomely: Gelon was remembered by the Greek historical tradition as a benevolent despot whose reign had brought social order and prosperity to the cities under his control (Diodorus 11.38).

The new tyrannical order was soon put to a serious test. The Carthaginians recognized the potential danger that the emergence of two cooperating and aggressive mini-empires, centered on Akragas and Syracuse, posed to allied Punic towns in northwestern Sicily and perhaps to its larger and long-term commercial interests. Things came to a head when, in 482 BCE, the tyrant of the important north-Sicilian polis of Himera (124: size 5) was deposed. The old tyrant had maintained friendly relations with the Punic towns to his west. Theron, the new tyrant of Himera, quickly allied himself with the Arkagas–Syracuse axis. Meanwhile, the tyrant who was then ruling Zancle–Messana, on the northeastern point of Sicily, allied himself with the Carthaginians. With both a new threat and a new ally, the Carthaginians were motivated to act. They gathered a large force of soldiers drawn from Carthage's extensive North African empire, supplemented by mercenaries from around the western Mediterranean.

Confronted with the prospect of a Carthaginian invasion of Sicily, Gelon pressed the wealthy new citizens of Syracuse to provide emergency funds. Given that they owed their positions to him, they had little choice other than to comply. The cash infusion enabled him to mobilize a very large army composed mostly, it seems, of Greek mercenaries. At just this moment, according to Herodotus (7.157–162), Gelon was approached by envoys from the Greek mainland, asking for his help against Persia. Gelon offered to loan the mainland Greeks 20,000 infantry, 2,000 cavalry, and many slingers and archers—but only if they would make him their commander-in-chief. The proud Spartans, as the obvious local leaders of the anti-Persian coalition, demurred, as Gelon surely guessed they would.

In 480 BCE, as the Persian land army was marching south into central Greece, the Carthaginian expeditionary force landed at one of the Punic towns in northwestern Sicily. The big army proceeded east, to the territory of Himera, where they made camp. Answering Theron's summons, Gelon brought up his army in an attempt to relieve Himera. After several skirmishes, in which the Carthaginians suffered substantial losses (including the death of their commander), a full-scale battle was joined. In later Sicilian legend, the land battle of Himera was fought on the same day in September as the naval battle of Salamis.

As on the mainland, Greek specialists in organized violence proved their worth. The Carthaginian land forces were routed and either massacred or captured and enslaved. The Carthaginian ships were burnt; only a few survivors made it home to report the disaster. In the aftermath, Carthage paid a massive war indemnity of 2,000 talents of silver (twice the annual income of the Athenian empire at its height: ch. 8), plus, it was said, a gigantic side payment of 100 talents of gold to Gelon's wife for brokering the deal (Diodorus 11.25.2). The indemnity money, along with booty in the form of equipment and slaves, provided Gelon with ample funds with which he could reward his loyal supporters. In return, Carthage retained its allies in northwestern Sicily. It would be three generations before Carthage again attempted to challenge the Greek domination of Sicily. Six years after the battle of Himera, in 474 BCE, Gelon's brother and successor-tyrant, Hieron, added to the tyrant family's military reputation by winning a great naval victory over the Etruscans, off Cumae on the west coast of Italy.

The victories over the Persians at Salamis, Plataea, and Mycale by the mainland Greeks were won by the citizens of independent city-states and were celebrated accordingly. The victories won by Sicilian forces over the Carthaginians and Etruscans, along with the booty reaped from them, were claimed by the tyrant and his family. The surviving stone base for what was reportedly a massive (16-talent) gold tripod was dedicated to Apollo at Delphi by "Gelon, son of Deinomenes . . . a Syracusan."[30] An epigram probably associated with this and other Delphic dedications states that Gelon and his three brothers, sons of Deinomenes, dedicated tripods, from a hundredth part of the "booty that they took, having been victorious over barbarian nations."[31] Only slightly more generously, two bronze Etruscan helmets dedicated at Olympia after the naval victory at Cumae in 474 were inscribed with a text that states that they were given by "Hieron, son of Deinomenes, and the Syracusans."[32]

The rich dedications made by Gelon and Hieron at Delphi and Olympia, along with their patronage of famous mainland Greek poets (notably Pindar and Simonides, who wrote flattering odes) and their active participation in athletic competitions at mainland Greek festivals (especially superexpensive chariot races), points to the Sicilian tyrants' evident desire to be seen as active participants in a wider Greek cultural koine.

Despite Gelon's massive population transfers, and those of Hieron after him, the tyrants of Sicily were never treated by their subjects as godlike kings. Nor did they ever seek to change the game by playing that role. No Sicilian tyrant put his own likeness or name on coins. Throughout the tyrannical period of the fifth century BCE, as before and after, the Syracuse mint produced silver coins "of the Syracusans." Diodorus of Sicily, the Roman-era historian to whom we owe most of our knowledge of the classical history of Greek Sicily, notes that when Gelon fell ill, he gave orders that he was to be buried according to the modest standard demanded by established Syracusan sumptuary legislation. The grateful citizens later built him an impressive tomb at which he was honored as a hero—but not as a god (Diodorus 11.38.2–5). The limits placed on the self-presentation of the hugely ambitious Sicilian tyrants testify to the strength that the Greek cultural norm of citizenship had achieved by the early fifth century. The Greek world had become robustly exceptional in respect to civic identity.

Gelon, Hieron, and their fellow Sicilian tyrants pragmatically placed coalition-building ahead of attempts to promote an ideology of kingship. They were successful insofar as they created and sustained extensive elite coalitions, included within their coalitions large numbers of skilled mercenaries, and kept the peace by preventing revolutionary uprisings by poorer citizens and serfs. Their methods were straightforward: a combination of payoffs to coalition members, credible threats against potential troublemakers, and *pluralistic ignorance* among the citizen population. Ignorance of each citizen about what other citizens really thought about the tyrant was fostered under Hieron by an extensive secret police.[33]

In the end, Greek tyrants on Sicily proved no more capable of creating a stable equilibrium than were earlier tyrants in the eastern Greek world. Sicilian tyrants were undermined, as were their eastern predecessors, by intraelite competition and intrafamilial conflict. Moreover, the very integration into a wider Greek cultural koine, sought so assiduously by the tyrants themselves, meant that Sicilian Greeks were aware of political developments on the mainland—including the success story of posttyrannical democracy at Athens.

SICILY AFTER THE TYRANTS

The era of the early Sicilian tyrants came to an abrupt end when one of the four sons of Deinomenes, who was the disgruntled ruler over the now second-tier town of Gela, joined the tyrant of Akragas in an attempt to unseat Hieron, Gelon's brother, who had inherited the imperial capital of Syracuse. Hieron survived the challenge, defeating his rivals' army, but his victory in turn precipitated the final collapse of the tyranny at Akragas, where a republican, probably broadly based oligarchic, government was instituted in 472. The Akragans did not have an easy regime transition: The many mercenaries previously hired by the tyrant and still resident in Akragas sought to seize control of the polis. Clearly they anticipated that the new regime, in which they were decidedly not to be citizens, would not honor the tyrant's commitments to them.

Despite these troubles, following the pattern of interstate emulation that had precipitated the wave of Sicilian tyrannies after 505, the emergence of a republican regime at Akragas triggered the end of tyranny at Syracuse and the other Sicilian Greek states. Shortly after the death of Hieron in 467, the last of the four sons of Deinomenes was expelled from Syracuse, and a democracy was soon established. Within a few years, Sicily was virtually free of tyrants. The mini-empires established by the tyrants of Akragas, Zancle–Messana, and Syracuse disintegrated; the Greek poleis of Sicily returned to the status of genuinely independent states, each of which adopted some variation of a republican (oligarchic or democratic) government.

The difficulties faced by the new regime at Akragas were far from unique. In Syracuse, after the tyrant was deposed, a citizens' assembly had voted to establish a democracy. Who had the right to attend the assembly is far from clear now, as perhaps it was then, but at any rate the assemblymen also voted to construct a colossal statue of Zeus the Liberator and to establish the Eleutheria, an annual freedom festival which would include athletic contests (like the Athenian Panathenaia) and would culminate in a great citizens' feast. The assembly then turned to more contentious matters and decided to limit eligibility for state offices (although perhaps not the right to attend assemblies) to the "old citizens," thus at least partially disenfranchising many, perhaps all, of those who had been brought to Syracuse and treated as citizens by the tyrants.

Among the disenfranchised were some 7,000 of the tyrant's mercenaries. The mercenaries rightly saw the decision about offices as signaling the end of their privileged position in a rent-seeking coalition and as proof that their interests could be ignored by the new government. Predictably, they chose to fight and, equally predictably, these experts in violence proved difficult opponents for the numerically superior Syracusans. Thanks to the efforts of an elite unit of 600 citizen-soldiers, the Syracusans eventually won out, but the war was long and debilitating (Diodorus 11.72–73, 76.1–2).

The civil war fought against mercenary forces in Akragas and Syracuse was an acute form of a general problem faced by every Greek city in Sicily after the fall of the tyrants: The tyrants' policy of moving populations and building up a few favored cities at the expense of others posed hard questions for the new posttyrannical regimes: Who was a citizen—and of what polis? Who had a rightful claim to what property? The mid-460s saw attempts by individual citizens and individual poleis to return to a pre-tyrannical *status quo ante*. A number of states, including Gela, Akragas, and Himera, witnessed episodes of what might be called civic cleansing: People who had been forced to emigrate from their homes by the tyrants now returned to their native cities, seized power, accused tyrant-era immigrants of having wrongfully taken other men's property, and sent the immigrants into exile (Diodorus 11.76.4).

Those exiled by posttyrannical regimes were unlikely to be welcomed home by the people currently occupying their (former) native cities, and the situation was highly volatile. The complex questions about who deserved what status, and what property, and where could not readily be answered on a polis-by-polis basis. Yet until these questions were answered, it was impossible to take the next essential step, that of defining, in a reasonably definitive way, rights related to civic membership and property: the immunities, participation rights, and right to control goods that would be assigned to various residents in each polis. In the meantime, while the Greek poleis were distracted by these sociopolitical matters, the inland Sikel population was being organized on a new military footing by an ambitious and competent Sikel leader. Some Greek states, including Syracuse, were initially willing to cooperate with the Sikels against Greek rivals if and when it allowed them to pursue a civic cleansing agenda (Diodorus 11.76.3).

After several years of strife, and in the face of the potential collapse of Greek Sicily's prosperity into a Hobbesian struggle of all against all, what might be described as a weakly federalist solution was put into place: According to Diodorus (11.76.5–6), almost all the poleis, eager to put an end to persistent civil conflicts, coordinated their citizenship policies according to a Common Resolution (*koinon dogma*). The terms of the Resolution called for a negotiated settlement with any former mercenaries still in residence, for a general recall of those people sent into exile during the posttyrannical incidents of civic cleansing, and for returning the poleis to the "old citizens" (i.e., the original pre-tyrannical era inhabitants).

The apparent contradiction between "recalling" exiles while simultaneously "returning" poleis to their original citizens may have been resolved by creating different gradations of citizenship, with different immunities and/or participation rights. Meanwhile, mercenary forces still in control of strongholds were induced to give them up by guarantees that their movable property would be inviolate, conjoined with the grant of control over Zancle–Messana, where ex-mercenaries would, collectively, be a majority of the citizen body. Finally, a mechanism was devised whereby the land in each polis was apportioned among people with legitimate claims to it under the Resolution. Like much else in Diodorus' compressed account, the details of this last measure remain obscure. Some kind of dispute resolution mechanism, rather than wholesale redistribution of land, seems, however, to be indicated: The well-documented rise of rhetorical expertise in Sicily was later attributed to the increase in legal disputation arising from the posttyrannical situation.[34]

How the poleis of Sicily managed to come to this remarkable regional accord is unknown. Diodorus' reference to a single Resolution and the arrangements for mercenaries to take over Zancle–Messana point to a unitary convention to which many states were signatories, rather than a one-state solution that was subsequently imposed upon or emulated by other states. But the way forward to the cooperative solution on citizenship status seems to have been prepared through the by-now-familiar tendency of the Sicilian Greek cities to move quickly, en bloc, in adopting new social and legal arrangements. In the event, the Common Resolution worked: At least some of the demographic results of tyrannical social engineering, including the dramatic increase in the population of Syracuse, were now accepted as established social facts. Diodorus (11.76.6) reports that the civil wars that had wracked the Sicilian poleis in the immediate posttyrannical era now came to an end. Although there is no legislator (mythic or real) whose name we can attach to this Sicilian Greek invention of a new approach to citizenship, the Common Resolution was of a piece with the Lycurgan reforms at Sparta and the Solonian/Cleisthenic reforms at Athens. And in each case, the result was a distinctive citizen-centered superpolis.

DEMOCRACY AT SYRACUSE

Syracuse's fifth century democracy is much less well documented than Athens', but what we do know points to an ongoing struggle to find an institutional design that would fit the distinctive form taken by citizenship in posttyrannical Sicily. The new government of Syracuse was centered on a citizen assembly with final authority over legislation, and it is, therefore, properly described as a democracy. It was not, however, a democracy that closely resembled the democracy established in Athens after 508. In comparison to Athens' federalist approach to popular self-government, Syracuse's fifth century democracy was at once more elitist and more populist. There is no evidence that Syracuse used a regionally representative, agenda-setting citizen council—the institution that, as we have seen, was a linchpin for the democracy in Athens. Syracuse seems never to have inscribed laws on stone for public display, as the Athenians did with increasing frequency. Unlike Athens, the Syracusans did not use a lottery when selecting magistrates. It is likely that elected officials, especially 15 annually elected generals, were more central to the government of Syracuse than they were to that of Athens. Overall, the Syracusan democracy appears to have been dominated by elites—although rarely by a unified elite coalition. Rivalry among men competing fiercely for positions of influence constantly risked compromising the stability of Syracusan government.[35]

Moreover, as Diodorus (11.85.3) acerbically notes, at Syracuse "many had been added to the roll of citizens without plan and in a haphazard fashion." There is no indication that Syracuse ever adopted a federalist model, despite having a big territory, many subsidiary villages and towns, and a population that was probably close to that of Athens. Demes and artificial tribes had proved effective in engaging Athenian citizens in the ongoing civic project of enrolling new citizens and in networking citizens from diverse regions and social backgrounds. Citizenship at Syracuse, by contrast, appears to have remained at the national level and to have been manifest politically only in the citizen assembly.[36]

With neither a citizen council nor the integrative levels of tribes and demes, Syracusan politics centered around individuals able to build temporarily powerful coalitions. The instability of the coalitions is signaled by reports of unruliness among the masses of ordinary citizens and the rise of "demagogues." These were charismatic leaders who gained influence by appealing directly to mass audiences through rousing speeches in the citizen assembly. As such, they posed a potential threat to the authority of elected officials. Athens too had its demagogues, but in light of the civic experience many citizens gained through Council service and the networks encouraged by the deme–tribe system, they frequently played a productive, rather than a disruptive role in the Athenian democracy.[37]

Diodorus (11.86.4–5) takes as exemplary of the troubles faced by Syracuse's new democracy the rise of a certain Tyndarides, who gathered a large

following of poorer citizens. He reportedly had armed them and was ru-
mored to be planning to use them in a bid to seize control of the government.
The Syracusan legal system at first seemed equal to the challenge: Tyndarides
was tried and sentenced to death. An attempt by his supporters to rescue him
on the way to the gallows led, however, to a violent counterattack by "respect-
able" citizens—i.e., elites and their retainers. These men seized and slaugh-
tered Tyndarides' supporters, along with the condemned man himself. Thus,
noted Diodorus, "as this sort of thing kept happening time and again," the
Syracusans sought to address the problem of political unrest by emulating
the Athenian law on ostracism (Diodorus 11.86–87).

Assuming that Diodorus had his facts right, the decision by the democrats
of Syracuse to emulate a specific institution developed by a prominent mainland state, in an attempt (unsuccessful, as it turned out) to redress a specific
sociopolitical problem, is an example of the general phenomenon of interstate
institutional transfer. Diodorus says that the goal of the Syracusan law was the
same as that of the Athenian law on ostracism: to allow the citizenry to expel,
by plurality vote, an influential man "most able through his influence to tyr-
annize over his fellow citizens" (Diodorus 11.86.5). As at Athens, the Syracusans did not envision a criminal procedure, but a preemptive move against a
potential threat to the democratic order. But Syracuse did not imitate ostracism in a slavish manner. Rather than writing the name of the most dangerous
man on a potsherd, the citizens of Syracuse wrote names on olive leaves, and
the period of exile was five years, as opposed to ten at Athens. Moreover, while
the Athenian ostracism law remained on the books through the late fourth
century, Syracuse's so-called "petalism" law was soon repealed.[38]

The reason for the repeal of petalism, according to Diodorus (11.87.4), was
that "since the most influential men were being sent into exile," there was a
general withdrawal from public affairs by elites capable of taking leadership
roles in the community. The frequency of petalism during its brief tenure must,
if we are to believe Diodorus, have been high enough to have had the undesir-
able result of dissuading at least some talented individuals from entering public
service. It therefore seems likely that, unlike Athens—where only one ostracism could be held each year, and where the practice was, as we have seen, used
sparingly—petalism could be used to expel a citizen whenever the Syracusan
assembly so chose. The inauguration of petalism can best be explained as the
result of an attempt by a broad-based coalition to preserve social order by imposing restraint on ambitious individuals—whether elected officials or demagogues. But the weapon proved impossible to control, as the citizen masses, led
on by ambitious elites, turned it on anyone they distrusted. The reform

coalition then was rebuilt for long enough to repeal the law—but not for long enough to bring long-term stability to Syracuse's government: Diodorus (11.87.5) reports that after the repeal, political strife remained endemic.

The divergent histories of Athenian ostracism and Syracusan petalism show that institutional transfer is not a simple affair: Because both the socio-cultural context and the details of mechanism design matter, superficially similar institutions may enhance the performance of one state's government while degrading that of another. Either the very different Syracusan political environment or the frequency of its use might have doomed petalism to failure. Together, they predictably led to a negative effect on elite choices regarding participation in public affairs. That negative effect was, however, not fatal to Syracuse's wealth. Despite all the political unrest, Syracuse in the mid-fifth century, like other Sicilian poleis in the same period, was economically prosperous. Syracuse had a large and increasingly urbanized population and substantial surpluses available for investment in major building projects. Those projects, as we see in the next chapter, included massive fortifications and improved military forces.

EXPLAINING SICILIAN WEALTH

The political and economic history of Syracuse in the early to mid-fifth century provides a counterpoint to that of Athens and Sparta in the sixth and early fifth century BCE. As such, it sets up a test whereby the explanatory hypotheses for the classical Greek efflorescence, offered in chapter 5, might be falsified. The Greek poleis of Sicily do seem to have participated in the wider Greek efflorescence from the pre-tyrannical mid-sixth century, through the tyrannical early fifth century, and into the posttyrannical mid-fifth century. At least one apparent case of institutional transfer, ostracism/petalism, was a signal failure. We might conclude, therefore, that political arrangements and institutional emulation had no discernible positive effects on Sicilian prosperity, and therefore that we ought to seek an explanation outside the organization of political order for the general phenomenon of classical efflorescence.

Before drawing any conclusions, however, we have to take into account the role of interdependence. Sicily's archaic and classical-era wealth was derived, in part, from surplus grain exported to the eastern Greek poleis. Without the growth of the eastern Greek population, and without the specialization of the eastern Greeks in economic activities that enabled them to pay for imported grain, Sicilian poleis would have had fewer markets for exported grain.[39] Syracusan wealth was to some degree bound up in eastern Greek development, just as eastern Greek development was furthered by the ready availability of Sicilian grain.

Any conclusions about whether the fair rules/low transaction costs and competition/innovation hypotheses introduced in chapter 5 are helped or hurt by the Sicilian case need to wait until the full historical quasi-experiment has been run. In the next three chapters, we complete the experiment by taking the narrative of wealthy Hellas down to the late fourth century—to the end of the era in which great independent Greek states made their own policy choices without being subject to the will of an imperial overlord. An important part of that story, told in the next chapter, is the rise and fall of the most promising native Greek attempt to sustain a Hellenic empire.

8

GOLDEN AGE of EMPIRE, 478–404 BCE

PREEMPTIVE WAR

In 478 BCE, as they surveyed the wreckage of their once-beautiful city, the Athenians reckoned the cost of victory in the Persian wars. There was much to celebrate: The bulk of the population had survived, evacuated in advance of the Persian attack to safe havens in the Peloponnesus. The bold choice of the young democratic regime to fight at sea had been vindicated. The tenuous alliance with Sparta had remained intact for the duration of the war. Athens' reputation had grown. Along with the Spartans, the Athenians were honored at Delphi by their fellow Greeks as having contributed decisively to the victories on land and sea. A great bronze tripod monument in the form of intertwined snakes had been inscribed with the names of the states that had defied the Persians. Punishment had been and would be meted out to Greeks who had too eagerly embraced the Persian side.[1]

On the other side of the ledger, Athens' losses, collective and individual, were profound. Many good men, hoplite infantrymen and rowers in the fleet, had died in battle; the elders who had made a desperate stand on the acropolis had been massacred. The urban center had been twice occupied by the invaders and twice looted and sacked, its temples and sanctuaries burned. The dozens of marble statues and other dedications that had graced the peak of the Acropolis had been defiled; they were tossed into a heap and buried. Sacred buildings were deliberately left in ruins as a reminder of Persian sacrilege. Towns in the countryside had been plundered. Agriculture, trade, and industry were disrupted. It would be a full generation before the Athenian mint would be ready to return to full production of silver coins.[2]

Worse yet, in 478, there was little reason for anyone in the Greek world to believe that the Persian threat had been eliminated by the victories at Salamis, Plataea, and Mycale. With the exception of the Aegean islands and the

Greek cities on the south coast of Thrace and along the western coasts of Anatolia, Persia's empire was intact. Persia still controlled vast capital resources and a huge population. The Persian Great King had made two serious attempts to conquer mainland Greece and was known not to tolerate failure. There was every reason for the Greeks to suppose that he would try again.

The Spartans had lost soldiers at the land battles of Thermopylae and Plataea, but their territory was untouched by the war. They had gained in prestige from their military leadership in the successful operations, and they regarded themselves as the natural leaders of Hellas. In what must have seemed to many Athenians a blatantly self-seeking ploy to extend their authority and to weaken rival states in central Greece, the Spartans now proposed that no Greek city north of the Isthmus of Corinth should be fortified—ostensibly to deny the Persians a base of operations when they next invaded. Returning to a plan that they had urged after the pass at Thermopylae had been turned in 480, Sparta proposed constructing a defensive wall across the isthmus—a plan that would explicitly sacrifice all Greek poleis north of the Peloponnese, including, of course, Athens (Thucydides 1.90).

Herodotus (7.139.3) had mocked Sparta's earlier isthmus wall plan as strategically absurd (the Persians could readily use transport ships to land expeditionary forces south of the wall). Moreover, it did not take strategic genius to recognize that the plan played directly to Sparta's relative advantage in military operations. Without urban fortifications, the states north of the isthmus would be endemically vulnerable to the Peloponnesian League armies, led by Sparta's crack army of hoplite warriors. The Spartans, backed by the allies, were formidable in open-field battle but had no deep experience in siege operations. Without fortifications, Sparta's rivals were much more vulnerable to coercion.[3]

Rejecting the Spartan plan, the Athenians quickly threw a circuit wall around their city, employing as some of their construction materials rubble from public buildings wrecked by the invaders. For the Athenians, the strategic question was not how to fight the Persians once they returned but how to preempt their return. Sea power was the key. The operations of the recent wars had demonstrated with stark clarity the essential role played by sea power in Persia's capacity to invade Greece in force. The first attack on the mainland, in 490, had come by sea, across the Aegean. The second attack, in 480, had come over land via Thrace and Thessaly, but the size and complexity of Persia's land forces required massive and continuous resupply by sea. The army was much too large for the invaders to count on "living off the land" by commandeering local food supplies along their route. So long as the Greeks had a credible navy, Persian supply ships (in the form of unarmed sailing vessels), upon which the invading army depended, had to be protected by Persian warships (oared galleys).[4]

The Greek naval victory at Salamis in 480 had turned the tide of the war by putting the Persian overseas logistical operation at risk. Without naval supremacy, the Great King had been constrained to evacuate the bulk of his army (along with himself). The Persian army that fought at Plataea in 479 was only a fragment of the original invasion force—albeit it was composed of elite troops and well led by top Persian commanders. The naval victory at Mycale had temporarily knocked out the bulk of the Persian navy. But with its store of treasure and a huge population that included many with experience in naval operations, the Persians could soon be ready to put a new naval force into the Aegean from bases in Phoenicia, Cyprus, and Egypt. Unless, that is, someone stopped them.

The Athenians had a plan for how to do that. Their own navy of triremes was largely intact. Moreover, the victory at Mycale had liberated the Greek poleis of the Aegean islands, southern Thrace, and western Anatolia. Whether they welcomed the liberation or not, the residents of these Aegean, Thracian, and Anatolian poleis knew that if the Persians returned, the king would be likely to take vengeance upon them as traitors to the Empire. As the hapless residents of Eretria and Miletus had learned, "Great King of Persia as taker of vengeance, in the name of god, against despicable traitors" was a central part of Persian royal ideology. No doubt there was a range of opinion among Persia's former subjects about the costs and benefits of having been part of the Persian Empire. While some former subjects certainly longed to be free of Persia (Herodotus 8.132), being subjects of the empire had certainly offered advantages for others. But with the Great King absent and assumed infuriated, and with the Athenians and Spartans in no mood to brook any expression of pro-Persian sentiment, the citizens of the liberated Greek states now had strong reasons to cooperate in a plan that would prevent a Persian reconquest.[5]

With these factors in mind, the Athenians proposed their plan: A new anti-Persian alliance, extended in membership and in duration, would be formed under the same joint Spartan–Athenian leadership that had brought victory in the recent war. Its goal would be to keep naval pressure on the Persians, through privateering and preemptive attacks on any organized force of Persian warships that dared show itself in Mediterranean waters, thereby preventing the reemergence of a Persian military presence substantial enough to threaten any part of the extended Greek world. But the Spartans demurred, as they had before in the face of Gelon of Syracuse's offer to support the eastern Greek cause against Persia at the price of his own participation in leadership—or at least they dragged their feet for so long that the Athenians proceeded without them.

Sparta's hesitancy to join in the naval confederation plan was determined at least in part by a *path dependency*—the constraint of current choices by past decisions—arising from their prior commitment to specialization in land warfare. Despite the success of Spartan naval commanders in the later phases of the war against Persia, seaborne operations were not Sparta's strong suit: Warships required big capital outlays and large crews of reliable men who were not needed for hoplite service. Sparta had neither: Those who were reliable were needed as hoplites; those who were not needed as hoplites were unreliable.[6]

Moreover, the Spartans needed to keep most of their military forces relatively nearby if they were to maintain *escalation dominance*—the capacity to win wars at increasing scale ("if the conflict escalates, we still win")—over both the numerous helots and potentially restive Peloponnesians.[7] Finally, to ice the cake of their disapproval, a Spartan king who had been posted in the north Aegean as part of the anti-Persian operations late in the war had gone seriously off the rails: Reportedly, he had conspired with the Great King of Persia. Whatever the truth of that accusation, he had certainly acted in a very un-Spartan fashion, dressing and feasting in the Persian manner and surrounding himself with a foreign bodyguard. This was clear enough evidence for the Spartans, had any been needed, that the social panopticon of the Lycurgan system was essential for maintaining Spartan society in its current equilibrium.

So Athens was left to implement the anti-Persian confederation on its own. Most of the Aegean and coastal Anatolian Greek states were quickly signed up, and other states joined, voluntarily or otherwise, in the years to come. The result was the Delian League (map 7), named after the tiny Aegean island (later a Roman-era trade center and notorious slave market) dedicated to Apollo. Here, at a site especially sacred to the Ionian Greeks who were, ethnolinguistically, the majority of the League's membership, a common treasury was to be established and league meetings would be held to discuss policy. The league's stated purpose was to build and man enough warships to maintain active naval patrols in the Aegean throughout the sailing season—winter operations were for the most part out of the question, due to weather.[8]

But who would build and who would man the warships? Many of the member states of the league were very small. Most had neither the local expertise nor the facilities to build, row, or store (in the off-season) the state-of-the-art trireme warships that would be the ships of the line in all major anti-Persian operations. Athens had both growing expertise and experience in ship-building and a large population with a proven willingness to take to the

MAP 7 *Athenian empire (maximum extent).*

sea in force. But the post-Persian War Athenians were obviously in no condition to pay for all necessary work themselves—Athens had taken a big hit in the war and already had heavy calls on whatever funds they could raise from their own pockets.

Ex post, the solution was obvious: Athenians, with their recognized specialization in naval architecture and naval warfare and a manpower base to match, would build and operate most of the ships. Several other major poleis would contribute their own ships and men. But most of the members of the league would contribute money instead. An Athenian named Aristeides came up with the schedule of payments—in ships or silver—for each polis in the league, famously earning himself the nickname, at least among Athenians (Plutarch *Life of Aristeides* 7.6), of "the Just" for the equitability of his arrangement.

The agreement that brought the new confederation into existence was sealed with solemn oaths that would be kept, it was promised, until iron ingots, ceremonially thrown into the sea, floated. The new league began operations immediately, reducing several important Persian strongholds in the north Aegean and forcing the south-Euboean polis of Karystos (i373), which had been pro-Persian during the war, into the league. The league's first decade was capped by a major victory in 469 BCE at the Eurymedon River on the southwest coast of Anatolia. The strategic plan was working: Persia had not come back. And meanwhile, a newly invigorated Aegean exchange economy was emerging. It was dispersed across many markets but more focused than before on Athens and its port at Piraeus.[9]

TROUBLE WITH SPARTA

There was, however, trouble almost from the beginning. Insofar as Persia was a real threat, the security provided by the Delian League against any potential resurgence by Persia was a *nonexcludable public good*, in the sense that every Greek state potentially vulnerable to Persian predation benefited from the league's activity in preventing Persian operations. Those states that contributed nothing to the effort to muzzle Persia reaped just as much of the benefit as did those that contributed much. Moreover, in an easily conceivable counterfactual, if Persia were someday to defeat the forces of the league and thus retake the eastern Aegean, those states that had refused to participate in anti-Persian military actions might be spared the full force of the Great King's righteous vengeance. Thus, there was a strong incentive for each of the league states to free ride on the security conditions produced by the collective action of the others, by failing to contribute to the league. If one state were successful in this self-interested strategy, it could precipitate an emulation cascade of defection, dooming the league and leaving Athens, and all Hellas, vulnerable to Persia.

The wealthy Aegean polis of Naxos (i507: size 4, fame 4) was the first Greek state to attempt to defect from the league. The response was swift: Naxos was besieged by an Athenian-led naval group and forced back into compliance. The pattern of attempted defection (through nonpayment of dues) followed by efficient reprisal was to be repeated on a fairly regular basis over the next two generations, generally with the same result. As Thucydides (1.98–99) notes, the Athenians, who built and manned the ships, also did most of the actual fighting. They were therefore constantly gaining in military experience—in, for example, naval operations, siegecraft, and logistics—relative to those league states that contributed only money.

It is not surprising that specifically Athenian interests were increasingly furthered by league-financed operations. As a positive (to Athens) externality arising from the necessity of preempting Persian naval power, Athens had taken the next big step as a superpolis by leveraging the resources of many other states. Athens had, in short, embarked on the road to empire.[10]

These developments were viewed with alarm in Sparta. Thucydides (1.101) reports that in 463 BCE the Spartans secretly offered to aid the defection from the Delian League of the prominent north Aegean island-polis of Thasos (i526: size 4, fame 5). They were, however, prevented from doing so by a major earthquake that killed many Spartans and triggered an uprising by the helots of Messenia.

The helots threw up improvised fortifications on the steep slopes of Mount Ithome in central Messenia, enabling them to defy the Spartans, whose skill in open-field battle was not matched by their siege technique. In a quick turnabout, Sparta appealed for aid to Athens, by now the Greek state with the deepest expertise in siege operations. An Athenian army headed south, led by the highly successful general Cimon, who had long advocated closer relations between the two former allies. But there was another surprising turnabout. The Spartans, who, according to Thucydides (1.102), were now alarmed by the Athenians "daring and revolutionary nature" and feared that they might side with the helots, abruptly informed the Athenians that their services were not needed. Deeply offended, the Athenians returned home—and ostracized the pro-Spartan Cimon.

The events of 462 are sometimes described as a watershed in Athenian political history. With the eclipse of Cimon came a constitutional reform that limited the judicial authority of the Areopagus council of former archons to a few categories of criminal trial, eliminating its role in reviewing (and possibly setting aside) legislation passed by the assembly. The way was opened for a new style of leadership, prominently exemplified by Pericles—who was related by birth and marriage to the Alcmaeonids—the family of Cleisthenes. The decades after 462 saw an intensification of the democratic features of the Cleisthenic system.[11]

Over the course of the next generation, the system of people's courts and the practice of paying citizens who held public office were expanded, enabling ordinary men to take an increasingly active role in polis governance. But those developments were hardly a revolutionary change of political direction. The increasingly important role of the navy in ensuring state security gave the ordinary-citizen rowers substantial bargaining power. But the growth of imperial wealth, conjoined with ever-deepening social networks made possible by the Cleisthenic tribal system, obviated for the time being any need for difficult bargains between elites and masses. Prodemocracy members of the elite, like Pericles, provided effective leadership for the state. Meanwhile, the ostracism of several prominent Athenians suspected of obstructionism undercut the ability of those elite Athenian who were opposed to deepening democracy to coordinate behind their own preferred leadership.[12]

The events of 462 showed that there would be no quick return to the Athens–Sparta alliance that had defeated the Persians, but there was no fundamental change in the direction in Athenian foreign policy. Like Cimon and Aristeides before him, Pericles and his political allies were ready and able to employ the Delian League to further Athenian policy goals. The decade following 462 saw ambitious operations in several theaters: against Persian bases in Cyprus and Phoenicia, in support of anti-Persian uprisings in Egypt, and against Athens' old rivals in mainland Greece. Megara and Aegina were among the major Greek states now added to the league. An effort to incorporate the poleis of Boeotia, to Athens' north, was, however, ultimately stymied by Spartan military opposition. Recognizing the status quo, the two superpolis rivals declared a five-year cessation of hostilities in 451; after another brief spate of hostilities, which included a Spartan incursion into Attica, a second armistice agreement was signed in 446 BCE. This time the peace was meant to last 30 years. In the event, it lasted for fewer than 15. The war that broke out in 431 BCE, recorded in great detail by Thucydides and usually known as the Peloponnesian War, would polarize the Greek world and convulse Hellas, on and off, for 27 years.[13]

ATHENIAN EMPIRE

Meanwhile, by the 450s, it was increasingly clear that the anti-Persia confederation was quickly morphing into an Athenian empire (map 7). In 454 BCE, following a major setback in which an Athenian expeditionary force was lost off Egypt, the Delian League's treasury was moved from Delos to Athens. After this, we hear of no further meetings of the league assembly, an institution that had, in any event, devolved to a rubber stamp for policy decisions made in Athens. The same year saw the inauguration of the so-called Athenian Tribute Lists, a monumental set of inscriptions on a great marble stele set up on the acropolis. The inscriptions record the goddess Athena's 1/60th share of the annual contributions of Athens' sometime allies. In 449, some sort of peace agreement was struck between Athens and Persia. It appears that by the terms of the agreement, the Athenians agreed to cease raiding Persian territory, and the Persians agreed to keep their military forces away from the Anatolian coast and out of the Aegean. The ostensible goal of the league, containment of Persia, would now seem to have been fulfilled. But the mandatory annual contributions to the league treasury by member states quickly resumed. The question, by this time, is no longer whether the league was an Athenian empire but rather what sort of empire was it?[14]

The most obvious imperial model was Persia. The Athenians adapted some features of Persian imperial imagery, along with the system of assessing tribute and perhaps some Persian techniques of rule.[15] But Persia's empire was, measured in population, some 20 times the maximum size of the Athenian empire. There were, moreover, structural differences that went well beyond the difference in scale. Persia's empire stretched across much of western and central Asia, encompassing a vast land area and a huge diversity of cultures and languages. Athens' empire was not only smaller, it was much more homogeneous, culturally and linguistically. Virtually all the states under Athens' control were at least Hellenized, if not fully Hellenic.[16]

Athens had another big advantage over Persia as an imperial power: Athens did not confront the intractable *principal-agent problem* faced by every extensive premodern continental empire. In light of slow overland communications and difficult logistics, the agents (local governors) must be granted considerable scope for independent decision and action by the principal (the central government or emperor). But, the greater an agent's independence (and thus his capacity to serve his own interests), the lower is his motivation loyally to advance the interests of the principal. Most of the states controlled by Athens were on or very near the Mediterranean coast, and because Athens had a dominant navy of fast and powerful warships, communication, command, and control were much simpler for Athens than for Persia or any great continental empire. As the events of the Peloponnesian War would soon show, Athens was able to concentrate military forces in trouble spots with great speed and devastating efficiency. By contrast, it might take months, even years, for a Persian army to respond to a distant uprising. As a result, the Athenians had no need to create a Persian-like system of quasi-autonomous, and thus potentially rebellious, provincial governors.[17]

On the other side of the imperial control ledger, the Athenians lacked a legitimating ideology that could stand in for the Great King's claim to have a special relationship to a great god. The closest thing the Athenians had to an imperial ideology was the claim that Athens was the mother-city of the Ionians—that is, the Greeks who spoke an Ionian dialect. It seems clear enough that the Athenians did make some efforts to assert an "ancestral" leadership over Ionians, claiming, for example, that Ion, the mythical ancestor of all Ionians, was the son of an Earth-born Athenian queen (see Euripides' tragedy *Ion*). Yet there is little evidence than anyone outside Athens ever behaved as if that claim were in any meaningful sense action-guiding. In order for an imperial ideology to function in the interests of the hegemonic power, those subject to it must act under moral constraint: They must behave in a dutiful manner out of something exceeding the cost–benefit reasoning of economically rational agents. I know of no evidence that any of Athens' imperial subjects ever acted out of a sense of duty to Athens arising from an ideology of "Ionicism." Moreover, it is not the case that Athens' empire was homogeneously Ionian—some subject states in northwestern Anatolia were Aeolic; others were Doric; yet others, notably in Caria in southwestern Anatolia, fell completely outside Greek ethnolinguistic subdivisions.[18]

The problems that could arise in the absence of a legitimating ideology of empire were exacerbated by the strong Greek commitment to the normative ideal of local citizenship. Although, as we have seen (table 2.3), many Greek states lacked full independence, at least in their ability to set their own foreign policy, there were limits to the degree of dependency that could be accommodated within a value system centered on citizenship. While ordinary citizens might see Athens as a supporter of local democracy, as a bulwark against domination by local oligarchs, there was some point at which at least part of the populace of a given state would push back against the devolution from "free and equal citizen of polis X" to "humbly obedient subject of imperial Athens." The option of exchanging "citizenship in polis X" for the status of "citizen (or even quasi-citizen) of a greater Athenian state"—the approach to imperial expansion that was being adopted by the Romans in Italy—was never on the table.[19]

The Athenians guarded the status of Athenian citizenship jealously. Indeed, in 451 BCE a new law, passed by the assembly on a proposal sponsored by Pericles, restricted Athenian citizenship to people who could demonstrate that each of their parents had been an Athenian native. Mixed marriages (which had usually been of the form native Athenian male with nonnative wife) were no longer recognized as legitimate. The male offspring of a mixed marriage was now legally a bastard. As such, he was ineligible to inherit an equal share in the family property or to be presented by his father before the demesmen as a candidate for inclusion in the ranks of the Athenians.[20]

In lieu of an imperial ideology based on divinity, shared ethnicity, or shared citizenship, the Athenians could, in some cases, lean on shared regime preferences. In the course of the fifth century BCE, more Greek states, and especially those within the Athenian empire, adopted some version of democratic government. We seldom know many of the details. As we have seen in the example of Syracuse's adoption of democracy in 465, the constitutional form taken by popular government might vary considerably from the Athenian model. But all democracies shared the common feature of being "not oligarchy."

As the Greek historian Matthew Simonton has demonstrated in recent work, in the Greek world the political form "oligarchy" is not best thought of as the generic background political condition of all nondemocratic Greek states. Rather, oligarchy, as it was understood by classical Greeks, was a specific reaction by "the few who were wealthy" to the emergence of democracy as a strong form of extensive citizenship and collective self-government. Thus, with the development of democracy came the possibility that democracy might be subverted—not only by a tyrant, but also by an organized effort on the part of local elites to establish a government in their own interest. Elite interests might overlap with, but were far from identical to, the interests of the masses of non-elite natives. The ordinary citizens of a democratic Greek polis could, therefore, expect to do substantially worse if and when their polis was transformed by elites into an oligarchy—and vice versa.[21]

While Athens never consistently required subject states to adopt democratic constitutions, the Athenians were obviously sympathetic to democracy as a form of government in ways that the Spartans and Persians, for example, were not. Among the advantages, then, that might be enjoyed by the ordinary citizens of a Greek polis in the Athenian empire was the expectation of a certain level of solidarity with the demos of Athens. In several high-profile cases, notably after a revolt by the great island state of Samos (1864: size 5) in the 440s, the Athenians did actively promote the establishment of a democratic regime. Democratic states within the empire could expect some measure of Athenian support were local elites to seek to overthrow a democratic regime in favor of oligarchy. And thus, democracy may have encouraged some Greeks to accept their position as subjects.[22]

The most widespread benefit that the Athenian empire offered to its subjects was, however, economic. Most obviously, by guaranteeing protection against Persian privateers and against the ordinary pirates that have historically infested the Mediterranean in the absence of a strong naval power determined to suppress them, the Athenians created the baseline conditions for peaceful trade. Smaller states no longer needed to fear predation by larger states, or raids on their ships or coastal settlements by pirates—which was an endemic problem when there was no power strong enough to keep piracy down to a minimum.[23]

Reliable security, along with reliable punishment of would-be free riders, encouraged rational submission to imperial rule: Unlike raid-and-grab pirates, the Athenians had a vested interest in keeping order and in protecting the economic interests of tribute-paying imperial subjects. In the face of the alternative, residents of weak states were relatively better off, all things considered, when they paid a reasonable and predictable level of protection money to a stable hegemon with relatively long time horizons. The long Athenian horizon was graphically expressed, for example, by the Athenian Tribute Lists: The great stone stele set up prominently on the Acropolis in 454, on which the lists were inscribed, had room for 15 or more years of records: Clearly by setting up that massive stele, the Athenians signaled that they planned to be in the empire business for many years to come.[24]

The logic of rational acquiescence to rule was not lost on Greeks of the fifth century. An inscription found in Athens dated around 445–430 details the relations between "the community (*koinon*) of the Eteokarpathians" (on the island of Karpathos, between Crete and Rhodes) and the Athenians. The Eteokarpathians (i488: size unknown but surely small) seem to have taken some initiative in getting themselves assessed for tribute, and they donated building materials (in the form of a cypress log from a sacred precinct) to a construction project on the Athenian acropolis. In turn, they had received Athenian military intervention in a local dispute, and thus their community's continued existence was guaranteed. The inscribed record of mutually beneficial interaction points to the self-consciousness on the part of a small community of the benefits it might receive by being under the control of a great state. Like most of the Greek states overall (figure 2.2), most states of the Athenian empire were small (size 3 or below).[25]

In the first book of his text, in an abbreviated analytic narrative of earliest Greek history, Thucydides theorized the relationship of rational acquiescence in a quasi-historical account of the rise of Greek civilization. He notes that in the distant past, before the Trojan War, there were no substantial coastal towns due to piracy.

> But after Minos [mythical king of Crete] had organized a navy, sea communications improved. . . . [he] drove out the notorious pirates, with the result that those who lived on the coasts were now in a position to acquire wealth and live a more settled life. Some of them, on the strength of their new riches, built walls for their cities. The weaker, because of the general desire to make profits, were content to put up with being governed by the stronger, and those who won superior power by acquiring capital resources brought the smaller poleis under their control.
> —*Thucydides 1.8, trans. Warner (Penguin), adapted*

Despite its setting in a mythic past, this passage is clearly meant to alert the reader to a central logic of empire—and especially of the kind of maritime empire that had been created by the Athenians during Thucydides' own lifetime.

ECONOMICS OF EMPIRE

In fact, the Athenians seem to have run their empire with a close eye to the balance sheet of interests reckoned as costs and benefits—in the first instance, their own interests but, because the imperial system was based on increasingly high levels of economic integration and interdependency, the interests of other states as well. Both the strength and, as we will see, one of the weaknesses of the Athenian empire was the historically unusual degree to which it was predicated on assumptions about rationality of behavior, understood as the pursuit of interests capable of being reckoned upon a cost–benefit basis. Lacking any very promising ideological justification for their rule, the Athenians went on the assumption that, so long as the subject poleis were net gainers from the existence of the empire, local rulers (whether democrats or oligarchs) would, under most conditions, act like the Eteokarpathians. They would realize that their collective interests were better served by cooperation with the hegemonic power than by defection.[26]

The Athenian empire did indeed provide very substantial economic benefits for the states and their residents within its ambit in exchange for the costs they were asked to bear in the form of imperial tribute and loss of foreign policy independence. The total tax burden of the empire was probably in the range of 3% to 6% of imperial GDP. If, counterfactually, this comparatively light burden had been shared across the entire population of the empire on a regressive per capita basis (in fact local elites bore most of the tax burden), an average family would have had to devote no more than one or two days of labor per month to paying the imperial taxes.[27] In return, in addition to security against rapacious states and pirates, Athens provided substantial economic services: First there was, at Piraeus and in the Athenian agora, a central market for exchange. The costs of entering that market were not exorbitant—a standard (as it appears insofar as we have comparative Greek evidence) 2% tax on imports and exports. Although many goods were exchanged through *cabotage*—i.e., local coasting voyages by small-scale merchants—and so did not need to go through a central market, there were obvious advantages to some traders to having a single major market to which bulk and luxury goods could be brought for exchange. Fifth century writers were explicit about the advantages that central exchange brought, both to Athenians and to those who traded in Athens.[28]

The advantage was multiplied when the central market was well regulated; was liquid (well-supplied with specie); employed standard weights, measures, and units of exchange; provided first-rate facilities (docks, storage areas, transport system); and when there was a great deal of local wealth. Athens made

major improvements in infrastructure and imposed regulations meant to reduce cheating by unscrupulous traders. The Athenians at first encouraged,
and ultimately required, throughout their empire, the use of standardized
weights and measures, and a standard coinage, in the form of Athenian owls.
Finally, because of the massive production of owls by the Athenian mint after
449 BCE, the Athenians effectively guaranteed market liquidity: With perhaps 12–24 million silver drachmae produced each year by the Athenian mint,
there was no lack of specie available with which to transact exchanges.[29]

The upshot of these several measures was to lower the costs of transactions and thereby to increase the value of voluntary and mutually beneficial
exchanges. Under the relatively high-security, low-transaction-cost conditions promoted by the Athenian empire, increasing investment in specialization to maximize relative advantage and increasing the percentage of production aimed at exchange relative to that aimed at subsistence were rational
behaviors. And thus, as we would expect, the part of Hellas controlled by
Athens became wealthier. Moreover, Athens had a very limited capacity to
impose a mercantilist policy that might have limited imperial subjects to
trading within the empire—even if the Athenians had formed a preference
for such a policy.[30] Because imperial subjects traded outside as well as inside
the empire, the growth of the imperial economy benefited all of Hellas—and
thus it promoted the efflorescence that we are seeking to explain.

The Athenians themselves, of course, benefited most of all. Athenians
benefited directly, as rentiers. Elite Athenians reaped rewards from military
leadership positions, especially when, as was often the case, military operations resulted in booty. Non-elite Athenians had the chance to raise their
socioeconomic status by sharing rents from distribution of goods, notably
when agricultural land was confiscated from a subject state that had failed
fully to grasp the rationality of acquiescence. Confiscated lands were divided
among Athenian "cleruchs" (*klerouchoi*: "shareholders"—the Greek root *kle-
ros* is the term that was used for the "allotment" of land and helots controlled
by each Spartan in the Lycurgan system). Cleruchs, often drawn from the
ranks of formerly poorer Athenians, might take up residence abroad to look
after their new landholdings in person. Alternatively, they might lease the
land on a sharecropping basis back to its original owner. Other Athenians
benefited from the imperial revenues that were plowed back into the Athenian economy: Athenian rowers, marines, and infantrymen were relatively
well compensated for military service on the annual naval patrols in the Aegean and for garrison duty among potentially restive subjects.[31]

Yet other Athenians, of all classes, benefited from pay for government and
legal service and from a surge in public building. That surge began in earnest

in the mid-440s: A series of extraordinary new temples and related sacred buildings were constructed on the Acropolis and in major towns of Attica. The Parthenon, the most technically advanced temple that had ever been constructed in Greece, was the masterpiece. But it was only one sacred building among many that went up in the city of Athens and at the demes of Rhamnous, Eleusis, and Sounion. The city and Piraeus fortification circuits were now connected with monumental long walls, which created a fortified corridor from the coast to the city, five miles inland. Piraeus was fitted out with monumental dockyards and shipsheds to protect the precious warships when they were not on active duty. The theater of Dionysus was for the first time built in stone. A new concert hall (the Odeon) was the largest roofed performance space ever contemplated in the Greek world. And a host of other public buildings, many of them constructed at an unprecedented level of grandeur and attention to artistic detail, went up in the agora and in other parts of the city and countryside. Based on the limited evidence preserved in inscriptions, the wages, even for unskilled or semiskilled construction work were good— well above the subsistence level that was the premodern norm (ch. 4).[32]

Athenian industry was growing apace: Silver production from the mines of south Attica reached all-time highs, as did the marble and limestone production of Athenian quarries and vase production in pottery workshops. It is a reasonable guess that other industries (weaving, leatherworks, bronze and iron foundries, etc.) flourished as well. Prominent Athenian politicians were reputed to have made their fortunes in industry—in, for example, tanning and the production of musical instruments.[33]

Meanwhile, the population of Athens was also growing. Athens was a highly desirable destination for economic migrants, both temporary and permanent. Despite casualties of war and a more restrictive citizenship policy, conditions of improved welfare also promoted increased natural population growth. By the mid-430s, Athenian (adult male) citizen population had reached its ancient peak of perhaps 50,000 or more. A good number of citizens lived abroad, as cleruchs or garrison soldiers, and Athens led a new wave of Greek colonization, collaborating in the founding of new poleis in Thrace (notably Amphipolis [i553: size 5]) and Italy (Thurii [i74: size 3]). Nonetheless, the total resident population of the polis certainly exceeded 250,000; if we add nonresident Athenians (cleruchs, garrison troops, etc.), the total probably exceeded 300,000.[34]

The growth of Athens was both spurred by and was a result of more intensive and more diversified specialization, both in Athens and across the Greek world. The imperial-era comedies of Aristophanes preserve a startlingly high number of names for work specializations in industry and service.[35]

Intensified specialization, in a context of competition and cultural conditions enabling ready emulation, drove innovation. The results are, today, vividly evident in the high-cultural products of what has often been described as
the Athenian Golden Age: These include the tragedies of Aeschylus, Sophocles, and Euripides; the comedies of Aristophanes; the architecture of Icti-
nus; the sculpture of Pheidias; the histories of Herodotus and Thucydides;
the moral philosophy of Socrates; the astronomy of Anaxagoras; the anthropology of Democritus; the medicine of Hippocrates—the list could be very
readily extended.[36] It would be even more impressive if so much had not
been lost since antiquity. Fifth century Athens was, for example, the center of
major innovations in large-format figurative painting and in musical compo-
sition and performance. These remarkable cultural results were, as we have
seen, the basis of Byron's (and many others') belief in Greek greatness. They
were produced both by native Athenians and by artists and intellectuals
drawn to Athens by its role as a cultural capital. As Ian Morris and Reviel
Netz have shown with simple statistics, Athens was unquestionably the intellectual and cultural hub of the Greek world through much of the fifth century BCE.[37]

Less visible to us than the products of high culture, but of great consequence for Athens and Hellas, were innovations in other domains. Athenian
warships were not only numerous, they were also capable of speed and maneuvers that were well in advance of those built and maintained by other
Greek states—the incremental results of ever-deepening expertise gained by
thousands of hours of experience by naval architects, captains, steersmen,
and rowers. The management of the empire led to deepening expertise in the
organization of state finances—the leadership of Pericles and other prominent Athenians of this era was in part based on their skill in the traditional
roles of generalship and public speech but in part on the new domain of organizing the finances of an imperial state.[38]

GREEK THEORIES OF WEALTH,
POWER, AND POLITICS

These dramatic changes did not go unnoticed—or untheorized—by contemporaries. The so-called sophists, a highly diverse group of Greek intellectuals,
wrote texts and offered to teach students (typically the offspring of elite Athenians capable of paying their fees), in fields of expertise relevant to political
leadership: broadly speaking, they taught "political science" (*politike techne*)—
which conjoined theories of human nature and the nature of power with the
theory and practice of rhetoric, music, mathematics, and ethics. Behind their

theorizing about politics lay a general theory of specialization and education: The sophists claimed to have mastered the essence of what it took to be a specialist and that they knew how to achieve genuine expertise.[39]

Some Athenians scoffed at the sophists' claims. Among their most prominent critics was Socrates, whose dialectical method was meant to show that (among other things) the sophists' pretensions to be masters of political science were spurious. But many others, like Socrates' young friend Hippocrates (ch. 5), took the sophists seriously and learned from them—or hoped to. Herodotus was clearly well aware of arguments developed by the sophists about the techniques that produced efficient centralized authority and about the strengths and weaknesses of various forms of government. But among surviving fifth century writers, it was Thucydides who most obviously and effectively adopted the techniques and arguments of the sophists (as well as those of other imperial-era intellectuals—notably including the Hippocratic medical writers), in his exposition of the origins and conduct of the Peloponnesian War.

While his text (as far as we know he produced just the one) is often read simply as a brilliant historical narrative of a terrible war, Thucydides goes beyond the discipline of history, as we now tend to think of it, in his analytic framework and aims. His expressed goal was not only to offer an accurate account of the course of events but also to enable readers to be effective political actors in the future. Thucydides' explanation for why the Peloponnesian War broke out, and why both powerful and weak states acted as they did in the course of the war, was based on a view of human political nature as, to a significant degree, rationally self-interested.[40]

Humans are, for Thucydides, driven by, on one side, fear of loss, and on the other by desire for wealth, power, and glory. States, as aggregates of human fears and desires, are likewise driven by their perceived self-interest. All states seek to survive; powerful states also seek rents and resources that enable them to dominate other states. All states, and all powerful states, therefore, shared some features in common with one another. But they also had salient features that made them differ from one another. For Thucydides, the three superpoleis of Athens, Sparta, and Syracuse—which were the most important (but certainly not the only) collective historical agents in his history—were at once relevantly alike and relevantly different. Both their similarities and their differences helped to determine the choices that in turn determined the course of the war—or helped to affect it, given that chance was also a major factor in Thucydides' narrative.[41]

Thucydides was intensely interested in precisely the puzzle that concerns us, that is, explaining the changing situation of Hellas in terms of both wealth and organized political power. Thucydides pointedly contrasts the impoverished and weak Greek communities of ancient times with the rich and powerful states of his own era. As we have already seen, he regarded it as rational for a small and weak state to choose to accept subjection to a powerful hegemon capable of providing security and welfare. This allowed him to explain the emergence and persistence of the coalitions of states that enabled Athens, Syracuse, and Sparta to leverage human and natural resources. Thucydides was especially interested in the phenomenon of the dramatic growth in Athenian wealth and power in the 50-year era between the Persian Wars and the Peloponnesian War. For Thucydides, Athens in the age of Pericles represented a new and fascinating condition of human possibility.[42]

The necessary conditions for Athens' dramatic rise were, in Thucydides' view, the massive and extensive fortifications that ensured security against hostile powers, a great navy that provided the capacity to enforce the will of a powerful hegemon with unmatched quickness and efficiency, and huge capital resources that funded both the walls and the navy. These three conditions were created and sustained by a large, highly experienced, highly motivated, and relatively cohesive citizen population. But these were still only necessary, not sufficient, conditions. The essential ingredient that propelled Athens into a new condition of human possibility was self-conscious human reason and leadership. Thucydides wrote his account of the great Peloponnesian War in part to demonstrate to readers the role of human knowledge and knowledge-based choices in the rise, and ultimately also in the fall, of Athens as a great imperial power.

Thucydides singled out Pericles as a leader who had come to understand the underlying factors that could and did, under his direction, make Athens into a new kind of superpolis—a Greek state that had moved to a higher level of achievement and that had the potential to bring much of the rest of the Greek world along for the ride. Three explanatory speeches are put into Pericles' mouth in Thucydides' history: The second and most famous is an inspiring funeral oration over Athenian soldiers who fell in the first year of the Peloponnesian War. In the funeral oration (2.35–46), Pericles celebrates the extraordinary achievements of Athens' post-Persian War generation, links Athens' present greatness to its democratic form of government and to the depth and diversity of individual Athenian skills, and suggests that Athens can and should be a model for all of Hellas. The first Periclean speech in the text (1.140–144) is delivered to Athens' citizen assembly. Here Pericles sets out the necessity of fighting Sparta and enumerates the unique resources that Athens would bring to the struggle and that, as he confidently predicted, would enable Athens to be victorious. The third and final speech is again delivered to the citizen assembly (2.60–64), but this time in the aftermath of a plague that had devastated Athens during the war's second year. In this speech, Pericles explains why the Athenians cannot afford to abandon the imperial project and emphasizes how each Athenian's private interests were inextricably conjoined to the collective fate of the Athenian state.[43]

Pericles is credited by Thucydides with extraordinary insight and talent as a leader, but he did not work in the shadows nor did he ever have anything like autocratic political authority: Each of his speeches in Thucydides' text was delivered to a mass audience, and in reality his policy recommendations, which were offered in the face of rival policies urged by other leaders, were deliberated and voted upon by Athenian citizen bodies. Pericles was a highly skilled player within a game with rules that were widely understood. Although Thucydides' analysis of Athenian power and wealth is unique in its depth and detail, other Athenian writers also grasped the essentials of the imperial age.[44]

A short text by Pseudo-Xenophon, an anonymous author, nicknamed "The Old Oligarch" by modern classicists, describes Athens as a democratic imperial state that was at once "bad" (because not dominated by the excellent few) and extremely effective at gaining and keeping wealth and power. The Old Oligarch's text is (or affects to be) by a politically disaffected Athenian (he speaks of Athenians as "we") writing for an audience ("you") that is antidemocratic in political sympathy and relatively ignorant of Athenian norms. The Old Oligarch assumes that his reader wants to understand how and why "bad" Athens rose to such a remarkable level of prominence in the Greek world. Athens' effectiveness is succinctly explained as a result of non-elite Athenians' capacity to recognize and to pursue their own best interests and of their development of expertise in naval operations. That expertise enabled them to exploit a favorable location and to leverage the talents of a large and diverse population at home and abroad. Moreover, noted the Old Oligarch, the Athenians were (unfortunately, in his view) not at risk of an oligarchic coup because both masses and elites benefited materially from the imperial order that their conjoined efforts maintained. Finally, our author recognized that the Athenians benefited by legally protecting not only their own interests but also those of slaves and noncitizens.[45]

While we can now see why the growth of the Athenian imperial economy would have had positive knock-on effects for the economies of other parts of the Greek world and thus we can begin to explain some part of the general phenomenon of efflorescence, the rise of Athens was a serious and growing problem for its rivals. The control Athens exercised over its imperial subjects meant that, even without implementing a general mercantilist strategy, Athens could punish trading states with which it was displeased. One of the triggers of the Peloponnesian War was the Athenian decision to exclude Megarian merchants from the harbors of the empire after Megara left the Athenian empire to rejoin the Peloponnesian League (Thucydides 1.139.1–2). Moreover, the fast and continued growth of Athenian wealth and power threatened the established position of Sparta. Because Sparta's economy was more or less a closed system, based primarily on extracting the surplus of the agricultural production of Laconia and Messenia, Sparta stood to one side of the system of economic integration and interdependency of the Athenian empire. After the falling out of 462, and in spite of the uneasy truce of 446, Athens' gain looked, at least potentially, to be Sparta's loss.

The demonstrated Athenian ability to take member states away from the Peloponnesian League degraded Sparta's alliance system and thereby its military capacity. Corinth was one of the most important poleis of Sparta's league due to its size, wealth, large navy, and strategic location on the isthmus, potentially controlling movement between southern and northern Greece. Corinth's threat to leave the Spartan alliance in favor of Athens (Thucydides 1.71.4), was, in Thucydides' account of the outbreak of the war, a matter of grave concern to Sparta. But the ultimate reason for the war was, according to Thucydides, deeper: The Spartans were terrified by the growth of Athenian power (Thucydides 1.23.6, 1.88.1).

The underlying reasons for the Spartans' fear are traced in detail by Thucydides through the device of a speech given by "the Corinthians" at a Peloponnesian League assembly held to debate recent Athenian moves against league members (Thucydides 1.68–71). The Corinthians argue, with devastating rhetorical force, that a new Athenian approach to state power and its uses was quickly rendering the Spartan approach to power politics obsolete. The Corinthians portray the Athenians as dynamic risk takers who had recognized that quickness, innovation, and an experimental approach to policy drove the continuous growth of wealth and power. Moreover, individual Athenians eagerly cooperated in collective state ventures because they recognized that their individual interests were bound up in that growth. In the Corinthians' assessment, the Spartans were, in every sense, the Athenians' opposites: Slow, conservative, risk-averse, and (contrary to Plutarch's vision of Lycurgus' Sparta as a state defined by virtuous common-good seeking) narrowly and selfishly self-interested. Athenian collective dynamism had potential downsides and might collapse under intense pressure, but only if the Spartans pressed the issue by declaring war. The main points of the Corinthians' argument in Thucydides' text are summed up in table 8.1.[46]

Although Thucydides' Corinthians tended to make their argument in terms of inherent Spartan and Athenian "national characters," their core ar-

TABLE 8.1 *Thucydides' "Corinthian Assessment"*

Growing Athens: Strong Performance	Stagnating Sparta: Weak Performance	Negative Side of Athenian Growth

Agility
• Speed
• Innovation
• Flexibility/versatility
  across domains
	Clumsiness
	• Slowness
	• Conservatism
	• Domain-specific
	  expertise
		Decision gridlock, as a
		result of too much
		information, conflicting
		information

Ambition • Hard work • Risk-taking • Future orientation	Complacency • Laziness • Risk aversion • Past orientation	Rashness, failure to calculate downside risk. Overambitious leadership
Common-ends seeking • Public goods • Long-term goals	Narrow, short-term self- interest seeking by groups and individuals	Free riding, factionalism

NOTE: Source: Thucydides 1.70.2–71. Adapted from table in Ober 2010b: 74.

gument—that the Athenian system was generative, influential, and capable of indefinite expansion (if not stopped in time)—suggests that Athens' success was not uniquely a matter of a peculiarly Athenian character. Rather, indirectly mirroring Pericles' claim in the funeral oration recorded by Thucydides (2.41.1.) that Athens could be "an education to Hellas," the Corinthians seem to regard the Athenian approach as both attractive to others and, at least in some senses, a model that other communities might successfully emulate. The implication was clear enough: While conservative Sparta stagnated, much of the rest of the Greek world, led by dynamic and aggressive risk-taking Athenians, would continue to grow. At some time, the tipping point would be reached and Sparta's military specialization would no longer be enough to maintain its superpolis status. And at that time, there would be a cascade of defection from the Peloponnesian League, ultimately leaving Sparta isolated in a world dominated by hostile rivals who had chosen, out of fear or desire, to follow the Athenian path of dynamic growth.

If the Corinthians' arguments were valid, then Sparta certainly did have a lot to worry about. Thucydides' claim that the ultimate cause of the Peloponnesian War was Sparta's fear at the growth of Athenian power appears entirely plausible as a rational explanation of a cost–benefit calculation: The Spartans were not afraid of a democratic bogeyman. They were afraid of the consequences of unusually rapid growth by a hostile rival and the prospect

that its growth was sustainable into the foreseeable future. Under these circumstances, unless they were willing to abandon the contest for preeminence, the Spartans had no choice but to attack before the power disparity
became too great. Whether that would be a matter of months, years, or decades was and still is an open question. The question of how long the attack
could be postponed was, according to Thucydides (1.79–87), hotly debated
by the Spartans in a closed meeting. But it came down to a question of when,
not whether, to attack. In this sense, Thucydides' claim that the war's origins
must be sought, not in particular incidents, but in deep structural changes in
the Greek world, in changes that were caused by what we can now characterize as an extended period of unusually robust efflorescence, seems well supported. And thus, for the first time but not the last, the prospects for an era
of Greek efflorescence that might continue indefinitely were put at risk by
the considerations of interstate rivalry and the politics of state power.

PELOPONNESIAN WAR TO 416 BCE

Thucydides' account leads us to believe that Pericles and the Spartans had
done the same math and had come to similar conclusions: Pericles realized
that war with Sparta was inevitable. But, as he assured the Athenian assembly
in the first of his speeches in Thucydides' text, it was winnable so long as the
Athenians did not overreach by seeking to grow the empire before Sparta had
given up the attempt to end it. Pericles' optimism about Athens' prospects
was not universally shared. Many Greeks apparently agreed with the Spartans that, given Sparta's unquestioned superiority in infantry forces and the
fact that Greek wars on the mainland tended to be decided by infantry battles, it would be a relatively short war: Within a few campaigning seasons, at
most, the highly trained Spartan hoplites, backed by the Peloponnesian infantry and Boeotian cavalry, would crush the Athenian land forces, deciding
the contest decisively in Sparta's favor (Thucydides 2.8.4, 5.14.3).

Pericles foresaw a very different war: The Peloponnesians would invade
Attica annually, but the Athenians would not meet them in the field. Since
the Peloponnesian allies had farms of their own to look after, the occupation
of the Athenian homeland would be fairly brief. The Athenian cavalry, along
with garrison troops at fortified outposts, would harry the invaders, preventing them from dispersing to plunder efficiently, and thus protecting, as well
as possible, Athenian extramural assets. The Athenians did not, in any event,
need to confront the Spartan–Peloponnesian army on land. Athens' extramural population would be evacuated from the villages and towns of Attica
and housed in the fortified city–Piraeus complex. The entire population could

readily be fed for as long as necessary with imported food, paid for by the unimpaired imperial economy. The Athenian fleet would keep order in the empire and would launch maritime raids on vulnerable targets along the Peloponnesian coasts. Megara would be subjected to biannual invasions and forced back into the Athenian fold. Eventually the Spartans would tire of the fruitless enterprise and retire to their strongholds in Laconia and Messenia, leaving the rest of the Greek world to be integrated into the empire and developed at leisure under Athenian leadership.[47]

The first year of the war, 431 BCE, went exactly according to Pericles' policy recommendations and plans. The Peloponnesians marched into Attica, but despite some grumbling by the residents of the very large deme of Acharnai, where the Spartans, not coincidentally, made their camp, there was no break in Athenian discipline. Harrying by Athenian cavalry and garrisons kept the invading forces relatively compact, and the damage done by the invaders was minimal. The counterraids and invasions of Megara went off like clockwork. Pericles' inspiring funeral oration, given over the bodies of the relatively few Athenian soldiers who fell in the course of the year, was offered at a high point of optimism and enthusiasm. The democratic political order, characterized by skillfully deployed expertise and rational planning, had brought Athens to its acme of wealth and power. Athens appeared to be a whole new kind of superpolis, capable, it seemed, of taking on the Spartans in a new kind of war.

The second year of the war was starkly different: In the summer of 430 BCE, the Peloponnesians stayed in Attica for longer (40 days) and were able to range more widely and to do more damage. But the real crisis came with the outbreak in Athens, although not among the Peloponnesians, of a highly contagious and usually fatal disease. Within two years, the plague had carried off at least a quarter of Athens' population, a total of perhaps 75,000 people. Neither scientific medicine in the new Hippocratic style nor old-fashioned prayers to the gods had any effect. This was a staggering blow to Athens' plans, in every possible sense. Pericles' second assembly speech in Thucydides' text was delivered in the aftermath of the first and worst outbreak of the disease. Pericles was indicted on legal charges, fined, and temporarily deposed from his position as general. But the surviving Athenians nonetheless took his advice to stay the imperial course. Meanwhile, democratic political order proved robust: The government continued to function, and military operations continued unabated.[48]

After Pericles died of plague in 429, his grand strategy for the war was initially adhered to by his political successors. In 428, the Athenians faced their next great test: the revolt of the major subject state of Mytilene (1798:

size 4, fame 5) on the eastern Aegean island of Lesbos and the threat of a simultaneous Peloponnesian land and sea attack on Athenian territory. Thucydides' vivid account of the Athenian response demonstrates the depth of Athenian military expertise and also the value of individual Athenians' adaptive versatility.[49]

Upon receiving news of the revolt, the Athenians dispatched 40 warships to Lesbos, where they established a naval blockade. The Peloponnesians, meanwhile, were slow to muster, "being both engaged in harvesting their grain and sick of making expeditions" (3.15.2). The Athenians responded to the Peloponnesian naval threat with a devastating show of force, manning 100 ships with which they descended upon the Peloponnesian coast, ravaging at will.[50] In order to pay for the necessary operations, the Athenians levied a 200-talent property tax upon themselves while also sending commanders abroad to collect imperial funds. When the discouraged Spartans disbanded their half-assembled invasion force, the Athenians dispatched a general to Mytilene with additional forces.

The Athenian reinforcements came in the form of an army of hoplites, who rowed themselves in triremes to Lesbos. When they arrived, they built a siege wall to complement the naval blockade. Hard pressed by the siege, the Mytilenean oligarchs armed the lower classes, who then demanded distributions of grain. Caught between a rock and a hard place, the Mytilenean oligarchs surrendered. More than 1,000 of them were executed. The agricultural land of Mytilene was turned over to Athenian cleruchs.

The Mytilene campaign of 428–427 seemed to confirm the Corinthian portrait of the agile, ambitious, and cooperative Athenians. After an informal intelligence network brought advance warning of hostile intentions, the Athenian military response to the revolt was masterful and multifaceted. The closely coordinated naval blockade of Mytilene, siegeworks, land operations against other Lesbian cities, and naval patrols in the Aegean accomplished Athens' goals with dispatch. The threat of a Peloponnesian land and sea invasion in late summer 428 failed to panic the Athenians. By digging deep into their reserves of human and material resources, they launched a huge naval force manned by heavy infantry: Athenian hoplites, it turns out, were capable oarsmen, and they took up oars without the foot-dragging that stymied plans for a Peloponnesian expedition.

The operations of 428–427 reveal that the all-important technical expertise of rowing warships at a high Athenian standard was widely dispersed across the Athenian citizen population.[51] When the occasion demanded it, there was no resistance on the part of "middling" hoplites to take on the oarsman's role usually fulfilled by poorer citizens. Neither technical incapacity nor social distaste stood in the way of generating the required level of projectible power at the right moment. There seems to be a clear connection between democratic culture, with its emphasis on basic equality among a socially diverse citizenry, the wide distribution of certain kinds of technical expertise, and Athenian military proficiency. Just as the Athenian hoplite accepted a poorer fellow citizen as an equal when sitting in assembly or on a jury, so too he accepted the "lower class" role of rower when the common good of the state demanded it. And upon arrival at his destination, he proved to be a willing and skilled wall builder in the bargain.[52]

The capacity of the individual Athenian to acquire a wide range of technical skills and to recombine various of his diverse abilities into new skill sets as the situation demanded meant that the Athenians could be flexible in deploying their manpower reserves. Thucydides' military narrative gives substance to the boast in Pericles' funeral oration: "I doubt if the world can produce a man, who where he has only himself to depend upon, is equal to so many emergencies, and graced by so happy a versatility as the Athenian. And that this is no mere boast thrown out for the occasion, but plain matter of fact, the power (*dunamis*) of the state acquired by these habits proves" (Thucydides 2.41.1). What is particularly striking about Thucydides' Mytilene narrative is that the Athenians' ability to excel is not limited to upward social mobility but implies mobility to any point on the "social status–labor map" that the situation demanded. Athens' democratic advantage was on full display.[53]

The Mytilene campaign demonstrated the extent of Athenian potential, but not all military operations went so smoothly; there were serious setbacks in Aetolia, Boeotia, and other theaters. Meanwhile, the Spartans produced in Brasidas a highly competent and strikingly innovative commander who saw that the best hope for breaking the impasse of the war was to take the war to Athens' imperial subjects. The result was a broadening of the conflict. Brasidas' new strategy not only put pressure on Athens; it exacerbated latent conflicts between prodemocratic and pro-oligarchic elements in Greek states, resulting in savage civil wars.[54]

The huge expense of fighting the long war led to a sharp increase in the imperial taxation rate, and in general to a more coercion-intensive approach to imperial control. Because, as we have seen, the nature of the maritime empire allowed an unusual degree of command and control compared to extensive continental empires with their principal-agent problems, Athens could readily increase tax and coercion rates, and, in the 420s, did so. Direct tribute taxes on states were raised in 425, and new indirect taxes on trade from the Black Sea were imposed. The total tax burden on the subject states of the empire must have doubled, at the very least. Meanwhile, in 428 the Athenians for the first time imposed substantial internal war taxes on themselves. In sum, the costs to both Athenians and their imperial subjects of imperial centralization were rising sharply, while the benefits were declining.[55]

After years of seesawing conflict and serious losses for both of the principal competitors and their allies, the rival powers were exhausted. A truce was declared in 421 BCE that reestablished something very like the prewar status quo. But many on each side remained unsatisfied: While Athens had taken a huge demographic hit and had spent down its capital surplus, the structural danger to Sparta of sustained Athenian growth had not gone away. On the Athenian side, the primary goal of reducing Sparta to a regional power incapable of standing in the way of expanding the empire had not been achieved. Ambitious men on both sides, and third-party opportunists, were eager to see hostilities recommenced.[56]

In 416, Athenian hawks persuaded the citizen assembly to vote for an attack on Melos (i505), a small (size 3), oligarchic, Aegean island polis. Melos was an ostensibly neutral state that had never been part of Athens' league or empire and may have provided some material support early in the war for Sparta. When an Athenian expeditionary force arrived at Melos, but before the commencement of hostilities, the Athenian commanders sought permission to speak to a full assembly of Melian citizens: Clearly they hoped to persuade the Melians of the rationality of acquiescing to Athenian rule. Melos' oligarchic leaders refused the request. Thucydides produces the resulting discussion between anonymous Athenian commanders and the equally anonymous Melian oligarchs in the form of a dialogue.[57]

In the Melian dialogue, the Athenians make arguments readily identifiable as sophistic in origin: Their premise is that their mission at Melos is entirely motivated by Athens' perceived interests in eliminating a neutral state in a region otherwise dominated by Athenian subjects. The anticipated benefits to Athens outweigh the cost of the operations that would be necessary to complete the conquest. The Athenians prefer that the Melians submit voluntarily but will eliminate the Melians if necessary. The cost–benefit calculation favoring conquest will not be changed by a Melian choice to resist. The Athenians pointedly refuse to listen to justice-based arguments. The Melians are left to assert that they will place their trust in the admittedly slim hope of succor by the Spartans or by the gods. The outcome, as the Athenians had pointed out, was never seriously in doubt. After the Melian resistance failed, the Athenians killed the male citizens and sold the rest of the population into slavery. The land was then redistributed to Athenian cleruchs.[58]

Thucydides' account of the Melian dialogue and its aftermath makes an important point about the limits of human rationality when it is understood in cost–benefit terms. By the strict economic accounting advanced by the Athenian commanders, the Melian leaders made a painfully irrational choice: giving up the opportunity to retain much of what they currently had for a vanishingly small chance of keeping everything by somehow defeating the superior Athenian forces. Yet, and I think this is Thucydides' point, the Melian choice to take an enormous risk of a catastrophic loss, in the vain hope of maintaining their status quo, followed from an entirely normal human decision process, in which the emotional attachment to what we have outweighs considerations of what we can actually expect. That process, which is described by the behavioral psychologist Daniel Kahneman in terms of "prospect theory," is irrational in the economic terms of risk assessment, probability, and cost–benefit payoffs. Yet it is the way most of us make decisions much of the time: Faced with the prospect of a substantial loss and a slight chance to avoid all loss, most people will choose to gamble at odds that no economically rational individual with a basic intuitive conception of mathematical probability would ever accept.[59]

The Melian oligarchs' "irrational" decision to fight demonstrated the limits of the rationality of acquiescence to Athenian rule. Ominously for the Athenians, if the rulers of enough states were similarly irrational in making their choices about resistance or submission, the Athenians would be unable to maintain their empire. They could take on only so many battles at one time, even assuming the high standard of military efficiency that they had manifested in the suppression of the Mytilenean revolt. The decision of the Melians to gamble on resistance pointed to a weakness in the sophistical "realist" analysis of power and human motivation. In the wake of Melos, Thucydides' text would seem to imply, the Athenians would do well to remember Pericles' cautious advice that there be no attempt to expand the empire until the war against the Peloponnesians had been concluded on terms favorable to Athens.

ATHENS VS. SYRACUSE

In the summer following the attack on Melos, the Athenians embarked on the most ambitious military operation of the war: a massive invasion of Sicily, aimed at conquest of the superpolis of Syracuse and at radically expanding the Athenian empire into the western Mediterranean. Thucydides (6.8–26) offers a detailed narrative of the assembly meeting at which the decision was made. Although a substantial Athenian force had campaigned in Sicily in the 420s in support of states friendly to Athens, Thucydides claims that the Athenian voters were largely ignorant of the physical size, demography, and political history of Sicily. He implies that they were misled by Alcibiades, the most prominent of the hawkish leaders who overemphasized divisions within and between Sicilian poleis. Others, by contrast, urged caution. The most prominent of the cautious leaders was Nicias, the general who had brokered the peace with Sparta in 421 and who, ironically, ended up as Athens' chief commander on Sicily. Nicias pointed to Sicilian manpower and material resources that could be brought to bear against an Athenian invasion and challenged the hawks' optimistic portrayal of Sicilian divisiveness.[60]

In fact, the situation in Sicily was complex. In the decades after the end of the tyrannies and the establishment of republican governments in the 460s, the Sicilian economy, still heavily based on agricultural exports, continued to grow. Carthage and the Aegean Greek world provided ready markets for Sicilian food products. Wealthy Syracuse and Akragas, and to a lesser degree other Sicilian poleis, spent lavishly on public buildings, minted large issues of silver coins, and became centers of culture and science. There were, however, deep political divisions—and not only between Greek poleis. In the 450s, Syracuse, Akragas, and the major Greek states had confronted an insurgent movement driven by ethnic nationalism among the native Sikels of east-central Sicily. That movement had been crushed and its leader coopted, leaving Syracuse free to rebuild a mini-empire in eastern and northern Sicily. Hostilities had flared anew between democratic Syracuse and oligarchic Akragas. Leontini in eastern Sicily was threatened by Syracuse's expansion. The major Elymian city of Segesta was threatened by Greek Selinous. And there were festering social tensions within Sicilian Greek cities, dating back to the fall of the tyrannies, centered on disputes over citizenship and property and on antagonism arising from stark inequalities between wealthy elites and ordinary residents.

Athenians who attended to Sicily's growing economic prosperity could have concluded either that it would be a tough opponent or a highly desirable prize. Those focusing on Sicilian politics might point either to endemic divisions that an invader might readily exploit or to the alliance among Sicilian poleis that had doomed the Carthagian invasion of 480. In the background was the historical tendency of the Sicilian Greek cities to exchange information and to follow regional trends in cascades of emulation—a factor that could tilt either in the invaders' favor or against them.

The original agenda of the Athenian assembly meeting at which the fateful decision was made to invade Sicily with a massive force was quite narrowly framed: The assembly was to decide on details of the logistics for a relatively modest military expedition to Sicily, of about the same magnitude as the Athenian force that had campaigned there in the 420s. The expedition's ostensible goals were defensive, to support Segesta and other Athenian allies against expansionism on the part of Syracuse and Selinous. But Nicias, who was an elected general in 415, feared that a modest expedition could quickly escalate, given the ambitions of the Athenian hawks.

In what proved to be a fateful speech to the assembly, Nicias unconstitutionally raised an issue that was not on the Council-approved agenda: the option of canceling the expedition altogether. He also ferociously attacked the character and motivations of Alcibiades, the prominent hawkish leader. Then, when the assembly evinced no interest in scuttling the planned expedition, Nicias tried a second ploy. He raised the stakes of the invasion, arguing that if there must be an expedition to Sicily, it must be a huge one, since only a super-sized force would be able to control the risk of failure. He gambled that the Athenians would prefer the no-expedition option to the high cost of guaranteeing the outcome by voting for a hugely expensive show of military might. As it turned out, he badly misjudged his audience.

In a logical inverse of the irrational (from a cost–benefit, probable-outcome perspective) choice to risk everything on a slight chance of saving everything, made a year before by the oligarchs of Melos, the democratic Athenians proved ready to pay an irrationally high "insurance rate" to lock in the gains they now felt confident they could reap from the expedition. Once again, as Kahneman's experimental work on prospect theory demonstrates, this is a common reaction of people facing the possibility of a large gain. They willingly spend heavily to ensure against a small chance of failure.

In this instance, as Thucydides pointedly noted, the common "prospective gain" response was so strong in the assembly that those citizens who remained opposed were unwilling to express criticism, lest they be labeled unpatriotic: Athens' most important single decision of the long Peloponnesian War was thus made under a cloud of constitutional violation, explicable but potentially disastrous irrationality, and false consensus bought at the cost of stifled dissent. In future years, the Athenians sought to correct the institutional design flaws that had made this decision possible (ch. 9). But for now the die was cast, and the expedition launched. After some setbacks, including the loss of Alcibiades, Athens' most hawkish—and most talented—general to a legal prosecution arising from charges of impiety, the Athenian force settled in to besiege the big and heavily fortified city of Syracuse.

Over the next two years, many things went wrong for the Athenian invaders, while things went right for Syracuse's defenders. In the end, the Sicilian expedition resulted in the greatest military catastrophe in Athenian history. Perhaps with better luck, the expedition could have succeeded. But, contrary to the Athenians' belief that their overinsurance had eliminated risk, the expedition was a very risky gamble from the start. Sicily was not Lesbos, and Syracuse was not Mytilene. As Thucydides points out, Syracuse was, in relevant ways, Athens' twin: The two superpoleis were similar in population; both had big navies; both were experienced at land warfare based on building and defending fortifications. And both were democracies. Although, as we have seen, they were quite different sorts of democracy, Syracuse manifested a very "Athens-like" resilience and social cohesion under conditions of extreme pressure, and likewise a capacity for strategic insight and ruthlessness in exploiting its advantages. Syracuse's population was as productively diverse and innovative as that of Athens. And Athens had no experience with an Athens-like opponent.[61]

The disunity of the Sicilians, anticipated by the Athenians based on their information regarding Sicily's ethnic diversity and its history of interstate rivalry, failed to materialize. Instead the invasion produced a typical Sicilian emulation cascade, in Syracuse's favor: The Athenians were regarded as outsiders, who were no more likely to pursue the interests of the Sicilian poleis if victorious than were the Carthaginians before them. Meanwhile, Athens' primary ally, Segesta, had wildly overrepresented the material support that Athens would be able to muster locally. As a result, the expedition had to be resupplied overseas from Athens—a daunting and hugely expensive prospect as the years dragged on.

The Syracusan defenders furthermore had the advantage of the advice of a Spartan military expert—and the sense to take it. After it became clear to the Spartans that the Sicilian invasion meant that the war with Athens was reengaged, they dispatched Gylippos to Sicily. Like Brasidas and a few other Spartan commanders in this war, Gylippos belied the Corinthian stereotype of the slow, conservative, risk-averse Spartan. A Spartan citizen, he had the standard intensive Spartan training and extensive field experience. But he seems also to have thought through the lessons of both Spartan and Athenian military campaigns of the mid-fifth century onward. In brief, fulfilling the boasts of fifth century sophists, he had mastered a great deal of technical knowledge and he was able to instruct others in what he knew in ways that made them much more effective at gaining their ends. The final outcome of the effective Syracusan resistance was the complete destruction of the Athenian land and sea forces in 413 BCE. Very few of the many thousands of soldiers and sailors who left Athens in 415 ever returned.[62]

FINAL PHASE OF THE WAR

Athens did not give up. Syracuse was slow in taking the war to the mainland: The victory over Athens was followed by resurgent social conflict, a roiling series of political reforms that ended in replacing the democracy with yet another tyranny, and a second Carthaginian attempt to conquer much of the island. Meanwhile, despite building a permanent base in Athenian territory, which denied the Athenians access to much of their land for the rest of the war, the Spartans failed to capitalize on Athens' gigantic setback in the west. Although individual Spartans, like Gylippos, were adroit at achieving tactical and strategic ends, Sparta as a state was as yet unable to act with enough decisiveness and speed to put an end to the war. Athens was still able to draw on a big capital fund that had been kept in reserve for just this sort of emergency. A new Athenian fleet was quickly built and manned. Revolts across the empire were contained. Work recommenced on public projects.

In the immediate aftermath of the catastrophe in Sicily, Athens' democratic government was temporarily replaced by a narrow oligarchy. The regime change followed a series of temporary constitutional adjustments and a terrorist campaign by antidemocratic Athenians. The terrorists assassinated democratic leaders and sought to create fear and suspicion among the citizenry. The coup initially succeeded, but the oligarchs never consolidated their authority. They were rightly suspected by the middling hoplites, the very men they claimed to represent, of planning to allow a Spartan takeover of Athens.

Meanwhile, the main Athenian fleet, now based in Samos, constituted itself as a democratic government in exile and continued military operations in the Aegean. The narrow oligarchy was soon replaced by a broad-based "hoplite republic," which then morphed back into full democracy. The Cleisthenic constitutional order once again proved its robustness in the face of severe shocks. The long-term result of the oligarchic interlude was the reorganization of the Athenian law code. The reform process was not completed until after the end of the war, but it eventually had major implications for the Athenian and, more generally, the Greek economy (ch. 9).[63]

Meanwhile, the Spartans finally realized that the war could not be won without access to capital sufficient to allow them to build and man a fleet capable of challenging the Athenian navy—thereby disrupting Athens' capacity to bring overwhelming force quickly to bear against defecting subjects. The only available source of capital was Persia, and so the Spartans cut a deal: Persia would supply the money. Once Athens was defeated, Sparta would allow subject states of the Athenian empire to be reincorporated into the Persian Empire. Sparta duly built fleets and found competent commanders and skilled rowers, but then, so did the Athenians, who welcomed back the brilliant general Alcibiades—only to expel him again. The war dragged on for years. Naval operations were focused in the northern Aegean and especially at the Hellespont, the vital choke point for Athenian imports of grain from the Black Sea.

Finally, in 406 BCE, the decision by several Athenian generals to pursue the Spartan fleet after a difficult Athenian naval victory led to the loss of many Athenian rowers in a storm.[64] The infuriated Athenian assembly violated ordinary legal procedure by convicting the generals en masse. The next year's college of elected generals was uncharacteristically risk averse. That all-too-predictable strategic quirk allowed the Spartan general to destroy much of Athens' main fleet on a Hellespontine beach at the battle of Aigospotamoi (map 7). This time, Athens lacked the resources to rebuild.[65]

The Athenians surrendered in 404 BCE. The city and its population were spared; the Spartans needed to maintain a counterweight to their sometime ally, Thebes, in central Greece. But Athens' walls were slighted, the fleet destroyed, the empire dismantled. Political authority in the polis was turned over to a hand-picked gang of pro-Spartan antidemocrats. Their leaders styled themselves students of Socrates but quickly proved themselves lawless kleptocrats who killed and exiled at will and confiscated the property of wealthy foreign residents.[66]

Athens' loss in the Peloponnesian War ended the most extensive, in duration and extent, and the most influential, in economic and cultural terms, Greek empire of the classical age. Successor mini-empires, led by Syracuse, Sparta, and Thebes were smaller and more ephemeral. With the defeat of Athens, the desire for strong citizenship and local autonomy seems to have trumped the cost–benefit logic of rational acquiescence to imperial rule. And so the Greek world continued on its path as an outlier in the world history of city-state ecologies, in terms of both extent and robustness of decentralized political authority. As it turned out, no Greek city-state would ever follow the trajectory of the imperial city-states of Babylon and Rome (for example), by successfully transforming a small-state ecology into a great and durable empire.

If the era of Greek efflorescence had coincided with the Athenian imperial age, classical Greece would not be such a notable outlier and we would not need to explain how efflorescence could be sustained in a decentralized ecology of states. The end of the golden age of Greek empire did not, however, mark either the beginning or the end of Greek economic growth and cultural accomplishment. The rise of imperial Athens stimulated growth across the Greek world, but the fall of Athens did not trigger an economic collapse. Indeed, the era that followed the Peloponnesian War, while catastrophically disordered from a Hobbesian "imperative of central authority" perspective, marked the apex of the classical Greek efflorescence.

9

DISORDER AND GROWTH, 403–340 BCE

In the century following the end of the Peloponnesian War, Hellas reached the peak of the classical-era efflorescence. That Hellas would be highly developed by the late fourth century BCE was, however, far from obvious to Greek observers of the immediate postwar generation: Xenophon, Plato, and Isocrates each characterized their Greek world as without leadership, lacking order, and plagued by chaotic wars and endemic civil strife. In the fourth century BCE, Hellas was in effect divided into three zones, each with its own political and economic trajectory. In the first half of the fourth century, each zone saw what look like signal failures when viewed from the perspective of the golden age of empire: In the west, polis republics collapsed and warlords reigned. In central Greece, grand imperial projects came to nothing. In Anatolia, the Great King reasserted Persian control over Greek states.[1]

Whereas the history of the Greek world for much of the fifth century was defined by the rise and fall of an empire in a power struggle among a few superpoleis, fourth century Greek history is a shifting collage, with many significant players engaged in a bewildering range of historically consequential enterprises. If the late classical peak was not the result of commands emanating from a central authority, neither can it be explained by rivalry among a handful of competitors for that role. It was produced by the choices and actions of millions of individuals and hundreds of collectivities, each pursuing advantage in an expanding ecology characterized by fierce competition, rational cooperation, and growing opportunities for profitable specialization.

In the west, the poleis of Sicily suffered an economic and demographic downturn. Major cities were reduced to villages; parts of the countryside were abandoned. Citizen-centered regimes that arose after the fall of the early fifth century tyrannies were overthrown. The political landscape was dominated by a volatile mix of exploitative autocratic states and predatory nonstate military organizations led by skilled and ruthless violence specialists with short time horizons. The sharp downturn in Sicily was, however, followed by a quick recovery in the decades after ca. 340 BCE. Cities were refounded and given republican constitutions. The population of Greek Sicily rebounded with immigration from Italy and central Greece, and agricultural productivity bounced back to fifth century levels. Meanwhile, the creation of new poleis and the Hellenization of native Sicilian settlements continued apace. Almost a third of the Sicilian communities listed in the *Inventory* as poleis (14 of 47) achieved that status between 400 and 323 BCE.

At the other end of the Greek world, the poleis of western Anatolia, formerly subject to Athens, became for a decade subjects of Sparta. With the quick collapse of Sparta's Aegean imperial project after 394 BCE, they reverted to their early fifth century status as imperial possessions of the Great King of Persia. The Anatolian poleis' economic standing was not, however, seriously degraded when they were reintegrated into the Persian Empire. Meanwhile, a substantial number of cities near the Anatolian coast became sufficiently culturally Hellenized to be ranked as Greek poleis in the *Inventory*. The island poleis of the central and northern Aegean were ruled early in the century by Sparta and later taxed by Athens, but in the half century after 355, they experienced an era of especially vigorous efflorescence.[2]

In mainland Greece, the first half of the fourth century was characterized by the surprisingly quick recovery of Athens and by failed attempts by Sparta and Thebes to build their own coercion-intensive empires. The ultimate failure of any fourth century city-state to create a viable system of domination resembling Athens' fifth century empire ensured the continuation of the dispersed-authority polis ecology. Athens was a leader in economically salient postimperial institutional innovations: law-based constitutionalism, opening access, and lowering transaction costs. These innovations helped to sustain economic growth insofar as successful Athenian institutional experiments were emulated by other states.

In the Euboean polis of Eretria in around 400 BCE, a set of reforms reorganized the territory on a deme-tribe basis; the new system was clearly modeled on Athens' Cleisthenic system but was adapted to local Eretrian needs.[3] Meanwhile, in Achaea and Aetolia, as in other regions of Hellas, informal cooperative intraregional relations deepened to become the institutional foundations of federal states. In one sense, federalist projects may be seen as recreating Athens' late sixth/early fifth century success in "getting and staying big" by implementing the system of demes and artificial tribes (ch. 7). But the fourth century Greek federal leagues had distinctive institutional fea-

MAP 8 *Aegean Greek world, early to mid-fourth century* BCE.

tures that were quite different from anything Athens had previously under-taken. The most successful of the Greek leagues developed new forms of two-tier (local and regional) citizenship and managed the fine balance be-tween assertive central authority and independent constituent states. As the American Founders realized in the late eighteenth century, and as contempo-rary political scientists have demonstrated, finding that balance is the key to creating a federal system capable of robust growth.[4]

Across Hellas, the fourth century saw deepening recognition on the part of people and states of the essential role played by specialization and exper-tise in gaining individual and collective ends, as well as an increasing self-consciousness about the value of relative advantage. Due to greater demand, experts were more mobile than ever. In at least some regions, increased ex-change, promoted by trade-friendly institutional changes, drove transaction costs lower. Elsewhere, as in Sicily before 340, transaction costs soared as a result of endemic political disorder and the collapse of rule-egalitarian constitutional regimes.

Heightened levels of individual expertise and technological innovation were especially apparent in military affairs. Strategic planning became more sophisticated as generals became more adept at integrating light infantry, cavalry, archers, and slingers into field armies. The availability of mercenaries made year-round campaigning easier and promoted the development of strategies aimed at undermining the enemy's economic infrastructure. The art of siegecraft advanced in technique and technology. Artillery was invented: First came nontorsion, crossbow-type catapults and then, by midcentury, more powerful torsion, spring-type catapults. In response to these advances in siegecraft, poleis adopted new forms of military architecture: City walls were rebuilt to accommodate higher towers, shuttered windows for artillery fire, and more elaborate outworks. In the countryside, fortresses and watchtowers were constructed in an attempt to protect rural populations and vital resources. Meanwhile, foreign policy decision-making became more sophisticated, and new institutions promoted interstate cooperation.[5]

The fourth century saw bold new experiments in the arts and letters, the flowering of moral thought, and the emergence of new perpetual nonstate civil organizations. The philosophical schools founded at Athens by Plato and Aristotle exemplified several of these trends. But Athens was not the only great center of learning and art: The postimperial era saw the multiplication of centers of enterprise that pioneered advances in architecture and the visual arts; in historiography and poetry; in philosophy and rhetoric; and in natural science and engineering.[6]

While the polis proved robust as a social, political, and cultural form, Greek elites, and some who expressly rejected elite values (e.g., Diogenes the Cynic), found more freedom to express their individuality. Individuals, rather than collectivities, were now more likely to be regarded by the Greeks as primary agents of historical change. Although tyranny and oligarchy remained viable alternatives, democracy became a more prevalent form of political organization. Meanwhile, democracy itself was evolving. As exemplified by Athens, democracies were more willing to offer extraordinary public honors to individuals whose actions benefited the community. At the same time, the state also placed greater emphasis on the outstanding individual's legal responsibility for the public effects of his public speech and actions. It was an enhanced conception of the individual's personal responsibility for the effects of his speech—not religious intolerance or fear of dissident intellectuals—that accounts for the conviction of Socrates by an Athenian court in 399 BCE.[7]

In this chapter, we look first at the historical development of mainland and Aegean Greece through mid-century. The apparent confusion and disorder arising from interstate conflict is counterpoised to the expansion of the Greek culture zone, more interstate emulation of successful institutional practices, deeper integration of regional confederations of poleis, and the opening of access that is especially evident at Athens. We then turn, more briefly, to the fall and rise of the poleis of Sicily and to the fate of the Anatolian poleis under Persian rule. In the next chapter (ch. 10), we consider the question of Greece's "political fall": Why and how, in the era of kings Philip II and Alexander III (359–323 BCE), did the Macedonian state come to dominate the poleis of the Greek mainland, and then, in the course of the conquest of the Persian Empire, the entirety of the eastern Greek world? In the final chapter (ch. 11), we answer the question of why the loss of independence in foreign policy by Athens and the other major classical poleis did *not* mark an abrupt end to the era of Greek efflorescence.

SPARTA'S FAILED EMPIRE

In the immediate aftermath of the Peloponnesian War, Sparta had improved its position dramatically: The victory over Athens had eliminated, so it appeared, the grave threat of the continued growth of a dynamic, democratic rival. The victory had been won at the cost of a distasteful deal with the minions of the Great King of Persia. The king had funded the buildup of a Sparta-controlled navy capable of taking on the naval forces of Athens—but his price was Persian control of the Greek poleis of western Anatolia. Immediately following Sparta's defeat of Athens, the King of Persia was, however, in no position to assert his claim. The old king had died in 405; his successor, Artaxerxes II, was immediately faced with an uprising in Egypt. The revolt broke out in 404 and would last for the whole of Artaxerxes' long reign; Egypt was not regained until 343 BCE.[8]

King Artaxerxes soon had an even more pressing problem: His ambitious younger brother, Cyrus II, sought the throne for himself. Cyrus had been chief of Persian operations for western Anatolia during the final stages of the Peloponnesian War, and he knew the Greek world very well. Most saliently, he had a keen appreciation for the capacities of Greek hoplite infantrymen. After the end of the Peloponnesian War, there was a buyer's market in experienced mercenaries. Cyrus bought himself a big army, including more than 10,000 Greeks. They were led by a Spartan general working ostensibly as a freelance but with the tacit approval of Sparta's government.

Cyrus's Greek troops were victorious in what could have been a decisive battle, fought in 401 BCE at Cunaxa in central Mesopotamia. Cyrus himself was, however, killed when, leading a cavalry charge, he was cut off from his army. The Greek commanders were subsequently assassinated in the course of negotiations with the king's agents. Bereft of leaders and a cause, the surviving Greeks fought their way north through Mesopotamia to Anatolia and the south coast of the Black Sea. The expedition was made famous by Xenophon's autobiographical narrative (*Anabasis*). The Greeks' victory at Cunaxa and their long march through the heart of the Persian Empire proved to anyone paying attention that military expertise was widely distributed among Greek mercenaries, available in bulk, and extremely effective in practice. That lesson was taken to heart by the Great King, his restless agent-governors, the rebels in Egypt, and the Carthaginians—among others.[9]

With Athens weakened and Persia distracted, Sparta seized control of Athens' former subject states, establishing garrisons and setting up tightly controlled pro-Spartan governments and garrisons. The Spartans thus cheerfully ignored both their agreement with the Persian king and their wartime rhetoric in which they had claimed to be fighting to liberate the Greeks from imperial despotism. When, beginning in 400 BCE, Artaxerxes reasserted his territorial claims on the basis of the deal with Sparta, a series of Spartan generals, leading mostly mercenary forces, successfully held off the royal proxy armies. Those armies were led by the Persian governors of the western Anatolian provinces, and the governors displayed a notable lack of consistent zeal. The Persian king's principal-agent problem (ch. 8) remained unsolved. And so it appeared for a time that Sparta might simply replace Athens as the master of the Aegean world.

This was not good news for the Greeks of western Anatolia. Sparta had all the bad features of an imperial overlord, with none of the redeeming features that had, for much of the fifth century, made acquiescence to hegemony a rational strategy for Athens' subjects. Unlike Athens, Sparta did not play the game of empire with a long time horizon. The newly established pro-Spartan governments were brutally exploitative—the Thirty at Athens (next section) were typical in their predatory policies. Nor did Sparta offer its subjects the compensation of low transaction costs: Sparta did not have its own coinage that might take the place of Athens' owls as a common currency. Nor was Sparta capable of providing the Aegean with a central market to replace Piraeus. Finally, although we have no evidence one way or another, there is little reason to believe that Sparta used its sea power to provide reliable security against piracy. In brief, if counterfactually Sparta had enjoyed a two-generation run as a master of the eastern Aegean, it seems unlikely that this would have sustained, much less promoted, the classical efflorescence. But, in actuality, Sparta's Aegean empire lasted no more than a decade.[10]

King Artaxerxes eventually responded to the Spartan threat by resorting to a tried-and-true approach to securing Persia's interests on its western frontier. He identified Greeks whose goals aligned with his own and incentivized them, with Persian funds, to act in ways that would achieve his ends. To carry out anti-Spartan naval operations, the king used the Athenian general Conon, who had been living in Cyprus, at the court of a semi-independent dynast, Evagoras, who held the important Cyprian city of Salamis in the king's name.[11] Conon was a skilled admiral and was happy to take command of a Persian-funded fleet that could be used to hurt the interests of the Spartans and to further those of his Athenian compatriots. The upshot was a naval battle fought off the coast of Knidos (1903: just southeast of the island of Cos: map 8) in 394, which broke Spartan sea power in the north Aegean at a stroke and ended Sparta's overseas imperial project. The Aegean island states went their own way; the Persian king retook the poleis of western Anatolia.

Conon was next dispatched to mainland Greece, where he dispensed Persian funds to those poleis that were by now finding Sparta's imperial ambitions and high-handed tactics intolerable: These included Sparta's old enemies Athens and Argos but also some of Sparta's former allies, including the major states of Thebes and Corinth. The resulting Corinthian War ensured that the Spartan king, Agesilaus, who had campaigned until 394 with some effect in western Anatolia against such of the Persian governors as remained loyal to Artaxerxes, would be tied up in Greece indefinitely. The Corinthian War continued indecisively until 387, when the Great King discovered another Greek state whose interests were now well aligned with his own . . . Sparta.[12]

The Spartans and the king of Persia were once again united by their opposition to the Athenians, who had made a quick recovery after the low point of 404. Athens' walls were rebuilt, and a new, albeit smaller, fleet was commissioned. Athenian generals began campaigning in the northern Aegean—where Athens was interested in regaining key strategic positions. These positions included the islands of Lemnos (1502–503), Imbros (1483), and Skyros (1521), which, together, enabled Athens to patrol the essential grain route from the Bosphorus to Piraeus, and, at least in aspiration, Amphipolis (1553), Sestos (1627), and other strategic towns on the south shore of Thrace and in the northern Aegean (map 8). Athens also reimposed a 10% tax on shipping coming through the Bosphorus and an additional 5% tax on at least Thasos (1526) and Klazomenai (1847). The revival of Athens' Aegean ambitions was not welcomed by Spartans or Persians, nor was the potential rise of a Boeotian superpolis in central Greece. Thebes, the biggest single polis in the region, had long sought to consolidate the poleis of Boeotia under Theban hegemony—and the Corinthian War was providing an impetus to that end.[13]

In 387, the king of Persia and the Spartans declared a "common (all eastern Hellas) truce." It became known as the "King's Peace" because its terms were to be enforced by the Great King, in conjunction with Sparta and any of the Greeks who saw fit to join him (willing, that is, to use his money to hire mercenaries). The terms of the peace called for the cessation of current hostilities and for perpetual self-rule for all east Greek poleis outside of Anatolia (Anatolian poleis remained subject to the king). The island poleis of the Aegean were to remain independent. An exception to the autonomy clause was allowed for Sparta's possession of the towns of Laconia and of Messenia (ch. 6). Another exception, granted to buy Athenian acquiescence, allowed Athens to keep Lembros, Imbros, and Skyros. But the Boeotian confederacy was to be broken up into its constituent poleis. Also disallowed was an innovative union of the two big poleis of Corinth and Argos. They had made substantial steps toward conjoining into what would have been a second Peloponnesian superpolis. Sparta was now back in the driver's seat in the Greek mainland: likely to cause trouble for its rivals but quite unlikely to bother the king, who was now securely in possession of the Anatolian poleis.[14]

The Spartans quickly moved to take advantage of the situation, attacking mainland states within and outside the Peloponnese, forcing regime changes when they suited Sparta's interest and seizing and garrisoning Thebes. Among Sparta's most aggressive moves was the breakup of the major Arcadian city of Mantinea (i281: size 4), employing a strong reading of the autonomy clause of the King's Peace to force the Mantineans to disperse to villages in the countryside. Sparta was beginning to demonstrate some of the taste for social engineering that had characterized the Sicilian tyrants of the early fifth century.

In response, the Athenians built a new anti-Spartan alliance. In 377, after an abortive invasion of Attica by a rogue Spartan commander went unpunished by Spartan authorities, Athens inaugurated a second naval league. This was a sort of anti-Delian League in that its target was Sparta, not Persia, and its charter was carefully designed to prevent the reemergence of Athenian imperialism. The league states, eventually numbering about 70, were to provide funds, as well as ships and men. The league prevented Sparta from rebuilding a credible naval force, but it never became an effective instrument of Athenian policy in the way that the Delian League had been, and it was never run at a profit to Athens.[15]

Meanwhile, in 378 BCE anti-Spartan Thebans, with Athenian help, expelled the Spartan garrison from Thebes. Under the dynamic leadership of the ambitious generals Pelopidas and Epaminondas, the Thebans set out to rebuild their Boeotian League and to challenge Spartan supremacy on land. Their timing was good. Sparta was by now an empty shell. The Lycurgan social system (ch. 6), devised in a very different era and aimed at securing somewhat more modest ends, proved a bad fit for the challenges of the fourth century. Sparta's soldiers were still, man for man, equal to their ancestors as warriors and in battlefield know-how—as proved by the frequency with which Spartan commanders were hired as mercenary commanders across and beyond the Greek world. But, having recently and repeatedly demonstrated their willingness to break interstate agreements as soon as it suited their interests, the Spartans were in a poor position to make the new and credible commitments that would have been necessary to sustain an extensive hegemony.

Like imperial Athens, the Spartans lacked a compelling ideology to support their transparently self-serving policies. The old claim to be the liberators of the Greeks had been shown up, time and again, for the lie it always had been. Spartans could not lean on the rationality of acquiescence. There was little reason for other states to find Sparta's commitments credible. Even their willingness to support ruling coalitions that they had themselves put into power was unreliable—as the Thirty at Athens discovered in 403 (next section). Worst of all, there were not many Spartan Equals left to do the fighting when it came down to physical coercion.

The numbers of Spartans had fallen catastrophically as a result of high war casualties, low birth rates, and downward status mobility—demotion from the status of Spartan to Inferior due to individual failures of duty on the battlefield or in provisioning the regimental dining clubs. Downward mobility was driven by growing economic inequality. Writing in the late fourth century, Aristotle noted that, "some Spartans have come to have far too many possessions, while others very few indeed; as a result, the land has fallen into the hands of a small number . . . although the land was sufficient to support 1500 cavalry and 30,000 hoplites, the number [of Spartans] fell to below 1000."[16] By the 370s, forty years before Aristotle wrote those lines, the ranks of the Spartan Equals had dropped from a high of some 9,000 in the sixth century, to perhaps 1,300. Increasingly, the burden of fighting Sparta's wars fell on non-Spartans: "marginals," liberated helots, or hired mercenaries. And thus, Sparta was quickly losing its one all-important relative advantage: the certainty that in an open-field infantry battle, the Spartan army would always win.

There had already been several skirmishes at which small units of Spartan hoplites had proved vulnerable, both to Athenian light-armed troops using sophisticated mobile tactics and to well-led Theban hoplites. But the day of reckoning came in 371, in Boeotia at the Battle of Leuctra. There, a Theban army, using a new wedge formation of heavy infantry and spearheaded by a crack unit of 300 highly trained citizen-soldiers ("the Sacred Band"), routed a Spartan army in the open field.

The era of Spartan supremacy in mainland Greece ended abruptly at Leuctra. Pericles' dream of knocking Sparta back to a modest regional power was achieved soon thereafter, when a Theban army marched into the Peloponnesus to found a new capital city for the Messenians—and fortified it with a spectacular state-of-the-art city wall. With the creation of Messene (i318), the Messenians were no longer helots but citizens of a substantial and defensible polis of their own. When added to the Peloponnesian states already prone to hostility toward Sparta—Arcadians, Eleans, Argives, Corinthians, and Achaeans—Messene proved an adequate counter to attempts at Spartan resurgence. With the eclipse of Sparta's hegemony, the poleis of the Peloponnese fully reentered the Greek world of dispersed authority—with substantial positive knock-on effects for overall Greek efflorescence.[17]

ATHENS' INSTITUTIONAL INNOVATIONS AND CIVIC CULTURE

Among the surprises of the post-Peloponnesian War era was the quick recovery of Athens. In 404, the crushing defeat in the war had been quickly followed by the imposition of a Spartan puppet government, "the Thirty." Like other postwar Sparta-imposed governments, the Thirty sought to impose a rough form of centralized autocracy. With a coalition that included as its enforcers young thugs and upper-class cavalrymen, the Thirty began a reign of terror. They confiscated property from wealthy resident foreigners, exiled thousands of their fellow citizens, and employed pseudojudicial processes to execute anyone who stood in their way. By some accounts, they killed more than 1,500 Athenians in a few months.

A democratic counterinsurgency quickly emerged, based initially at the deme of Phyle in northern Attica (map 5). Gaining momentum with early victories over field armies sent against them by the Thirty, the democratic rebels shifted their base of operations to Athens' port town of Piraeus. At a major battle in central Piraeus, the forces of the Thirty were again defeated, and their leader, Critias (Plato's uncle and a sometime student of Socrates), was killed. Divisions among Sparta's ruling elite prevented a decisive Spartan response. Athens' democracy was restored. Proposals to expand and to restrict the citizen body were defeated. The restored citizen assembly undertook to pay back the debts that had been incurred by the Thirty to pay for a Spartan garrison.

To the surprise of many, who expected tit-for-tat retaliation by the democrats against their enemies, an amnesty was declared. The events of the civil war were officially (if not actually) to be forgotten. The amnesty forbade the use of the courts or other state institutions by those seeking vengeance on Athenian supporters of the Thirty.[18]

Meanwhile, legal reforms that had begun in 410, after the first oligarchic coup, were recommenced. The main work was largely complete by 399, by which time the laws of Athens were codified and made accessible in a new public archive and the legislative process was significantly revised. The Solonian–Cleisthenic system was largely retained, but according to the new constitutional rules, all decrees of the assembly must now be in conformity with the written (and now properly codified and archived) fundamental laws of the state. Those basic laws could be revised: Each year, the assembly held a vote on the laws, deciding section by section whether revision was called for. But new fundamental law would now be made, not by the assembly directly, but by a large, lottery-chosen, jurylike, body of "lawmakers" (*nomothetai*), over age 30.

Any proposed new law must be advertised for a statutory period on whitened boards in the agora, where any citizen who wished could review the proposal. The new lawmaking procedure was triallike, in that proposed legal changes were publicly debated between advocates of change and state-appointed defenders of the existing law. The lawmakers then voted to determine the result. The proposer of any decree of the assembly thought to be in contradiction of the laws (*paranomon*) could be indicted before the people's court, as could the proposer of a new law thought to be inexpedient (*me epitedeion*). If the proposer was condemned by the court, the decree or law in question was invalidated. The upshot was a democratic brake on the legislative process of democracy.

The legal changes were motivated, at least in part, by Athenians' recognition that the fifth century democratic process had led to some bad outcomes that might have been avoided by better process. The new procedure clarified and codified the fundamental rules, subordinated day-to-day decisions of democratic bodies to those rules, and set up incentives that discouraged clever and articulate public speakers from seeking to end-run the rules. The constitutional reforms of the late fifth and early fourth century are sometimes characterized as a moderation of, or retreat from, the original radical spirit of participatory democracy, but they are better understood as a refinement of the Athenians' understanding of democracy as collective self-governance by citizens. By limiting the authority of the assembly, the Athenians were not limiting the authority of the demos. Rather they were seeking to enable the demos, as a collectivity, to judge well—to choose the course of action most consonant with the deeper principles of the democracy and most likely to further the common interests of the citizenry—and of the polis.[19]

The new constitutional order precipitated changes in the nature of the game played between elite speakers and mass audiences. As before, the Council of 500, with its membership chosen by lot from across the regions of Attica, set the agenda for meetings of the citizen assembly and often made recommendations on policy. And, as before, social networks encouraged by Council and magisterial service helped a large and diverse citizen body to make good use of expertise (ch. 7). But over the course of the fifth century, a weakness had appeared in the original system: a potentially perverse relationship between skilled speakers and mass audiences. As Thucydides, Plato, and other Athenian writers critical of democracy pointed out, the skills of public speakers were being sharpened by the kinds of expertise taught by the sophists. Meanwhile, mass audiences developed a taste for rhetorical pyrotechnics. With no brake on the process, the dynamic of public speakers seeking influence and honors, and mass audiences eager to be entertained and willing to be flattered sometimes led to catastrophic policy mistakes.[20]

Before the constitutional changes, an assembly speaker who did not like the Council's agenda or its recommendations might break the rules by introducing a topic outside the agenda. Or he might propose a superficially attractive but dangerous alternative to the Council's proposal—relying on his expert skills in the arts of rhetoric to sway the assemblymen in his favor. With hindsight, the decision to send a supersized expedition to Sicily in 415 could be recognized as a prime example of constitutional violation, one that was accompanied by rhetorical excess and levels of popular enthusiasm that suppressed dissident voices (ch. 8). But now, assembly speakers confronted the likelihood that if they broke the procedural rules or proposed a measure that was either illegal (contravening the standing laws) or inexpedient (retrospectively seen as rashly imprudent policy), they would be brought to trial by their political rivals. The judges would be drawn from the same citizen body as were the assemblymen, but the young citizens (under age 30) were excluded, and the fever-pitch excitement of the assembly meeting would have cooled. The new rules, in short, encouraged each politician to anticipate the consequences of his actions in light of others' likely responses—to "look a little further down the game tree," recognize that if he violated the rules his rivals had a winning move, and act accordingly.[21]

Athenian mass audiences could for their part collectively use the revised rules of the game to make better use of expertise. We may assume that, given the high stakes of policy-making and the absence of organized political parties, most Athenian citizens attending an assembly charged with deciding a matter of grave moment were sincerely seeking the best outcome: That is, they were there to promote what they took to be common interests, rather than a narrowly partisan agenda, in the assumption that their private interests would be furthered by the public goods of collective security and welfare. As Thucydides' Pericles had repeatedly pointed out, there would be no chance for Athenians to pursue private interests if the polis failed as a collective enterprise.

That said, the opinions of the wealthy elite and the mass of ordinary citizens concerning, for example, what would constitute optimal levels of taxation, were not identical. Speakers in the assembly were drawn primarily from the ranks of the elite—men who were considerably richer and also more highly educated than the median assemblyman. Highly educated, well-informed speakers offered a potential advantage to the state: As we have seen (ch. 7), if and when the Athenians attended properly to true experts, the polis stood to do better. But on the other hand, if the educated elite used their near-monopoly as assembly speakers to warp debates in the direction of the interests of the wealthy and against those of ordinary citizens, the democracy would quickly unravel.

In the course of the fourth century, the two-way communication of elites and masses at Athens was refined through regular interchanges in Council, assembly, and courtroom against the background of the new constitutional rules. What emerged from these interchanges was a set of informal but clearly articulated discursive rules of expression. By sticking to the rules, elite speakers had the opportunity to win the respectful attention, and the votes, of the citizen masses. In order to win that chance, each speaker was required to demonstrate, by the everyday conduct of his life and by his rhetorical self-presentation, over time and in both legislative and legal forums, that he was worthy of the citizens' trust. He must prove himself to be at once elite and democratic: He must show that he was both a highly educated expert in the relevant policy area and that he was fully committed to the core democratic values of personal liberty, political equality, and civic dignity. He must demonstrate that his loyalties were to the democratic constitution, the polis, and the demos—not an elite class or to aristocratic cronies. He must show himself to be an independent statesman, not a spokesman for a clique of powerful men. And he must prove himself to be incorruptible: His public opinions must be his own, not those of some shadowy paymaster.

Those Athenian politicians who successfully walked the tightrope by presenting themselves as both sufficiently elite and staunchly democratic were granted considerable privilege by their fellow citizens: They were accorded the status of recognized political leaders: treated as reliable experts, worthy advisors, loyal statesmen—and rewarded accordingly. Those who failed the test were discarded. The game was tough and the stakes high. Many failed, but, given the competitive culture of the democratic city, there were always other elite competitors ready to enter the lists in hopes of gaining influence, honor, and the respectful attention of the demos.

The upshot of iterated play of the mass–elite game of public speech was that the increasingly sophisticated governmental institutions of the democratic polis were complemented by an equally sophisticated culture of public discourse. Democratic institutions and culture were, on the whole, effective at achieving two ends essential to the long-term success of the polis: making good (innovative, but not excessively risky) policy and reducing the level of discord and dissonance between elites who were intensely engaged in public affairs and the masses of ordinary citizens. Individual Athenians could count on a reasonable stability in the basic rules (institutional and discursive) and thus could calculate risks and make reasonable personal decisions about the future accordingly. The community of citizens could look forward to the chance to consider innovative policy options arising from brisk competition between would-be leaders, without being too worried about falling prey to a dangerously charismatic leader.[22]

There was ongoing tension between Athenian elites and masses, as well as among rivalrous elites. And it is not the case that all fourth century Athenian policy was wise. But the overall positive feedback loop between democratic institutions and democratic discursive culture did mean that the way was open to innovative and effective policy-making and that postwar Athens was able to achieve a high-level, productive, and stable social and political equilibrium. That equilibrium appears striking when it is contrasted, for example, with the extreme volatility of fourth century Syracuse—which had seemed to be Athens' twin in the mid-fifth century as a superpolis democracy.

We consider, in the section of this chapter on opening access to institutions, a few key Athenian innovations that were instrumental in enabling the democratic polis to rebuild its economy, finance public programs, and thereby to maintain security relative to dangerous rivals and to enhance the welfare of residents. Meanwhile, there was no internal challenge by disaffected elites to Athens' democratic order in the 80 years between the overthrow of the Thirty and the top-down replacement of democracy with a broad-based oligarchy by ruling Macedonians after the Lamian War in 322 BCE (ch. 11). In his analytic history of Athenian political development (*Ath. Pol.* 41.2), Pseudo-Aristotle describes this period as a single constitutional era and as the culmination of democracy as he knew it.

CONFUSION AND DISORDER: MAINLAND AND
AEGEAN GREECE TO 352 BCE

The dramatic victory of Thebes at Leuctra was won without Athens' help. Athens and Thebes had found common ground in the early fourth century, when faced with the machinations of an expansionist Sparta. But the quick rise of Theban power in the mid-370s rebooted the old and deep rivalry between the two central Greek neighbors. Athens had, after all, tried to force all Boeotia into its empire in the mid-fifth century. Thebes had reciprocated by stripping rural Attica of movable assets in the late Peloponnesian War and by urging the Spartans to reduce Athens to a sheep walk in 404. Relations worsened when, in 372, Thebes for the second time sacked Plataea, Athens' traditional ally in southwestern Boeotia. The town had only recently been refounded after its destruction early in the Peloponnesian War.

Thebes had long sought to achieve superpolis status by asserting authority over the poleis of Boeotia. A Boeotian confederation of a sort had existed in the sixth century, before the Persian Wars; it was reinvented on federalist lines in the fifth century. That federation had been broken up by the terms of the King's Peace of 387. Now the Thebans were determined to rebuild it once again—but this time with an organizational structure that would enable Thebes to control the smaller poleis of Boeotia and to mobilize Boeotia's military capacity under Theban generals. As in the origins of the Delian League, the founding ideal of the new Boeotian League was cooperative defense against a common enemy. As with the Delian League and Athens, the Boeotian League quickly became an instrument wielded to ends determined by its dominant member.[23]

With Sparta out of the way after Leuctra, Thebes grew more actively belligerent toward Athens. In the 360s, Thebes' leader, Epaminondas, threatened invasion of Attica by land and was reported to be planning a 100-ship navy that could potentially disrupt Aegean trade routes. The second Athenian naval league, which had been formed with the purpose of resisting imperial Sparta, might have been dissolved now that Spartan power had been broken, but it was not. The league remained important for the security of Athens and that of other grain-importing states. Athens was a regular importer of large quantities of wheat and was therefore dependent on maintaining the overseas routes from grain-producing regions around the Black Sea, through the Bosphorus and Hellespont, to Piraeus.

There were other threats to Aegean states that valued their independence and depended on the free movement of people and goods across the eastern Mediterranean: Persia was now ready and able to exert its power beyond the

Anatolian coast, as demonstrated by its takeover of Samos, in contravention of the autonomy clause of the King's Peace, some time before 366. In that year, Athens wrested Samos from Persian control. Athens had developed an especially close relationship with Samos during the late Peloponnesian War; now the Athenians settled a group of cleruchs on Samos. In the 360s, Athens also attempted, but failed, to regain control of Amphipolis (i553), its former colony on the south Thracian coast. Athens had more success at Potidaia (i598) on the Chalkidike Peninsula, (map 9) which accepted Athenian cleruchs in 362. Athens also took Sestos (i672) on the Thracian Chersonese on the west side of the Bosphorus (map 8). Each of these cities occupied a strategic location on the grain route. Athens' aims in these military actions could be interpreted in two ways. For the Athenians, it may have been primarily a matter of regaining key strategic assets. For nervous allies and suspicious rivals, it might appear that Athens was seeking to rebuild an overseas empire.[24]

Persian governors of the empire's western provinces were, for their part, becoming more independent and ambitious. A protracted series of revolts against the authority of the king in Anatolia (the so-called Satraps' Revolt) drew in large numbers of Greek mercenaries—and provided employment for expert Greek generals, including several from Athens. Although the revolt was eventually suppressed, the Persian king's principal-agent problem clearly had not yet been solved.

Among Persia's restless governors was Mausolus, who ruled Caria in southwestern Anatolia during the second quarter of the fourth century. Under Mausolus, many cities of Caria became more Hellenized than before; they were becoming poleis and increasingly were viewed as such by their residents and by other Greek cities. Mausolus not only allowed but actively encouraged the process of Hellenization. He was in the forefront of a group of powerful Persian governors who adapted various aspects of Greek culture to their own purposes—spectacularly so in his great tomb: the original Mausoleum. But Hellenization in Caria went deeper, including the active employment by the dynast himself of standard practices of interpolis Greek diplomacy; in essence in his interactions with Greek poleis, Mausolus acted as if he himself *were* a polis. Mausolus proved adept at playing the game of Aegean power politics, building diplomatic relations with some of Athens' key allies and challenging the Athenian navy for supremacy in the Aegean.[25]

Thebes meanwhile sought to expand its influence into various parts of the Greek mainland. In northern Greece, Theban armies fought on the side of Thessalian cities against Alexander of Pherai, a dynast who, following the lead of his father, Jason, sought to unite Thessaly under his leadership. The king of Macedon got involved, leading ultimately to an imposed settlement according to which, in 368, the Macedonian king was forced to offer hostages to the Thebans. Among the noble Macedonians sent to Thebes was an observant teenager named Philip. After spending several years in the close company of resourceful and experienced Theban military commanders, Philip was allowed to return to Macedon. Years later, as Philip II, King of Macedon, he would radically change the power equation of the Greek world (ch. 10). Meanwhile, in central Greece, the Thebans seized Oropos, a disputed district on the eastern Athenian–Boeotian border that was home to an important sanctuary (map 5). In southern Greece, Thebes extended its zone of influence into Achaea and Arcadia. Pushback by Athens and a coalition of Peloponnesian states set up what could have been a decisive battle near Mantinea in 362. The Thebans came out ahead in the battle, but Epaminondas, their dominant and charismatic leader, was killed.[26]

In the concluding words of his narrative of this period of Greek history, the Athenian polymath, Xenophon, offered what might be read as an obituary for the dream that a hegemonic polis might impose order on the Greek world:

[After the battle of Mantinea] the opposite of what everyone believed would happen came to pass. For since nearly all the peoples of Greece had foregathered and formed themselves into opposing lines, there was no one who did not suppose that if a battle were fought, those who proved victorious would be the rulers and those who were defeated would be their subjects. Yet the god so ordered it that . . . neither side was found to be any better off, in regards to territory, or city, or empire . . . indeed, there was even more confusion and disorder in Greece after the battle than before.

—*Hellenica 7.5.26–27, trans. Brownson (Loeb) adapted*

The confusion and disorder to which Xenophon alluded included a long drawn-out conflict between Athens and Philip II, who became King of Macedon in 359, initially centered on the control of Amphipolis. We consider Philip's remarkable rise in the next chapter (ch. 10). Suffice it to say here that he outmaneuvered the Athenians and seized Amphipolis in 358. Athens made up for that defeat with a quick campaign that induced the states of Euboea, divided between pro-Theban and pro-Athenian factions, to rejoin the Athenian alliance. But this success was in turn overbalanced by a costly war (the so-called "Social War") against a coalition of major Aegean states, including Rhodes (11000), Chios (1640), Cos (1497), and Byzantion (1674). Athens' former allies were now allied with Mausolus of Caria. The fighting went against the Athenians; they acknowledged their failure to hold together the league with a truce in 355. The Social War was a wake-up call for any Athenian who might still have dreamed of a restored empire. For his part, Mausolus incorporated a number of former states of Athens' league into his own sphere. Apparently having realized that strict control of the western governors was impossible, the Great King allowed his ostensible agent to act as a principal in his own interest—so long as those interests remained directed outward, toward the Aegean.

Meanwhile, in central Greece, war broke out between Thebes and the loosely confederated poleis of Phocis (region 9: map 9). The Phocians, who controlled the territory around the Panhellenic sanctuary of Delphi, had neither the capital nor the population (ca. 85,000 among some 26 poleis: appendix I) to take on Thebes with their own resources. They resorted, however, to taking treasure (characterized as loans) from the rich store of dedications at Delphi. This enabled the Phocians to hire enough mercenaries to fight the Thebans to a virtual standstill. The war expanded into Thessaly, with Athens coming in on the side of the Phocians and Philip II against them. Philip won a major victory in Thessaly at the Battle of the Crocus Field in 352, but the Athenians held the pass of Thermopylae against him. Once again, what might have been a decisive battle appeared only to add to disorder and confusion.[27]

EXPANSION AND INTEGRATION

As the quote from Xenophon in the previous section suggests, it is easy to regard the postimperial fourth century as a descent into chaos, a sad failure after the high hopes of the golden age of empire. Descent was no doubt a possible historical trajectory, as is evident from the section of this chapter that traces the fall and rise of Syracuse and Greek Sicily. Historians of classical Greece once embraced a descent narrative for fourth century Hellas as a whole. But a general decline is sharply at odds with the evidence, reviewed in chapter 4, demonstrating that the fourth century saw the acme of the classical-era Greek efflorescence.

When we look beyond the roiling surface of battles and personalities, we can see that there were, in the fourth century, several important and related developments that promoted flourishing: The ongoing expansion of the Greek culture zone, institutionalization of productive interdependence among states, opening access to institutions, and expanded employment of experts to further public purposes. While these developments had quite uneven effects across the Greek world, taken together they conduced to promote the conditions of specialization and human capital investment, productive competition, low-cost emulation, and growth of social capital—all in a context of lower transaction costs. Those conditions in turn sustained and enhanced the classical efflorescence.[28]

First, and at the most general level, the Greek decentralized ecology of states was growing—due not only to natural demographic increase but also to the embrace of salient elements of Greek culture by societies at the expanding frontiers of the Greek world. In the far west, the colony of Massalia was the conduit for Greek exports, especially wine, into what is now southern France. In Italy, the Etruscans had long been eager importers of Greek art and other artifacts of Greek culture; now that taste was extending to the Romans, who would prove, over the next centuries, to be ardent (if often conflicted) consumers of Greek culture. In Macedonia, the royal family, and the elite generally, were increasingly culturally Hellenized. Further to the north and east, fourth century Greek coins and artifacts have been found in substantial numbers in hoards in Bulgaria, Romania, and Ukraine. The Greek cities on the coasts of the Black Sea promoted a taste for Greek goods among populations in what is now south Russia and Georgia. That taste could be satisfied by production and sale of grain for the Greek market: Around the Black Sea, new states were emerging, at least in part as a result of the potential opened up by a lucrative exchange of grain (among other products, including slaves) for Greek goods and services. The rulers of some of these emerging states were deeply involved in diplomacy with the Greek poleis—notably with Athens.

In Anatolia, Greek culture was likewise moving inland and down the coast. Syria and Egypt (still in revolt from Persia) were increasingly drawn into a Greek sphere of exchange—local Egyptian and Syrian dynasts minted massive numbers of imitation Athenian owls, many of which circulated in Aegean markets—including Athens. Carthage, while often at war with Greeks in the fourth century, was considered by Aristotle to be sufficiently Greek-like to be discussed in his *Politics* and included in his survey of polis constitutional histories. As we have seen, at the margins of the Greek world, Hellenization proceeded far enough for the editors of the *Inventory* to regard a number of "barbarian" cities as properly reclassified as Greek poleis.

The adoption of Greek culture by non-Greek peoples tended to be, at least at first, at the elite level. Even among the most ardently philhellenic elites, Greek culture was never simply taken up wholesale: Hellenization was a process of selective adaptation rather than wholesale cultural adoption. And it is important to remember that influence went both ways—Greeks were well aware that they themselves had borrowed and adapted many aspects of non-Greek culture. Yet, while "Hellenization" is inevitably a subjective judgment resting on imperfect evidence, it captures something very real and historically important about the Mediterranean world of the fourth century BCE. For our purposes, the main point is that markets for Greek goods and services were expanding more quickly than was the core Greek population itself. To the extent that these expanded markets enabled Greeks to intensify specialization and exploit relative advantages, the expansion of the ecology favored continued growth of the Greek economy—as well as, at least potentially, increasing the wealth of non-Greek elites.[29]

Next, states within several regions of the Greek world developed more sophisticated forms of federalism that both emerged from and promoted deeper intraregional economic integration. The poleis of Boeotia had been early movers in creating a federal league (*koinon*). A united Boeotia, with a total population that probably exceeded 200,000 (appendix I: region 10) was a formidable power, economically and militarily. The first Boeotian League had dissolved after the Persian Wars; the second was dissolved by the King's Peace in 387. In its fourth century iteration, as we have seen, the presence of Thebes as a would-be superpolis had tilted the balance toward centralization and thus coerced, rather than voluntary, cooperation. Thebes' willingness to use deadly force within Boeotia was demonstrated by the destruction of the poleis of Plataea in 372 and Orchomenos (I213) in 364 (the men killed; women and children enslaved).[30]

The coercion-intensive Boeotian League was, however, aberrant among fourth century Greek federal leagues. Federations that emerged in the fifth century and reached early maturity in the fourth century in Achaea (region 12) and Aetolia (region 7) were better balanced. Both regions were characterized by a number of relatively small poleis and considerable geographic diversity. Achaea had 16 poleis and a total fourth century population of ca. 70,000. Aetolia had 15 poleis with a total population of perhaps 60,000 (appendix I). Considered as a single polis, neither Achaea nor Aetolia would reach the level of superpolis, but each would be in the same category (size 6) as a handful of great poleis, for example, Argos or Eretria. There was no plausible way to unify either region into a single polis. Instead, the poleis of each region developed deeper intraregional social relations and new political institutions.

Federal leagues remained citizen-centered, but rights of citizenship were effectively doubled. A citizen of the Achaean polis of Dyme (I234), for example, would retain special participation rights within Dyme but would also have participation rights, via representation, in the Achaean *koinon* and civil rights in Pellene (I240), Patrai (I239), and the 13 other Achaean poleis. Federalism allowed small states to retain the advantages arising from *subsidiarity*: That is, many decisions could be addressed at a local level by those most directly affected. But at the same time, the members of a federal state gained the security and welfare advantages of "getting big." In each case, the intensi-fication of political relations among states in a region built upon, and subse-quently fostered, productive intraregional economic relations, for example, between upland and coastal towns. Some degree of economic cooperation had long existed in each region, arising from shared interests and a sense of regional identity encouraged by attending religious ceremonies at regional sanctuaries. In the fourth century, and continuing through the third and into the second centuries, the federal leagues became increasingly capable of act-ing as political entities, diplomatically and militarily.

By credibly committing the member states to cooperative trade relations and by increasing security, the leagues were incubators of productive eco-nomic specialization. Pastoralists in upland poleis could, for example, plan to raise more sheep whose wool could be exported through coastal ports, without worrying about restrictions on movement across polis borders, or extortionate taxes. The leagues also helped to provide for better regional se-curity, as potential counterweights to the hegemonic ambitions of their larger neighbors. The Achaean and Aetolian leagues seem to have been espe-cially well managed and are relatively well documented, but the idea of fed-eralism spread across much of the polis ecology in the course of the fourth and subsequent centuries. By the later fourth century, half of mainland Greek poleis were organized in federal leagues (table 2.3).

OPENING ACCESS TO INSTITUTIONS AT ATHENS

A third development that, along with continued expansion of the Greek world and federalism, helped to maintain economic growth in the face of the apparent disorderly struggles for supremacy among great poleis and Persian dynasts was a trend toward more open access to institutions. That trend can be traced in detail only at Athens, where it can be seen as a logical outgrowth of the political reforms discussed above. Constitutional changes clarifying the law and establishing a distinction between fundamental law and day-to-day legislation, along with the productive equilibrium struck between elites and masses through the elaboration of a political language of mutual accom-modation, produced a social order that was robust enough for the Athenians to begin opening access to legal and other institutions to noncitizens.

Access was never opened unilaterally: Political participation rights (vot-ing in the assembly, serving as a judge or magistrate) remained, for the most part, a monopoly of native-born adult males. Where we see access opening to a wider body of people is in the realms of civil law and civil association. In the course of the fourth century, the Athenians introduced a degree of status-blind impartiality in certain categories of legal judgment, expanded the right to initiate litigation, and granted authority to create perpetual organizations to groups with no connection to the state.[31]

Various open-access reforms may be explained, at least in part, by reference to the financial challenge that confronted Athens after the loss of the empire. As we have seen (ch. 8), for much of the fifth century Athens had used superior military power to extract rents, in the form of tribute and other remunerative taxes and imposts, from an extensive Aegean empire. After losing their empire and regaining their democracy, the Athenians confronted the difficult question of how to pay for citizen self-government, state defense, and social welfare. That Athens succeeded in doing so is evident. The democratic government continued to function throughout the period in question; fortifications, dockyards, and warships were built; important new public buildings were erected for a variety of civic purposes; the safety net of government-supported social welfare was expanded. The total cost of state expenditures was considerable (table 9.1). Where, in the absence of imperial rents, did the money come from to pay for it all?

Wealthy Athenians were taxed through the *eisphora* (occasional levies on large properties) and the system of liturgies, whereby the wealthiest residents paid for the outfitting of a warship or the financing of some aspect of a religious festival. But there were limits to how much the wealthy could be asked to pay before they would defect—if not by attempting violent regime change, then by hiding their wealth. The growth of Athenian trade, especially in grain, had led to the development of increasingly sophisticated forms of credit, managed by family-run companies that functioned as banks. This was very good news for the liquidity of Athenian markets, but on the other hand it meant that wealth could become "invisible"—existing in the elusive form of credit instruments rather than in the highly visible form of landed property. If taxes on locally owned wealth were set too high, the Athenians faced the prospect of driving money underground, and, in a worst-case scenario, crashing the essential grain market. As in the case of the legal reforms of the early fourth century, the financial needs of the state imposed certain limits on government. The challenge was how to acknowledge those limits without fatally undermining democratic authority.[32]

The solution was to increase revenues from indirect taxes. The fourth century Athenian state raised revenues from various sources, but indirect taxes on trade were, by all accounts, especially important. This taxation meant, however, that Athens had to find ways to attract more traders to its markets. Institutional innovations aimed at opening access appear to be essential in ensuring that trade remained robust and thus that taxes on trade could sus-

TABLE 9.1 *Estimated Athenian State Spending and Income*

	Ca. 435	Ca. 425	Ca. 370	354	Ca. 340	330s
Spending						
Military	400	1,500	350	130	200	400
Government & law	100	100	100	75	100	120
Festivals	100	100	100	100	100	150
Welfare	50	50	40	30	50	100
Building	350	100	75	0	50	200
TOTAL	*1,000*	*1,850*	*665*	*335*	*500*	*970*
Income						
General	1,000	1,500	600	130	400	1,200
Mint (max)	300	100	50	150	100	150
TOTAL	*1,300*	*1,600*	*650*	*280*	*500*	*1,350*
Loans (internal)		250				
Surplus/deficit	300	0	−15	−55	0	380

NOTES: Source data: Ober forthcoming. All dates are BCE. General income is as reported in ancient sources except for ca. 370, which is a guess. Mine leases are included in General Income, but minting fees are not. One-time windfall minting profit from coinage recall in 355 (Kroll 2011b) is included in 354. Pritchard 2012 estimate for ca. 425 military expenses is adopted here. Pritchard 2012 estimate for 370s–360s "public and private" expenses is reduced to reflect public only. Hansen 1999 estimate for 330s government expense increased by 20–30 T (Gabrielsen 2013; Pritchard 2014). Substate (deme, tribe) spending and income are excluded.

tain essential state services: Athens would be a magnet for trade only if Athens provided a superior environment for traders. Athens certainly benefited from natural advantages: its location and an exceptionally fine natural harbor at Piraeus. But the long history of Piraeus from the archaic period through early modernity shows that the harbor was often a backwater. Clearly a good location alone was insufficient to generate flourishing trade. If Piraeus were to be a center of Aegean trade in the postimperial era, the state would need to intervene in ways that would lower transaction costs.[33]

In the course of the fourth century, the Athenian state became more willing to forgive the head tax paid by some noncitizen long-term residents (*isoteleia*) and to extend the right to own real estate in Attica to noncitizens (*enktesis*). More rarely, individuals who had been especially helpful to the state were naturalized as full citizens. But probably more important in terms of the incentives of traders were changes in the system of market regulations that tended to lower information asymmetries between buyers and sellers in the Athenian marketplace.

Notable among institutional innovations was the establishment, in the 370s, of public "approvers" of silver coinage. The great popularity of Athenian "owls" as a means of exchange in eastern Mediterranean markets meant that Athenian coinage was widely imitated. Some of the imitations were similar to genuine Athenian coins in weight and purity; others were not. The Athenian approvers were publicly provided market officials charged with detecting counterfeits. Sellers in the market offering goods in exchange for silver could demand that buyers present their coins to the approver as a condition for concluding the sale. "Bad" counterfeits (coins with substandard silver content) were confiscated; "good" counterfeits (correct weight and purity, but minted outside Athens) were returned to the buyer; coins issued by the Athenian mint were "approved"—meaning that their acceptance by the seller was now mandatory. The publicly displayed law governing the approval procedure makes it clear that the service was freely available to all traders in Athenian markets: to citizens, foreigners, and slaves alike.[34]

In the 340s, the section of the Athenian law code regulating enforcement of contracts for overseas trade was revised in ways that substantially opened access to litigation over contracts and legal dispute resolution to non-Athenians. The reform leveled, at least in principle, the legal playing field between citizens and noncitizens in contract disputes. In the restructured "commercial cases" (*dikai emporikai*), the procedural rules now limited the legitimate basis of judicial judgment to the question of whether the terms of a written contract had been violated. This reform substantially reduced the discretion of the jurors (Athenian citizens) to judge on the basis of arguments about litigants' origins, character, or their histories of public generosity or private misbehavior. Moreover, a contract violation case could now be initiated by a noncitizen—certainly by free foreigners and probably by slaves, some of whom worked in banks and engaged in large-scale financial transactions.[35]

Open access requires that the right to form publicly recognized civil associations be made widely available. As we have seen (ch. 7), classical Athens had a rich infrastructure of civil associations, some of which performed important civic functions. By the later fifth century, and continuing through the fourth century, associations of foreigners in Athens were granted official perpetual charters. These charters provided the foreigners with public land on which they could construct their own sanctuaries and where they were free to practice their religions as they saw fit. An Athenian document from 333 BCE, for example, records a state land grant to a group of Athens-resident merchants from the town of Citium on Cyprus for a sanctuary to be dedicated to Cyprian Aphrodite "just as also the Egyptians have built the sanctuary of Isis." The mention in the document of the Egyptian Isis sanctuary as a precedent suggests that grants to associations of foreigners were being advertised as standard state policy.[36]

Open access also applied to ideas, including ideas used to criticize the state. The establishment of philosophical schools—for example, those of Plato, Isocrates, and Aristotle—which included citizens and noncitizens among their memberships—is one example of open access in ideas. It is also a well-documented example of the formation of perpetual nonstate civil associations. The school of the rhetorician Isocrates apparently ended with his death, but the Academy and Lyceum, founded respectively by Plato and Aristotle, had very long histories. These schools were formal organizations, with their own internal bylaws and elected officials. State acceptance of the philosophical schools is especially noteworthy given the highly critical stance toward democracy taken by their founders.[37]

The net effect of Athenian investment in infrastructure that was likely to be valuable and accessible to residents and visitors to Athens, and institutional innovations opening access and lowering transaction costs, helped to make Athens a relatively more desirable location for Greek and non-Greek traders. While there were other factors involved in Athens' postimperial revival, for example, the renewed productivity of the silver mines, it seems undeniable that more open access contributed to the growing strength of the Athenian economy.

While it remains impossible to quantify the economic value of Athenian open access, it seems reasonable to postulate that the performance of the Athenian state in the post-Peloponnesian War era would have been substantially worse had the Athenians—counterfactually—moved to restrict access to valuable public institutions and to forbid the establishment of new nonstate civil associations. Moreover, the Aegean economy would in general have fared worse under the counterfactual closed-access order. Brian Rutishauser, an expert in the economic history of the ancient Aegean, notes that the period from 355 (end of the Social War) to 314 (Athenian loss of Delos) was a period of especially vibrant economic activity in the island poleis of the central and northern Aegean. He attributes this in part to their symbiotic relationship, based on mutual economic interests, with Athens and its big and open market.[38]

Given the limits of our documentation, we can detail the move to more open access only in Athens, and it is probable that open-access institutions were most fully developed there. But at least some market-enhancing institutions best documented at Athens were adopted elsewhere—an inscription from Olbia (i690: size 5) on the north shore of the Black Sea, for example, mandating the use of Olbian coinage in the Olbian market is likely to be adapted from Athenian law.[39] We cannot trace the specific mechanisms by which institutions were borrowed, but the idea that opening access could enrich the state was available through literary works that readily circulated through the Greek world.

Xenophon's mid-fourth century pamphlet, *Revenues,* argues that Athens should and could enlarge its tax base by making the city more desirable to foreigners, thereby increasing "imports and exports, sales, rents, and customs" (Xenophon *Revenues* 3.5). Among other measures, Xenophon emphasizes the value of open and fair access to public institutions: He urges that state officials responsible for adjudicating disputes over commercial exchanges be given prizes when they produced especially just and prompt settlements (3.3). Xenophon notes that this remedy would cost nothing beyond "benevolent legislation and regulations" (3.6). But he also recommends substantial state capital investment in infrastructure—in hotels, mercantile halls, an increased stock of available houses, and shops in both Piraeus and in the central city. These "would be an ornament to the state, and at the same time the source of considerable revenue." They could readily be paid for by loans to the state by individuals, who would, Xenophon assures his reader, be ready to loan funds in light of the state's reputation for stability (3.12–13). To what extent Xenophon's proposals were influenced by, or influential upon, actual policy is unknown. But he clearly articulated the relationship between open access, the incentives of foreign traders, and the value of increased trade to the state.

EXPERTISE AND STATE PERFORMANCE

Institutional reforms that served to open access in ways likely to make markets especially desirable to traders were paralleled by reforms that enabled the state to make better use of expertise. As in the case of open access, the trend is best documented at Athens. It is quite likely that Athens was in the forefront of the trend but highly unlikely that Athens was unique. We have seen that military expertise, both at the level of expert generals and at the level of experienced mercenaries, had a substantial effect on the conduct of war in the postimperial era. Xenophon's manual on how and why to open access in order to stimulate trade and increase indirect tax revenues has its military analogue in his essay on the command of cavalry forces. Another

highly literate military expert, Aeneas, nicknamed "the Tactician," was probably an Arcadian mercenary captain from Stymphalos (i296). Aeneas wrote
a number of manuals about various aspects of military operations. His one
preserved text, *On the Defense of Fortified Positions*, shows a deep awareness
of the interrelationship between social order and state military security and
draws on empirical cases from around the Greek world.[40]

The fourth century Athenians were certainly well aware of the potential
value of military expertise. They employed expert generals (both Athenian
citizens and foreigners), hired mercenaries, and developed a formal system,
the *ephebeia*, that employed experts in the military training of young Athenians. By the 330s, if not before, their training included hoplite tactics, projectile weapons, and the operation of catapults. In the fifth century, there had
been much overlap between the sets "leading Athenian politicians" and
"leading Athenian generals." In the fourth century, there was much less overlap: Politicians who frequently addressed the assembly were much less likely
to serve as generals. With both domestic and foreign policy, and military tactics and strategy becoming specialized fields, each domain was now dominated by experts. Ten Athenian generals were annually elected, as before.
But, whereas in the fifth century the duties of individual generals remained
unspecified, by the mid-fourth century, several of the generals were elected to
serve in specialized roles: A general "for the defense of the countryside" is
attested by 357; by the later fourth century, the Aristotelian *Ath. Pol.* (61.1)
attests, in addition, two generals for Piraeus, one for foreign expeditions, and
one with responsibility for the financing of the fleet.[41]

The Athenian general elected to be responsible for fleet finance must have
worked closely with other public officials with responsibility for state finance. The Athenians were, by the mid-fourth century, acutely aware of the
need for expertise in the domain of money and finance. We have already considered the law of 375, concerning approvers of silver coinage. In this case, as
in some others considered in this section, the Athenians literally bought experts: The approvers were salaried public slaves, with connections to the
Athenian mint. They clearly were expected to be expert in the identification
of real and fake Athenian owls. The high level of expertise that was demanded
of them is suggested by the continuing disputes among modern numismatists
over the attribution of some owls to Athenian or foreign mints.

In 354, two decades after the approvers law was passed, all Athenian silver
coinage was recalled and quickly reminted in a recognizably new format (the
"*pi*-style" owls). The reminting had the double effect of allowing the state a
windfall from minting fees and making it much easier, at least for a time, for
nonexperts to distinguish between genuine and imitation owls. The drafters of

the recall law, like the writers of the approvers law, were acutely sensitive to the concerns of traders in the Athenian market. The recall law, like the law on the approvers, the "grain tax law" of 375, and other fourth century legislation concerning state finance, bears the mark of input by individuals who had become relatively expert in what we would now call transaction cost economics.[42]

State finances were put on a new footing in the fourth century: The overall state budget was reorganized, so that various spending authorities (Council, assembly, various boards of magistrates) were issued a fixed sum per year, each as a portion (*merismos*) of the annual budget. Before this time, the budget had been a single pot from which all authorities had dipped as needed. The new *merismos* system would have allowed those individuals responsible for managing the budget of the different branches of the government to plan ahead, and it eliminated perverse incentives to overspend early in the budget cycle. The system for collecting direct taxes, both *eisphora* and naval liturgies (the special responsibility of the general in charge of fleet finance), were repeatedly tweaked, in what appears to be an iterative process, drawing on a growing pool of financial expertise. Changes seem to be aimed at finding an optimal position between maximizing compliance and income, and avoiding the necessity of building up an intrusive and costly state bureaucracy.[43]

In the years after the financial emergency precipitated by the Social War, the Athenians concentrated duties for state-level financial planning and management in a central elective office that, like the generalship, could be held in consecutive years. While we lack many of the details, it seems clear that a series of competent managers, beginning in the late 350s and continuing into the 320s, helped to put Athenian finances on a sound footing, such that annual state income and expenditures were brought into better alignment (table 9.1). The eventual result of successful measures to increase indirect taxes and to collect direct taxes in a way that was relatively fair and not too costly to the state, in the context of good financial management, was that annual state income and spending increased dramatically. By ca. 335 BCE, state income (reportedly 1,200 talents) seems to have been roughly equal to what it had been in the imperial era a hundred years previously—with the notable difference that fourth century state income was not predicated on big imperial rents. The strong income stream allowed Athens to engage in various high-profile public projects, including civil and military construction and increasing the number of ships available for naval operations.[44]

The Athenian state's recognition of the value of experts is particularly evident in the domains of war and finance, but it extended into other domains as well. Some time between 368 and 362 BCE, the chief secretary of the Council of 500, a position that had previously rotated according to the 10-tribe system among the year's Councilors, was appointed, as a lotteried official, from the general citizen population to serve for an entire year: As Peter Rhodes of the University of Durham points out, this reform was certainly intended to increase efficiency in the conduct of the office, which included the publication of laws and decrees. By the later fourth century, the Council had another secretary, in this case an elected official, who was responsible for reading out documents when called upon to do so at meetings of the Council and the assembly (Pseudo-Aristotle *Ath. Pol.* 54.5). In the course of the century, a number of other secretaries were added to various administrative bodies; some were citizens (the politician Aeschines began his public career in this way). Others were public slaves. These included the approvers; Nicomachus, a late fifth century archivist of the Athenian laws; and a man named Eukles, who was for some 20 years an assistant to public officials at Eleusis.[45]

While Athenian government remained predicated on the assumption that many citizen-amateurs could, under the right conditions, make relatively wise decisions on matters of common interest, there appears to be a growing willingness to make use of experienced individuals—citizens and noncitizens alike—whose specialized knowledge could be tapped to make the system more effective. There is no way for us to determine the value added (or lost) by the increased employment of experts by the Athenian state. But in light of the complexity of the tasks undertaken by the state, and the inefficiencies arising from all-amateur government when, for example, an otherwise competent lottery-chosen magistrate was illiterate, it seems reasonable to guess that the addition of a certain number of experienced officials and secretaries, each subject to public scrutiny at the end of every year's service, pushed in the direction of increased governmental productivity rather than bureaucratic bloat.

To the extent that greater use of experts in government enhanced the capacity of the Athenian government to raise funds and to spend them wisely, government expertise would have promoted Athenian economic flourishing. Annual Athenian state spending in the fourth century was very substantial, probably in the range of 10–15% of Athens' gross domestic income (GDI). Although that is a substantially lower percentage than is spent by developed modern states, Athens' level of government spending was probably very high by the standards of most premodern states.[46] Substantial government spending that resulted in better security enabled Athenians to plan ahead, as they could not do if they lived in constant fear of invasion or piracy. State investment in infrastructure (water, roads, harbors, storage facilities), as well as on provision of services such as market officials and the approvers of coins, had positive knock-on effects.

Even with the increase in indirect tax revenues, part of Athenian spending took the form of transfer payments from the rich to poorer Athenians as military pay, state pay for offices, orphan relief, and welfare payments to handicapped citizens—all of which increased in the course of the fourth century. These transfers reduced income inequality and provided a kind of baseline social insurance that allowed non-elite citizens to take somewhat greater risks in the knowledge that there was at least a minimal safety net in the case of individual catastrophe. So long as state spending had the net effect of (1) increasing security, (2) lowering inequality and dampening social conflict without engendering significant levels of moral hazard or triggering elite defection, and (3) enabling individuals to invest more deeply in themselves and their families and thereby building the overall social stock of human capital, it would have promoted economic growth—as well as limiting economic inequality. As noted in chapter 5, getting that balance right was not easy; erring on either side (too much inequality, too much moral hazard) would have dampened economic growth. The Athenian institutional system of the later fourth century was the result of much experimentation, not all of which was successful.[47]

Athens was obviously in some ways exceptional but also in some ways exemplary of the Greek state's approach to finance and expertise. The British historian John K. Davies has documented the later adoption of Athenian financial methods by Hellenistic kingdoms.[48] It seems likely that emulation of successful Athenian uses of expertise by Greek city-states, combined with independent developments along similar lines, promoted state performance outside Athens and that enhanced state performance was one factor driving the classical efflorescence.

The employment of experts did not invariably promote growth across the Greek world. The history of the Greek poleis of Sicily from the late-fifth through the mid-fourth century demonstrates how an overdose of military experts could help push a once-productive region into economic decline.

FALL AND RISE OF SYRACUSE AND GREEK SICILY

In the aftermath of their victory over the Athenian invaders in 413 BCE, the Syracusans had much to celebrate. Thucydides (7.87.5) described the destruction of the Athenian fleet and ground forces in Sicily as the greatest event of the greatest war in Hellenic history. But soon thereafter, it appeared that the imminence of the Athenian threat had been a linchpin of Syracuse's political stability. In 412, constitutional changes were introduced, evidently in favor of a stronger form of democracy. For the first time, some magistrates at Syracuse were chosen by lot. Hermocrates, who had been a principal military leader, was exiled while in command of a small squadron of Syracusan warships sent to the Aegean to aid in the war against Athens; he quickly defected to Persia.

Meanwhile, ongoing disputes between Sicilian cities created an opening for Carthage to expand its sphere of influence on the island. A long series of ultimately inconclusive but horrifically bloody and debilitating wars followed, pitting Carthage and its various Sicilian allies against an unstable coalition of Sicilian Greek poleis. Early in the course of those wars, all Carthaginian traders were summarily expelled from Syracuse and the other Greek poleis. Eventually, many of the major cities of Sicily—Greek, native, and Carthaginian alike—along with some Greek cities of south Italy, were sacked; many of their residents were killed, enslaved, or transported. Some cities were refounded or founded anew with forcibly relocated populations. Others were stripped of fortifications and left vulnerable. The miseries of war were compounded by intensified social conflicts. As in the early fifth century, these conflicts were stoked by ethnic antagonism and social inequality.

Greek and south Italian mercenaries did much of the fighting. Freelance military experts—especially Spartans—provided military leadership. Some mercenary forces fought under the direction of polis governments that aimed at self-preservation or aggrandizement. But elsewhere, mercenary bands evolved into nonterritorial, nonstate organizations, specializing in the use of violence to extract resources from settled populations. Unlike the mainland, there was no critical mass of reasonably stable republican states ready and able to field citizen armies large enough to counterbalance the negative externalities of a burgeoning market in organized violence provision.[49]

Sicily's republican governments were replaced by tyrannies. Syracuse's reformed democratic government proved fragile in the face of the pressure of the ongoing war with Carthage and Carthage's Sicilian allies. The tyrant Dionysius I had assumed power at Syracuse by 405 BCE, on the strength of his military skills and by his skillful manipulation of social conflict. While unable to defeat the Carthaginians decisively, he was a skilled general, capable of defending Syracuse from attack, building up its fortifications and often taking the war to the Carthaginians. Among the accomplishments with which Dionysius is credited is the invention of the nontorsion (cross-bow type) catapult. According to Diodorus (14.42.1), by offering a mix of high wages and prizes, Dionysius attracted a number of skilled mechanics to Syracuse. They were provided with work spaces and encouraged to develop new engines of war. The story of the invention of the catapult in Syracuse is lent plausibility by the account of the use of catapults, as well as extremely tall siege towers, in Dionysius' successful siege of the Carthaginian stronghold of Motya in 397 (Diodorus 14.50.4–51.7).[50]

As in the mainland, the allure of empire proved strong. When he was not fighting Carthage, Dionysius sought to rebuild and extend the Syracusan mini-empire in eastern Sicily, making war on both native Sicilian and Greek towns. By the mid-380s, he had achieved considerable success in eastern Sicily, sacking Hipponium (i53: size 3) and Rhegium (i68: size 6) on the toe of Italy and gaining control of a number of south Italian cities. He launched raids further north in Italy, against the Etruscans, and established outposts and diplomatic ties in Epirus (region 5: modern Albania). It appeared, for a time, that he might be an empire builder on a substantial scale, exceeding even the early fifth century accomplishments of Gelon and Hieron (ch. 7). Unlike imperial Athens, however, Syracuse under Dionysius I neither created a peaceful zone of imperial control nor encouraged rational acquiescence by signaling long time horizons and extracting a sustainable level of rents. Syracuse's fourth century mini-empire remained at the level of smash and grab—with dire consequences for the Sicilian economy. Wars between Syracuse and Carthage, and involving Sicilian cities and the poleis of south Italy, continued intermittently until Dionysius I's death in 368.

He was succeeded by his son, Dionysius II. In one of the more bizarre experiments in fourth century politics, Plato now returned to Syracuse. He had previously visited there in the 380s, during the reign of Dionysius I—his interview with the old tyrant had not gone well. As before, the invitation had come from Plato's philosophical adherent, Dion, who was intimately connected to the tyrant's household. Plato's idea seems to have been that he would convert the young tyrant into a sort of philosopher-ruler.

That plan predictably failed, Plato got out of Sicily by the skin of his teeth, and Dion engineered a coup against Dionysius II. Disputes among the "liberators" over offices, spoils, and regime type led to a messy and protracted civil war in Syracuse. Dionysius II survived it; Dion did not. Through the 350s and into the 340s, Syracuse was ruled by a series of predatory warlords, culminating in the return in 346 of an increasingly bloody-minded Dionysius II. The external wars continued.[51]

According to our literary sources, 60 years of killing and plunder wreaked havoc on Sicily's economy. Plutarch offers a vivid description of Syracuse and Sicily in the mid 340s:

> . . . some [residents of Syracuse] had perished in their external and civil wars, while others had fled into exile from tyrannical governments. Indeed, for lack of population the market place of Syracuse had produced such a quantity of dense grass that horses were pastured in it, . . . and the other [Sicilian] poleis, with almost no exceptions, were full of deer and

wild swine, while in their suburbs and around their walls those who had
leisure for it went hunting, and not one of those who were barricaded in
fortresses and strongholds would attend to any summons, or come down
into the urban center, but fear and hatred kept all away from market place
and civic life . . .

—*Timoleon 22.4–6, trans. Perrin (Loeb) adapted*

Diodorus (16.83.1) tells a similar story of how Sicily's population responded
to endemic instability by fleeing, hiding, and digging in. Although the archaeological record is less clear and the literary accounts obviously highly
colored, the numismatic evidence, and some archaeological evidence, is consistent with a period of economic decline. While rhetorically embellished,
Plutarch's and Diodorus' detailed accounts of infrastructure destruction and
decay are plausible enough and unlikely to be simple fictions.[52]

Sicily had undergone previous periods of war without economic decline,
and as we have seen, the eastern Greek world experienced conflict along with
continued efflorescence. But the fourth century Sicilian situation was different in various ways: Carthage was, from the late fifth century onward, willing
to pour its resources, gained from its imperial and trading enterprises, into a
protracted attempt to gain control of Sicilian cities. Ethnic differences between Greeks and native Sicilians were exacerbated and exploited by Carthaginians and Greeks alike. Mature citizen-centered governments—relatively stable oligarchies and democracies—were less common in the Sicilian
cities than in the Greek east.

The Sicilian Greek poleis had long been marked by social conflict driven
by high levels of wealth and income inequality. Military expertise imported
from abroad had, in the person of Gylippos of Sparta, enabled Syracuse to
resist imperial Athens. In the fourth century, however, foreign military experts became warlords. Finally, and underlying other factors, the Sicilian
Greek cities had specialized in grain production for export. That had produced high-value surpluses but lacked regional (island-level) economic integration. Compared with the mainland, there were few economic incentives
for the rulers of Sicilian cities to avoid debilitating warfare and there were
large rents to be reaped by victors—or so it seemed.

By the mid-fourth century BCE, Sicily had more rent-seekers than rent-
producers. The collapse of the lucrative wine trade with Carthage, after the
expulsion of Carthaginian traders from the Greek cities early in the century,
left grain-growing as the primary rent-producing activity. Arable agriculture
was robust to the ordinary conditions of Greek warfare, but it did require
cultivators with a reasonable expectation of reaping what they had sown.

And it required a substantial agricultural labor force. After two generations of warfare, there were neither expectations of decent harvests nor enough laborers. The warlords of fourth century Sicily, with their short time horizons, employed violent methods of expropriation that both discouraged cultivation and encouraged laborers to exit.[53]

Many residents of Sicily were killed or enslaved and sold abroad. Many others availed themselves of the opportunities that Hellas offered to migrants. As the Berkeley historian Emily Mackil has shown, the world of the poleis often proved willing and able to absorb surviving populations from failed poleis. Because Hellas remained a net importer of labor in the fourth century (ch. 4), Sicilians who fled the island could expect to make a living elsewhere, in Greek Italy or the mainland. Greek labor mobility may have pushed forward the tipping point for the Sicilian economy.[54]

If we are to believe our literary sources, the tipping point had been reached by mid-century. If we were to take Plutarch's description at face value, Sicily might have seemed ready for a descent into conditions resembling the Early Iron Age nadir. But, unlike the system-level collapse at the end of the Bronze Age, Sicily's economic difficulties were regional and stemmed from political problems that could potentially be rectified. Indeed, by the last third of the fourth century BCE, Sicily's economic fortunes were on the mend. The downturn was reversed and Sicily rejoined the world of wealthy Hellas.

In 344 BCE, answering an appeal from surviving residents of Syracuse to the ancestral mother city, Corinth dispatched one of its citizens, Timoleon, with a small army to Sicily. Although we hear little of his earlier career (other than his killing of his brother, who had sought tyranny at Corinth), Timoleon proved adept as a general, politician, and diplomat. As in the case of the arrival of Gylippos at Syracuse in 414 BCE, an outsider with particular skills and disengaged from local factional politics proved capable of intervening successfully at a moment of acute crisis. Like Gylippos, and Solon before him (and for reasons unexplained in our sources), throughout his Sicilian career Timoleon remained uninterested in seeking personal power, at least through the familiar route of using autocratic military authority as a springboard to tyranny. By playing on very real fears of a Carthaginian takeover of the island, and by rallying a populace desperately tired of tyrants, Timoleon eventually came out ahead in a struggle between the tyrant of Leontini, the Carthaginians, and Dionysius II for the control of Syracuse. No doubt to the surprise of many, Syracuse was then given a new republican constitution. At least parts of the new constitution were designed by Timoleon's associate, a Corinthian named Cephalus. The Corinthians, like the Athenians, seem to have recognized the value of distinguishing between expertise in military affairs and constitutional reform.

With Syracuse secured, Timoleon successfully campaigned against tyrants in other Sicilian cities and against the Carthaginians. Again, contrary to what many Sicilians must initially have expected, this did not prove to be a prelude to renewed Syracusan empire building. Timoleon resembled the warlords in that he employed mercenaries and resorted to booty raiding to pay them. But each tyrant he overthrew was replaced by a republican regime; each polis he took was treated as an independent ally, rather than as a subject state. Meanwhile, Timoleon gained a series of military victories against Carthage, resulting in a negotiated settlement that limited Carthage's sphere in Sicily to the northwestern third of the island. Seven years after arriving in Sicily, having gone blind, Timoleon retired from active politics.[55]

The upside to an economic decline that had been compounded, if not caused, by labor mobility is that when the underlying conditions that led to large-scale emigration changed, such that agricultural cultivation for export was again a rational strategy, there would be good reason for Greeks to return to the fertile fields of Sicily. The incentive would be especially strong insofar as labor shortage, as a result of depopulation, put upward pressure on wages.[56] By 337 BCE, the warlords and tyrants were gone, Syracusan and Carthaginian imperialistic ambitions were on hold, and Timoleon had resigned his military command. Greek immigrants flooded into Sicily—some 60,000, according to Diodorus and Plutarch.

Some archaeological evidence supports the literary accounts of the rapid revival of Sicily's economy, both in the cities and the countryside, in the wake of Timoleon's campaigns. Grain exports seem to have recovered; large numbers of coins from Corinth and Corinthian colonies in Sicilian hoards from this era are most readily explained as payments for grain. Minting of coins by Sicilian poleis, which (other than at Syracuse) had been at a near standstill for most of the fourth century, now revived, with close to half (20/47) of the poleis in Sicily for the first time issuing bronze coins for purposes of local exchange.[57]

The economic fall and rise of Sicily in the fourth century shows both the potential fragility of regional economies—especially those that depended on the export of grain—but also the resilience of the larger economy of Hellas. The dispersed-authority ecology proved capable of responding to changes in local political conditions in ways that we can see, *ex post*, were at once unfavorable to polis-centered empires and favorable to long-term economic growth. The ecology-level response—including the short-term depopulation and the repopulation of Greek Sicily—was an emergent phenomenon. It arose from the behavior of a great many individuals who made their choices based on simple assumptions—e.g., the likelihood of being able to move freely about Hellas and find work outside Sicily, and then the likelihood that republican regimes would be nonexploitative relative to tyrannies. Although the choices made by, for example, Dionysius I, the Carthaginian government, Corinth, and Timoleon had significant consequences, there was no central power setting policy or determining outcomes.

THE ANATOLIAN GREEKS UNDER PERSIA

Among the headlines of the history of mainland Greece and Sicily in the fourth century BCE is the failure of imperial states to subordinate free Greek city-states. In western Anatolia, however, the story was quite different. As both Athens and Sparta stumbled in their expansionist projects by the mid-390s, Persia stepped into the breach. Picking up where his royal predecessors had left off after the war of 480–478, Artaxerxes II reasserted an ancestral sovereignty over the coastal cities of Anatolia. The history of the fourth century Anatolian Greek cities is not well documented in our surviving literary sources, but the gap is at least partially filled by documentary and archaeological evidence.

For our purposes, the important point was made by the eminent American historian, Chester Starr 40 years ago: Contrary to what classical historians had long supposed—based in part on highly colored accounts by the rhetorician Isocrates, who hoped to persuade Philip II of Macedon to invade the Persian Empire—there is good reason to believe that the Anatolian Greeks were at least as prosperous in the fourth century under the Persians as they had been in the mid-fifth century under the Athenians. Almost certainly they were better off than they would have been if, counterfactually, Sparta's imperial project had been prolonged for two generations. Starr emphasized the archaeological evidence for public building and the expansion of minting activity by a number of the Anatolian poleis. He also noted that the Anatolian Greek cities seem not to have joined revolts against the king by western Anatolian governors. A generation of scholarship has tended to confirm Starr's main points, while substantially deepening and broadening our understanding of the history of western Anatolia in the fourth century BCE.[58]

A major study of the Anatolian Greek world from the late fifth through late fourth centuries BCE by the French historian, Pierre Debord, concludes that at least some Anatolian poleis fared better in this period than did some parts of mainland Greece. Like Starr, Debord points to the evidence of a spate of architectural construction: temples, civic buildings, and fortifications. In Ionia (region 38), for example, Priene (i861) was refounded, probably around mid-century, on the slopes of Mt. Mycale, with a full complement of civic buildings and a monumental city wall. Much of the city plan of Neandreia (i785) in the Troas (region 35) was reorganized, as was the entirety of Priene, on a grid plan. And, as at Priene, Neandreia's new building included massive city walls. Debord also details increased minting activity. Ephesus (i844), Miletus, Cos, and Rhodes issued substantial quantities of silver coins; other poleis under Persian control minted in gold and electrum.

On the whole, the Anatolian Greek poleis seem to have accepted the rationality of acquiescence to an imperial power that had demonstrated its commitment to long time horizons and reasonable taxes. While most of the Anatolian Greek cities were ruled by pro-Persian oligarchies, there were notable exceptions; Erythrai (i845) had democratic institutions by ca. 400 BCE, and Kyme (i817) was democratic by 350 BCE. As in the mainland, institutional innovations were linked to the growth of civic populations. The king and his governors generally respected local autonomy. Cities that paid their taxes were left in peace.

Meanwhile, the fourth century saw a hastened pace of Hellenization, especially but not uniquely in Caria in southwestern Anatolia. Formerly "barbarian" towns increasingly took on the institutional and architectural forms of Greek poleis in a process whose importance for the expansion of Greek horizons has been emphasized by the historian John Ma. As more of western Anatolia became more Hellenized, in part as a result of choices made by the king's semi-independent governors, the transaction costs incurred by Greeks engaged in diplomacy and exchange with those regions dropped accordingly. At the same time, as Ma emphasizes, residents of newly Hellenized towns benefited as their towns were drawn into a large and robust network of peer polities. Along with inland Sicily, fourth century Anatolia represented the expanding frontier of the Greek world: A considerable part of the growth of the total Greek population in this period (ch. 4) can be attributed to the adoption of Greek culture and institutions by Anatolian cities under Persian rule. The expansion of polis culture into Asia continued after the conquest of Persia by Alexander, but the process was well advanced before Alexander set foot on Asian soil.[59]

The Anatolian Greek cities, old and new, were in a good position to profit from trade across an extensive zone of Persian imperial control. Not only did a number of Anatolian cities mint their own coinage in this period, but they also converged on a common weight standard. Unlike the harrowing history of Sicilian poleis in the fourth century, few of the Anatolian poleis were sacked; their populations were seldom killed, enslaved, or transported. The king controlled naval forces adequate to suppress pirates—and insofar as his tax revenues from the coastal cities depended on their financial solvency, he had an incentive to do so.[60]

The king demanded the "traditional" payment of tribute, but the tax rate seems on the whole not to have been excessive. It remained true that, as an absolute monarch, the king could arbitrarily try to increase taxes to exorbitant rates. But he had even less incentive to attempt to do so than had the Athenians in the fifth century, before the crises of the 420s. The king's incentives were affected by the costs of enforcement. By the later fourth century, almost all of the larger (over size 2) Greek cities of the Anatolian coast were protected by substantial fortified circuits—as at least some had not been in the mid-fifth century.[61] While the Persian king's army could certainly take any one of these walled cities by force, it would be expensive to do so. In general, therefore, well-fortified Greek cities found that they could negotiate reasonable taxation levels. As we will see (ch. 11), this dynamic continued well into the second century BCE.

The negotiations between the king's agents and a Greek city need not have been formal. We may perhaps imagine discussions as being carried on in an early version of the polite language of friendship and mutual accommodation that was later perfected by the Anatolian cities under the rule of Macedonian Seleucid kings—the dynasty that came to rule much of western Asia in the era after the death of Alexander the Great. In this way, as in others, the history of the Anatolian Greek cities under fourth century Persian rule pointed to the later history of much of Hellas under the rule of Macedonian monarchs.[62]

10

POLITICAL FALL,
359–334 BCE

THE TERMINATION OF THE
CLASSICAL ERA

LOOKING AHEAD

Warfare was rife in the half century after the Peloponnesian War. Yet, with the exception of Leuctra, where Sparta's long run as a superpolis abruptly ended in 371 BCE, there were few truly decisive battles. That changed in the seventh decade of the fourth century, when a series of battlefield decisions remade the Greek world: In 338, at Chaeronea, Philip II of Macedon defeated a Greek alliance led by Athens and Thebes. His victory ended the era in which great and independent poleis dominated the Aegean world. Philip's son, Alexander III "The Great," then brought down the once-mighty Persian Empire in three battles in 334, 333, and 331. Having spent the next decade expanding and partially consolidating an empire that eventually stretched east to the Indus River, Alexander returned to Mesopotamia, where he died in Babylon in June 323. Revolts against Macedonian rule that broke out in Greece upon the news of the king's death were quickly suppressed.

The Hellenistic era of Greek history, from the death of Alexander to the Roman takeover in the second century BCE, was dominated by Macedonian dynasts and, in Sicily and south Italy, by their Greek imitators. A few city-states, notably Rhodes, remained fully independent and centrally important in Mediterranean affairs. Syracuse became the capital of a Sicilian kingdom. The Achaean and Aetolian federal leagues (ch. 9) periodically broke free of Macedonian royal control. But from the later fourth century into the early second century, many poleis paid tribute taxes to one or another of the Hellenistic kings. Some key cities, including Athens, Chalkis, and Corinth, periodically received Macedonian garrisons.

The diminution of the role of great and independent Greek poleis in Mediterranean history in the late fourth century BCE is the *political fall* that had been averted by the successful fifth century resistance to Persia and Carthage. This chapter answers the question of why and how Philip and Alexander of Macedon succeeded in defeating a Greek coalition led by two great poleis, whereas Darius and Xerxes of Persia had failed in their earlier attempts. The political fall of Hellas in the later fourth century was precipitated, at least in part, by the Macedonian kings' masterful appropriation of the by-now familiar instruments that had driven Hellas' economic rise in the preceding centuries: specialization and expertise, developed as a result of the deep investments in human capital, along with competitive emulation of successful technological and institutional innovations. In the final chapter (ch. 11), we explore the relationship between the political fall and the robust persistence of economic growth, federalism, and democracy in a transformed ecology of city-states.

THE "OPPORTUNISTS"

The sudden rise of Macedon in the mid-fourth century was not the historical equivalent of a "crater of doom" meteor strike, terminating a thriving ecology at a stroke.[1] Rather, Philip emerged as the most successful of a group of very effective, highly ambitious, and at least semi-Hellenized dynasts who ruled territories on the fringes of the Greek world in the early to mid-fourth century BCE. Several of these rulers posed serious problems (as well as employment opportunities) for certain of their Greek neighbors, and they shared some methods in common. John K. Davies of the University of Liverpool aptly dubbed the members of this informal club "the opportunists" because each of them borrowed opportunistically (that is, selectively, seeking their own advantage and that of their community) from Greek culture and institutions. Each made extensive use of Greek experts—notably including mercenary soldiers, commanders, and designers of military systems. "Opportunist" is not meant here as a derogatory term—we might just as well call the Hellenized dynasts of the fourth century "the entrepreneurs." And of course they were hardly unique in their opportunistic borrowing: As we have seen, the emulation of institutions and technology among Greek states was a primary driver of the classical efflorescence.[2]

Prominent dynasts on the margins of Hellas included Evagoras and Nicocles, rulers of Salamis on Cyprus; Jason and Alexander of Pherai (1414), each sometime master of Thessaly; Mausolus and Artemisia II of Caria; and Hermias of Atarneus (1803) in northwestern Anatolia, Aristotle's father-in-law and patron. The opportunists' club also included other ambitious and semi-independent governors of Anatolian provinces in the Persian Empire; the Thracian and Scythian rulers of new and emerging Black Sea states from which the Greek poleis imported great quantities of wheat; Tachos of Egypt, and other rebels who from time to time broke free of the Great King of Persia. At a further remove, but in the category of states beyond the Greek world that made effective and selective use of Greek expertise, were the Carthaginians and the Great King himself.

The opportunists' employment of Greek experts would threaten the Greek world (rather than the ambitions of specific Greek states) only if it put the overall ecology of independent poleis at risk. As it turned out, the danger posed by most of the opportunists, even to individual Greek states, was episodic. The Great King had retaken the Anatolian poleis, and, for a time, major Aegean island states, including Samos and Rhodes. As we have seen (ch. 9), some poleis suffered under the Persians, but overall the Persian-ruled Anatolian Greeks did quite well in the fourth century. The Carthaginians were fought to a standstill by the tyrants of Sicily and then by Timoleon; Carthage ended up controlling about a third of Sicily, but no more. Jason and later Alexander of Pherai were assassinated before realizing their full potential as leaders of a united Thessaly. Mausolus died soon after launching his challenge to Athens in the Social War of 357–355; his successors were less threatening to Athenian interests.

Philip of Macedon stood out among the fourth century opportunists. He shared their taste for selective features of Greek culture, and, like them, he employed Greek experts to his own ends. But he went his fellow dynasts one better in various ways. As a leader, Philip possessed many of the characteristics that Thucydides had so admired in Pericles: He was a subtle diplomat, a superb manager of men and money, a bold and astute military strategist. He had a focused and a far-sighted vision of what his state might accomplish and of what natural and human resources would be required in order for his vision to be fulfilled.

Like Dionysius I of Syracuse, Philip made creative use of advances in military technology and actively pursued new technological advances. Like Epaminondas of Thebes, Philip saw the value of military training and experimented successfully with novel battlefield formations. Philip innovated in combining cavalry, light infantry, and heavy infantry. He employed both strategic pursuit of defeated enemies and strategic foundation of cities. Moreover, Philip was lucky, if not in his total life span (born in 382, he died in 336 at age 46), then both in his relatively long reign and in his heir. Unlike the other leading opportunists, Philip ruled for long enough (23 years: 359–336 BCE) both to expand and to consolidate his state. Moreover, upon Philip's death, his son, at age 20, was ready to assume control. Alexander quickly proved to be his father's equal as a ruler, diplomat, strategist, and field commander.[3]

The Macedonian conquest of Greece was not inevitable. Philip's career might have followed an arc similar to that of other opportunists: He suffered at least two life-threatening battlefield wounds before arriving on the plain of Chaeronea; either incident could have killed him before Alexander was ready to take over as Macedon's ruler. Like Jason and Alexander of Pherai, Philip was assassinated by a trusted member of his inner circle. His death came two years after he had beaten the Greek allies at Chaeronea, but had an assassin struck a few years earlier, the Macedonian imperial state might have fallen apart before any decisive encounter with the great poleis of central Greece had taken place. If, upon coming to the throne in 336, Alexander had proven less than superbly competent, the effects of Philip's victory at Chaeronea might have proved ephemeral.

Philip did very well in the domain of leveraging Greek expertise—his choice of Aristotle as a tutor for his son is exemplary. Each of the earlier opportunists, however, had also been skilled in the domain of borrowing expertise, as they were in various other domains (strategy, management) relevant to hegemonic ambitions. Had one of the earlier opportunists been luckier in regard to his length of reign and heir, Philip might have been beaten to the punch; Macedon might have been absorbed into someone else's empire. On the other hand, in counterfactual worlds in which one imagines that Philip died before consolidating the Macedonian state, or that his heir was not his equal, other opportunists could have emerged as existential threats to the Greek world— Darius III, as Great King of Persia, is among the plausible candidates.

In sum, we ought not imagine that the political fall of Greece had to happen just when and just as it did—or that the loss of Greek independence was nothing more than a bizarre twist of fortune that sequentially placed two world-class military and organizational geniuses on the Macedonian throne. While the rapid rise of Macedon and the political fall of classical Greece could not have been predicted *ex ante*, they are certainly explicable *ex post*, when viewed against the wider context of the development of expertise relevant to empire-building and the mobility of that expertise in the late classical Greek world.[4]

MACEDON BEFORE PHILIP

Macedonia was a large and resource-rich region north and east of Thessaly and the Chalkidike Peninsula (map 9). It had long been connected culturally, economically, and politically to the mainland Greek world. But Macedonia also had historical and geographic connections with Epirus to the west, with

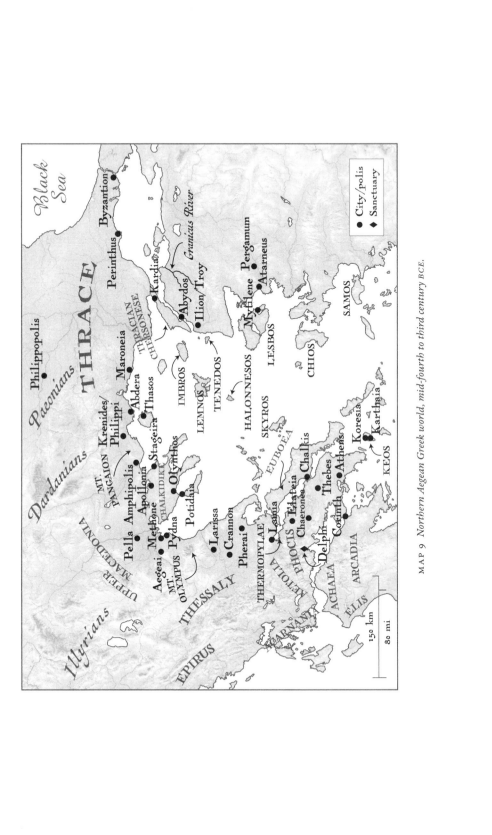

MAP 9 *Northern Aegean Greek world, mid-fourth to third century* BCE.

tribal regions of inland Eurasia to the north, and with Thrace and Persian-ruled Anatolia to the east. Topographically, Lower Macedonia was centered on the fertile lowland plain formed by the Axios River in the south and east, while Upper Macedonia was an extensive zone of mountainous highlands extending west and north from Mt. Olympus. While Lower Macedonia lay within the Mediterranean climatic zone, Upper Macedonia lay outside it. Indeed, the Macedonian highlands may be generally defined as that part of the Greek peninsula lying outside the Mediterranean zone. As such, much of Macedonia was colder and wetter than the Mediterranean Greek world.

The history and culture of Upper Macedonia, especially, was nearly as foreign to the Greeks as that of Thrace or Scythia. Macedonia was rich in natural resources that were rare in the rest of Greece. Upper Macedonia was especially famous for its timber, producing in abundance the large trees essential for ship-building and for the ceiling elements of monumental buildings, including temples, stoas, shipsheds, and military towers. Poleis like Athens that regularly constructed warships and large public buildings had strong reasons to seek access to Macedonian resources.[5]

The *Inventory* lists 17 poleis as having been established in the region of Macedonia by 323 BCE. I estimate the population of these poleis at 145,000, but the total population of Macedonia was certainly higher. Many Macedonians, especially residents of Upper Macedonia, lived in settlements not categorized as poleis. By the end of his reign in 336 BCE, Philip had created a Greater Macedonia that incorporated the coastal plain west of the Thermaic Gulf, the whole of the Chalkidike Peninsula, and much of coastal Thrace. Greater Macedonia was the core of an empire that, by 336, also included Thessaly, inland Thrace, Epirus, and the Greek mainland (map 9).

Philip sent an expeditionary force to establish a beachhead in northwestern Anatolia shortly before his untimely death. This move made it abundantly clear that he intended to continue Macedon's imperial expansion to the east, into regions controlled by Persia. Although we cannot say how much of the Persian Empire Philip imagined he might conquer, Alexander went after the entirety of the Great King's domain—and more. By the time of Alexander's death in 323 BCE, the king of Macedon ruled over the largest empire the Western world had ever seen. But none of that could have been foreseen when Philip came to the throne in 359 at age 23. Before Philip, the king of Macedon had not been a major player, even on the Greek scene—much less an existential threat to the greatest of the Greek poleis and to the Great King himself.

As early as the Persian Wars of the early fifth century, the Greeks regarded the king of Macedon as within their orbit—if not exactly as one of themselves. Alexander I (who ruled ca. 498–454 BCE) was reputed to have brought the Greeks intelligence of the Persian advance early in the great Persian Wars of 481–478. By the end of the fifth century, the Macedonian court was sufficiently Hellenized to have become the "off-off Broadway" of Greek tragedy: Euripides ended his career by producing his plays for Macedonian audiences. Some elite Macedonian social customs were, however, still regarded as typically "barbarous" by the Greeks—notably the Macedonian symposium, at which heavily armed men downed mass quantities of undiluted wine (wine was always mixed with water in a proper Greek symposium). The impression of barbarism was not reduced when, as sometimes happened, drunken arguments escalated into murderous violence.

Much of Macedonian society before Philip appears to have been essentially feudal. Macedonian nobles were in some ways reminiscent of Homeric heroes, glorying in hunting, feasting, and war. They were willing to follow a king into battle if he was a strong leader but limited in their loyalty to the weak Macedonian state. While most Macedonians practiced monogamy, as did the Greeks, the Macedonian king (at least as exemplified by Philip and Alexander) might take multiple wives, perhaps in imitation of the practice of Persian royalty. How culturally or linguistically "Hellenic" the general Macedonian population was in the age before Philip II, or even a generation after his death, remains controversial. It is in any event unlikely that most Greeks in the fourth century regarded most Macedonians as truly Greek—or for that matter that most Macedonian elites regarded the citizens of Greek city-states as their own social peers.[6]

Unlike the polis-dwelling Greeks to their south, the Macedonians had long been at least nominally ruled by kings. The royal capital was, by the early fourth century, located at the town of Pella (1543: size 4) on the Axios River plain. Aigeai (1529: size 2), the former capital, was situated some 35 km to the southwest and remained an important ritual center. It was also the royal burial ground and the site of some extraordinary late fourth century tombs, one of which has been (somewhat dubiously) identified as that of Philip II. Macedonian kings were invariably drawn from the extended Argead lineage. In a familiar bit of specious and self-serving mythologizing (cf. the Athenian myth of Ion as founder of the Ionian ethnos: ch. 8), the Argead clan traced its ancestry to Herakles. The royal succession did not, however, necessarily pass from father to son. The succession seems to have been based on "necessary if insufficient" conditions of bloodline and competence. When there were multiple plausible heirs, the choice was presumably made by a coalition of powerful Macedonian elites. Kings were acclaimed, but not elected, by the Macedonian army.[7]

Macedon can best be understood as a basic "natural state," centered on a ruler and his elite coalition, in which rents were distributed according to the potential for violence. Although "Macedonian" was a recognized status and some Macedonians were citizens of poleis, Macedon as a state certainly had no pretentions to being a citizen-centered order. Any movement in the direction of more open access was carefully controlled. The authority of a king of Macedon was not based on a formal constitutional system but on the king's personal capacity to mobilize an army and to command the loyalty of other powerful Macedonian families. Although there had been occasional strong Macedonian rulers—notably Archelaus I (417–399: Thucydides 2.100.2), most kings before Philip II had been relatively ineffective. The king's authority was often undercut by bloody dynastic struggles. Plato (*Gorgias* 471a–d) offers a colorful account of how Archelaus I murdered his way to the throne. Royal authority was further undercut by the independence of the barons of Upper Macedonia and by strategic meddling by major poleis of central Greece.

In the earlier decades of the fourth century, both Athens and Thebes maneuvered to place their own chosen pretenders on the Macedonian throne. The resources of Macedonia, especially its abundant stands of timber, were highly valuable, and those resources were more accessible when Macedonian central authority was weak enough to be readily manipulated. The Macedonian state was, moreover, periodically threatened by Persia to the east, and by Illyrian, Triballian, and Paeonian tribes to the west and north. In the early fourth century, there were new threats to Macedon's standing: the emergence to the south of the Chalkidike confederation, led by the great polis of Olynthos (i588: size 5); the consolidation of independent kingdoms in Thrace and Scythia; and the growing ambitions of the Thessalian dynasts, Jason and Alexander.[8]

PHILIP AND THE RISE OF MACEDON (359–346 BCE)

In 359 BCE, King Perdiccas III was killed on the western Macedonian frontier in a battle against Illyrian tribes. His brother, Philip II, took over as king. The new king faced challenges on multiple fronts. He bought time: first by paying off the Illyrians and Paeonians (presumably using reserves from timber sales and harbor dues, see the section in this chapter on "explaining Philip's success"), and then by diplomatically false-footing Athens with vague assurances about his support for their claim to Amphipolis. Meanwhile, Philip took his first steps in the program of military reform that would, within a decade, fundamentally realign the power structure of the Greek world. Before Philip, the Macedonian king had only limited military forces on which he could dependably rely: perhaps a small body of infantry and the "mounted companions"—an elite unit of light cavalry. Given the weaponry and tactics of the classical era, light cavalry was trumped by heavy infantry—especially when the infantrymen were well trained and backed up by light-armed slingers, archers, javelin throwers, and accompanied by their own light cavalry. Having been fostered to Thebes as a teenager, Philip knew all that. He recognized that without an army capable of taking on a sizable phalanx of Greek hoplites, Macedon would always be forced to serve the interests of better-organized states.[9]

Building a bigger, better trained, and more loyal army was the essential prerequisite to Philip's ambitious plans for Macedon. The key to expanding the army was, first, more secure frontiers, and then successful imperial expansion into territories with fertile agricultural land. Spear-won land could be distributed to Macedonian families from the hardscrabble uplands in the form of grants of real estate contingent on the provision of young men for military service. Since conquered land belonged to the king, implementing this strategy made Philip the patron of a growing body of clients, thus bypassing the feudal relations that had bound ordinary Macedonians to local chiefs. When the barons realized that they could be end-run and thus made socially redundant, they chose to join the king's coalition as their best remaining option.

The dynamic of growing royal power, driven by the imperative to recruit and train more armed men, and to distribute more land to them, meant that a logic of continuous territorial expansion underlay Philip's reign. The king's capacity to keep most of the barons in his coalition, working with him rather than plotting against him, depended on continuously growing the army, which in turn depended on building a Greater Macedonia. And build he did.[10]

Within a year of coming to power, Philip had recruited and trained an infantry force of 10,000 men. He used this force, in close coordination with several hundred cavalry, to win a major battle against the Illyrian tribes. That victory stabilized Macedonia's western frontier and thereby helped Philip to lay the groundwork for at least somewhat greater royal control over Upper Macedonia. That in turn gave Philip access to a substantially increased population, from which he could recruit more soldiers—assuming he could pay them. Paying recruits with land (or promises of land) meant expanding to the east and south, where there were fertile agricultural tracts that might be distributed to Macedonian families who provided the king with soldiers. Those fertile lands were, however, controlled or claimed by powerful poleis.

In 357, in a surprise move, Philip besieged Amphipolis, the big (size 5), strategically located former Athenian colony that dominated the Strymon River valley—the region that lay immediately to the east of Lower Macedonia. The Athenians, who had never given up their claims to a city that had been independent for two generations, were shocked and outraged. But, as Philip must have known, they were tied up with their Social War against their former allies (who were being backed by Mausolus of Caria) in the north Aegean and unable to respond effectively to Philip's gambit. Amphipolis fell; Philip took the Strymon valley and over the next three years systematically extended Greater Macedonia south and further east.

To the south, on the eastern and western shores of the Thermaic Gulf, Philip took, among other places, the cities of Pydna (1544: size 3), Potidaia (1598: size 2), and Methone (1454: size 1). In the east, on the south Thracian coast, he seized Apollonia (1627), Abdera (1640: size 5), and Maroneia (1646: size 5). In addition to his military victories, Philip also made strategic alliances, often cemented with dynastic marriages: In Illyria (wife Audata), in Epirus (wife Olympias), in Thessaly (wives Nikesipolis and Philinna), with the Chalkidikean League, and with certain of the Thracian kings (wife Meda). As we have seen (ch. 9), in the later 350s Philip campaigned against the Delphi-robbing Phocians in support of his allies in Thessaly. Philip beat the Phocians at the Battle of the Crocus Field in 352 but was turned back at the pass of Thermopylae by the Athenians when he sought to move south in order to consolidate his victory. This was, as events soon showed, only a temporary setback.[11]

In 356, Philip had made one of the most fiscally significant territorial acquisitions of his reign. The town of Krenides (1632), located 45 km east of Amphipolis and 15 km inland from the Thracian coast, between Mt. Pangaion to the west and a southern spur of the Rhodopian range, was the primary processing center of a productive gold- and silver-mining region. Control of the mines had been hotly contested since the sixth century by Athens, Thasos, and various Thracian dynasts. Philip refounded the town a few kilometers to the east and renamed it Philippi (1637: size 2)—among the first known instances in the extended Greek world of a founder naming a city for himself. According to Diodorus (16.6.6–7) Philip's control of the Pangaion mining region substantially enriched the Macedonian king, increasing his revenues by more than 1,000 talents per annum—a sum equivalent to Athens' annual revenues in the high imperial era preceding the Peloponnesian War.

The main part of the new mineral resource revenue stream may not have come on line immediately, but in the mid-340s Philip was minting silver tetradrachms on a large scale. Instead of the Athenian weight standard (tetradrachm weight 17.15 g), Philip used the weight standard that had previously been employed by the Chalkidikean League and Amphipolis (tetradrachm weight 14.5 g). Philip's silver coinage circulated within Greater Macedonia and northward into inland Europe. But Alexander, Philip's successor, switched to the Athenian weight standard, and within a generation, Macedonian coinage had overtaken Athenian coinage as the dominant form of exchange in the eastern Mediterranean world. Philip added to his repertoire by minting gold staters (weight 9.5 g). Greeks associated gold coins with the mints of the Great King, a fact that is unlikely to have been lost on Philip. Philip's gold coinage was both voluminous and popular; it soon became the dominant gold coinage in the Aegean. Philip and Alexander were, in effect, at once emulating and competing with the minting practices of the Athenians and the Great King alike.[12]

Philip's coins, both silver and gold, were produced to high standards; they were reliable in weight and precious metal content. They were also superb examples of the engraver's art and must have made a splash when they first appeared in northern Aegean markets. Philip's coins portray a god (Zeus or Apollo) on the obverse, and a mounted rider (generally believed to be Philip himself) on the reverse. They resemble the finest Greek coins in fabric, iconography, and craftsmanship. Yet unlike any of the coins issued by the city-states, even those minted under the auspices of the grandiose tyrants of Syracuse, Philip's coins advertised the ruler's own name: each was stamped *Philippou*—belonging to (i.e., minted by) Philip. Greek coins were typically stamped with an abbreviated form of the name of the minting state (e.g., AΘE: Athe[nians]). By the age of Philip, if not before, the Macedonian state *was* the king. Philip's style of silver and gold royal coinage set the standard for the gigantic coinages of Alexander and later Hellenistic kings. In his coinage, as in other ways, Philip both built upon classical Greek practice and introduced innovations pointing toward the postclassical era of Greek history.

By 352, just eight years after Philip's accession to the kingship, Macedon had moved out of the shadows and had joined the ranks of the greatest powers of the extended Greek world. Over the next six years, Philip consolidated and extended his position. After the collapse of his alliance of convenience with the cities of Chalkidike, he besieged and, in 348, captured Olynthos, giving him effective control of the entire peninsula. The surviving population of Olynthos was enslaved or expelled; the city itself was looted and sacked. Because the site was never substantially reoccupied, excavations at the ancient site of Olynthos have provided archaeologists an extraordinarily comprehensive example of fourth century Greek domestic architecture and assemblages. Prominent among the small finds are Macedonian arrowheads and sling bullets engraved with Philip's name.[13]

Having failed to relieve either Amphipolis in 357 or Olynthos in 348, the Athenians now faced up to the new reality of Macedonian power, signing a treaty with Philip in 346 that is traditionally called the "Peace of Philocrates,"

after one of the Athenian ambassadors. In the course of the protracted negotiations, the cities of Phocis surrendered to Philip. Although allied with Athens, they had been excluded from the truce at Philip's insistence. The population of the cities of Phocis, like that of Mantinea earlier in the century (ch. 9),
was dispersed to villages—thus angering the Thebans who had thought Phocis would be theirs to plunder.

Macedon was, by the mid-340s, the most powerful state in the Greek
world—comparable to Athens in the 430s or Sparta in the 380s. Eight years
later, at Chaeronea, when the Macedonian army proved superior to the
united forces of Athens and Thebes, it would be clear that Macedon had exceeded all earlier city-state-based hegemonies. But in the immediate aftermath of the truce of 346 and the humbling of the Phocians, Philip focused
on expanding his empire west, north, and east and on diplomacy aimed at
preventing (or at least delaying) the formation of a potentially dangerous
Athens–Thebes alliance.[14]

TO CHAERONEA (346–336 BCE)

In the eight years between the Peace of Philocrates and the battle of Chaeronea, Philip was busy consolidating the Macedonian Empire and extending it
on several fronts. After suppressing restive poleis in Thessaly, he reorganized
that large region under Macedonian-appointed governors. He campaigned
in the north against the Illyrians and Paeonians. In the southwest, he extended his influence south of Epirus. In the east, he deposed Thracian and
Scythian kings and incorporated much of inland Thrace into his empire. By
early 338, as king of Greater Macedonia and *archon* of Thessaly, Philip ruled
perhaps 1.25 to 2 million subjects.[15]

Meanwhile, Macedonian relations with Athens had worsened after the
signing of the Peace of Philocrates. Some Athenian leaders, notably the orator Demosthenes, were never reconciled to Philip's incorporation of Amphipolis into Greater Macedonia or with treating Macedon as Athens' peer polity. Rightly or wrongly, Demosthenes and other Athenian hawks interpreted
Philip's ongoing campaigns in Thrace and his conquest of the small north
Aegean island of Halonessos—a notorious pirate lair that lay about 30 km
south of the Athenian-controlled island of Lemnos—as deliberate provoca-
tions. Philip offered to give Halonessos to Athens and proposed an expedition against Aegean pirates, to be carried out by the Athenian navy and financed by Macedon. Ambassadors went back and forth, but negotiations
bogged down over, among other things, the question of whether Philip
would be "giving" or "giving back" (as the Athenians insisted) Halonessos.

Philip sought to build alliances with leading central and southern Greek states—activity that Demosthenes interpreted in the worst possible light. In fact, Philip's diplomatic successes in Greece south and east of Phocis were limited: For a short time in the late 340s, it appeared that Philip would bring the poleis of Euboea, the big island off Athens' east coast, into his sphere. But Athenian diplomacy and military intervention turned the situation around, with the result that an independent Euboean League was formed that was friendly toward, if not formally allied with, Athens. Philip found some friends among the Peloponnesians, but there was no Peloponnesian state on which he could rely for military aid.

Exactly what Philip was aiming at in his "Greek policy" during this period has been much debated. It has been argued that he was already focused on the invasion of the Anatolian provinces of the Persian Empire, which offered the prospect of rich booty and fertile lands. Under this interpretation, his goal in central and southern Greece was stable peace rather than conquest, given that the cost of the conquest of Greece was likely to be higher than any possible payoff and that the payoff for invading Asia was likely to be high. This interpretation suggests that Philip's negotiations with Athens were sincere and that the breakdown of the treaty was primarily due to warmongering Athenian leaders.

The alternative view is that Philip could not afford to contemplate an expedition into Asia until he had definitively eliminated the endemic and serious danger to Macedonian security represented by the independent states of central Greece, especially Athens and Thebes. The Peace of Philocrates had been a delicate balancing act that, from Philip's perspective, avoided the unhappy prospect of Athens and Thebes uniting against Macedon. But that danger would remain until both great poleis had been defeated in battle. According to this latter interpretation, Philip was biding his time with insincere negotiations, waiting for the opportunity to crush his Greek rivals militarily. On the whole, this second interpretation makes more sense. Assuming that Philip did plan to invade Persia, and that such an invasion would take the Macedonian army a long way from Macedon and Greece, it is hard to see how the undefeated Greek states could have credibly committed not to exploit the situation.[16]

In the event, Philip's imperial expansion eastward across Thrace and toward the Hellespont, along with Athenian determination to retain a strong presence in exactly this region, precipitated the final collapse of the Peace of Philocrates. By 341, Athenian generals stationed in the Thracian Chersonese on the west shore of the Hellespont were raiding Macedonian shipping and fighting what amounted to a proxy war against Thracian poleis allied with

Philip. In 340 BCE, continuing his drive to the east, Philip threw an army of 30,000 into a siege of Perinthus (i678: size 5) on the south shore of Propontic Thrace. When Perinthus held out, he split his forces and extended his siege operations to nearby Byzantion (i674: size 5), thereby threatening to take control of the Bosphorus straits. If Philip took Byzantion, he would control the entrance to the Black Sea and could deny Athens access to its primary source of imported grain.

Athens now dispatched a fleet to reinforce Byzantion. The Great King independently sent aid to the two besieged cities, as did Chios, Rhodes, and Cos—the Aegean island states that had been Athens' primary foes in the recent Social War. In the face of massive fortification walls, determined resistance, and substantial external support, both of Philip's sieges failed. But in autumn of the year, his navy, still too small to engage the Athenian fleet in battle, managed to capture a big convoy of mostly Athenian grain ships. The transport ships were mustering at the Bosphorus, awaiting an Athenian military escort to take them, down the Propontis, through the Hellespont, into the Aegean, and onward to Piraeus. Philip appropriated the timber and grain from 180 Athenian ships. He let free the other 50 ships, bound for non-Athenian ports.

Athens and Macedon were by this point unquestionably at war.

The question now was which central and southern Greek states would join Athens against Philip—or vice versa. For his part, Philip found no new allies. Demosthenes led the Athenian diplomatic effort. Most Greek states chose to stay on the fence. The anti-Philip alliance included the Achaean League, Corinth, Megara, the Ionian Sea island states of Corcyra and Leukas (i126), and some of the poleis of Euboea and Acarnania (Demosthenes 18.237). But by far the most important addition to the Athenian alliance was Thebes. Philip had reportedly offered the Thebans the right to plunder Athens if they joined him. Demosthenes claimed that the Theban alliance was his own doing, the product of his persuasive skills. No doubt the initiative was his. But Thebes had a long and troubled history with Macedon. The Theban leadership must have realized that if Philip defeated Athens, Thebes would be left without significant allies. Philip would have little incentive to fulfill his promises and ample incentive to take down the last of the great independent states of mainland Greece.

Athens' diplomatic efforts had resulted in an alliance of states with a total estimated population of something under 1 million people.[17] As we have seen, Philip now probably controlled a population of 1.25–2 million. At least as important as total population, however, was the strategy dictated by the alliance. Athens' success in creating a multistate alliance that included Thebes meant that the showdown with Philip would take the form of a land battle—rather than a war of attrition in which protracted sieges and naval maneuvers might play a major role in the outcome: Unlike Athens, Thebes' strength lay in its heavy infantry rather than in its fortification walls or navy; the defense line must now be drawn in northwestern Boeotia, in advance of the city of Thebes. Demosthenes' approach to alliance building either forced or enabled Philip to risk a major land battle against a substantial coalition—a battle that Philip might have lost but was probably quite confident that he could win.[18]

The Athens–Thebes axis meant that Philip was denied the option of continuing to pursue the incremental strategy of capacity building and imperial expansion that he had employed successfully since the early 350s. But on the other hand, a protracted war of attrition and maneuver might have made things more difficult for Philip: His last two major sieges had failed, and his navy was vastly inferior to that of Athens. Counterfactually, Athens might have chosen to employ against Philip a variant of Pericles' strategy in the Peloponnesian War—that is, trusting to the walled city–Piraeus circuit to keep Philip at bay while seeking allies to help fund large-scale naval operations against his imperial assets in the north. Such a strategy would mean that, in the place of Thebes, Athens would have sought as its main allies the major poleis of the northern Aegean and the Great King—i.e., the states that had rallied against Philip during the sieges of Perinthus and Byzantion. It is impossible to predict what would have happened had that strategy been pursued; the point is that the breakdown of the Peace of Philocrates by 340 did not necessarily mean that the fate of the independent poleis of Greece would be decided by a set-piece land battle.

In the event, the showdown came in August 338. After a barrage of charges and countercharges of impious state behavior (reminiscent, *mutatis mutandis*, of the religious charges leveled by both Athens and Sparta before the Peloponnesian War: Thucydides 1.126–128), Philip was summoned to march in arms into central Greece by the Amphyctions of Delphi—the sanctuary's managing board that Philip had effectively controlled since becoming master of Thessaly. Once south of Thessaly, Philip diverted his forces from his ostensible target (Locrian Amphissa: i158, accused of having impiously built on sacred lands) and seized the strategic Phocian town of Elateia (i180). The way into the Boeotian plain now lay open.

The anti-Macedonian allies responded quickly, mustering in the narrows of the plain, near the small Boeotian town of Chaeronea (i201: size 2). The opposing forces were similar in size, and each was primarily composed of heavy infantry and cavalry: Philip fielded some 24,000 Macedonian infantry, 6,000 allied infantry, and 2,000 cavalry. On the Greek side there were

12,000 Thebans, 6,000 Athenians, and 12,000 allied infantry, along with 3,800 cavalry. Altogether, there were on the order of 65,000 combatants on the field, certainly more than any in any land battle ever contested between Greek city-states.[19]

The battle was hard fought but never in doubt. The Macedonians were better led, well trained, armed with novel weapons (the sarissa), and battle-hardened. Thousands of allied troops were captured or killed—the dead included 1,000 Athenians and the entire Theban Sacred Band of 300 picked men. The surviving allied soldiers (including Demosthenes, who fought as an ordinary hoplite) fled the field. In stark contrast to the confused aftermath of the battle of Mantinea in 362 (ch. 9), Philip's victory was decisive. As the historian Justin (9.3.71) put it, "For the whole of Greece, this day marked the end of its glorious supremacy and its ancient independence."[20]

LEAGUE OF CORINTH

Thebes was forced to accept a Macedonian garrison, a narrowly oligarchic pro-Macedonian government, and the reconstitution of the Boeotian League on genuinely federal (rather than Thebes-dominated) lines. Corinth also surrendered and was garrisoned. The Athenians, by contrast, prepared for a siege. But Philip had little to gain from a protracted siege of a huge and heavily fortified city: We may assume that the 30,000 infantry he had brought to Chaeronea was as large an army as he could safely muster while leaving Macedon and Thrace properly garrisoned. A Macedonian army of similar size had failed to take Perinthus. Besieging Athens would be a more daunting undertaking than Perinthus and Byzantion combined—and all the more so if the Great King saw it in his own interest to support the besieged city, as he had two years before. It is hardly surprising, then, that Philip offered to negotiate a truce with Athens on reasonable terms: There would be no garrison or new government. Athens would cede control of the cleruchies on the Thracian Chersonese but would retain the strategic and productive islands of Lemnos, Imbros, and Skyros, along with Delos and the cleruchy on Samos. Athens accepted the terms.[21]

That winter (338–337 BCE), all major Greek mainland states, other than the now-irrelevant Spartans, sent representatives to meet with Philip at the headquarters he had established at Corinth. Here the Greeks agreed to a common peace, reminiscent of the King's Peace of 387 (ch. 9). They also joined a Macedonian-led Hellenic federation known to history as the League of Corinth. Philip's new arrangements borrowed freely from earlier and contemporary Greek practices, conjoining mechanisms familiar from Sparta's fifth century Peloponnesian League, from the fourth century Athenian naval league, and from the central Greek federal leagues that had emerged in the late fifth and fourth centuries.

The peace and federation agreement signed by the member states specified that no state would act so as to harm the interests of Philip, or his descendants, or any of the other league states. Moreover, interstate constitutional meddling was strictly forbidden: Each state was to continue indefinitely with the constitutional arrangements it currently enjoyed—whether oligarchy or democracy. As had been the case in Sparta's consistent support of Peloponnesian oligarchies in the fifth century, this entrenchment of existing regimes gave the ruling coalition in every member state a strong reason to prefer the Macedonian-guaranteed status quo. The league was to be headed by a leader (*hegemon*), but like the Athenian fourth century naval league, its council (*sunedrion*), made up of representatives from each of the constituent states, excluded the hegemon. Like contemporary federal leagues, the decrees of the league's council regarding war, peace, and interstate relations were binding on its member states, but each state retained its autonomy in local affairs. As in these other successful federalized systems, the member states of the League of Corinth agreed, jointly, to punish defectors. Those who failed in the duty of punishment could expect to be treated in their turn as defectors by the other member states and, when necessary, by the hegemon.[22]

In its first formal meeting, in spring of 337, to no one's surprise, the council of the League of Corinth elected Philip as its hegemon, and he announced his plan for invading the Persian Empire. The ideological justification offered for the proposed attack was, first, borrowing from the Athenian playbook of the early fifth century, vengeance for Persian sacrilege and destruction during the Persian Wars. Next, borrowing from the Spartan playbook of the later Peloponnesian War, Philip proposed to liberate the poleis of western Anatolia from Persian domination.

There can have been little doubt in anyone's mind that the actual purpose of the invasion was booty and land for Macedonians: The imperative to continuous imperial expansion, the dynamic Philip had set in train in the early 350s, had not changed. But expansion had been stalled during the last few years, while Philip had been settling affairs in Greece—whatever Philip's true motives after 346, it was true that the cost of pacifying Greece exceeded any immediate material gains. Macedon needed to resume the full-throated imperialism that had been interrupted, at considerable expense to the king's treasury, by the relatively muted (and not lucrative) imperialism represented by the League of Corinth.[23]

In spring of 336, Philip, who now controlled the Thracian Chersonese, established an Asian base of operations by moving 10,000 men across the

Hellespont to Abydos (1765) in northwestern Anatolia. Several Anatolian poleis, including Ephesus (1844), some 260 km (straight line) to the south, broke with the Great King and declared for Philip. But the Great King had hired his own highly competent Greek military expert, Memnon of Rhodes, who defeated Philip's lieutenants in several engagements.

Then, in July of 336, Philip himself was assassinated by a member of his bodyguard while officiating at his daughter's wedding in the theater at Aegeai. The Athenians cheerfully passed a resolution honoring the assassin but otherwise stood pat: Having grasped the fact that their best hope for striking a favorable bargain was an impregnable city, they had spent the two years following Chaeronea modernizing their fortifications and building warships. The Thebans were bolder, expelling the Macedonian garrison and deposing the pro-Macedonian government.

Philip's heir was up to the challenge. Upon being acclaimed as king of Macedon, Alexander moved quickly south to Corinth, where the council of the league duly declared him hegemon. In 335, after a lightning campaign in the northern empire against restive Illyrian tribes, he returned to central Greece, where he successfully besieged and then eliminated Thebes. The resident population of the polis was killed or enslaved. As with the destruction of Eretria and Miletus by the Great King in the early fifth century (ch. 7), Alexander demonstrated that he had no qualms about destroying one of the greatest of the Greek poleis if and when he was defied.

The next year, at the head of a large army that included substantial contingents from the states of the League of Corinth, Alexander crossed the Hellespont into Asia, declaring the continent to be his spear-won domain. Within three years, and after as many battles, the Persian Empire had fallen and the Greek world was about to be transformed. The classical era was ending; the Hellenistic about to begin. [24]

EXPLAINING PHILIP'S SUCCESS

How are we to explain the political fall of Greece? Appeal to Hellenic decline, in the form either of the putative weakness of individual Greek states or of divisions among them, does not get us far. It is certainly true that individually each of the greatest of the eastern Greek states—Sparta, Athens, and Thebes—was in 338 less militarily powerful than it had been at its historical peak: Sparta after Leuctra was a shadow of its sixth–fifth century self. Thebes had suffered in the wars of the 360s and 350s but still commanded a very large army as the dominant state of the Boeotian League. Athens, with a citizen population of about 30,000, was less populous than it had been a hundred

years earlier, and state income was probably still well below that of the imperial peak. But Athens' finances had recovered substantially from the Social
War era low, and there were as many triremes in the shipsheds as there had
been in the mid-fifth century. Overall, as we have seen (ch. 4), the population
of mainland Greece appears to have reached all-time highs, and Hellas was
remarkably wealthy by historical standards.

It is also true that Greece was far from united in 338: As we have seen, the
states in the anti-Philip alliance had a total population of under a million;
something on the order of 1.5 million Greeks in central and southern mainland Greece and the islands stood aloof.[25] But division among the Greek
states was nothing new. As we have seen in previous chapters, Greece had
always been divided, insofar as there was never a "Leviathan" central authority capable of coercively coordinating the actions of "the Greeks" at scale and
over time. Cooperative action among coalitions of Greek states was always
predicated on shared interests, not obedience. After the Persian Wars, some
29 other Greek states had their names inscribed on the Serpent Column at
Delphi as having joined Sparta and Athens in opposing the invasion. That
coalition represented only a fraction of the total manpower of the mainland
Greek world. In 338, the anti-Macedonian coalition put an army into the field
that was equal in size to that of the invaders—something that the Greek allies had certainly not managed to do when faced with the Persian invasion.
There is no reason to believe that the Greek soldiers in 338 fought any less
well than their ancestors had done when facing the Persians at Thermopylae,
Marathon, and Plataea. In brief, in seeking to explain the "political fall of
Greece," it is more informative to ask what Philip did right, rather than what
his Greek opponents did wrong.

Philip took Macedon from relative weakness to greatness in a very short
time. By defeating a coalition of leading Greek poleis, and then by bringing
all of mainland Greece, along with Thrace, under a coherent hegemonic order,
Philip succeeded where a sequence of empire-building city-states, with imperial populations roughly comparable to that of imperial Macedon before
Chaeronea (table 2.3), had failed (chs. 8 and 9). Many details of how he accomplished all that remain murky, due to the fragmentary nature of our
sources. But we can dispel much of the fog by making informed guesses based
on the evidence we do have.

In many particulars Philip must be seen as a ruler of a continental (as opposed to coastal), resource-rich autocratic state (as opposed to a human capital rich, citizen-centered state). As such, he took an approach to empire-
building that differed markedly from that taken by any Greek polis. Philip
saw the possibilities offered by his world in different terms than did his

southern neighbors. Unlike the polis-dwelling Greeks, Philip was not bound, culturally or otherwise, to a coastal littoral (ch. 2). He exploited inland natural resources (especially timber and, later, minerals), and he founded cities deep inland in Thrace—some 150–200 km inland from the coast—in order to promote overland trade.[26]

Once he had built a strong coalition that included the formerly independent barons of Upper Macedonia and an army of soldiers bound to him by patronage and grants of land, Philip possessed a degree of centralized control over state policy that no government of a citizen-centered state could hope to match. Philip's authority, unlike a democratic or oligarchic polis government, was in principle indefinitely scalable, at least insofar as social cooperation was based on obedience and hierarchy (ch. 3). Unlike the natives of the Greek city-states, Macedonians were not used to thinking of themselves as citizens; the centralization of Philip's authority does not seem to have been a problem for his Macedonian subjects. Philip certainly needed to attend to the concerns of the barons and soldiers in his extensive coalition. Like Alexander after him, Philip participated in the social-capital-building rituals of the Macedonian symposium and the military camp—joining in the dangers and pleasures of the men he led. He surrounded himself with talented individuals and depended on loyal lieutenants. But he did not need to clear his policy plans with a representative council, nor did he have to move legislation through a large assembly of independent and critical-minded citizens.

Philip's position as Argead king gave him a degree of legitimacy as sole ruler that no Greek leader could aspire to. Since the king effectively *was* the Macedonian state, he was able to act more quickly and with less advance publicity than was conceivable in the world of the city-states. This was, as his polis-based opponents realized at the time, a substantial advantage in war and diplomacy. While he devoted a great deal of time and energy to military affairs, Philip was famous for his diplomatic acumen and was said to prefer a victory won by ruse to one gained by open combat. Moreover, the king was not bound by the rules that constrained the social behavior of ordinary mortals. Royal polygamy enabled him to cement political alliances through marriage alliances with other dynasts and to display his affinity for other regions. Unlike Greek leaders of citizen-centered states, or even Greek tyrants who ruled over men accustomed to citizenship, Philip could advantageously adopt some of the ideological apparatus of godlike kingship. While it is debatable how far he went in portraying himself as godlike, and exactly who were the intended audiences for his performances of divinity or near-divinity, there is no doubt that he went further in this direction than any Greek leader had ever dared.[27]

These various deviations from polis norms help to explain certain of Philip's advantages in pursuing his imperial project—advantages that were denied to Athens, Sparta, Thebes, and Syracuse. But these deviations do not adequately answer a second question: Why did Philip succeed in the conquest of central and southern Greece, when the Great Kings of Persia, who would seem to have similar advantages and vastly greater resources, had failed? This question is more pointed insofar as once-popular explanations, based on the discredited assumption that the fourth century Greek poleis were impoverished or somehow degenerate, must be rejected in light of the evidence for classical efflorescence.

In order to answer the question of why Philip succeeded where Darius and Xerxes had failed, we need to look at the other side of the comparative coin—that is, how Philip's Macedon was *like* an advanced fourth century Greek polis. The core similarity lay in a capacity to identify and recruit specialized expertise that could be useful for state purposes. Given the thinness of our sources for Philip's reign, this claim rests as much on inference as it does on evidence. But there seems good reason to infer that Philip employed Greek expertise and that it was important to his success. The Liverpool historian, John K. Davies, has shown that in the Hellenistic period Macedonian dynasts borrowed extensively from fourth century Athenian fiscal institutions, especially in the area of taxation. This is especially clear in Egypt, where the documentary record is exceptionally rich (thanks to a climate that preserves scraps of papyrus). I suggest that the Macedonian adaptation of useful Greek expertise began earlier. Philip, who anticipated the practices and methods of his royal Macedonian successors in so many areas, was also a leader in the essential domain of opportunistic emulation. As we will see, however, in this domain Philip was himself anticipated by Perdiccas III, his royal predecessor.[28]

Some of the skilled experts recruited by Philip were talented Macedonians, but others were Greek. The availability of Greek expertise is not a sufficient explanation for the rise of Macedon or the political fall of Greece. As noted above, there were in the fourth century any number of states at the margins of the Greek world, ruled by aggressive "opportunists" who were eager and able employers of Greek expertise. In the end, of course, it was Macedon alone that posed an existential threat to the independence of the great poleis of the Greek world. Although the ready availability of Greek expertise cannot be *sufficient* to explain Philip's success, it is entirely plausible to suppose that it was a *necessary* condition for it. Pushing the argument one step further, the availability of Greek expertise and a recognition of how to use it to advantage may be regarded not only as the key similarity between

Philip and the other fourth century opportunists, but also as the key differentiator between imperial Macedon in the fourth century BCE and imperial Persia in the fifth.

Unlike Xerxes, who took on an alliance of Greek states at the head of military forces (at least insofar as the land army is concerned) organized and armed in the tradition of multiethnic Persian armies, Philip led a state that was, in various ways, Greek-like in its financial and military organization. When Greek armed forces confronted Macedonians in the mid-fourth century, they had none of the advantages in arms, armor, unit cohesion, training, maneuver, or morale that their ancestors had enjoyed relative to the armies of Darius and Xerxes in the fifth century. In a meaningful sense, when they faced Philip's Macedonians, Greek soldiers were confronted with more experienced, better-armed, better-trained, and better-led versions of themselves.

I suggest that the two key areas in which Philip's Macedon benefited from Greek expertise were financial administration and military organization and technology. But those specific areas were developed against a general background of Greeks in Macedonian service and the related phenomenon of elite Macedonian uptake of Greek culture. There is no doubt that Greek language, literature, art, and architecture were increasingly incorporated into elite Macedonian society during Philip's reign. Elite Macedonians in the king's court spoke Greek and were at home in the greater Greek world. While we know regrettably little about Philip's civil administration, we do know that he employed Greeks as ambassadors (e.g., Python of Byzantion) and at least one Greek secretary: the ferociously competent Eumenes, a citizen of Kardia (i665), a small (size 2) but important (fame rank 3) polis on the northern shore of the Thracian Chersonese. Eumenes' role in Philip's administration is unknown, but under Alexander he became a principal secretary. After Alexander's death Eumenes became a first-tier military commander in an age otherwise dominated by ethnically Macedonian warlords and soldiers.[29]

Perhaps most telling is Philip's selection of Aristotle as tutor to his son, and presumptive heir. Aristotle, the son of a Greek physician who had attended Philip's father, Amyntas III, was born in 384 BCE in Stageira (i613), then a prominent (size 4, fame 3) polis on the northeast coast of the Chalkidike Peninsula. Stageira was probably destroyed by Philip, in or around 348 when the Chalkidike was absorbed into the Macedonian empire, although the city may later have been refounded by him. Since about 366 BCE Aristotle had lived in Athens, as a member of Plato's Academy. He left Athens after Plato's death in 347. After a few years in Atarneus on the northwestern coast of Anatolia, as the guest of the local dynast/Persian governor Hermias, and then in nearby Mytiline on Lesbos, Aristotle was invited by Philip to Macedon to be Alexander's tutor. Plutarch mentions instruction in Homeric poetry, but he also supposed that Aristotle offered his pupil political counsel.

The canonical list of Aristotle's writings includes two lost treatises that were said to have been specifically written for Alexander, one "on behalf of colonists" and another "on kingship." I have suggested elsewhere that the treatise on behalf of colonists should be understood in light of Aristotle's development in book 7 of the *Politics* of a design for a "best practically achievable" polis. The lost treatise may have specified the sort of men Aristotle believed should be recruited for at least one of the new colonial foundations that he knew Philip and Alexander were planning. While Philip's aims in hiring Aristotle as a tutor were certainly very far from Dion of Syracuse's specious plan for having Plato transform the tyrant Dionysius II into a philosopher-king (ch. 9), Philip must have believed that immersion in aspects of Greek rational thought, including Greek political theory, would be of value to his heir (see further, below). Alexander himself presumably agreed on the value; in any event when he set off to conquer Asia, he brought with him Aristotle's nephew, the historian Callisthenes, who had been born in Olynthos before its sack by Philip, along with other Greek experts in various aspects of science and administration.[30]

We may readily imagine that Philip recruited useful Greek experts both from free Greeks willing to be paid for their services, like Aristotle, and from enslaved Greek populations; Callisthenes may not have been the only talented Greek from Olynthos in Philip's employ. There was, in any event, no lack of accomplished Greeks eager to bring themselves to Philip's attention. Our fragmentary literary record includes genuine letters addressed to Philip by the Athenian orator Isocrates and by the Athenian philosopher Speusippos, as well as spurious letters to Alexander by Aristotle. At any given time, there would be a number of Greeks resident in the court; Speusippos' letter implies, for example, that the historian and rhetorician, Theopompus, had made himself unpopular at Philip's court.[31] Philip had, as it were, a number of Greek resumes in hand from which he could pick and choose if and when he sought to recruit new talent. Among the Greeks he would have been particularly eager to recruit were individuals with deep experience in taxation and state finance, and in the related areas of mining, coinage, and minting. As we have seen (ch. 9) there is good reason to think that such individuals existed at Athens (and probably in other major poleis) and that the employment of experts by the Athenian state was a key element in sustaining Athens' economy and influence in the fourth century.[32]

Philip was certainly well aware of the power of money. He was as famous in the Greek world for his clever use of money for diplomatic purposes as he was for his military innovations and victories. He was believed to have used his money freely to bring individuals and communities over to his side and was said to have quipped that there was no citadel to which one could not "send up a little donkey laden with gold" (Cicero *ad Atticum* 1.16.12). Although according to the historian Theopompus, Philip was a poor manager of state funds, this is contradicted by the evidence of his accomplishments and is probably the result of a polemical tradition conjoined with ignorance of how late-classical-era state finances actually worked.[33] There is some reason to believe that the Macedonian state was, in the age of Philip, able to raise money through the mechanism of sovereign debt. The Macedonian treasury was thought to be in the red when Alexander took over as king, and Alexander was said to have borrowed heavily before embarking for Asia. If these reports have a basis in truth, they would account for Philip's reputation as a bad manager among historians who failed to grasp the value of deficit financing. The same reports likewise point to the sophistication of Macedonian state finances.[34]

While Philip probably made especially good use of Greek experts, he was not the first Macedonian king to recognize that Macedon needed the kind of fiscal expertise that the Greek world could readily supply. We get a hint of the use of Athenian financial experts by a Macedonian king shortly before the reign of Philip from a late fourth century text wrongly attributed to Aristotle:

> Callistratus, when in Macedonia, caused the harbor-dues, which were usually sold for twenty talents, to produce twice as much. For noticing that only the wealthier men [among the Macedonians] were accustomed to buy them because the sureties for the twenty talents were obliged to show [provide collateral] talent for talent, he issued a proclamation that anyone might buy the dues on furnishing securities for one-third of the amount, or as much more as could be procured in each case.
> —*Pseudo-Aristotle,* Economics *2.1350a, trans. Armstrong (Loeb) adapted*

Callistratus of the Athenian deme of Aphidna was a prominent politician who was in exile from Athens in the mid-360s. He was apparently employed as a sort of financial consultant by Perdiccas III, Philip's immediate predecessor, and was set to work on the problem of how to increase royal revenues. Callistratus' innovation, allowing tax farmers to leverage their collateral, evidently broke the monopoly of a few extremely wealthy Macedonians. Once the tax auction was opened to men outside the superwealthy few able to put up twenty talents of collateral, the resulting competition drove up the bidding for the right to farm the relevant taxes to what we may guess was closer to its market price (i.e., just below the amount that could prospectively be realized by the tax farmer).[35]

Assuming that the story is true, it is a vivid example of opening access in ways that benefited the state—i.e., the king. The opening of access was done in a carefully controlled and limited way that appears calculated to expand the king's revenues without upsetting his coalition: The very rich now could participate in an institution formerly monopolized by the super-rich. It is tempting (albeit entirely speculative) to link the passage in the *Economics* concerning Callistratus to Philip's success in buying off the Illyrian tribes upon the death of Perdiccas III. A recent increase in the revenues from farming the export taxes could have left enough in the state treasury to give Philip, as incoming king, the means to purchase the time he needed in order to recruit and drill his first substantial army—and thus to begin the process that led to the rise of Greater Macedonia.

As we have seen, Macedon became a major gold- and silver-minting state after Philip's takeover of the Pangaion mines in 356. The production and distribution of coinage—including the mining and refining of precious metals, minting of high quality (standard weight, high purity, iconographically distinctive) coins in large quantities, and circulating them through northern Aegean markets—required specialized knowledge at each stage. When recruiting experts to operate his mining and minting operations, Philip could have looked to Athens, the state that had, since the mid-fifth century, been the leading silver-coin producer of the Mediterranean. Athens, like Macedon, controlled rich silver mines. The fourth century was a period of innovation in Athenian practices of mining and refining silver ores. In the middle decades of the century the production of the Laurion mines increased substantially, a result both of new technology and legislation that encouraged mineral exploration. The Athenian mint produced great numbers of high quality coins, which circulated at a premium in Aegean markets (ch. 9). As we have seen, Philip adopted the tetradrachm form (although at a different weight standard) as a standard large-denomination coin. Although we lack direct evidence that Philip brought in Greek experts in mining, processing ores, and minting, it is altogether likely that he did, perhaps, as at Athens, acquiring experienced slaves for some of the work.[36]

Along with state finance and resource management, the military is the most obvious area in which Philip's reforms catapulted Macedon to preeminence in the mid-fourth century. Here, Philip's innovations not only resemble, but ultimately transcend, the state of the art in the leading Greek poleis of the era. And once again, there is reason to think that Philip self-consciously and selectively employed Greek expertise in achieving his own ends. As his revenues increased, Philip augmented his Macedonian army with Greek mercenaries, but, unlike the armies of the Sicilian tyrants, there is no reason to believe that Macedonian forces were ever predominantly mercenary, nor did Philip hire Greek mercenary generals to command his armies. The most prominent military commanders who fought for Philip were native Macedonians. Yet, as suggested above, the principles on which Philip's military was organized—heavy infantry, in massed ranks, supported by cavalry and other arms—was adapted from techniques developed in fourth century Greece, and especially Thebes, where Philip had spent several years as a privileged hostage.

Philip's ability to build on and ultimately to transcend Greek military practices is demonstrated by the development of a new offensive infantry weapon: the *sarissa*. The standard heavy infantry weapon of the Greek world had long been the thrusting spear: about 8 feet (2.4 m) long, with wood shaft, iron point and butt spike, weighing about 2.2 lbs (1 kg). The Greek spear was wielded in the hoplite's right hand; his left hand and arm carried a heavy round shield. Under Philip, the Macedonian infantry began using a much longer and heavier thrusting spear, 15 to 18 feet (4.6–5.5 m) long, weighing about 12–14.5 lb (5.5–6.5 kg), and wielded with both hands. A light shield that could be slung over one shoulder replaced the heavy hoplite shield, leaving both hands free to manage the heavy sarissa. The sarissa was at some point, perhaps as early as the reign of Philip, adopted by Macedonian cavalrymen. As shown by the famous Alexander mosaic, the Macedonian cavarlyman held his long pike low over his horse's withers, employing an underhand thrust that used the horse's forward momentum, rather than the rider's strength, to deliver the blow.

The sarissa reform involved a rethinking of long-canonical approaches to warfare. Far from a simple incremental improvement ("long spear good, longer spear better"), incorporating the sarissa into military operations involved fundamental changes in armor, shield, battlefield formation, and training methods, for infantry and cavalry alike. The idea of a long thrusting spear may have been borrowed from the equipment of light-armed Thracian peltasts.[37] Yet the new approach was based solidly on the fundamentals of Greek land warfare as they had been modified in the course of the later fifth and fourth centuries: a deep and maneuverable phalanx of trained and reliable heavy infantrymen, each armed with a thrusting spear and shield, closely supported by smaller numbers of trained and reliable light arms and cavalry.

While the inventor of the sarissa is not preserved in the ancient tradition, we may imagine the sarissa reform as the product of a self-conscious project of military innovation driven by Philip and carried out by experts in arms, armor, and training. Given that the sarissa reform was a direct development of the contemporary Greek approach to warfare—as opposed to, for example, being based on masses of bowmen and cavalry supported by light infantry (as in fifth century Persia), or mounted archers, backed up by warriors armed with long swords and battle axes (as in Scythia)—it is reasonable to suppose that Philip employed Greek military experts in designing and implementing the reforms.[38]

By the 340s Philip was able to deploy a small navy of triremes. The Macedonian navy under Philip remained too small to challenge even a modest, 20-ship Athenian naval squadron, but it was sufficient to capture an Athenian grain fleet at the Bosphorus in 340. Since there was no Macedonian navy before Philip, he was required to build from scratch. Thus, there is circumstantial reason to suppose that Philip enlisted expert advice in ship construction and naval operations. The most obvious source of that advice would be from within the Greek world, although the Phoenicians and Carthaginians were also highly experienced in trireme construction and operations.[39]

We lack direct evidence to show that Philip hired Greek experts to restructure the Macedonian infantry and cavalry, or to build the Macedonian navy. We are on firmer footing with siegecraft. Philip clearly saw, from the very beginning, that having an effective siege train was essential to his plans: The successful siege of Amphipolis in 357 was the essential first step in the expansion of Greater Macedonia. Philip was not always successful in taking walled cities. In 340, as we have seen, he failed in his assaults of Perinthus and Byzantion (both size 5). But Philip did successfully take a number of Greek cities by storm, including Potidaia (size 2) and Methone (size 3). By his sieges of Amphipolis and Olynthos, he demonstrated that the Macedonian forces were sufficiently disciplined and determined to take very large (size 5) and well-fortified Greek cities.

Part of Philip's success in siegecraft, but also in open-field battle, can be attributed to technological and operational innovations in artillery. Philip certainly made use of the nontorsion (crossbow-type) catapults that were probably invented in Syracuse at the beginning of the fourth century (ch. 9). It is, moreover, very likely that the torsion (hair- or sinew-spring-type) catapult was invented, around mid-century, by engineers in Philip's pay. Torsion springs allowed for a major advance in the power of ancient artillery, and pointed to the potential for further advances. Torsion catapults proved to be a big factor in Alexander the Great's campaigns in Asia. Increasingly tall and massive, yet mobile, siege towers were a related development. Siege towers allowed artillery to be used to maximum advantage, and enabled soldiers to gain access to circuit walls without resorting to flimsy ladders.

Philip is known to have employed several Greek designers of siege machinery. Like Xenophon and Aeneas the Tactician earlier in the fourth century (ch. 9), at least three of Philip's poliorcetic experts wrote technical manuals. Polyidus, a Thessalian, the author of *On Machines*, was with Philip at the siege of Byzantion in 340, where he reportedly devised a huge mobile siege tower that was (somewhat prematurely) dubbed the "city-taker" (*helepolis*). At the siege of Perinthus, in 340, one Macedonian siege tower is reported to have reached a height of 37 meters. Polyidus had at least two Greek students who were also associated with Philip: Charias and Diades, another Thessalian. Like their teacher, each wrote a treatise on siege machines and both of these men accompanied Alexander to Asia.[40]

In addition to the marquee developments in artillery and siege towers, Philip's siege engineers may be responsible for more subtle innovations: Not only are the catapult javelin heads, from bolts shot from Macedonian catapults and found in the ruins of Olynthos, heavier than earlier javelin heads, but Macedonian arrow heads and sling bullets are somewhat heavier than those used by the Olynthians. It is possible that Macedonian siege troops were using projectiles specifically designed for siege warfare.

PHILIP AND ALEXANDER BETWEEN ARISTOTLE AND HOBBES

In sum, one reason that Macedon under Philip succeeded in conquering the mainland Greek city-states, whereas Persia under Darius and Xerxes had failed, was because Macedon took on some, but only some, of the characteristics of a Greek superpolis. Macedon was like Athens and Syracuse in making effective use of experts and seizing a first-mover advantage from institutional and technical innovations. Even at the level of political institutions and culture, Philip's Macedon was in certain ways more like a polis than was the Persia of Xerxes or Darius. Of course Macedon remained very *unlike* any great polis in that it was a monarchy, ruled by a king who could keep his own counsel, make his own policy, and did not need to worry about challenges to his legitimacy—at least so long as he was militarily successful.

As subjects of the king, Macedonians were never citizens of Macedon in the strong political sense that Athenians or Spartans were citizens of their respective states. Yet, like the citizens of a leading Greek polis, many Macedonians must actively have supported the regime at least in part because they saw that doing so was in their own interest, as rational people, capable of cost–benefit reasoning, and concerned (although not uniquely) with maximizing their own utility. While power played a part, Macedonians (unlike, say, the helots of Sparta) were not merely coerced into obedience. Nor did they obey only because they accepted a state ideology claiming for the king a godlike status. The Macedonians in Philip's and Alexander's armies expected to do better for themselves and their families than their ancestors in Upper Macedonia could ever have hoped to do. Alexander was not exaggerating wildly when he (reportedly) dressed down restive Macedonian troops by reminding them where they had come from and what they had gained:

> Philip took you over when you were helpless vagabonds, mostly clothed in skins, feeding a few animals on the mountains and engaged in their defense in unsuccessful fighting with Illyrians, Triballians, and the neighboring Thracians. He gave you cloaks to wear instead of skins; he brought you down from the mountains to the plains; he made you a match in battle for the barbarians on your borders. . . . He made you city dwellers and established the order that comes from good laws and customs. It was due to him that you became masters and not slaves and subjects. . . . He annexed the greater part of Thrace to Macedonia and, by capturing the best placed positions by the sea, he opened up the country to trade.
> —*Arrian,* Anabasis *7.9.2–3, trans. Brunt (Loeb) adapted*[41]

Macedonians fought, not only for king and country, but also for themselves.

Like Cleisthenes of Athens, Philip was a sociopolitical innovator in that he created a vastly expanded coalition that included tens of thousands of ordinary (non-elite) men. In a move that is in some ways analogous to the radical expansion of the Athenian navy in the era of the Persian wars, Philip's military reforms incentivized a great many more individuals to undertake service in the armed forces and enabled them to see themselves as primary stakeholders in the outcomes of state-directed military operations.

A rational commitment to advancing a community's common interest in welfare and security, well aligned with the self-interest of many members of that community, had undergirded the reforms of Lycurgus of Sparta and of Solon, Cleisthenes, and Themistocles of Athens. That alignment of collective and individual interests was made explicit in the speeches put into Pericles' mouth by Thucydides. It was the key to the rise of Thebes in the age of Epaminondas, to the rebuilding of Athens after the Peloponnesian War, and to the rise of the Greek federal leagues. The failure to align collective and individual interests at a scale beyond that of the city-state ultimately doomed the various imperial projects of Athens, Sparta, Syracuse, and Thebes. A similar failure led the poleis of Sicily into a cycle of tyranny and economic downturn in the mid-fourth century. Timoleon revived the Sicilian economy by aligning the interests of many Greeks around a common project of resisting Carthaginian expansionism and ending an era of warlord exploitation.

Any reasonably attentive student of Greek social and political history might well have come to the conclusion that, in the absence of a state monopoly of coercive force conjoined with a compelling ideology of godlike kingship (the package that Greeks supposed, rightly or wrongly, the Great King of Persia offered his subjects), alignment of collective and individual interests was the only plausible route to high state performance. Herodotus, Thucydides, Xenophon, and Diodorus were attentive students of history, and their texts make the point clearly enough.

Aristotle was an astute student of history and a world-class theorist of politics. The alignment of the collective interest of the whole community (the state) with the interest in the flourishing of each of its essential constituent parts (individual citizens) lay at the center of Aristotle's discussion in the *Politics* of both justice and the practical measures that could be employed to preserve regimes.

For Aristotle, the key features of an uncorrupted regime were, first, the alignment of the interests of the ruler (individual or collective) with the common good of the community as a whole, and next the reliable deference of rulers to law—that is, to established rules guaranteeing the alignment of interests. None of this is surprising if we think of Aristotle in the tradition of Greek historical and political thought. But it is puzzling if we think of Philip as an absolute and lawless sovereign, on the model of Hobbes' Leviathan—a model that Hobbes used to refute Aristotle (ch. 3). Why on Earth, we may ask, would *Leviathan* hire *Aristotle* to tutor his prospective heir?

It is possible, but surely unlikely, that Philip was entirely ignorant of Aristotle's political (including social and ethical) commitments when he appointed him as Alexander's tutor. Yet assuming Philip *did* do a background check, and therefore *did* have an inkling of Aristotle's political thought, we may assume that Philip found Aristotle's thought worthwhile. Surely he would *not* have hired a tutor whose ideas about social order he found repugnant. So what was he thinking of?

Philip certainly did *not* hire Aristotle to tell him how to run his kingdom. Aristotle may have been working on the *Politics* (among other works) in the late 340s, when he was in residence in Macedon. But there can be no causal story leading from Aristotle's political philosophy to Philip's success. Aside from the absurdity of imagining Philip as playing Dion of Syracuse to his own Dionysius II, Philip had embarked on the reforms that led to his victory at Chaeronea long before Aristotle arrived. Yet, much in the philosopher's political theory would, I think, have resonated with the Macedonian king for the reasons suggested above: Philip's approach to ruling a kingdom relied on intuitions about aligning the interests of the state with those of rational men concerned with their own welfare. Whatever the source of those intuitions, Philip shared them with Greek institutional designers since the sixth century, with Greek political theorists since the fifth century, and with Aristotle himself.

It seems likely, then, that Philip's selective borrowing from Greek culture and expertise included not only techniques of state finance and military organization but also a general conception of social order that was based on the rational alignment of the interests of a great many individuals, rather than just a few elites, with the interests of the state. In Philip's Macedon, the state was personified by the king, and Philip might therefore be imagined as a Hobbesian sovereign. But in order to achieve his ambitious goals, Philip had to be able to commit credibly to social conditions that were regarded as advantageous by the tens of thousands of ordinary Macedonians who made up the bulk of the army. The question of whether that commitment meant that the king was bound by rules (per Aristotle) or that he ruled as a lawless third-party enforcer of agreements among his subjects (per Hobbes) was probably not fully articulated in the time of Philip. And that ambiguity later contributed to sometimes-violent confrontations between Alexander and certain members of his supercoalition during the conquest of Asia.

Wherever we situate Philip and Alexander between Aristotle and Hobbes, the social equilibrium that was struck between the kings of Macedon and their Macedonian subjects is central to any explanation for the rise of Macedon and thus for the political fall of the independent Greek city-states. As we see in the next chapter, a secondary equilibrium, between kings and poleis, is a key to explaining the persistence of the high-performing Greek economy in the generations after the fall.

11

CREATIVE DESTRUCTION
AND IMMORTALITY

Immortal, though no more! though fallen, great!
—BYRON 1812

In the poetic lines with which we began, Byron described Greece as immortal, fallen, and great. We have followed the rise of classical Greece to greatness, understood as efflorescence. We have traced the fall, understood as the loss of full independence by the major city-states. This concluding chapter reviews the causes of greatness and fall and turns to the question of immortality.

FALLEN, GREAT . . .

Both greatness and fall had similar causes: high levels of specialization, innovation, and mobility of people, goods, and ideas as the result of distinctive political conditions. I characterized those political conditions as fair rules and competitive emulation. Those conditions were emerging in the eight century BCE, had crystallized by the sixth century, and continued to develop through the fourth century in self-governing citizen-centered polities within a decentralized marketlike ecology of many small states sharing a common language and background culture.

In the most developed Greek city-states, relatively impartial rules, backed by the willingness of citizens to act in their defense, protected citizens (and some noncitizens) from historically common forms of domination and expropriation. That gave individuals and communities reason to invest in themselves. Investments included acquiring education, perfecting skills, and deferring short-term payoffs in favor of anticipated long-term rewards. The Greek world was characterized by intense competition between individuals and between communities but also by institutions and cultural norms that enabled extensive interpersonal and interstate cooperation and that lowered the costs of transactions. Competition, along with growing human capital and lower transaction costs, drove continuous innovation, both institutional and technological. Successful institutions and technologies, along with goods and ideas, were readily transferred within and among states. Because transaction costs were low, the value gained from the exchange of specialized goods and services was high. These political conditions promoted economic growth that was driven by a large middle class of consumers: non-elite families living well above subsistence. Economic growth in turn underpinned spectacular levels of cultural achievement. The same conditions paved the way, however, for an entrepreneurial and opportunistic authoritarian leader to borrow selectively from Greek institutions and technological innovations and thereby to conquer the mainland Greek states, ending the era of full great-polis independence.

Fair rules and competitive emulation in an ecology of small states do not explain every historical example of efflorescence. The historical sociologist Jack Goldstone's survey, discussed in chapter 1, shows that premodern societies with different political trajectories have experienced efflorescence.[1] But in Greece, the distinctive political situation that arose beginning around 800 BCE and persisted for at least the next half-millennium was the differentiator that enabled the world of the city-states to perform economically and culturally at a level much higher than the premodern normal, defined by conditions in the Late Bronze, Early Iron, and early modern periods of Greek history—and indeed, at a level that in some respects matched the exceptionally high-performing early modern societies of Holland and Britain.

Those conclusions are important to us in modernity, not because Greece was the unique origin of the Western tradition or the spark that ignited a putative "great divergence" between East and West but because classical Greece is the earliest documented case of "democratic exceptionalism plus efflorescence"—a historically rare combination of economic, cultural, and political conditions pertaining among developed countries in the contemporary world.

Insofar as we value democracy and prefer wealth to poverty, then we have good reason to care about explaining the rise of the society in which the wealth and democracy package is first documented. We have equally good reasons for wanting to explain why the major states within that society failed to maintain their full independence in the face of entrepreneurial authoritarians willing and able to appropriate institutions and technology. In the long run, the loss of city-state independence was coincident with a long economic decline. By the seventh century CE, core Greece had reverted to the relatively impoverished condition of the "premodern normal." The world of Greek antiquity was obviously very different from our own, and some of the factors that led to both the rise and fall of classical Greece are unlikely to be repeated. Yet for those who do recognize certain features of our modernity in the history of classical Greece, that history may serve as a cautionary tale.

. . . BUT WHY IMMORTAL?

We have one more puzzle to solve: Whence Greek immortality? How is it that Byron (and we) could know so much about the history and cultural accomplishment of classical Greece? If the political fall had coincided with the end of Greek greatness—if Greece had quickly reverted to the depressed economic situation of the premodern normal after Philip's victory at Chaeronea, Byron could not have learned enough about ancient Greece to regard it as immortal. Much of the literature, science, art, and architecture that are associated with "immortal Greek greatness" were indeed produced during the classical era. Even more was, however, produced in the subsequent Hellenistic period, drawing on that classical heritage. Self-consciously classicizing Greek literature continued vibrant during the high Roman Empire with the literary renaissance called the "Second Sophistic." In late antiquity, Greek philosophers and historians were still producing important work, actively drawing on classical models. Moreover, the cultural achievement that was a primary basis for Byron's belief in Greek greatness was preserved and canonized, as well as built upon, in the postclassical era: We would be severely limited in our knowledge of the history of the Greek world in the era 800–300 BCE if it were not for the sustained efforts of librarians and copyists during the centuries that followed the fall.[2]

Neither Byron's famous lines nor this book would have been written if the political fall of classical Greece had meant an abrupt end of efflorescence. But if the fall did not terminate economic growth and cultural achievement, we must ask *why* it did not. I have argued that distinctive classical-era political conditions that supported fair rules and competitive emulation—conditions not pertaining during the Bronze or Early Iron Ages nor in the medieval through early modern periods of Greek history—produced the sustained specialization and innovation that drove efflorescence. Then why did the loss of full independence *not* precipitate a quick and steep decline?

The answer is that the initial loss of Greek independence turned out to be only partial: Although the power of the Macedonian dynasts was real, many postclassical Greek poleis enjoyed considerable independence in the Hellenistic period. Some smaller Greek states were *more* independent than they had been in the classical era of hegemonic city-states. We now know that, contrary to what most scholars of Greek antiquity long believed, important aspects of Greece's political exceptionalism survived the classical fall.[3]

The political conditions of the postclassical Hellenistic world included the persistence of a multistate ecology: Until the Roman takeover of Greece in the second century BCE, there were always multiple rulers rather than a unitary empire. Meanwhile, ongoing institutional innovations promoted new forms of interstate cooperation. The political institutions and values of classical Greek democratic exceptionalism—federalism, rule of law, citizen self-government, and civic values of freedom, equality, and dignity persisted long after the fall, albeit sometimes in modified forms. As a spate of new scholarship has proved, many polis governments were democratic well into the second century BCE, and robustly so.[4]

Under these conditions, enough of the Greek poleis were able to preserve sufficient levels of rule egalitarianism and competitive emulation to sustain efflorescence for some two centuries after the "fall": Economic growth, while harder to measure after 323, appears to have continued long after Chaeronea. Cultural production certainly remained high. Important new advances were made in the fields of Greek historiography, drama, philosophy, science, technology, medicine, art, and architecture. While Athens remained an important cultural center, Hellenistic cultural production was widely dispersed across a large number of major cities. Cultural centers now included royal capitals—including Egyptian Alexandria, Anatolian Pergamum, and Syrian Antioch, each functioning as a polis with its own laws, citizens, and local government—along with poleis that had already been major centers in the classical period: Rhodes, Cos, Corinth, Sicyon, Kyrene—as well as Syracuse, Athens, and others. The political fall of classical Greece proved, in short, to be yet another example of creative destruction, rather than a ruinous destruction leading to quick economic and cultural collapse.

By the time imperial Rome took over a still-flourishing Greek world, Romans had become eager consumers of Greek culture. By the second century BCE, Roman elites were deeply enough Hellenized to ensure the subsequent preservation and dissemination of Greek thought and culture throughout the huge and still-growing Roman Empire and across the next several hundred years. Having jumped scale to become a dominant imperial culture in one of the two biggest empires of the premodern world (the other was Han China), the immortality of Greece was, if not ensured, at least made possible.

After the collapse of the western Roman Empire in the fifth to seventh centuries CE, classical Greek culture was sustained by the successor Eastern (Byzantine) empire and by scholars and scientists in the medieval Arabic-speaking world. When, in the fourteenth and fifteenth centuries CE, in the face of Ottoman Turkish imperial expansion, Greek literature was reexported to the West during the Italian Renaissance, and when Greek learning was popularized in northern Europe by Erasmus and other luminaries in the sixteenth century, its immortality was ensured.[5]

None of that was inevitable in the late fourth century BCE: Not every empire has encouraged, or even allowed, the preservation of the intellectual heritage of conquered small-state ecologies.[6] The immortality of Greek culture hinged on its uptake by the Hellenistic kingdoms after the political fall. That uptake was in turn predicated, at least in part, on the capacity of a number of the Greek poleis, in the two centuries after the fall, to negotiate terms of local independence and reasonable tax rates with powerful and rapacious Hellenistic dynasts. The dynasts were forced to concede more independence and to charge lower rents than they would have preferred because Greek cities were hard targets: While a given dynast often had the power to capture a given city, the cost of doing so was likely to be high (appendix II). Greek cities were hardened through Greek institutional and technical innovations—especially democracy, federalism, and military architecture—devised in the classical era and robustly sustained and further developed in the Hellenistic period.

ALEXANDER'S CAMPAIGN AND ANOTHER FALL

Alexander the Great's invasion of the Persian Empire had immediate and profound effects on the Greek world. The Greek cities of western Anatolia were liberated from Persian imperial control—whether or not they wished to be—following Alexander's battle with Persian satraps at the Granicus River (map 9). The battle, fought just east of Abydos in northwestern Anatolia in May 334, was a great victory for the young Macedonian king. Things might, however, have gone otherwise. There would have been no battle to win had the Great King Darius III accepted the strategic advice of his Greek general, Memnon of Rhodes. Memnon advocated a scorched earth policy aimed at starving the invaders while avoiding direct battle. Moreover, in the course of the battle, Alexander was nearly killed. Leading a cavalry charge, he was cut off from most of his men, and his helmet was cleaved by a Persian axe. Alexander thus came close to suffering the fate of the brilliant would-be usurper of the Persian throne, Cyrus II, who died leading a cavalry charge at the battle of Cunaxa in 401 (ch. 9). The near-doublet need not have been happenstance: Persian tactics in both instances seemed well designed to isolate an impetuous commander. Only a fortuitous spear thrust by Alexander's companion, Cleitus "the Black," saved the young Macedonian king from suffering Cyrus' fate.

The history of a counterfactual world in which Cleitus had been just a bit slower would have diverged radically from what in fact followed.[7]

After his victory at Granicus, Alexander moved inland and replaced the Persian governors of Lydia and Phrygia with men of his own choosing. He left intact the existing Persian satrapal system of local governance, however, perpetuating the principal-agent problem that had long bedeviled the governance of the Persian Empire. Once the Macedonian army returned to the coast, most of the Anatolian Greek poleis accepted their liberation, but Miletus in central Ionia resisted, as did Halicarnassus in Caria. Miletus fell fairly quickly to Alexander's siege machines. Halicarnassus, though, whose defense was led by the redoubtable Memnon, held out for much longer by making effective use of catapults mounted on the city walls. Each of the Anatolian Greek cities, now subject to Alexander, paid taxes to him in the form of *suntaxis*—the Greek term was borrowed from the "contribution" system of the Athenian naval league of the fourth century—and avoided the coercive associations of the "tribute" (*phoros*) system of the fifth century Athenian empire.[8]

Alexander actively promoted democracy in the Anatolian poleis, in place of Persia-supported oligarchies. He thus broke with Philip's Corinthian League regime policy, guaranteeing that subject states kept their existing constitutions. He also broke with Philip's preference for oligarchy, a preference that had been expressed in the new government imposed on Thebes after Chaeronea. Presumably Alexander felt that he had good reason to distrust the Greek elites who had gained most from Persian rule. New democracies would be more likely to support the new king—especially if the alternative was the return of the oligarchs with bloody reprisals to follow. The incumbent satrap of Caria, Ada (sister of Mausolus and wife of the previous satrap), was left in control of her province. The Greek cities of Ionia and Aiolis (regions 37 and 38: map 1 and appendix I) seem, however, to have arranged the terms of their allegiance directly with the Macedonian king, thus anticipating the situation of many Anatolian Greek poleis in the Hellenistic period.[9]

Meanwhile, after leaving Halicarnassus, Memnon, Darius' Greek commander, moved west into the Aegean, where he quickly gained control of Cos, Chios, and four of the poleis of Lesbos. He besieged the fifth and most important Lesbian city: Mytilene, the site of the Athenian campaign in 427 BCE (ch. 8). Alexander now faced the prospect of losing the Aegean. He hastily regrouped naval forces that had been prematurely dismissed after his victory at Miletus. Memnon, however, fell ill and died before the walls of Mytilene. Persian commanders carried on with Memnon's Aegean strategy, eventually taking Mytilene and the island of Tenedos (i793). But Alexander's lieutenants contained the Persian advance and later retook the north Aegean islands.

Once again, Alexander had dodged a bullet and thus was free to continue his fast-paced advance south to Syria and Egypt and then east across Asia.[10]

The rest of Alexander's extraordinary campaign—from the victory at Issus to the great sieges of Tyre and Sidon, to the conquest of Egypt, and to his greatest victory at Gaugemela; the burning of Persepolis, the pursuit of Darius and then of Darius' murderers, the difficult Afghan and Indian campaigns, the voyage down the Indus River, and the horrific march back through the Gedrosian Desert to Babylon—falls outside the ambit of this book. What matters for our purposes is that, during his lifetime, the diplomatic arrangements that followed the Macedonian victories over the Greeks in 338 and 334 remained for the most part intact. There was one dangerous challenge to Macedonian authority while Alexander was still campaigning deep inside Asia: By spring of 331 BCE, King Agis III of Sparta had built an anti-Macedonian Peloponnesian alliance that included most of the poleis of Arcadia, Elis, and Achaea. Megalopolis (i282) stood by Macedon and was besieged by Agis. Athens hesitated but eventually stood aloof, as did Corinth and other major poleis. The uprising was crushed by the Macedonian general, Antipater, after a big battle before the walls of Megalopolis (reportedly some 65,000 combatants: equivalent to the number who fought at Chaeronea). Sparta, defeated, was forced to join the League of Corinth.[11]

Upon Alexander's death in 323 BCE, there was another uprising, this time led by Athens. Relations between the king and the city had soured when, in 324, Alexander had ordered the return of political exiles to the Greek cities—thereby threatening Athens' cleruchy on Samos. Alexander had also demanded that he be offered divine honors as a godlike king in each of the Greek cities. When, soon thereafter, news came of the king's death at Babylon, the Athenians had already raised funds and gathered a large mercenary army. There were several hundred warships (triremes, and the new quadriremes and quinqueremes) ready for action in the shipsheds. Athens declared war, joined by Rhodes, the Aetolians, Phocians, Locrians, and some states of the Peloponnese. Leosthenes of Athens was elected commander by the council of the allies. The Boeotians, most of the poleis of Euboea, and many other Greek states remained loyal to Macedon.

Leosthenes gained quick victories over Antipater, besieging him in the southern Thessalian city of Lamia (i431)—the town that would give its name to the war. But the siege was broken by Macedonian reinforcements. The Athenians meanwhile launched a fleet of 170 ships—an armada comparable in size to the great imperial navies Athens had put to sea during crises of the Peloponnesian War. But in July 322, the Athenian fleet was destroyed by the Macedonian navy in battles fought off Abydos at the Hellespont and the island of

Amorgos in the central Cyclades. The Macedonian victories at sea were sealed a month later by a big land battle (again with about 65,000 combatants) at Crannon (1400) in central Thessaly (map 9).

After the Macedonian victory at Crannon, there was another negotiated settlement, but this time, with its fleet lost and vulnerable to being starved (as in 404 at the end of the Peloponnesian War), Athens was forced to accept a new government: The robust democracy of the fifth and fourth centuries was abolished. Athens was to be ruled as a moderate oligarchy in which citizenship was determined by a property qualification of 2,000 drachmas. The cleruchy on Samos was disbanded. In September 322, a Macedonian garrison took up residence in Piraeus. Athens' political fall appeared complete. Yet a few years later, the democracy was briefly restored. For the next century, the Athenians would repeatedly struggle, sometimes successfully, to regain democracy and a measure of independence.[12]

AFTER THE FALL: HELLENISTIC WORLD

The possibility that the era in which great and independent Greek city-states dominated the eastern Medieterranean might be rebooted after 338 was shut down by the Macedonian victories against Agis in 330 and in the Lamian War of 322. In 304, however, a failed siege of the island-polis of Rhodes by Demetrius "the Besieger" proved that even the most redoubtable of the Hellenistic warlords risked failure when they sought to capture the greatest of the fortified Greek cities. Then, in 301, at Ipsus in central Anatolia, an epic battle was contested by more than 130,000 infantry, 25,000 cavalry, and 500 war elephants. It pitted several of Alexander's ambitious former commanders against one another. The victory of Seleucus "the Victorious" and his allies at Ipsus determined that Alexander's mega-empire would not survive to be governed by a single emperor but rather would be subdivided into several rival kingdoms, each ruled by a Macedonian warlord.[13]

By the beginning of the third century, the framework of the postclassical Hellenistic world had been set. Which colorfully nicknamed dynast would control what territory remained in doubt. But by 300 BCE, in the wake of Ipsus, it was certain that at any given moment several kings, most of them Alexander's former generals or their descendants, would share in ruling the eastern Greek world.

Sicily quickly followed the lead of the Greek east. After the collapse of the constitutional order established by Timoleon (ch. 9) and a brief oligarchic interlude, the military adventurer and mercenary general, Agathocles, had become tyrant of Syracuse. He eventually became master of eastern Sicily along with (occasionally) parts of south Italy. In 304, Agathocles declared himself king. Breaking with the practice of earlier Sicilian tyrants and emulating the practice of the Macedonian kings, Agathocles issued coins featuring his own image in his own name and with the royal title that the Greeks had ordinarily reserved for legendary heroes and eastern monarchs: *basileus.* By the third century, the main Hellenistic kingdoms were centered in Syria and Mesopotamia, ruled by descendants of Seleucus "the Victorious"; in Egypt, ruled by descendants of Ptolemy "the Savior"; and in Macedonia, ruled by descendants of Antigonus "the One-Eyed." Substantial second-tier kingdoms were centered in Pergamon, Pontus, and Syracuse.[14]

These were extremely important developments for the city-state ecology. Rather than a single empire, able to bring matchless resources to bear on dissidents, the greatest power holders of the Hellenistic world were both limited and counterbalanced by rivalry with one another. With authority divided and the now much-expanded Greek world remaining in many ways decentralized, there were ample openings for city-states and federal leagues to play the Macedonian dynasts against one another. While there was no question of most Greek city-states remaining fully independent of the will of kings, the citizens of the poleis were not reduced to the status of docile royal subjects. Meanwhile, as the noted historian of the ancient Greek world, John Ma, has emphasized, the end of city-state hegemonies left many smaller poleis (for example, the poleis of Boeotia) with *more* freedom of action than they had experienced in the classical era.[15]

While the citizen-centered world of city-states that Aristotle had described in the *Politics* was certainly changed in many ways, the new world that emerged from the dramatic late fourth century era of creative destruction did not bring forth a Leviathan of the sort that would have satisfied Thomas Hobbes (ch. 3). Just as the destruction of the Athenian empire had brought into being new and creative political and economic possibilities (ch. 9), so too the end of the hope and the fear that Alexander's empire could be consolidated as a single state spurred the creation of new polis and interpolis institutions.

There had been, in the course of the later fourth century, reason to fear that the end of the political conditions that had sustained the classical efflorescence would precipitate a quick and severe economic decline. As we have seen, Philip's Macedon was far from an open-access order. Whatever grand plans Alexander might have had for the cities of his empire were lost in the struggles that culminated at Ipsus. Alexander's successors were, as the British historian of the Hellenistic era, M. M. Austin, has emphasized, warlords: pirates writ large. By the third century BCE, several of the dynasties founded by Alexander's generals were able to maintain control over core regions. But in the generation immediately following Alexander's death, the Macedonian kings treated much of the extended Greek world as up for grabs and a source of booty. An early Hellenistic warlord's two primary policy goals were closely related: gain control of an army of well-trained, well-armed Greeks and Macedonians, and find the means to pay them.[16]

Under these conditions, we would expect ferocious rent-seeking. Cities would be plundered to pay mercenaries. Extortionate taxes on surviving cities, arbitrarily collected, would drive up transaction costs, reducing individual and collective incentives to invest in human capital. Increased costs of trade and declining economic specialization would result in a long-term drop in the value of exchange and thus economic contraction. Places where central authority was strong, notably Egypt under the Ptolemies, settled quickly into an equilibrium that was productive in the long run for the ruling elites. But in Asia and the mainland, with authority contested, armies large, and the stakes high, we might expect an economic decline similar to that suffered by the poleis of Sicily in the mid-fourth century (ch. 9). Yet this grim scenario was not played out—or at least not consistently enough to put an end to Greek efflorescence.

Because the data on Greek poleis in the *Inventory* do not extend beyond 323 BCE, the conventional end point of the classical era, it becomes more difficult to measure the performance of the Greek economy in the late fourth and third centuries. There was considerable migration of Greeks, east and south out of mainland Greece, as Macedonian kings established new cities in Egypt and other former provinces of the Persian Empire. This movement presumably reduced population density in core Greece. But it seems highly unlikely that late fourth or third century saw a general or sustained economic decline across Hellas. Indeed, in at least some parts of the Greek world, notably in western Anatolia, the Greek poleis probably reached new economic peaks.[17]

EMULATION, CONVERGENCE, AND COOPERATION AFTER CHAERONEA

Athens in the era after Chaeronea provides a particularly well-documented and exhaustively studied example of the postclassical economic and cultural potential of a leading Greek state. As we have seen, after Chaeronea Philip II negotiated a diplomatic settlement with Athens rather than seeking to force submission by besieging the city. Athens joined the League of Corinth and thereby lost its independence in foreign policy. But there was no change in government, no garrison, no extortionate taxes. In the years between 338 and 322, Athens was robustly and actively democratic. Politicians debated policy

in the Council and citizen assembly and prosecuted one another in the people's courts over alleged breaches of public trust. The democratic government
passed numerous laws and decrees and ordered them published on marble
stelae. Many public documents from this era have been unearthed by archaeologists, including the law passed on the motion of Eukrates in 336, which
reiterated the legality of tyrant killing and specified punishment for magistrates who collaborated with a nondemocratic government.[18]

Athens also flourished economically. Under the expert financial management of the statesman Lycurgus and his associates, annual state income rose to
the point that it roughly equaled that of the high imperial era before the Peloponnesian War. Public funds were expended on important building projects,
civic and military alike: The city and Piraeus fortification walls were modern-
ized, and more warships were built, along with shipsheds and dockyards to
house them. A monumental new arsenal for the storage of naval equipment was
constructed in Piraeus. Among major civic projects was a new stadium for the
Panathenaia festival. The Theater of Dionysus was given a massive overhaul, as
was the civic assembly place of the Pnyx. This was also the period in which Athenian wages—at least for laborers (including slaves) on public projects—reached
levels similar to those of Golden Age Holland (table 4.7). Similarly high wages
were offered for especially important forms of public service. The civic education and military training of 18- and 19-year old Athenian citizens was formalized and intensified through the institution known as the *ephebeia*.[19]

Athens in the 17 years after Chaeronea serves as a model for the semi-
independent postclassical Greek city-state. The Greek historian John Ma has
documented what he calls the "great convergence" of the Hellenistic poleis
around institutions that were especially associated with, and in some cases directly borrowed from, classical Athens. Greek states in the Hellenistic period
took on signature democratic institutions, including elimination of property
qualifications, people's courts, pay for public service, and formal accountability procedures for magistrates.[20] The Athenian "epigraphic habit" of publishing democratically enacted laws and decrees on stone spread widely across the
Hellenistic world. Hellenistic Greek cities have provided modern epigraphers
with extensive dossiers of public decisions on a variety of matters—including
detailed records of negotiations with the kings to whom taxes were paid.
Young citizens were trained in military skills and civic values in institutions
modeled on the Athenian *ephebeia*. Wealthy citizens were expected to contribute generously to public goods. They were honored publicly, with inscriptions
and sometimes with statues, when they did so with sufficient enthusiasm. New
public buildings were erected. Many states now constructed theaters, stadi-
ums, and stoas—as well as new temples and religious sanctuaries. Special

attention was lavished on military architecture. Some states, most notably Rhodes, built navies of modern warships.[21]

Meanwhile, although in certain respects subject to the constraints imposed by membership in the League of Corinth, Athens, like other Greek poleis, remained actively engaged in cooperative interstate relations that remained unregulated by royal authority and yet essential for sustained prosperity. In the late 330s, Greece was hit by a severe grain shortage, probably as the result of an especially bad harvest in Egypt—a big and reliable exporter of grain in normal years. A unique document from Kyrene (i1028), the leading Greek polis in North Africa west of Egypt, records shipments of grain to 43 beneficiaries, 41 of them Greek city-states. In each case, the beneficiary state would have sent commissioners to Kyrene, requesting a specific amount of grain; the government of Kyrene in turn bought grain (wheat or barley) locally and granted export licenses to various poleis. Under the circumstances, the authorities in Kyrene could set the price of grain wherever they wished. As the University of Chicago's Alain Bresson argues in his definitive analysis of the document, the actual price charged by the Kyrenean state authorities was probably well below what they could have demanded in light of the grain shortage.[22]

Athens received the biggest shipment (100,000 medimnoi: 12.4% of the total grain recorded in the inscription). If distributed across the entire Athenian population, this would be about 21 L (at ordinary prices, about 1.5 days' wages for an adult male) per capita.[23] Other major poleis (Argos, Larissa, Corinth, Rhodes, Sicyon, Megara) received 30,000–50,000 medimnoi; relatively tiny poleis, including Karthaia and Koresia on Keos, also received several thousand medimnoi. In every case, this must represent substantially more grain per capita than was exported to Athens.

As Alain Bresson cogently argues, the Kyreneans erected the inscription because they were proud of having saved the other Greeks from a potential famine. They did not exploit the grain shortage by charging extortionate prices, but they did not lose from the deal either. Both the local farmers of Kyrene and the state itself stood to gain, financially as well as in prestige, from the evidently well-managed relief effort. The point is that the Greek world remained decentralized and productively interdependent after the political fall. Interstate exchange of information and goods buffered what could have been severe local conditions of famine. There was no intervention, or need of intervention, by an imperial Leviathan. The effective response was predicated on good information (identifying local deficits and surpluses across the ecology) and on a form of rational cooperation that used market mechanisms while rejecting profit maximization as the only relevant value.[24]

Several years later, in 325, the Athenians erected an inscription detailing the dispatch of a number of warships to a naval base that Athens had established somewhere in the Adriatic. The inscription states that the purpose of the expedition was "so that the demos may for all future time have its own commerce and transport in grain and that the establishment of their own naval station may result in a guard against the Etruscan pirates . . . and that those Greeks and barbarians sailing the sea, and themselves sailing into the Athenians' naval station, will have their ships and all else secure. . . ." Athens was obviously continuing its policy of using its naval power to suppress pirates and thereby push down the costs of exchange, especially for the essential trade in grain. The primary beneficiaries are the Athenian citizens themselves (the demos). But the decree is explicit in recognizing that the interests of the Athenians were conjoined to those of their trading partners, both Greek and non-Greek ("barbarian") and that those interests involved security in respect to property: "[they] will have their ships and all else secure." The inscription points to the continuation of actions by a Greek state, acting independently to secure overseas trading routes as a public good. That public good was among the underlying cooperative conditions that had sustained the classical efflorescence.[25]

After the Lamian War of 322 had effectively eliminated Athenian naval power, Athens could no longer defend interstate commerce against pirates. But Athens was not the only Greek polis concerned with trade: In the later fourth and third centuries, Rhodes, which had a huge trade in wine, grain, and other commodities, took on the responsibility of patrolling the Aegean and thus keeping the costs of exchange reasonably low.[26]

Meanwhile, the relatively independent Greek cities of the postclassical era continued to compete vigorously with one another. But competition was carried out in the context of an increasingly rich array of cooperative interstate institutions. Some disputes were still settled by interpolis warfare, but other interstate conflicts were resolved by resort to formal and binding third-party arbitration. Sometimes the arbitrator was a king, but often it was a peer polity—another city-state or federal league. The results of arbitration clarified which states had a recognized claim to what borderland territories. Such clarification reduced the border disputes that had been a perennial source of violent interstate conflict in the classical period. Piracy and privateering were at least to some extent controlled by formal interstate agreements banning the compensatory seizure of assets from residents of one state by the residents of another community. Once again, the upshot was to keep transaction costs relatively low. And once again, all this was accomplished without the intervention of a central authority.[27]

Interstate cooperation included the refoundation of important cities. When Thebes was rebuilt in 316, some 20 years after its destruction by Alexander, and with the collusion of the League of Corinth, a number of Greek poleis contributed to the cost—including Thebes' one-time rival and sometime ally, Athens. The Athenian contribution was focused on the reconstruction of the Theban city walls. A half century before, after the battle of Leuctra, Messene had been refounded as a polis under the auspices of the Thebans, as a counterweight to a potentially resurgent Sparta. A big part of the refoundation of Messene had been the construction of a massive, state-of-the-art, stone city circuit wall, complete with towers designed to house catapult artillery. So too, 22 years after the fall of 338, the refounding of Thebes began with the construction of a fortification wall capable of protecting citizens against coercive threats.[28]

DEMOCRACY, FEDERALISM, FORTIFICATIONS

Insofar as decentralized forms of interstate cooperation, along with fair rules and competitive emulation, remained the norm for the poleis of Hellas— after as well as before the political fall—the continued vitality of Greek economy and culture after the loss of full independence by most of the great poleis does not falsify the causal explanation that I have offered for the classical efflorescence. Many Hellenistic Greek states remained, by comparative historical standards, surprisingly independent and surprisingly democratic. Their ability to remain so owed little to charity on the part of the Macedonian kings. Rather it was because rent-seeking kings were unable to impose a settlement more heavily weighted in their own favor.[29]

The creative potential of a postclassical Greek world was realized, and the classical efflorescence gave way to a Hellenistic efflorescence, rather than collapsing into economic and cultural decline, both because interstate cooperation continued in the absence of a unitary empire and because the Greek cities were able to defend themselves against the warlords—well enough, at least, to secure a high level of independence and low rents. The poleis were able to make coercive rent extraction difficult for the Hellenistic kings in part by playing the dynasts off against one another. But the cities would not have been in a position to play that diplomatic game had they been unable to defend themselves when necessary. The Hellenistic poleis' capacity to look after their own security was, in large measure, the result of three related developments: the consolidation of democracy as the local government for many of the Greek poleis; the expansion and consolidation of federal leagues; and continued innovations in military architecture and technology. Together, those three developments tipped the offense–defense balance back in favor of the defenders of cities and against would-be attackers.

As we have seen, Greek democracy did not perish in the fall; many Greek poleis of the Hellenistic period adopted signature institutions and cultural norms familiar from classical Athens. Indeed, by the end of the fourth century BCE, it is likely that *more* Greek poleis were democracies than ever before. Based on the evidence collected in the *Inventory*, David Teegarden, a historian at the University of Buffalo, counted the number of Greek states recorded as experiencing different regime types in each half century from the early seventh to the late fourth century BCE. The number and percent of poleis known to have experienced oligarchy increased every half century from the early seventh to the late fifth century (from 40% to 59%) and decreased (to 37%) thereafter. By contrast, the number and percentages of states known to have experienced democracy increased markedly from the early sixth to the late fourth century (from 4% to 46%).[30] Extrapolating from these trends, we may guess that as many as half the poleis of the Greek world were democracies by 300 BCE.

While Hellenistic democracies were in some ways different from classical Greek democracies, they were democratic in the meaningful sense of being states that were collectively self-governing, ruled by an extensive and socially diverse body of citizens. The trend toward democracy seems not to have been reversed in the course of the third and early second centuries.[31] There are various ways to explain this postclassical floruit of citizen self-governance, including Alexander's strategic choice to depose Persian-supported oligarchs in the poleis of western Anatolia. The question remains why the trend was not reversed over time: Why did the new democracies prove so robust against oligarchic and tyrannical coups d'etat?

David Teegarden has provided an answer: By emulating legal institutions that had helped to stabilize classical democracies, notably legislation legitimating the killing of tyrants, democrats in postclassical Greek poleis in effect set up an "oligarchs and democrats game" that favored the perpetuation of democracy. The rules of the game were established by legislation that was partially modeled on classical Athenian antityranny laws. The new rules reduced the level of pluralistic ignorance among citizens regarding one another's regime preferences, provided strong incentives for first movers to initiate attacks on antidemocratic revolutionaries, and thereby enabled a cascade of cooperative action in defense of the regime by prodemocracy citizens. Would-be oligarchs, looking back down the "oligarchs and democrats" game tree to that unhappy (for them) outcome, were rationally dissuaded from revolutionary activity and chose instead to cooperate with the democrats. The resulting social equilibrium stabilized the democratic regime.[32] This equilibrium was clearly an important part of the story of postclassical democracy. In this section I suggest a similar and complementary argument for why self-interested elites in cities threatened by warlords might choose to support democracy despite relatively high internal tax rates.

A Hellenistic version of the classical Athenian democratic solution to the "mass and elite game" (ch. 9) helped to bring the interests of elite and ordinary citizens into closer convergence. The elaboration of a public language of reciprocity, reinforced by institutionalized practices of civic honoring, at once encouraged high levels of generosity on the part of elites and imposed restraint on the democratic majority's impulse to tax the wealthy minority at extortionate rates. Stable regimes promoted polis security because attackers were less able to take advantage of internal divisions by holding out a credible option of regime change. Democratic poleis also enjoyed advantages in respect to mobilization and morale, as well as in disclosure and aggregation of useful knowledge dispersed across the citizenship. Those democratic advantages, as we have seen, helped to make Athens a preeminent polis in the classical period.[33]

The late fourth through early second centuries BCE saw the fulfillment of the potential of Greek federal leagues (*koina*). As we have seen (ch. 9), the Greek *koinon* was a new and innovative form of strong interstate cooperation, predicated on shared identities, religious practices, and economic interests among the member states. As the Berkeley historian Emily Mackil has shown, *koina* of the late classical and Hellenistic eras were not throwbacks to primitive forms of prestate, tribal association. The Boeotian League of the mid-fourth century was aberrant in being the hegemonic instrument of a single imperial state. For most of their history, Greek *koina* were innovative and adaptive voluntary associations of peer polities. Each *koinon* managed regional affairs among states that treated one another as political equals and promoted strong forms of citizenship, both locally and regionally.[34]

The federal leagues fostered economic welfare at a regional level by lowering transaction costs among member states. They also promoted the welfare of member states through military organization. The league charter enabled each member state to commit credibly to defending the interests of the other member states—thus solving the commitment problem that had doomed so many Greek classical-era alliances and peace treaties. *Koina* were thus, on the whole, able to provide a measure of security for small states against external threats by much larger predatory states. The Achaean and Aetolian leagues, the most powerful of the Greek *koina* in the Hellenstic era, never managed to displace the kingdom of Macedon as the single most powerful player on the Greek mainland. But they did serve to limit the Macedonian king's power to dominate the states of central and southern Greece and to extract rents from them.

By the end of the classical era, almost all relatively large and prominent Greek poleis were heavily fortified (table 2.5). For many large and mid-sized poleis, fortifications served a function similar and complementary to that of democracy and federalism: providing a measure of security against the predatory tendencies of Hellenistic warlords, based on an improved negotiating position. Relatively low rents and royal acquiescence to relatively high levels of local polis independence were, in part, the products of a balance struck between the offensive potential of the warlords' armies to take fortified cities by force and the ability of the cities to defend themselves against sieges.

The political role of military mobilization and investment in fortification has been a recurring theme in this book: Although siege technology and technique advanced in the classical era, so long as there were enough well-motivated men to defend them, well-built fortifications markedly increased an attacker's costs. In the Hellenistic period, the costs of offensive siege operations remained high enough to induce the kings to negotiate a reasonable level of taxation with the cities within their zones of control. Kings could not afford to use too much coercion, too often, against heavily fortified and well-defended Greek cities—especially when the kings remained in fierce competition with one another. A king might offer aid to a city besieged by a rival—as the Great King had done when Philip II besieged Perinthus and Byzantion in 340 (ch. 10), and as Ptolemy I had done (thus gaining his nickname of "Savior") when Demetrius besieged Rhodes in 304.

The equilibrium that emerged from the game played by the democratic, federalized, and fortified Greek cities and the kings of the Hellenistic age left many of the Greek poleis as self-governing and free to continue to compete with one another—militarily as well as in other ways. The resulting "king–polis" equilibrium was superior in terms of economic performance to a counterfactual equilibrium predicated on unlimited royal coercive power (i.e., closer to the "Pareto optimal" condition in which at least one player gains and none loses). This robust Hellenistic equilibrium extended the efflorescence of "wealthy Hellas" well past the end of the classical era.

In seeking to explain the persistence of efflorescence after the classical fall, the factors of federation, heavy local investment in city fortifications, and the prevalence and stability of democracy are not entirely separate. Substantial manpower was required to take on a royal army in the field or to defend an extensive system of fortifications against a concerted attack by a large army with a big siege train. Defenders must be reliable, which meant that mercenaries were less than desirable. Democracy was a proven way for a beleaguered Greek city to mobilize a large part of its potential manpower. As we have seen (ch. 7), Syracuse proved to be a more formidable opponent than imperial Athens had expected during the long siege of 415–413—in part because Syracuse was at the time a democracy. On the other hand, while there were a number of reasons for residents of Greek states to favor democracy and federation, poleis chose to invest heavily in bigger and better fortifications specifically in response to an evolving military threat: the presence of predatory warlords with big armies, who were capable of making full use of late classical and early Hellenistic advances in artillery and siegecraft.[35]

KINGS, DEMOCRATIC CITIES, ELITES: THE HELLENISTIC EQUILIBRIUM

There is no space, in a book devoted to explaining classical Greece, to offer a detailed account of the centuries between the political fall and the final Roman takeover of the Greek world. Instead, I offer a simple model to illustrate certain Hellenistic-era relations relevant to political and economic exceptionalism. By constructing a game played by a Hellenistic king, a democratic Greek city, and an elite citizen of that city, it is possible to model choices of kings about whether to attack a fortified city, the choices of citizens about whether to invest in fortifications and military training, and the choices of elite citizens in respect to supporting or subverting a democratic regime. Although some of the particulars would be different, a similar game could be constructed to model the choices of a king, a federation of cities, and elite citizens of the federation. Indeed, as my Stanford colleague, the political scientist Barry Weingast, and I show in collaborative work in progress, analogous games can readily be constructed to illustrate other equilibria discussed in this book: between elites and ordinary citizens in Solon's Athens, between hoplites and poorer citizens in Themistocles' Athens, and between elite orators and ordinary citizens in Demosthenes' Athens.[36] Our King, City, and Elite Game, is presented more formally in appendix II.

In this kind of game, each player moves (makes a choice) in turn. When no player has a move to make that would better his or her situation, in light of moves he or she knows could be made by other players, the game ends. The (Nash subgame perfect) equilibrium outcome of this game is a negotiated settlement in which the King declines to attack the fortified city, the city pays to the king a reasonable rate of taxes (substantially lower than would be demanded if the city submitted), and the elite citizen chooses to support democracy, despite a relatively high internal taxation rate.

Of course, simple games do not capture the complexity of historical reality. In many real-world situations, the outcome would differ from that of the game sketched in appendix II. In the real Hellenistic world, kings did sometimes choose to besiege even very well fortified cities. Sometimes cities were destroyed or forced to submit and pay high taxes. Sometimes elites chose revolution rather than cooperation with democratic regimes. The game offers only a general model, not a reliable prediction of what would happen in a specific instance. But the model's historical realism is affirmed both by general trends in Hellenistic military, political, and economic history, and by consideration of an often-overlooked passage in Aristotle's *Politics*.

Writing in the later fourth century, at the cusp of the classical and Hellenistic eras, Aristotle, in books 7 and 8 of the *Politics*, developed his own model for a "best practically achievable polis." Most of his discussion regarding the "polis of our prayers" concerns social, political, and educational institutions. Notably, his best polis, although in many ways aristocratic, is also democratic insofar as all native free males turn out to be citizens. The best polis' citizens possess both civil rights to property and legal redress, and participation rights, in the sense of "ruling and being ruled over in turns."[37]

A central part of the duty of these citizens is to defend the state as soldiers. Like Plato, in the *Republic* and *Laws*, Aristotle was very concerned to ensure that the citizen-warriors of his best polis had the right motivation (to this end, Aristotle specified that each citizen would own property in militarily sensitive border zones) and the right training. The goal was to ensure full mobilization of a military that was effective in time of war. Unlike Plato, Aristotle also specifically advocates for city walls. Moreover, he insists that fortifications be militarily advanced and defended by the best available technology. His reason is the necessity of deterring aggressors:

> As regards walls, those [i.e., Plato] who aver that cities which pretend to valor should not have them hold too old-fashioned a view—and that though they see that the cities that indulge in that form of vanity are refuted by experience. . . . [Because] the superior numbers of the attackers may be too much for the human valor of a small force, if the city is to survive and not to suffer disaster or insult, the securest fortification of walls must be deemed to be the most warlike, particularly in view of the inventions that have now been made in the direction of precision with missiles and artillery for sieges. . . . not only must walls be put round a city, but also attention must be paid to them in order that they may be suitable . . . in respect of military requirements, especially the new devices recently invented. For just as the attackers of a city are concerned to study

the means by which they can gain the advantage, so also for the defenders some devices have already been invented and others they must discover and think out; *for [potential aggressors] do not even start attempting to attack those who are well prepared.*
—Aristotle, Politics *7.1330b–1331a, trans. Rackham (Loeb) adapted*

The King, City, and Elite Game described in appendix II explains the relationship among four distinctive features of the Hellenistic Greek world—more democratic states, lower than expected levels of rent extraction by warlords, heavy investment in fortification by city-states, and elite cooperation with local democratic regimes. The key to their relationship is called out in the italicized phrase of Aristotle's *Politics*: potential aggressors "do not even start attempting to attack those who are well prepared." That disinclination of the potential aggressor to begin an attack is an important outcome of the game.

Aristotle is sometimes criticized for being excessively "polis-centric"—for putatively failing to attend to the great changes that were already well advanced when he was writing the *Politics*. I have argued elsewhere that, quite to the contrary, Aristotle's "best practical polis" was designed with the emerging world of Macedonian hegemony very much in mind.[38] If this is right, then we may suppose that among the unnamed aggressors who will not "even start attempting to attack" the presumptively well-prepared (with fortifications, artillery, and defenders) polis is, as in our game, a potentially predatory Macedonian king.

Among Aristotle's primary goals in the *Politics* is to show that the autonomous polis is the best, indeed the only possible, environment for the pursuit of an essential moral end: the fulfillment of human flourishing (*eudaimonia*). I would suggest that Aristotle was very well aware of the military developments of his age. He took those developments into account in designing his best polis and, most particularly, when writing the passage cited here. If the morally essential (as he supposed) autonomous polis were to continue into the era that had been set in train by Aristotle's employer, Philip II, and by his pupil, Alexander, the polis would have to be able to defend itself against levels of coercion that could destroy its autonomy and thus ruin the environment in which human lives might be perfected.

Aristotle knew from experience that Macedonian kings could often, although not always, expect to win when they chose to besiege major Greek cities. He knew that Philip, Alexander, and their warlord successors put a great deal of energy into developing technology (torsion catapults, siege towers) and techniques of siegecraft. Their sieges, when attempted, were frequently successful. Aristotle's hometown of Stageira had, like its neighbor

Olynthos in 348, been razed as a result of Philip's effectiveness as a besieger of cities. Aristotle also knew, however, that there had been some spectacular failures: Philip failed to capture either Byzantion or Perinthos, despite major sieges, in 340. Moreover, even a successful siege was likely to be costly—tying up essential manpower and resources for months—Alexander's famous siege of Tyre, a prominent Phoenician city-state, delayed him for seven months in 332. All of these facts were readily available to Aristotle when he was writing and revising the *Politics*.

Aristotle imagines his best polis as a new colonial foundation but one that will exist in an ecology of other poleis—potential partners in exchange and allies in war, as well as potential rivals. Aristotle also knew that the major Greek cities were well fortified and well defended, and that there were many of them. While it goes beyond the text of the *Politics*, Aristotle might well have reasoned that if a king attacked cities within his realm without provocation in an obviously predatory manner, the rest of the fortified cities in his realm would lose their incentive to cooperate with him. They might stop paying taxes, coordinate with other cities in revolt, or invite in a rival king (as Perinthus and Byzantion had done in receiving aid from the Great King of Persia). Given these conditions, a potentially predatory king had good reason, on the face of it, not to "even start attempting to attack" a well-fortified, well-defended city—so long as he could gain the revenue he needed to pursue his ends by other, less risky means.

Aristotle certainly knew all that. Importantly, the Hellenistic kings who dominated the Greek world in the era after Aristotle also knew it, as did the residents of the fortified Greek cities within their realms. Moreover, each participant knew that the others knew it, and so on. That is to say, the predatory king's disincentive to attack, if a city were well fortified and well defended, was a matter of common knowledge.[39]

Common knowledge regarding the probability that a king's attack would succeed and concerning the costs he incurred in mounting an attack is a premise of the game between a predatory King, a democratic fortified City, and a potentially revolutionary Elite citizen of the City (formalized in appendix II). The game predicts that the King will decline to attack the City; the City will agree to pay moderate taxes to the King; and the Elite will support the democracy. The King declines to attack because, although he has a good chance of taking the City if he does attack, he also faces a significant chance of failure. In light of that chance, the cost of attacking is prohibitively high. The City willingly pays some tax because to refuse to do so would change the King's cost–benefit assessment in the direction of an attack that really does have a good chance of succeeding, leading to plunder and higher taxes.

The Elite citizen supports democracy because an oligarchic city would be less able to defend against the King's attack. Because the King also knows that, the taxes the King could demand from the City might be proportionately higher if the City were oligarchic.

These outcomes generally track historical trends across much of the Hellenistic world in the third and early second centuries. Moreover, if we change the assumptions of the game in ways that violate Aristotle's recommendations for the defense of his best city, the outcomes of the game change in ways that track historical reality less well. Appendix II offers a fuller defense of the claim that the equilibrium solution of the game is a reasonable approximation of historical relationships between cities, kings, and elites in the early Hellenistic era.

There are various possible contributory causes of continued growth after the classical fall: Most importantly, with Alexander's conquests the greater Greek world continued on the path, traced in chapter 9, of expanding in size while converging on a common polis culture—and this increased the potential payoff to Greek cities from specialization and exploitation of relative advantages in production and distribution of goods. Counterfactually, however, had predatory early Hellenistic warlords been free to tax the Greek cities at very high rates, the underlying conditions that had (so I have argued) produced the classical efflorescence—vigorous competition between relatively wealthy and relatively independent city-states in the context of social orders that encouraged individual and collective investments in human capital—would have come to an end.

Most of the early Hellenistic kings had short time horizons and were ready to forego the uncertain prospect of long-term gains for short-term payoffs in the form of booty and high rents. The conjunction of fortifications and/or federalism with democracy forced upon the kings a certain level of restraint in coercive rent extraction. That restraint helped to create the conditions that sustained a strong economy and thereby enabled the Greek world to continue to make substantial cultural advances long after the fall of classical Greece.

ENVOI

The victories of imperial Macedon and the loss of full independence in the later fourth century were very painful for great city-states like Athens, and at least temporarily eliminated others, including Thebes. But by the end of the fourth century BCE, it was clear that the fall had not been fatal for the polis ecology overall. The Hellenistic equilibrium maintained both political exceptionalism and efflorescence through the third century and well into the second century. That equilibrium was the enabling condition for the survival of Greek culture in the vibrant form in which it was taken up by the Romans, when they conquered the Greek world. Because Greek culture flourished for long enough to be adopted by the imperial Romans, it was eventually, albeit in fragmentary form, passed along to us.

While Greek city-states remained in existence long after the Roman take-over, the Hellenistic equilibrium did not endure indefinitely. Roman military capacity was of a different order from that of any Greek state, so a different game was to be played in the Greek world after Rome arrived as imperial hegemon. The Greek cities, like most of the cities of the Roman Empire, were eventually stripped of their fortifications.[40] The federal leagues were disbanded. But by that time, they had done their work: Greek political culture, in the form of democratic exceptionalism, had survived the fall and had been deeply embedded into a developing literary canon. Greece, once great and though fallen, was on its way to immortality.

Because of the immortality of classical Greece, democratic exceptionalism has been preserved as a real-world possibility ever since. Because that which once was could again be, domination could no longer be authoritatively presented as the only secure form of social order, as the only route to economic growth and cultural achievement, or as the inevitable fate of humanity. Although autocracy and domination have remained historically common, whenever and wherever domination is challenged, political theorists and legislators know that there is an alternative. They know that the alternative could be a brilliant age of citizen-centered politics and high culture. Readers of history also know that regression to the historical mean of elite domination is possible, that citizen-centered regimes can be oppressive in their own right and can be overthrown, and that political, economic, and cultural development can be reversed.

The purpose of this book has been to present anew the inspiring story and cautionary tale of the rise and fall of classical Greece, using newly available evidence and the explanatory tools of twenty-first century scholarship. I have thereby sought to keep faith with my predecessors: the generations of scholars and writers—from Herodotus, Thucydides, and Aristotle onward—who made the political history of ancient Greece a living resource for all who aspire to end domination and to advance toward citizenship.

APPENDIX I

REGIONS OF THE GREEK WORLD:
POPULATION, SIZE, FAME

The 45 regions of the Greek world are those listed in the *Inventory*, although names of regions have in in some cases been anglicized: thus Sicily for Sikelia. Region numbers are assigned according to order of regions in the *Inventory*. Regions are located by number on map 1. Numbers of the poleis within each region are per the *Inventory*. For each region, I estimate a total population, list the number of known (i.e., listed in the *Inventory*) poleis in the region, and calculate the size and fame of an average polis of the region.

Each region's population is calculated as follows: Multiply poleis of known size by estimated population per size category (see table 2.1). Add known poleis of unknown size according to the formula used to generate table 2.1. Estimate the total number of unknown-size poleis of each size category (the standard size of a polis of unknown size calculated at $(0.3 \times 1,000) + (0.53 \times 3,500) + (0.114 \times 7,000) + (0.04 \times 17,000) + (0.14 \times 35,000) = 4,125$). Add 6 unlocated poleis and 64 hypothesized poleis, each assumed to be of the standard size, to reach the hypothetical polis total of 1,100 (per table 2.1). Unlocated and hypothesized poleis are assigned to regions 5, 25, 27, 33, 35, 37, and 39. Total population thereby added = 288,750. Population added to some regions is based on the high average size of known poleis and the large number of unknown poleis (regions 2 and 3), on the basis of literary and/or documentary population figures cited in Hansen 2008 or on other evidence suggesting undercount (regions 4, 7, 10, 11, 18–20, 30, 36, 39, and 40). Total population thereby added = 439,375. Population of region 30 (Inland Thrace) is a guess, since there are no known-size poleis in that region. Population is reduced in region 44 (Cyprus), based on unusual distribution of size 5 poleis. Sum of regional totals = 8,248,500, per table 2.1. "Average Size" (based on 7 size categories in table 2.1) is of known-size poleis only. "Average Fame" (based on the raw data of *Inventory* text columns rather than the five categories of table 2.2) is of all *Inventory* poleis.

TABLE 1.1 45 Regions of the Greek World: Population, Average Polis Size, and Fame

Region (Polis Inventory Nos.)	Region Name	Estimated Region Population	No. of Known Poleis	No. of Poleis of Known Size	Average Polis Size	Average Polis Fame
1 (1–4)	Spain & France	18,125	4	3	2.33	2.03
2 (5–51)	Sicily	655,625	47	18	4.00	2.26
3 (52–74)	Italy & Campania	307,000	23	19	3.11	4.04
4 (75–85)	Adriatic	139,625	11	6	3.50	1.46
5 (86–111)	Epeiros	230,750	26	7	3.00	0.61
6 (112–141)	Acarnania & Adjacent	207,875	30	27	2.26	1.40
7 (142–156)	Aetolia	60,375	15	8	1.75	0.56
8 (157–168)	West Locris	35,125	12	7	1.43	0.73
9 (169–197)	Phocis	83,750	29	23	1.61	1.34
10 (198–223)	Boeotia	202,625	26	25	2.20	1.64
11 (224–228)	Megaris, Corinthia, Sikyonia	121,000	5	5	3.00	3.12
12 (229–244)	Achaea	69,375	16	13	2.00	0.96
13 (245–265)	Elis	143,125	20	7	2.14	0.84
14 (266–303)	Arcadia	283,125	39	26	2.65	1.32

15 (304–311)	Triphylia	29,375	8	5	1.8	0.76
16 (312–322)	Messenia	47,125	11	10	1.8	1.44
17 (323–346)	Lakedaimon (Laconia)	217,125	24	19	1.54	1.57
18 (347–357)	Argolis	170,000	11	11	2.91	2.67
19 (358–360)	Saronic Gulf	30,000	3	3	1.67	2.00
20 (361–364)	Attica	251,500	3	3	2.67	8.33
21 (365–377)	Euboea	153,375	14	11	2.27	2.03
22 (378–388)	East Locris	19,125	11	10	1.20	1.08
23 (389–392)	Doris	4,000	4	4	1.00	1.21
24 (393–470)	Thessaly & Adjacent	318,625	78	54	1.98	0.88
25 (471–527)	Aegean	296,250	57	55	2.24	1.63
26 (528–544)	Macedonia	145,375	17	10	3.40	1.09
27 (545–626)	Thrace: Axios–Strymon	495,125	82	38	2.11	0.74
28 (627–639)	Thrace: Strymon–Nestos	78,250	13	11	2.82	1.33
29 (640–651)	Thrace: Nestos–Hebros	127,375	12	9	3.11	1.57
30 (652–657)	Thrace: Inland	40,000	6	0	NA	1.39
31 (658–672)	Thracian Chersonesos	61,125	15	10	2.10	0.91

(continued)

TABLE 1.1 *45 Regions of the Greek World: Population, Average Polis Size, and Fame (continued)*

Region (Polis Inventory Nos.)	Region Name	Estimated Region Population	No. of Known Poleis	No. of Poleis of Known Size	Average Polis Size	Average Polis Fame
32 (673–681)	Propontic Thrace	159,500	9	9	2.78	1.69
33 (682–734)	Black Sea	610,375	53	29	3.10	1.24
34 (735–764)	Propontic Asia Minor	283,875	30	11	3.36	1.27
35 (765–793)	Troas	227,500	29	22	2.45	0.91
36 (794–799)	Lesbos	93,500	6	6	3.67	3.19
37 (800–835)	Aiolis & Southwest Mysia	164,500	35	12	1.67	0.67
38 (836–869)	Ionia	383,125	34	25	2.48	2.33
39 (870–941)	Caria	351,625	72	27	1.59	0.66
40 (942–943)	Lycia	24,125	2	1	4.00	2.31
41 (944–992)	Crete	256,625	49	48	2.25	1.56
42 (993–1,000)	Rhodes	150,500	8	4	4.50	2.64
43 (1,001–1,011)	Pamphylia & Cilicia	127,750	11	5	4.20	1.20
44 (1,012–1,021)	Cyprus	268,375	9	9	5.00	1.04
45 (1,022–1,035)	Syria to Pillars of Herakles	105,875	8	5	3.00	2.47

APPENDIX II

KING, CITY, AND ELITE GAME

Josiah Ober and Barry Weingast

This game models the choices of a Hellenistic King, the democratic government of a well-fortified Hellenistic Greek City, and an Elite resident of that
City. The King must decide whether to threaten to attack; if he chooses to
threaten, the City must decide whether to defend or submit. If the City
chooses to defend, the Elite individual must choose whether to support or
subvert the democratic government. Depending on those choices, there will
be subsequent choices made by the three players. The game assumes rational
(expected utility maximizing) decisions from the stylized players, who make
their moves in the game under conditions of incomplete but symmetric information: That is, the outcome of the lottery that decides, in the case of an
attack, whether the attack will succeed cannot be known with certainty in
advance. But all players have the same level of knowledge about the lottery—
that is, they calculate the likelihood of the attack succeeding in the same way,
reaching the same conclusions about probabilities of outcomes. Other than
the lottery, players are assumed to have complete information.

The game is obviously an abstraction from the much messier real world of
politics and decision-making, where there are many actors, decisions are not
formally rational, and information is often assymetrical and incomplete at
every step. However, as the application of game theory to the problem of why
wars are ever fought has shown (Fearon 1995), formalization may be useful
insofar as it offers a framework for explaining puzzling phenomena. In our
case, the puzzles are the counterintuitive correlation between more democracy and more investment in military architecture, the relatively low rents
demanded from Greek cities by the kings, and the acceptance of democracy
by Greek elites.

In this game, the three players are the King (K), the walled democratic
City-state (C), and an Elite citizen of that state (E). The King moves first,
deciding either to threaten the City with attack (demanding that the City

submit and thus pay high rents as the price of peace) or alternatively to negotiate a relatively low-rent agreement (Q) with the City; Q may be the status quo or some adjustment to the status quo but will be lower than the rent level that the King could demand if the City submitted unconditionally.[1] If K chooses to negotiate a low-rent agreement, the game ends and the outcome is Q. If K chooses to threaten, C (that is, the democratic majority of the currently democratic city) decides whether to resist or submit. If C decides to submit, the game ends, and the outcome (S) is that C and E pay high rents to K. If C decides to resist (or, more plausibly, if C had formulated a general policy of "resistance if and when threatened" in advance of K's decision), then E must choose either to support the existing democracy or to subvert the democracy, transforming the City's regime into an oligarchy. If E chooses not to support democracy, K now decides whether to carry through on his threat or to back down. If K attacks, then with probability p', K's attack succeeds, and with probability $1 - p'$, the now-oligarchic City, without the support of the democratic masses, beats back K's attack. If E instead chooses to support democracy, K again decides whether to carry through on his threat or to back down. If K attacks, then with probability $p < p'$, the attack

TABLE II.I *King, City, and Elite Game: Payoffs to Each Player*

	Outcome	King (K)	City (C)	Elite (E)
S	C submits	9	−9	−9
A_O	K attacks C not democratic	6	−10	−10
N	Negotiate	>2/<5	<−2/>−5	<−4/>−7
A_D	K attacks C democratic	2	−5	−7
B_D	K backs down C democratic	0	5	3
B_O	K backs down C not democratic	0	5	5

NOTES: Explanations of the abbreviations in this table and in the game form.
A_O = King attacks (city is oligarchic because Elite has defected).
A_D = King attacks (city is democratic because Elite has cooperated).
B_O = Bluff of the King is called by the City (city is oligarchic), King backs down.
B_D = Bluff of the King called by the City (city is democratic), King backs down.
L = Lottery. If the King attacks, a Lottery decides the final outcome, based on p, p'.
N = City and King negotiate King's rents/tax on the City at moderate rate Q.
S = City submits to the King without negotiation, King sets high rent/tax rate.
p = probability A_D succeeds. $1 - p$ = probability A_D fails.
p' = probability A_O succeeds. $1 - p'$ = probability A_O fails.

succeeds and with probability $1 - p > 1 - p'$, the democratic City (Elites and democratic masses working together) beat back the attack.

Each player's choices are determined by expected payoffs for each outcome. The payoffs for each player for each possible outcome are listed in table II.1. The game is illustrated as a decision tree in figure II.1.

The payoffs to the players are calculated as follows:

S: C submits. In this case, K can demand that C weaken its fortifications (Herodotus 1.164, 6.46–47 for early examples; cf. Frederiksen 2011: 45 with n. 56), can set a very high tax rate, and can change the rate when and as he wishes. This is a very good outcome for K, who gets high rents at low cost, but inversely and equally bad for C and E, who pay those rents.

A_D: K attacks and C is democratic. If, counterfactually, there was no cost to K in mounting the attack, and if his probability (p) of success in the attack were 1, then K's payoff would be 15. But he must pay the costs of carrying out

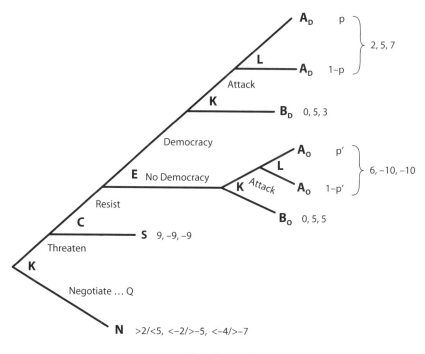

FIGURE II.1 *King, City, and Elite game.*

NOTES: K = King. C = City. E = Elite. L = Lottery. N = Negotiate. S = Submit. B_O = King backs down (city oligarchic). B_D = King backs down (city democratic). A_O = King attacks (city oligarchic). A_D = King attacks (city democratic). p = probability A_D succeeds. $1 - p$ = probability A_D fails. p' = probability A_O succeeds. $1 - p'$ = probability A_O fails. Assumed value of p = 0.6. Assumed value of p' = 0.8.

the attack, so his net $(p = 1)$ payoff is $15 - 5 = 10$. In this version of the game, we assume that $p = 0.6$: K has a better than even chance of success because of highly developed Hellenistic siegecraft. But p is substantially less than 1 because C is well walled and well defended. If K attacks and fails, his payoff is -10 because C will pay no rents and K's failure will motivate other cities to revolt. K's payoff is the average of the payoffs he can expect based on p being the probability of success and $1 - p$ being the probability of failure. Thus, K's expected payoff for the lottery (L) is calculated as $0.6(10) + 0.4(-10) = 2$. C's payoff is calculated in the same way. If K's attack succeeds, C's payoff is -15; if K's attack fails, C's payoff is 10. Under the assumed probability $(1 - p = 0.4)$, C's expected payoff for the lottery is calculated as $0.6(-15) + 0.4(10) = -5$. E's payoff is indexed to that of C, but because E must pay higher taxes in a democratic City, E's payoff is always 2 points lower than that of C if C is democratic.

A_O: K attacks and C is *not* democratic. Payoffs to K, C, and E are calculated in the same way as above. p' (the probability that K's attack succeeds if C is not democratic) $> p$ (the probability that K's attack succeeds if C is democratic) because the oligarchic city has fewer well-motivated defenders. Here p' is set at 0.8, which yields an expected payoff to K of 6. C's payoff is -10. Because C is not democratic, E's payoff is identical to that of C.

B_D or B_O: K backs down. K receives a payoff of 0 because he receives no rents from C, but he does not face revolts in other cities. C receives a payoff of 5, being relieved of taxes but not having the spoils of victory. E's payoff is, as usual, 2 points lower than that of C if C is democratic.

N: K chooses to negotiate. In this case, C and E may offer a tax rate Q as K's payoff. C's payoff is the inverse of K's. E's payoff is 2 points below that of C. K accepts C and E's offer if Q is higher than his other available payoffs. C and E make an offer Q that K will accept if Q leaves both C and E with better payoffs than are otherwise available to them.[2]

The solution to the game is as follows: K would most prefer S, but C will submit only if the alternative is A_O. A_O is K's second-best outcome. E, however, prefers A_D and B_D to A_O. K's best payoff (other than N) is therefore $A_D = 2$. C and E can accept Q at any level <5 because a payoff of >-5 leaves both C and E better off than other available options. C and E thus offer Q at a rate between 2 and 4.5. Since this is >2, K accepts the offer, and N (negotiated settlement at level Q) is thus the Nash (subgame perfect) equilibrium solution.

We calculate the equilibrium of this game through the usual method of backward induction. At the penultimate node of the game, K must decide whether to attack or to back down. Given the payoffs under the assumed conditions of the lottery, he will always choose to attack over backing down.

At one node back, E must decide between democracy and oligarchy. Although, all other things being equal, E prefers oligarchy to democracy, because K's attack is less likely to succeed if C is democratic, E prefers A_D to A_O, so E chooses democracy. Backing up a node, C must decide whether to resist K's threats or to submit. Because C prefers A_D to S, C chooses to resist. At the first node of the game, K must choose between N, resulting in Q, the relatively low negotiated rent, or threatening the city in an effort to gain higher rents. K knows that if he chooses to threaten the city, the city will resist and will remain democratic, leading to the lottery A_D. K knows that C and E will offer Q higher than his expected payoff in the lottery, so he chooses to negotiate: N.

The solution to the game, i.e., the King negotiates a low rent rather than threatening attack, depends on the expected payoff-based preference orderings of the players (table II.1). Those payoffs include their expectations about the outcome of the lottery and their shared belief that the King's attack has a higher probability of failing if the walled City is democratic. The reasons for that belief are not mysterious: Aristotle had pointed out in the *Politics* that democracy was in general more stable than democracy (see Ober 2005a); recent work by historians of Greek antiquity has helped to show why that was true (Simonton 2012, Teegarden 2012, 2014a). Democracy, both ancient (Scheidel 2005b) and modern (Reiter and Stamm 2002), has been correlated with success at war as a result of higher mobilization rates and higher morale among soldiers. High mobilization rates have been correlated, for modern democracies, with more progressive tax rates, and that correlation can be explained by the assumption that citizen masses believe that, in times of high mobilization, elites ought to pay more (Scheve and Stasavage 2012). Elites evidently agree, insofar as democracies are not overthrown during or in the aftermath of periods of high mobilization.

There are at least six reasons to suppose that the stylized game presented here tracks the historical reality of the early Hellenistic period.

First, as Aristotle clearly implies in the passage cited in chapter 11, if we change the second player in the game from well-walled City to unfortified City, the nature of the City's regime becomes irrelevant. The King can threaten the City with confidence because the unwalled City's forces must confront the King in the open field. Given the King's much superior army, the City will certainly lose. Since that is also (as Aristotle points out) a matter of common knowledge ("cities that indulge in that form of vanity are refuted by experience"), the unwalled City will submit and will have to pay high rents. Thus, in an unwalled city, the elite had less incentive to support democracy. Under the conditions pertaining in at least some Hellenistic cities, therefore, we see that democracy is related to fortifications in a specific way: Insofar as the conditions modeled in the game are relevant for elite choices and insofar as elite choices determine democratic stability, it is *only* when there are fortifications in place—or when a federation does the work of fortifications by increasing the scale of field armies—that democracy is stably sustained.

Democracy is not *caused by* fortifications or federalism, but, according to the logic of the game (which oversimplifies reality by assuming that the players are formally rational, expected-utility maximizers), either fortifications or federalism provide necessary conditions for stable democracy—at least insofar as it is a matter of self-interested elite choices about whether or not to revolt. On the other side, insofar as fortifications are ineffectual without defenders and democracy increases the effectiveness of defenders by increasing rates of mobilization and raising morale, then having democracy makes the choice to invest in fortifications (i.e., to pay taxes to support fortified defenses) a more rational one.

Defense of walls required many reliable men. To be effective in defense, those men must be well trained in the use of catapults and projectile weapons—as Aristotle notes in the *Politics* passage and as, in reality, were the Athenian 18- and 19-year-old participants in the *ephebeia* by the mid-330s (Aristotle *Ath. Pol.* 42.3: bow, javelin, catapult). They must, moreover, be capable of deploying effectively and must not be treasonous. This means, in the first instance, that the defenders should be citizens rather than mercenaries and that the citizens should have good reason to support the current regime. Each of these factors was emphasized by Aeneas Tacticus, the mid-fourth century writer on defense of cities (ch. 9).

Second, the payoffs change when the probability of the King succeeding in his attack changes: The higher (or lower) the probability that the King's attack will succeed, the higher (or lower) the negotiated tax rate (i.e., the King's rents) will be. This means that, unless King and City can credibly commit to disarmament (I assume that they cannot), King and City each will have an incentive to continue investing in siege equipment and artillery and military architecture, respectively. The democratic citizens of the City (who are assumed to prefer democracy to oligarchy) also have an incentive to continue to mobilize and to train for city defense. Each of these conditions is demanded by Aristotle in the quoted passage and is manifest in the history of Hellenistic military developments.

Third, if the probability that the attack will succeed or fail, which depends in part on whether the City is democratic or not, is changed, then the payoffs to Elites will change as well. If the probability of attack success increases significantly (e.g., if the democratic citizens refuse to train or mobilize), then the Elite may prefer an attack by the King under the conditions of oligarchy to an attack on the City under conditions of democracy and so will choose to subvert the democracy. Likewise, if the spread between the City's payoffs and the Elite's payoffs is increased significantly (e.g., if the democratic masses increase the Elite's tax burden or decrease the Elite's access to civic honors), then the Elite will once again choose to subvert the democracy.

Insofar as the mass of citizens prefer that the democracy *not* be subverted, they have a correspondingly strong incentive to continue to train and mobilize, to exercise restraint in setting the tax rate on the Elites, and to continue to offer honors to patriotic and generous elites. Masses and elites thus have good reason to stay in communication regarding expectations and duties. As we have seen (ch. 9), a sophisticated discourse of reciprocal gratitude did in fact develop and was sustained between elites and masses in democratic Greek cities.

Fourth, the probability of the King succeeding in taking the City if he does attack, even when the City is well walled and democratic, remains substantial. The likelihood that, were the King to threaten an attack, the threat would be real and that his siege would succeed, means that the City must always expect to pay some rents to the King. As the likelihood of the King's attack succeeding increases, so too, as a general rule, do his expected rents, although the strength of that correlation varies with other factors. The negotiations between the City and the King over the level of taxation are, in sum, real negotiations—each side has something to gain and something to lose.

Yet, under plausible scenarios, there *is* an equilibrium solution that all can agree to—once again supposing that all players share common knowledge of the probability of the King's chance for success, should he choose to conduct a siege.[3] The idea that there is a solution that can be agreed upon is the background condition against which there developed the performative language of king–city communication that was explored in detail by John Ma.[4] The background assumption that there is an equilibrium solution is an enabling condition of the performative language, although it is not, of course, adequate fully to explain the richness and variety of the diplomatic language and practices that structured relations of kings and cities.

Fifth, I have assumed in setting up the game that the information relevant to forming expectations about the result of the "attack lottery" (that is, if the King attacks, the probability that he will succeed) is symmetrical, and thus that all players make the same calculations of probabilities. But this assumption does not always hold in the real world. The City or the King may make a mistake in estimating probabilities (perhaps by overestimating its own strength) or may possess information that the other side does not have (e.g., a secret advance in siege technology or military architecture), leading to differing expectations about the probable outcome of the lottery.[5]

As estimates of probabilities become increasingly divergent, the equilibrium solution of "negotiate a reasonable tax rate" is destabilized. The likelihood that the King will attack increases: either because he rates his chances of success higher than does the City or because the City, overrating its own chances of foiling the attack, offers a tax rate that is below the King's reserve price (i.e., the calculated value of his chances of victory). Mistakes are potentially very costly to either side. Both King and City therefore have strong incentives to keep lines of communication open and to share information. This situation is manifest in the diplomatic language studied by Ma. But it also explains the cases in which kings did choose to besiege cities.

Sixth, and finally, although the negotiated rent level is not the first choice of any of the players, that equilibrium solution arguably had positive effects on economic growth—perhaps *more* positive than any given player's first choice would have had. Although, as noted (ch. 11), we do not yet have good data for measuring Greek economic growth after 323 BCE, it seems likely that the surprisingly robust growth (by premodern standards) of the Greek economy in the previous half-millennium was sustained in the Hellenistic period.

NOTES

PREFACE

1. Centralized, autocratic "natural state": North, Wallis, Weingast 2009. Empires and godlike kings: Morris and Scheidel 2009. Tribal identities and unaccountable leaders: Fukuyama 2011.

2. Recent work, led by scholars at Australian universities, notably Benjamin Isakhan, Stephen Stockwell, and John Keane, seeks to uncover a "secret history of democracy" by searching for "democratic tendencies" (limits to the absolute authority of elite rulers) and ephemeral or local "democratic moments" across a number of historical societies typically regarded as autocracies: Keane 2009; Isakhan and Stockwell 2011, 2012. This research is valuable insofar as it reminds us that the categories "democracy" and "domination" are ideal types and that the historical reality is more complex. But highlighting and celebrating "tendencies" and "moments" risks obscuring fundamental differences between autocracy and democracy as a system of collective self-governance by citizens, sustained over generations by a complex of formal institutions and a widely shared political culture.

3. Morris 2010.

4. Value of democracy: Ober 2007, 2012. Reasons for the preference may be instrumental (democracy brings desired outcomes) or intrinsic (democracy valued for its own sake).

5. Murray 1990.

6. Runciman 1990: 364.

7. Rejection of quantification: Hobson 2014.

8. Big history, at various scales: Diamond 1999; Morris 2010; Christian 2011.

9. Ginzburg 1980 is an influential early example of microhistory.

10. Conjunction of quantitative and qualitative approaches to social science: King, Keohane, and Verba 1994.

11. Goldstone 2013 critically reviews recent literature on the supposed "great divergence" of East and West. This book addresses Goldstone's call (p. 59) for the study of "smaller divergences that arose in different times and places."

CHAPTER 1   *The Efflorescence of Classical Greece*

1. *Childe Harold's Pilgrimage*, Canto II, stanza 73.

2. Byron 1812. Byron in Greece: Minta 1998; Beaton 2013. Greece in the Roman Empire: Alcock 1993. Poorest European country before World War II: Allbaugh 1953: 15. The recent Greek economic crisis: Lynn 2010. Greece did experience other, if less remarkable, efflorescences in the middle Bronze Age and in the early Byzantine era of the later fifth and sixth centuries CE. See note 3 in this chapter.

3. Goldstone 2002: 333–334: An efflorescence is "a relatively sharp, often unexpected upturn in demographic and economic indices, usually accompanied by political expansion and . . . cultural synthesis and consolidation." Efflorescence is, however, "distinct from Kuznetzian 'modern' economic growth founded on the continual and conscious application of scientific and technological progress to economic activity." Cf. de Vries and van der Woude 1997, who call Golden Age Holland of the late sixteenth and seventeenth centuries "the First Modern Economy." Relative brevity (to date) and possible fragility of the nineteenth to twenty-first century efflorescence: Deaton 2013: 78.

4. Figure 4.3 breaks out population and consumption estimates. Dates at which modern Greek development achieved classical peak levels: figure 4.1. Figures 1.1, 4.1, and 4.3 are restricted to core Greece because an exceptionally full body of documentary and archaeological evidence, discussed in chapter 4, allows rough estimates of population and consumption rates for this territory over the long run (1300 BCE–1900 CE). For a comparison of the population of core Greece and the wider Greek world, see figure 2.1, with further discussion in chapter 4.

5. Cultural features are detailed in chapter 2. Because of "Hellenization"—the tendency of non-Greek communities to adopt Greek cultural features, especially in the fourth century BCE (see chs. 9–10)—some Greeks had non-Greek ancestors; others could claim a Greek ancestry back to the Bronze Age. It is meaningless to speak of a "Greek race."

6. By "middle class" I mean a demographic category of people who fall below elite levels of consumption but who are able to consume at levels comfortably above subsistence; see ch. 4. I do not mean to imply anything substantive about self-identification, class consciousness, or place in the mode of production.

7. Precocious modernity of Athens: Carugati, Ober, and Weingast forthcoming.

8. Hansen and Nielsen 2004.

9. Bintliff 2012.

10. The *Inventory* (Hansen and Nielsen 2004) is the source of many of the numbers concerning size, prominence, persistence, and regimes of Greek states that are cited in this book. The *Inventory* was the culmination of the work of the Copenhagen Polis Center, which produced many important studies of individual Greek states and addressed a wide range of historical issues. For some of the limitations of the *Inventory*'s framework, see the critical review of Fröhlich 2010. de Callataÿ 2012, 2014a surveys recent quantitative work on ancient Greek and Roman economies and its effect on the study of ancient economic history. Morley 2014 critically assesses the uses of quantification in ancient history, pointing both to its potential and its limits.

11. Unitary, essentially unchanging ancient economy: Finley 1999, with foreword by Ian Morris. New institutional economics: North 1981, 1990. North and Weingast 1989 (on why England was able to raise more money to fight wars than was France in the seventeenth and eighteenth centuries) and Acemoglu, Johnnson, and Robinson 2002 (on the "reversal of fortune" of rich and poor colonized regions of the New World from the sixteenth to the eighteenth centuries) are classics of the institutional economics field. Bresson 2007 is an impressive example of recent ancient-historical work in institutional economics. See further Christensen 2003; Eich 2006; Scheidel, Morris, and Saller 2007; Osborne 2009a; Ober 2010c; Halkos and Kyriazis 2010; de Callataÿ 2014a, and the works cited in ch. 4. On the other side: Hobson 2014 urges a poststructuralist, postcolonialist approach to archaeology and ancient history. He argues that quantification and institutional economics should be "exorcize[d]" (p. 13), along with deductive reasoning and hypothesis

testing, on the grounds that they are neo-liberal, imperialist, ideological "relics" (p. 12) that import "concerns from outside the discipline" (p. 14) of ancient history. De Ste. Croix 1983 and Rose 2012 offer Marxist accounts of economic development in the Greek world, predicated on structural conditions of exploitation and class struggle; each presents a detailed argument for the applicability of Marx's economic theory to the Greek world.

12. Forsdyke 2012.

13. Encyclopedic surveys of ancient Greek culture: Brunschwig and Lloyd 2000; Grafton, Most, and Settis 2010. The *genetic* impact of ancient Greeks on populations in Sicily, Italy, Corsica, and southern France: King et al. 2011, with literature cited.

14. Number of poleis and population of Hellas: Hansen 2006b, 2008; with discussion in this book, chs. 2 and 4. As we will see (table 2.4), about four-fifths of the states listed in the *Inventory* as "Greek poleis" were unambiguously Greek communities; some scholars would not count all or even many of the remaining one-fifth as Greek. But reducing the total Greek population by 20% would not change the overall picture in any substantial way. Today's population of the nation of Greece is about 11.3 million.

15. Peer polity interaction: Renfrew and Cherry 1986; Ma 2003. On the Greek world as a decentralized network of states, see further Malkin 2011.

16. Definition and primary features of the polis: Hansen 2006a. While most Greek poleis lacked some features found in the most highly developed modern nation-states, the attempt to define the polis as an "acephalous society" rather than as a state (Berent 1996, 2000) is misguided (Rhodes 1995, Hansen 2002b). Disappearance of poleis: *Inventory* pp. 120–123, Index 20.

17. Small-state systems: Spruyt 1994. Comparative studies of city-state cultures: Molho and Raaflaub 1991; Hansen 2000, 2002a; Parker 2005. Long duration of the polis ecology: Ma (in progress b). Ancient Phoenicia: ch. 5. Tilly 1975: 15 notes that Europe in 1500 had some 500 more or less independent political units, but by 1900 only 25. For Tilly, the challenge was explaining consolidation. For a historian of ancient Greece, the challenge is explaining persistent decentralization. Comparison of Rome and China as cases of successful imperial states: Scheidel 2009b.

18. Problem of violence as central to social order: North, Wallis, and Weingast 2009.

19. Hobbes 1996 [1651], with discussion here in ch. 3. Contemporary Hobbesianism: Anderson 2009; Morris 2014. Contrast van der Vliet 2011.

20. Logic of centralized authority systems and godlike rulers, and role of war: Morris 2014. Empire as the standard ancient form of large-scale state organization: Morris and Scheidel 2009.

21. Scheidel 2006, with discussion here, ch. 3 note 15.

22. Cooptation or destruction of deliberative associations at all levels by centralizing royal authority, during in the seventeenth century: Tilly 1975: 21–22.

23. Natural state: North, Wallis, Weingast 2009; proportionality of violence potential and privilege: Cox, North, and Weingast 2012. Development and emergence of large, centralized states, and their association with development: Tilly 1975, 1990; Morris 2010, 2014; Fukuyama 2011. The question then becomes, Whence modern democracy (and its associated values and rights)? Acemoglu and Robinson 2006 develop an influential theory, based on rational bargaining and elite choice, for how democracy arises from autocracy. We consider the Greek case of democratic emergence in detail in chapters 6–7.

24. Importance of exchange: Bresson 2000. Harris 2002 discusses the prevalence of horizontal specialization in the Greek world but underestimates vertical specialization in

some important Greek industries, e.g., pottery, architecture, shipbuilding, and mining. Greek understanding of core principles: Ober 2009.

25. Schumpeter 1942. On innovation, as opposed to rent-seeking, as the engine of growth, see Baumol 1993, 2004. Baumol and Strom 2010 underline the essential role of historical examples (and counterexamples) in studying the history of entrepreneurship.

26. Role of Mediterranean microclimates and geographic diversity in building networks of exchange: Horden and Purcell 2000. Role of rainfall in political development: Haber 2012; Haber and Elis 2014. Beneficial location relative to nearby societies: Ian Morris personal communication. See, further, ch. 5.

27. Tilly 1975: 18 points to Europe's "vital and prosperous cultural homogeneity" in ca. 1500, noting the "ease it gave to the diffusion of organizational models, to the expansion of states into new territories, to the transfer of populations from one state to another, and to the movement of administrative personnel from one government to another." For Tilly, cultural homogeneity is a background condition that fostered consolidation of large states; insofar as that is right, cultural homogeneity does not provide us with an adequate explanation for the persistence and efflorescence of a small-state ecology.

28. Smith 1776. Ford, Taylorism, and industrial production: Rothschild 1973.

29. Contemporary knowledge-based organizations and the polis as a knowledge-based organization: Manville and Ober 2003. Common knowledge: Chwe 2001. Wisdom of the crowd: Landemore 2012; Landemore and Elster 2012.

30. Aggregation, alignment, codification as collective knowledge processes, and their association with political institutions: Ober 2008. Stock of knowledge, modern science, and modern development: Mokyr 2002.

31. Civic rights, immunities, and risk-taking: Ober 2012.

32. Incentive compatibility and choice of amateurism in Athenian courts: Fleck and Hanssen 2012.

33. This epistemic approach to the question of why democratic institutions are positively correlated with economic growth weighs in on the long-standing debate, inaugurated by Lipset 1959, over whether democracy causes growth (and if so, how) or vice versa; cf. metastudy by Doucouliagos and Ulubaşoğlu 2008. For a recent argument that democracy *does* cause growth, see Acemoglu et al. 2014; for the other side: Boix 2011.

34. Plato, *Republic*, especially book 6, with discussion of Reeve 1988. Expertise in democratic systems of aggregated knowledge: Ober 2013a. See further, ch. 9.

35. "Opportunist" states and their adoption of Greek expertise: Davies 1993 (ch. 12), 2004; Pyzyk forthcoming. See further ch. 10.

36. The long history of the postclassical Greek polis: Ma in progress b.

CHAPTER 2 *Ants around a Pond*

1. On the demography of the Greek world, see Hansen 2006b, 2008, with discussion here, ch. 4. Roman population; world population: Scheidel 2007. The population of the United States is currently about 4.25% of the world's population.

2. Milanovic, Lindert, and Williamson 2011: Table 1.

3. West of Sicily: 4 poleis in region 1 (total population under 20,000); south of Crete: 6 poleis in region 45 (total population under 100,000); Black Sea (including Marmara): 92 poleis (total population just under one million).

4. The only noteworthy exception is region 30: Inland Thrace—where a half-dozen towns were sufficiently Hellenic by the later fourth century BCE to qualify as poleis. See discussion here, ch. 10.

5. Overall correlation of elevation/size = Pearson–0.19; elevation/prominence: Pearson–0.13. In Sicily, the correlations of both elevation to size and prominence = Pearson–0.48. Pearson correlations are common statistical measures of the linear relationship between data sets, ranging from–1 (complete negative correlation) to 1 (complete positive correlation); correlations greater than 0.5 (or less than–0.5) are considered quite strong. Note that polis location, where precision is possible, is measured at the center of the central city; large poleis, like Athens, included in their regions considerable high-elevation territory, and some villages lay at elevations considerably higher than the main city.

6. Designated "Csa" (temperate/dry summer/hot summer) in the standard Köppen-Geiger climate classification system: Peel, Finlayson and McMahon 2007. Per below, "dry summer" includes rainfall averages up to about 5 cm per month. Total average precipitation across most of the Greek world ranges from ca. 20 to 50 cm (Attica, Cycladic islands, parts of Sicily and Cyprus), to 50–75 cm (Argolis, Laconia, Corinthia, Boeotia, Thessaly, Thrace, Sporades and Dodecanese islands, Macedonia, Eastern Crete), and up to 75–125 cm (Western Peloponnese, Epirus, Acharnania, Adriatic islands, Rhodes, Western Crete, Caria). Source: http://www.bestcountryreports.com. Precipitation maps for Greece, Italy, Turkey. Accessed November 7, 2013.

7. Source: http://www.pacificbulbsociety.org/pbswiki/index.php/DrySummerClimates = Pacific Bulb Society. Map of Mediterranean summer rainfall: http://www.pacificbulb society.org/pbswiki/files/00_others/Europe_climate.gif (accessed Sept. 23, 2013). On this map, the range of Mediterranean climates is subdivided from A ("extreme desert": 5–15 cm total annual rainfall) to G ("wetter": rainfall of more than 2.3 cm/month in 2 summer months but less than 5.1 cm in the driest month), and from 1 ("frigid": winter lows average below–1°C) to 4 ("temperate": lows average 7–15°C). Greeks outside the Black Sea region inhabit almost uniquely zones C3, C4, D3, D4, E2, E3, E4, F2, F3, F4. Notable exceptions to the "very dry summer" rule are Neapolis and Massalia, both in zone G2. Bresson 2014 argues that the Mediterranean climate of ca. 500–1 BCE was on the whole cooler and wetter than in the twentieth century CE. On long-term climate change, see, further, ch. 5.

8. The relationship between specific climatic and/or agricultural regimes and the potential for the historical emergence of specific political and economic outcomes is the subject of important ongoing research; see Haber 2012; Haber and Elis 2014. The Greek world scores high in three measures (storability of crops, absence of aggregate shocks, and easy transport) that seem to open the way (while not determining it) to democracy, law, and growth.

9. The question of when Greek-speakers first arrived in mainland Greece (i.e., when mainland Greece became "the Greek homeland") need not concern us here: the arrival was in any event before the Late Bronze Age.

10. Steppe nomads: Morris 2014; Mayor 2014. The ancient geographer Strabo (11.3–5) notes that in the Caucasus region fertile land went uncultivated because of systematic raiding by nomads.

11. Of a total of 1,035, 84 poleis are known to have employed a street grid (*Inventory* Index 22), but since the street plan of many urban centers remains archaeologically

undetermined, this number certainly underestimates the total number of grid-planned Greek cities. See further Cahill 2000, 2002. Greek houses: Nevett 1999, 2005.

12. Food ways: Foxhall and Forbes 1982; Dalby 1997; Davidson 1997; Garnsey 1999.

13. Greek religion: Parker 1996; Cole 2004.

14. Greek warfare: Strauss 1996; van Wees 2000a, 2000b, 2004, 2013a; Pritchard 2010; Kagan and Viggiano 2013.

15. Aside from Vatican City, the smallest independent modern nation-states, Nauru and Tuvalu, have populations around 10,000; some 10 other countries have populations under 100,000. China's population is in excess of 1.3 billion. Alesina and Spolaore 2003 discuss (with reference to modern states) the trade-off between the economic and security advantages of large size and the costs associated with diverse preferences among large populations.

16. Hansen 2006b and 2008.

17. Regional variation in size: *Inventory* 70–73 with Index 9. Hansen 2008 adds 32 poleis to the "plausibly estimated size" group; four others were added by Emily Mackil (personal communication). Distribution of population into small, medium, and large poleis: table 2.1.

18. Herodotus 8.25.1–2 tells a similar story, in which Belbina (i326: size 1, fame score 2) plays the role of the obscure polis.

19. Although a diverse array of scholars wrote the individual *Inventory* entries, editorial oversight ensured a good level of consistency in treatment. Comparison of the space allotted to a sample of poleis in the *Inventory* and two other recent and distinguished encyclopedic works on Greek antiquity shows high correlation: Ober 2008: Appendix.

20. Coin data: see note 24. The evidence of coins as a category of archaeological evidence: de Callataÿ 2011b; van Alfen 2012. Victories: *Inventory* Index 16.

21. Scheidel 2006 offers a helpful discussion of the terms *hegemony* and *empire* in the context of ancient Mediterranean city-states. He suggests that *hegemony* is (at a minimum) a state's control over the foreign policy of other, autonomous, polities. An *empire*, by contrast, is (at a minimum) a very large state, generally created by conquest, divided between a dominating central core and subordinate peripheries.

22. On the challenges of finding a balance between the most prominent poleis and the rest, see Gehrke 1986; Brock and Hodkinson 2000.

23. Mackil 2013: 1.

24. Discussion of certainty of polis attribution and "hellenicity" and definitions for each category: *Inventory* 7.

25. Silver coinage: 340 poleis (of 1,035) are known to have minted silver coins, 94 of these by the end of the sixth century; 285 poleis also issued bronze coins. Coinage figures: *Inventory*, Index 26, with corrections of Peter van Alfen (American Numismatic Society, personal communication). Coinage and autonomous state identity: Martin 1986.

26. Most local Greek historiography has failed to survive intact; the very substantial fragments are collected in Jacoby et al. 1957 (and following), now available with English translation, in e-form as *Brill's New Jacoby*.

27. Greek colonization: Graham 1964; Malkin 1987, 1994, 2011. Osborne 2009c: 106–123, 220–230, while rejecting the term "colonization" in favor of "settlement abroad," offers a concise survey; his figure 32 and table 5 helpfully tabulate and map major Greek settlments outside core Greece. Data: *Inventory* Index 27.

28. Frederiksen 2011: 1.

29. Frederiksen (2011: 111) counts 121 poleis with evidence of having had fortifications by 480 BCE. Per table 2.5, by 323 BCE the count (based on Hansen and Nielsen 2004) was 537. On Greek fortifications and their historical development, see Maier 1959; Winter 1971; Lawrence 1979; Ober 1985, 1991; McNicoll 1997; Camp 2000.

CHAPTER 3 *Political Animals*

1. On the science of emergence, see for example Jensen 1998; M. Mitchell 2009; S. Mitchell 2009.

2. Couzin et al. 2005.

3. Olson 1965:2 (original emphasis).

4. See, for example, Bowles and Gintis 2011; Boehm 2012a.

5. Ober 2013b seeks to demonstrate that these "useless" arguments do *not* render Aristotle's naturalistic political theory as a whole useless for contemporary political theory. I do not seek to "save Aristotle" by claiming he did not make bad arguments (he certainly did), but I show that the bad arguments are not fundamental for a recognizably Aristotelian (as opposed to "Aristotle's own") political theory. Ryan 2013 offers an assessment of Aristotle's political thought along similar lines.

6. Aristotle's work in the *Politics* makes better sense when read in light of certain of his works on biology; see Depew 1995.

7. Aristotle's king bee (*History of Animals* 5.21) was actually the queen: i.e., the common mother of all bees in the hive; but queen bees no more direct the activity of a hive than do queen ants in a nest. And the cooperating individuals are females, not, as Aristotle apparently thought, males. On the surprisingly complex forms of cooperation achieved by honey bees, notably in the vital project of finding a new nest site, see Seeley 2010.

8. Aristotelian fair distribution is predicated not only on need but also on the differential levels of virtue possessed by different individuals, and by different categories of people. His theory is not egalitarian in an "equal shares to each" sense. It notoriously allows for very unequal distributions of certain goods to slaves and women, based on Aristotle's peculiar beliefs about moral psychology. See further Ober 2013b.

9. On these questions, see Murray 1993b and Ober 2005a.

10. In the real world, of course, all other things are *not* held constant—so that it is *not* the case that every citizen-centered community has outperformed, or even provided a better environment for individual or collective flourishing, than rival autocratic or hierarchical communities.

11. The Aristotelian approach sketched here is admittedly incomplete, in that it focuses primarily on the choices and behavior of adult male citizens. If we are fully to grasp the workings of the Greek polis, more work is needed on the roles played by women (wives of citizens), foreigners (long- and short-term), and slaves in the production of public goods (e.g., security, welfare) through shared knowledge, and in the consumption of those public goods.

12. Agonistic competition as definitive of Greek society: Burckhardt 1998 [1898]; Lendon 2005, 2010; Skultety 2009. Duplouy 2006 places agonism at the center of Greek social life. He focuses on the various strategies used to acquire prestige by those aspiring to elite status. He argues that the agon was generalized insofar as there was no ossified Greek aristocracy, meaning that elite status could potentially be attained by non-elite competitors.

13. Yoffee 2004 criticizes "neo-evolutionary" approaches to the study of early states (notably in Mesopotamia). He rejects the idea that rulers of early states are adequately characterized as godly despots and urges a greater focus on social relationships outside the realm of the state, while accepting (ch. 2) that early states were indeed typically organized around centralized authority of a ruler with special relationship to the gods, and (p. 3) "new ideologies . . . that insisted that such leadership was not only possible but the only possibility."

14. Egyptian royal authority: Frankfort 1948; O'Connor and Silverman 1994. In practice, of course, things were not so seamless: The Egyptian king faced principal-agent problems (misalignment among the incentives of those taking and giving orders), struggled to keep a big bureaucracy in line, and faced pushback from powerful priesthoods. See further Manning 2003, 2010; Kemp 2006.

15. Phoenician cities and Carthage: Aubet 1993; Krings 1998; Niemeyer 2000: 101–109; Ameling 2013. Stockwell 2011, 2012 seeks democratic elements in Phoenician political organization. Etruscan aristocracy and oligarchy: Torelli 2000: 196–205. Scheidel 2006: 6, drawing on the evidence collected in Hansen 2000: 619 nn. 81 and 82, notes the historical prevalence of republican (oligarchic and democratic) government in city-state ecologies and the fact that monarchical city-states sometimes feature deliberative assemblies and voting. Scheidel 2006 also notes the relative rarity of city-state empires. Etruscan imports of Greek vases: Osborne 2001.

16. We must always keep in mind that even in democratic poleis—where citizenship was held by almost all resident adult native males—citizens were a minority of the total resident population (see for example, population model for fourth century BCE Athens: table 4.4). In oligarchic poleis, empowered decision-makers were a minority of the resident native adult males. And yet, even Greek oligarchies appear strikingly "citizen-centered" when compared to most premodern societies; see Simonton 2012.

17. In practice, of course, it is more complicated: see n. 14, on the practical problems faced by Egyptian kings. What follows describes an ideal type of monarchical authority; in chapters 7–10 we consider some of the problems that ancient kings (notably the king of Persia) actually faced in asserting their unitary will across time and space.

18. In social choice theory, rationality is defined as a preference ordering among three choices, A, B, and C, taking the form A > B > C but *not* C > A. The impossibility of eliminating C > A in voting systems under plausible rules (Arrow 1963) is the basis of a large literature arguing that democracy is unworkable; see Riker 1982.

19. Morris 2014 is a notable example of an explicitly Hobbesian argument by a prominent historian (who happens to be my friend, colleague, and collaborator) who seeks to explain economic growth in the very long term. On Hobbes and the "personality" of the polis, see Anderson 2009.

20. The effort by Tuck 2008 to show that free riding is a uniquely modern idea seems to me to be wrong on the face of it; see Ober 2009. Likewise, Tuck's (2007) attempt to show that Hobbes embraced an Aristotelian conception of democracy is chimerical: Hoekstra 2007; Skinner 2007.

21. Performance of Greek states: Ober 2008. Tyranny and state performance in the Greek world: Fleck and Hanssen 2013, showing how tyrants inadvertently promoted conditions favorable to democracy.

22. Gordon 1999, 2010, 2014. My thanks to Deborah Gordon for many helpful and enjoyable discussions of ant behavior and how it might help us to think about features of ancient Greek history.

23. Forel 1930 offers an entrancing and detailed (if now outdated in its science) description of the varied "social worlds" of many different ant species.

24. Bernard Werber's engaging sci-fi fantasy, *Empire of the Ants* (1996), in which ants from many nests and across species do indeed form an empire under the leadership of a charismatic queen, points to the strength of the Hobbesian idea.

25. Gordon's breakthrough, demonstrated through careful observation of individuals and now generally accepted by ant scientists, was that the *same* ant did *different* tasks—individuals are not genetically programmed to do just one task—tasks are assigned by "collective intelligence" rather than by genetic distinctions among conspecifics. This is, of course, what makes harvester ants a good analogy for real Greek poleis and a poor analogy for Plato's ideal state.

26. From different perspectives, see Horden and Purcell 2000; Bresson 2000.

27. See, in detail, Ober 2008.

28. As Hoekstra (forthcoming) demonstrates, despite Hobbes' memorable rhetoric about human life being "solitary" in the state of nature, local cooperation is possible in the Hobbesian state of nature (in the form of gangs: which is why even the most powerful individual must live in fear), but large-scale cooperation, necessary to advance *beyond* the state of nature, requires Leviathan—that is, a third-party enforcer.

29. Before a new nest is established, the future queen mates with several males in a swarm, reserving the sperm of these short-lived founder-males for the remainder of the life of the queen and nest.

30. On Greek ethnic identity and fictive kinship in the classical period, see Hall 1997, 2002.

31. Altruistic punishment: Gintis et al. 2004, with literature cited.

32. Allen 2000.

CHAPTER 4 *Wealthy Hellas*

1. Demographics of modern Greece: Valaoras 1960. Impoverished conditions 1880–1912: ibid. 136. Poorest nation in Europe: Allbaugh 1953: 15. The question of efflorescence in the Hellenistic period of the third and second centuries BCE is more complex: See, for example, Reger 1994, 2007: 481–482. We return to this question in chapter 10. This chapter and the next are adapted and expanded from Ober 2010c.

2. The economy of core Greece in the Roman period of the first century BCE to fourth century CE: Alcock 1993 and 2007. Medieval Greece: Cheetham 1981; relative poverty of medieval Greece, compared to antiquity: Morris 2013b: 66–73; fifteenth to eighteenth century (Ottoman era) Greek economic conditions, with special reference to rent-seeking by the Turkish overlords and subsistence agriculture: Asdrachas 2005. Greek development from the Roman era to the nineteenth century, with special reference to archaeological evidence: Bintliff 2012: chs. 13–22. Populations of Peloponnese and Boeotia in ca. 1600: ibid. 438–439, 441. The drop in population of the Peloponnese by 1685 but the Aegean islands doing relatively better in this period: ibid. 447–448. Choniates quote: cited by Minta 1998: 119.

3. Survey of LBA economy: Bennet 2007; cf. Bintliff 2012, ch. 7. Numbers and sizes of LBA states; population estimates and levels of imports in LBA and Early Iron Age (EIA) Greece: Murray 2013: 134–145. See, further, ch. 6.

4. Minoan material culture: Shelmerdine 2008, chs. 5B, 6, 8, 9; Minoan palace administration: ibid. ch. 7. For the later history of Crete (twelfth to fifth centuries BCE),

which diverged markedly, both politically and economically, from the norms of the wider Greek world, see Wallace 2010.

5. Murray 2013 effectively refutes earlier arguments for a larger LBA population of around 1 million people and also demolishes arguments that the EIA decline, following the LBA collapse, was less than severe, demographically and economically. See, further, Bintliff 2012, ch. 8 and in this book, ch. 6.

6. Non-elite populations in premodern economies typically hover near subsistence: Scheidel 2010, with discussion below, this chapter, section on "equitable distribution."

7. Zimmern 1931: 219. Zimmern's line about the "doom of Athens" is borrowed from a comment about poverty and impossibility attributed by Herodotus to the self-description of residents of the Aegean island-polis of Andros/i475 (*Histories* 8.iii.3). Ironically, the Andrians were explicitly contrasting their own impoverished situation with that of "great and prosperous" Athens. Modern citations of Herodotus 7.102.1 and collection of the "standard ancient premise" in Greek writers: Desmond 2006. Not all historians of Greek antiquity bought into the standard modern premise: Chester Starr (1977) believed that economic growth was a key factor in Greek social history, but the no-growth argument, canonized in Finley 1999 [1973], largely carried the day. The "standard modern premise" is a staple of contemporary political theory: Ryan 2012: vol. 1, p. xii.

8. Athenian exemplarity or exceptionalism: Ober 2008: 276–80. Athenian performance compared to other leading poleis: Ober 2008: ch. 2.

9. Long recognized: e.g., Morris 2004: 22.

10. Economies in modern developed countries compared to ancient economies: Saller 2005, Morris 2010.

11. Wages: Scheidel 2010, discussed below, this chapter. The prosperous sixth century Babylonian period was terminated by 500 BCE, presumably at least in part by the focused rent-seeking of the ruling Persian imperial ethnoelite; see Ma 2013c and in progress a.

12. Ancient Middle Eastern economies: Bedford 2007; Babylonia in the late seventh to early fifth centuries BCE: Jursa 2010. Babylonia in the fourth–first centuries: van der Spek and van Leeuwen 2014. Roman economy: de Callataÿ 2005, 2014b; Bang 2007; Hopkins 2009; Bowman and Wilson 2009, 2011, 2013; and parts V–VIII of Scheidel, Morris, and Saller 2007. It is important to keep the diversity of the Roman Empire in mind; certain regions of the Roman Empire, including Italy, North Africa, and western Anatolia, were highly urbanized (Wilson 2011) and prosperous; these regions might have outperformed the Greek economy on the measures noted above.

13. Allen 2001 is a detailed study of wages, prices, and welfare levels in a number of early modern European cities. His conclusions (2001: 427–430, 433–435; cf. Allen 2009: 338, adding Delhi and Beijing) are clear: between 1500 and 1800, only Holland and England managed to avoid the Malthusian trap in which a rising population led to falling wages and lower welfare for most people.

14. Morris 2004, 2005, 2007; cf. Reden 2007; Kron 2014. It is important to keep in mind that no estimate of ancient economic change (aggregate or per capita) is fine grained. What can be estimated is change over relatively long periods of time. These long periods would certainly have included short-term eras of negative growth as well as eras of positive growth. For the mix of positive-growth and negative-growth years in modern societies, see North, Wallis, and Weingast 2009: 5–6 with Table 1.2. Thus, although the general trend of Greek economic growth was positive over the 500-year period 800–300 BCE, a given generation might have experienced substantial overall negative growth.

15. Beloch 1886, 1993 [1889]. Quote, Morris 2004: 727; high rate of growth: Morris 2004: 728; cf. Scheidel 2003.

16. Hansen's (2006b, 2008) estimation method is based, like that of many other ancient demographers, on calculating intramural (urban) areas and extramural (rural) areas and estimating settlement densities for each category. Price 2011 argues for substantially lower settlement densities for ancient Greek sites than those used by Hansen and other archaeologists, in part by employing Cretan and Ottoman-era comparanda. But, per above, there is good reason to believe that Ottoman-era Greek populations were much lower than the classical peak, and Cretan economic development was quite different from that of most of the rest of the ancient Greek world.

17. As noted in chapter 1, Hansen's figures are reduced by about 20% if we exclude partially Hellenized communities (table 2.4). This leaves a total "culturally Greek" population of ca. 6.6 million, and thus a 20-fold nadir-to-peak increase.

18. Change in house size: Morris 2004: 721; quote, 723–724. Morris has recently (2013b: 66–73) estimated Greek growth by energy capture; see ibid. 72–73 with literature cited, 279 n. 48, for the stark contrast in quality of housing and artifacts between classical and medieval/early modern Greece.

19. Saller 2005.

20. Morris 2004: 728.

21. My thanks to Elaine Matthews of the Lexicon for Greek Personal Names, who provided access to beta versions of the on-line database; see http://www.lgpn.ox.ac.uk/. Breakdown of numbers by century BCE (men/women): seventh: 75/9, sixth: 1,062/124, fifth: 5,234/436, and fourth: 14,714/2,424.

22. *Inventory of Greek Coin Hoards*: Thompson, Mørkholm, and Kraay 1973. These data were collected and analyzed, beginning in 2005, by David Teegarden and me; cf. discussion in Ober 2008: 285–286. Much more accurate data on Greek coins in hoards are currently being compiled at the American Numismatic Society. See http://admin.numismatics.org/igch/.

23. Turchin and Scheidel 2009.

24. Urbanization and total population as proxies for economic growth: Acemoglu, Johnson, and Robinson 2002; Wilson 2011: 161; Stasavage 2014: 344–345.

25. Hansen 2006b, 2008.

26. By my lower bound estimates (based on a variation of Hansen's shotgun method, but somewhat lower than Hansen's, for the relevant regions: appendix I in this book for figures), the regions apparently included in the Morris 2004 estimate of 4 million would have had a population of more than 5 million. Hansen 2008 offers new empirical evidence that suggests that his original "shotgun method" estimates, offered in Hansen 2006b, were too low, both in the number of poleis and in the total population of the Greek world.

27. As noted above, Hansen's "catchment area" for mainland Greece is different from that of Morris (2004: Aegean, south Italy, and Sicily). My own lower bound estimate for the late fourth-century BCE population of the 1889 census region is 2.75 million people, but that figure would increase to within Hansen's on the assumption of a total Greek population of about 9 million (the median of Hansen's "probable total" population figures). Hansen's estimate of the population of mainland Greece in the classical era is not radically different from that of earlier demographers: Scheidel 2008b. Densities: ch. 2 with note 2.

28. Valaoras 1960, with discussion above.

29. My lower bound estimate of 2.75 million would leave a surplus of 450,000.

30. Other Greek states, including Corinth, Megara, Aegina, and Samos, as major grain importers: Bissa 2009: ch. 9. Definition of rents: Krueger 1973.

31. Hansen 2006b: 24, 28. For size ranges and distributions, see table 2.1 in chapter 2. For the Malthusian trap, see Clark 2007; Goldstone 2002 notes examples of ancient societies that escaped the "trap" for extended periods of time.

32. Hansen 2006b: 26–29.

33. Roman urbanization: Wilson 2009, 2011. Of course, because the Roman world was much larger, the total number of Romans living in towns (ca. 7–8.5 million) was much greater than the number of urban Greeks (ca. 2.5–3 million); as noted above, some regions of the Roman Empire may have been more urbanized than Hellas overall. Moreover, the largest Roman cities, Rome and Alexandria, were much larger than any classical Greek city. Premodern comparisons: Milanovic, Lindert, and Williamson 2011: Table 1, and below, table 4.3.

34. The alternative demographic standard for measuring urbanization is the percentage of total population living in cities of more than 10,000 people. Assuming (based on table 2.1) that about a third of size 4 poleis, most size 5 poleis, and all size 6 and 7 poleis had total populations over 20,000, if Hansen's intramural estimate is correct, then some 20–24% of Hellas' late fourth century population lived in 100–113 cities of 10,000 or more. Based on de Vries 1984, Table 3.7 (p. 39), figures for European urbanization in 1600 (at the 10,000+ standard), Hellas was comparable to Holland (24.3%: 19 cities: de Vries 1984, Table 3.1), which was the most urbanized part of Europe in 1600. Hellas was substantially more urbanized at the 10,000+ standard than any other European region in 1600: Northern Italy = 16.6% (30 cities); Mediterranean = 13.7% (101 cities); Europe overall = 7.6% (220 cities).

35. Bresson 2000, 2007. Horden and Purcell 2000 characterize ancient Mediterranean trade as defined by intricate networks of interdependent regional exhange, based on a multiplicity of microenvironments.

36. Bloom, Canning, and Fink 2008.

37. Population growth leads to substantially lower living standards in most of the cities of Europe in 1500–1800: Allen 2001; Deaton 2013: 94–95. Disease: Scheidel 2007. Squalid conditions in the advanced economies of England and Holland: Kron forthcoming. Greek life expectancy: Morris 2004: 714–720, Kron 2005; von Reden 2007: 388–390. Improved life expectancy for those surviving childhood: Morris 2004: 715, Fig. 2.

38. On the question of life expectancy at birth, see Morris 2004: 7; Scheidel 2009a. Kron 2005, 2012 argues for longer life expectancies at birth for Roman and especially Greek populations than have other investigators. Deaton 2013: 82–83, drawing on exceptionally fine-grained data, shows that disease, rather than nutrition, was the primary limit to life expectancy in England in 1550–1850.

39. See, by way of contrast, Mayne and Murray 2002, on the archaeology of modern slums; Scobie 1986 on Roman slums.

40. Scheidel and Friesen 2009: 72–73 discuss the literature on egalitarian distribution of income and economic growth. Milanovic, Lindert, and Williamson (2011) examine inequality in 28 premodern societies (not classical Greece) on the basis of the the "extraction frontier," thus measuring inequality by how close elites in a given society approached the feasible maximum of resource extraction, beyond which the non-elite would perish.

41. Morris 2004: 722–723.

42. Kron 2014, forthcoming. For Olynthos houses, Kron 2014: 129, table 2 estimates the Gini coefficient of inequality at 0.14, considerably lower (i.e., more equal) than later Hellenistic and Roman era Greek cities.

43. Cost of houses: Morris 2004: 723.

44. Kron 2011, 2014. Calculation is based on Athens citizen male population of ca. 31,000. Of these, 9,000 met the 2,000 drachma census in 322 BCE. Cost of a typical large Greek house: ca. 1,000–2,000 dr; house prices in inscriptions range as low as 200 dr.

45. Kron 2011, 2014. It is important to keep in mind that the overall Gini wealth index for Athenian society as a whole, including slaves and metics, would surely be substantially higher—I cannot say how much higher because I know no way to calculate wealth of metics or slaves. Wealth inequality, as measured by the Gini coefficient, is typically much higher than income inequality, which is considered below.

46. Foxhall 1992, 2002; Osborne 1992.

47. Morris 1998: 235–236. Quote, ibid. 236.

48. Scheidel and Friesen 2009: 84–85. By way of early modern comparisons, Milanovic, Lindert, and Williamson 2011 (Table 2) report the income Gini for Tuscany in 1427 = 0.46; Holland in 1561 = 0.56; England and Wales in 1688 = 0.45; France in 1788 = 0.56.

49. Scheidel 2010, figures p. 452; Scheidel and Friesen 2009. Of course, most people were not paid in wheat, and in many ancient societies they may not have eaten wheat as a staple. The method is similar to the converting of modern incomes from different countries and over time into, e.g., "1990 dollars per annum."

50. Scheidel 2010: 454. Scheidel and Friesen 2009: 83 posit a bare subsistence minimum level of 335 kg of wheat equivalent per annum (i.e., 429 L wheat wage) per person in a tax-free environment, which translates to 1,716 L (4 × 429) for a family of four. This comes to 4.7 L/day/family. These figures are consistent with the calculations of Markle 1985, who argued that 3 obols/day (a juror's pay in Athens = a wheat wage of ca. 4.5 L) was adequate to sustain a nuclear family at a subsistence level. Allen 2009 uses a somewhat different calculation (assuming a family as three rather than four "adult-consumption equivalents" and 250 rather than 365 wage-days per year), but he arrives at similar results for what he describes as a "bare bones" existence (2009: 340). In sum, an adult male wage earner at the "floor of the core" 3.5 L/day level might provide about two-thirds to three-quarters of his family's minimum subsistence, meaning that women's and children's contributions to family income would be essential; see further, Scheidel 2010: 433–435, 454. Foxhall and Forbes 1982 offer a detailed examination of the role of grain in ancient diets—a key factor in any attempt to calculate actual subsistence minima.

51. Scheidel and Friesen 2009.

52. Scheidel and Friesen 2009: 71. Cf. Scheidel 2014, concluding, p. 191: "What little evidence we do have strongly suggests that Roman rule failed to deliver substantial benefits to workers in developed parts of the Mediterranean. . . . Roman economic development would not have differed greatly from that of most other pre-modern economies." Allen 2009: 42–43 reaches similar results, based on the figures in Diocletian's price edict of 301 CE. It is clear, however, that at least some regions of the Roman Empire in some eras of Roman rule performed well when compared to other ancient economies. The Roman economy is currently a very active research area; Scheidel's conclusions are more pessimistic than those of some other scholars: see Bowman and Wilson 2009, 2011, 2013; Scheidel 2012a, 2012b; Temin 2013.

53. Scheidel and Friesen 2009: 74, 90.

54. Athenian figures cited and discussed by Scheidel 2010: 441–442, 455–456 are taken from epigraphic and literary sources collected and discussed in Loomis 1998: 111–113 and Markle 1985.

55. Scheidel 2010: 441–442, 453–458; Scheidel 2014: 188.

56. In Delos in the third century BCE, the wheat wage was 8 L/day—thus a multiplier of 2.3—just below the "middling" floor: Scheidel 2010: 442–443.

57. Half-day meetings: Hansen 1999: 136–137. Pay for assembly service: Hansen 1999: 150. Pay for other kinds of public service: Gabrielsen 1981; Hansen 1999: 314; Pritchard 2014.

58. Data summed up in Scheidel 2010; Allen 2009.

59. Optimistic and pessimistic estimates: Scheidel and Friesen 2009: 84–87. I focus on the late fourth century population because Hansen's (2006b, 2008) "shotgun method" demographic model focuses on that period. Moreover, Athens did not have an empire in the late fourth century and was thus, in this way at least, more similar to other large poleis. For detailed discussion of fourth century Athenian demography, see Hansen 1986a, 1988, 2006c.

60. Definition: Davies 1971: xx–xxiv.

61. The limitation on rents and taxes exacted from farmers in Athens is emphasized by Wood 1988.

62. On Greek labor markets and interpolis movement of workers, see Davies 2007. My thanks to Barry Weingast for discussion of the labor market problem.

63. See, further, Whitehead 1977 (on Athenian metics), 1984 (on foreign residents in other Greek poleis, arguing that most poleis did have long-term foreign populations and that the conditions of their residency were formalized); McKechnie 1989.

64. Correlation: Bloom, Canning, and Fink 2008.

65. Roman growth rate: Saller 2005.

66. The estimates in Figure 4.3 are quite different from those suggested for Greece from 1—1900 CE by Angus Maddison (http://www.ggdc.net/maddison/Maddison.htm: accessed 2014.05.04). Maddison estimates long term historical population, total GDP, and GDP per capita for many countries, including Greece. His estimates for the population of Greece in 1000, 1500, 1700, 1800, 1900 seem to me much too high for "core Greece," based on the archaeological and tax record information cited in Bintliff 2012 and on actual census data from the nineteenth century (it is unclear what geographic area Maddison's Greece data is meant to cover). Maddison's Greek GDP per capita estimates for ca. 1500 to the mid-twentieth century also appear too high, and the basis for his early GDP estimates is mysterious. The standard CNTS data (Banks and Wilson 2013) for per Greek capita GDP begins only in 1940, when annual per capita GDP was $90 (in 1940 dollars), which converts to $840 in 1990 dollars. Using Geary-Khamis 1990 dollars (which factors in power of purchasing power parity: PPP), Maddison estimates annual per capita GDP for Greece in 1940 at $2223. Allowing for a PPP rate of 1:1.5 (based on comparing CNTS and Maddison figures for 1990) brings the CNTS 1940 figure close to $1300. But Maddison's 1940 figure of $2223 still seems too high. Maddison's population and GDP per capita figures for later decades of the twentieth century converge with the CNTS data, suggesting that his overestimates may be more extreme in the earlier, pre-twentieth century data.

CHAPTER 5 *Explaining Hellas' Wealth*

1. The important role of action-guiding rules (institutions and political culture) in regulating market exchanges, and thereby addressing the failure of markets to deal adequately with "negative externalities" (e.g., toxic waste produced as a side effect of manufacturing being dumped into public waters) is a central feature of the "new institutional economics" (ch. 1). Valuing rules and regulation distinguishes institutional economics from free market fundamentalism, which generally rejects the idea of market failure, holding that negative externalities will be adequately dealt with by the market itself (i.e., people who can afford to will move away from the toxic zone; cheap enough real estate will attract less affluent others). Osborne 2009a goes further in embedding economics in social relations by positing that changes in *ideas* about political entitlement, citizenship, and elite standing can explain ancient Greek and Roman economic growth. This notion has obvious similarities to the arguments developed here, and Osborne rightly underlines the importance of the substitution of social capital for material wealth (e.g., through euergetism: voluntary public payments and services by the wealthy, who thereby gain in public esteem). But the mechanisms and microfoundations of the "changing ideas drive growth" theory remain underspecified. Bresson 2014 argues that assessing ancient economies in the terms of "capitalism" is justified.

2. Harris 2002. Cf. chapter 1 on the issue of the degree of horizontal vs. vertical specialization in the Greek world. I know of no comparable list for other ancient societies. Unfortunately, even if such lists were available, given the nature of the literary sources of the evidence for many of Harris' specializations, and the lack of similar sources for most other ancient cultures, comparison would be difficult.

3. Cartledge 1998: 13.

4. List and Spiekermann 2013 demonstrate that a methodological focus on individuals as choice-making agents (in the form of "supervenience individualism") is compatible with some forms of causal-explanatory "holism" in respect to considering institutions as collective actors. My two hypotheses assume that their compatibility thesis is correct.

5. Rawls 1999 [1971].

6. Emergence and the relationship between microlevel and high-level phenomena: Petitot 2010.

7. The reasons that a severe, long-duration collapse of civilization at the dawn of the Iron Age, in the context of distinctive geography, resource endowments, and climate, produced conditions especially conducive to the emergence of many small states (rather than a unitary empire) and of a norm of citizen-centered government (rather than monarchy) are discussed in chapter 6.

8. Here, I use "nature" in the thin sense employed by game theorists: exogenous facts about the world that set the framework in which human agents make strategic choices.

9. Meta-study: Finné et al. 2011.

10. Causal role of climate change in the EIA collapse: Kaniewski et al. 2010; Drake 2012. Cline (2014: 143–147) provides an excellent review of recent literature, concluding (2014: 170) that climate change was one of a number of factors that conjoined into a "perfect storm" to sink the Bronze Age.

11. Roman Warm: McCormick et al. 2012.

12. See further, Morris 2013b: 71 and literature cited; Bresson 2014: 51–52 suggests that climatic conditions cooler and moister than recorded for modernity could have

favored agriculture in the Aegean by 500 BCE. My thanks to Ian Morris for bibliography and helpful discussion of these issues. He points out that we still need to explain why populations from Spain to China increased substantially in the first millennium BCE. Both climate studies and population estimates for the relevant periods are multiplying, and it is to be hoped that new data will enable us to better specify the extent, timing, and causes of population growth beyond the Greek world.

13. The modern Greek state's coastline is 13,676 km. Among European countries, Greece's coast/area ratio (104.68); is second only to Denmark (172.4); contrast Italy (26.0), Spain (9.95), and the United States (2.17): source of data: World Factbook, cited in http://en.wikipedia.org/wiki/List_of_countries_by_length_of_coastline. About 80% of Greece is mountainous; see discussion of polis elevations in chapter 2: http://www.nationsencyclopedia.com/Europe/Greece-TOPOGRAPHY.html. Mediterranean climate: ch. 2. Diversity and networks: Horden and Purcell 2000. Geophysics and the art of not being governed: Scott 2009.

14. Advantages in respect to location and climate: Xenophon *Poroi* 1.6–8 (specifically Athens). Aristotle *Politics* 7.1327b29 notes Hellas' central location between Asia and Europe; Pseudo-Plato. *Epinomis* 987d regards the Greek climate, balanced between summer and winter, as optimal for the development of virtue.

15. Independence is, of course relative; per table 2.3; divergences in prosperity within regions of Hellas, in some cases linked to independence or its lack, are discussed in chapters 6–11.

16. On the problem of endogeneity in explanation, see King, Keohane, and Verba 1994: 185–194. Another test would be to ask if other, non-Greek, societies that shared the advantageous location were also standouts in 800–300 BCE (or other periods); Cyprus, Thrace, and Sardinia are possible test cases.

17. Slavery and unfree labor: Scheidel 2005a, 2008a; Bang 2009.

18. Athenian empire and rents: Morris 2009; and this book, ch. 8.

19. Thrace and Athenian rents: Moreno 2008; and this book ch. 9.

20. Scheidel 2008a: 123–125.

21. My neologistic phrase "rule egalitarianism" (conceptually similar to what North, Wallis, and Weingast 2009 call "impersonality") is modeled on the term "rule consequentialism," commonly used by ethicists. The rule consequentialist focuses on social rules (as opposed to individual acts) that maximize aggregate welfare (or alternatively, aggregate preference satisfaction).

22. Eighth century egalitarianism: Morris 1987; and this book, ch. 6.

23. Greek egalitarianism: Morris 1996; Raaflaub 1996; Cartledge 1996. Runciman 1990 emphasizes the historically remarkable level of Greek egalitarianism. Foxhall 2002: 218 by contrast, regards "substantial inequalities in landholding" as a "paradox" that "I have never been able to resolve in my own mind." The paradox arises, of course, if one supposes that egalitarianism requires either equal outcomes or equal opportunities (measured by equal access to all valuable resources). But, per above, rule egalitarianism assumes neither.

24. There is, of course, a good deal of specialization in centralized hierarchies—the complex monarchical civilizations of, e.g., Mesopotamia, Egypt, and Persia would have not been possible without specialists. Rational people may specialize because they are ordered to do so or because they are born into a social group traditionally assigned some

specialized task. Such systems may work well, but they lack the marketlike features that, so I argue, drove classical Greek era innovation and creative destruction.

25. *Histories* 5.78. This passage is discussed in more detail in chapter 7.

26. Strategic calculation based on formal rationality in Greek thought: Ober 2009. Cf. North, Wallis, and Weingast 2009, who emphasize the behavioral implications of individuals being treated impersonally in institutional contexts. Note that I assume here not only formal equality of standing but also some degree of freedom of choice in respect to occupation. Obviously in practice the extent of free choice varied considerably, but it is the overall effect of differences in opportunities and incentives that produces the result of relatively greater investment in human capital. See further Ober 2012.

27. Xenophon, *Memorabilia* 2.7.7–10, esp. 2.7.10. Whether the women themselves would have concurred with Socrates' assessment, we cannot say.

28. See, for example, Xenophon, *Memorabilia* 2.7.3–6.

29. This sort of investment in political, rather than specifically economic, skills may be a driver of increased use of slaves and other forms of unfree labor: Scheidel 2008a: 115–123. On the other hand, Xenophon (*Memorabilia* 3.4) points out that certain skills required for success in private business affairs are also valuable for managing public affairs. Public goods are in general nonrival (i.e., not a fixed quantity, so that that their use is not subject to zero-sum competition) and nonexclusionary (i.e., all relevant people have free access).

30. Hansen 1999: 314, and ch. 9 in this book.

31. Bankruptcy laws that limit personal losses and rules of incorporation that protect individual investors are familiar modern examples. Patron–client relationships and voluntary associations (e.g., burial societies) provided alternative, civil society, routes to similar ends in some ancient societies.

32. Gallant 1991 assumes high levels of risk aversion on the part of ancient Greek subsistence farmers and suggests possible family risk-buffering strategies, based in part on evidence from subsistence farming in early modern Greece. However, if the arguments presented here are correct, the classical Greek economy was not predicated on the risk aversion of families of subsistence farmers. Public insurance and risk: Burke 2005; Möller 2007: 375–383; Ober 2008: 254–258. Mackil 2004 shows how a somewhat similar risk insurance mechanism operated in some interpolis relations.

33. Numeracy: Netz 2002; banking and credit instruments: Cohen 1992; rhetoric etc. and social networks: Ober 2008 ch. 4.

34. Transaction cost economics applied to antiquity: Frier and Kehoe 2007; Ober 2008: 115–116, 214–220, 234–239; Kehoe, Ratzan, and Yiftach-Firanko forthcoming.

35. North, Wallis, and Weingast 2009, with discussion above, ch. 1.

36. Innovation and growth: Baumol 1993. Energy capture and growth: Morris 2010. Technology in the Greek world: Greene 2000; Schneider 2007; Oleson 2008. Oil lamps, terra cotta lamps, and wine: Ian Morris, personal communication.

37. High stakes of interstate conflict: Ober 2008: 80–84. Prevalence and costs of ancient Greek civil wars: Gehrke 1985. Thucydides on Corcyra's civil war: Ober 2000; Thucydides on rational cooperation and competitive advantage: Ober 2010b.

38. Institutions and coordination: Weingast 1997; Greek awareness: Ober 2009, 2012.

39. Greek embrace of novelty: D'Angour 2011, arguing against, especially, van Groningen 1953.

40. Ober 2010b, and ch. 8 in this book.

41. Interstate learning among democracies: Teegarden 2014a. Among oligarchies: Simonton 2012. Institutional borrowing by non-Greek authoritarian states, especially in the fourth century, and role of mobile experts: Pyzyk forthcoming, and this book, ch. 10.

42. Athens' imperial coinage policy: Figueira 1998, and this book, ch. 8.

43. Modern impediments: Laitin 2007.

44. Innovative adaptations of the institution of coined money is a good case in point; for some particularly interesting innovations in this domain, see Mackil and van Alfen 2006.

45. Stasavage 2014. We lack time-series data for the populations of independent or dependent cities of antiquity, but, per chapter 4, we have proxies for measuring Greek economic growth over time, including intensive per capita proxies as well as extensive demographic proxies. It is certainly the case that some individual Greek cities did *not* continuously increase their populations from 800 to 300 BCE. But the overall population of the ecology of independent Greek cities certainly did grow across that period, and there is good reason to believe that per capita income did as well. We consider the economic trajectory of some dependent Greek cities in chapters 9 and 11.

CHAPTER 6 *Citizens and Specialization before 500 BCE*

1. For a general history of the ancient Greek world, see Morris and Powell 2009. Dillon and Garland 2010 is a useful collection of documents in translation; Erskine 2009 and Kinzl 2010 offer introductory essays on many relevant topics. The historical era covered in this chapter is treated in depth by Snodgrass 1971, 1980a; Murray 1993a; Hall 2006; Osborne 2009c; Rose 2012. See also note 17, this chapter.

2. Invention of new forms of citizenship and civic identity: Manville 1990.

3. Greece in the Bronze Age: *CAH* vols. 2.1, 2.2; Bennet 2007; Shelmerdine 2008; Burns 2010; Cline 2010, 2014: chs. 2, 3; Demand 2011.

4. Thuesen 2000 traces the the cycles of development (from small towns, to independent states, to city-state-empires, to domination by external empires) of the Bronze and Early Iron Age city-states of western Syria—including the major cities of Ugarit, Elam, and Hama.

5. Lupack 2011 surveys the economic role of the palace, relative to sanctuaries and local towns, calling for an adjustment of the view, represented by Killen 2008, of the Mycenaean palace as the unique center of political authority and economic redistribution. But the adjustment to the standard model still leaves the Mycenaean state as economic entity very different from the classical Greek polis. Natural state: North, Wallis, and Weingast 2009, and see ch. 1.

6. Bronze Age collapse and Greek migrations: Morris 2006 (disputing "gradualist" accounts of the EIA); Wallace 2010; Middleton 2010. Cline 2014: chs. 4, 5 offers a detailed account of the collapse and a balanced discussion of the multiple factors contributing to it.

7. Early Iron Age history and social structure: *CAH* vol. 3.1; Snodgrass 1971; Whitley 1991; Morris 2007. Continuity not collapse: Raaflaub and van Wees 2009: ch. 3 (by C. Morgan), but contrast ibid. ch. 4 (by I. Morris).

8. Control of cult by EIA chiefs: Mazarakis Ainian 1997.

9. Political leadership and war in EIA Greece: Donlan 1985; van Wees 1992.

10. Lefkandi hero: importance and rarity: Morris 2000, ch. 6.

11. By way of contrast, Tilly 1975: 25 notes that Europe in 1500 had a very long tradition of royal power, stretching back to the Roman Empire, that almost all Europeans in this era were already subject to one crown or another, and that European state makers were usually kings or their agents.

12. Snodgrass 1980b.

13. I assume that the shock was violent enough to knock Greek communities back to the norms of rough egalitarianism that presumptively pertained in human communities until the development of large-scale agriculture and that persisted until recently in some foraging and pastoral societies: Boehm 2012b.

14. The coordination mechanism was developed as a theory of democratic collective action by Weingast 1997 and was applied to classical Athenian law by Ober 2012. Early Greek law: Gagarin 2005, 2008. The assumption of considerable variation in early polis social organization, ranging from elite domination (van Wees 2004, 2013a) to protocitizenship (Hanson 1995, 2013), accommodates sharply contrasting scholarly views on the nature of the early polis.

15. Superior mobilization and morale are identified as causes of the statistical advantage modern democracies have held over autocracies: Reiter and Stam 2002. See, further, Ober 2010b. The relationship between military and social development in Greece is often described in terms of either relatively quick archaic-era "hoplite revolution" or a longer (EIA to early classical) process of "hoplite gradualism"; see Kagan and Viggiano 2013 for the debate. I agree with the gradualists in considering mass infantry fighting as already important in the EIA, while accepting the revolutionaries' claim that hoplite equipment and tactics crystallized into a more disciplined and standardized form some time in the seventh to sixth centuries BCE.

16. Greek state formation at the end of the EIA: Runciman 1982; van der Vliet 2011; Karachalios 2013.

17. Starr 1977. History of archaic Greece and cultural accomplishment: *CAH* vol. 3.3. Snodgrass 1980a; Murray 1993a; Osborne 2009c; Fisher, van Wees, and Boedeker 1998; Mitchell and Rhodes 1997; Raaflaub and van Wees 2009. Ancient evidence for archaic Greek history is collected in Crawford and Whitehead 1983; Fornara 1983; Stanton 1990. Climate change, ch. 5.

18. Scheidel 2003: 120–126, writing before the *Inventory* data were available (and thus assuming a lower "core Greece" late classical population of ca. 2 million), offers a useful model of population change in the Greek world from the Bronze Age through the late classical era. The War of the Lelantine Plain, mentioned by both Herodotus and Thucydides, among other ancient sources: *Inventory* 652; detailed study: Parker 1997; Hall 2006: 1–7. While the emergence of Greek states in this period conforms to Charles Tilly's (1975: 42) famous maxim that "War made the state, and the state made war," the question remains why the Greek state-formation process did not result in the consolidation of Hellas into a handful of large states, on the model of Europe 1500–1900.

19. Greek colonization and its motivations: Graham 1964; Malkin 1987; Dougherty 1993; Osborne 1998 (emphasizing entrepreneurial initiative). Scheidel 2003: 131–135 analyzes the demographics of overseas colonization, concluding that emigration could have had only a moderate effect on the whole of core Greek population growth but could have had substantially stronger effects locally in regions (e.g., Euboea).

20. Sicily's relative advantage in respect to agriculture (especially grain): De Angelis 2000, estimating that classical era Sicily had the capacity to produce twice the food its

own population required. Metapontum and agricultural production: Carter 2006. Genetic impact: King et al. 2011, with discussion above, ch. 1 n. 13.

21. Egyptian and west Asian effects on early Greek culture: Burkert 1992, 2004; West 1997. New crops and agricultural techniques: Sallares 1991. De Angelis 2006 contests earlier accounts of Sicilian–mainland exchange based on a colonialist model of Sicilian inferiority but reiterates the importance of agricultural exports to the Sicilian economy.

22. Seventh century BCE developments in Greek religion: Osborne 2009c: 190–201, concluding (p. 201) that stone temples and large statues, "will have been beyond the means of individuals to produce on their own and so were increasingly the preserve of a community." Greek religion and priests: Zaidman and Schmitt-Pantel 1992; Hägg 1996; Parker 1996; Price 1999.

23. For differing interpretations of the motivation and chronology of hoplite warfare and armor, see, for example, Hanson 1991; van Wees 2004; Schwartz 2009. Kagan and Viggiano 2013 is a helpful recent survey; see note 15.

24. Hesiod, *Works and Days,* in Edwards 2004. Of course, Tellus' wealth may have placed him in (say) the upper quintile of Athenian society; the question of exactly how deep mobilization would need to go in order to ensure state security was certainly answered differently at different times and places in the Greek world; the point is that Greek military development generally favored greater inclusivity.

25. Early Greek tyrants: Kinzl 1979; McGlew 1993; Raaflaub and van Wees 2009 ch. 6. Early Greek mercenaries: Parke 1933; Trundle 2004; Luraghi 2006; their employment by Greek tyrants: van Wees 2013b: 69–73. Hale 2013 emphasizes the entrepreneurial character of early Greek mercenaries and argues that mercenaries fighting abroad for pay, rather than citizen-warriors fighting for their poleis, were responsible for key innovations in Greek warfare.

26. Sparta and Laconia, politics, economics, and general history: Cartledge 1979, 1987, 2001; Hodkinson and Powell 1999; Hodkinson 1983, 2000. As we will see, economic specialization was limited at Sparta, and thus there was less room for demographic growth from the seventh to fourth centuries BCE than there was in some other parts of the Greek world.

27. Helots: Ducat 1990; Hodkinson 2000: ch. 4, 2008. Cartledge 2001 ch. 10; Luraghi and Alcock 2003. Bare subsistence: Cartledge 1987: 174. Hodkinson (2000: 135) argues for some "better off helots," but also notes that Spartan masters were fined by the state if any of their helots were *not* stunted in growth (presumably as a result of systematic malnutrition): Hodkinson 2000: 114 with reference cited. On the role of systematic violence in lowering labor costs in agricultural regimes, and in the formation of long-lasting social attitudes (with special reference to the southern United States post-1865), see Acharya, Blackwell, and Sen 2014, with literature cited.

28. Spartan army: Lazenby 1985. Spartan "mirage": Tigerstedt 1965; Cartledge 2001 ch. 12.

29. It is fairly certain that after the Spartan victory in the Messenian wars, the land of Messenia was made public, somehow divided among the Spartans (Hodkinson 2000: 104), and that the population of Messenia was enslaved as helots. Hodkinson 2000 argues at length that after (as before) the Messenian conquest, Spartan land was privately owned by individual Spartans, rather than collectively by the state and that women could inherit land. Helots were managed by individual Spartans, although they were collectively controlled by the Spartan state, and they could not be exported from Spartan

territory. Many residents of Laconia were helots; whether they were native Laconians, conquered early on by the Spartans, or imported Messenians, is debated.

30. I am assuming that the combined population of Laconia and Messenia was distributed somewhat as follows: Spartans and their families: 35,000–40,000; perioikoi and Spartan slaves: 50,000–60,000; helots: 150,000–160,000. Obviously these are very rough estimates, but the basic point of relatively low helot-labor rents per Spartan is robust to quite substantial adjustment of the figures, which are in any event quite close to those that other scholars have reached by other means. Hodkinson 2000: 385–386, estimates 162,000–187,000 helots; Cartledge 1987: 174 estimates 175,000–200,000. Rents were further reduced by problems of supervision: Fleck and Hanssen 2006 (many *kleroi* [lands distributed by the state to individual Spartans] were distant from Sparta, and Spartans were unlikely to be deeply involved in day-to-day management) and by the fact that helots had negative incentives to innovate or produce extra surplus through extraordinary efforts: Helots thought to stand out in any way made themselves targets for state terror killing. The proportion of helots to Spartans would have increased as the numbers of Spartan citizens declined; see further ch. 9.

31. A reference in a poem by the archaic Spartan poet Tyrtaeus (F 6 West) implies that fully half of a helot family's agricultural production was paid in rent to the Spartans; Hodkinson 2000: 126–127 argues that helots were sharecroppers and that they were indeed made to give over at least half their produce.

32. Spartan austerity: Holladay 1977. Spartan egalitarianism might be understood as a perverted (based on violence-enforced social inequality between citizens and helots) variant of John Rawls' (1999 [1971]) well-known egalitarian "difference principle," which holds that inequality should be tolerated only insofar as it benefits the least advantaged citizen.

33. Sparta's social panopticon: Plutarch, *Life of Lycurgus*; Hodkinson 2000: ch. 7. The term *panopticon* is taken from Jeremy Bentham's late eighteenth century design for a prison in which the prisoners believe themselves to be under constant scrutiny.

34. Spartan education: Ducat 2006.

35. On ways in which the state discouraged economic activity and limited circulation of coinage within Spartan territory, see Hodkinson 2000: 154–179.

36. Disappearance of ambitious helots: Thucydides 4.80.3.

37. Spartan demography: Cartledge 1979 ch. 14, and ch. 9 in this book.

38. Natural state and proportionality principle: ch. 1.

39. Sixth century Spartan imperialism and the formation of the Peloponnesian League: Cawkwell 1993.

40. Athenian cult centers: Parker 1996. Contrast with Argos: de Polignac 1995.

41. Eleusis (i362), which was a polis briefly, in 403–401 BCE, is the exception. Salamis (i363) and Athenai Diades (i364), despite their inclusion in the *Inventory*, did not have polis status in the classical era.

42. Pre-Solonian Athens, and the evidence of burials: Morris 1987. Treasurers of Athena: Bubelis 2014.

43. Solon and his patriotic poetry: Anhalt 1993. van Wees 2013b: 53–61 surveys the history of Athenian conflicts with neighbors and seeks to show that early Athens was somewhat more militarily formidable than is often assumed, but the evidence he musters primarily relates to the sixth century BCE.

44. Self-enslavement and sale abroad of Athenians: Lewis 2004. Athens was not yet minting coins; wages for labor could have been either in kind or in monetary silver (cut

fragments of bullion, found in some early Greek coin hoards). Kroll 2008 (and in earlier work) has argued that monetary silver was widely used in the archaic Greek world, including early sixth century Attica. Davis 2012 argues, against Kroll, for the dominance of in-kind exchange until the mid-sixth century BCE.

45. Kylon and Drakon: Ober 1989: 55–60.

46. Solon's reforms and his aims: Linforth 1919; Blok and Lardinois 2006; Lewis 2006; Raaflaub, Ober, and Wallace 2007 ch. 3.

47. Solon between elite and mass: Loraux 1984; Ober 1989: 60–65.

48. Solon and the invention of Athenian citizenship: Manville 1990.

49. Solon and the horoi: Ober 2006a.

50. Hubris law: Ober 2005b ch. 5. Cf. the use of intimidation, violence, and legal chicanery to create slavelike peonage ("neoslavery") in parts of the U.S. south after 1865: Blackmon 2009.

51. Assembly as law court (*Heliaia*): Hansen 1999: 30. On the profound significance of imposing legal equality on magistrates, see Gowder 2013.

52. The denomination of "measures" (200/300/500) defining the three upper classes is very tightly grouped: Foxhall 1997. The distribution makes sense, however, if we assume that Solon was seeking to carve out a middling class with an identity that was distinct from that of the wealthiest members of the elite.

53. Kelcy Sagstetter, in unpublished work in progress, has emphasized the lack of property equalization in Solon's laws and its potential consequences.

54. Solon's political and economic reforms: Blok and Lardinois 2006, chs. 9, 13–16. Exactly how quickly the reforms might have had substantial economic effects remains unclear. Cf. note 44, on the debate over the use of monetarized silver in exchanges in Attica before the Peisistratid era of the later sixth century BCE.

55. Solon's poetry: Blok and Lardinois 2006: chs. 1–6.

56. Peisistratid era: Lavelle 1993, 2005; Sancisi-Weerdenburg 2000. Panathenaic prizes: Shear 2003. Athenian pottery industry: this book, ch. 7 n. 3. Oil and wine production: Amouretti and Brun 1993.

57. Fleck and Hanssen 2013. Fleck and Hanssen's formal model and empirical demonstration, using a version of the *Inventory* data, is different in method from earlier attempts, based on the literary record, to link tyranny with specific political and economic changes.

58. Chios and other experiments with strong citizen regimes: Robinson 1997. Intraelite rivalry: Forsdyke 2005; Duplouy 2006.

CHAPTER 7   *From Tyranny to Democracy, 550–465 BCE*

1. The ancient literary and documentary evidence for the events of this chapter is collected in Crawford and Whitehead 1983; Fornara 1983; Stanton 1990. Athens' twin: this book, ch. 8.

2. "Natural state": this book, ch. 1. The Greek word *tyrannos*: tyrant was borrowed by the Greeks from an Anatolian language; early usage lacks the moral opprobrium of later fifth century literary usage, e.g., by Herodotus.

3. Athenian pottery industry: Arafat and Morgan 1989; Cook 1997: 259–262, concluding (p. 262) that the total of workmen in the painted pottery industry was "in the order only of hundreds"; Osborne 2001.

4. On the Peisistratid tyranny at Athens, see Lavelle 1993, 2005; Sancisi-Weerdenburg 2000. Athenians in the northern Aegean and the drive to control strategic resources: Davies 2013; Kallet 2013: 52–54. Trireme building: van Wees 2013b.

5. Persian Empire: Briant 2002; Kuhrt 2007; Ma in progress a, drawing on documents in Ma, Tuplin, and Allen 2013, on the violence and rent-seeking of the Persian ruling elite. Carthage and the Greeks: Krings 1998.

6. The tyrant killers: Taylor 1991.

7. The end of the Peisistratid tyranny is related by Herodotus 5.62–65 and by Pseudo-Aristotle *Ath. Pol.* 18.2–19.4.

8. Athenian revolution: Ober 1996 ch. 4, 2007, drawing on Herodotus and Pseudo-Aristotle, *Ath. Pol.* The Council that resisted Isagoras was either the Areopagus, a Solonian Council of 400, or a newly instituted Council of 500, on which, see this chapter, section "Democratic Federalism." Teegarden 2014b reviews the literature on the Solonian law on *stasis*, concluding that it is not genuinely Solonian.

9. For a range of views on Cleisthenes, the revolution, and the reforms, see Lévêque and Vidal-Naquet 1996 [1964]; Siewert 1982; Fornara and Samons 1991; Anderson 2003 with review of Pritchard 2005; Hammer 2005; Azoulay and Ismard 2012.

10. Regional population estimates are from the fourth century data: appendix I; late sixth century numbers were probably lower in each case.

11. The fundamental works on the Attic demes and deme/trittys/tribe organization are Traill 1975, 1986; Osborne 1985; Whitehead 1986. The geography of the demes has now been modeled in a brilliant new study: Fachard 2014.

12. Rhodes 1985a remains the fundamental account of the historical development and functioning of the Council of 500. On the Council's role in building social networks and useful knowledge, see Ober 2008, ch. 4, with literature cited.

13. In 462 BCE, the Areopagus was relegated to a court that tried certain murder cases; see ch. 8.

14. The word *demokratia* was probably coined some time in the early to mid-fifth century, although it is not impossible that it was used as a slogan during the revolution itself; see Hansen 1986b.

15. On the evidence for other early Greek democracies, some of which might antedate Athens, but none of which is well documented, see Robinson 1997.

16. The events of 506: Herodotus 5.74–78. No regular Athenian army before this date: Frost 1984. My mental image of the Athenian army of 506 is the ragtag thirteenth century Russian peasant army that confronts Teutonic invaders on a frozen lake in Sergei Eisenstein's great 1938 Soviet propaganda film, *Alexander Nevsky*.

17. A slightly different claim is made a few chapters earlier, at Herodotus 5.66.1: "Athens, which had been great before, now grew even greater when her tyrants had been removed." While, in the earlier passage, Herodotus seems to offer a more positive assessment of Athens' earlier standing, the association of growth with liberation is the point of both passages.

18. The puzzlement has quite often led to mistranslations, or even to philologically unwarranted emendations of the Greek text.

19. The developed "Cleisthenic" constitution: Hansen 1999. On the boom in Athenian public building after 508 BCE, see Paga 2012.

20. Battle of Marathon: Herodotus 6.94–117, with Krentz 2011. Importance: Mill 1846. The decision about the silver windfall: Herodotus 7.144.1–2 with Labarbe 1957. van Wees 2013b: 66–67 argues that Athens had built a navy of 50 triremes in the era of the Cleisthenic reforms and thus that the decision of 483 was a continuation of earlier policy, rather than a change of direction.

21. Athenian decision-making in 481: Ober 2013a; the battle of Salamis and its historical context: Strauss 2004.

22. Civic associations and trust: Kierstead 2013. Oath-taking: Teegarden 2012. The regional "thirds" by which each tribe was constituted remained essential administrative units but never developed strong identities of their own. Olson (1965, quoted in ch. 3) notes the relative ease with which collective action is achieved within groups small enough to ensure mutual monitoring.

23. Athens as a polis defined by its social networks: Ober 2008, ch. 4 (building on the fundamental work of Granovetter 1973 and Burt 1992); Ismard 2010. Absence of patronage in classical Athens: Millett 1989.

24. The discussion of knowledge and expertise in this section draws on Ober 2008, 2013a. The problem of (rational) collective ignorance: Caplan 2007. The problem of how best to use expert judgments along with "collective wisdom" within a democratic framework continues to be a research frontier; see for example http://www.goodjudgment project.com/.

25. Collective wisdom drawing on elite experts without elite capture, with reference to the decision of 481: Ober 2013a: 115–118.

26. This is the argument of Forsdyke 2005, the best and fullest recent discussion of ostracism and its origins. Notably, the ostracized man's family was not expelled with him, nor was his property confiscated, and he resumed full citizen status upon his return.

27. Histories of ancient Greek Sicily: Finley 1968; Berger 1992; Luraghi 1994; De Angelis 2003. The most important single source for ancient Sicilian history before the late fifth century is the historian of the first century BCE, Diodorus Siculus; on Diodorus as a historian and his sources, see Sacks 1990. Thucydides and Herodotus are earlier and vitally important but less comprehensive sources. The history of Greek Sicily is augmented by rich numismatic and archaeological evidence, but the Greek cities of Sicily left very few inscriptions.

28. Sicilian agriculture and its role in economic and political development: De Angelis 2000, 2006, 2010.

29. History of the tyrants of fifth century Sicily and their epicracies: *CAH* 4 ch. 16 (by D. Asheri), 5 ch. 7 (by D. Asheri); Luraghi 1994.

30. Meiggs and Lewis 1988, no. 27.

31. Simonides F 106 Diehl. See note by W. Oldfather on pp. 194–195 of the (1946) Loeb edition of Diodorus.

32. Meiggs and Lewis 1988, no. 29.

33. Pluralistic ignorance as a goal of modern authoritarian governments: Kuran 1995; pluralistic ignorance as a problem that ancient democracies sought to overcome: Teegarden 2014a.

34. *Koinon dogma*: Teegarden in progress. Rise of rhetoric in Sicily: Kennedy 1994.

35. On the fifth century democracy at Syracuse, see Rutter 2000; Robinson 2000, 2011: 67–89. Syracuse instituted a lottery for some offices in a constitutional reform in 412 BCE and instituted a council in the mid-fourth century: ch. 9.

36. D. Asheri in *CAH* 5 p. 167 estimates Syracuse's mid-fifth century population as 20,000 citizens, with a total population of ca. 250,000. Syracuse seems to have employed the three traditional Dorian tribes in organizing its army (147: p. 228), but these did not have the civic functions of the Cleisthenic tribes in Athens. Contrast the establishment of Athens-like demes, grouped into tribelike organizations, at Eretria: Knoepfler 1997; Fachard 2014, and this book, ch. 9.

37. The generally salutary role played by public speakers at Athens: Ober 1989; see also this book, ch. 9.

38. Forsdyke 2005, Appendix 2, pp. 285–289, suggests first (contra Diodorus), that petalism might have been an independent Syracusan invention and, next, that petalism might have been used whenever the Syracusan demos felt that a public figure was acting inappropriately. She surveys possible evidence for ostracism and ostracismlike institutions at Argos, Miletus, Megara, Ephesus, Chersonesus, and Kyrene.

39. As we see (this book, ch. 9), the contrary proposition, that eastern Greece could not have foregone grain production at a level high enough to feed its population without Sicily, is false: in the mid-fourth century, when Sicilian production declined, the eastern Greek poleis found a ready supply of grain from other sources.

CHAPTER 8 *Golden Age of Empire, 478–404*

1. History of Greece in the fifth century BCE: *CAH* 5. Ehrenberg 1973; Osborne 2000; Hornblower 2002; Rhodes 2010. Ancient sources: Crawford and Whitehead 1983; Fornara 1983. Meiggs and Lewis 1988.

2. Wreckage of Athens: Thucydides 1.89.3; Athenian minting, 480–449 BCE: Starr 1970.

3. The ordinary equipment and training of hoplites were not well suited to siege operations: Ober 1991. The role of mobilization and fortifications in sustaining state independence is a recurring theme in this book: see especially ch. 11.

4. Persian wars and Athenian strategy: Strauss and Ober 1990: ch. 1.

5. The conflicted relationship of Persia's sometime Greek subjects with the Persian Empire: Starr 1975; Debord 1999; see further this book, ch. 9.

6. Some of Sparta's Peloponnesian League allies did, however, command considerable naval forces: Kelly 1982.

7. The concept of escalation dominance is applied to Roman history by Luttwak 1976.

8. Foundation of the Delian League, first tax assessment: Meiggs 1972 chs. 3–4; funding ship-building and naval operations with taxes on allies: van Wees 2013b: 104–106.

9. Kallet 2013 surveys the early history of the Delian League and emphasizes that the league's naval forces were, from the beginning, employed to further specifically Athenian interests, notably in the northern Aegean.

10. Early operations against defectors from the Delian League: Meiggs 1972 ch. 5; Kallet 2013.

11. Azoulay 2014 is an excellent biography of Pericles, covering his political career and opponents in detail. Intensification of democracy: Fornara and Samons 1991; Raaflaub, Ober, and Wallace 2007: ch. 5.

12. Ostracisms of the fifth century: Forsdyke 2005: 165–177.

13. The high imperial era of the 450s and 431: Meiggs 1972 chs. 6–10.

14. On the empire as a "greater Athenian state," see Morris 2009, 2013a, emphasizing smallness of scale and ethnic homogeneity of rulers and ruled. Scheidel 2006: 8–9 describes Athens' relationship with subject poleis as a hybrid of hegemony and empire (see this book, ch. 2 n. 21 for definitions), suggesting that the completion of Athens' development as an imperial state was preempted by military defeat in the course of the Peloponnesian War. Important studies of the empire include Meiggs 1972; Rhodes 1985b; Mattingly 1996; Boedeker and Raaflaub 1998; Constantakopoulou 2007; Ma, Papazarkadas, and Parker 2009.

15. Persian influences in fifth century Athens: Miller 1997. Raaflaub 2009 goes further, arguing (p. 97): "with few exceptions, the entire range of Athenian instruments of empire was derived from Persian models." Athenian emulation of some Persian techniques is plausible, but the instruments in question (tribute, garrisons, destruction as punishment for rebellion, imposition of officials and regimes, use of naval power) are common to empires very widely separated in time and space.

16. Some 51, or about 1/6 of the poleis of the Delian League are ranked as less than fully Hellenic, i.e., "Hellenicity" β or γ. See table 2.4 for discussion.

17. The principal-agent problem, first identified as an issue in the management of business firms, has been generalized to a wide range of both economic and political environments: Stiglitz 2008. Cf. Xenophon (*Anabasis* 1.5.9): The king's empire is strong in size and population yet weakened by the fact that it is "dependent on the length of roads and the inevitable dispersion of defensive forces." See further Starr 1975: 69–71.

18. Ionic ideology: Connor 1993; Morris 2009. Greek ethnic identity: Hall 1997.

19. Roman citizenship: Sherwin-White 1973. Difficulties in creating city-state empires and distinctiveness of the Roman approach: Scheidel 2006.

20. The Athenian citizenship law: Patterson 2005; Blok 2009. Girls born to mixed marriages might be offered in marriage with a dowry but were very unlikely to find an Athenian husband.

21. Simonton 2012. De Ste. Croix 1954 inaugurated a long scholarly debate (discussed in De Ste. Croix 1972) by arguing that democracy, as protection against exploitation by oligarchs, was more valuable to most people within the empire than was local autonomy.

22. Athenian imperial policy and democracy: Brock 2009; Robinson 2011: ch. 4.

23. Mediterranean piracy in antiquity and its effects on economic activity: De Souza 1999; Gabrielsen 2003.

24. Hedrick 1994 discusses the monumental nature of the "first stele" and its role as an imperial monument, but, to my knowledge, its potential role as a long-horizon signaling device has not been noticed.

25. Of the 318 known states of the Delian League, 209 have size estimates. Of these, 154 were size 3 or below; 55 were size 4 or above. Eteokarpathians: Anderson and Dix 2004.

26. Rational calculation in classical Greek thought: Ober 2009. Economics of the empire: Finley 1978; Kallet-Marx 1993; Kallet 2001, 2007; Figueira 1998; Samons 2000; Erickson 2005.

27. Assuming total imperial taxes at 1,000 T (talents) (Xenophon *Anabasis* 7.1.27); ca. 550,000 families with daily income of 0.5–1.0 dr/day. Morris 2009, using different figures, suggests that Athens' subjects paid for security about half of what was paid by the subjects of imperial Rome.

28. Value of trade and markets: Bresson 2000, 2007. Cabotage: Horden and Purcell 2000.

29. Standardized weights, measures, and coinage: Figueira 1998; Johnstone 2011: ch. 3. Minting: van Alfen 2011; Ober forthcoming: n. 16 with references cited.

30. Greek navies were not good at large-scale and sustained naval blockades for operational reasons discussed by Gomme 1937; Harrison 1999.

31. Athens' imperial cleruchy system: Meiggs 1972: ch. 14; Moreno 2009.

32. Imperial era Athenian building: Boersma 1970; Wycherley 1978; Camp 2001: 59–116. Labor and wages: Loomis 1998.

33. Athenian mining and industry: Hopper 1953, 1979; Conophagos 1980; Bissa 2008.

34. Athenian demography in the fifth century: Hansen 1986a, 1988, 2006c.

35. Ehrenberg 1973; Harris 2002.

36. Culture in imperial Athens: Boedeker and Raaflaub 1998.

37. Morris 2009; Netz in progress.

38. Warships: Ober 2010b. Finance: Davies 1994; Kallet-Marx 1993, 1994; Samons 2000.

39. Sophists and their claims to expertise: de Romilly 1992; Cole 1991. Pyzyk forthcoming considers the question of Greek theories of expertise in detail.

40. Thucydides as a political scientist: Ober 2006b; Ober and Perry 2014. Cf. Reynolds 2009 for Thucydides' epistemology.

41. Chance and intelligence in Thucydides: Edmunds 1975.

42. Newness of Athenian power and its conditions: Ober 2001.

43. These Periclean speeches are analyzed in more detail in Ober 1998: ch. 2.

44. Limits of Pericles' authority: Ober 1996: ch. 6. On Pericles leadership, see further Azoulay 2014.

45. Pseudo-Xenophon, *Ath. Pol.* The arguments of the "Old Oligarch" are analyzed in more detail in Ober 1998: 14–27.

46. The "Corinthian assessement" is discussed in detail in Ober 2010b. Different evaluations of the origins of the war and the events leading up to it: Kagan 1969; De Ste. Croix 1972; Hanson 2005; Lendon 2010.

47. Pericles' strategy: Ober 1996: ch 6. The early stages of the war: Kagan 1974.

48. The Athenian plague was identified as typhoid on the basis of DNA tests by Papagrigorakis et al. 2006, but their identification has been challenged by other specialists; see Littman 2009 for discussion.

49. Mytilene was among the handful of states within the empire that still contributed ships rather than tribute. It was also, like Chios (1840) and Miletus (1854), for example, both big and oligarchic.

50. Thucydides notes that this summer (428) saw a record number of Athenian ships in service, some 250 in all, and that the expense was immense (3.17): The passage is regarded by some as spurious or misplaced. Cf. discussion by Hornblower 1991 ad loc.

51. On the high level of skills demanded of the trireme rower, see Coates, Platis, and Shaw 1990; Rankov 1993; Strauss 1996.

52. The ideology of the fifth century Athenian hoplites is sometimes imagined as sharply distinguished from the ideology of the lower class citizens who served as rowers, e.g., by Raaflaub 1996 and Samons 1998. But see Hanson 1996; Pritchard 1998; Strauss 2000.

53. See, further, Ober 2010b, from which the previous several paragraphs on the Mytilenean campaign are adapted.

54. See further Price 2001.

55. Development of the tribute system under the empire: Meiggs 1972: chs. 13, 18; internal *eisphora* war tax on Athenians: Thucydides 3.19.1.

56. Kelly 1972 explores the complex maneuvers by various parties interested in renewing hostilities.

57. On the Melian dialogue, see Morrison 2000.

58. The destruction of Melos was long remembered by the Greeks as a particularly brutal moment in Athens' imperial history, but it was not unique: Skione (i609, size 2) had been treated similarly after a revolt five years before (421 BCE): Thucydides 5.32.

59. Kahneman 2011: ch. 26, and Ober and Perry 2014 on Thucydides as a prospect theorist *avant la lettre*. On the Melians' choice, see further Orwin 1994: ch. 5, emphasizing the emotion of shame (at the prospect of loss of independence).

60. Thucydides on the Sicilian debate: Ober 1998: 104–113.

61. Similarities of Athens and Syracuse: Thucydides 7.55.2 and Ober 1996: 79–80.

62. Campaign in Sicily and the role of Gylippos: Thucydides books 6–7 and Kagan 1981.

63. Athens in the wake of the Sicilian disaster, and the oligarchic interlude: Thucydides book 8 and Kagan 1987.

64. Xenophon *Hellenica* 1.6.31 claims that in 406 BCE Athenian crews were inferior to the Peloponnesian counterparts: It is unclear whether the change was due more to the loss of skilled rowers on the Athenian side, or the growing experience of their opponents.

65. The late stages of the Peloponnesian War: Xenophon *Hellenica* Books 1–2.

66. Athens in the immediate aftermath of the war: Strauss 1986.

CHAPTER 9 *Disorder and Growth, 403–340 BCE*

1. Detailed histories of the Greek world in the fourth century include Hammond and Griffith 1979; Tritle 1997; Rhodes 2010; *CAH* 6; Buckler 2003. Documents: Harding 1985; Rhodes and Osborne 2003.

2. New poleis on Anatolian coast: 19/115 (9%). Island poleis: Rutishauser 2012.

3. Knoepfler 1997; Fachard 2012: 47–49, 2014. Like Athens, each citizen was a member of a deme and tribe, citizens were called by their demotic, deme membership was hereditary, and each deme was governed by a *demarchos*.

4. Greek federalism: Shipley and Hansen 2006; Mackil 2013. Role of market-preserving federalism in economic development: Weingast 1995.

5. Expertise and mobility: Pyzyk forthcoming. Artillery: Marsden 1969; Campbell 2011. Military architecture responds to artillery: Ober 1987. Military innovations of the fourth century and rural fortifications in Attica: Ober 1985; rural fortifications in Eretria: Fachard 2012. Rational foreign policy at Athens: Hunt 2010. Interstate cooperation: Ryder 1965; Low 2007.

6. The diffusion of Greek science in the fourth century. Netz in progress.

7. Individual expression: Morris 1992: 128–144. Individuals as opposed to collectivities regarded as agents of change: Ferrario 2014. Spread of democracy: Teegarden 2014a.

Honors to individuals: Shear 2011. Individual responsibility, example of the trial of Socrates: Ober 2010a.

8. History of Persia to 334 BCE: Briant 2002; Kuhrt 2007; Llewellyn-Jones 2013.

9. The expedition is described, in first-person detail and with great verve, by Xenophon, *Anabasis*. See further Lee 2007.

10. Imperial Sparta: Cartledge 1987; Hamilton 1991; Debord 1999: 233–253.

11. Evagoras was later to prove another untrustworthy agent, but for the time being was doing the king's bidding.

12. Corinthian War: Hamilton 1979; Debord 199: 253–258.

13. Athenian operations in the north Aegean: Badian 1995; Heskell 1997. Taxes: Xenophon *Hellenica* 4.8.27 and Figueira 2005. The 10% tax is mentioned again in 355 by Demosthenes 20.60.

14. King's Peace: Ryder 1965.

15. Second Athenian naval league: Cargill 1981. Income from the league ca. 195 talents per annum in the 370s, down to about 66 talents by 346: Brun 1983: 138–141. Costs of warfare in this period: Cook 1990. Harding 1995: 112–119 argues that Athenian foreign policy in the fourth century was consistently defensive, rather than imperialistic.

16. Aristotle, *Politics* 2.1270a. According to Aristotle, the situation was worsened by inheritance laws that allowed women to gain control over large tracts of real estate, claiming that by his time some two-fifths of Spartan territory was owned by women.

17. Sparta's successes and failure in the fourth century: Cartledge 1987. Rise of Thebes and foundation of Messene: Buckler 1980; Buckler and Beck 2008.

18. Quick recovery: French 1991. The Thirty: Krentz 1982, Wolpert 2002; Németh 2006. Amnesty: Carawan 2013; Ober 2005b: ch. 5.

19. Constitutional reforms at Athens: Harrison 1955; Ostwald 1986; Hansen 1999: ch. 7; Carugati forthcoming. Public archive: West 1989; Sickinger 1999.

20. Athenian critics of democratic rhetoric: Ober 1998: esp. chs. 2, 4.

21. Fleck and Hanssen 2012 show how Athenian courtroom procedure provided clear information about collective preferences and thereby allowed for closer alignment of incentives.

22. The previous paragraphs, on democratic discourse as a serious game played by masses and elites, and its social and political effects, draw on Ober 1989.See further Lanni 2009 on the role played by jurors in Athenian law courts in enforcing social norms.

23. Theban league as a *koinon* unusually dominated by a central state: Mackil 2013; the error of describing fourth century Thebes or the Boeotian League as democratic: Rhodes 2010: 291. History of the Theban attempt at hegemony: Buckler 1980; Buckler and Beck 2008.

24. Persian threat, fourth century Athenian cleruchies, and the "ghost of empire": Rhodes 2010: 229; Griffith 1978; Cargill 1995; Badian 1995. Special relationship with Samos: Rhodes and Osborne 2003 no. 2.

25. Satraps' Revolt: Weiskopf 1989 with review of Graf 1994. Origins and growth of the satrapy of Caria in early fourth century: Debord 1999: 357–358. Mausolus: Hornblower 1982. Mausolus and Hellenization: Ma 2014.

26. Theban belligerence and expansionism to 362: Buckler 1980; Philip at Thebes: Aymard 1954; Hammond 1997.

27. The complex international situation of 362–352: Buckler 2003.

28. Descent narrative: Pečírka 1976; descent narrative questioned: Eder 1995. The confusing name "Social War" derives from the Latin term for allies (*socii*), not from any role played by social class in the conflict.

29. Grain trade and state emergence: Moreno 2008. Imitation owls: van Alfen 2005. Selective Hellenization: Boardman 1994 and further discussion, this chapter and ch. 10.

30. This section draws on Mackil 2013. Focusing on the examples of Boeotia, Achaea, and Aetolia, and with reference to studies of federalism by contemporary institutional economists, Mackil's book is the best available history of Greek federalism.

31. On the analytic distinction between limited-access "natural states" and open-access orders, and the conditions necessary for moving to and across the "doorstep" of open access, see North, Wallis, and Weingast 2009. This section draws on Carugati, Ober, and Weingast forthcoming, as well as on Ober 2008, 2010c.

32. Banks: Cohen 1992; Shipton 1997. Invisible wealth: Gabrielsen 1986. Lyttkens 1992 and Gabrielsen 2013 are helpful treatments of Athenian taxation and finance.

33. Athenian finances: Ober forthcoming. See further, Pritchard 2012, forthcoming; Lyttkens 2012; Rhodes 2013. Piraeus history: Carugati forthcoming.

34. *Isoteleia*: Whitehead 1977; *enktesis*: Pečírka 1966; naturalization: Osborne 1981. On the many variations in legal and social status in Athens, see Kamen 2013. Approvers: Stroud 1974; Ober 2008: 220–240.

35. *Dikai emporikai*: Cohen 1973, 1992; Lanni 2006: ch. 6. The doubts raised by Todd 1994 do not change the picture substantially.

36. Civil associations: Ismard 2010; Kierstead 2013. Religious association charters: Ober 2008: 252.

37. Philosophical schools as civil associations: Kierstead 2013. Formal bylaws and officials: Lynch 1972. Criticism of democracy by founders of these schools: Ober 1998.

38. Rutishauser 2007, 2012: ch. 6.

39. Osborne 2009b: 341, "the Olbians observe practice in another Greek city, see its relevance to their own particular interests and concerns, and adapt it for their own use." Adoption of Athenian taxation practice in Thespiai: Schachter and Marchand 2013.

40. Aeneas' text is translated and helpfully annotated by Whitehead 1990.

41. *Ephebeia* and other changes in Athenian military organization: Ober 1985: ch. 5. Changing roles of politicians and generals: Hansen 1983. Hamel 1998: 194–195 shows that a fifth century BCE Athenian general "in charge of ships" is a fiction of modern scholarship.

42. Disputes over attribution of owls to mints: Ober 2008: 237–238. The reminting of owls in 354: Kroll 2011a and 2011b. The stone on which the law mandating the recall was inscribed is badly damaged and the law still awaits definitive publication. Grain tax law: Stroud 1998, and Ober 2008: 260–263.

43. *Merismos,* first attested in 386 (Rhodes and Osborne 2003: no. 19): Rhodes 2013; reforms of *eisphora* rules: Christ 2007.

44. Financial management of Eubulus and Lycurgus: Cawkwell 1963; Lewis 1997; Davies 2004; Burke 2010. Public projects of the 330s and 320s: this book, ch. 11.

45. Rhodes 2010: 299–301. Public slaves: Ismard 2013. Nicomachus: Todd 1996; Eukles: Clinton 2005: no. 159 line 60.

46. Ober forthcoming: 500–505. GDI is, for our purposes, a reasonable proxy for GDP. Other premodern fiscal regimes: Monson and Scheidel forthcoming.

47. Transfers as risk insurance, leading to growth: Ober 2008: 254–258. Transfers in the fifth century BCE: van Wees 2013b: 144–145. Reduced political inequality in the fourth century: Taylor 2007, 2008.

48. Davies 2004, and this book, ch. 11.

49. Syracuse after 413, constitutional change and war: *CAH* 6 ch. 5 (by D. M. Lewis), 13 (by H. D. Westlake).

50. Reign of Dionysius I: Sanders 1987; Caven 1990. Dionysius' pay and prize scheme is also credited by Diodorus (14.42.1) with stimulating the development of the first quadrireme and quinquereme warships—the larger and heavier versions of the trireme that became the standard "ships of the line" in the Hellenistic period. Given that there is no reliable account of their use until the second half of the fourth century, this seems unlikely. Pliny (7.207) cites a lost work by Aristotle making the quadrireme a Carthaginian invention.

51. Dionysius II and "the legend of Dion": Sanders 2008. Dion was Dionysius I's brother-in-law and son-in-law: Dion's sister married Dionysius I; Dion in turn married their daughter, his first cousin.

52. Archaeological evidence of economic crisis in Sicily: Talbert 1974: esp. 146. De Angelis' book in progress on the social and economic history of archaic and classical Sicily is eagerly awaited by historians of Greek antiquity and is likely to nuance the stark picture offered by the literary sources of mid-century crisis and recovery.

53. Warfare and agriculture: Hanson 1983.

54. Mackil 2004. On mobility of Greeks, including laborers: McKechnie 1989; Purcell 1990; Garland 2014.

55. Timoleon's life was recorded by Plutarch, Diodorus, and the Roman biographer Cornelius Nepos. While each of these accounts is clearly intended to draw a black and white contrast between a virtuous reformer and wicked tyrants, and while we cannot say whether things would have gone otherwise had Timoleon been in full health in 337 BCE, there is good reason to associate Timoleon's victories and his reforms with the revival of Greek Sicily: Talbert 1974; Davies 1993: 246–249.

56. Cf. sharp, although temporary (in most areas; Britain and Holland are the exceptions) rise in wages in Europe after the Black Death: Allen 2001.

57. Talbert 1974: ch. 8; cf. Smarczyk 2003. Bronze coinage: data from *Inventory* Index 26; another 14 Sicilian poleis had first issued bronze coins in the fifth century. By comparison, 31% (64/206) of the western Anatolian poleis and 28% (110/388) of mainland and Aegean Greek poleis began minting bronze coins in the fourth century.

58. Starr 1975: 85–87. Earlier assumption of economic decline: *CAH* 2, ch. 38 (by J. M. Cook: 1961). Starr was my graduate advisor at the University of Michigan from 1975 to 1980.

59. Prosperity, pro-Persian oligarchies, institutional innovations and civic population growth: Debord 1999: 397–399, 495–498. Kyme: Hamon 2008. Evidence for democracy in Anatolian Greek cities in the fourth century: Robinson 2011: ch. 3. Hellenization and its effect on Greek as well as non-Greek peoples; Ma 2014.

60. Adoption of Chian weight standard: Meadows 2011.

61. Exceptions to the fortified large-polis rule: Zeleia (i764: size 4), Prokonessos (i759: size 3), and Adramyttion (i800: size 4).

62. Diplomatic language: Ma 1999, and this book, ch. 11.

CHAPTER 10 *Political Fall*

1. Contrast the meteor strike that many scientists believe ended the Cretaceous period with a mass extinction of nonavian dinosaurs, among other species: Alvarez 1997.

2. Davies 1993.

3. Biographies of Philip: Cawkwell 1978; Hammond 1994; Worthington 2008. Detailed histories of the era: Ellis 1976; Hammond and Griffith 1979; Buckler 1989.

4. The role of "mobile experts" in the rise of Macedon is thoroughly documented and analyzed in Pyzyk forthcoming.

5. On Macedonian resources and history before the reign of Philip II, see Hammond and Walbank 1972; Borza 1990; Hatzopoulos 1996; Roisman and Worthington 2010: chs. 4, 7, 8. Timber: Meiggs 1982; Bissa 2009: chs. 4, 5.

6. The fraught question of "how Greek were the Macedonians" in language, ethnicity, social structures, and culture is reviewed, with somewhat different conclusions, by Borza 1990 and Haztopoulos 2011. Cf. Roisman and Worthington 2010: chs. 5, 6. Elite Macedonian society: Roisman and Worthington 2010: ch. 19.

7. Pella, Aegeai, and royal burials: Lane Fox 2011a: introduction and chs. 15, 18. On the "constitutionality" of the Macedonian kingship, I follow Borza 1990 against Hammond and Walbank 1972 and earlier scholars who tended to see Philip as a constitutional monarch. Full discussion in Hatzopoulos 1996; cf. Roisman and Worthington 2010: ch. 18.

8. On Macedonian kings and the Greeks in the fifth and early fourth century, see Lane Fox 2011a: chs. 4, 10, 13.

9. On the career of Philip, his impact on the development of Macedonia, and relations with the Greek world, see works cited in n. 2; Roisman and Worthington 2010: ch. 9; Lane Fox 2011b.

10. Land grants to soldier families and logic of continuous expansionism: Samuel 1988; Borza 1990: 239. Macedonian army: Roisman and Worthington 2010: ch. 22. Millett 2010 emphasizes the driving role of the army, imperial expansion, and plunder in the Macedonian economy under Philip.

11. Philip's wives; Satyrus *apud* Athenaeus 3.557b–e. Borza 1990: 206–208.

12. The standard works on Philip's coinage and mints is Le Rider 1977, with update in 1996. See also Borza 1990: 214; Worthington 2008: 197; Kremydi 2011; Millett 2010: 492–496.

13. Philip and Chalkidike: Lane Fox 2011a: chs. 7, 8. Excavations at Olynthos: Robinson and Mylonas 1929. Architecture, town planning, houeholds: Cahill 2002.

14. Athenian–Macedonian relations to 346, and the Peace of Philocrates: Montgomery 1983; Harris 1995; Hunt 2010.

15. Montgomery 1983 remains a good introduction to the main events, although Harding 1995 correctly points out that he underestimates the consistency and coherence of Athenian foreign policy. My lower bound for the empire's population is established by the aggregate population of the poleis of regions 24 and 26–31 (Thessaly, Macedonia, Thrace) = ca. 1.25 million; (appendix I). I assume that many people in the empire lived outside poleis. Note that this estimate includes Thessaly (ca. 320,000) but excludes Epirus (ca. 230,000). The upward bound is set by extrapolating from early twentieth century census figures. In 1917, some 2 million people lived in the regions encompassed by Greater Macedonia (Lane Fox 2011b, citing Hammond and Griffith 1972: 16). In 1913 (before the incorporation of Macedonia), the population of the modern Greek state reached ca. 2.75 million, a number

that matches the estimated population of the same region in the later fourth century (figure 4.1). I assume that, in contrast to central Greece, Macedonia and Thrace were somewhat less densely populated in the fourth century BCE than in the early twentieth century.

16. Philip's Greek policy: Ellis 1976 argued for the "secure peace" interpretation; Worthington 2008, among others, against it. Demosthenes and his policies: Mossé 1994; Worthington 2012.

17. The estimated population of the entirety of regions 6, 10–12, 20, and 21 comes to just over 1 million (appendix I), but the alliance did not include all of the poleis of regions 6, 11, or 21.

18. The course of events leading up to Chaeronea: Montgomery 1983.

19. Krentz 1985 offers the basis for estimating (albeit roughly) the total combatants in major "Greek vs. Greek" infantry/cavalry battles of the fifth and early fourth centuries: Akragas (472 BCE), 40,000; Tanagra (457), 25,500; Delium (424), 14,000; Mantinea (418), 17,000; Nemea (394), 46,500; Coronea (394), 40,000; Leuctra (371), 17,000.

20. The battle of Chaeronea: Ma 2008 with full bibliography of earlier literature.

21. Alexander's expeditionary force in 334 was of similar size. See Engels 1978 for discussion. Athens refortifies after Chaeronea: Habicht 1997: 10–12, noting (p. 11) that Philip was "wise enough not to seek further hostilities" with Athens.

22. League of Corinth: Ryder 1965; Habicht 1997: 12.

23. Allen 2003 points to the emptiness of the vengeance rhetoric.

24. Events of 337–334 BCE: Worthington 2008: 152–193. Habicht 1997: 14–15 notes that Athens came close to joining Thebes in revolt.

25. Estimated by aggregating the estimated populations of regions 4, 7, 8, 13–19, 22, 23, and 25. See appendix I.

26. Philippopolis (i655) lay 138 km (straight line) north of the site of Abdera (i640: on the south Thracian coast); Kabyle (i654) was 222 km north of Kardia (i655: northern Chersonese). Alexandropolis (i652)—reputedly founded in interior Thrace by Alexander in 34 BCE remains unlocated.

27. Philip's advantages in warfare: Demosthenes 11.47–50. The literature on the degree to which Philip sought to portray himself as a godlike king is reviewed by Borza 1990: 248–51; Worthington 2008: 194–203.

28. Davies 2004. On the role of imported experts in the political economy of Macedonia, especially in the age of Philip, see the informative discussion by Millet 2010, esp. 479 with n. 24.

29. Career of Eumenes of Kardia: Anson 2004.

30. On possible Aristotelian, and other fourth century Greek, influences on Alexander's demonstrated talent as a decision-maker, see Ma 2013b. Aristotle's tracts directed to Alexander: Ober 1998: 347–350.

31. Pyzyk forthcoming provides a full assessment of Greek experts in Philip's employ. Among earlier studies, see Berve 1926.

32. Isocrates' and Speusippos' letters: Markle 1976.

33. Lane Fox 2011b: 367–368 argues that, contrary to Theopompus (*FGrH* no. 115 F 224), Philip must be regarded as a very good manager of finances.

34. Debt and borrowing: Millett 2010: 495–496, with references cited. See further, Hammond and Griffith 1979 442–443, on budgeting. The problem of sovereign debt in fourth century Greek state finance: Ober forthcoming.

35. Career of Callistratus: Sealey 1956.

36. Athenian state regulation of mining, evolution of mining technology, and state minting policy: Bissa 2008; 2009: ch. 2.

37. Best 1969.

38. Markle 1977, 1978 discusses the evidence for the form and the early use of the sarissa, arguing that Philip armed cavalry with the sarissa, and that infantry sarissas were a later development. But the scholarly *communis opinion* is that Diodorus 16.3.2 ([Philip] "devised the compact order and equipment of the phalanx in imitation of the close-order fighting of the heroes at Troy, and he was the first to establish the Macedonian phalanx") is evidence for Philip's sarissa-armed infantry. See Rahe 1981 for discussion of the infantry sarissa and its relationship to fourth century Greek military developments.

39. Athenian shipbuilders sent to Macedonia to build triremes on the spot: Meiggs and Lewis 1988: no. 91. Philip's navy: Hauben 1975, arguing that the ships were built in Macedonian shipyards. We have the names of two of Philip's admirals: Alkimos and Demetrios, but their origins and backgrounds are unknown.

40. Philip's artillery, siege towers, Greek experts: Marsden 1977; *CAH* 6, ch. 12*e* (by Y. Garlan).

41. Nagle 1996 suggests, reasonably, that the speech is based on Macedonian court propaganda. But the sentiments it expresses were a matter of rhetorically colored exaggeration, not simple invention.

CHAPTER 11 *Creative Destruction and Immortality*

1. Goldstone 2002.

2. Hellenistic literature, Second Sophistic, and preservation of classical culture: Goldhill 2001; Whitmarsh 2005; Clauss and Cuypers 2010.

3. Hellenistic polis independence: Ma 1999, 2014, both building on Gauthier 1985, 1993; Fröhlich 2010.

4. Democracy in Hellenistic poleis: Dmitriev 2005; Grieb 2008; Carlsson 2010; Mann and Scholz 2012 with Ma 2013c; Teegarden 2014a. Literature review with critical discussion: Hamon 2010.

5. Arabic engagement with Greek texts: Pines 1986; Gutas 2000. European uptake of Greek literary culture: Goldhill 2002; Grafton, Most, and Settis 2010.

6. For example, the alleged systematic destruction of the texts and teachings of the non-Legalist "One Hundred Schools of Thought" by the First Emperor in Qin China after the consolidation of the empire in ca. 221 BCE.

7. The counterfactual world: Ober 1999: "Alexander dies young." Ironically, years later Cleitus was himself speared to death by Alexander in the course of a drunken symposium. Alexander's career and campaigns: Wilcken 1967; Bosworth 1988, 1996; Bosworth and Baynham 2000; Green 1991; Cartledge 2004; Roisman 2003.

8. Alexander's adoption of the satrapal system; sieges of Miletus and Halicarnassus: Bosworth 1988.

9. Alexander's arrangements in western Anatolia: Wilcken 1967: 81–95.

10. Ruzicka 1988 offers a detailed account of the sources and a plausible reconstruction of Persian strategy in 333 to 331 BCE.

11. Agis' uprising: Wilcken 1967: 131, 138, 145; Habicht 1997: 20–21. Of the combatants, some 40,000 were on the Macedonian side. Agis' Peloponnesian alliance would

have had a population base of about 600,000, assuming that he had most of the poleis of regions 12–14, 17.

12. Lamian War and Athenian history after 322 BCE: Habicht 1997: 36–66. The population base for the Lamian War alliance was perhaps about 600,000 (assuming regions 7, 8, 20, 22, 42, and some of the states of the Peloponnesus)—thus roughly comparable in size to the estimated population base of the revolt led by Agis III in 331; see previous note. Neither alliance was equal in population base to the anti-Macedonian alliance of 338, but if (counterfactually) combined, the alliances of 331 and 322 would have had a population base substantially larger than that of the 338 alliance.

13. Hellenistic Rhodes and the siege: Gabrielsen 1997, 1999; battle of Ipsus: Billows 1990.

14. Hellenistic history and culture: Walbank 1993; Shipley 2000; Erskine 2003; Bugh 2006. Political history of the Hellenistic world: Will 1979.

15. Ma 2000, 2003, 2014a.

16. Austin 1986 concluded (pp. 465–466) that Augustine's (*City of God* 4.4) description of kingdoms without justice as nothing more than "large robber bands" is "strikingly appropriate to the Hellenistic monarchies."

17. Hellenistic economy: Reger 2007; Archibald 2001; Archibald, Davies, and Gabrielsen 2011.

18. Law of Eukrates: Teegarden 2014a, with literature cited. List of speeches preserved from this period by Aeschines, Demosthenes, Dinarchus, Hyperides, and Lycurgus: Ober 1989: 349. Public laws and decrees: Schwenk 1985.

19. History of the period: Habicht 1997: 22–35.

20. Ma forthcoming. By contrast, Tilly 1975: 24 notes that in 1500 CE governments in Europe bore considerably greater resemblance to one another than they did 200–300 years later. Tilly attributes the divergence to power struggles between kings seeking to centralize authority on one side and existing deliberative assemblies and other forms of dispersed governance on the other. The struggle was, for the most part, won by the kings, who largely succeeded in destroying or coopting deliberative institutions: ibid. 22.

21. Epigraphic dossiers: Ma 1999; public honors to generous elites: Ma 2013a; advances in military architecture: Ober 1992; McNicoll 1997.

22. Bresson 2011. What follows is based on Bresson's interpretation of the inscription. The other two beneficiaries of grain were royal kinswomen of Alexander III: his mother Olympias, and his sister Cleopatra, who was at the time ruling Epirus.

23. This assumes that the standard was the Attic medimnos of ca. 52.4 L (as argued by Bresson 2011: 86–87); if instead it was the larger Aeginetan medimnos, then each individual's share was about 30 L. The monetary value would be lower if the grain was barley rather than wheat. Labor value in wheat wages: table 4.6. We do not actually know how the grain was distributed in Athens or elsewhere. The 100,000 medimnoi is about 1/8 of the grain production of Attica plus Lemnos, Imbros, and Skyros in 329–328 BCE—which may also have been a bad year: ibid 87.

24. Amartya Sen (1981) famously demonstrated that modern democracies respond to famine threats more reliably and effectively than autocracies, citing the open exchange of relevant information as the operative mechanism. Although we cannot be certain that the Kyrenean response prevented famine conditions, it seems certain that it at least lessened the severity of those conditions.

25. The naval base: Rhodes and Osborne 2003: no. 100, with discussion in Ober 2008: 124–133.

26. Rhodes, trade, and Aegean security: Gabrielsen 1997, 1999.

27. Hellenistic interpolis warfare: Ma 2000; interstate arbitrations: Ager 1996. Non-seizure (*asylia*) agreements: Rigsby 1996.

28. Refoundation of Thebes: Habicht 1997: 61–62; catapult-ready towers in the new city circuit of Messene: Ober 1987, 1992.

29. Blockmans 1989 analyzes the contest between rent-seeking "voracious states" and independence-seeking "obstructing cities" in medieval and early modern Europe, detailing the conditions (notably the level of urbanization) under which more and less favorable bargains were struck between kings and cities in different regions. Bargains in which cities retained some independence and paid relatively low taxes appear to have stimulated economic growth; arrangements that led to the complete subordination of cities appear to have depressed growth.

30. Teegarden 2014a: 221–238, illustrated on p. 223, figure A1. The other two regimes measured are kingship (peaking at 27% in the early sixth century) and tyranny (peaking at 53% in the late sixth century). Note that a given polis might experience more than one regime type in a given half century and the quantity and quality of information for regime type generally increases over time (many more observations in the fifth and fourth centuries than in the seventh and sixth centuries). But there is no reason to believe that the later data are biased in favor of democracy or that democratic interludes were especially short. The same historical trends held when Teegarden looked at the percentage of regions with at least one recorded instance of the relevant regime: ibid. Figure A2. The editors of the *Inventory* (Hansen and Nielsen 2004: 84) point to the continued prevalence of oligarchy and tyranny in the earlier fourth century, concluding that "it is first in the age of Alexander that democracy becomes the predominant type of constitution."

31. See literature cited in note 4.

32. Teegarden 2014a.

33. Public languages of reciprocal generosity: Ober 1989; Ma 2013a; Athenian classical preeminence: Ober 2008.

34. Mackil 2013.

35. Marsden 1969; Winter 1971: 157; Campbell 2011; Frederiksen 2011: 94.

36. For an example, see Ober 2012.

37. Aristotle's polis a kind of democracy: Ober 2005.

38. Ober 1998: 347–351.

39. On common knowledge, see Chwe 2001, with discussion here in ch. 1. Simonton 2012 demonstrates the importance of common knowledge for explaining ancient Greek regime change and persistence.

40. On the Roman policy of defortification of Greek towns, see Frederiksen 2011: 1 n. 6, 45–46.

APPENDIX II *King, City, and Elite Game*

1. Some idea of the "submission level" is suggested by the demands of the Roman senator Marcus Brutus when raising money for a war against the Caesareans in the mid-first century BCE: Brutus demanded that the cities of western Anatolia pay immediately the equivalent of 10 years of taxes. Cities that resisted were attacked. Rhodes was

compelled to surrender all gold and silver in the city, public, private, or sacred. Xanthos was stormed and almost completely destroyed: Appian *Civil Wars* 4.63, Dio Cassius 47.33.1.

2. The negotiations between the splendidly walled Anatolian city of Herakleia under Latmos with Zeuxis, the envoy of King Antiochus III, provide an example: Ma 1999: 169–170, 185–186, 198–199.

3. It is not necessary that the actual probability be known, of course; what matters is that assumptions about the probability are shared.

4. Ma 1999.

5. On the role of information asymmetry in the origin of war in the modern world, see Fearon 1995.

BIBLIOGRAPHY

Acemoglu, Daron, and James A. Robinson. 2006. *Economic Origins of Dictatorship and Democracy*. New York and Cambridge: Cambridge University Press.

Acemoglu, Daron, Simon Johnson, and James A. Robinson. 2002. "Reversal of Fortune: Geography and Institutions in the Making of the Modern World Income Distribution." *Quarterly Journal of Economics*. 117.4:1231–1294.

Acemoglu, Daron, Francisco A. Gallego, and James A. Robinson. 2014. *Institutions, Human Capital and Development*. Cambridge, MA: National Bureau of Economic Research.

Acharya, Avidit, Matthew Blackwell, and Maya Sen. 2014. "The Political Legacy of American Slavery." Working paper (draft of October 1): http://www.mattblackwell .org/files/papers/slavery.pdf.

Ager, Sheila L. 1996. *Interstate Arbitrations in the Greek World, 337–90 B.C.* Berkeley, CA: University of California Press.

Alcock, Susan E. 1993. *Graecia Capta: The Landscapes of Roman Greece*. Cambridge and New York: Cambridge University Press.

———. 2007. "The Eastern Mediterranean." *The Cambridge Economic History of the Greco-Roman World*, edited by Walter Scheidel, Ian Morris, and Richard P. Saller. Cambridge: Cambridge University Press, 671–697.

Alesina, Alberto, and Enrico Spolaore. 2003. *The Size of Nations*. Cambridge, MA: MIT Press.

Allbaugh, Leland G. 1953. *Crete*. Princeton, NJ: Princeton University Press.

Allen, Danielle S. 2000. *The World of Prometheus: Politics of Punishing in Democratic Athens*. Princeton, NJ: Princeton University Press.

Allen, Katarzyna Hagemajer. 2003. "Becoming the 'Other': Attitudes and Practices at Attic Cemeteries." *The Cultures within Greek Cultures: Contact, Conflict, Collaboration*, edited by Carol Dougherty and Leslie Kurke. Cambridge: Cambridge University Press, 207–236.

Allen, Robert C. 2001. "The Great Divergence in European Wages and Prices from the Middle Ages to the First World War." *Explorations in Economic History*. 38:411–447.

———. 2009. "How Prosperous Were the Romans? Evidence from Diocletian's Price Edict (AD 301)." *Quantifying the Roman Economy: Methods and Problems*, edited by Alan K. Bowman and Andrew Wilson. Oxford and New York: Oxford University Press, 327–345.

Alvarez, Walter. 1997. *T. Rex and the Crater of Doom*. Princeton, NJ: Princeton University Press.

Ameling, Walter. 2013. "Carthage." *The Oxford Handbook of the Ancient State: Near East and Mediterranean*, edited by P. Bang and Walter Scheidel. Oxford: Oxford University Press, 361–382.

Amouretti, Marie-Claire, and Jean-Pierre Brun, eds. 1993. *La production du vin et de l'huile en Méditerranée.* Athens and Paris: Ecole française d'Athènes, Diffusion de Boccard.

Anderson, Greg. 2003. *The Athenian Experiment: Building an Imagined Political Community in Ancient Attica, 508–490 B.C.* Ann Arbor, MI: University of Michigan Press.

———. 2009. "The Personality of the Greek State." *Journal of Hellenic Studies.* 129:1–22.

Anderson, Carl A., and T. Keith Dix. 2004. "Small States in the Athenian Empire: The Case of the Eteokarpathioi." *Syllecta Classica.* 15:1–31.

Anhalt, Emily Katz. 1993. *Solon the Singer: Politics and Poetics.* Lanham, MD: Rowman & Littlefield Publishers.

Anson, Edward. 2004. *Eumenes of Cardia: A Greek among Macedonians.* Boston: Brill Academic Publishers.

Arafat, Karim, and Catherine Morgan. 1989. "Pots and Potters in Athens and Corinth: A Review." *Oxford Journal of Archaeology.* 8:341–386.

Archibald, Zofia. 2001. *Hellenistic Economies.* London and New York: Routledge.

Archibald, Zofia, John Kenyon Davies, and Vincent Gabrielsen, eds. 2011. *The Economies of Hellenistic Societies, Third to First Centuries BC.* Oxford and New York: Oxford University Press.

Arrow, Kenneth Joseph. 1963. *Social Choice and Individual Values.* New Haven, CT: Yale University Press.

Asdrachas, Spyros I. 2005. "An Introduction to Greek Economic History, Fifteenth to Nineteenth Centuries: Fields of Observation and Methodological Issues." *Historical Review. Institute for Neohellenic Research.* 2:7–30.

Aubet, María Eugenia. 1993. *The Phoenicians and the West: Politics, Colonies, and Trade.* Cambridge: Cambridge University Press.

Austin, M. M. 1986. "Hellenistic Kings, War, and the Economy." *Classical Quarterly.* 36:450–466.

Aymard, A. 1954. "Philippe de Macedoine, otage à Thèbes." *Revue des Etudes Anciennes.* 56:25–26.

Azoulay, Vincent. 2014. *Pericles of Athens.* Translated by Janet Lloyd. Princeton, NJ: Princeton University Press.

Azoulay, Vincent, and Paulin Ismard. 2012. *Clisthène et Lycurgue d'Athènes: Autour du politique dans la cité classique.* Paris: Publications de la Sorbonne.

Badian, E. 1995. "The Ghost of Empire. Reflections on Athenian Foreign Policy in the Fourth Century B.C." *Die athenische Demokratie im 4. Jahrhundert v. Chr.: Vollendung oder Verfall einer Verfassungsform?* edited by Walter Eder. Stuttgart, Germany: F. Steiner, 79–106.

Bang, Peter F. 2007. "Trade and Empire—In Search of Organizing Concepts for the Roman Economy." *Past and Present.* 195 (1):3–54.

———. 2009. "Labor: Free and Unfree." *A Companion to Ancient History*, edited by Andrew Erskine. Chichester, U.K., and Malden, MA: Wiley-Blackwell, 447–461.

Banks, Arthur S., and Kenneth A. Wilson. 2013. *Cross-National Time-Series Data Archive.* Jerusalem: Databanks International. http://www.databanksinternational.com.

Baumol, William J. 1993. *Entrepreneurship, Management, and the Structure of Payoffs.* Cambridge, MA: MIT Press.

———. 2004. "On Entrepreneurship, Growth and Rent-Seeking: Henry George Updated." *American Economist.* 48 (1):9–16.

Baumol, William J., and Robert J. Strom. 2010. "'Useful Knowledge' of Entrepreneurship: Some Implications of the History." *The Invention of Enterprise: Entrepreneurship from Ancient Mesopotamia to Modern Times*, edited by David S. Landes, Joel Mokyr, and William J. Baumol. Princeton, NJ: Princeton University Press, 527–542.

Beaton, Roderick. 2013. *Byron's War: Romantic Rebellion, Greek Revolution*. Cambridge: Cambridge University Press.

Bedford, Peter. 2007. "The Persian Near East." *The Cambridge Economic History of the Greco-Roman World*, edited by Walter Scheidel, Ian Morris, and Richard P. Saller. Cambridge: Cambridge University Press, 302–329.

Beloch, Julius. 1886. *Historische Beiträge zur Bevolkerungslehre*. Leipzig, Germany: Duncker & Humblot.

———. 1893. *Griechische Geschichte*. Strassburg, Germany: K. J. Trübner.

———. 1993 [1889]. *La popolazione antica della Sicilia*. S. Cristina Gela, Italy: E.L.S.

Bennet, John. 2007. "The Aegean Bronze Age." *The Cambridge Economic History of the Greco-Roman World*, edited by Walter Scheidel, Ian Morris, and Richard P. Saller. Cambridge: Cambridge University Press, 175–210.

Berent, Moshe. 1996. "Hobbes and the 'Greek Tongues.'" *History of Political Thought*. 17:36–59.

———. 2000. "Anthropology and the Classics: War, Violence and the Stateless Polis." *Classical Quarterly*. 50:257–289.

———. 2006. "The Stateless Polis: A Reply to Critics." *Social Evolution & History*. 5 (1):140–162.

Berger, Shlomo. 1992. *Revolution and Society in Greek Sicily and Southern Italy*. Stuttgart, Germany: Steiner.

Berve, Helmut. 1926. *Das Alexanderreich auf prosopographischer Grundlage*. Munich, Germany: Beck.

Billows, Richard A. 1990. *Antigonos the One-Eyed and the Creation of the Hellenistic State*. Berkeley, CA: University of California Press.

Bintliff, John. 2012. *The Complete Archaeology of Greece: From Hunter-Gatherers to the 20th Century A.D.* Chichester, U.K., and Malden, MA: Wiley-Blackwell.

Bissa, Errietta M. A. 2008. "Investment Patterns in the Laurion Mining Industry in the Fourth Century BCE." *Historia*. 57 (3):263–273.

———. 2009. *Governmental Intervention in Foreign Trade in Archaic and Classical Greece*. Leiden, Netherlands, and Boston: Brill.

Blackmon, Douglas A. 2009. *Slavery by Another Name: The Re-Enslavement of Black Americans from the Civil War to World War II*: Anchor: New York.

Blockmans, Wim. 1989. "Voracious States and Obstructing Cities: An Aspect of State Formation in Preindustrial Europe." *Theory and Society*. 18:733–755.

Blok, Josine. 2009. "Perikles' Citizenship Law: A New Perspective." *Historia*. 58:141–170.

Blok, Josine, and André Lardinois, eds. 2006. *Solon: New Historical and Philological Perspectives*. Leiden, Netherlands: E. J. Brill.

Bloom, David E., David Canning, and Günther Fink. 2008. "Urbanization and the Wealth of Nations." *Science*. 319:772–775.

Boardman, John. 1994. *The Diffusion of Classical Art in Antiquity*. Princeton, NJ: Princeton University Press.

Boedeker, Deborah Dickmann, and Kurt A. Raaflaub, eds. 1998. *Democracy, Empire, and the Arts in Fifth-Century Athens*. Cambridge, MA: Harvard University Press.

Boehm, Christopher. 2012a. *Moral Origins: Social Selection and the Evolution of Virtue, Altruism, and Shame*. New York: Basic Books.

———. 2012b "Prehistory." *The Edinburgh Companion to the History of Democracy*, edited by Benjamin Isakhan and Stephen Stockwell. Edinburgh, U.K.: Edinburgh University Press, 29–39.

Boersma, Johannes Sipko. 1970. *Athenian Building Policy from 561/0 to 405/4 B.C.* Groningen, Germany: Wolters-Noordhoff Publishing.

Boix, Carles. 2011. "Democracy, Development, and the International System." *American Political Science Review*. 105:809–828.

Borza, Eugene N. 1990. *In the Shadow of Olympus: The Emergence of Macedon*. Princeton, NJ: Princeton University Press.

Bosworth, A. B. 1988. *Conquest and Empire: The Reign of Alexander the Great*. Cambridge and New York: Cambridge University Press.

———. 1996. *Alexander and the East: The Tragedy of Triumph*. Oxford and New York: Oxford University Press.

Bosworth, A. B., and Elizabeth Baynham. 2000. *Alexander the Great in Fact and Fiction*. Oxford and New York: Oxford University Press.

Bowles, Samuel, and Herbert Gintis. 2011. *A Cooperative Species: Human Reciprocity and Its Evolution*. Princeton, NJ: Princeton University Press.

Bowman, Alan K., and Andrew Wilson, eds. 2009. *Quantifying the Roman Economy: Methods and Problems*. Oxford and New York: Oxford University Press.

———, eds. 2011. *Settlement, Urbanization, and Population*. Oxford: Oxford University Press.

———, eds. 2013. *The Roman Agricultural Economy: Organization, Investment, and Production*. Oxford: Oxford University Press.

Bresson, Alain. 2000. *La cité marchande*. Paris: Diffusion De Boccard.

———. 2007. *L'économie de la Grèce des cités*. Paris: A. Colin (forthcoming. *The Making of the Ancient Greek Economy: Institutions, Markets, and Growth in the City-States*. Princeton, NJ: Princeton University Press).

———. 2011. "Grain from Cyrene." *Hellenistic Economies III*. Oxford: Oxford University Press, 66–95.

———. 2014. "The Ancient World: A Climatic Challenge." *Quantifying the Greco-Roman Economy and Beyond, Pragmateiai*, edited by François de Callataÿ. Bari, Italy: Edipuglia, 39–55.

Briant, Pierre. 2002. *From Cyrus to Alexander: A History of the Persian Empire*. Winona Lake, IN: Eisenbrauns.

Brock, Roger. 2009. "Did the Athenian Empire Promote Democracy?" *Interpreting the Athenian Empire*, edited by John Ma, Nikolaos Papazarkadas, and Robert Parker. London: Duckworth, 125–148.

Brock, Roger, and Stephen Hodkinson, eds. 2000. *Alternatives to Athens: Varieties of Political Organization and Community in Ancient Greece*. Oxford: Oxford University Press.

Brun, Patrice. 1983. *Eisphora-syntaxis-stratiotika: Recherches sur les finances militaires d'Athènes au IVe siècle av. J.-C.* Paris: Les Belles Lettres.

Brunschwig, Jacques, and G.E.R. Lloyd. 2000. *Greek Thought: A Guide to Classical Knowledge*. Cambridge, MA: Harvard University Press.

Bubelis, William. 2014. *Hallowed Stewards: Solon and the Sacred Treasurers of Ancient Athens*. Ann Arbor: University of Michigan Press.

Buckler, John. 1980. *The Theban Hegemony, 371–362 BC*. Cambridge, MA: Harvard University Press.

———. 1989. *Philip II and the Sacred War*. Leiden, Netherlands, and New York: E. J. Brill.

———. 2003. *Aegean Greece in the Fourth Century BC*. Leiden, Netherlands, and Boston: E. J. Brill.

Buckler, John, and Hans Beck. 2008. *Central Greece and the Politics of Power in the Fourth Century BC*. Cambridge: Cambridge University Press.

Bugh, Glenn Richard, ed. 2006. *The Cambridge Companion to the Hellenistic World*. Cambridge: Cambridge University Press.

Burckhardt, Jacob. 1998 [1898]. *The Greeks and Greek Civilization*, edited by Oswyn Murray. Translated by Sheila Stern. New York: St. Martin's Press.

Burke, Edmund M. 2005. "The Habit of Subsidization in Classical Athens: Toward a Thetic Ideology." *Classica et Mediaevalia*. 56:5–47.

———. 2010. "Finances and the Operation of Athenian Democracy in the Lycurgan Era." *American Journal of Philology*. 131:393–423.

Burkert, Walter. 1992. *The Orientalizing Revolution: Near Eastern Influence on Greek Culture in the Early Archaic Age*. Cambridge, MA: Harvard University Press.

———. 2004. *Babylon, Memphis, Persepolis: Eastern Contexts of Greek Culture*. Cambridge, MA: Harvard University Press.

Burns, Bryan E. 2010. *Mycenaean Greece, Mediterranean Commerce, and the Formation of Identity*. New York: Cambridge University Press.

Burt, Ronald S. 1992. *Structural Holes: The Social Structure of Competition*. Cambridge, MA: Harvard University Press.

Byron, George Gordon, Lord. 1812. *Childe Harold's Pilgrimage: A Romaunt*. London: John Murray.

Cahill, Nicholas. 2000. "Olynthus and Town Planning." *Classical World*. 93:497–515.

———. 2002. *Household and City Organization at Olynthus*. New Haven, CT: Yale University Press.

Cambridge Ancient History (CAH), 2nd ed. (vols. 3–14) or 3rd ed. (vols. 1–2), 1970–2005. Cambridge: Cambridge University Press.

Camp, John McK. II. 2000. "Walls and the *Polis*." *Polis and Politics [Festschrift Hansen]*, edited by P. Flensted-Jensen, T. H. Nielsen, and L. Rubinstein. Copenhagen, Denmark: Munksgaard, 41–57.

———. 2001. *The Archaeology of Athens*. New Haven, CT: Yale University Press.

Campbell, Duncan B. 2011. "Ancient Catapults: Some Hypotheses Reexamined." *Hesperia*. 80:677–700.

Caplan, Bryan. 2007. *The Myth of the Rational Voter*. Princeton, NJ: Princeton University Press.

Carawan, Edwin. 2013. *The Athenian Amnesty and Reconstructing the Law*. New York: Oxford University Press.

Cargill, Jack. 1981. *The Second Athenian League: Empire or Free Alliance?* Berkeley, CA: University of California Press.

———. 1995. *Athenian Settlements of the Fourth Century B.C.* Leiden, Netherlands: E. J. Brill.

Carlsson, Susanne. 2010. *Hellenistic Democracies: Freedom, Independence and Political Procedure in Some East Greek City-States*. Stuttgart, Germany: F. Steiner.

Carter, Joseph Coleman. 2006. *Discovering the Greek Countryside at Metaponto*. Ann Arbor, MI: University of Michigan Press.

Cartledge, Paul. 1979. *Sparta and Lakonia: A Regional History, 1300–362 BC*. London: Routledge & Kegan Paul.

———. 1987. *Agesilaos and the Crisis of Sparta*. London: Duckworth.

———. 1996. "Comparatively Equal." *Dēmokratia: A Conversation on Democracies, Ancient and Modern*, edited by Josiah Ober and Charles W. Hedrick. Princeton, NJ: Princeton University Press, 175–186.

———. 1998. "The Economy (Economies) of Ancient Greece." *Dialogos*. 5:4–24.

———. 2001. *Spartan Reflections*. London: Duckworth.

———. 2004. *Alexander the Great: The Hunt for a New Past*. Woodstock, NJ: Overlook Press.

Carugati, Federica. Forthcoming. "In Law We Trust (Each Other). Legal Institutions, Democratic Stability and Economic Development in Classical Athens." Stanford, CA: Classics, Stanford University.

Carugati, Federica, Josiah Ober, and Barry Weingast. Forthcoming. "Is Democracy Uniquely Modern? Athens on the Doorstep." Working paper: Stanford University, Stanford, CA.

Caven, Brian. 1990. *Dionysius I: War-Lord of Sicily*. New Haven, CT: Yale University Press.

Cawkwell, George L. 1963. "Eubulus." *Journal of Hellenic Studies*. 83:47–67.

———. 1978. *Philip of Macedon*. London and Boston: Faber & Faber.

———. 1993. "Sparta and Her Allies in the Sixth Century." *Classical Quarterly*. 43(2): 364–376.

Cheetham, Nicolas. 1981. *Mediaeval Greece*. New Haven, CT: Yale University Press.

Christ, Matthew R. 2007. "The Evolution of the *Eisphora* in Classical Athens." *Classical Quarterly. 57:53–69.*

Christensen, Paul. 2003. "Economic Rationalism in Fourth-Century Athens." *Greece and Rome.* 50:1–26.

Christian, David. 2011. *Maps of Time: An Introduction to Big History*. Berkeley, CA: University of California Press.

Chwe, Michael Suk-Young. 2001. *Rational Ritual: Culture, Coordination, and Common Knowledge*. Princeton, NJ: Princeton University Press.

Clark, Gregory. 2007. *A Farewell to Alms: A Brief Economic History of the World*: Princeton, NJ: Princeton University Press.

Clauss, James Joseph, and Martine Cuypers, eds. 2010. *A Companion to Hellenistic Literature*. Chichester, U.K., and Malden, MA: Blackwell.

Cline, Eric H., ed. 2010. *The Oxford Handbook of the Bronze Age Aegean (ca. 3000–1000 BC)*. New York and Oxford: Oxford University Press.

———. 2014. *1177 B.C.: The Year Civilization Collapsed*. Princeton, NJ: Princeton University Press.

Clinton, Kevin. 2005. *Eleusis, the Inscriptions on Stone: Documents of the Sanctuary of the Two Goddesses and Public Documents of the Deme*. Athens: Archaeological Society at Athens.

Coates, J. F., S. K. Platis, and J. T. Shaw. 1990. *The Trireme Trials 1988: Report on the Anglo-Hellenic Sea Trials of Olympias*. Oxford: Oxbow.

Cohen, Edward E. 1973. *Ancient Athenian Maritime Courts*. Princeton, NJ: Princeton University Press.

———. 1992. *Athenian Economy and Society: A Banking Perspective*. Princeton, NJ: Princeton University Press.

Cole, Susan Guettel. 2004. *Landscapes, Gender, and Ritual Space: The Ancient Greek Experience*. Berkeley, CA: University of California Press.

Cole, Thomas. 1991. *The Origins of Rhetoric in Ancient Greece*. Baltimore: Johns Hopkins University Press.

Connor, W. Robert. 1993. "The Ionian Era of Athenian Civic Identity." *Proceedings American Philosophical Society*. 137.3:194–206.

Conophagos, C. E. 1980. *Le Laurium antique, et la technique grecque de la production de l'argent*. Athens: Ekdotike Hellados.

Constantakopoulou, Christy. 2007. *The Dance of the Islands: Insularity, Networks, the Athenian Empire, and the Aegean World*. Oxford: Oxford University Press.

Cook, Margaret L. 1990. "Timocrates' 50 Talents and the Cost of Ancient Warfare." *Eranos*. 88:69–97.

Cook, Robert M. 1997. *Greek Painted Pottery*. London: Routledge.

Couzin, Iain D., Jens Krause, Nigel R. Franks, and Simon A. Levin. 2005. "Effective Leadership and Decision-Making in Animal Groups on the Move." *Nature*. 433: 513–516.

Cox, Gary, Douglass C. North, and Barry R. Weingast. 2012. "The Violence Trap: A Political-Economic Approach to the Problems of Development." Working paper: Stanford University, Stanford, CA.

Crawford, Michael H., and David Whitehead. 1983. *Archaic and Classical Greece: A Selection of Ancient Sources in Translation*. Cambridge: Cambridge University Press.

D'Angour, Armand. 2011. *The Greeks and the New: Novelty in Ancient Greek Imagination and Experience*. Cambridge and New York: Cambridge University Press.

Dalby, Andrew. 1997. *Siren Feasts: A History of Food and Gastronomy in Greece*. London: Routledge.

Davidson, James N. 1997. *Courtesans & Fishcakes: The Consuming Passions of Classical Athens*. Hammersmith, London: HarperCollins.

Davies, John Kenyon. 1971. *Athenian Propertied Families, 600–300 B.C.* Oxford: Clarendon Press.

———. 1993. *Democracy and Classical Greece*. Cambridge, MA: Harvard University Press.

———. 1994. "Accounts and Accountability in Classical Athens." *Ritual, Finance, Politics: Athenian Democratic Accounts Presented to David Lewis*, edited by Robin Osborne and Simon Hornblower. Oxford: Clarendon Press, 201–212.

———. 2004. "Athenian Fiscal Expertise and Its Influence." *Mediterraneo Antico*. 7 (2):491–512.

———. 2007. "Classical Greece: Production." *The Cambridge Economic History of the Greco-Roman World*, edited by Walter Scheidel, Ian Morris, and Richard P. Saller. Cambridge: Cambridge University Press, 333–361.

———. 2013. "Corridors, Cleruchies, Commodities, and Coins: The Pre-History of the Athenian Empire." *Handels- und Finanzgebaren in der Ägäis im 5. Jh. v. Chr.* (*Trade and Finance in the 5th c. BC Aegean World, BYZAS 18*, edited by Anja Slawisch. Istanbul, Turkey: German Archaeological Institute (DAI), 1–24.)

Davis, Gil. 2012. "Dating the Drachmas in Solon's Laws." *Historia*. 61 (2):127–158.

De Angelis, Franco. 2000. "Estimating the Agricultural Base of Greek Sicily." *Papers of the British School at Rome*. 68:111–148.

———. 2003. *Megara Hyblaia and Selinous: The Development of Two Greek City-States in Archaic Sicily*. Oxford: Oxford University, School of Archaeology.

De Angelis, Franco. 2006. "Going against the Grain in Sicilian Greek Economics." *Greece & Rome.* 53.1:29–47.

———. 2010. "Re-Assessing the Earliest Social and Economic Developments in Greek Sicily." *Mitteilungen des Deutsches Archäologisches Institut. Rome.* 116:21–53.

———. In progress. *Archaic and Classical Greek Sicily: A Social and Economic History.* New York: Oxford University Press.

de Callataÿ, François. 2005. "The Graeco-Roman Economy in the Super Long Run: Lead, Copper, and Shipwrecks." *Journal of Roman Archaeology.* 18:361–372.

———, ed. 2011a. *Quantifying Monetary Supplies in Greco-Roman Times.* Bari, Italy: Edipuglia.

———. 2011b. "Quantifying Monetary Supplies in Greco-Roman Times: A General Frame." *Quantifying Monetary Supplies in Greco-Roman Times,* edited by François de Callataÿ. Bari, Italy: Edipuglia, 7–29.

———. 2012. "Le retour (quantifié) du « miracle grec »." *Stephanèphoros. De l'économie antique à l'asie mineure. Hommages à Raymond Descat,* edited by Koray Kornuk. Bordeaux, France: Ausonius.

———. 2014a. "Long-Term Quantification in Ancient History: A Historical Perspective." *Quantifying the Greco-Roman Economy and Beyond,* edited by François de Callataÿ. Bari, Italy: Edipuglia, 13–27.

———, ed. 2014b. *Quantifying the Greco-Roman Economy and Beyond.* Bari, Italy: Edipuglia.

de Polignac, François. 1995. *Cults, Territory, and the Origins of the Greek City-State.* Chicago: University of Chicago Press.

de Romilly, Jacqueline 1992. *The Great Sophists in Periclean Athens.* Oxford and New York: Oxford University Press.

de Souza, Philip. 1999. *Piracy in the Graeco-Roman World.* Cambridge and New York: Cambridge University Press.

De Ste. Croix, G.E.M. 1954. "The Character of the Athenian Empire." *Historia.* 3:1–41.

———, 1972. *The Origins of the Peloponnesian War.* London: Duckworth.

———, 1983. *The Class Struggle in the Ancient Greek World: From the Archaic Age to the Arab Conquests.* London: Duckworth.

de Vries, Jan. 1984. *European Urbanization 1500–1800.* Cambridge, MA: Harvard University Press.

de Vries, Jan, and A. M. van der Woude. 1997. *The First Modern Economy: Success, Failure, and Perseverance of the Dutch Economy, 1500–1815.* Cambridge and New York: Cambridge University Press.

Deaton, Angus. 2013. *The Great Escape: Health, Wealth, and the Origins of Inequality*: Princeton, NJ: Princeton University Press.

Debord, Pierre. 1999. *L'Asie mineure au IVe siècle (412–323 a.C.): Pouvoirs et jeux politiques.* Bordeaux, France: Ausonius.

Demand, Nancy H. 2011. *The Mediterranean Context of Early Greek History.* Chichester, U.K., and Malden, MA: Wiley-Blackwell.

Depew, David. 1995. "Humans and Other Political Animals in Aristotle's *History of Animals." Phronesis.* 40:156–181.

Desmond, William D. 2006. *The Greek Praise of Poverty: Origins of Ancient Cynicism.* Notre Dame, IN: University of Notre Dame Press.

Diamond, Jared M. 1999. *Guns, Germs, and Steel: The Fates of Human Societies.* New York: W. W. Norton & Company.

Dillon, Matthew, and Lynda Garland. 2010. *Ancient Greece: Social and Historical Documents from Archaic Times to the Death of Alexander.* London and New York: Routledge.

Dmitriev, Sviatoslav. 2005. *City Government in Hellenistic and Roman Asia Minor.* Oxford and New York: Oxford University Press.

Donlan, Walter. 1985. "The Social Groups of Dark Age Greece." *Classical Philology.* 80:293–308.

Doucouliagos, Hristos, and Mehmet Ali Ulubaşoğlu. 2008. "Democracy and Economic Growth: A Meta-Analysis." *American Journal of Political Science.* 52.1:61–83.

Dougherty, Carol. 1993. *The Poetics of Colonization: From City to Text in Archaic Greece.* New York: Oxford University Press.

Drake, Brandon L. 2012. "The Influence of Climatic Change on the Late Bronze Age Collapse and the Greek Dark Ages." *Journal of Archaeological Science.* 39:1862–1870.

Ducat, Jean. 1990. *Les hilotes.* Athens and Paris: École française d'Athènes. Diffusion De Boccard.

———. 2006. *Spartan Education: Youth and Society in the Classical Period.* Translated by Emma Stafford, Pamela-Jane Shaw, and Anton Powell. Swansea, U.K.: Classical Press of Wales.

Duplouy, Alain. 2006. *Le prestige des élites: Recherches sur les modes de reconnaissance sociale en Grèce entre les Xe et Ve siècles avant J.-C.* Paris: Belles Lettres.

Eder, Walter, ed. 1995. *Die athenische Demokratie im 4. Jahrhundert v. Chr.: Vollendung oder Verfall einer Verfassungsform?* Stuttgart, Germany: F. Steiner.

Edmunds, Lowell. 1975. *Chance and Intelligence in Thucydides.* Cambridge, MA: Harvard University Press.

Edwards, Anthony T. 2004. *Hesiod's Ascra.* Berkeley, CA: University of California Press.

Ehrenberg, Victor. 1973. *From Solon to Socrates; Greek History and Civilization during the Sixth and Fifth Centuries B.C.* London: Methuen.

Eich, Armin. 2006. *Die politische Ökonomie des antiken Griechenland.* Cologne, Germany: Böhlau.

Ellis, John R. 1976. *Philip II and Macedonian Imperialism.* London: Thames and Hudson.

Engels, Donald W. 1978. *Alexander the Great and the Logistics of the Macedonian Army.* Berkeley, CA: University of Califronia Press.

Erickson, Brice. 2005. "Archaeology of Empire: Athens and Crete in the Fifth Century B.C." *American Journal of Archaeology.* 109:619–693.

Erskine, Andrew, ed. 2003. *A Companion to the Hellenistic World.* Oxford: Blackwell Publishing Ltd.

———. 2009, ed. *A Companion to Ancient History.* Chichester, U.K., and Malden, MA: Wiley-Blackwell.

Fachard, Sylvian. 2012. *Eretria fouilles et recherches 21: La défense du territoire. Etude de la chora et de ses fortifications.* Gollion, Switzerland: Infolio.

———. 2014. "Modeling the Territories of Attic Demes: A Computational Approach." Working paper.

Fearon, James. 1995. "Rationalist Explanations for War." *International Organization.* 49.3: 379–414.

Ferrario, Sarah Brown. 2014. *Historical Agency and the "Great Man" in Classical Greece.* Cambridge: Cambridge University Press.

Figueira, Thomas J. 1998. *The Power of Money: Coinage and Politics in the Athenian Empire.* Philadelphia: University of Pennsylvania Press.

———. 2005. "The Imperial Commercial Tax and the Finances of the Athenian Hegemony." *Incid Antico.* 3:83–133.

Finley, M. I. 1968. *A History of Sicily.* London: Chatto & Windus.

———. 1978. "The Fifth-Century Athenian Empire: A Balance Sheet." *Imperialism in the Ancient World,* edited by P.D.A. Garnsey and C. R. Whittaker. Cambridge: Cambridge University Press, 103–126, 306.

———. 1999 [1973]. *The Ancient Economy.* Berkeley, CA: University of California Press.

Finné, Martin, et al. 2011. "Climate in the Eastern Mediterranean, and Adjacent Regions during the Past 6000 Years—A Review." *Journal of Archaeological Science.* 28:3153–3173.

Fisher, N.R.E., Hans van Wees, and Deborah Boedeker. 1998. *Archaic Greece: New Approaches and New Evidence.* London: Duckworth and Classical Press of Wales.

Fleck, Robert K., and F. Andrew Hanssen. 2006. "The Origins of Democracy: A Model with Application to Ancient Greece." *Journal of Law and Economics.* 49:115–146.

———. 2012. "On the Benefits and Costs of Legal Expertise: Adjudication in Ancient Athens." *Review of Law and Economics.* 8.2:367–399.

———. 2013. "How Tyranny Paved the Way to Wealth and Democracy: The Democratic Transition in Ancient Greece." *Journal of Law and Economics.* 56: 389–416.

Forel, Auguste. 1930. *The Social World of the Ants Compared with That of Man.* New York: Albert & Charles Boni.

Fornara, Charles W. 1983. *Archaic Times to the End of the Peloponnesian War.* Cambridge: Cambridge University Press.

Fornara, Charles W., and Loren J. Samons. 1991. *Athens from Cleisthenes to Pericles.* Berkeley, CA: University of California Press.

Forsdyke, Sara. 2005. *Exile, Ostracism, and Democracy: The Politics of Expulsion in Ancient Greece.* Princeton, NJ: Princeton University Press.

———. 2012. *Slaves Tell Tales: And Other Episodes in the Politics of Popular Culture in Ancient Greece.* Princeton, NJ: Princeton University Press.

Foxhall, Lin. 1992. "The Control of the Attic Landscape." *Agriculture in Ancient Greece,* edited by Berit Wells. Stockholm, Sweden: Paul Åströms Förlag, 155–159.

———. 1997. "A View from the Top: Evaluating the Solonian Property Classes." *The Development of the Polis in Archaic Greece,* edited by Lynette G. Mitchell and P. J. Rhodes. London and New York: Routledge, 113–136.

———. 2002. "Access to Resources in Classical Greece: The Egalitarianism of the Polis in Practice." *Money, Labour and Land: Approaches to the Economies of Ancient Greece,* edited by Paul Cartledge, Edward E. Cohen, and Lin Foxhall. London and New York: Routledge, 209–220.

Foxhall, Lin, and H. A. Forbes. 1982. "*Sitometreia*: The Role of Grain as a Stable Food in Classical Antiquity." *Chiron.* 12:41–90.

Frankfort, Henri. 1948. *Kingship and the Gods, a Study of Ancient Near Eastern Religion as the Integration of Society and Nature.* Chicago: University of Chicago Press.

Frederiksen, Rune. 2011. *Greek City Walls of the Archaic Period, 900–480 BC.* New York: Oxford University Press.

French, Alfred. 1991. "Economic Conditions in Fourth-Century Athens." *Greece and Rome.* 38:24–40.

Frier, Bruce, and Dennis P. Kehoe. 2007. "Law and Economic Institutions." *The Cambridge Economic History of the Greco-Roman World,* edited by Walter Scheidel, Ian Morris, and Richard P. Saller. Cambridge: Cambridge University Press, 113–143.

Fröhlich, P. 2010. "L'inventaire du monde des cités grecques. Une somme, une méthode et une conception de l'histoire." *Revue Historique.* 302.3:637–677.

Frost, Frank J. 1984. "The Athenian Military before Cleisthenes." *Historia.* 33:283–294.

Fukuyama, Francis. 2011. *The Origins of Political Order: From Prehuman Times to the French Revolution.* New York: Farrar, Straus and Giroux.

Gabrielsen, Vincent. 1981. *Remuneration of State Officials in Fourth Century B.C. Athens.* Odense, Denmark: Odense University Press.

———. 1986. "*Phanera* and *Aphanes Ousia* in Classical Athens." *Classica et Mediaevalia.* 37:99–114.

———. 1997. *The Naval Aristocracy of Hellenistic Rhodes.* Aarhus, Denmark: Aarhus University Press.

———. 1999. *Hellenistic Rhodes: Politics, Culture, and Society.* Aarhus, Denmark, and Oakville, CT: Aarhus University Press.

———. 2003. "Piracy and the Slave Trade." *A Companion to the Hellenistic World,* edited by Andrew Erskine. Oxford: Blackwell Publishing Ltd., 389–404.

———. 2013. "Finance and Taxes." *Blackwell's Companion to Ancient Greek Government.* Oxford: Blackwell, 332–348.

Gagarin, Michael. 2005. "Early Greek Law." *The Cambridge Companion to Ancient Greek Law,* edited by Michael Gagarin and David Cohen. Cambridge and New York: Cambridge University Press, 82–94.

———. 2008. *Writing Greek Law.* Cambridge and New York: Cambridge University Press.

Gallant, Thomas W. 1991. *Risk and Survival in Ancient Greece: Reconstructing the Rural Domestic Economy.* Stanford, CA: Stanford University Press.

Garland, Robert. 2014. *Wandering Greeks: The Ancient Greek Diaspora from the Age of Homer to the Death of Alexander the Great.* Princeton, NJ: Princeton University Press.

Garnsey, Peter. 1999. *Food and Society in Classical Antiquity.* Cambridge and New York: Cambridge University Press.

Gauthier, Philippe. 1976. *Un commentaire historique des Poroi de Xénophon.* Geneva and Paris: Droz and Minard.

———. 1985. *Les cités grecques et leurs bienfaiteurs.* Athens and Paris: Ecole Française d'Athènes. Diffusion De Boccard.

———. 1993. "Les cités hellénistiques." *The Ancient Greek City-State,* edited by Mogens Herman Hansen. Copenhagen, Denmark: Munksgaard, 211–231.

Gehrke, Hans-Joachim. 1985. *Stasis: Untersuchungen zu den inneren Kriegen in den griechischen Staaten des 5. und 4. Jahrhunderts v. Chr.* Munich, Germany: Beck.

———. 1986. *Jenseits von Athen und Sparta: Das dritte Griechenland und seine Staatenwelt.* Munich, Germany: Beck.

Gintis, Herbert, et al., eds. 2004. *Moral Sentiments and Material Interests: The Foundations of Cooperation in Economic Life.* Cambridge, MA: MIT Press.

Ginzburg, Carlo. 1980. *The Cheese and the Worms: The Cosmos of a Sixteenth Century Miller.* London: Routledge and Kegan Paul.

Goldhill, Simon, ed. 2001. *Being Greek under Rome: Cultural Identity, the Second Sophistic and the Development of Empire.* Cambridge and New York: Cambridge University Press.

———. 2002. *Who Needs Greek? Contests in the Cultural History of Hellenism.* Cambridge and New York: Cambridge University Press.

Goldstone, Jack. 2002. "Efflorescences and Economic Growth in World History." *Journal of World History.* 13:323–389.

———. 2013. "The Origins of Western Superiority: A Comment on Modes of Meta-History and Duchesne's Indo-Europeans Article." *Cliodynamics: The Journal of Theoretical and Mathematical History.* 4.1:54–66.

Gomme, A. W. 1937. *Essays in Greek History and Literature.* Oxford: B. Blackwell.

Gordon, Deborah. 1999. *Ants at Work: How an Insect Society Is Organized.* New York: The Free Press.

———. 2010. *Ant Encounters: Interaction Networks and Colony Behavior.* Princeton, NJ: Princeton University Press.

———. 2014. "The Ecology of Collective Behavior." *PLOS Biology.* DOI: 10.1371/journal. pbio.1001805.

Gowder, Paul. 2013. "The Rule of Law and Equality." *Law and Philosophy.* 32:565–618.

Graf, David F. 1994. "Review of Weiskopf 1989." *Journal of the American Oriental Society.* 114.1:99–101.

Grafton, Anthony, Glenn W. Most, and Salvatore Settis, eds. 2010. *The Classical Tradition.* Cambridge, MA: Harvard University Press.

Graham, A. J. 1964. *Colony and Mother City in Ancient Greece.* Manchester, U.K.: Manchester University Press.

Granovetter, Mark S. 1973. "The Strength of Weak Ties." *American Journal of Sociology.* 78.6:1360–1380.

Green, Peter. 1991. *Alexander of Macedon, 356–323 B.C.: A Historical Biography.* Berkeley, CA: University of California Press.

Greene, K. 2000. "Technical Innovation and Economic Progress in the Ancient World: M. I. Finley Reconsidered." *Economic History Review.* 53:29–59.

Grieb, Volker. 2008. *Hellenistische Demokratie: Politische Organisation und Struktur in freien griechischen Poleis nach Alexander dem Grossen.* Stuttgart, Germany: F. Steiner.

Griffith, G. T. 1978. "Athens in the Fourth Century." *Imperialism in the Ancient World*, edited by Peter Garnsey and C. R. Whittaker. Cambridge and New York: Cambridge University Press, 127–144.

Grote, George. 1846. *A History of Greece. From the Earliest Period to the Close of the Generation Contemporary with Alexander the Great.* London: J. Murray.

Gutas, Dimitri. 2000. *Greek Philosophers in the Arabic Tradition.* Aldershot, U.K., and Burlington, VT: Ashgate.

Haber, Stephen H. 2012. "Where Does Democracy Thrive: Climate, Technology, and the Evolution of Economic and Political Institutions." Working paper: Stanford University, Stanford, CA.

Haber, Stephen H., and Roy Elis. 2014. "Geography, Endogenous Institutions, and the Well Being of Nations." Working paper: Stanford University, Stanford, CA.

Habicht, Christian. 1997. *Athens from Alexander to Antony.* Cambridge, MA: Harvard University Press.

Hägg, Robin, ed. 1996. *The Role of Religion in the Early Greek Polis: Proceedings of the Third International Seminar on Ancient Greek Cult.* Stockholm, Sweden: Svenska Institutet i Athen.

Hale, John R. 2013. "Not Patriots, Not Farmers, Not Amateurs: Greek Soldiers of Fortune and the Origins of Hoplite Warfare." *Men of Bronze: Hoplite Warfare in Ancient Greece,* edited by Donald Kagan and Gregory Viggiano. Princeton, NJ: Princeton University Press, 176–193.

Halkos, George E., and Nickolas C. Kyriazis. 2010. "The Athenian Economy in the Age of Demosthenes: Path Dependence and Change." *European Journal of Law and Economics.* 29:255–277.

Hall, Jonathan M. 1997. *Ethnic Identity in Greek Antiquity.* Cambridge; New York: Cambridge University Press.

———. 2002. *Hellenicity: Between Ethnicity and Culture.* Chicago: University of Chicago Press.

———. 2006. *A History of the Archaic Greek World: ca. 1200–479 BCE.* Chichester, U.K., and Malden, MA: Wiley-Blackwell.

Hamel, Debra. 1998. *Athenian Generals: Military Authority in the Classical Period.* Leiden, Netherlands, and Boston: Brill.

Hamilton, Charles D. 1979. *Sparta's Bitter Victories: Politics and Diplomacy in the Corinthian War.* Ithaca, NY: Cornell University Press.

———. 1991. *Agesilaus and the Failure of Spartan Hegemony.* Ithaca, NY: Cornell University Press.

Hammer, Dean. 2005. "Plebescitary Politics in Archaic Greece." *Historia.* 54 (2):107–131.

Hammond, N.G.L. 1994. *Philip of Macedon.* London: Duckworth.

———. 1997. "What May Philip Have Learnt as a Hostage at Thebes?" *Greek, Roman, and Byzantine Studies.* 38.4:355–372.

Hammond, N.G.L., and G. T. Griffith. 1979. *A History of Macedonia, vol. 2. 550–336 B.C.* Oxford: Clarendon Press.

Hammond, N.G.L., and F. W. Walbank. 1972. *A History of Macedonia.* Oxford: Clarendon Press.

Hamon, Patrice. 2008. "Kymè d'Éolide, cité libre et démocratique, et le pouvoir des stratèges." *Chiron.* 38:63–106.

———. 2010. "Démocraties grecques après Alexandre. À propos de trois ouvrages récents." *Topoi* 16:389–424.

Hansen, Mogens Herman. 1983. "*Rhetores* and *Strategoi* in Fourth-Century Athens." *Greek, Roman, and Byzantine Studies.* 24:151–180.

———. 1986a. *Demography and Democracy: The Number of Athenian Citizens in the Fourth Century B.C.* Herning, Denmark: Systime.

———. 1986b. "The Origin of the Term *Demokratia.*" *Liverpool Classical Monthly.* 11:35–36.

———. 1988. *Three Studies in Athenian Demography.* Copenhagen, Denmark: Munksgaard.

———. 1999. *The Athenian Democracy in the Age of Demosthenes: Structure, Principles and Ideology.* Norman, OK: University of Oklahoma Press.

———, ed. 2000. *A Comparative Study of Thirty City-State Cultures: An Investigation.* Copenhagen, Denmark: Kongelige Danske Videnskabernes Selskab.

———, ed. 2002a. *A Comparative Study of Six City-State Cultures.* Copenhagen, Denmark: Kongelige Danske Videnskabernes Selskab.

Hansen, Mogens Herman. 2002b. "Was the *Polis* a State or a Stateles Society?" *Even More Studies in the Ancient Greek Polis. Papers from the Copenhagen Polis Centre 6*, edited by Thomas Heine Nielsen. Stuttgart, Germany: F. Steiner, 17–47.

———. 2006a. *Polis: An Introduction to the Ancient Greek City-State*. Oxford: Oxford University Press.

———. 2006b. *The Shotgun Method: The Demography of the Ancient Greek City-State Culture*. Columbia, MO: University of Missouri Press.

———. 2006c. *Studies in the Population of Aigina, Athens and Eretria*. Copenhagen, Denmark: Kongelige Danske Videnskabernes Selskab.

———. 2008. "An Update on the Shotgun Method." *Greek, Roman, and Byzantine Studies*. 48:259–286.

Hansen, Mogens Herman, and Thomas Heine Nielsen, eds. 2004. *An Inventory of Archaic and Classical Poleis*. Oxford: Oxford University Press.

Hanson, Victor Davis. 1983. *Warfare and Agriculture in Classical Greece*. Pisa, Italy: Giardini.

———, ed. 1991. *Hoplites: The Classical Greek Battle Experience*. London and New York: Routledge.

———. 1995. *The Other Greeks: The Family Farm and the Agrarian Roots of Western Civilization*. New York: Free Press.

———. 1996. "Hoplites into Democrats: The Changing Ideology of Athenian Infantry." *Dēmokratia: A Conversation on Democracies, Ancient and Modern*, edited by J. Ober and C. W. Hedrick. Princeton, NJ: Princeton University Press, 289–312.

———. 2005. *A War Like No Other: How the Athenians and Spartans Fought the Peloponnesian War*. New York: Random House.

———. 2013. "The Hoplite Narrative." *Men of Bronze: Hoplite Warfare in Ancient Greece*, edited by Donald Kagan and Gregory Viggiano. Princeton, NJ: Princeton University Press, 256–271.

Harding, Phillip. 1985. *From the End of the Peloponnesian War to the Battle of Ipsus*. Cambridge: Cambridge University Press.

———. 1995. "Athenian Foreign Policy in the Fourth Century." *Klio*. 77:105–125.

Harris, Edward M. 1995. *Aeschines and Athenian Politics*. New York: Oxford University Press.

———. 2002. "Workshop, Marketplace and Household: The Nature of Technical Specialization in Classical Athens and Its Influence on Economy and Society." *Money, Labour and Land: Approaches to the Economies of Ancient Greece*, edited by Paul Cartledge, Edward E. Cohen, and Lin Foxhall. London and New York: Routledge, 67–99.

Harrison, A.R.W. 1955. "Law-Making at Athens at the End of the Fifth Century B.C." *Journal of Hellenic Studies*. 75:26–35.

Harrison, Cynthia M. 1999. "Triremes at Rest: On the Beach or in the Water?" *Journal of Hellenic Studies*. 119:168–171.

Hatzopoulos, Miltiades V. 1996. *Macedonian Institutions under the Kings*. Paris: Diffusion De Boccard.

———. 2011. "Macedonians and Other Greeks." *Brill's Companion to Ancient Macedon*, edited by Robin J. Lane Fox. Leiden, Netherlands: Brill, 51–78.

Hauben, H. 1975. "Philippe II, fondateur de la marine macédonienne." *Ancient Society*. 6:51–59.

Hedrick, Charles W. 1994. "Writing, Reading, and Democracy." *Ritual, Finance, Politics: Athenian Democratic Accounts Presented to David Lewis*, edited by Robin Osborne and Simon Hornblower. Oxford: Clarendon Press, 157–174.

Heskel, Julia. 1997. *The North Aegean Wars, 371–360 B.C.* Stuttgart, Germany: F. Steiner.

Hobbes, Thomas. 1996 [1651]. *Leviathan*, edited by Richard Tuck. Cambridge: Cambridge University Press.

Hobson, Matthew S. 2014. "A Historiography of the Study of the Roman Economy: Economic Growth, Development, and Neoliberalism." *TRAC 23, Theoretical Roman Archaeology Conference. Vol. 23*, edited by Hannah Platts et al. Oxford: Oxbow Books, 11–26.

Hodkinson, Stephen. 1983. "Social Order and the Conflict of Values in Classical Sparta." *Chiron.* 13:239–281.

———. 2000. *Property and Wealth in Classical Sparta*. London: Duckworth.

———. 2008. "Spartiates, Helots and the Direction of the Agrarian Economy: Toward an Understanding of Helotage in Comparative Perspective." *Slave Systems: Ancient and Modern*, edited by Enrico Dal Lago and Constantina Katsari. Cambridge and New York: Cambridge University Press, 285–320.

Hodkinson, Stephen, and Anton Powell, eds. 1999. *Sparta: New Perspectives*. London: Duckworth.

Hoekstra, Kinch. 2007. "A Lion in the House: Hobbes and Democracy." *Rethinking the Foundations of Modern Political Thought*, edited by Annabel Brett and James Tully. Cambridge: Cambridge University Press, 191–218.

———. forthcoming. *Thomas Hobbes and the Creation of Order*. Oxford: Oxford University Press.

Holladay, A. J. 1977. "Spartan Austerity." *Classical Quarterly.* 27.1:111–126.

Hopkins, Keith. 2009. "The Political Economy of the Roman Empire." *The Dynamics of Ancient Empires: State Power from Assyria to Byzantium*, edited by Ian Morris and Walter Scheidel. Oxford and New York: Oxford University Press, 178–204.

Hopper, R. J. 1953. "The Attic Silver Mines in the Fourth Century B.C." *Annual of the British School at Athens.* 48:200–254.

———. 1979. *Trade and Industry in Classical Greece*. London: Thames and Hudson.

Horden, Peregrine, and Nicholas Purcell. 2000. *The Corrupting Sea: A Study of Mediterranean History*. Oxford and Malden, MA: Blackwell.

Hornblower, Simon. 1982. *Mausolus*. Oxford: Clarendon Press.

———. 1991. *A Commentary on Thucydides*. vol. 1. Oxford: Clarendon Press.

———. 2002. *The Greek World, 479–323 B.C.* London and New York: Routledge.

Hunt, Peter. 2010. *War, Peace, and Alliance in Demosthenes' Athens*. Cambridge and New York: Cambridge University Press.

Inventory. See Hansen and Nielsen 2004.

Isakhan, Benjamin, and Stephen Stockwell, eds. 2011. *The Secret History of Democracy*, New York: Palgrave Macmillan.

———, eds. 2012. *The Edinburgh Companion to the History of Democracy*, Edinburgh, U.K.: Edinburgh University Press.

Ismard, Paulin. 2010. *La cité des réseaux. Athènes et ses associations, VIe–Ier siècle avt. J.-C.* Paris: Publications de la Sorbonne.

———. 2013. "Public Slavery, Politics and Expertise in Classical Athens." *Center for Hellenic Studies Research Bulletin.* 1.2.

Jacoby, Felix, et al. 1957 and following. *Die Fragmente der griechischen Historiker*. Leiden, Netherlands, and New York: E.J. Brill (*Brill's New Jacoby*. http://referenceworks.brill online.com/browse/brill-s-new-jacoby).

Jensen, Henrik Jeldtoft. 1998. *Self-Organized Criticality: Emergent Complex Behavior in Physical and Biological Systems*. Cambridge and New York: Cambridge University Press.

Johnstone, Steven. 2011. *A History of Trust in Ancient Greece*. Chicago: University of Chicago Press.

Jursa, Michael. 2010. *Aspects of the Economic History of Babylonia in the First Millennium BC: Economic Geography, Economic Mentalities, Agriculture, the Use of Money and the Problem of Economic Growth*. Münster: Ugarit-Verlag.

Kagan, Donald. 1969. *The Outbreak of the Peloponnesian War*. Ithaca, NY: Cornell University Press.

———. 1974. *The Archidamian War*. Ithaca, NY: Cornell University Press.

———. 1981. *The Peace of Nicias and the Sicilian Expedition*. Ithaca, NY: Cornell University Press.

———. 1987. *The Fall of the Athenian Empire*. Ithaca, NY: Cornell University Press.

Kagan, Donald, and Gregory Viggiano. 2013. *Men of Bronze: Hoplite Warfare in Ancient Greece*. Princeton, NJ: Princeton University Press.

Kahneman, Daniel. 2011. *Thinking, Fast and Slow*. New York: Farrar, Straus and Giroux.

Kallet, Lisa. 2001. *Money and the Corrosion of Power in Thucydides: The Sicilian Expedition and Its Aftermath*. Berkeley, CA: University of California Press.

———. 2007. "The Athenian Economy." *The Cambridge Companion to the Age of Pericles*, edited by Loren J. Samons. Cambridge and New York: Cambridge University Press, 70–95.

———. 2013. "The Origins of the Athenian Economic *Arche*." *Journal of Hellenic Studies*. 133:43–60.

Kallet-Marx, Lisa. 1993. *Money, Expense, and Naval Power in Thucydides' History, 1–5.24*. Berkeley, CA: University of California Press.

———. 1994. "Money Talks: Rhetor, Demos, and Resources of the Athenian Empire." *Ritual, Finance, Politics: Athenian Democratic Accounts Presented to David Lewis*, edited by Robin Osborne and Simon Hornblower. Oxford: Clarendon Press, 227–252.

Kamen, Deborah. 2013. *Status in Classical Athens*. Princeton, NJ: Princeton University Press.

Kaniewski, D., et al. 2010. "Late Second–Early First Millennium BC Abrupt Climate Changes in Coastal Syria and Their Possible Significance for the History of the Eastern Mediterranean." *Quaternary Research*. 74:207–215.

Karachalios, Foivos Spyridon. 2013. "The Politics of Judgment in Early Greece: Dispute Resolution and State Formation from the Homeric World to Solon's Athens." Stanford, CA: Classics, Stanford University.

Keane, John. 2009. *The Life and Death of Democracy*. New York: W.W. Norton & Co.

Kehoe, Dennis P., David Ratzan, and Uri Yiftach-Firanko, eds. forthcoming. *Law and Transaction Costs in the Ancient Economy*. Ann Arbor, MI: University of Michigan Press.

Kelly, Thomas. 1972. "Cleobulus, Xenares, and Thucydides' Account of the Demolition of Panactum." *Historia*. 21.2:159–169.

———. 1982. "Thucydides and Spartan Strategy in the Archidamian War." *American Historical Review*. 87:25–54.

Kemp, Barry J. 2006. *Ancient Egypt: Anatomy of a Civilization*. London: Routledge.

Kennedy, George A. 1994. *A New History of Classical Rhetoric*. Princeton, NJ: Princeton University Press.

Kierstead, James. 2013. "A Community of Communities: Associations and Democracy in Classical Athens." Stanford, CA: Classics, Stanford University.

Killen, J. T. 2008. "Mycenaean Economy." *A Companion to Linear B: Mycenaean Greek Texts and Their World*, edited by Yves Duhoux and Anna Morpurgo Davies. Louvain-la-Neuve, Belgium, and Dudley, MA: Peeters, 241–305.

King, Gary, Robert O. Keohane, and Sidney Verba. 1994. *Designing Social Inquiry: Scientific Inference in Qualitative Research*. Princeton, NJ: Princeton University Press.

King, Roy J., et al. 2011. "The Coming of the Greeks to Provence and Corsica: Y-Chromosome Models of Archaic Greek Colonization of the Western Mediterranean." *BMC Evolutionary Biology*. 11.69. http://www.biomedcentral.com/1471-2148/11/69.

Kinzl, Konrad. 1979. *Die ältere Tyrannis bis zu den Perserkriegen: Beiträge zur griechischen Tyrannis*. Darmstadt, Germany: Wissenschaftliche Buchgesellschaft.

———. 2010, ed. *A Companion to the Classical Greek World*. Chichester, U.K., and Malden, MA: Wiley-Blackwell.

Knoepfler, Denis. 1997. "Le territoire d'Erétrie et l'organisation politique de la cité (*dēmoi, chōroi, phylai*)." *The Polis as an Urban Centre and as a Political Community*, edited by Mogens Herman Hansen. Copenhagen, Denmark: Munksgaard, 352–449.

Kremydi, S. 2011. "Coinage and Finance." *Brill's Companion to Ancient Macedon*, edited by Robin J. Lane Fox. Leiden, Netherlands: Brill, 159–78.

Krentz, Peter. 1982. *The Thirty at Athens*. Ithaca, NY: Cornell University Press.

———. 1985. "Casualties in Hoplite Battles." *Greek, Roman, and Byzantine Studies*. 26:13–20.

———. 2011. *The Battle of Marathon*. New Haven, CT: Yale University Press.

Krings, Véronique. 1998. *Carthage et les Grecs c. 580–480 av. J.-C.: Textes et histoire*. Leiden, Netherlands, and Boston: Brill.

Kroll, John H. 2008. "The Monetary Use of Weighed Bullion in Archaic Greece." *The Monetary Systems of the Greeks and Romans*, edited by William V. Harris. Oxford: Oxford University Press, 12–37.

———. 2011a. "Athenian Tetradrachm Coinage of the First Half of the Fourth Century BC." *Revue Belge de Numismatique*. 157:3–26.

———. 2011b. "The Reminting of Athenian Silver Coinage, 353 BC." *Hesperia*. 80:229–259.

Kron, Geoffrey. 2005. "Anthropometry, Physical Anthropology, and the Reconstruction of Ancient Health, Nutrition, and Living Standards." *Historia*. 54 (1):68–83.

———. 2011. "The Distribution of Wealth in Athens in Comparative Perspective." *Zeitschrift für Papyrologie und Epigraphic*. 179:129–138.

———. 2012. "Nutrition, Hygiene, and Mortality: Setting Parameters for Roman Health and Life Expectancy Consistent with Our Comparative Evidence." *L'impatto della "peste antonina,"* edited by E. Lo Cascio, Bari, Italy: Edipuglia, 193–252.

———. 2014. "Comparative Evidence and the Reconstruction of the Ancient Economy: Greco-Roman Housing and the Level and Distribution of Wealth and Income." *Quantifying the Greco-Roman Economy and Beyond*, edited by François de Callataÿ. Bari, Italy: Edipuglia.

———. Forthcoming. "Growth and Decline. Forms of Growth. Estimating Growth in the Greek World." *The Oxford Handbook of Economies in the Classical World*, edited by Elio Lo Cascio, Alain Bresson, and F. Velde. Oxford: Oxford University Press.

Krueger, Anne O. 1973. "The Political Economy of the Rent-Seeking Society." *American Economic Review.* 64:291–303.

Kuhrt, Amélie. 2007. *The Persian Empire.* London and New York: Routledge.

Kuran 1995. *Private Truths, Public Lies: The Social Consequences of Preference Falsification.* Cambridge, MA: Harvard University Press.

Labarbe, Jules. 1957. *La loi navale de Thémistocle.* Paris: Société d'Édition "Les Belles Lettres".

Laitin, David D. 2007. *Nations, States, and Violence.* Oxford and New York: University Press.

Landemore, Hélène. 2012. *Democratic Reason: Politics, Collective Intelligence, and the Rule of the Many.* Princeton, NJ: Princeton University Press.

Landemore, Hélène, and Jon Elster, eds. 2012. *Collective Wisdom: Principles and Mechanisms.* Cambridge: Cambridge University Press.

Lane Fox, Robin J., ed. 2011a. *Brill's Companion to Ancient Macedon.* Leiden, Netherlands: Brill.

——. 2011b. "Philip's and Alexander's Macedon." *Brill's Companion to Ancient Macedon,* edited by Robin J. Lane Fox. Leiden, Netherlands: Brill, 367–391.

Lanni, Adriaan M. 2006. *Law and Justice in the Courts of Classical Athens.* Cambridge: Cambridge University Press.

——. 2009. "Social Norms in the Courts of Ancient Athens." *Journal of Legal Analysis.* 1:691–736.

Lavelle, Brian M. 1993. *The Sorrow and the Pity: A Prolegomenon to a History of Athens under the Peisistratids, c. 560–510 B.C.* Stuttgart, Germany: F. Steiner.

——. 2005. *Fame, Money, and Power: The Rise of Peisistratos and "Democratic" Tyranny at Athens.* Ann Arbor, MI: University of Michigan Press.

Lawrence, A. W. 1979. *Greek Aims in Fortification.* Oxford: Clarendon Press.

Lazenby, J. F. 1985. *The Spartan Army.* Warminster, U.K.: Aris & Phillips.

Le Rider, Georges. 1977. *Le monnayage d'argent et d'or de Philippe II frappé en Macédoine de 359–294.* Paris: Bourgey.

——. 1996. *Monnayage et finances de Philippe II: Un état de la question.* Athens and Paris: Boccard.

Lee, John W. I. 2007. *A Greek Army on the March: Soldiers and Survival in Xenophon's Anabasis.* Cambridge and New York: Cambridge University Press.

Lendon, J. E. 2005. *Soldiers & Ghosts: A History of Battle in Classical Antiquity.* New Haven, CT: Yale University Press.

——. 2010. *Song of Wrath: The Peloponnesian War Begins.* New York: Basic Books.

Lévêque, Pierre, and Pierre Vidal-Naquet. 1996 [1964]. *Cleisthenes the Athenian: An Essay on the Representation of Space and Time in Greek Political Thought from the End of the Sixth Century to the Death of Plato.* Translated by David Ames Curtis. Atlantic Highlands, NJ: Humanities Press.

Lewis, David M. 1997. "On the Financial Offices of Eubulus and Lycurgus." *Selected Papers in Greek and Near Eastern History,* edited by P. J. Rhodes. Cambridge and New York: Cambridge University Press, 212–229.

Lewis, John David. 2004. "Slavery and Lawlessness in Solonian Athens." *Dike.* 7:19–40.

——. 2006. *Solon the Thinker: Political Thought in Archaic Athens.* London: Duckworth.

Linforth, Ivan Mortimer. 1919. *Solon the Athenian.* Berkeley, CA: University of California Press.

Lipset, Seymour Martin. 1959. "Some Social Requisites of Democracy: Economic Development and Political Legitimacy." *American Political Science Review.* 53:69–105.

List, Christian and Kai Spiekermann. 2013. "Methodological Individualism and Holism in Political Science: A Reconciliation." *American Political Science Review.* 107.4:629–643.

Littman, Robert J. 2009. "The Plague of Athens: Epidemiology and Paleopathology." *Mount Sinai Journal of Medicine.* 76:456–467.

Llewellyn-Jones, Lloyd. 2013. *King and Court in Ancient Persia 559 to 331 BCE.* Edinburgh, U.K.: Edinburgh University Press.

Loomis, William T. 1998. *Wages, Welfare Costs, and Inflation in Classical Athens.* Ann Arbor, MI: University of Michigan Press.

Loraux, Nicole. 1984. "Solon au milieu de la lice." *Aux origines de l'hellénisme: La Crète et la Grèce: hommage à Henri van Effenterre.* Paris: Publications de la Sorbonne, 199–214.

———. 2007. *Interstate Relations in Classical Greece.* Cambridge: Cambridge University Press.

Lupack, Susan. 2011. "Redistribution in Aegean Palatial Societies. A View from Outside the Palace: The Sanctuary and the Damos in Mycenaean Economy and Society." *American Journal of Archaeology.* 115:207–217.

Luraghi, Nino. 1994. *Tirannidi arcaiche in Sicilia e Magna Grecia: Da Panezio di Leontini alla caduta dei Dinomenidi.* Florence, Italy: L. S. Olschki.

———. 2006. "Traders, Pirates, Warriors: The Proto-History of Greek Mercenary Soldiers in the Eastern Mediterranean." *Phoenix.* 60:21–47.

Luraghi, Nino, and Susan E. Alcock, eds. 2003. *Helots and Their Masters in Laconia and Messenia: Histories, Ideologies, Structures.* Washington, DC: Center for Hellenic Studies.

Luttwak, Edward. 1976. *The Grand Strategy of the Roman Empire from the First Century A.D. to the Third.* Baltimore: Johns Hopkins University Press.

Lynch, John Patrick. 1972. *Aristotle's School; A Study of a Greek Educational Institution.* Berkeley, CA: University of California Press.

Lynn, Matthew. 2010. *Bust: Greece, the Euro, and the Sovereign Debt Crisis.* London: Bloomberg Press.

Lyttkens, Carl Hampus. 1992. "Effects of the Taxation of Wealth in Athens in the Fourth Century B.C." *The Scandinavian Economic History Review.* 40:3–20.

———. 2012. *Economic Analysis of Institutional Change in Ancient Greece: Politics, Taxation and Rational Behaviour.* New York: Routledge.

Ma, John. 1999. *Antiochos III and the Cities of Western Asia Minor.* Oxford and New York: Oxford University Press.

———. 2000. "Fighting Poleis of the Hellenistic World." *War and Violence in Ancient Greece,* edited by Hans van Wees and Paul Beston. London: Duckworth, 337–376.

———. 2003. "Peer Polity Interaction in the Hellenistic Age." *Past and Present.* 180 (1):9–39.

———. 2008. "Chaironeia 338: Topographies of Commemoration." *Journal of Hellenic Studies.* 128:72–91.

———. 2013a. *Statues and Cities: Honorific Portraits and Civic Identity in the Hellenistic World.* Oxford: Oxford University Press.

———. 2013b. "Alexander's Decision-Making as Historical Problem." *Revue des Etudes Militaires Anciennes.* 6:113–125.

———. 2013c. "Review of Mann and Scholz, *"Demokratie" im Hellenismus.*" *Sehepunkte. Rezensionsjournal für Geschichtswissenschaften.* 13. http://www.sehepunkte.de/2013/07/21837.html.

Ma, John. 2014. "La cité grecque et les transferts culturels." *Dialogues d'histoire ancienne.* 40:251–269.

———. Forthcoming. "Whatever Happened to Athens? Perspectives on the Political History of Post-Classical Greece." *The Hellenistic and Early Imperial Greek Reception of Classical Athenian Democracy and Political Thought,* edited by Benjamin Gray and Mirko Canevaro. Oxford: Oxford University Press.

———. In progress a. "Arshama the Vampire." *Arshama and Egypt: The World of an Achaemenid Prince.* Oxford: Oxford University Press.

———. In progress b. *Polis 800 BC–AD 600. A Biography of a Social Form.* Princeton, NJ: Princeton University Press.

Ma, John, Nikolaos Papazarkadas, and Robert Parker, eds. 2009. *Interpreting the Athenian Empire.* London: Duckworth.

Ma, John, Christopher Tuplin, and Lindsay Allen. 2013. *The Arshama Letters from the Bodleian Library.* Vol. I. Oxford: Oxford University.

Mackil, Emily. 2004. "Wandering Cities: Alternatives to Catastrophe in the Greek Polis." *American Journal of Archaeology.* 108:493–516.

———. 2013. *Creating a Common Polity: Religion, Economy, and Politics in the Making of the Greek Koinon.* Berkeley, CA: University of California Press.

Mackil, Emily, and Peter G. van Alfen. 2006. "Cooperative Coinages." *Agoranomia: Studies in Money and Exchange Presented to John Kroll,* edited by Peter G. van Alfen. New York: American Numismatic Society, 201–246.

Maier, Franz Georg. 1959. *Griechische Mauerbauinschriften.* Heidelberg, Germany: Quelle & Meyer.

Malkin, Irad. 1987. *Religion and Colonization in Ancient Greece.* Leiden, Netherlands, and New York: Brill.

———. 1994. *Myth and Territory in the Spartan Mediterranean.* Cambridge and New York: Cambridge University Press.

———. 2011. *A Small Greek World: Networks in the Ancient Mediterranean.* New York: Oxford University Press.

Mann, Christian, and Peter Scholz, eds. 2012. *"Demokratie" im Hellenismus. Von der Herrschaft des Volkes zur Herrschaft der Honoratioren?* Mainz, Germany: Verlag Antike.

Manning, Joseph Gilbert. 2003. *Land and Power in Ptolemaic Egypt: The Structure of Land Tenure.* Cambridge: Cambridge University Press.

———. 2010. *The Last Pharaohs: Egypt under the Ptolemies, 305–30 BC.* Princeton, NJ: Princeton University Press.

Manville, Philip Brook. 1990. *The Origins of Citizenship in Ancient Athens.* Princeton, NJ: Princeton University Press.

Manville, Philip Brook, and Josiah Ober. 2003. *A Company of Citizens: What the World's First Democracy Teaches Leaders about Creating Great Organizations.* Boston: Harvard Business School Press.

Markle, Minor M. 1976. "Support of Athenian Intellectuals for Philip: A Study of Isocrates' Philippus and Speusippus' Letter to Philip." *Journal of Hellenic Studies.* 96:80–99.

———. 1977. "The Macedonian Sarissa, Spear, and Related Armor." *American Journal of Archaeology.* 81.3:323–339.

———. 1978. "Use of the Sarissa by Philip and Alexander of Macedon." *American Journal of Archaeology.* 82.4:483–497.

————. 1985. "Jury Pay and Assembly Pay at Athens." *Crux: Essays Presented to G.E.M. De Ste. Croix*, edited by Paul Cartledge and F. D. Harvey. London: Duckworth, 265–297.

Marsden, Eric William. 1969. *Greek and Roman Artillery: Historical Development*. Oxford: Oxford University Press.

————. 1977. "Macedonian Military Machinery and Its Designers under Philip and Alexander." *Ancient Macedonia*. 2:211–223.

Martin, Thomas R. 1986. *Sovereignty and Coinage in Classical Greece*. Princeton, NJ: Princeton University Press.

Mattingly, Harold B. 1996. *The Athenian Empire Restored: Epigraphic and Historical Studies*. Ann Arbor, MI: University of Michigan Press.

Mayne, A.J.C., and Tim Murray. 2002. *The Archaeology of Urban Landscapes: Explorations in Slumland*. Cambridge: Cambridge University Press.

Mayor, Adrienne. 2014. *The Amazons: Lives and Legends of Warrior Women across the Ancient World*. Princeton, NJ: Princeton University Press.

Mazarakis Ainian, Alexander. 1997. *From Rulers' Dwellings to Temples: Architecture, Religion and Society in Early Iron Age Greece (1100–700 B.C.)*. Jonsered, Sweden: Paul Åstroms Förlag.

McCormick, Michael, et al. 2012. "Climate Change during and after the Roman Empire: Reconstructing the Past from Scientific and Historical Evidence." *Journal of Interdisciplinary History*. 43.2:169–220.

McGlew, James F. 1993. *Tyranny and Political Culture in Ancient Greece*. Ithaca, NY: Cornell University Press.

McKechnie, Paul. 1989. *Outsiders in the Greek Cities in the Fourth Century B.C.* London and New York: Routledge.

McNicoll, A. W. 1997. *Hellenistic Fortifications from the Aegean to the Euphrates*. Oxford: Oxford University Press.

Meadows, Andrew. 2011. "The Chian Revolution: Changing Patterns of Hoarding in 4th-Century BC Western Asia Minor." *BCH Supplement*. 273–295.

Meiggs, Russell. 1972. *The Athenian Empire*. Oxford: Clarendon Press.

————. 1982. *Trees and Timber in the Ancient Mediterranean World*. Oxford: Clarendon Press.

Meiggs, Russell, and David M. Lewis. 1988. *A Selection of Greek Historical Inscriptions to the End of the Fifth Century B.C.* Oxford: Oxford University Press.

Middleton, Guy D. 2010. *The Collapse of Palatial Society in LBA Greece and the Postpalatial Period*. Oxford: Archaeopress.

Milanovic, Branko, Peter H. Lindert, and Jeffrey G. Williamson. 2011. "Pre-Industrial Inequality." *The Economic Journal*. 121 (551):255–272.

Mill, John Stuart. 1846. "Grote's History of Greece [I]." *Edinburgh Review*. 84:343–377.

Miller, Margaret Christina. 1997. *Athens and Persia in the Fifth Century B.C.: A Study in Cultural Receptivity*. Cambridge and New York: Cambridge University Press.

Millett, Paul C. 1989. "Patronage and Its Avoidance in Classical Athens." *Patronage in Ancient Society*, edited by A. Wallace-Hadrill. London: Routledge, 15–48.

————. 2010. "The Political Economy of Macedonia." *A Companion to Ancient Macedonia*, edited by Joseph Roisman and Ian Worthington. Chichester, U.K., and Malden, MA: Wiley-Blackwell, 472–504.

Minta, Stephen. 1998. *On a Voiceless Shore: Byron in Greece*. New York: Henry Holt and Co.

Mitchell, Lynette G., and P. J. Rhodes, eds. 1997. *The Development of the Polis in Archaic Greece*. London: Routledge.

Mitchell, Melanie. 2009. *Complexity: A Guided Tour*. Oxford and New York: Oxford University Press.

Mitchell, Sandra D. 2009. *Unsimple Truths: Science, Complexity, and Policy*. Chicago: Chicago University Press.

Mokyr, Joel. 2002. *The Gifts of Athena: Historical Origins of the Knowledge Economy*. Princeton, NJ: Princeton University Press.

Molho, Anthony, and Kurt A. Raaflaub, eds. 1991. *City-States in Classical Antiquity and Medieval Italy*. Ann Arbor, MI: University of Michigan Press.

Möller, Astrid. 2007. "Classical Greece: Distribution." *The Cambridge Economic History of the Greco-Roman World*, edited by Walter Scheidel, Ian Morris, and Richard P. Saller. Cambridge: Cambridge University Press, 362–384.

Monson, Andrew, and Walter Scheidel, eds. forthcoming. *Fiscal Regimes and Political Economy of Premodern States*. Cambridge: Cambridge University Press.

Montgomery, Hugo. 1983. *The Way to Chaeronea: Foreign Policy, Decision-Making, and Political Influence in Demosthenes' Speeches*. Bergen, Norway: Universitetsforlaget.

Moreno, Alfonso. 2008. *Feeding the Democracy: The Athenian Grain Supply in the Fifth and Fourth Centuries B.C.* Oxford: Oxford University Press.

———. 2009. "'The Attic Neighbour': The Cleruchy in the Athenian Empire." *Interpreting the Athenian Empire*, edited by John Ma, Nikolaos Papazarkadas, and Robert Parker. London: Duckworth, 211–222.

Morley, Neville. 2014. "Orders of Magnitude, Margins of Error." *Quantifying the Greco-Roman Economy and Beyond, Pragmateiai*, edited by François de Callataÿ. Bari, Italy: Edipuglia, 29–42.

Morris, Ian. 1987. *Burial and Ancient Society: The Rise of the Greek City-State*. Cambridge: Cambridge University Press.

———. 1992. *Death-Ritual and Social Structure in Classical Antiquity*. Cambridge and New York: Cambridge University Press.

———. 1996. "The Strong Principle of Equality and the Archaic Origins of Greek Democracy." *Dēmokratia: A Conversation on Democracies, Ancient and Modern*, edited by Josiah Ober and Charles W. Hedrick. Princeton, NJ: Princeton University Press, 19–49.

———. 1998. "Archaeology as a Kind of Anthropology (A Response to David Small)." *Democracy 2500? Questions and Challenges*, edited by Ian Morris and Kurt A. Raaflaub. Dubuque, IA: Kendall/Hunt, 229–239.

———. 2000. *Archaeology as Cultural History: Words and Things in Iron Age Greece*. Malden, MA: Blackwell.

———. 2004. "Economic Growth in Ancient Greece." *Journal of Institutional and Theoretical Economics*. 160 (4):709–742.

———. 2005. "Archaeology, Standards of Living and Greek Economic History." *The Ancient Economy: Evidence and Models*, edited by Joseph Gilbert Manning and Ian Morris. Stanford, CA: Stanford University Press, 91–126.

———. 2006. "The Collapse and Regeneration of Complex Society in Greece, 1500–500 B C." *After Collapse: The Regeneration of Complex Societies*, edited by Glenn M. Schwartz and John J. Nichols. Tucson, AZ: University of Arizona Press, 72–84.

———. 2007. "Early Iron Age Greece." *The Cambridge Economic History of the Greco-Roman World*, edited by Walter Scheidel, Ian Morris, and Richard P. Saller. Cambridge: Cambridge University Press, 211–241.

———. 2009. "The Greater Athenian State." *The Dynamics of Ancient Empires*, edited by Ian Morris and Walter Scheidel. Oxford: Oxford University Press, 99–177.

———. 2010. *Why the West Rules—For Now: The Patterns of History and What They Reveal about the Future*. New York: Farrar, Strauss, and Giroux.

———. 2013a. "Greek Multicity States." *The Oxford Handbook of the State in the Ancient Near East and Mediterranean*, edited by Peter Fibiger Bang and Walter Scheidel. Oxford: Oxford University Press, 279–303.

———. 2013b. *The Measure of Civilization: How Social Development Decides the Fate of Nations*. Princeton, NJ: Princeton University Press.

———. 2014. *War! What Is It Good For? Conflict and the Progress of Civilization from Primates to Robots*. New York: Farrar, Straus and Giroux.

Morris, Ian, and Barry B. Powell. 2009. *The Greeks: History, Culture, and Society*. Upper Saddle River, NJ: Pearson Prentice Hall.

Morris, Ian, and Walter Scheidel, eds. 2009. *The Dynamics of Ancient Empires: State Power from Assyria to Byzantium*. Oxford and New York: Oxford University Press.

Morrison, James. 2000. "Historical Lessons in the Melian Episode." *Transactions of the American Philological Association*. 130:119–148.

Mossé, Claude. 1994. *Démosthène, ou, Les ambiguités de la politique*. Paris: A. Colin.

Murray, Oswyn. 1990. "Cities of Reason." *The Greek City: From Homer to Alexander*, edited by Oswyn Murray and S.R.F. Price. Oxford and New York: Clarendon Press.

———. 1993a. *Early Greece*. Cambridge, MA: Harvard University Press.

———. 1993b. "*Polis* and *Politeia* in Aristotle." *The Ancient Greek City-State*, edited by Mogens Herman Hansen. Copenhagen, Denmark: Munksgaard, 197–210.

Murray, Sarah C. 2013. "Trade, Imports, and Society in Early Greece: 1300–900 B.C.E." Stanford, CA: Classics, Stanford University.

Nagle, D. Brendan. 1996. "The Cultural Context of Alexander's Speech at Opis." *Transactions of the American Philological Association*. 126:151–172.

Németh, György. 2006. *Kritias und die Dreissig Tyrannen: Untersuchungen zur Politik und Prosopographie der Führungselite in Athen 404/403 v. Chr*. Stuttgart, Germany: Steiner.

Netz, Reviel. 2002. "Counter Culture: Towards a History of Greek Numeracy." *History of Science*. 40 (3):321–352.

———. In progress. *Scale, Space and Canon: Parameters of Ancient Literary Practice*.

Nevett, Lisa C. 1999. *House and Society in the Ancient Greek World*. Cambridge: Cambridge University Press.

———. 2005. "Between Urban and Rural: House Form and Social Relations in Attic Villages and *Deme* Centers." *Ancient Greek Houses and Households: Chronological, Regional, and Social Diversity*, edited by Bradley A. Ault and Lisa C. Nevett. Philadelphia: University of Pennsylvania Press, 83–98.

Niemeyer, Hans Georg. 2000. "The Early Phoenician City-States on the Mediterranean: Archaeological Elements of Their Description." *A Comparative Study of Thirty City-State Cultures: An Investigation*, edited by Mogens Herman Hansen. Copenhagen, Denmark: Kongelige Danske Videnskabernes Selskab, 89–115.

North, Douglass Cecil. 1981. *Structure and Change in Economic History*. New York: Norton.

North, Douglass Cecil. 1990. *Institutions, Institutional Change, and Economic Performance.* Cambridge and New York: Cambridge University Press.

North, Douglass Cecil, and Barry R. Weingast. 1989. "Constitutions and Commitment: The Evolution of Institutions Governing Public Choice in Seventeenth Century England." *Journal of Economic History.* 49:803–832.

North, Douglass Cecil, John Joseph Wallis, and Barry R. Weingast. 2009. *Violence and Social Orders: A Conceptual Framework for Interpreting Recorded Human History.* Cambridge: Cambridge University Press.

O'Connor, David, and David P. Silverman. 1994. *Ancient Egyptian Kingship.* Leiden, Netherlands: E. J. Brill.

Ober, Josiah. 1985. *Fortress Attica: Defense of the Athenian Land Frontier, 404–322 B.C.* Leiden, Netherlands: E. J. Brill.

———. 1987. "Early Artillery Towers: Messenia, Boiotia, Attica, Megarid." *American Journal of Archaeology.* 91 (4):569–604.

———. 1989. *Mass and Elite in Democratic Athens: Rhetoric, Ideology, and the Power of the People.* Princeton, NJ: Princeton University Press.

———. 1991. "Hoplites and Obstacles." *Hoplites: The Classical Greek Battle Experience,* edited by Victor D. Hanson. London and New York: Routledge, 173–196.

———. 1992. "Towards a Typology of Greek Artillery Towers: The First and Second Generations (c. 375–275 B.C.)." *Fortificationes Antiquae, McGill University Monographs in Classical Archaeology and History. No. 12,* edited by Symphorien Van de Maele and John M. Fossey. Amsterdam, Netherlands: J. C. Gieben, 147–169.

———. 1996. *The Athenian Revolution: Essays on Ancient Greek Democracy and Political Theory.* Princeton, NJ: Princeton University Press.

———. 1998. *Political Dissent in Democratic Athens: Intellectual Critics of Popular Rule.* Princeton, NJ: Princeton University Press.

———. 1999. "The Premature Death of Alexander the Great." *What If? The World's Foremost Military Historians Imagine What Might Have Been,* edited by Robert Cowley. New York: G. P. Putnam, 37–56.

———. 2000. "Political Conflicts, Political Debates, and Political Thought." *The Shorter Oxford History of Europe I: Classical Greece,* edited by Robin Osborne. Oxford: Oxford University Press, 111–138.

———. 2001. "Thucydides Theoretikos/Thucydides Histor: Realist Theory and the Challenge of History." *Democracy and War: A Comparative Study of the Korean War and the Peloponnesian War,* edited by D. R. McCann and B. S. Strauss. Armonk, NY, and London: M. E. Sharpe, 273–306.

———. 2005a. "Aristotle's Natural Democracy." *Aristotle's Politics: Critical Essays,* edited by Richard Kraut and S. Skultety. Lanham, MD: Rowman and Littlefield, 223–243.

———. 2005b. *Athenian Legacies: Essays in the Politics of Going on Together.* Princeton, NJ: Princeton University Press.

———. 2006a. "Solon and the *Horoi*: Facts on the Ground in Archaic Athens." *Solon: New Historical and Philological Perspectives,* edited by Josine Blok and André Lardinois. Leiden, Netherlands: E. J. Brill, 441–456.

———. 2006b. "Thucydides and the Invention of Political Science." *Brill's Companion to Thucydides,* edited by Antonios Rengakos and Antonis Tsakmakis. Leiden, Netherlands: E. J. Brill, 131–159.

———. 2007. "'I Besieged That Man': Democracy's Revolutionary Start." *The Origins of Democracy in Ancient Greece*, edited by Kurt Raaflaub, Josiah Ober, and Robert W. Wallace. Berkeley and Los Angeles: University of California Press, 83–104.

———. 2008. *Democracy and Knowledge: Innovation and Learning in Classical Athens.* Princeton, NJ: Princeton University Press.

———. 2009. "Public Action and Rational Choice in Classical Greek Political Theory." *A Companion to Ancient Political Thought*, edited by Ryan K. Balot. Oxford: Blackwell, 70–84.

———. 2010a. "Socrates in Democratic Athens." *Cambridge Companion to Socrates*, edited by D. Morrison. Cambridge: Cambridge University Press, 136–175.

———. 2010b. "Thucydides on Athens' Democratic Advantage in the Archidamian War." *War, Democracy and Culture in Classical Athens*, edited by David Pritchard. Cambridge: Cambridge University Press, 65–87.

———. 2010c. "Wealthy Hellas." *Transactions of the American Philological Association.* 140:241–286.

———. 2012. "Democracy's Dignity." *American Political Science Review.* 106.4:827–846.

———. 2013a. "Democracy's Wisdom: An Aristotelian Middle Way for Collective Judgment." *American Political Science Review.* 107.1:104–122.

———. 2013b. "Political Animals Revisited." *Good Society.* 22:201–214.

———. forthcoming. "Fiscal Policy in Classical Athens." *Fiscal Regimes and Political Economy of Premodern States*, edited by Andrew Monson and Walter Scheidel. Cambridge: Cambridge University Press, 492–522.

Ober, Josiah, and Tomer Perry. 2014. "Thucydides as a Prospect Theorist." *Polis.* 31:206–232.

Oleson, John Peter. 2008. *Oxford Handbook of Engineering and Technology in the Classical World*. Oxford and New York: Oxford University Press.

Olson, Mancur. 1965. *The Logic of Collective Action: Public Goods and the Theory of Groups*. Cambridge, MA: Harvard University Press.

Orwin, Clifford. 1994. *The Humanity of Thucydides*. Princeton, NJ: Princeton University Press.

Osborne, Michael J. 1981. *Naturalization in Athens*. Brussels, Belgium: Paleis der Academiën.

Osborne, Robin. 1985. *Demos, the Discovery of Classical Attika*. Cambridge and New York: Cambridge University Press.

———. 1992. "Is it a Farm? The Definition of Agricultural Sites and Settlements in Ancient Greece." *Agriculture in Ancient Greece*, edited by Berit Wells. Stockholm, Sweden: Paul Åströms Förlag, 22–27.

———. 1998. "Early Greek Colonization? The Nature of Greek Settlement in the West." *Archaic Greece: New Approaches and New Evidence*, edited by N.R.E. Fisher, Hans van Wees, and Deborah Boedeker. London: Duckworth & Classical Press of Wales, 251–270.

———. 2000. *Classical Greece, 500–323 BC*. Oxford and New York: Oxford University Press.

———. 2001. "Why Did Athenian Pots Appeal to the Etruscans?" *World Archaeology.* 33.2:277–295.

———. 2009a. "Economic Growth and the Politics of Entitlement." *Cambridge Classical Journal.* 55:97–125.

Osborne, Robin. 2009b. "Reciprocal Strategies: Imperialism, Barbarism and Trade in Archaic and Classical Olbia." *Meetings of Cultures between Conflicts and Coexistence*, edited by P. G. Bilde and J. H. Petersen. Aarhus, Denmark: Aarhus University Press, 333–346.

———. 2009c. *Greece in the Making, 1200–479 BC*, 2nd ed. New York: Routledge.

Ostwald, Martin. 1986. *From Popular Sovereignty to the Sovereignty of Law: Law, Society, and Politics in Fifth-Century Athens*. Berkeley, CA: University of California Press.

Paga, Jessica. 2012. "Architectural Agency and the Construction of Athenian Democracy." Princeton, NJ: Art and Archaeology, Princeton University.

Papagrigorakis, Manolis J., et al. 2006. "DNA Examination of Ancient Dental Pulp Incriminates Typhoid Fever as a Probable Cause of the Plague of Athens." *International Journal of Infectious Diseases*. 10 (3):206–214.

Parke, H. W. 1933. *Greek Mercenary Soldiers, from the Earliest Times to the Battle of Ipsus*. Oxford: Clarendon Press.

Parker, Geoffrey. 2005. *Sovereign City: The City-State Ancient and Modern*. London: Reaktion Books.

Parker, Robert. 1996. *Athenian Religion: A History*. Oxford: Oxford University Press.

Parker, Victor. 1997. *Untersuchungen zum Lelantischen Krieg und verwandten Problemen der frühgriechischen Geschichte*. Stuttgart, Germany: F. Steiner.

Patterson, Cynthia. 2005. "Athenian Citizenship Law." *The Cambridge Companion to Ancient Greek Law*, edited by Michael Gagarin and David Cohen. Cambridge and New York: Cambridge University Press, 267–289.

Pečírka, Jan. 1966. *The Formula for the Grant of Enktesis in Attic Inscriptions*. Prague, Czech Republic: Universita Karlova.

———. 1976. "The Crisis of the Athenian Polis in the Fourth Century B.C." *Eirene*. 14:5–29.

Peel, M. C., B. L. Finlayson, and T. A. McMahon. 2007. "Updated World Map of the Köppen-Geiger Climate Classification." *Hydrology and Earth System Sciences*. 11:1633–1644.

Petitot, Jean. 2010. "Reduction and Emergence in Complex Systems." *Questioning Nineteenth-Century Assumptions about Knowledge: Reductionism, (Fernand Braudel Center Studies in Historical Social Science)*, edited by Richard F. Lee. Binghamton, NY: State University of New York Press, 107–159.

Pines, Shlomo. 1986. *Studies in Arabic Versions of Greek Texts and in Mediaeval Science*. Jerusalem and Leiden, Netherlands: Magnes Press, Hebrew University and E. J. Brill.

Price, Jonathan J. 2001. *Thucydides and Internal War*. Cambridge and New York: Cambridge University Press.

Price, Simon R. F. 1999. *Religions of the Ancient Greeks*. Cambridge and New York: Cambridge University Press.

———. 2011. "Estimating Ancient Greek Populations: The Evidence of Field Survey." *Settlement, Urbanization, and Population*, edited by Alan K. Bowman and Andrew Wilson. Oxford: Oxford University Press.

Pritchard, David. 1998. "The Fractured Imaginary: Popular Thinking on Military Matters in Fifth Century Athens." *Ancient History*. 28 (1):38–61.

———. 2005. "Kleisthenes and Athenian Democracy: Vision from Above or Below?" *Polis*. 22 (1):136–157.

———, ed. 2010. *War, Democracy and Culture in Classical Athens*. Cambridge: Cambridge University Press.

———. 2012. "Costing Festivals and War: Spending Priorities of the Athenian Democracy." *Historia.* 61:18–65.

———. 2014. "The Public Payment of Magistrates in Fourth-Century Athens." *Greek, Roman, and Byzantine Studies.* 54.1:1–16.

———. Forthcoming. *Public Spending and Democracy in Classical Athens.* Austin, TX: University of Texas Press.

Purcell, Nicholas. 1990. "Mobility and the Polis." *The Greek City: From Homer to Alexander*, edited by Oswyn Murray and S.R.F. Price. Oxford and New York: Clarendon Press, 29–58.

Pyzyk, Mark. forthcoming. "Economies of Expertise: Knowledge and Skill Transfer in Classical Greece." Stanford, CA: Classics, Stanford University.

Raaflaub, Kurt. 1996. "Equalities and Inequalities in Athenian Democracy." *Dēmokratia: A Conversation on Democracies, Ancient and Modern*, edited by Josiah Ober and Charles W. Hedrick. Princeton, NJ: Princeton University Press, 139–174.

———. 2009. "Learning from the Enemy: Athenian and Persian "Instruments of Empire." *Interpreting the Athenian Empire*, edited by John Ma, Nikolaos Papazarkadas, and Robert Parker. London: Duckworth, 89–124.

Raaflaub, Kurt, and Hans van Wees, eds. 2009. *A Companion to Archaic Greece.* Chichester, U.K., and Malden, MA: Wiley-Blackwell.

Raaflaub, Kurt, Josiah Ober, and Robert W. Wallace. 2007. *The Origins of Democracy in Ancient Greece.* Berkeley and Los Angeles: University of California Press.

Rahe, Paul Anthony. 1981. "The Annihilation of the Sacred Band at Chaeronea." *American Journal of Archaeology.* 85.1:84–87.

Rankov, N. B. 1993. "Rowing *Olympias*: A Matter of Skill." *The Trireme Project*, edited by J. T. Shaw. Oxford: Oxbow, 50–57.

Rawls, John. 1999 [1971]. *A Theory of Justice.* Cambridge, MA: Harvard University Press.

Reeve, C.D.C. 1988. *Philosopher-Kings: The Argument of Plato's Republic.* Princeton, NJ: Princeton University Press.

Reger, Gary. 1994. *Regionalism and Change in the Economy of Independent Delos, 314–167 B.C.* Berkeley, CA: University of California Press.

———. 2007. "Hellenistic Greece and Western Asia Minor." *The Cambridge Economic History of the Greco-Roman World*, edited by Walter Scheidel, Ian Morris, and Richard P. Saller. Cambridge: Cambridge University Press, 460–483.

Reiter, Dan, and Allan C. Stam. 2002. *Democracies at War.* Princeton, NJ: Princeton University Press.

Renfrew, Colin, and John F. Cherry, eds. 1986. *Peer Polity Interaction and Socio-Political Change.* Cambridge: Cambridge University Press.

Reynolds, Joshua J. 2009. "Proving Power: Signs and Sign-Inference in Thucydides' Archaeology." *Transactions of the American Philological Association.* 139.2:325–368.

Rhodes, P. J. 1985a. *The Athenian Boule.* Oxford: Clarendon Press.

———. 1985b. *The Athenian Empire.* Oxford: Oxford University Press.

———. 1995. "The 'Acephalous' Polis?" *Historia.* 44:153–167.

———. 2010. *A History of the Classical Greek World: 478–323 BC*, 2nd ed. Malden, MA: Blackwell.

———. 2013. "The Organisation of Athenian Public Finance." *Greece & Rome.* 60:203–231.

Rhodes, P. J., and Robin Osborne. 2003. *Greek Historical Inscriptions: 404–323 BC.* Oxford: Oxford University Press.

Rigsby, Kent J. 1996. *Asylia: Territorial Inviolability in the Hellenistic World*. Berkeley, CA: University of California Press.

Riker, William H. 1982. *Liberalism against Populism: A Confrontation between the Theory of Democracy and the Theory of Social Choice*. San Francisco: W. H. Freeman.

Robinson, David M., and George E. Mylonas. 1929. *Excavations at Olynthus*. Baltimore and London: Johns Hopkins Press and H. Milford, Oxford University Press.

Robinson, Eric W. 1997. *The First Democracies: Early Popular Government outside Athens*. Stuttgart, Germany: F. Steiner.

———. 2000. "Democracy in Syracuse, 466–412 B.C." *Harvard Studies in Classical Philology*. 100:189–205.

———. 2011. *Democracy beyond Athens: Popular Government in the Greek Classical Age*. Cambridge: Cambridge University Press.

Roisman, Joseph. 2003. *Brill's Companion to Alexander the Great*. Leiden, Netherlands, and Boston: Brill.

Roisman, Joseph, and Ian Worthington. 2010. *A Companion to Ancient Macedonia*. Chichester, U.K., and Malden, MA: Wiley-Blackwell.

Rose, Peter W. 2012. *Class in Archaic Greece*. Cambridge: Cambridge University Press.

Rothschild, Emma. 1973. *Paradise Lost: The Decline of the Auto-Industrial Age*. New York: Random House.

Runciman, W. G. 1982. "Origins of States: The Case of Archaic Greece." *Comparative Studies in Society and History*. 24.3:351–377.

———. 1990. "Doomed to Extinction: The Polis as an Evolutionary Dead-End." *The Greek City*, edited by Oswyn Murray. Oxford: Oxford University Press, 348–367.

Rutishauser, Brian. 2007. "A Dark Wine in the Wine Dark Sea: Production, Trade and Athenian Policy in the Northern Aegean." *Revue des Etudes Anciennes*. 109:465–473.

———. 2012. *Athens and the Cyclades: Economic Strategies 540–314 BC*. New York: Oxford University Press.

Rutter, N. K. 2000. "Syracusan Democracy: 'Most Like the Athenian'?" *Alternatives to Athens: Varieties of Political Organization and Community in Ancient Greece*, edited by Roger Brock and Stephen Hodkinson. Oxford: Oxford University Press, 137–151.

Ruzicka, Stephen. 1988. "War in the Aegean, 333–331 B.C.: A Reconsideration." *Phoenix*. 42.2:131–151.

Ryan, Alan. 2012. *On Politics: A History of Political Thought from Herodotus to the Present*. New York: Liveright.

———. 2013. *On Aristotle: Saving Politics from Philosophy*. New York: Liveright.

Ryder, T.T.B. 1965. *Koine Eirene*. London and New York: Oxford University Press.

Sacks, Kenneth. 1990. *Diodorus Siculus and the First Century*. Princeton, NJ: Princeton University Press.

Sallares, Robert. 1991. *The Ecology of the Ancient Greek World*. London: Duckworth.

Saller, Richard P. 2005. "Framing the Debate over Growth in the Ancient Economy." *The Ancient Economy: Evidence and Models*, edited by Joseph Gilbert Manning and Ian Morris. Stanford, CA: Stanford University Press, 223–238.

Samons, Loren J. 1998. "Mass, Elite, and Hoplite-Farmer in Greek History." *Arion*. Winter: 100–123.

———. 2000. *Empire of the Owl: Athenian Imperial Finance*. Stuttgart, Germany: Steiner.

Samuel, Alan E. 1988. "Philip and Alexander as Kings: Macedonian and Merovingian Parallels." *American Historical Review*. 93.5:1270–1286.

Sancisi-Weerdenburg, Heleen, ed. 2000. *Peisistratos and the Tyranny: A Reappraisal of the Evidence.* Amsterdam, Netherlands: J. C. Gieben.

Sanders, Lionel Jehuda. 1987. *Dionysius I of Syracuse and Greek Tyranny.* London and New York: Croom Helm.

———. 2008. *The Legend of Dion.* Toronto: Edgar Kent Inc.

Schachter, Albert, and F. Marchand. 2013. "Fresh Light on the Institutions and Religious Life of Thespiai: Six New Inscriptions from the Thespiai Survey." *Epigraphical Approaches to the Post-Classical Polis: Fourth Century BC to Second Century AD,* edited by Paraskevi Martzavou and Nikolaos Papazarkadas. Oxford and New York: Oxford University Press, 277–299.

Scheidel, Walter. 2003. "The Greek Demographic Expansion: Models and Comparisons." *Journal of Hellenic Studies.* 123:120–140.

———. 2005a. "Real Slave Prices and the Relative Costs of Slave Labor in the Greco-Roman World." *Ancient Society.* 35:1–17.

———. 2005b. "Military Commitments and Political Bargaining in Ancient Greece." *Princeton/Stanford Working Papers in Classics.* http://www.princeton.edu/~pswpc /pdfs/scheidel/110501.pdf.

———. 2006. "Republics between Hegemony and Empire: How Ancient City-States Built Empires and the USA Doesn't (Anymore)." *Princeton/Stanford Working Papers in Classics.* http://www.princeton.edu/~pswpc/pdfs/scheidel/020601.pdf.

———. 2007. "Demography." *The Cambridge Economic History of the Greco-Roman World,* edited by Walter Scheidel, Ian Morris, and Richard P. Saller. Cambridge: Cambridge University Press, 38–86.

———. 2008a. "The Comparative Economies of Slavery in the Greco-Roman World." *Slave Systems: Ancient and Modern,* edited by Enrico Dal Lago and Constantina Katsari. Cambridge and New York: Cambridge University Press, 105–126.

———. 2008b. "Review of M. H. Hansen, *The Shotgun Method: The Demography of the Ancient Greek City-State Culture,* Columbia Mo. and London 2006; *Studies in the Population of Aigina, Athens and Eretria,* Copenhagen 2006." *Klio.* 90:487–489.

———. 2009a. "New Ways of Studying Incomes in the Roman Economy." *Quantifying the Roman Economy: Methods and Problems.* edited by Alan K. Bowman and Andrew Wilson. Oxford and New York: Oxford University Press 346–352.

———. 2009b. *Rome and China: Comparative Perspectives on Ancient World Empires.* Oxford and New York: Oxford University Press.

———. 2010. "Real Wages in Early Economies: Evidence for Living Standards from 1800 BCE to 1300 CE." *Journal of the Social and Economic History of the Orient.* 53: 425–462.

———, ed. 2012a. *The Cambridge Companion to the Roman Economy.* Cambridge: Cambridge University Press.

———. 2012b. "Roman Wellbeing and the Economic Consequences of the Antonine Plague." *L'impatto della "peste antonina,"* edited by E. Lo Cascio. Bari, Italy: Edipuglia, 265–295.

———. 2014. "Roman Wages in Context." *Quantifying the Greco-Roman Economy and Beyond, Pragmateiai,* edited by François de Callataÿ. Bari, Italy: Edipuglia, 185–192.

Scheidel, Walter, and Steven J. Friesen. 2009. "The Size of the Economy and the Distribution of Income in the Roman Empire." *Journal of Roman Studies.* 99:61–91.

Scheidel, Walter, Ian Morris, and Richard P. Saller, eds. 2007. *The Cambridge Economic History of the Greco-Roman World.* Cambridge: Cambridge University Press.

Scheve, Kenneth and David Stasavage. 2012. "Democracy, War, and Wealth. Lessons from Two Centuries of Inheritance Taxation." *American Political Science Review.* 106:81–102.

Schneider, Helmuth. 2007. "Technology." *The Cambridge Economic History of the Greco-Roman World*, edited by Walter Scheidel, Ian Morris, and Richard P. Saller. Cambridge: Cambridge University Press, 144–171.

Schumpeter, Joseph A. 1942. *Capitalism, Socialism, and Democracy.* New York: Harper.

Schwartz, Adam. 2009. *Reinstating the Hoplite: Arms, Armour and Phalanx Fighting in Archaic and Classical Greece.* Stuttgart, Germany: F. Steiner.

Schwenk, Cynthia J. 1985. *Athens in the Age of Alexander: The Dated Laws and Decrees of "The Lykourgan Era" 338–322 B.C.* Chicago: Ares.

Scobie, Alex. 1986. "Slums, Sanitation, and Mortality in the Roman World." *Klio.* 68:399–433.

Scott, James C. 2009. *The Art of Not Being Governed: An Anarchist History of Upland Southeast Asia.* New Haven, CT: Yale University Press.

Sealey, Raphael. 1956. "Callistratus of Aphidna and His Contemporaries." *Historia.* 5:178–203.

Seeley, Thomas D. 2010. *Honeybee Democracy.* Princeton, NJ: Princeton University Press.

Sen, Amartya. 1981. *Poverty and Famines: An Essay on Entitlement and Deprivation.* Oxford: Clarendon Press.

Shear, Julia L. 2003. "Prizes from Athens: The List of Panathenaic Prizes and the Sacred Oil." *Zeitschrift für Papyrologie und Epigraphik.* 142:87–105.

———. 2011. *Polis and Revolution: Responding to Oligarchy in Classical Athens.* Cambridge: Cambridge University Press.

Shelmerdine, Cynthia W., ed. 2008. *The Cambridge Companion to the Aegean Bronze Age.* Cambridge: Cambridge University Press.

Sherwin-White, A. N. 1973. *The Roman Citizenship.* Oxford: Clarendon Press.

Shipley, D. Graham J., and Mogens H. Hansen. 2006. "The *Polis* and Federalism." *The Cambridge Companion to the Hellenistic World*, edited by Glenn Richard Bugh. Cambridge: Cambridge University Press, 52–72.

Shipley, Graham. 2000. *The Greek World after Alexander, 323–30 B.C.* London and New York: Routledge.

Shipton, Kirsty. 1997. "The Private Banks in Fourth-Century B.C. Athens: A Reappraisal." *Classical Quarterly.* 47:396–322.

Sickinger, James P. 1999. *Public Records and Archives in Classical Athens.* Chapel Hill, NC: University of North Carolina Press.

Siewert, Peter. 1982. *Die Trittyen Attikas und die Heeresreform des Kleisthenes.* Munich, Germany: C. H. Beck.

Simonton, Matthew S. 2012. "The Rules of the Few: Institutions and the Struggle for Political Order in Classical Greek Oligarchies." Stanford, CA: Classics, Stanford University.

Skinner, Quentin. 2007. "Surveying the *Foundations*: A Retrospect and Reassessment." *Rethinking the Foundations of Modern Political Thought*, edited by Annabel Brett and James Tully. Cambridge: Cambridge University Press, 236–261.

Skultety, Steven C. 2009. "Competition in the Best of Cities: Agonism and Aristotle's *Politics.*" *Political Theory.* 37 (1):44–68.

Smarczyk, Bernhard. 2003. *Timoleon und die Neugründung von Syrakus.* Göttingen, Germany: Vandenhoeck & Ruprecht.

Smith, Adam. 1981 [1776]. *An Inquiry into the Nature and Causes of the Wealth of Nations*. Vol. 1. Indianapolis: Liberty Fund.

Snodgrass, Anthony M. 1971. *The Dark Age of Greece: An Archaeological Survey of the Eleventh to the Eighth Centuries BC*. Edinburgh, U.K.: University Press.

———. 1980a. *Archaic Greece: The Age of Experiment*. London and Toronto: J. M. Dent.

———. 1980b. "Iron and Early Metallurgy in the Mediterranean." *The Coming of the Age of Iron*, edited by Theodore A. Wertime and James David Muhly. New Haven, CT: Yale University Press, 335–374.

Spruyt, Hendrik. 1994. *The Sovereign State and Its Competitors: An Analysis of Systems Change*. Princeton, NJ: Princeton University Press.

Stanton, G. R. 1990. *Athenian Politics, c. 800–500 B.C.: A Sourcebook*. London and New York: Routledge.

Starr, Chester G. 1970. *Athenian Coinage, 480–449 B.C.* Oxford: Clarendon Press.

———. 1975. "Greeks and Persians in Fourth Century BC: A Study in Cultural Contacts before Alexander. Part I." *Iranica Antiqua*. 11:39–99.

———. 1977. *The Economic and Social Growth of Early Greece, 800–500 B.C.* New York: Oxford University Press.

Stasavage, David. 2014. "Was Weber Right? The Role of Urban Autonomy in Europe's Rise." *American Political Science Review*. 108.2:337–354.

Stiglitz, Joseph E. 2008. "Principal and Agent." *New Palgrave Dictionary of Economics*. New York: Palgrave Macmillan. http://www.dictionaryofeconomics.com/article?id =pde2008_P000183.

Stockwell, Stephen. 2011. "Before Athens: Early Popular Government in Phoenicia and Greek City-States." *The Secret History of Democracy*, edited by Benjamin Isakhan and Stephen Stockwell. New York: Palgrave Macmillan, 35–48.

———. 2012. "Israel and Phoenicia." *The Edinburgh Companion to the History of Democracy*, edited by Benjamin Isakhan and Stephen Stockwell. Edinburgh, U.K.: Edinburgh University Press, 71–84.

Strauss, Barry S. 1986. *Athens after the Peloponnesian War: Class, Faction and Policy 403–386 BC*. London: Croom Helm.

———. 1996. "The Athenian Trireme, School of Democracy." *Dēmokratia: A Conversation on Democracies, Ancient and Modern*, edited by Josiah Ober and Charles W. Hedrick. Princeton, NJ: Princeton University Press, 313–326.

———. 2000. "Democracy, Kimon, and the Evolution of Athenian Naval Tactics in the Fifth Century B.C." *Polis and Politics [Festschrift Hansen]*, edited by P. Flensted-Jensen, T. H. Neilsen, and L. Rubinstein. Copenhagen, Denmark: Munksgaard, 315–326.

———. 2004. *The Battle of Salamis: The Naval Encounter That Saved Greece—and Western Civilization*. New York: Simon & Schuster.

Strauss, Barry S., and Josiah Ober. 1990. *The Anatomy of Error: Ancient Military Disasters and Their Lessons for Modern Strategists*. New York: St. Martin's Press.

Stroud, Ronald S. 1974. "An Athenian Law on Silver Coinage." *Hesperia*. 43:157–188.

———. 1998. *The Athenian Grain-Tax Law of 374/3 B.C.* Princeton, NJ: American School of Classical Studies at Athens.

Talbert, Richard J. A. 1974. *Timoleon and the Revival of Greek Sicily, 344–317 B.C.* Vol. Cambridge classical studies. London and New York: Cambridge University Press.

Taylor, Claire. 2007. "From the Whole Citizen Body? The Sociology of Election and Lot in the Athenian Democracy." *Hesperia*. 76:323–346.

Taylor, Claire. 2008. "A New Political World." *Debating the Athenian Cultural Revolution: Art, Literature, Philosophy, and Politics 430–380 BC*, edited by Robin Osborne. Cambridge: Cambridge University Press, 72–90.

Taylor, Michael W. 1991. *The Tyrant Slayers: The Heroic Image in Fifth Century B.C. Athenian Art and Politics.* Salem, NH: Ayers.

Teegarden, David. 2012. "The Oath of Demophantos, Revolutionary Mobilization, and the Preservation of the Athenian Democracy." *Hesperia.* 81.3:433–465.

———. 2014a. *Death to Tyrants! Ancient Greek Democracy and the Struggle against Tyranny.* Princeton, NJ: Princeton University Press.

———. 2014b. "The Inauthenticity of Solon's Law against Neutrality." *Buffalo Law Review.* 61 (1):157–175.

———. In progress. "The *Koinon Dogma* and the Consolidation of the Democratic Revolutions in Mid-Fifth Century Sicily." Working Paper: University at Buffalo: Buffalo, NY.

Temin, Peter. 2013. *The Roman Market Economy.* Princeton, NJ: Princeton University Press.

Thompson, Margaret, Otto Mørkholm, and Colin M. Kraay, eds. 1973. *An Inventory of Greek Coin Hoards.* New York: American Numismatic Society.

Thuesen, Ingolf. 2000. "The City-State in Ancient Western Syria." *A Comparative Study of Thirty City-State Cultures: An Investigation*, edited by Mogens Herman Hansen. Copenhagen, Denmark: Kongelige Danske Videnskabernes Selskab, 55–65.

Tigerstedt, Eugene Napoleon. 1965. *The Legend of Sparta in Classical Antiquity.* Stockholm, Sweden: Almqvist & Wiksell.

Tilly, Charles. 1975. "Reflections on the History of European State-Making." *The Formation of National States in Western Europe*, edited by Charles Tilly and Gabriel Ardant. Princeton, NJ: Princeton University Press, 3–83.

———. 1990. *Coercion, Capital, and European States, AD 990–1990.* Cambridge, MA: B. Blackwell.

Todd, S. C. 1994. "Status and Contract in Fourth-Century Athens." *Symposion 1993: Vorträge zur griechische under hellenistische Rechtsgeschichte*, vol. 10, edited by Gerhard Thür. Cologne, Germany, and Vienna, Austria: Böhlau, 125–140.

———. 1996. "Lysias, *Against Nikomachos*: The Fate of the Expert in Athenian Law." *Greek Law in Its Political Setting: Justifications Not Justice*, edited by Lin Foxhall and A.D.E. Lewis. Oxford: Clarendon Press, 101–131.

Torelli, Mario. 2000. "The Etruscan City-State." *A Comparative Study of Thirty City-State Cultures: An Investigation*, edited by Mogens Herman Hansen. Copenhagen, Denmark: Kongelige Danske Videnskabernes Selskab, 189–205.

Traill, John S. 1975. *The Political Organization of Attica: A Study of the Demes, Trittyes, and Phylai, and Their Representation in the Athenian Council.* Princeton, NJ: American School of Classical Studies at Athens.

———. 1986. *Demos and Trittys: Epigraphical and Topographical Studies in the Organization of Attica.* Toronto: Athenians Victoria College.

Tritle, Lawrence A. 1997. *The Greek World in the Fourth Century: From the Fall of the Athenian Empire to the Successors of Alexander.* London and New York: Routledge.

Trundle, Matthew. 2004. *Greek Mercenaries: From the Late Archaic Period to Alexander.* London: Routledge.

Tuck, Richard. 2007. "Hobbes and Democracy." *Rethinking the Foundations of Modern Political Thought*, edited by Annabel Brett and James Tully: Cambridge University Press, 171–190.

———. 2008. *Free Riding*. Cambridge, MA: Harvard University Press.

Turchin, Peter. 2006. *War and Peace and War: The Life Cycles of Imperial Nations*. New York: Pi Press.

Turchin, Peter, and Walter Scheidel. 2009. "Coin Hoards Speak of Population Declines in Ancient Rome." *Proceedings of the National Academy of Science*. 106 (41):17276–17279.

Valaoras, Vasilios G. 1960. "A Reconstruction of the Demographic History of Modern Greece." *Milbank Memorial Fund Quarterly*. 38.2:115–139.

van Alfen, Peter G. 2005. "Problems in Ancient Imitative and Counterfeit Coinage." *Making, Moving, and Managing: The New World of Ancient Economics, 323–31 B.C*, edited by Zofia Archibald, John Davies, and Vincent Gabrielsen. Oxford: Oxbow, 322–354.

———. 2011. "Hatching Owls: Athenian Public Finance and the Regulation of Coin Production." *Quantifying Monetary Supplies in Greco-Roman Times*, edited by François de Callataÿ. Bari, Italy: Edipuglia, 127–149.

———. 2012. "Problems in the Political Economy of Archaic Greek Coinage." *Notae Numismaticae*. 7:13–36.

van der Spek, Robartus J., and Bas van Leeuwen. 2014. "Quantifying the Integration of the Babylonian Economy in the Mediterranean World Using a New Corpus of Price Data, 400–50 BCE." *Quantifying the Greco-Roman Economy and Beyond, Pragmateiai*, edited by François de Callataÿ. Bari, Italy: Edipuglia, 79–101.

van der Vliet, E. 2011. "The Early Greek Polis: Regime Building, and the Emergence of the State." *State Formation in Italy and Greece: Questioning the Neoevolutionist Paradigm*, edited by Donald Haggis and Nicola Terrenato. Oxford: Oxbow Books.

van Groningen, B. A. 1953. *In the Grip of the Past: Essay on an Aspect of Greek Thought*. Leiden, Netherlands: E. J. Brill.

van Wees, Hans. 1992. *Status Warriors: War, Violence, and Society in Homer and History*. Amsterdam, Netherlands: J. C. Gieben.

———. 2000a. "The City at War." *Classical Greece, 500–323 BC*, edited by Robin Osborne. Oxford and New York: Oxford University Press, 81–110.

———. ed. 2000b. *War and Violence in Ancient Greece*. London: Duckworth and the Classical Press of Wales.

———. 2004. *Greek Warfare: Myth and Realities*. London: Duckworth.

———. 2013a. "Farmers and Hoplites: Models of Historical Development." *Men of Bronze: Hoplite Warfare in Ancient Greece*, edited by Donald Kagan and Gregory Viggiano. Princeton, NJ: Princeton University Press, 222–255.

———. 2013b. *Ships and Silver, Taxes and Tribute: A Fiscal History of Archaic Athens*. London: I. B. Tauris.

von Reden, Sitta. 2007. "Consumption." *The Cambridge Economic History of the Greco-Roman World*, edited by Walter Scheidel, Ian Morris, and Richard P. Saller. Cambridge: Cambridge University Press, 385–406.

Walbank, F. W. 1993. *The Hellenistic World*. Cambridge, MA: Harvard University Press.

Wallace, Saro. 2010. *Ancient Crete: From Successful Collapse to Democracy's Alternatives, Twelfth–Fifth Centuries BC*. Cambridge: Cambridge University Press.

Weingast, Barry R. 1995. "The Economic Role of Political Institutions: Market-Preserving Federalism and Economic Development." *Journal of Law, Economics, and Organization*. 11 (1):1–31.

———. 1997. "The Political Foundations of Democracy and the Rule of Law." *American Political Science Review*. 91:245–263.

Weiskopf, Michael. 1989. *The So-Called "Great Satraps' Revolt," 366–360 B.C.: Concerning Local Instability in the Achaemenid Far West.* Stuttgart, Germany: F. Steiner.

Werber, Bernard. 1996. *Empire of the Ants.* Translated by Margaret Rocques. London and New York: Bantam.

West, M. L. 1997. *The East Face of Helicon: West Asiatic Elements in Greek Poetry and Myth.* Oxford and New York: Clarendon Press.

West, W.C. 1989. "The Public Archives in Fourth Century Athens." *Greek, Roman, and Byzantine Studies.* 30:529–543.

Whitehead, David. 1977. *The Ideology of the Athenian Metic.* Cambridge: Cambridge Philological Society.

———. 1984. "Immigrant Communities in the Classical Polis. Some Principles for a Synoptic Treatment." *L'Antiquité Classique.* 53:47–59.

———. 1986. *The Demes of Attica, 508/7–ca. 250 B.C.: A Political and Social Study.* Princeton, NJ: Princeton University Press.

———, ed. 1990. *Aeneas: How to Survive under Siege.* Oxford and New York: Oxford University Press.

Whitley, James. 1991. *Style and Society in Dark Age Greece: The Changing Face of a Pre-Literate Society, 1100–700 BC.* Cambridge and New York: Cambridge University Press.

Whitmarsh, Tim. 2005. *The Second Sophistic.* Oxford: Oxford University Press.

Wilcken, Ulrich. 1967. *Alexander the Great.* New York: W. W. Norton.

Will, Edouard. 1979. *Histoire politique du monde hellénistique: 323–30 av. J.-C.* Nancy, France: Presses Universitaires de Nancy.

Wilson, Andrew. 2009. "Approaches to Quantifying Roman Trade." *Quantifying the Roman Economy: Methods and Problems*, edited by Alan K. Bowman and Andrew Wilson. Oxford and New York: Oxford University Press, 2013–2049.

———. 2011. "City Sizes and Urbanization in the Roman Empire." *Settlement, Urbanization, and Population*, edited by Alan K. Bowman and Andrew Wilson. Oxford: Oxford University Press, 161–193.

Winter, Frederick Elliott. 1971. *Greek Fortifications.* Toronto: University of Toronto Press.

Wolpert, Andrew. 2002. *Remembering Defeat: Civil War and Civic Memory in Ancient Athens.* Baltimore: The Johns Hopkins University Press.

Wood, Ellen Meiksins. 1988. *Peasant-Citizen and Slave: The Foundations of Athenian Democracy.* London and New York: Verso.

Worthington, Ian. 2008. *Philip II of Macedonia.* New Haven, CT, and London: Yale University Press.

———. 2012. *Demosthenes of Athens and the Fall of Classical Greece.* New York: Oxford University Press.

Wycherley, R. E. 1978. *The Stones of Athens.* Princeton, NJ: Princeton University Press.

Yoffee, Norman. 2004. *Myths of the Archaic State: Evolution of the Earliest Cities, States, and Civilizations.* New York: Cambridge University Press.

Zaidman, Louise Bruit, and Pauline Schmitt-Pantel. 1992. *Religion in the Ancient Greek City.* Cambridge and New York: Cambridge University Press.

Zimmern, Alfred Eckhard. 1931. *The Greek Commonwealth: Politics and Economics in Fifth-Century Athens.* Oxford: Oxford University Press.

INDEX

NOTE: Figures, maps, and tables are indicated by *f*, *m*, and *t*, respectively, following page numbers. Definitions of key terms are indicated by page numbers in bold type.

siege warfare, 197, 226, 253, 287–88, 309,
313, 353n3
Sikels, 184, 218
silphium, 44
silver, 168–69, 270, 285
Simonides, 182
Simonton, Matthew, 201
Skione, 356n58
Skyros, 229, 230
slavery, 113
slums, 89
small-state cultures, 7–10
Smith, Adam, 11, 14
Snodgrass, Antony, 129
social capital, 16–17
social insects, 49, 58. *See also* ants; bees
social mobility, 142–43, 215
social networks, development of, 170–71
social norms, citizen-centered regimes
arising from, 131
social panopticon, **141**, 170, 194
social science, xvii–xviii
Social War, 239–40, 270
Socrates, 165, 206–7, 222, 232
Solon, 78, 146, 148–49, 152
Solonian reforms, 124, 148–53, 161, 289
sophists, **206**–7, 234
Sophocles, 206
Sounion, 205
Sparta: advantages of, 123; Athenian conflicts with, 160, 166, 196–98, 210–17;
and Athenian tyranny, 160–61; Athens
compared to, 210–11, 211*t*; austerity of,
141; in Bronze Age, 125–26; citizenship
in, 123, 143; and colonization, 139; conflicts involving, 69; defense plan of,
192; development of, 132; economy of,
139, 210; education in, 141–42; and
empire, 227–32; equality in, 140–41,
349n32; ideology of, 231; infantry of,
124, 138–39, 231; influence and prominence of, 37, 144; land area of, 33,
137–38; land holdings in, 357n16; as
land power, 31; language of, 137; life-
styles in, 141, 142; Lycurgan system in,
124, 139–44, 194, 231, 289; Macedon
challenged by, 299; as model for

city-state, 155; navy of, 119, 194, 221–22,
229; Persian alliance with, 221, 227–30;
and Persian invasion, 168, 169, 192–94;
political regime in, 142; population of,
231, 349n30; private wealth in, 140–41;
resistance to innovation in, 118–19; in
seventh and sixth centuries, 137–44;
size of, 33, 37; social crisis in, 124; social
mobility in, 142–43; specialization in,
31, 124, 139, 142; state-sponsored violence in, 139; as superpolis, 140, 143,
211; and trade, 142; warfare central to,
140. *See also* Peloponnesian War
spears, 130, 136, 286
specialization: in Athens, 124; in Bronze
Age, 125; centralized authority and,
14–15, 17, 344n24; in classical Greece,
11–14, 17–18, 31, 205; in Early Iron
Age, 127; economic growth dependent
on, 11–14; federal leagues and, 243; in
fourth century, 225; market exchange
and, 204; military, 139; occupational,
102, 205; rejection of, 17–18, 214–15;
and slavery, 113; in Sparta, 31, 124, 139,
142
Speusippos, 283
standard ancient premise, about Greek
economic development, **76**, 80, 107
standard modern premise, about Greek
economic development, **76**, 80, 88, 118,
338n7
standard of living. *See* living standards
Starr, Chester, 132, 258
Stasavage, David, 122
state performance, Athenian: access as
factor in, 247; elite incentives as factor
in, 174–75; expertise as factor in,
171–74, 248–52; federalism as factor
in, 170–71; political regime type as
factor in, 166–67
states. *See* Greek states
steppe cultures, 28
Stockwell, Stephen, 329n2
strong ties, in networks, **171**
subsidiarity, **242**
subsidies, 115
subsistence minimum baseline, **93**, 341n50